MATH TEACHING SERIES
STUDENTS • TEACHERS • PARENTS

A step-by-step
MATH TEACHING SERIES
for
Students, Teachers, **AND** Parents

GRADE LEVEL

5

ABOUT THE AUTHOR:

Nicholas Aggor is a parent and an ex-senior engineer with a master's degree in engineering, fully trained in the prestigious Six Sigma Blackbelt of Problem Solving, and a National Dean's List Scholar

www.MathTeachingSeries.com
Published by Nicholas Aggor Publisher, LLC.

Welcome to the Math Teaching Series

IF YOU ARE AN EDUCATOR...

This text and every text in the Math Teaching Series provide new "tools" designed to assist you in teaching mathematics. After listening and working with educators to assist all students, even those who struggle with math, we were able to build a step-by-step method to improve the delivery of effective instruction.

IF YOU ARE A PARENT...

We will guide your student to build skills and they will become competent. Study will progress with less stress and more peace as the student and you are able to work together toward success. Pride in accomplishment can come early and stay during the study effort with the system.

IF YOU ARE A STUDENT...

These texts were built to assist all students and allow them to earn respect for their efforts. Those who struggle can get the help they need in a process built to avoid becoming lost and stuck. You are guided and the course is designed to allow you to build competence in skills, which will allow you to feel confident!

Nicholas Aggor, an Author, an Engineer, a Parent

This series of texts is dedicated to making the playing field a more fair and equal process to all students with a well-constructed platform to deliver the lessons.

I believe there are always at least three parties to the success of education. With the student supported with a text built to this level of support, we are confident that the educators of the world will now receive "hands on" help as well for the student with parents, relatives, and others who are dedicated to the journey that can use this text.

I wish to thank all the teachers who help in the real life struggle to teach.

We have designed a new set of tools for students, teachers, and parents.

Nicholas Aggor

ISBN: 978-0-9840609-0-0

School to Home Connection

You promise to work and I promise you will not get lost.

Math Teaching Series Lesson One

LEARN WHY TO WORK AND YOU WILL SUCCEED

- You are as rich and as intelligent as anyone while studying this book.
- Stay with me and work daily and you will see improved results.
- This is all about effort, so follow the pathways and you will improve.

LEARN HOW TO WORK AND YOU WILL SUCCEED

- Peace and quiet will allow focus. NO radio, television, games, and phones.
- Expect to win, to progress and keep score daily and results will improve.
- Your teachers are there to help and teach, so show them your work daily.

Daily Score Card

1. Students grade parents for providing scheduled studies time, homework time, bed time, quiet place to study, quiet place to do homework, and food.
2. Parents grade students for the effort the students make during the scheduled studies time, homework time, and bed time.
3. Teachers grade students during quizzes, homework, and tests.

| Days | Studies Time | Quality Control at Home | | Quality Control at School | Steps to Improve |
		Students' Grading	Parents' Grading	Teachers' Grading	Improvement
Mon					
Tue					
Wed					
Thu					
Fri					
Sat					
Sun					

- Students earn good results with good work habits. Take pride in your efforts.
- Share your daily effort with your parents, guardians, your family, and friends.
- Seek advice and help from your math teachers on your journey to success.
- Parents should make copies of the score card for monitoring progress.

How to Use This Book Most Effectively

There is a consistent teaching method in the text to follow.

Your book contains Examples, with step-by-step demonstration of "how to" do the math problems. As you study, focus on learning the "how to" properly and the solutions offered throughout your text will teach you the methods to use.

Practice the Examples and come to know how to do the work. The Examples section will "teach you" the process in a step-by-step manner. This way, learning the correct methods will prevent you from getting lost or stuck. You will find each step to be connected and the pace will allow you to progress with confidence.

After following the Examples offered with understanding, work the chapter Exercise Problems. As you do the Exercise Problems, use the "hints" provided, as you need them, sending you back to the Examples. This will allow you to advance, and as you learn the steps properly, your confidence will strengthen.

Challenge questions are designed for you to excel in the area of study. Allow yourself time to work the Challenge Questions as they will strengthen your skills.

Word Problems provide Real World applications of the methods you are learning. You are provided with the "how to" method again, showing the step-by-step solutions to solve these questions properly. This will help to improve your math reasoning skills.

Learn to use the Table of Contents (front) and the Index of Terms (back) in this book. These are reference aids to quickly direct you to solutions.

TABLE OF CONTENTS - Grade 5

Chapter 4: Estimating Quotients... 76

Chapter 5: Test for Divisibility... 80

Chapter 6: Average, Mean, Range, Mode, And Median 86

Chapter 7: Fractions... 97

xiii

CHAPTER 1

MULTIPLICATION OF WHOLE NUMBERS

I can solve the problems too if only
I understand the concepts.

Cumulative Review

1. 4 + 17 =   **2.** 3 - 3 =   **3.** 5 + 3 =   **4.** 12 - 7 =

5. 23 - 17 =   **6.** 12 ÷ 4 =   **7.** 18 × 2 =   **8.** 15 ÷ 5 =

9. 12   **10.**   4   **11.** 9 ÷ 3 =   **12.** 7 + 8 =
    × 2   × 3

13. 15 + 8 =   **14.** 12 ÷ 3 =   **15.** 16 - 8 =   **16.** 9 × 2 =

17. 25 ÷ 5 =   **18.** 21 - 13 =   **19.** 30 ÷ 6 =   **20.** 17 - 8 =

21.   25   **22.**   16   **23.**   37   **24.**   17
     × 3   + 19   - 13   × 4

25. 48 ÷ 3 =   **26.** 24 ÷ 8 =   **27.** 12 + 38 =   **28.** 36 - 17 =

The symbol for multiplication is ×.
Let us do the addition:

$$4 + 4 + 4 + 4 + 4 = 20$$

We can also say that 4 × 5 = 20. So, multiplication is a shortcut method of doing
addition. Notice that when you multiply numbers, you are really adding groups
of the same numbers. For example, 4 × 5 = 20 is read "4 times 5," and it is the
same as adding five 4s.
So, 4 × 5 = 20 is the same as 4 + 4 + 4 + 4 + 4 = 20. Multiplication may be considered
as the repetition of the addition of the same number.
So, multiplication can be used to find the total when you know the number of equal
groups and the number in each group.

Example 1
Find the total number of counters in the diagram by:
a. addition
b. multiplication

Solution

a. The sum of the counters is:

$5 + 5 + 5 = 15$ counters   (There are 3 rows that contain 5 counters each.)

b. The total number of counters is:

$5 \times 3 = 15$ counters   (There are 3 rows that contain 5 counters each.)

Example 2

How can you use multiplication to find $2 + 2 + 2 + 2$?

Solution

$2 + 2 + 2 + 2 = 2 \times 4$, because the number of equal groups and the number in each group is known. The number of equal groups is 4, and the number in each group is 2. So, there are 4 2s or $2 \times 4 = 8$.

Example 3

A box of pencils contains 6 pencils. What is the total number of pencils in:

a. 2 similar boxes

b. 3 similar boxes

c. 4 similar boxes

Solution

a. 1 box of 6 pencils represents 1 row of 6 pencils. So, 2 boxes of pencils represent 2 rows of pencils. The total number of pencils in 2 boxes or two rows of 6 pencils is:

$2 \times 6 = 12$ pencils, or $6 + 6 = 12$ pencils.

b. 3 boxes of 6 pencils represent 3 rows of 6 pencils.
The total number of pencils in 3 boxes or 3 rows of 6 pencils is:

$3 \times 6 = 18$ pencils or $6 + 6 + 6 = 18$ pencils.

c. 4 boxes of pencils represent 4 rows of pencils. The total number of pencils in 4 boxes or 4 rows of 6 pencils is:

$4 \times 6 = 24$ pencils or $6 + 6 + 6 + 6 = 24$ pencils.

Example 4

Why do you think that you can multiply to find the total number of pencils in the boxes in Example 3?

Solution

You can multiply to find the total number of pencils in the boxes because the number of pencils in each box is the same.

Example 5

Write an addition sentence and a multiplication sentence for each picture.

a.

b.

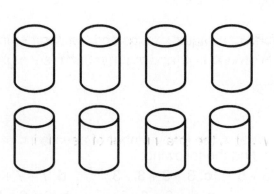

Solution

a. There are two groups of stars and each group contains 7 stars. **The addition sentence is** 7 stars plus 7 stars equal 14 stars. (7 + 7 = 14 stars)
The multiplication sentence is 7 stars times 2 equal groups equal 14 stars. (7 × 2 = 14 stars)

b. There are two groups of cylinders and each group contains 4 cylinders. **The addition sentence is** 4 cylinders plus 4 cylinders equal 8 cylinders. (4 + 4 = 8 cylinders)
The multiplication sentence is 4 cylinders times 2 equal groups equal 8 cylinders. (4 × 2 = 8 cylinders)

The notes and the generous examples have provided me with the conceptual understanding and the computational fluency to do my homework.

Exercises

1. What is multiplication?
2. Explain what multiplication is used for.

3. Find the total number of counters in the rows by:
    a. addition
    b. multiplication

    Hint: See Example 1.

4. Find the total number of stars in the rows by:
    a. addition
    b. multiplication

    Hint: See Example 1.

5. How could you use multiplication to find the following:
    a. 4 + 4 + 4   **b**. 5 + 5 + 5 + 5 + 5   **c**. 3 + 3 + 3 + 3   **d**. 7 + 7 + 7
    e. 12 + 12 + 12   **f**. 8 + 8 + 8   **g**. 6 + 6 + 6 +6   **h**. 9 + 9 + 9 + 9
    Hint: See Example 2.

6. A box contains 8 pens. What is the total number pens in:
    a. 3 similar boxes?
    b. 4 similar boxes?
    c. 6 similar boxes?
    Hint: See Example 3.

7. An envelope contains 3 pictures. What is the total number of pictures in 5 similar envelopes? Hint: See Example 3.

8. A bag contains 4 cookies. What is the total number of cookies in 8 similar bags? Hint: See Example 3.

9. Mary said that multiplication can be used to find the total when you know the number of equal groups and the number in each group. Is her statement correct?

10. Why do you think that you can multiply to find the total number of cookies in the bags in Exercise 8? Hint: See Example 4.

11. Write an addition sentence and a multiplication sentence for the pictures.
    Hint: See Example 5.

a.

b.

12. Each row of seats in the Hila Theater has 36 chairs. If the first 4 rows are completely filled with people, how many people are in the first 4 rows? Hint: See Example 1b.

13. Each row of seats in the Vicki Theater has 18 chairs. If the first 9 rows are completely filled with people, how many are in the first 9 rows? Hint: See Example 1b.

Challenge Questions

14. How could you use multiplication to find the following:
   a. 2 + 2 + 2 + 2   **b.** 11 + 11 + 11   **c.** 9 + 9   **d.** 6 + 6 + 6

15. A box contains 7 apples. What is the total number of apples in:
   a. 2 similar boxes?
   b. 5 similar boxes?
   c. 8 similar boxes?
   Assume that the number of apples in each box is the same.

16. An envelope contains 5 pictures. What is the total number of pictures in 7 similar envelopes? .

17. A bag contains 3 cookies. What is the total number of cookies in 6 similar bags?

18. Write an addition sentence and a multiplication sentence for the diagram.

19. Write an addition sentence and a multiplication sentence for the diagram.

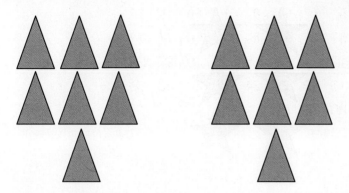

20. 7 + 7 + 7 + 7 + 7 + 7 = 7 × ?

21. A farmer has 12 rows of apple trees. If each row has 12 apple trees, how many apple trees does the farmer have?

22. 10 + 10 + 10 + 10 = 10 × ?

23. A box contains 10 apples. What is the total number of apples in:

   a. 3 similar boxes?

   b. 6 similar boxes?

   c. 8 similar boxes?

   Assume that the number of apples in each box is the same.

Answers to Selected Questions

   5a. 4 + 4 + 4 = 4 × 3 = 12   **6a**. 8 × 3 = 24 pens   **12**. 36 × 4 = 144 people

Patterns in Multiplying

For speed in some computations such as multiplication and division, it is recommended that the student should know the number facts for multiplying whole numbers up to at least 12 × 12. A calculator can be used to check yourself.

Group Exercise - Multiplication Table 1

The multiplication table is partially completed. Each group should copy and complete the Multiplication Table by using the first row at the top and the first column at the left side as guides. **Multiplication is repeated addition of the same number** as shown by the numbers in row 3 or column 3.

3 + 3 = 6, 6 + 3 = 9, 9 + 3 = 12, 12 + 3 = 15, 15 + 3 =18, 18 + 3 = 21, 21 + 3 =24, ...

Use a similar idea of **repeated addition** to complete the Multiplication Table.

Multiplication Table

	1	2	3	4	5	6	7	8	9	10	11	12
1	1	2	3	4	5	6	7	8	9	10	11	12
2	2	4	6	8	10	12	14	16	18	20	22	24
3	3	6	9	12	15	18	21	24	27	30	33	36
4					20							
5	5				25							
6			18				42					
7												
8					40			64				96
9												
10												
11	11						77					
12												144

1. Compare all of the completed Multiplication Tables of each team.
2. Are all the Multiplication Tables the same?
3. What are the common mistakes made and why?
4. Every member of each group should make his/her own Multiplication Table.

How to Read the Multiplication Table

1. 2 in the table is obtained by multiplying 1 in the first row by the 2 in the first column.
2. 25 in the table is obtained by multiplying 5 in the first row by the 5 in the first column.
3. Similarly, all the other numbers in table are obtained by multiplying the numbers in the first row by the numbers in the first column respectively.
4. The Group Exercise shows that multiplication tables can also be constructed using repeated addition of the same number. Recall that multiplication is the shortcut for repeated addition. Knowing the **pattern of repeated addition** can help you recall multiplication facts and also be used to construct the multiplication table.

Group Exercise - Multiplication Table 2

The class should be divided into 4 groups.

1. Each group should construct the multiplication table by using repeated addition of the same number and also by multiplication.
2. Compare the four multiplication tables. Are the tables the same? Correct any error found.
3. Each group should report their multiplication table on the overhead to the class.
4. What is the pattern by multiplying by 10? Is the last digit of each product 0?
5. What is the pattern by multiplying by 5? Is the last digit of each product 5 or 0?

Mental Quiz

1. $3 \times 4 =$ **2**. $7 \times 7 =$ **3**. $9 \times 9 =$ **4**. $5 \times 5 =$

5. $6 \times 6 =$ **6**. $8 \times 8 =$ **7**. $8 \times 6 =$ **8**. $4 \times 9 =$

9. $3 \times 9 =$ **10**. $12 \times 12 =$ **11**. $8 \times 3 =$ **12**. $11 \times 11 =$

Chanting of the Multiplication Facts

Multiplication is repeated addition of the same number, similarly **chanting** is the repetitive melody in which several words are sung to one tone as a celebration. Let us celebrate that we understand the multiplication facts by chanting the multiplication table from 2 to 12. (You may need to use the Math Teaching Series' CD or DVD which may be released shortly for sale.)

REAL WORLD APPLICATION - WORD PROBLEMS

Example 1

Pens cost $3 each. How much will 9 pens cost?

Solution

Cost of 1 pen = $3

Cost of 9 pens = $3 \times 9 = $27   **Note that every pen costs $3.**

Example 2

Mary can bake 8 cakes each day. How many similar cakes can she bake in 6 days?

Solution

Number of cakes baked in 1 day = 8

Number of cakes baked in 6 days = $8 \times 6 = 48$

Note that 8 cakes are baked each day.

Example 3

Mary earns $6 an hour for baby-sitting. How much does she earn in:

     a. 4 hours?   **b**. 5 hours?   **c**. 7 hours?

Solution

a. Money earned in 1 hour = $6

     Money earned in 4 hours = $6 \times 4 = $24   **Note that $6 is earned each hour.**

b. Money earned in 1 hour = $6

     Money earned in 5 hours = $6 \times 5 = $30   **Note that $6 is earned each hour.**

c. Money earned in 1 hour = $6

     Money earned in 7 hours = $6 \times 7 = $42   **Note that $6 is earned each hour.**

The notes and the generous examples have provided me with the conceptual understanding and the computational fluency to do my homework.

Exercises

1. Pens cost $4 each. How much will 7 similar pens cost? Hint: See Example 1
2. Calculators cost $6 each. How much will 8 similar calculators cost? Hint: See Example 1.
3. How much will 12 shirts cost if a shirt costs $9 each? Hint: See Example 1.
4. Joan can bake 9 cakes each day. How many similar cakes can she bake in 4 days? Hint: See Example 2.
5. Cookies cost $7 per box. How much will 11 similar boxes of cookies cost? Hint: See Example 2.
6. How much will 7 books cost if 1 book costs $5? Hint: See Example 1.
7. John earns $7 an hour for baby-sitting. How much does she earn in:
   a. 2 hours?   **b**. 5 hours?   **c**. 8 hours?
   Hint: See Example 3.

Challenge Questions

8. Pens cost $2 each. How much will 5 similar pens cost?
9. Calculators cost $5 each. How much will 5 similar calculators cost?
10. Erica earns $6 an hour for baby-sitting. How much does she earn in:
    a. 1 hour?   **b**. 3 hours?   **c**. 6 hours?

Answers to Selected Questions
1. $28   **7b**. $35

Zero Property of Multiplication
The product of zero and any number is zero. The product of any number and zero is zero.

Example 1
Find the products:
a. $0 \times 4 =$ **b**. $8 \times 0 =$ **c**. $99 \times 0 =$
Solution
a. $0 \times 4 = 0$ Because of the zero property of multiplication.
b. $8 \times 0 = 0$ Because of the zero property of multiplication.
c. $99 \times 0 = 0$ Because of the zero property of multiplication.

Critical Thinking: If the product of two numbers is zero, then at least one of the numbers is zero.

9

Identity Property of Multiplication

The product of any number and one is the same number. The product of one and any number is the same number.

Example 2

Find the products:

a. $22 \times 1 =$ **b.** $1 \times 8 =$ **c.** $99 \times 1 =$

Solution

a. $22 \times 1 = 22$ Because of the identity property of multiplication.

b. $1 \times 8 = 8$ Because of the identity property of multiplication.

c. 99×1 Because of the identity property of multiplication.

Commutative Property of Multiplication

Two numbers can be multiplied in any order and the product is the same.

Example 3

Find the products:

a. $3 \times 8 =$ **b.** $7 \times 4 =$ **c.** $6 \times 5 =$

$8 \times 3 =$ $4 \times 7 =$ $5 \times 6 =$

What property does the products confirm?

Solution

a. $3 \times 8 = 24$

$8 \times 3 = 24$

The products are the same which confirm the commutative property of multiplication.

b. $7 \times 4 = 28$

$4 \times 7 = 28$

The products are the same which confirm the commutative property of multiplication.

c. $6 \times 5 = 30$

$5 \times 6 = 30$

The products are the same which confirm the commutative property of multiplication.

 The notes and the generous examples have provided me with the conceptual understanding and the computational fluency to do my homework.

Exercises

1. John said that the product of any number and zero is zero. Is his statement correct? What property of mathematics supports your answer? Hint: See Example 1.

2. Find each product:

   a. $10 \times 0 =$ **b.** $66 \times 0 =$ **c.** $3 \times 0 =$

Hint: See Example **1**.

3. Nick said that the product of any number and 1 is not the same number.

   a. Is his statement correct?

   b. What property of mathematics can you state to show that he is correct or wrong?

   Hint: See Example **2**.

4. Find the following products:

   a. $18 \times 1 =$ **b**. $1 \times 24 =$ **c**. $9 \times 1 =$

   Hint: See Example **2**.

5. Find the missing number:

   a. $? \times 4 = 0$ **b**. $3 \times ? = 0$ **c**. $? \times 1 = 0$

   d. What property of mathematics did you use to find the missing numbers in 5**a**, 5**b**, and 5**c**.

   Hint: See Example **1**.

6. What property of mathematics can you use to show that if $9 \times 2 = 18$, then $2 \times 9 = 18$. Hint: See Example **3**.

7. Jane said that if the product of two numbers is zero, then at least one of the numbers is zero. Is her statement correct? Explain your answer.

Challenge Questions

8. Find each product:

   a. $9 \times 5 =$ **b**. $6 \times 0 =$ **c**. $98 \times 1 =$

   d. $6 \times 6 =$ **e**. $7 \times 7 =$ **f**. $0 \times 8 =$

9. Find each missing number. Tell which property of mathematics that can help you.

   a. $? \times 9 = 0$ **b**. $4 \times 3 = 3 \times ?$ **c**. $1 \times ? = 36$ **d**. $1 \times ? = 20$ **e**. $6 \times 7 = 7 \times ?$

10. The product of two number is 0. What is one of the numbers?

Answers to Selected Questions

2a. 0   **4a**. 18   **8a**. 45   **9a**. 0

Multiplying Horizontally and Vertically

Multiplication problems can be written horizontally or vertically as shown:

7 × 2 = 14 is the same as   Vertical multiplication

Horizontal multiplication

The notes and the generous examples have provided me with the conceptual understanding and the computational fluency to do my homework.

Exercises
Review the multiplication table your group has made, and answer the following:

1. $6 \times 3 =$ **2.** $8 \times 3 =$ **3.** $9 \times 2 =$ **4.** $3 \times 8 =$ **5.** $7 \times 2 =$

6. $\begin{array}{r} 8 \\ \times\ 4 \\ \hline \end{array}$ **7.** $\begin{array}{r} 6 \\ \times\ 3 \\ \hline \end{array}$ **8.** $\begin{array}{r} 7 \\ \times\ 4 \\ \hline \end{array}$ **9.** $\begin{array}{r} 6 \\ \times\ 2 \\ \hline \end{array}$ **10.** $\begin{array}{r} 10 \\ \times\ 2 \\ \hline \end{array}$

11. $8 \times 4 =$ **12.** $7 \times 5 =$ **13.** $5 \times 5 =$ **14.** $10 \times 3 =$ **15.** $4 \times 9 =$

16. $\begin{array}{r} 5 \\ \times\ 12 \\ \hline \end{array}$ **17.** $\begin{array}{r} 11 \\ \times\ 3 \\ \hline \end{array}$ **18.** $\begin{array}{r} 7 \\ \times\ 10 \\ \hline \end{array}$ **19.** $\begin{array}{r} 12 \\ \times\ 12 \\ \hline \end{array}$ **20.** $\begin{array}{r} 11 \\ \times\ 9 \\ \hline \end{array}$

21. $11 \times 4 =$ **22.** $6 \times 6 =$ **23.** $10 \times 5 =$ **24.** $9 \times 7 =$ **25.** $5 \times 7 =$

26. $\begin{array}{r} 8 \\ \times\ 11 \\ \hline \end{array}$ **27.** $\begin{array}{r} 9 \\ \times\ 12 \\ \hline \end{array}$ **28.** $\begin{array}{r} 8 \\ \times\ 9 \\ \hline \end{array}$ **29.** $\begin{array}{r} 12 \\ \times\ 4 \\ \hline \end{array}$ **30.** $\begin{array}{r} 7 \\ \times\ 8 \\ \hline \end{array}$

Challenge Questions
31. $11 \times 7 =$ **32.** $7 \times 8 =$ **33.** $10 \times 3 =$ **34.** $8 \times 6 =$ **35.** $9 \times 7 =$

36. $\begin{array}{r} 9 \\ \times\ 11 \\ \hline \end{array}$ **37.** $\begin{array}{r} 9 \\ \times\ 7 \\ \hline \end{array}$ **38.** $\begin{array}{r} 9 \\ \times\ 9 \\ \hline \end{array}$ **39.** $\begin{array}{r} 7 \\ \times\ 4 \\ \hline \end{array}$ **40.** $\begin{array}{r} 7 \\ \times\ 8 \\ \hline \end{array}$

Answers to Selected Questions
1. 18   6. 32   11. 32   16. 60   21. 44   26. 88

Review
1. Describe a rule that shows how to find each multiple of 5. Hint: Multiples of a whole number are all the whole numbers that are products of the given number. Describe a rule that shows how to find each multiple of 10.
3. Describe a rule that shows how to find each multiple of 11.
4. Write a multiplication sentence for $6 + 6 + 6 + 6$.

Using Known Facts to Find Unknown Facts
Recall that during the group exercise involving the multiplication table, it is easier

to recall the patterns of the multiples of 1, 2, 5, 10, and 11 than the multiples of other numbers. For example:

a. 1 × any number equals the same number. 1 × 1 = 1, 1 × 2 = 2, 1 × 3 = 3,...

b. 2 × any number equals twice the number. 2 × 1 = 2, 2 × 2 = 4, 2 × 3 = 6,...

c. 5 × any number that can be divided by 2, equals a product with a last digit of 0.
   5 × 2 = 10, 5 × 4 = 20, 5 × 6 = 30,...

d. 5 × any number that cannot be divided by 2, equals a product with a last digit of 5.
   5 × 1 = 5, 5 × 3 = 15, 5 × 5 = 25,...

e. 10 × any number equals a product with a last digit of 0. 10 × 1 = 10, 10 × 2 = 20,
   10 × 3 = 30,...

f. 11 × any number equals a product with mainly the repetition of the digit of the
   number. 11 × 1 = 11, 11 × 2 = 22, 11 × 3 = 33,...

The multiplication facts for the multiples of 1, 2, 5, 10, and 11 are shown with their patterns.

1 × 1 = 1	2 × 1 = 2	5 × 1 = 5	10 × 1 = 10	11 × 1 = 11
1 × 2 = 2	2 × 2 = 4	5 × 2 = 10	10 × 2 = 20	11 × 2 = 22
1 × 3 = 3	2 × 3 = 6	5 × 3 = 15	10 × 3 = 30	11 × 3 = 33
1 × 4 = 4	2 × 4 = 8	5 × 4 = 20	10 × 4 = 40	11 × 4 = 44
1 × 5 = 5	2 × 5 = 10	5 × 5 = 25	10 × 5 = 50	11 × 5 = 55
1 × 6 = 6	2 × 6 = 12	5 × 6 = 30	10 × 6 = 60	11 × 6 = 66
1 × 7 = 7	2 × 7 = 14	5 × 7 = 35	10 × 7 = 70	11 × 7 = 77
1 × 8 = 8	2 × 8 = 16	5 × 8 = 40	10 × 8 = 80	11 × 8 = 88
1 × 9 = 9	2 × 9 = 18	5 × 9 = 45	10 × 9 = 90	11 × 9 = 99
1 × 10 = 10	2 × 10 = 20	5 × 10 = 50	10 × 10 = 100	11 × 10 = 110
1 × 11 = 11	2 × 11 = 22	5 × 11 = 55	10 × 11 = 110	11 × 11 = 121
1 × 12 = 12	2 × 12 = 24	5 × 12 = 60	10 × 12 = 120	11 × 12 = 132

So, we can break apart one unknown multiplication fact into two known multiplication facts to solve problems.

Example 1

John has 3 rows of 6 counters. How many counters does he have?

Solution

The number of counters = 3 × 6. But how can we find 3 × 6?

The 3 rows of 6 counters are shown:

3 rows of 6 counters ← → 2 rows of 6 counters

→ 1 row of 6 counters

Notice that 3 rows of 6 counters is the same as 2 rows of 6 counters and 1 row of 6 counters.

2 rows of 6 counters = 2 × 6 = 12 counters.   Known fact (partial product)
1 row of 6 counters = 1 × 6 = 6 counters.   Known fact (partial product)
Add the partial products together to get the total product.

12 + 6 = 18 counters so, 3 × 6 = 18.

Two Ways to Break Apart a Fact

The two ways of breaking apart a fact are:

1. By breaking the first factor (which represents the number of rows).

2. By breaking the second factor (which represents the number of columns).

Factors   Product

3 × 12 = 36

First factor   Second factor
(Represents rows)   (Represents columns)

3 rows —

12 columns

Example 2

Find 3 × 12:

a. By breaking apart the first factor (which is the number of rows).

b. By breaking apart the second factor (which is the number of columns).

Solution

3 × 12 = 36

First factor   Second factor
(Represents rows)   (Represents columns)

a. From Example 1, 3 × 12 = 2 × 12 + 1 × 12
$$= 24 + 12$$
$$= 36$$

b. The second factor, 12, can be broken apart into 10 and 2. Notice that 10 is selected because it is easier to multiply by 10 than to multiply by 12, or we know the multiplication facts involving 10.

10 columns
3 × 10 = 30 counters)

2 columns
(3 × 2 = 6 counters)

To find 3 × 12, I think of 12 columns as 10 columns and 2 columns.
    3 × 10 = 30 counters   Known fact (partial product)
    3 × 2 = 6 counters   Known fact (partial product)
Add the partial products together to get the total product.
    30 + 6 = 36 counters, so 3 × 12 = 36.

Notice that Examples **2a** and **2b** produce the same answer.

How You Can Use Facts You Know to Break Apart a Fact That You Do Not Know

Example 3
Find 7 × 9
a. By breaking apart the first factor (which is the number of rows).
b. By breaking apart the second factor (which is the number of columns).
Solution
Let us use counters to help us to understand the solution of the problem. Let 7 × 9 represents 7 rows of 9 counters.
a. 7 rows of 9 counters is the same as 5 rows of 9 counters and 2 rows of 9 counters.

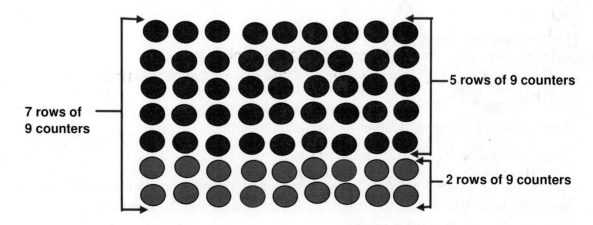

7 rows of 9 counters

5 rows of 9 counters

2 rows of 9 counters

First factor (Number of rows)

Second factor (Number of columns)

7 × 9

Break apart into 5 and 2.

5 × 9 = 45   Known fact (partial product)
2 × 9 = 18   Known fact (partial product)
Add the partial products together to get the total product.
       45 + 18 = 63, so 7 × 9 = 63.

b. 9 columns of 7 counters is the same as 5 columns of 7 counters and 4 columns of 7 counters.

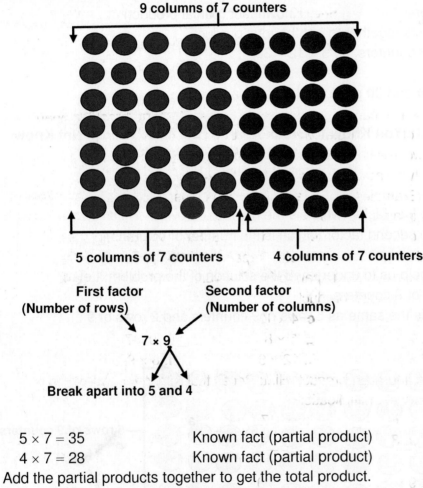

9 columns of 7 counters

5 columns of 7 counters   **4 columns of 7 counters**

First factor (Number of rows)

Second factor (Number of columns)

7 × 9

Break apart into 5 and 4

5 × 7 = 35   Known fact (partial product)
4 × 7 = 28   Known fact (partial product)
Add the partial products together to get the total product.
       35 + 28 = 63, so 7 × 9 = 63.

Notice that we select 5 columns because we know the multiplication facts of 5, or it is easier to multiply by 5 than to multiply by 9. Notice also that the answers to Example **3a** and **3b** are the same.

Check for Understanding

Example 4
Explain how you can use breaking apart to find 9×12.
Solution
To find 9×12, I know that 12 is $10 + 2$.
$9 \times 10 = 90$ Partial product
$9 \times 2 = 18$ Partial product
Add the partial products to get the total product.
      $90 + 18 = 108$, so $9 \times 12 = 108$

═══════════════════════════ The notes and the generous examples have provided me with the conceptual understanding and the computational fluency to do my homework.

Exercises
1. Mary said that known facts can be used to find unknown facts by breaking apart unknown or difficult facts. Is her statement true? Explain your answer.
2. In Example **1**, what two known facts were used to find 3×12?
3. In Example **2b**, what two known facts were used to find 3×12?
4. John said that either Example **2a** or Example **2b** can be used to find 3×12. Is his statement correct? Explain your answer.
5. Explain how you would find 3×9 by breaking apart 3. Hint: See Example **2a**.
6. Explain how you would find 3×9 by breaking apart 9. Hint: See Example **2b**.
7. Explain how you can use breaking apart to find 7×12. Hint: See Example **4**.
8. Use breaking apart to find each product.
      a. 6×8 **b.** 4×7 **c.** 4×12 **d.** 7×8
      e. 8×6 **f.** 9×9 **g.** 5×8 **h.** 9×7
      i. 9×5 **j.** 6×4 **k.** 12×6 **l.** 8×9
9. Use breaking apart to find each product. Hint: Recall that horizontal multiplication is the same as the vertical multiplication.

      a.   9   **b.**   6   **c.**   7   **a.**   9
         $\times\,3$ $\times\,3$ $\times\,9$ $\times\,6$

      e. 8×6 **f.** 9×8 **g.** 8×9 **h.** 7×7
10. A farmer plants 4 rows of 12 apple trees. How many apple trees does he have? Hint: See Example 1.

Challenge Questions
11. Erica plants 6 rows of 10 orange trees. How many orange trees does she have?

12. Multiply.

a. 8
× 4

b. 7
× 2

c. 8
× 8

a. 12
× 6

13. Multiply.

e. 9 × 6 =   **f.** 4 × 7 =   **g.** 6 × 8 =   **h.** 5 × 7 =

Answers to Selected Questions

8a. 48   **8b.** 28   **9a.** 27   **9b.** 54

Cumulative Review

Find each product

1. 3 × 12   **2.** 8 × 6   **3.** 7 × 6   **4.** 9 × 3
5. 9 × 9   **6.** 7 × 7   **7.** 10 × 4   **8.** 5 × 11
9. Write a multiplication sentence for 3 + 3 + 3 +.3
10. Write a multiplication sentence for 5 + 5 + 5 + 5 + 5
11. Write a multiplication sentence for 9 + 9 + 9

Challenge Questions

1. To find a number that is three times as great as 9, I will multiply 3 by 9.
   Find the number that is 6 times as great as 11.
2. Find: 12 × 9 =
3. John wants to plant 20 flowers in 5 rows. How many flowers should he put in
   each row? Hint: You may use counters to represent flowers. Think of what number
   multiplied by 5 equals 20.

Multiplying Two-Digit and One-Digit Numbers
Multiplication problems are set up like this:

Notice that the bottom number is the multiplier and the top number is the
multiplicand. Notice also that the ones digits are aligned, as in addition and
subtraction. Knowing the multiplication facts is important, because you can multiply
any two numbers together.

Multiplication Rule

To solve a problem in multiplication, always multiply from right to left, starting with the ones digit in the multiplicand.

Example 1

Find

Solution

To solve a problem in multiplication, always multiply from right to left, starting with the ones digit in the multiplicand.

Step 1: Multiply the ones. Regroup if necessary.

2 times 3 equals 6. Write the 6 under the ones column.

Step 2: Multiply the tens. Add any extra tens carried over from Step 1, and regroup if necessary.

2 times 2 equals 4. There is no extra tens carried over from Step 1. Write the 4 under the tens column.

Tens column ⟶ ┃ ┃ ⟵ Ones column

```
    23
  ×  2
  ----
    46    Answer
```

Shortcut Method

A detailed explanation for solving the problem is provided step-by-step so that the student can understand the concept. Once the concept is understood, only the summary of Step 2 (as shown below) may be provided as the solution to similar problems during homework and tests.

```
    23
  ×  2
  ----
    46
```

Example 2

Find 34 × 3

Solution

Set up the problem and then multiply from right to left.

Step 1: Multiply the ones. Regroup if necessary.

3 times 4 equals 12. Regroup, write the 2 under the ones column, and carry the 1 to the next digit, the 3 (at the tens column).

(Notice that $3 \times 4 = 12$ ones. **Regroup 12 ones as 1 ten 2 ones.** The 1 ten is carried over to the tens column.)

Step 2: Multiply the tens. Add any extra tens carried over from Step 1, and regroup if necessary.

3 times 3 equals 9, plus the 1 you carried over from Step 1, equals 10. Regrouping is not necessary because there is no next digit (no digit in the hundreds column to work with). Write the 0 under the tens column and the 1 under the hundreds column, or just write the 10 in front of the 2.

Shortcut Method

A detailed explanation for solving the problem is provided step-by-step so that the student can understand the concept. Once the concept is understood, only the summary of Step 2 (as shown below) may be provided as the solution to similar problems during homework and tests.

```
      1
     34
   ×  3
    102
```

Example 3

Find   564
       ×   3

Solution

Step 1: Multiplying the ones. Regrouping if necessary.
3 times 4 equals 12. Regroup, write 2 under the ones column and carry the 1 to the next digit, the 6 (at the tens column).

(Notice that $3 \times 4 = 12$ ones. **Regroup 12 ones as 1 ten 2 ones.** The 1 ten is carried over to the tens column.)

Step 2: Multiply the tens. Add any extra tens carried over from Step 1, and regroup if necessary.
3 times 6 is 18, plus the 1 you carried from Step 1, equals 19. Regroup, write the 9 under the tens column and carry the 1 to the next digit, the 5 (at the hundreds column).

(Notice that $3 \times 6 = 18$ tens. 18 tens plus 1 ten carried over from Step 1 equals 19 tens. **Regroup 19 tens as 1 hundred 9 tens.** The 1 hundred is carried to the hundreds column. 9 tens is written in the tens column.)

Step 3: Multiply the hundreds. Add any hundreds carried over from Step 2, and regroup if necessary
3 times 5 equals 15, plus the 1 you carried from Step 2, equals 16. Regrouping is not necessary because there is no next digit (no digit in the hundreds column to work with). Write the 6 under the hundreds column and write 1 in the thousands column or simply write the 16 in front of the 9.

Shortcut Method

A detailed explanation for solving the problem is provided step-by-step so that the student can understand the concept. Once the concept is understood, only the summary of Step 3 (as shown below) may be provided as the solution to similar problems during homework and tests.

$$\begin{array}{r} 11 \\ 564 \\ \times \quad 3 \\ \hline 1692 \end{array}$$

Critical Thinking

1. In Example **3**, Step 3, the 3 times 5 is really 3×500 because the 5 in the multiplicand is in the hundreds column.
2. In Example **1**, Step 2, the 2 times 2 is really 2×20 because the 2 in the multiplicand is in the tens column.

The notes and the generous examples have provided me with the conceptual understanding and the computational fluency to do my homework.

Exercises

1. Describe regrouping.

2. Find each product. Hint: See Example 1.

a. 22	**b.** 14	**c.** 33	**d.** 44
× 4	× 2	× 3	× 2

3. Find each product. Hint: See Example 2.

a. 24	**b.** 15	**c.** 12	**d.** 55
× 3	× 4	× 9	× 3

e. 27	**f.** 19	**g.** 21	**h.** 49
× 6	× 4	× 7	× 4

i. 56	**j.** 78	**k.** 99	**l.** 64
× 7	× 2	× 2	× 3

4. Find each product. Hint: See Example 2.

22

a. 553 × 4	b. 125 × 7	c. 234 × 8	d. 349 × 9
e. 148 × 4	f. 718 × 4	g. 389 × 7	h. 174 × 9
i. 642 × 6	j. 408 × 5	k. 636 × 2	l. 709 × 8
m. 934 × 8	n. 606 × 6	o. 844 × 7	p. 438 × 4
q. 884 × 6	r. 196 × 7	s. 346 × 4	t. 564 × 8

Answers to Selected Questions

2a. 88   **2b.** 28   **3a.** 72   **3b.** 60   **4a.** 2212   **4b.** 875

Challenge Questions

1. Find each product.

a. 339 × 4	b. 65 × 6	c. 26 × 9	d. 846 × 4
e. 24 × 9	f. 62 × 4	g. 21 × 9	h. 874 × 3

2. Find 8×437. Hint: 8×437 may be written as:

$$\begin{array}{r} 437 \\ \times 8 \\ \hline \end{array}$$

3. Find 943×6. Hint: 943×6 may be written as:

$$\begin{array}{r} 943 \\ \times 6 \\ \hline \end{array}$$

Multiplying Four-Digit and One-Digit Numbers

The steps for multiplying a 3-digit number by a 1-digit number can be extended to multiplying a 4-digit number by a 1-digit number.

Example 1

Find: 8,403
         ×   7
         ―――――

Solution

To provide a detailed understanding, the problem is written showing the place values of the multiplicand.

Step 1: Multiply the ones. Regroup if necessary.

    7 times 3 equals 21. Regroup, write 1 under the ones column and carry the 2 to the next digit, the 0 (at the tens column).

    (Notice that $7 \times 3 = 21$ ones. **Regroup 21 ones as 2 tens 1 one.** The 2 tens is carried over to the tens column.)

Step 2: Multiply the tens. Add any extra tens carried over from Step 1 and regroup if necessary.

    $7 \times 0 = 0$, plus the 2 you carried from Step 1, equals 2. Write the 2 under the tens column.

    (Notice that $7 \times 0 = 0$, so there is no hundreds to be carried over to the hundreds column, and therefore, regrouping is not necessary.)

Step 3: Multiply the hundreds. Add any extra hundreds carried over from Step 2 and regroup if necessary

    7 times 4 equals 28. We did not carry over any hundreds from Step 2, so, write the 8 under the hundreds column and carry the 2 to the next digit, the 8 (at the thousands column).

Tens column
Ones column
Carry 2 to the next digit
2 2
8,403
× 7
821

(Notice that $7 \times 4 = 28$ hundreds. **Regroup 28 hundreds as 2 thousands 8 hundreds.** The 2 thousands is carried to the thousands column and the 8 hundreds is written in the hundreds column.)

Step 4: **Multiply the thousands. Add extra thousands carried over from Step 3 and regroup if necessary.**

7 time 8 equals 56, plus the 2 you carried from Step 3, equals 58. Write the 8 under the thousands column and write the 5 under the ten thousands column or simply write the 58 in front of the 8 in the answer (product).

Ten thousands column
Tens column
Ones column
2 2
8,403
× 7
58,821   **Answer**

Shortcut Method

A detailed explanation for solving the problem is provided step-by-step so that the student can understand the concept. Once the concept is understood, only the summary of Step 4 (as shown below) may be provided as the solution to similar problems during homework and tests.

2 2
8,403
× 7
58,821   **Answer**

Example 2 - Group Exercise

A theater sold 5704 tickets at $6 each. How much money was received from the sale of the tickets?

Solution

Set up the solution as follows:

Money received from the sale of the tickets = 5,704 × $6

5704 × $6 may be written as:

5,704
× 6

25

Hint: Multiply as in Example 1.

Example 3 - Group Exercise

There are 2,462 packages of hamburgers in a store. If there are 4 frozen hamburgers in a package, how many frozen hamburgers are in the store?

Solution

Set up the solution as follows:

The number of frozen hamburgers in the store = 2,462 × 4.

2,462 × 4 may be written as:

$$
\begin{array}{r}
2{,}462 \\
\times \quad 4 \\
\hline
\end{array}
$$

Hint: Multiply as in Example 1.

The notes and the generous examples have provided me with the conceptual understanding and the computational fluency to do my homework.

Exercises

1. Find the product. Hint: See Example 1.

a. $\begin{array}{r}2{,}324 \\ \times \quad 4 \\ \hline\end{array}$	**b.** $\begin{array}{r}6{,}842 \\ \times \quad 3 \\ \hline\end{array}$	**c.** $\begin{array}{r}7{,}035 \\ \times \quad 3 \\ \hline\end{array}$	**d.** $\begin{array}{r}1{,}648 \\ \times \quad 9 \\ \hline\end{array}$
e. $\begin{array}{r}8{,}115 \\ \times \quad 7 \\ \hline\end{array}$	**f.** $\begin{array}{r}6{,}567 \\ \times \quad 4 \\ \hline\end{array}$	**g.** $\begin{array}{r}1{,}762 \\ \times \quad 3 \\ \hline\end{array}$	**h.** $\begin{array}{r}3{,}481 \\ \times \quad 3 \\ \hline\end{array}$

2. Find the product.

6 × 3489

Hint: 6 × 3489 is the same as:

$$
\begin{array}{r}
3489 \\
\times \quad 6 \\
\hline
\end{array}
$$

Hint: See Example 1.

3. Find the product.

4672 × 3

Hint: 4672 × 3 is the same as:

$$
\begin{array}{r}
4672 \\
\times \quad 3 \\
\hline
\end{array}
$$

Hint: See Example 1.

4. A copier can copy 2,849 pages per day. How many pages can the copier copy in 4 days? Hint: Set up the solution as in Example 2 and solve with the help of Example 1.
5. A book is sold for $3. Find the cost of the following numbers of similar books.
   a. 3,745   **b.** 2,148   **c.** 7,119   **d.** 2,043
   Hint: Set up the solution as in Example 3 and solve with the help of Example 1.
6. A copier can copy 3,746 pages per day. How many pages can the same copier copy in:
   a. 2 days?   **b.** 3 days?   **c.** 4 days?   **d.** 5 days?
   Hint: Set up the solution as in Example 2 and solve with the help of Example 1.

Challenge Questions

7. The cost of a school lunch is $3. How much is the cost of a similar school lunch for:
   a. 2,984 students?   **b.** 1,408 students?   **c.** 6,781 students?
8. Find the product.

   a. 1,734   **b.** 2,847   **c.** 9,436   **d.** 8,345
   $\times$ 4 $\times$ 2 $\times$ 3 $\times$ 7

9. Find the product.
   $4 \times \$2,364$
   Hint: $4 \times \$2,364$ is the same as:
   $\$2,364$
   $\times$ 4

   Hint: Do the multiplication and then attach a dollar symbol to your answer.
10. Find the product.
   $\$4,165 \times 6$
   Hint: $\$4,165 \times 6$ is the same as:
   $\$4,165$
   $\times$ 6

Hint: Do the multiplication and then attach a dollar symbol to your answer.

Answers to Selected Questions
1a. 9,296   **5a.** $11,235   **6a.** 7,492   **9.** $9,456

Cumulative Review
1. Add.

   a. 234   **b.** 629   **c.** 178   **d.** 234
   + 375   +   86   + 211   + 178

27

2. Subtract.

   a.   74   **b.**   97   **c.**   400   **d.**   368
      - 56   - 36   - 214   - 149

3. Multiply.

   a.   79   **b.**   63   **c.**   468   **d.**   2416
      ×   9   ×   6   ×   7   ×   3

4. Find the missing numbers.

   a. $? \times 5 = 45$ **b.** $9 \times ? = 63$ **c.** $12 \times ? = 144$ **d.** $8 \times 9 = ?$

   e. $7 \times 4 = ?$ **f.** $7 \times ? = 49$ **g.** $6 \times ? = 12$ **h.** $3 \times 11 = ?$

Answers to Selected Questions

1a. 609   **2a.** 18   **3a.** 711

Multiplying by 2-Digit Numbers
How to multiply by 2-digit numbers.

When a multiplier has two or more digits, you must multiply each digit of the multiplier separately by the multiplicand (the top number). Each multiplication then gives a partial product or answer. When the partial products or answers are added, the product is obtained. Example of a problem multiplied by 2-digit numbers is:

        45 ◄――― **Multiplicand**
     × 27 ◄――――― **Multiplier (two digit number)**

Example 1
Find the product: 45×27
Solution
Set Up: Set up the problem by lining up the ones digit of the multiplicand.

        45
     × 27

Step 1: Multiply the ones. Regroup if necessary.

    Using the ones digit of the multiplier, multiply from right to left.
    $7 \times 5 = 35$. Regroup, write the 5 directly under the 7, the digit you are multiplying with. Carry the 3 to the next digit of the multiplicand, the 4 (at the tens column).

28

Carry 3 to the next digit, 4.

Write 5 directly under the 7, the digit you are working with.

$7 \times 4 = 28$, plus the 3 you carried from Step 1, equals 31. Write the 31 in front of the 5. The number 315 is the first partial answer.

$$
\begin{array}{r}
3 \\
45 \\
\times\ 27 \\
\hline
315
\end{array}
$$
← **First partial product**

(Notice that $7 \times 5 = 35$ ones. Regroup 35 ones as 3 tens 5 ones. The 3 tens is carried over to the tens column and the 5 ones is written in the ones column under the 7.)

Step 2: **Place a zero in the ones place as a place holder**. **Multiply the tens. Regroup if necessary.**

Place a zero in the ones place as a place holder. Using the tens digit of the multiplier, 2, multiply from right to left. Align the right-hand digit of this partial product ($2 \times 5 = 10$) under the digit (2) you are multiplying with.

$2 \times 5 = 10$. Write the 0, aligned under the 2 you are multiplying with. Carry the 1 to the next digit, the 4 (at the tens column).

Carry I to the next digit, 4.

Align this 0 with the 2 (tens column), the digit you are multiplying with.

Always place a zero at the ones column as a place holder before you multiply by the tens digit of any multiplier.

$2 \times 4 = 8$, plus the 1 you carried equals 9. Write the 9 in front of the 00. The 900 is the second partial product.

$$
\begin{array}{r}
1 \\
3 \\
45 \\
\times\ 27 \\
\hline
315 \\
900
\end{array}
$$

315 ← First partial product (7 ones $\times 45 = 315$)
900 ← Second partial product (2 tens $\times 45 = 90$ tens $= 90 \times 10 = 900$)
↑ Write the 9 in front of the 00 (at the hundreds column.)

Step 3: Add the partial products.

```
      1
      3
     45
 ×   27
    315
    900
   1215 ←——  Answer
                Product
```

Shortcut Method

A detailed explanation for solving the problem is provided step-by-step so that the student can understand the concept. Once the concept is understood, only the summary of Step 3 (as shown below) may be provided as the solution to similar problems during homework and tests.

```
      1
      3
     45
 ×   27
    315
    900
   1215
```

Example 2

Find 28 × 376

Solution

Set up:

28 × 376 can be written as:

```
   376
 ×  28
```

Step 1: **Multiply by the ones. Regroup if necessary. Using the ones digit of the multiplier, multiply from right to left.**

8 × 6 = 48. Regroup, write the 8, aligned with the 8 in the multiplier (the ones column), the digit you are multiplying with. Carry the 4 over to the next digit of the multiplicand, the 7 (at the tens column).

Carry the 4 to the next multiplicand, the 7 (at the tens column.)

```
          →4
       376 ←—— Multiplicand
 ×      28 ←—— Multiplier
         8
         ↑
```
Write 8, aligned with the digit you are working with in the multiplier, the 8 (aligned with the ones column.)

(Notice that 8 × 6 = 48 ones. Regroup 48 ones as 4 tens 8 ones. The 4 tens is carried over to the tens column and the 8 ones is written in the ones column.) $8 \times 7 = 56$, plus the 4 you carried over equals 60. Regroup, write the 0, aligned with the tens column and carry the 6 to the next digit, the 3 (at the hundreds column).

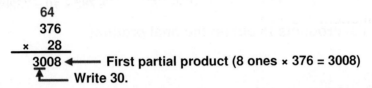

Carry the 6 to the next multiplicand, the 3 (at the hundreds column.)

64
376 ← Multiplicand
× 28 ← Multiplier
08
↑ Write 0.

$8 \times 3 = 24$, plus the 6 carried over from the tens column, equals 30. There is no number next to 3 (at the thousands column) for us to regroup, so write 30 in front of 08 (or write 30 so that the last digit of the 30 is aligned with the hundreds column.)

64
376
× 28
‾‾‾‾
3008 ← First partial product (8 ones × 376 = 3008)
↑ Write 30.

Step 2: Place a zero in the ones place or column as a place holder before multiplying by the tens digit of the multiplier. Multiply the tens. Regroup if necessary.

Place a zero in the ones place or column as a place holder before multiplying by the tens digit of the multiplier, the 2.

2 tens × 6 = 12 tens. Regroup, write the 2, aligned with the digit in the multiplier that you are working with, the 2 (at the tens column.) Carry the 1 over to the next digit of the multiplicand, the 7 (at the tens column.)

Carry the 1 to the next multiplicand, the 3 (at the hundreds column.)

1
64
376
× 28
‾‾‾‾
3008
20
↑↑ Always put 0 here as a place holder before multiplying by the tens digit of the multiplier.

Write the 2 tens in the tens column as 2 or write the 2, aligned with the digit of the multiplier you are working with, the 2.

(Notice that 2 tens × 6 = 12 tens. Regroup 12 tens [12 × 10 = 120] as 1 hundred 2 tens. Carry the 1 hundred, as 1, to the next digit of the multiplicand, the 3, in the hundreds column. The 2 tens is written as 2 in the tens column.)

$2 \times 7 = 14$, plus the 1 carried over from the tens column equals 15. Regroup, write 5 in the hundreds column and carry 1 to the thousands column.

Carry the 1 to the thousands column.

```
        11
        64
       376
   ×    28
      3008
       520
```
↳ **Write 5.**

$2 \times 3 = 6$, plus the 1 carried over equals 7. Write the 7.

```
        11
        64
       376
   ×    28
      3008  ← First partial product (8 ones × 376 = 3008)
      7520  ← Second partial product (2 tens × 376 = 752 tens
Write 7 ↑              = 752 × 10 = 7520)
```

Step 3: Add the partial products to obtain the final product

```
        11
        64
       376
   ×    28
      3008  ← First partial product (8 ones × 376 = 3008)
      7520  ← Second partial product (2 tens × 376 = 752 tens
     10528  Answer       = 752 × 10 = 7520)
```

So 376 × 28 = 10528

Shortcut Method

A detailed explanation for solving the problem is provided step-by-step so that the student can understand the concept. Once the concept is understood, only the summary of Step 3 (as shown below) may be provided as the solution to similar problems during homework and tests.

```
        11
        64
       376
   ×    28
      3008
      7520
     10528
```

The notes and the generous examples have provided me with the conceptual understanding and the computational fluency to do my homework.

Exercises

1. Describe how you can multiply by a 2-digit number. Hint: Summarize the steps in solving the problem.
2. John said that to multiply by the digit at the tens column of a multiplier, you should first write 0, as a place holder. Is this statement correct? Explain your answer.
3. Multiply. Hint: See Example 1.

a. $\begin{array}{r}37\\ \times\,37\\ \hline\end{array}$	**b.** $\begin{array}{r}94\\ \times\,25\\ \hline\end{array}$	**c.** $\begin{array}{r}72\\ \times\,29\\ \hline\end{array}$	**d.** $\begin{array}{r}63\\ \times\,58\\ \hline\end{array}$
e. $\begin{array}{r}53\\ \times\,24\\ \hline\end{array}$	**f.** $\begin{array}{r}19\\ \times\,29\\ \hline\end{array}$	**g.** $\begin{array}{r}78\\ \times\,64\\ \hline\end{array}$	**h.** $\begin{array}{r}48\\ \times\,29\\ \hline\end{array}$
i. $\begin{array}{r}81\\ \times\,23\\ \hline\end{array}$	**j.** $\begin{array}{r}27\\ \times\,28\\ \hline\end{array}$	**k.** $\begin{array}{r}46\\ \times\,45\\ \hline\end{array}$	**l.** $\begin{array}{r}34\\ \times\,23\\ \hline\end{array}$
m. $\begin{array}{r}61\\ \times\,16\\ \hline\end{array}$	**n.** $\begin{array}{r}72\\ \times\,17\\ \hline\end{array}$	**o.** $\begin{array}{r}94\\ \times\,64\\ \hline\end{array}$	**p.** $\begin{array}{r}19\\ \times\,38\\ \hline\end{array}$
q. $\begin{array}{r}86\\ \times\,17\\ \hline\end{array}$	**r.** $\begin{array}{r}28\\ \times\,19\\ \hline\end{array}$	**s.** $\begin{array}{r}34\\ \times\,16\\ \hline\end{array}$	**t.** $\begin{array}{r}49\\ \times\,29\\ \hline\end{array}$

u. $94 \times 33 =$ **v.** $23 \times 74 =$ **w.** $13 \times 79 =$ **x.** $39 \times 58 =$

4. Multiply. Hint: See Example 2.

a. $\begin{array}{r}648\\ \times\,34\\ \hline\end{array}$	**b.** $\begin{array}{r}589\\ \times\,23\\ \hline\end{array}$	**c.** $\begin{array}{r}237\\ \times\,14\\ \hline\end{array}$	**d.** $\begin{array}{r}634\\ \times\,19\\ \hline\end{array}$
e. $\begin{array}{r}137\\ \times\,27\\ \hline\end{array}$	**f.** $\begin{array}{r}390\\ \times\,25\\ \hline\end{array}$	**g.** $\begin{array}{r}685\\ \times\,15\\ \hline\end{array}$	**h.** $\begin{array}{r}138\\ \times\,17\\ \hline\end{array}$
i. $\begin{array}{r}636\\ \times\,95\\ \hline\end{array}$	**j.** $\begin{array}{r}272\\ \times\,25\\ \hline\end{array}$	**k.** $\begin{array}{r}146\\ \times\,48\\ \hline\end{array}$	**l.** $\begin{array}{r}734\\ \times\,39\\ \hline\end{array}$
m. $\begin{array}{r}188\\ \times\,27\\ \hline\end{array}$	**n.** $\begin{array}{r}904\\ \times\,39\\ \hline\end{array}$	**o.** $\begin{array}{r}423\\ \times\,19\\ \hline\end{array}$	**p.** $\begin{array}{r}662\\ \times\,17\\ \hline\end{array}$

q. 807	r. 714	s. 934	t. 593
× 34	× 22	× 12	× 54

u. 399	v. 834	w. 178	x. 245
× 63	× 45	× 72	× 46

5. Multiply. Hint: See Example 2.
   a. 344 × 29 =   b. 246 × 34 =   c. 628 × 17 =   d. 164 × 95 =

6. Multiply. Hint: See Examples 2.
   a. 32 × 246 =   b. 19 × 568 =   c. 47 × 217 =
   d. 13 × 798 =   e. 99 × 348 =   f. 58 × 291 =

Challenge Questions

7. Multiply.

a. 79	b. 287	c. 54	d. 9041
× 32	× 78	× 16	× 26

e. 14 × 438 =   f. 714 × 33 =   g. 274 × 75 =   h. 69 × 709 =

i. 28 × 228 =   j. 963 × 13 =   k. 4 × 867 =   l. 34 × 19 =

Answers to Selected Questions

3a. 1,369	3b. 2,350	4a. 22,032	4b. 13,547
5a. 9,976	5b. 8,364	6a. 7,872	6b. 10,792

REAL WORLD APPLICATIONS - WORD PROBLEMS

Example 1 - Group Exercise

Eric can type 43 words per minute. How many words can he type in 38 minutes, if he types at the same speed?

Solution

Set up the solution as shown:

In 1 minute, he types 43 words.

In 38 minutes, he will type 38 × 43 words.

38 × 43 may be written as:

     38
  × 43

Hint: Use the solution method under the section "Multiplying by 2-Digit Numbers," Example 1, to perform the multiplication in detail.

So, Eric can type 1,634 words in 43 minutes.

Example 2

There are 128 oranges in a bag. How many oranges are in 45 similar bags?

Solution

1 bag contains 128 oranges.

45 bags will contain 45 × 128 oranges.

45 × 128 can be written as:

```
    128
×    45
```

Hint: Use the solution method under the section "Multiplying by 2-Digit Numbers," Example 2, to perform the multiplication in detail.

```
     13
     14
    128
×    45
    640 ◄──── First partial product (5 ones × 128 = 640)
   5120 ◄──── Second partial product (4 tens × 128 = 512 tens
   5760  oranges                                  = 512 × 10 = 5120)
```

So, there are 5,760 oranges in 45 similar bags.

Example 3

A school buys 66 pairs of running shoes. If it costs $19 per a pair of shoes, how much did the school pay for the 66 pairs of shoes?

Solution

1 pair of shoes cost $19.

66 pairs of shoes will cost 66 × $19.

66 × $19 may be written as:

```
    66
×   19
```

Hint: Use the solution method under the section "Multiplying by 2-Digit Numbers," Example 1, to perform the multiplication in detail.

```
       5
      66
  ×   19
     594 ◄──── First partial product (9 ones × 66 = 594
     660 ◄──── Second partial product (1 ten × 66 = 66 tens
   $1254                              = 66 × 10 = 660)
     ▲
     └──── Attach the dollar symbol.
```

So, 66 pairs of shoes will cost $1,254.

The notes and the generous examples have provided me with the conceptual understanding and the computational fluency to do my homework.

Exercises

1. Mary can type 37 words per minute. How many words can she type in 23 minutes? Hint: See Example 1.

2. James can type 26 words per minute. How many words can he type in 42 minutes? Hint: See Example 1.

3. There are 246 apples in a bag. How many apples are in 19 similar bags? Hint: See Example 2.

4. There are 138 pencils in a box. How many pencils are in 35 similar boxes? Hint: See Example 1.

5. There are 93 pens in a box. How many pens are in 17 similar boxes? Hint: See Example 2.

6. An auditorium has 134 rows of seats, with 43 seats in each row. What is the total number of seats. Hint: See Example 2.

7. A calculator is sold for $28. What is the cost of 32 similar calculators? Hint: See Example 3.

8. Ama makes $56 per week for baby-sitting. How much money does she make in 12 weeks? Hint: See Example 3.

9. John makes $42 per month for baby-sitting.
   a. How much does he make in 14 months?
   b. How much does he make in one year?
      (12 months = 1 year). Hint: See Example 3

10. Multiply: 16 × $246. Hint: See Example 3.

Answers to Selected Questions

1. 851 words   **6.** 5762 seats

Challenge Questions

11. John can type 30 words per minute. How many words can he type in 19 minutes?

12. Elizabeth can type 28 words per minute. How many words can she type in 37 minutes?

13. There are 146 apples in a bag. How many apples are in 26 similar bags?

14. There are 108 pencils in a box. How many pencils are in 12 similar boxes?

15. An auditorium has 121 rows of seats, with 29 seats in each row. What is the total number of seats.

16. A calculator is sold for $13. What is the cost of 19 similar calculators?

17. Ama makes $46 per week for baby-sitting. How much money does she make in 14 weeks?

18. John makes $66 per month for baby-sitting.
   a. How much does he make in 16 months?
   b. How much does he make in one year?
      (12 months = 1 year).

19. Multiply: 14 × $274

Cumulative Review

1. Add.

a. 99	**b.** 64	**c.** 126	**d.** 341
+ 145	+ 28	+ 248	+ 299

2. Subtract.

a. 74	**b.** 36	**c.** 401	**d.** 658
- 29	- 9	- 198	- 246

3. Multiply.

a. 12	**b** 418	**c.** 141	**d.** 49
× 3	× 3	× 19	× 56

4. 7 × 0 =   **5.** 0 × 7 =   **6.** 86 - 49 =   **7.** 87 + 173 =

8. Find the missing numbers.
   a. 6 × ? = 36   **b.** ? × 7 = 49   **c.** 9 × ? = 63
   d. 12 × 10 = ?   **e.** 12 × 12 = ?   **f.** 12 × ? = 144

9. The product of two numbers is 0, what is one of the numbers?

10. Multiply.
   a. 7 × $148 =   **b.** $296 × 36 =   **c.** 48 × 249 =

Answers to Selected Questions

1a. 244   **2a.** 45   **3a.** 36   **8a.** 6   **10a.** $1036

CHAPTER 2

ESTIMATING PRODUCTS

New Terms: compatible numbers, rounding

Compatible Numbers and Rounding
There are several methods of estimation. We will discuss estimations using **compatible numbers** and **rounding**.
Compatible numbers are two or more numbers that are easy to compute with mentally. You can estimate using compatible numbers. First, change a factor or factors of a product (number) to compatible numbers by changing a factor or factors to a number or numbers that will make the numbers easy to compute with mentally.

Rounding is to change a factor or factors to the nearest ten, hundred, thousand, ..., so that we can easily compute with the factors mentally. (Hint: Read the section on Place Values and Rounding before reading the examples). You can estimate products by rounding one or both of the factors of the product to the nearest ten, hundred, thousand,..., so that the multiplication can be done mentally.

Note: In general,   **Product**

$$a \times b = c$$

        Factor   **Factor**

Example 1
Estimate 4×27 using:
a. compatible numbers. Is the answer an underestimate or an overestimate?
b. rounding. Is the answer an underestimate or an overestimate?
Solution
a. We can replace 27 with 25, because we can mentally multiply 4 by 25 to obtain 100 as shown:
        4×27 is about 4×25
        $4 \times 25 = 100$
So 4×27 is about 100.
Notice that 27 was adjusted to 25, which is less than 27, so the answer is an **underestimate**. So, the exact answer must be greater than 100.
b. We can round 27 to 30. Note that the rounding is done to the nearest ten.
(Hint: See the chapter/section on Rounding and Place Values.)

Round 27 to 30.

4×27 is about 4×30

↓

$4 \times 30 = 120$ Rounded to the nearest ten

So, 4×27 is about 120.

Notice that 27 was rounded to 30, which is greater than 27.

So, the answer is an **overestimate**. So the exact product (answer) must be less than 120.

Example 2

Estimate 8×253 using compatible numbers.

Solution

We can replace 253 with 250 because four 250s is 1,000 ($4 \times 250 = 1000$ and $8 \times 250 = 2000$). Recall that we are looking for compatible numbers.

8×253

↓

$8 \times 250 = 2000$

⌄

Compatible numbers

So, 8×253 is about 2,000.

Example 3

Estimate $3 \times 2{,}194$ using rounding.

Solution

Round 2,194 to the nearest thousand, which is 2000. Multiply as shown:

$3 \times 2{,}194$

↓

$3 \times 2{,}000 = 6{,}000$ Rounded to the nearest thousand
                                     Note: $3 \times 2 = 6$, and then attach the three 0s to obtain 6,000.

So, $3 \times 2{,}194$ is about 6000.

Example 4

Estimate 187×313 using rounding.

Solution

Round each number to the nearest hundred, and then multiply as shown:

$$
\begin{array}{rcl}
187 & \rightarrow & 200 \\
\times \ 313 & \rightarrow & \times \ 300 \\
\hline
& & 60{,}000
\end{array}
$$

Rounded to the nearest hundred
Rounded to the nearest hundred
Note: $3 \times 2 = 6$, and then attach the four 0s to obtain 60,000.

So, 187×313 is about 60,000.

Notice that in this example, both factors were rounded to the nearest hundred.

39

Example 5

Estimate 72×866 using rounding.

Solution

Round 72 to the nearest ten to obtain 70, round 866 to the nearest hundred to obtain 900, and then multiply as shown:

$$
\begin{array}{rcl}
72 & \rightarrow & 70 \\
\times\ 866 & \rightarrow & \times\ 900 \\
\hline
& & 63,000
\end{array}
$$

Rounded to the nearest ten
Rounded to the nearest hundred
Note: $9 \times 7 = 63$, and then attach the three 0s to obtain 63,000.

So, 72×866 is about 63,000.

Note: In this solution, both factors were rounded. One factor (72) was rounded to the nearest ten and the other factor (866) was rounded to the nearest hundred.

The notes and the generous examples have provided me with the conceptual understanding and the computational fluency to do my homework.

Exercises

1. Explain compatible numbers.
2. Explain rounding. Hint: You may read the chapter/section on Place Values and Rounding.
3. Explain an overestimate in estimating a product. Hint: See Example 1(a).
4. Explain an underestimate in estimating a product. Hint: See Example 1(b).
5. Estimate 4×26 using:
    a. Compatible numbers.
    b. rounding.
    c. Is your answer to 5(a) an overestimate or an underestimate? Explain your answer.
    d. Is your answer to 5(b) an overestimate or an underestimate? Explain your answer.
    Hint: See Example 1.
6. Estimate each product using rounding.
    a. 4×92 **b.** 77×3 **c.** 2×388
    Hint: See Example 1
7. Estimate 4×244 using compatible numbers. Hint: See Example 2.
8a. Estimate 4×256 using compatible numbers. Hint: See Example 2.
8b. Explain whether your answer to exercise **8a** is an overestimate or an underestimate. Hint: See Example 1.

9. Estimate the following products using rounding.
  a. 3×315 **b.** $4 \times 2{,}204$ **c.** $2{,}181 \times 3$
  d. $5 \times 1{,}234$ **e.** 709×5 **f.** $8{,}109 \times 3$
  Hint: See Example 3. (Do you have to round to the nearest hundred or to the nearest thousand as needed in order to solve each problem? The answer is yes.)
10. Estimate the following using rounding.
  a. 199×202 **b.** 189×295 **c.** 212×204 **d.** 219×305
  Hint: See Example 4.
11. Estimate each product using rounding
  a. 92×714 **b.** 604×62 **c.** 102×42

  d. $\begin{array}{r} 294 \\ \times\ \ 19 \\ \hline \end{array}$ **e.** $\begin{array}{r} 320 \\ \times\ \ 87 \\ \hline \end{array}$ **f.** $\begin{array}{r} 305 \\ \times\ \ 12 \\ \hline \end{array}$

  Hint: See Example 5.

Real World Application - Word Problem
12. A rectangular garden is 406 feet long and 27 feet wide. Estimate the area of the rectangle by rounding. Hint: See Example 5.
  The formula for finding the area of a rectangle is:
      Area = **Length** × **Width**.
  Read the chapter/section on the Area of a Rectangle before solving this problem.)

Challenge Questions
13. Estimate each product:
  a. 33×122 **b.** 5×970 **c.** 92×52

  d. $\begin{array}{r} 301 \\ \times\ \ 13 \\ \hline \end{array}$ **e.** $\begin{array}{r} 292 \\ \times\ \ 8 \\ \hline \end{array}$ **f.** $\begin{array}{r} 321 \\ \times\ \ 86 \\ \hline \end{array}$

14. Explain whether your answer to each of the exercises 13**a** to 13f is an overestimate or an underestimate.

Answers to Selected Questions
6a. About 360 **7.** About 1000 **9a.** About 900 **10a.** About 40,000

41

CHAPTER 3

DIVISION OF WHOLE NUMBERS

Whole numbers are numbers that we use for counting. All whole numbers are formed from the digits 0, 1, 2, 3, 4, 5, 6, 7, 8, and 9. For example, the number 25 contains the digits 2 and 5.

Division Without a Remainder

Division is the process to find out how many times a number (the **divisor**) is contained in another number (the **dividend**). The answer to any division question is called the **quotient**.

The division symbols are ÷, ⌐ , and ——

A division number sentence may be written in three ways as shown:

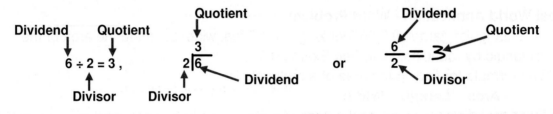

Example 1

$6 \div 2 =$

Solution

The question $6 \div 2 =$ can be read as six divided by two is equal to what? The question means how many 2s are there in 6? Since $2 \times 3 = 6$, there are 3 of the 2s in 6. So, $6 \div 2 = 3$. (Knowing the multiplication tables is helpful in understanding and solving division problems because division is the opposite of multiplication.)

Group Exercise 1

The class should be divided into four groups. Each group should be given 6 counters.

1. The goal in this Group Exercise 1 is to solve Example 1 by dividing 6 counters equally into 2 groups of 3 counters as shown below. This represents $6 \div 2$. The 6 counters can be divided into 2 equal groups of 3 counters as shown:

6 counters

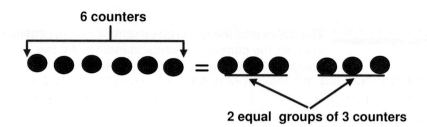

2 equal groups of 3 counters

Therefore, 6 ÷ 2 = 3. This Group Exercise 1 confirms that using multiplication to solve division problem as in Example **1** is correct. Think about division as equally sharing.

2. Each group should find the answer to 6 ÷ 3 by using 6 counters. Note that 6 ÷ 3 means 6 divided by 3. This also means how many 3s are there in 6. The answer can be found by dividing 6 counters into 3 equal groups to obtain 2 counters in each group as shown:

6 counters

3 equal groups of 2 counters

Think about division as equally sharing.

3. Each group should model the solution of 6 ÷ 2 = 3, and 6 ÷ 3 = 2 as in the Group Exercise 1 and also as in Example 1, using multiplication facts to solve:

    a. 12 ÷ 3 = ?   Hint: Divide 12 counters equally into 3 groups such that each group contains the same number of counters. How many counters are in each of the 3 groups? Now use the related multiplication facts to confirm your answer by finding the number that can be multiplied by 3 to obtain 12. The number is 4. Since 3 × 4 = 12, so, 12 ÷ 3 = 4.

    b. 15 ÷ 5 = ?
    c. 20 ÷ 4 = ?
    d. 24 ÷ 6 = ?
    e. 30 ÷ 5 = ?
    f. 36 ÷ 4 = ?
    g. 56 ÷ 8 = ?

4. Each group will demonstrate how it solved each division problem.

Critical Thinking

Example 1 and the Group Exercise 1 confirm that **multiplication facts can be used to find division facts**.

The notes and the generous examples have provided me with the conceptual understanding and the computational fluency to do my homework.

Exercises

Solve each question. Hint: See Example **1**. Use multiplication facts.

1. $9 \div 3 =$ **2.** $8 \div 2 =$ **3.** $28 \div 7 =$ **4.** $48 \div 6 =$

5. $39 \div 3 =$ **6.** $40 \div 8 =$ **7.** $54 \div 9 =$ **8.** $64 \div 8 =$

9. $72 \div 9 =$ **10.** $81 \div 9 =$ **11.** $45 \div 5 =$ **12.** $64 \div 8 =$

13. Describe how you can use multiplication facts to divide.

14. Thirty oranges are to be divided equally among 6 students. How many oranges will each student get? Hint: Set up the question as shown:
What number multiplied by 6 equals 30? or $30 \div 6 = ?$

15. Twelve dollars is to be divided equally among 3 boys. How many dollars will each boy receive?

16. $36 \div 6 =$ **17.** $21 \div 3 =$ **18.** $21 \div 7 =$ **19.** $9 \div 3 =$

20. Three girls are to share nine pens equally. How many pens will each girl get?
Hint: "Share equally" is the same as "Divide equally."

Challenge Questions

21. You need to arrange 12 people into rows of 3. How many rows can you make?
Hint: You may use counters to represent people in rows. Think of what number multiplied by 3 equals 12.

22. John wants to plant 15 flowers in 5 rows. How many flowers should he put in each row? Hint: You may use counters to represent flowers. Think of what number multiplied by 5 equals 15.

Answers to Selected Questions

1. 3   **4.** 8

Exploring Division as Sharing

The goal in the Group Exercise 1 is to solve Example **1** by dividing 6 counters equally into 2 groups of 3 counters. The 6 counters can be divided into 2 equal groups of 3 counters. This division problem can similarly be stated as "To **share** 6 counters equally between 2 people, and the result is 3 counters per person or 2 equal groups of 3 counters. The **critical thinking is that division is the same as sharing**.

Exploring Division as Repeated Subtraction

Suppose that Nicholas eats 2 cookies a day. He wants to know how many days it will take him to eat 12 cookies. This problem can be solved by taking away groups of 2 cookies from 12 cookies. There will be 6 equal groups of 2 cookies. So he will take 6 days to eat 12 cookies. This solution is shown below using 12 counters instead of 12 cookies.

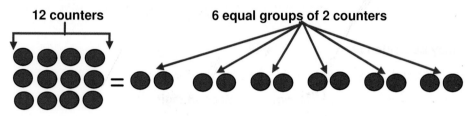

Notice that 12 ÷ 6 = 2, which is similar to 6 equal groups of 2 counters. So **repeated subtraction** is another way to understand division.

Group Exercise 2

Suppose that Mary eats 3 cookies a day. She wants to know how many days it will take her to eat 9 cookies.

1. Describe how to solve this problem using division as repeated subtraction.
   Hint: See the section under "Exploring Division as Repeated Subtraction."
2. Use counters to solve the problem.
   Hint: See the section under "Exploring Division as Repeated Subtraction."
3. Each group should write their answer on the overhead. Are the answers from each group the same? Explain if there is any difference.

How can you tell where to start dividing?

Move from left to right along the dividend as many digits as is necessary to be equal or greater than the divisor, then begin to divide. Explain how the following divisions should be started:

Explanations

a.

Move from left to right along the dividend as many digits as is necessary to be as large as or larger than the divisor, then begin to divide.

The divisor is 4, and moving along the dividend 48, from left to right, the first digit is 4. Since the divisor is as large as the first digit of the dividend, the division should be started by dividing 4 by 4.

b.

Move from left to right along the dividend as many digits as is necessary to be equal or greater than the divisor, then begin to divide.

The divisor is 4, and moving along the dividend 16, from left to right, the first digit is 1. Since the first digit of the dividend is smaller than the divisor, 1 cannot be divided by 4 to result in a whole number or a number greater than a whole number. So combine the first and the second digits of the dividend, which is 16. Since 16 is larger than the divisor, the division should be started by dividing 16 by 4.

c.

Move from left to right along the dividend as many digits as is necessary to be as large as or larger than the divisor, then begin to divide.

The divisor is 5, and moving along the dividend 624, from left to right, the first digit is 6. Since the first digit of the dividend is larger than the divisor, the division should be started by dividing 6 by 5.

d.

Move from left to right along the dividend as many digits as is necessary to be as large as or larger than the divisor, then begin to divide.

The divisor is 8, and moving along the dividend 104, from left to right, the first digit is 1. Since the first digit of the dividend is smaller than the divisor, 1 cannot be divided by 8 to result in a whole number or a number greater than a whole number. So combine the first and the second digits of the dividend, which is 10. Since 10 is larger than the divisor, the division should be started by dividing 10 by 8.

e.

Move from left to right along the dividend as many digits as is necessary to be as large as or larger than the divisor, then begin to divide.

The divisor is 12, and moving along the dividend 118, from left to right, the first digit is 1. Since the first digit of the dividend is smaller than the divisor, 1 cannot be divided by 12 to result in a whole number or a number greater than a whole number. So combine the first and the second digits of the dividend, which is 11. Since 11 is still smaller than the divisor, combine the first three digits of the dividend, which is 118. Since 118 is larger than the divisor, the division should be started by dividing 118 by 12.

(Are you having fun with the mathematics?)

f.

Move from left to right along the dividend as many digits as is necessary to be as large as or larger than the divisor, then begin to divide.

The divisor is 28, and moving along the dividend 2046, from left to right, the first digit is 2. Since the first digit of the dividend is smaller than the divisor, 2 cannot be divided by 28 to result in a whole number or a number greater than a whole number. So combine the first and the second digits of the dividend, which is 20. Since 20 is still smaller than the divisor, combine the first three digits of the dividend, which is 204. Since 204 is larger than the divisor, the division should be started by dividing 204 by 28.

Group Exercise 3

The class should be divided into four groups.

1. Using the concept/section on "How can you tell where to start dividing," each member of the group should explain how to tell where to start dividing.

2. Each group should write where to start dividing in the following division problems, and then put the answers on the overhead. Are all the answers for each group the same, and why?

1.	**2.**	**3.**	**4.**
2⟌26	3⟌15	4⟌92	5⟌120

5.	**6.**	**7.**	**8.**
9⟌828	28⟌2744	7⟌91	12⟌2412

Dividing with One - Digit Divisors
Example 2

Divide: 3⟌36

The problem asks, "How many 3's are there in 36?" We have already solved similar problems using counters in Example 1. Let us establish **a rule** and **five steps** for solving this problem.

Rule: **Move from left to right along the dividend as many digits as is necessary to be equal or greater than the divisor, then begin to divide.**

Divisor   **Dividend**

Step 1: **Divide**

The first digit in the dividend is 3, and since 3 is as large as the divisor which is 3, instead of asking, "How many 3's are there in 36?" you ask, "How many 3's are there in 3?" The answer is 1. So you place the 1 directly above the digit of the dividend you are using, which is 3.

The first digit in the dividend is as large as the divisor.

"How many 3's are there in 3?"
The answer is 1.

1
3⟌36

We can also state that 3 ÷ 3 = 1

Step 2: **Multiply**

Multiply this answer, 1, as stated in Step 1 by the divisor 3. The product is 3. Place the product, 3, under the 3 of the dividend.

       1
    3⟌36   **Place the product under the 3 of the dividend.**
       3

Step 3: **Subtract**

Subtract the bottom number (3) from the top number (3). The result of the subtraction is 0 (3 - 3 = 0).

       1
    3⟌36
      −3
       0 ⟵——— 3 - 3 = 0

Step 4: **Compare**

          1
       3⟌36   **Difference**
         −3
          0 ⟵——— 3 - 3 = 0
Divisor

Compare the divisor with the difference, 3 > 0.
The divisor is greater than the difference, so bring down the next digit of the dividend as shown in Step 5.

Step 5: **Bring down the next digit**

Bring down the next digit of the dividend, which is 6, in a straight line as

49

shown.

Bring the 6 down so that the division can continue.

Repeat Steps 1 through 5 to find:

$$3\overline{)6}$$

Step 1: Divide

The new problem is: "How many times does 3 go into 6?" The answer is 2.
Place the 2 directly above the 6 in the dividend as shown.

"How many times does 3 go into 6?"
The answer is 2.

We can state that $6 \div 3 = 2$

Step 2: Multiply

Multiply this answer, 2, as stated in Step 1 by the divisor 3. The product is 6.
Place the product, 6, under the 6 which is brought down from the dividend.

```
   12
3⃒36
  -3
   06
   6
```

The 6 which is brought down from the dividend.

The product of $3 \times 2 = 6$

Step 3: Subtract

Subtract 6 from 6, and the result is 0.

```
   12
3⃒36
  -3
   06
  - 6
    0
```

50

Step 4: Compare

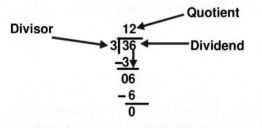

**Compare the divisor with the difference, 3 > 0.
The divisor is greater than the difference, but there are no
more of the digit of the dividend to bring down. So go to
Step 5.**

Step 5: Bring down the next digit

Since there are no more digits to bring down, the dividing is completed.
So we say that, "there are twelve (12) threes (3) in 36."

Check: Division is the opposite of multiplication. So a division problem can be
checked by multiplying the answer to the problem (quotient) by the divisor.
The formula for checking division problem is:

Quotient × Divisor = Dividend

To check this division problem, substitute Quotient = 12, Divisor = 3, and
Dividend = 36 into the formula:

$$\text{Quotient} \times \text{Divisor} = \text{Dividend}$$
$$12 \times 3 = 36$$
$$36 = 36$$

The solution to the division problem is correct because the left side of the
equation is equal to the right side of the equation.

Note: The five steps (Step 1: Divide, Step 2: Multiply, Step 3: Subtract,
Step 4: Compare, and Step 5: Bring down next digit) can be used to solve
division problems.

Shortcut Method

The step-by-step solution of Example 2 provides detailed information for conceptual
understanding and computational fluency. Once the student understands the detailed
solution, the student can then use a shortcut method in solving the problems during
homework and tests by producing a solution similar to that shown in the final Step 4.

The notes and the generous examples have provided me with the conceptual understanding and the computational fluency to do my homework.

Exercises

1. Describe how to divide a number by using multiplication facts.
2. What is the rule for starting division problems?
3. What are the 5 steps in solving division problems?
4. Divide, hint: See Example 2. Check your answers.

a. 4⟌48	b. 2⟌24	c. 2⟌66	d. 3⟌39
e. 2⟌48	f. 3⟌96	g. 4⟌84	h. 3⟌69
i. 5⟌55	j. 3⟌93	k. 7⟌77	l. 3⟌66

5. Divide 28 books equally between 2 girls. How many books does each girl get?
   Hint: Divide 28 by 2.
6. John says, "6 × 4 is 24, so 24 ÷ 6 is 4." Do you agree or disagree? Explain.

Answers to Selected Questions
4a. 12   **4c**. 33

Challenge Questions

7. Divide 33 apples equally among 3 girls. How many apples does each girl get?
8. Divide 36 pens equally among 4 boys. How many pens does each boy get?
9. Divide.

a. 3⟌69	b. 4⟌44	c. 2⟌42	d. 3⟌39
e. 2⟌44	f. 3⟌93	g. 4⟌84	h. 3⟌66

Example 3

Divide: 5⟌635

Solution
Use the **Rule** and the **five steps** for solving division problems.

Rule: Move from left to right along the dividend as many digits as is necessary to be as large as or larger than the divisor, then begin to divide.

Step 1: Divide

The first digit in the dividend is 6, and since 6 is larger than the divisor which is 5, instead of asking, "How many 5's are there in 635?" you ask, "How many 5's are there in 6?" The answer is 1. So you place the 1 directly above the digit of the dividend you are using, which is 6.

The first digit in the dividend is larger than the divisor.

"How many 5's are there in 6?"
The answer is 1.

We can also state that 6 ÷ 5 = 1 remainder 1

Step 2: Multiply

Multiply this answer, 1, as stated in Step 1 by the divisor 5. The product is 5. Place the product, 5, under the 6 of the dividend.

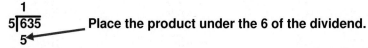

Place the product under the 6 of the dividend.

Step 3: Subtract

Subtract the bottom number (5) from the top number (6). The result of the subtraction is 1 (6 - 5 = 1).

6 - 5 = 1

Step 4: Compare

Divisor

Difference

6 - 5 = 1

Compare the divisor with the difference, 5 > 1.
The divisor is larger than the difference, so bring down the next digit of the dividend as shown in Step 5.

Step 5: Bring down the next digit

Bring down the next digit of the dividend, which is 3, in a straight line as shown.

Bring the 3 down so that the division can continue.

Repeat Steps 1 through 5 to find:

5⟌13

Step 1: Divide

The new problem is: "How many times does 5 go into 13?" The answer is 2 remainder 3.

Place the 2 directly above the 3 in the dividend as shown.

"How many times does 5 go into 13?"
The answer is 2 remainder 3.

We can state that 13 ÷ 5 = 2 remainder 3.

Step 2: Multiply

Multiply this answer, 2, as stated in Step 1 by the divisor 5. The product is 10. Place the product, 10, under the 13 as shown

$5 \times 2 = 10$

Step 3: Subtract

Subtract the bottom number (10) from the top number (13). The result of the subtraction is 3 (13 - 10 = 3).

13 - 10 = 3

Step 4: Compare

Divisor

Difference

13 - 10 = 3

Compare the divisor with the difference, 5 > 3.
The divisor is larger than the difference, so bring down the
next digit of the dividend as shown in Step 5.

Step 5: Bring down the next digit

Bring down the next digit of the dividend, which is 5, in a straight line as shown:

Bring the 5 down so that the division
can continue.

54

Repeat Steps 1 through 5 to find:

5⟌35

Step 1: Divide

The new problem is: "How many times does 5 go into 35?" The answer is 7. Place the 7 directly above the 5 in the dividend as shown:

"How many times does 5 go into 35?"
The answer is 7.

```
    127
5⟌635
  -5↓
   13
  -10↓
  035
```

We can say 35 ÷ 5 = 7

Step 2: Multiply

Multiply this answer, 7, as stated in Step 1 by the divisor 5. The product is 35. Place the product, 35, under the 35 as shown:

```
    127
5⟌635
  -5↓
   13
  -10↓
  035
   35
```

5 × 7 = 35

Step 3: Subtract

Subtract the bottom number (35) from the top number (35). The result of the subtraction is 0 (35 - 35 = 0).

Divisor

```
    127
5⟌635
  -5↓
   13
  -10↓
  035
  -35
   00
```

35 - 35 = 0

Step 4: Compare

Compare the divisor with the difference, 5 > 0.
The divisor is larger than the difference, but there are no
more digits of the dividend to bring down as shown in Step 5.

Step 5: Bring down the next digit

Since there are no more digits to bring down, the dividing is completed.
So we say that, "there are 127 5s in 635."

Check: Division is the opposite of multiplication. So a division problem can be
checked by multiplying the answer to the problem (quotient) by the divisor.
The formula for checking division problem is:

Quotient × Divisor = Dividend

To check this division problem, substitute Quotient = 127, Divisor = 5, and
Dividend = 635 into the formula:

Quotient × Divisor = Dividend

$$127 \times 5 = 635$$
$$635 = 365$$

The solution to the division problem is correct because the left side of the
equation is equal to the right side of the equation.

Note: The five steps (Step 1: Divide, Step 2: Multiply, Step 3: Subtract,
Step 4: Compare, and Step 5: Bring down next digit) can be used to solve
division problems.

Shortcut Method

The step-by-step solution of Example 3 provides detailed information for conceptual
understanding and computational fluency. Once the student understands the detailed

solution, the student can then use a shortcut method in solving the problems during homework and tests by producing a solution similar to that shown in the final Step 4.

▬▬▬▬▬▬▬▬▬ The notes and the generous examples have provided me with the conceptual understanding and the computational fluency to do my homework.

Exercises

1. What is the rule for starting division questions?
2. What are the 5 steps in solving division problems?
3. Divide, hint: See Example 3. You may use multiplication facts to solve the division problems. Check your answers.

a. $5\overline{)640}$ b. $4\overline{)564}$ c. $2\overline{)376}$ d. $3\overline{)489}$

e. $5\overline{)815}$ f. $6\overline{)798}$ g. $4\overline{)544}$ h. $3\overline{)693}$

i. $5\overline{)635}$ j. $3\overline{)936}$ k. $7\overline{)854}$ l. $4\overline{)648}$

4. Describe how you solved Exercise 3a.
5. Divide 462 students into 3 equal groups. How many students are there in each group? Hint: Divide 462 by 3.

Answers to Selected Questions

3a. 128   **2b.** 141

Challenge Questions

6. Divide 544 students into 4 equal groups. How many students are there in each group?
7. Divide 462 students into 3 equal groups. How many students are there in each group?
8. Divide.

a. $5\overline{)635}$ b. $4\overline{)572}$ c. $2\overline{)342}$ d. $3\overline{)429}$

e. $5\overline{)775}$ f. $6\overline{)744}$ g. $4\overline{)552}$ h. $3\overline{)636}$

i. $5\overline{)665}$ j. $3\overline{)963}$ k. $7\overline{)952}$ l. $4\overline{)584}$

Example 4

Divide: $6\overline{)498}$

Solution

Use the **Rule** and the **five steps** for solving division problems.

Rule: **Move from left to right along the dividend as many digits as is necessary to be as large as or larger than the divisor, then begin to divide.**

Step 1: Divide

The first digit in the dividend is 4, and since 4 is less than the divisor, which is 5, the 5 cannot divide into the 4 to produce a quotient that is a whole number. To maintain the rule, move from left to right along the dividend as many digits as is necessary to be as large as or larger than the divisor, then begin to divide. So, select 49. Since 49 is larger than the divisor, begin to divide. Instead of asking, "How many 6's are there in 498?" you ask, "how many 6's are there in 49?" The answer is 8 remainder 1. So you place the 8 directly above **the last digit** of the dividend you are using, which is 9.

"How many times does 6 go into 49?"
The answer is 8 remainder 1.

$$\begin{array}{r} 8 \\ 6\overline{\smash{)}498} \end{array}$$

Step 2: Multiply

Multiply this answer, 8, as stated in Step 1 by the divisor 6. The product is 48. Place the product, 48, under the 49 in the dividend.

$$\begin{array}{r} 8 \\ 6\overline{\smash{)}498} \\ 48 \end{array}$$

Place the product of 48 under 49.

Step 3: Subtract

Subtract the bottom number (48) from the top number (49). The result of the subtraction is 1 (49 - 48 = 1).

$$\begin{array}{r} 8 \\ 6\overline{\smash{)}498} \\ -48 \\ \hline 01 \end{array}$$

49 - 48 = 1

Step 4: Compare

Divisor

Difference

$$\begin{array}{r} 8 \\ 6\overline{\smash{)}498} \\ -48 \\ \hline 01 \end{array}$$

49 - 48 = 1

Compare the divisor with the difference, 6 > 1.
The divisor is larger than the difference, so bring down the next digit of the dividend as shown in Step 5.

Step 5: Bring down the next digit

Bring down the next digit of the dividend, which is 8, in a straight line as shown.

Divisor

8
6)498
−48↓
018

Bring the 8 down so that the division can continue.

Repeat Steps 1 through 5 to find:

6)18

Step 1: Divide

The new problem is: "How many times does 6 go into 18?" The answer is 3. Place the 3 directly above the 8 in the dividend as shown:

"How many times does 6 go into 18?"
The answer is 3.

83
6)498
−48↓
018

Step 2: Multiply

Multiply this answer, 3, as stated in Step1 by the divisor 6. The product is 18. Place the product, 18, under 18 as shown:

83
6)498
−48↓
018
18 ⟵ Place the product, 18, under 18 as shown.

Step 3: Subtract

Subtract the bottom number (18) from the top number (18). The result of the subtraction is 0 (18 - 18 = 0).

Step 4: Compare

Compare the divisor with the difference, 6 > 0.
The divisor is larger than the difference, but there are no
more digits of the dividend to bring down as shown in Step 5.

Step 5: Bring down the next digit

Since there are no more digits to bring down, the dividing is completed.
So we say that, "There are 83 sixes (6s) in 498."

Check: Division is the opposite of multiplication. So a division problem can be
checked by multiplying the answer to the problem (quotient) by the divisor.
The formula for checking division problems is:

Quotient × Divisor = Dividend

To check this division problem, substitute Quotient = 83, Divisor = 6, and
Dividend = 498 into the formula:

Quotient × Divisor = Dividend
$$83 \times 6 = 498$$
$$498 = 498$$

The solution to the division problem is correct because the left side of the
equation is equal to the right side of the equation.

Note: The five steps (Step 1: Divide, Step 2: Multiply, Step 3: Subtract,

Step 4: Compare, and Step 5: Bring down next digit) can be used to solve division problems.

Shortcut Method

The step-by-step solution of Example 4 provides detailed information for conceptual understanding and computational fluency. Once the student understands the detailed solution, the student can then use a shortcut method in solving the problems during homework and tests by producing a solution similar to that shown in the final Step 4.

The notes and the generous examples have provided me with the conceptual understanding and the computational fluency to do my homework.

Exercises

1. State the rule for starting a division problem.

2. What are the 5 steps for dividing?

3. Divide, hint: See Example 4. You may use multiplication facts to solve the division problems. Check your answers.

a. $6\overline{)564}$	b. $5\overline{)485}$	c. $4\overline{)388}$	d. $2\overline{)118}$
e. $3\overline{)279}$	f. $7\overline{)588}$	g. $6\overline{)546}$	h. $3\overline{)258}$
i. $5\overline{)375}$	j. $3\overline{)117}$	k. $7\overline{)644}$	l. $4\overline{)372}$

Answers to Selected Questions

3a. 94   **3b**. 97

Challenge Questions

4. Divide and check your answers.

a. $6\overline{)576}$	b. $5\overline{)365}$	c. $4\overline{)396}$	d. $2\overline{)116}$
e. $3\overline{)219}$	f. $7\overline{)658}$	g. $6\overline{)552}$	h. $3\overline{)264}$

Dividing With Two - Digit Divisors

Example 5

Divide: $12\overline{)1032}$

Solution

Use the **Rule** and the **five steps** for solving division problems.

Rule: **Move from left to right along the dividend as many digits as is necessary to be as large as or larger than the divisor, then begin to divide.**

Step 1: Divide

The first digit in the dividend is 1, and since 1 is less than the divisor, which is 12, the 12 cannot divide into the 1 to produce a quotient that is a whole number. To maintain the Rule, move from left to right along the dividend as many digits as is necessary to be as large as or larger than the divisor, then begin to divide. So select 10, but the 10 is still less than 12, therefore, select 103. Since 103 is larger than the divisor, begin to divide. Instead of asking, "How many 12's are there in 1032?" you ask, "How many 12's are there in 103?" The answer is 8 remainder 7. So you place the 8 directly above **the last digit** of the dividend you are using, which is 3.

"How many times does 12 go into 103?"
The answer is 8 remainder 7.

$$\frac{8}{12\overline{)1032}}$$

Step 2: Multiply

Multiply this answer, 8, as stated in Step 1 by the divisor 12. The product is 96. Place the product, 96, under the 03 in the dividend. Note that the last digit of the product should be under the last digit of the dividend you are using, which is 3.

$$\frac{8}{12\overline{)1032}}$$
96 ◄────── Place the product of 96 under 03.

Step 3: Subtract

Subtract the bottom number (96) from the top number (103). The result of the subtraction is 7 (103 - 96 = 7).

$$\begin{array}{r} 8 \\ 12\overline{)1032} \\ -96 \\ \hline 7 \end{array}$$ ◄────── 103 - 96 = 7

Step 4: Compare

Divisor ────► $12\overline{)1032}$ with quotient 8, -96, 7 ◄──── 103 - 96 = 7, and "Difference" arrow pointing to the 7.

Compare the divisor with the difference, 12 > 7.
The divisor is larger than the difference, so bring down the next digit of the dividend as shown in Step 5.

Step 5: Bring down the next digit

Bring down the next digit of the dividend, which is 2, in a straight line as

62

shown:

Bring the 2 down so that the division can continue.

Repeat Steps 1 through 5 to find:

12⟌72

Step 1: Divide

The new problem is: "How many times does 12 go into 72?" The answer is 6. Place the 6 directly above the 2 in the dividend as shown:

"How many times does 12 go into 72?" The answer is 6.

Step 2: Multiply

Multiply this answer, 6, as stated in Step 1 by the divisor 12. The product is 72. Place the product, 72, under 72 as shown:

Place the product of 72 under 72.

Step 3: Subtract

Subtract the bottom number (72) from the top number (72). The result of the subtraction is 0 (72 - 72 = 0).

72 - 72 = 0

Step 4: Compare

Compare the divisor with the difference, 12 > 0.
The divisor is larger than the difference, but there are no
more digits of the dividend to bring down as shown in Step 5.

Step 5: **Bring down the next digit**

Since there are no more digits to bring down, the dividing is completed.
So we say that, "There are 86 12s in 1032."

Check: Division is the opposite of multiplication. So a division problem can be
checked by multiplying the answer to the problem (**quotient**) by the **divisor**.
The formula for checking division problems is:

Quotient × Divisor = Dividend

To check this division problem, substitute Quotient = 86, Divisor = 12, and
Dividend = 1032 into the formula:

$$\text{Quotient} \times \text{Divisor} = \text{Dividend}$$
$$86 \times 12 = 1032$$
$$1032 = 1032$$

The solution to the division problem is correct because the numbers are the
same on both sides of the equal sign.

Note: The **five steps** (Step 1: Divide, Step 2: Multiply, Step 3: Subtract,
Step 4: Compare, and Step 5: Bring down next digit) can be used to solve
division problems.

Shortcut Method

The step-by-step solution of Example **5** provides detailed information for conceptual
understanding and computational fluency. Once the student understands the detailed
solution, the student can then use a shortcut method in solving the problems during
homework and tests by producing a solution similar to that shown in the final Step 4.

Exercises

1. What is the rule for starting division questions?
2. What are the 5 steps in solving division problems?
3. Divide. Hint: See Example **5**. Check your answers.

a. 11$\overline{)1067}$ b. 12$\overline{)1140}$ c. 12$\overline{)1164}$ d. 10$\overline{)9120}$

e. 11$\overline{)7249}$ f. 10$\overline{)5880}$ g. 11$\overline{)5742}$ h. 12$\overline{)1128}$

i. 13$\overline{)156}$ j. 13$\overline{)1196}$ k. 12$\overline{)960}$ l. 11$\overline{)957}$

Answers to Selected Questions

3a. 97   **3b**. 95

Challenge Questions

4. Divide and check your answers.

a. 11$\overline{)1023}$ b. 12$\overline{)1176}$ c. 12$\overline{)1188}$ d. 10$\overline{)9120}$

e. 11$\overline{)7238}$ f. 10$\overline{)5240}$ g. 11$\overline{)5786}$ h. 12$\overline{)1164}$

i. 13$\overline{)1144}$ j. 13$\overline{)1235}$ k. 12$\overline{)972}$ l. 11$\overline{)913}$

Zeros in the Quotients
Example 6

Divide: 4$\overline{)436}$

Solution

Use the **Rule** and the **five steps** for solving division problems.

Rule: Move from left to right along the dividend as many digits as is necessary to be as large as or larger than the divisor, then begin to divide.

Step 1: Divide

The first digit in the dividend is 4, and since 4 is as large as the divisor which is 4, instead of asking, "How many 4's are there in 436?" you ask, "How many 4's are there in 4?" The answer is 1. So you place the 1 directly above the digit of the dividend you are using, which is 4.

$4\overline{)436}$

The first digit in the dividend is as large as the divisor.

"How many 4's are there in 4?"
The answer is 1.

$$1$$
$$4\overline{)436}$$

We can also state that 4 ÷ 4 = 1

Step 2: Multiply

Multiply this answer, 1, as stated in Step 1 by the divisor 4. The product is 4. Place the product, 4, under the 4 in the dividend as shown.

$$1$$
$$4\overline{)436}$$
$$4$$ ◄────── **Place the product, 4, under 4.**

Step 3: Subtract

Subtract the bottom number (4) from the top number (4). The result of the subtraction is 0 (4 - 4 = 0).

$$1$$
$$4\overline{)436}$$
$$-4$$
$$0$$ ◄─── 4 - 4 = 0

Step 4: Compare

Divisor ──────►   **Difference**

4 - 4 = 0

Compare the divisor with the difference, 4 > 0.
The divisor is larger than the difference, so bring down the next digit of the dividend as shown in Step 5.

Step 5: Bring down the next digit

Bring down the next digit of the dividend, which is 3, in a straight line as shown:

Bring the 3 down so that the division can continue.

Repeat Steps 1 through 5 to find:

$$4\overline{)3}$$

Step 1: Divide

The new problem is: "How many times does 4 go into 3?" The answer is 4 cannot go into 3 to result in a quotient that is a whole number because 4 is larger than 3. Since the divisor (4) is larger than 3, write 0 in the quotient directly above the number in the dividend that you are working with, which is 3. (**Note**:

Apart from the start of divisions, when the divisor is larger than the number being divided, write a zero in the quotient.)

Write 0 in the quotient directly above 3 in the dividend.

```
   10
4)436
 -4
   03
```

Step 2: Multiply

Multiply the 0 as stated in Step1 by the divisor 4. The product is 0.
Place the product, 0, under the 3 as shown:

```
   10
4)436
 -4
   03
    0        4 × 0 = 0
```

Step 3: Subtract

Subtract the bottom number (0) from the top number (3). The result of the subtraction is 3 (3 - 0 = 3).

```
   10
4)436
 -4
   03
  -0
    3        3 - 0 = 3
```

Step 4: Compare

Divisor

```
        10
   4)436
    -4
      03               Difference
     -0
       3 ←— 3 - 0 = 3
```

Compare the divisor with the difference, 4 > 3.
The divisor is larger than the difference, so bring down the
next digit of the dividend as shown in Step 5.

Step 5: Bring down the next digit

Bring down the next digit of the dividend, which is 6, in a straight line as shown.

```
     10
  4⎡436
   −4↓
    03
   −0↓
     36
```

Bring the 6 down so that the division can continue.

Repeat Steps 1 through 5 to find:

```
  4⎡36
```

Step 1: Divide

The new problem is: "How many times does 4 go into 36?" The answer is 9. Place the 9 directly above the 6 in the dividend as shown:

"How many 4's are there in 36?" The answer is 9.

```
    109
  4⎡436
   −4↓
    03
   −0↓
     36
```

Step 2: Multiply

Multiply this answer, 9, as stated in Step1 by the divisor 4. The product is 36. Place the product, 36, under 36 as shown:

```
    109
  4⎡436
   −4↓
    03
   −0↓
     36
     36 ◄——— Place the product, 36, (4 × 9 = 36) under 36.
```

Step 3: Subtract

Subtract the bottom number (36) from the top number (36). The result of the subtraction is 0 (36 - 36 = 0).

```
    109
  4⎡436
   −4↓
    03
   −0↓
     36
    −36
     00 ◄——— 36 - 36 = 0
```

Step 4: Compare

Compare the divisor with the difference, 4 > 0.
The divisor is larger than the difference, but there are no
more digits of the dividend to bring down as shown in Step 5.

Step 5: Bring down next digit

Since there are no more digits to bring down, the division is completed.
So we say that, "There are 109 4s in 436, or 436 ÷ 4 = 109."

Shortcut Method

The step-by-step solution of Example 6 provides detailed information for conceptual understanding and computational fluency. Once the student understands the detailed solution, the student can then use a shortcut method in solving the problems during homework and tests by producing a solution similar to that shown in the final Step 4.

The notes and the generous worked examples have provided me with conceptual understanding and computational fluency to do my homework.

Exercises

1. Mary said that apart from the start of divisions, when the divisor is larger than the number being divided, write a zero in the quotient. Is her statement correct? Explain your answer by dividing one number by another.
2. What is the rule for dividing one number by another?
3. What are the **5 steps** in dividing one number by another?
4. Divide. Hint: See Example **6**. Check your answers.

   a. 5⟌545   b. 4⟌416   c. 7⟌763   d. 8⟌816

   e. 9⟌936   f. 2⟌216   g. 3⟌324   h. 8⟌872

   i. 4⟌408   j. 5⟌525   k. 7⟌749   l. 3⟌327

5. Richard and James want to share 202 pencils equally. How many pencils will each get? Hint: To share equally is the same as to divide equally. Check your answer.
6. Divide 432 cookies equally among 4 students. Hint: Divide 432 by 4. Check your answer.

Answers to Selected Questions

4a. 109   **4b**. 104

Challenge Questions

7. Divide 927 counters equally among 9 students. How many counters does each student get?

8. Divide 404 counters equally between Judith and Erica. How many counters does each get?

9. Divide and check your answers.

a. $5\overline{)515}$ b. $4\overline{)436}$ c. $7\overline{)735}$ d. $8\overline{)824}$

e. $9\overline{)945}$ f. $2\overline{)218}$ g. $3\overline{)315}$ h. $8\overline{)864}$

i. $4\overline{)412}$ j. $5\overline{)545}$ k. $7\overline{)763}$ l. $3\overline{)318}$

Division With Remainders

The answer to a subtraction problem is called the **difference**. In the preceding sections, when you performed the final subtraction in each division problem, the difference was 0. When you perform division and the final difference is not 0, this difference is called a **remainder**. The **remainder is always less than the divisor**. The remainder is denoted by R.

Example 1

Divide 7 counters into 2 parts:
  a. by using counters.
  b. by using multiplication facts.
  c. Relate the division of 7 with the remainder to the form $a = bq + r$, where **a** is the dividend, **b** is the divisor, **q** is the quotient, and **r** is the remainder. Check your answer.

Solution

The question can be stated as shown:

$7 \div 2 = ?$ (**This is referred to as a division problem**).

a. Let us use counters to solve the problem. Notice that $7 \div 2$ means put 7 counters into 2 equal groups of counters. When 7 counters are separated into 2 equal groups of counters, there are 3 counters in each group, with 1 counter leftover as shown.

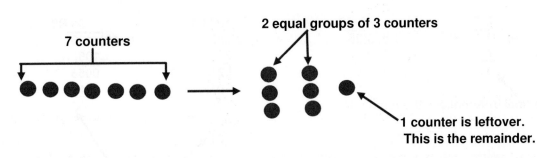

7 counters

2 equal groups of 3 counters

1 counter is leftover.
This is the remainder.

So, $7 \div 2 = 3$ R1, where R1 means remainder 1. **Notice that the remainder (1) is less than the divisor (2).**

b. Let us use multiplication facts to solve the problem. Since division is the opposite of multiplication, we can ask, "what whole number multiplied by 2 will give a 7 or a number nearest to 7 but less than 7. So, $3 \times 2 = 6$. Subtract the 6 from 7 and the difference is 1. We can write $7 \div 2 = 3$ R1.

c. Relate the division of 7 with the remainder to the form $a = bq + r$, where **a** is the dividend, **b** is the divisor, **q** is the quotient, and **r** is the remainder as shown:

Substitute $a = 7$, $b = 2$, $q = 3$, and $r = 1$ into the equation $a = bq + r$.
So $7 = 2 \times 3 + 1$, which is similar to $a = bq + r$.

Check the answer

$7 = 2 \times 3 + 1$

$7 = 6 + 1$ $2 \times 3 = 6$ (See the chapter on Order of Operations.)

$7 = 7$ $6 + 1 = 7$

Since the left side of the equation is equal to the right side of the equation, the answer is correct. Note that the equation $a = bq + r$ **can also be used to check your answer and if there is no remainder, $r = 0$.**

Example 2
Divide:

     a. $2\overline{)7}$ b. $3\overline{)26}$ c. $3\overline{)322}$ d. $12\overline{)1136}$

Solution
The shortcut of the solutions are shown. The students can use the **Rule** and the **five steps** for dividing whole numbers to solve the problems. Similar detailed solutions have already been provided in the preceding sections without remainders. Notice that the **remainders are the final difference during the division.**

The final difference is the remainder.

The final difference is the remainder.

═══════════════════════════ The notes and the generous examples have provided me with the conceptual understanding and the computational fluency to do my homework.

Exercises

1. John said that, during division, the final difference is the remainder. Is his statement correct? Explain your answer.
2. Divide 9 oranges into 2 parts. Hint: See Example **1**.
3. Divide 14 apples into 3 parts. Hint: See Example **1**.
4. Mary said that during division, the remainder is always less than the divisor. Is her statement correct? Explain your answer by dividing 11 by 3.
5. Relate the division of 11 by 3 with the remainder to the form **a** = **bq** + **r**, where **a** is the dividend, **b** is the divisor, **q** is the quotient, and **r** is the remainder: Hint: See Example **1**. Note that the equation **a** = **bq** + **r**, can be used **to check your answer**.
6. Divide. Hint: You may use multiplication facts to solve the problems.
   - **a.** $23 \div 4 =$
   - **b.** $18 \div 4 =$
   - **c.** $19 \div 3 =$
   - **d.** $10 \div 3 =$
   - **e.** $21 \div 2 =$
   - **f.** $13 \div 3 =$
   - **g.** $24 \div 5 =$
   - **h.** $20 \div 3 =$
7. Divide. Hint: See Example **2**. Match similar problems. Check your answers.

   - a. $4\overline{)49}$
   - b. $2\overline{)25}$
   - c. $3\overline{)65}$
   - d. $7\overline{)39}$

   - e. $5\overline{)48}$
   - f. $3\overline{)95}$
   - g. $4\overline{)86}$
   - h. $3\overline{)67}$

   - i. $4\overline{)55}$
   - j. $3\overline{)91}$
   - k. $7\overline{)79}$
   - l. $3\overline{)29}$

8. Divide. Hint: See Example **2**. Match similar problems. Check your answers.

a. $5\overline{)643}$ b. $4\overline{)561}$ c. $2\overline{)373}$ d. $3\overline{)488}$

e. $6\overline{)814}$ f. $6\overline{)799}$ g. $4\overline{)543}$ h. $3\overline{)691}$

i. $5\overline{)637}$ j. $3\overline{)930}$ k. $7\overline{)850}$ l. $4\overline{)645}$

9. Divide. Hint: See Example **2**.
Match similar problems. Check your answers.

a. $11\overline{)1068}$ b. $12\overline{)1145}$ c. $12\overline{)1163}$ d. $10\overline{)9121}$

e. $11\overline{)7245}$ f. $10\overline{)5884}$ g. $11\overline{)5749}$ h. $12\overline{)1129}$

i. $13\overline{)158}$ j. $13\overline{)1191}$ k. $12\overline{)965}$ l. $11\overline{)959}$

Challenge Questions

10. Divide, and check your answers.

a. $13 \div 4 =$ **b**. $35 \div 6 =$ **c**. $19 \div 9 =$ **d**. $28 \div 9 =$
e. $17 \div 3 =$ f. $68 \div 8 =$ g. $45 \div 6 =$ h. $73 \div 12 =$

11. Divide, and check your answers.

a. $11\overline{)49}$ b. $8\overline{)25}$ c. $12\overline{)1125}$ d. $10\overline{)9128}$

e. $8\overline{)7245}$ f. $10\overline{)5884}$ g. $11\overline{)5740}$ h. $12\overline{)1129}$

i. $13\overline{)158}$ j. $4\overline{)547}$ k. $12\overline{)975}$ l. $11\overline{)958}$

12. Divide, and check your answers.

a. $9\overline{)55}$ b. $4\overline{)29}$ c. $12\overline{)1325}$ d. $10\overline{)6125}$

e. $7\overline{)2461}$ f. $11\overline{)5584}$ g. $11\overline{)5690}$ h. $12\overline{)1429}$

i. $13\overline{)160}$ j. $4\overline{)549}$ k. $12\overline{)775}$ l. $11\overline{)466}$

Answers to Selected Questions

6a. 5 R3 **6b**. 4 R2 **7a**. 12 R1 **7b**. 12 R1
8a. 128 R3 **8b**. 140 R1 **9a**. 97 R1 **9b**. 95 R5

Dividing 0 by Another Number, **Dividing a Number by Itself**,
Dividing a Number by 1, and **Dividing a Number by 0**

1. Zero divided by any number (that is not zero) equals 0.

Example 1

$0 \div 4 = 0$ Zero divided by 4 equals 0 because there is nothing to be divided by 4. So, **0 divided by any non-zero number equals 0.**

2. Any number (which is not 0) divided by itself equals 1.

Example 2

$3 \div 3 = 1$ $3 \div 3$ means 3 objects are to be divided into 3 equal groups. Each of the 3 groups will have 1 object.

$4 \div 4 = 1$ $4 \div 4$ means 4 objects are to be divided into 4 equal groups. Each of the 4 groups will have 1 object.

So, **any non-zero number divided by itself equals 1.**

3. Any number divided by 1 equals the same number.

Example 3

$3 \div 1 = 3$ $3 \div 1$ means 3 objects to be divided into 1 group. All the 3 objects will belong to 1 group.

$4 \div 1 = 4$ $4 \div 1$ means 4 objects to be divided into 1 group. All the 4 objects will belong to 1 group.

So, **any number divided by 1 equals the same number.**

4. You cannot divide by zero.

Example 4.

$3 \div 0 = ?$ You cannot divide by 0. (You will learn more about dividing by 0 in the higher grade level books of the Math Teaching Series.)

━━━━━━━━━━━━━━━ The notes and the generous examples have provided me with the conceptual understanding and the computational fluency to do my homework.

Exercises
1. Zero divided by any number (that is not zero) equals ____.
2. Divide, hint: See Example 1.

a. $0 \div 2 =$ **b.** $0 \div 6 =$ **c.** $0 \div 99 =$ **d.** $0 \div 1000 =$

3. Eric said that any number (which is not 0) divided by itself equals 1. Is his statement correct? Explain your answer by using $6 \div 6$. Hint: See Example 2.

4. Divide, hint: See Example 2.

     a. $2 \div 2 =$ **b.** $7 \div 7 =$ **c.** $25 \div 25 =$ **d.** $300 \div 300 =$

5. Any number divided by 1 equals the same _____.

6. Divide, hint: See Example 3.

     a. $6 \div 1 =$ **b.** $7 \div 1 =$ **c.** $295 \div 1 =$ **d.** $350 \div 1 =$

7. Ama said that she cannot divide by 0. Is her statement correct?

8. Divide, hint: See Example 4.

     a. $2 \div 0 =$ **b.** $9 \div 0 =$ **c.** $180 \div 0 =$ **d.** $237 \div 0 =$

Cumulative Review

1. Describe how you can divide 12 oranges among 3 people.

2. Divide, and check your answers.

     a. $16 \div 4 =$ b. $19 \div 4 =$ c. $27 \div 3 =$ d. $55 \div 4 =$

     e. $7 \div 7 =$ f. $38 \div 6 =$ g. $64 \div 8 =$ h. $72 \div 6 =$

3. Describe when a zero is written in the quotient while dividing whole numbers.

4. List the **five steps** for dividing whole numbers.

5. Divide, and check your answers:

     a. $9\overline{)36}$ b. $3\overline{)29}$ c. $12\overline{)108}$ d. $4\overline{)417}$

     e. $5\overline{)245}$ f. $11\overline{)588}$ g. $11\overline{)1199}$ h. $12\overline{)1529}$

     i. $13\overline{)160}$ j. $4\overline{)549}$ k. $12\overline{)775}$ l. $11\overline{)1129}$

     m. $7\overline{)2161}$ n. $12\overline{)61014}$ o. $11\overline{)5690}$ p. $13\overline{)1429}$

6. $3 \div 1 =$ **7.** $0 \div 2 =$ **8.** $3 \div 3 =$ **9.** $8 \div 8 =$

10. $0 \div 7 =$ **11.** $2 \div 0 =$ **12.** $11 \div 11 =$ **13.** $7 \div 0 =$

14. The three parts to any division problem are:

                 divisor, dividend, and _____

15. What is the relationship regarding quotient, divisor, and dividend?

CHAPTER 4

ESTIMATING QUOTIENTS

Compatible numbers can be used to estimate quotients. Recall from the chapter on the Division of Whole Numbers that a **quotient** is the answer to a division problem. Recall from the chapter on Estimating Products that **compatible numbers are numbers that are easy to compute with mentally**. (Review the chapter on Estimating Products.)

Example 1
Estimate 110 ÷ 4
Explain whether your answer is an underestimate or an overestimate.
Solution
Adjust 110 to 100 because 100 ÷ 4 = 25. Notice that using compatible numbers, we can adjust 110 to 100. Notice also that adjusting 110 to 100 is the same as rounding to the nearest hundred.

$$110 ÷ 4$$
$$\downarrow$$
$$100 ÷ 4 = 25 \qquad \text{Adjust 110 to 100.}$$

So, 110 ÷ 4 is about 25.
Since 110 is adjusted to 100, the answer is an underestimate because 100 is less than 110. The exact answer must be greater than 25.

Example 2
Estimate 117 ÷ 4 by using compatible numbers. Explain whether your answer is an underestimate or an overestimate.
Solution
Adjust 117 to 120 because 12 ÷ 4 = 3 and 120 ÷ 4 = 30.

$$117 ÷ 4$$
$$\downarrow$$
$$120 ÷ 4 = 30 \qquad \text{Adjust 117 to 120.}$$

So, 117 ÷ 4 is about 30.
Since 117 was adjusted to 120, and 120 is greater than 117, the answer is an overestimate. The exact answer must be less than 30.

Example 3
Estimate using compatible numbers.
330 ÷ 8

Solution

Adjust 330 to 320 because $32 \div 8 = 4$ and $320 \div 8 = 40$.

$$330 \div 8$$
$$\downarrow$$
$$320 \div 8 = 40 \qquad\qquad \text{Adjust 330 to 320.}$$

So, $330 \div 8$ is about 40.

Example 4

Estimate $437 \div 4$.

Solution

Adjust 437 to 440 because $44 \div 4 = 11$ and $440 \div 4 = 110$.

$$437 \div 4$$
$$\downarrow$$
$$440 \div 4 = 110 \qquad\qquad \text{Adjust 437 to 440.}$$

So, $437 \div 4$ is about 110.

Example 5

Estimate $508 \div 7$

Solution

Adjust 508 to 490 because $49 \div 7 = 7$ and $490 \div 7 = 70$.

$$508 \div 7$$
$$\downarrow$$
$$490 \div 7 = 70 \qquad\qquad \text{Adjust 508 to 490.}$$

So, $508 \div 7$ is about 70.

Example 6

Estimate $4{,}102 \div 8$.

Solution

Adjust 4,102 to 4,000 because 40 is close to 41 and 40 is divisible by 8.
Notice that 4,000 is divisible by 8 to obtain 500.

$$4{,}102 \div 8$$
$$\downarrow$$
$$4{,}000 \div 8 = 500 \qquad \text{Adjust 4,100 to 4,000.}$$
$$\text{Notice that } 40 \div 8 = 5 \text{ and } 4{,}000 \div 8 = 500.$$

So, $40{,}102 \div 8$ is about 500.

Example 7

Estimating by using compatible numbers.

$76 \div 24$

77

Solution

Adjust 76 to 75 and adjust 24 to 25 because $75 \div 25 = 3$.

$$76 \div 24$$
$$\downarrow \quad \downarrow$$
$$75 \div 25 = 3$$

Notice that in this solution, both numbers (76 and 24) are adjusted to form compatible numbers.

Real World Application
Example 8

a. The population of students in a school district is 3,104. If the school district decides to divide the student population into 3 equal groups during sports and games. Estimate the number of students in each group.

b. Explain whether your answer to Example **8a** is an underestimate or an overestimate.

Solution

a. The solution to the problem can be written as:

$$3{,}104 \div 3$$

Adjust 3,104 to 3,000 because 30 is close to 31 and 30 is divisible by 3.
$3{,}000 \div 3 = 1{,}000$.

$$3{,}104 \div 3$$
$$\downarrow$$
$$3{,}000 \div 3 = 1{,}000 \qquad \text{Adjust 3,104 to 3,000.}$$

So, $3{,}104 \div 3$ is about 1000.

Notice that adjusting 3,104 to 3,000 is the same as rounding 3,104 to the nearest thousand. (Hint: Read the chapter/section on Rounding.)

b. 3,104 was adjusted to 3,000. Since 3,000 is less than 3,104, the answer is an underestimate. So the exact answer must be greater than 1,000.

Exercise

1. Explain how you can estimate quotients.
2. Explain compatible numbers.
3. Estimate each quotient:

a. $105 \div 4$	b. $209 \div 4$	c. $111 \div 4$
d. $311 \div 3$	e. $312 \div 5$	f. $421 \div 8$
g. $312 \div 8$	h. $310 \div 8$	i. $115 \div 4$
j. $760 \div 8$	k. $171 \div 8$	l. $59 \div 3$
m. $288 \div 5$	n. $638 \div 7$	o. $366 \div 4$
p. $491 \div 7$	q. $804 \div 9$	r. $804 \div 9$

Hint: See Example 1, 2, 3, 4, and 5.

(In Examples 1 to 5, notice that adjusting a number to another number is the same as rounding the number to the nearest ten or the nearest hundred that can be easily divisible.)

4. Explain if each solution to Example 3 is an underestimate or an overestimate. Hint: See Examples 1 and 2.
5. Estimate the following quotients.

   a. $4,119 \div 8$ b. $5,117 \div 5$ c. $4,108 \div 4$
   d. $2,071 \div 4$ e. $3,089 \div 3$ f. $5,111 \div 5$

   Hint: See Example 6. Notice in Example 6 that adjusting 4,102 to 4,000 is the same as rounding 4,102 to the nearest thousand that can easily be divisible (by 8).
6. Explain whether each of your answers to Exercise 5 is an underestimate or an overestimate. Hint See Examples 1 and 2.
7. Estimate each quotient using two sets of compatible numbers.

   a. $77 \div 26$ b. $7,041 \div 6$ c. $107 \div 9$
   d. $208 \div 9$ e. $4,101 \div 6$ f. $4,018 \div 3$
   Hint: See Example 7.

8. The population of the students in a school district is 4,111. The school district decides to divide the student population into four groups. Estimate the number of students in each group. Hint: See Example 8.

Answers to Selected Questions
3a. about 25   5a. about 500   7a. about 3

(Are you having fun with mathematics? There is a champion in every student. In order to become a champion, every student needs to work both hard and smart. I believe that working hard is the constant determination to succeed, working smart is to understand how the examples are solved step-by-step, and you can use the concept to solve similar problems.)

CHAPTER 5

TEST FOR DIVISIBILITY

Objective: In this section, we will explore the rules for a number to be divided by 2, 3, 4, 5, 6, 8, 9, or 10.

How Can You Tell if One Number is Divisible by Another?
If 8 is divided by 2, the answer or the quotient is 4 and the remainder is 0. **Since the remainder is 0, 8 is divisible by 2** as shown:

$$2\overline{)8} \quad \begin{array}{r} 4 \\ \underline{-8} \\ 0 \end{array}$$

Therefore, if a number can be divided evenly (**without a remainder**) by another number, it is **divisible** by that number. A number is **divisible** by another number if after division there is **no remainder**.

Rules for divisibility
The **divisibility rules** are used to decide if one number is divisible by another.
Rule 1: If a whole number is divisible by 2, then its last digit is divisible by 2.

Example 1
Is 398 divisible by 2?
Solution
Since the last digit of 398 is 8 and 8 is divisible by 2, then 398 is divisible by 2.
Let us show that 398 is divisible by 2 by dividing 398 by 2 as shown:

Since 398 is divided evenly by 2, **Rule 1** is confirmed.
What is the name given to numbers which can be divided evenly by 2?
Answer: **Even numbers**.
What is the name given to numbers that cannot be divided evenly by 2?
Answer: **Odd numbers**.

Rule 2: If a number is divisible by 3,then the sum of the digits of the number is divisible by 3.

Example 2

Is 105 divisible by 3?

Solution

The digits of 105 are 1, 0, and 5.

Let us add up the digits of 105 as shown:

$1 + 0 + 5 = 6$

Using the rule, since the sum of the digits is 6 and 6 is divisible by 3, 105 is divisible by 3. Let us show that 105 is divisible by 3 by dividing 105 by 3 as shown:

$$
\begin{array}{r}
35 \\
3\overline{)105} \\
-9 \\
\hline
15 \\
-15 \\
\hline
00
\end{array}
$$

Since 105 is divided evenly by 3, **Rule 2** is confirmed.

Rule 3: If a number is divisible by 4, then its last two digits are divisible by 4.

Example 3

Is 216 divisible by 4?

Solution

The last two digits of 216 are 1 and 6 and 16 is divisible by 4 ($\dfrac{16}{4} = 4$), and

therefore, 216 is divisible by 4.

Let us show that 216 is divisible by 4 by dividing 216 by 4 as shown:

$$
\begin{array}{r}
54 \\
4\overline{)216} \\
-20 \\
\hline
016 \\
-16 \\
\hline
00
\end{array}
$$

Since 216 can be divided evenly by 4, **Rule 3** is confirmed.

Rule 4: If a number is divisible by 5, then the last digit number is either 5 or 0.

Example 4

(a) Is 115 divisible by 5?

(b) Is 110 divisible by 5?

Solution

(a) Using Rule 4, since the last digit of 115 is 5, 115 is divisible by 5.

Let us show that 115 is divisible by 5 by dividing 115 by 5 as shown:

Since 115 can be divided evenly by 5, **Rule 4** is confirmed.

(b) Using Rule 4, since the last digit of 110 is 0, then 110 is divisible by 5.

Let us show that 110 is divisible by 5 by dividing 110 by 5 as shown:

Since 110 can be divided evenly by 5, **Rule 4** is confirmed.

Rule 5: If a number is divisible by 6, then the number is divisible by both 2 and 3.

Example 5

Is 114 divisible by 6?

Solution

Let us divide 114 by 2 and by 3 as shown:

Using Rule 5, since 114 can be divide by both 2 and 3 evenly, then 114 is divisible by 6.
Let us show that 114 is divisible by 6 by dividing 114 by 6 as shown:

Since 114 can be divided evenly by 6, **Rule 5** is confirmed.

Rule 6: If a number is divisible by 8, then the last three digits of the number are divisible by 8.

Example 6
Is 2104 divisible by 8?
Solution
Using Rule 6, let us check the divisibility of 2104 by 8 by dividing the last three digits of 2104 which are 1, 0, and 4 (104) by 8 as shown:

Using the Rule 6, 2104 is divisible by 8 because the last three digits of 2104 which are 1, 0, and 4 (104) is divisible by 8. Let us show that 2104 is divisible by 8 by dividing 2104 by 8 as shown:

Since 2104 can be divided evenly by 8, **Rule 6** is confirmed.

Rule 7: If a number is divisible by 9, then the sum of the digits of the number is divisible by 9.

Example 7
Is 117 divisible by 9?

Solution

The sum of the digits of 117 is $1 + 1 + 7 = 9$. Using Rule 7, since the sum of the digits is 9 which can be divided by 9, then 117 is divisible by 9.

Let us show that 117 is divisible by 9 by dividing 117 by 9 as shown:

Since 117 can be divided evenly by 9, **Rule 7** is confirmed.

Rule 8: If a number is divisible by 10, then the last digit of the number is 0.

Example 8

Is 210 divisible by 10?

Solution

Using Rule 8, since the last digit of 210 is 0, then 210 is divisible by 10.

Let us show that 210 is divisible by 10 by dividing 210 by 10 as shown:

Since 210 can be divided evenly by 10, **Rule 8** is confirmed.

Exercises

1. Are the numbers divisible by 2? Hint: See Rule 2 and Example 2. Show your method.
   (a) 144 (b) 123 (c) 96 (d) 99 (e) 48
2. Are the numbers divisible by 3? Hint: See Rule 3 and Example 3. Show your method.
   (a) 111 (b) 223 (c) 39 (d) 8102 (e) 117
3. Are the numbers divisible by 4? Hint: See Rule 4 and Example 4. Show your method.
   (a) 316 (b) 56 (c) 112 (d) 117 (e) 1416

4. Are the numbers divisible by 5? Hint: See Rule 5 and Example 5. Show your method.
   (a) 555   (b) 310   (c) 134   (d) 229   (e) 1225
5. Are the numbers divisible by 6? Hint: See Rule 5 and Example 5. Show your method.
   (a) 168   (b) 148   (c) 138   (d) 186   (e) 588
6. Are the numbers divisible by 8? Hint: See Rule 6 and Example 6. Show your method.
   (a) 1760   (b) 2101   (c) 7104   (d) 1784   (e) 1512
7. Are the numbers divisible by 9? Hint: See Rule 7 and Example 7. Show your method.
   (a) 324   (b) 577   (c) 882   (d) 1098   (e) 1154
8. Are the numbers divisible by 10? Hint: See Rule 8 and Example 8. Show your method.
   (a) 2210   (b) 4515   (c) 1110   (d) 9418   (e) 4410

Challenge Questions

9. What is the difference between an even number and an odd number?
10. Are these numbers divisible by 5? Explain your answer.
    (a) 496   (b) 125   (c) 530   (d) 217   (e) 475
11. Are these numbers divisible by 10? Explain your answer.
    (a) 1100   (b) 2194   (c) 6115   (d) 493   (e) 2240
12. Test each number to determine if it is divisible by 2, 3, 4, 5, 6, 8, 9, or 10.
    (a) 65   (b) 119   (c) 64   (d) 220   (e) 675
13. Explain why 144 is divisible by 2 but not by: (a) 5   (b) 10
14. John said that 21117 is divisible by 2. Is his statement correct? Explain your answer.

Answers to Selected Questions

1(a) Yes, because if a whole number is divisible by 2, then its last digit is divisible by 2. The last digit of 144 is 4, and 4 is divisible by 2.

2(a) Yes, because if a number is divisible by 3, then the sum of the digits of the number is divisible by 3. The sum of the digits of 111 is 1 + 1 + 1 = 3, and 3 is divisible by 3.

4(d) No, because if a number is divisible by 5, then the last digit number is either 5 or 0. The last digit number of 229 is 9, and 9 is neither 5 nor 0.

AVERAGE, MEAN, RANGE, MODE, AND MEDIAN

Average

Explanation 1

In its simplest form, an average is to share or divide anything equally. For example, how can we share or divide 6 oranges equally between 2 girls? We can share the 6 oranges equally such that each girl will receive 3 oranges as shown:

Six oranges to be shared equally.

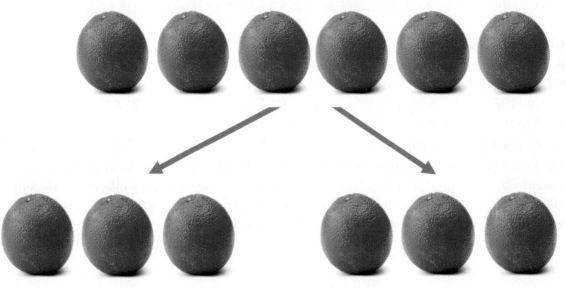

Equal share of 3 oranges   **Equal share of 3 oranges**

From the above picture, we are able to divide 6 oranges equally between 2 girls by dividing the total number of the oranges by the number of people who are to receive the share. Similarly, **an average is the total number divided by the number of the numbers**, and in this case the number of the numbers involves 2 girls which can be written as shown:

$$\text{Average} = \frac{\text{Total number of oranges}}{\text{Number of people}} = \frac{6}{2} = 3 \text{ oranges}$$

Explanation 2

Assume that a girl has 2 oranges and another girl has 4 oranges and they are requested to share the oranges equally, then they have to add the oranges together and then divide the total number of the oranges or the sum of the oranges by 2 or the number of the girls. Similarly, sharing the oranges equally is the same as finding the average which can be stated as shown: **an average is the sum of numbers divided by the number of the numbers**. This average can be written as shown:

$$\text{Average} = \frac{\text{Sum of oranges}}{\text{Number of people}} = \frac{2+4}{2} = \frac{6}{2} = 3$$

Conclusion from Explanations 1 and 2.
In Explanation 1, we find the average by dividing "Total number of oranges" by "Number of people," but in Explanation 2, the average is found by dividing the "Sum of oranges" by "Number of people." We can then combine Explanations 1 and 2 together to write that **an average is the total or the sum of the numbers divided by the number of the numbers**. Therefore, there are two methods of finding averages as explained by Examples 1 and 2, and stated in the rule below:

Rule: An average can be found by dividing the total number by the number of the numbers if the total number is given in the question, otherwise the average can be found by dividing the sum of the numbers by the number of the numbers if the individual numbers are given in the question.

Understanding Average
When students from schools take part in the external examinations, the schools are rated by the average performance of the students in each school by dividing the sum of the test scores of all the students in a specific school by the number of students who took the test. The average test score can be written as shown:

$$\text{Average test score} = \frac{\text{Sum of the test scores}}{\text{Number of the students who took the test}} \qquad \qquad [A]$$

Group Exercise
The class should be divided into four groups and without using any students' names, each group should be given the test scores of the last weekly test. Each group should find the average test score of the last weekly test by completing the tables as shown and using the average equation, which is equation $[A]$.

Test Scores:

Student #	1	2	3	4	5	6	7	8	. . .	N
Test score	?	?	?	?	?	?	?	?	. . .	?

Each group should report out the average test score to the whole class.
Each group should discuss the following 4 questions and to list and report out their answer with reasons to the whole class.
1. Are the average test scores from the 4 groups the same?

2. How could the average test score be improved? When each student's test score is increased by 2, what happens to the average test score? Is the average test score higher when the individual test score is increased by 2?
3. Could you name some external tests that your school participates in?
4. What factors will lower the average test score? When the individual test score is lowered by 2, does the average test score become lower?

Example 1
(**a**). The test scores of five students out of a maximum score of 10 are 8, 7, 9, 10, and 6. Find the average test score of the students.
(**b**). The total age of 5 boys is 20 years. What is their average age?
Solution
(**a**). Using the formula, the average test score is:

$$\text{Average test score} = \frac{\text{Sum of the test scores}}{\text{Number of the students that took the test}} \quad\text{———— [A]}$$

Sum of the test scores $= 8 + 7 + 9 + 10 + 6 = 40$
Number of the students that took the test $= 5$

$$\text{Average test score} = \frac{40}{5} \qquad \text{See equation } [A]$$

$$= \frac{\overset{8}{\cancel{40}}}{\underset{1}{\cancel{5}}} \qquad \text{Divide by 5.}$$

Therefore, the average test score is 8.
(**b**). The total age of the 5 boys $= 20$ years
　　 The number of the boys $= 5$
　　 Using the formula:

$$\text{Average} = \frac{\text{Total number (ages)}}{\text{Number of people}} = \frac{20}{5}$$

$$= \frac{\overset{4}{\cancel{20}}}{\underset{1}{\cancel{5}}} \qquad \text{(Divide by 5).}$$

Therefore, the average age of the 5 boys is 4 years.

88

Example 2

Find the average of the following numbers:

$$1\frac{1}{2}, 2\frac{3}{4}, 3\frac{2}{3}, 2\frac{1}{2}$$

Solution

Using the formula, the average of the numbers is:

$$\text{Average number} = \frac{\text{Sum of the numbers}}{\text{Number of the numbers}} \qquad\qquad [A]$$

$$\text{Sum of the numbers} = 1\frac{1}{2} + 2\frac{3}{4} + 3\frac{2}{3} + 2\frac{1}{2}$$

Number of the numbers = 4   (There are 4 numbers involved.)

Add the numbers as follow: (Review the addition of mixed numbers).

$$1\frac{1}{2} = 1\frac{1}{2} \times \frac{6}{6} = 1\frac{6}{12}$$

$$2\frac{3}{4} = 2\frac{3}{4} \times \frac{3}{3} = 2\frac{9}{12}$$

$$3\frac{2}{3} = 3\frac{2}{3} \times \frac{4}{4} = 3\frac{8}{12}$$

$$2\frac{1}{2} = 2\frac{1}{2} \times \frac{6}{6} = 2\frac{6}{12}$$

$$8\frac{29}{12} = 8 + 2\frac{5}{12} = 10\frac{5}{12} \quad \text{(Review division of fractions)}$$

$$\text{Sum of the numbers} = 10\frac{5}{12}$$

Using equation $[A]$:

$$\text{Average number} = \frac{10\frac{5}{12}}{4} \qquad \text{(There are 4 numbers.)}$$

$$= 10\frac{5}{12} \div 4$$

$$= 10\frac{5}{12} \times \frac{1}{4} \qquad \text{(Review the division of fractions - multiply by reciprocal of 4.)}$$

Note: The reciprocal of any number = 1 ÷ the number

$$= \frac{125}{12} \times \frac{1}{4} \qquad \text{(Review the multiplication of mixed fractions.)}$$

$$= \frac{125}{48} = 2\frac{29}{48}$$

Therefore, the average number is $2\frac{29}{48}$

Example 3

The average age of 8 children is 9 years. If the ages of seven of the children are 6, $8\frac{1}{2}$, 4, 10, 11, 12, and 9, how old is the 8th child?

Solution

Sum of the ages of the 7 children $= 6 + 8\frac{1}{2} + 4 + 10 + 11 + 12 + 9 = 60\frac{1}{2}$ years.

Total ages of the 8 children $= 8 \times$ average age of the 8 children.
$$= 8 \times 9 \text{ years}$$
$$= 72 \text{ years.}$$

Age of 8th child $=$ Total age of the 8 children $-$ Sum of the ages of the 7 children

$$= 72 \text{ years} - 60\frac{1}{2} \text{ years}$$

$$= 11\frac{1}{2} \text{ years.}$$

Therefore, the age of the 8th child is $11\frac{1}{2}$ years.

Mean, Range, Mode, and Median.

The **mean** is the same as the average.

The **range** is the difference between the biggest number and the smallest number in a data.

Example 4

The table shows the ages of 9 students.

Students #	1	2	3	4	5	6	7	8	9
Ages	16	14	13	14	17	15	14	12	11

a. Find the range of the ages of the students.

b. Find the mean age of the students.

c. By conducting a group exercise, find the range of the data by using a line plot.

d. Find the mode of the data.

e. By using the line plot in Example 4c, how would you find the mode of the data?

90

f. Find the median age of the students.

g. By using the line plot of Example 4c, how would you find the median age of the students?

Solution

a. From the table, the student # 5 has the highest age of 17 years and the student # 9 has the lowest age of 11 years.

Therefore, the range = Highest age - Lowest age

$$= 17 \text{ years} - 11 \text{ years } = 6 \text{ years.}$$

b. Let us find the mean age of the students as follows:

Sum of the ages of the students = 16 + 14 13 + 14 + 17 + 15 + 14 + 12 + 11

$$= 126 \text{ years}$$

The number of students = 9   From the table, 9 students are listed.

$$\text{The mean of the ages of the students} = \frac{\text{Sum of the ages of the students}}{\text{Number of the students}}$$

$$= \frac{126 \text{ years}}{9}$$

$$= 14 \text{ years}$$ Review the division of integers.

Therefore, the mean age of the students is 14 years.

c. Group Exercise

The class should be divided into four groups. Each group should complete the line plot of the ages of all the 9 students, using x for each mark as started below.

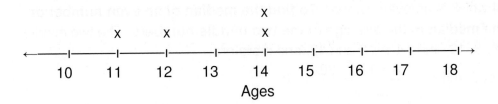

Ages

How could the range be determined from the line plot?

Answer: The x at the extreme left side of the line plot indicates the lowest age and the x at the extreme right side of the line plot indicates the highest age. **Subtract the lowest age from the highest age to obtain the range.**

d. The **mode** is the number that occurs most often. From the table, the age 14 years occurs 3 times which is the age that occurs most often, and therefore, 14 is the mode.

e. Group Exercise
From the completed line plot, how could you find the mode?
Answer: **The age column which has the most "x" indicates the mode**. Which age column has the most "x"? What is then the mode from the line plot? The mode is the data that appears most.

f. The **median** is the middle number when data is listed in numerical order. Numerical order means to list the data from the least number to the greatest number, in order without omission. We can write the ages of the 9 students in numerical order as follow:

11, 12, 13, 14, 14, 14, 15, 16, 17

↑

This 14 is the middle number when the data is listed in numerical order, and therefore, this 14 is the median.

g. Group Exercise
From the completed line plot, how could you find the median?
Answer: The xs on the line plot are already in numerical order, and therefore, by counting the x from left to right on the line plot, **we should be able to locate the x which is at the middle of the data and this middle x is the median.** What is the median from the line plot?

Special Method for Finding Median
The median is the middle number when data is listed in numerical order. However, if the data is an even number of numbers, there will be no middle number as the median as shown:

6, 8, 12, 14

The numbers 6, 8, 12, and 14 have no middle number because the number of the numbers is 4 which is an even number. **To find the median of an even number of numbers, the median is the average of the two middle numbers**. The two middle numbers of 6, 8, 12, and 14 are 8 and 12, and therefore,

the average of 8 and 12 $= \dfrac{8 + 12}{2} = \dfrac{20}{2} = 10.$

Therefore, the median of 6, 8, 12, and 14 is 10.

How to Solve Multi-Step Problems Involving Mean.

Example 5
The mean of the ages of 3 boys is 5 years. How old should the fourth boy be such that the mean of the 4 boys will be 8 years?
Solution
The method of solving this problem involves finding the total ages of the 3 boys and

then let x represent the age of the fourth boy. We can then find the sum of the ages of all the 4 boys, we can also find the mean of the ages of all the four boys. Finally, we can equate the mean of the ages of the 4 boys to 8 years, and then solve for x which is the age of the fourth boy as shown:

Total ages of the 3 boys = 3 × Mean age of the 3 boys.

$$= 3 \times 5 \text{ years} \qquad \text{Mean age of the 3 boys} = 5 \text{ years.}$$
$$= 15 \text{ years}$$

Let the age of the fourth boy = x years

Total age of all the 4 boys = 15 years + x years

$$\text{Mean of the ages of the 4 boys} = \frac{\text{Sum of the ages of the 4 boys}}{\text{Total number of boys}}$$

$$= \frac{15 + x}{4}$$

Since the question gives us the mean of the 4 boys is 8 years, we can equate $\frac{15 + x}{4}$ to 8 and then solve for x which is the age of the fourth boy as shown:

$$\frac{15 + x}{4} = 8$$

$$\frac{15 + x}{4} = \frac{8}{1} \qquad \text{8 is the same as } \frac{8}{1}.$$

Cross products of a proprotion are equal. A proportion is a statement that two ratios are equal. Review the chapter on proportion.

$\frac{15 + x}{4} \times \frac{8}{1}$

(15 + x) × 1 = 4 × 8	Review the chapter on proportion.
15 × 1 + x × 1 = 4 × 8	Multiply to eliminate the bracket.
15 + x = 32	4 × 8 = 32.
15 - 15 + x = 32 - 15	Subtract 15 from both sides of the equation 15 + x = 32 in order to obtain x.
0 + x = 17	15 - 15 = 0 and 32 - 15 = 17.
x = 17	

Therefore, the fourth boy should be 17 years.

Exercises

1. (a) Explain what is meant by average, mean, range, mode, and median.
   (b) Six boys are given $24. What is the average amount each boy will receive? Hint: See Example **1(a)**.
   (c). If 8 students are to share 16 apples, what is the average number of the apples each student receives? Hint: See Example **1(b)**.

2. What is the average of 4, 5, 2, and 1? Hint: See Example **1(a)**.

3. Find the average of the following numbers: Hint: See Examples **1(a)** and **2**.

(a) 2.1, 6.4, 2.8, 1.2, 2.5   (b) $1\frac{1}{2}$, $6\frac{2}{3}$, $1\frac{5}{6}$

(c) 22, 5, 14, 6, 8   (d) 4, 7, 8, 11, 2, 6, 3, 9, 13

(e) 14, 16, 8, 10, 7, 5   (f) 77, 43

(g) $2\frac{2}{3}$, $1\frac{3}{4}$, $3\frac{1}{4}$, $\frac{1}{3}$ (h) 1, 3, 9, 11, 4, 3, 12

(i) 14, 24, 31, 16   (j) 5, 10, 12, 14, 6

4. From the given data, find the range. Hint: See the section under Range. See Example **4a**.

(a) 3, 4, 7, 28   (b) 101, 7, 2, 94
(c) 38, 49, 86, 99, 31, 2   (d) 2, 8, 4, 35, 44
(e) 39, 98, 401, 30, 11   (f) 15, 25, 7, 5

5. Find the median. Hint: See the section on Median, see Example **4f**.

(a) 4, 8, 1, 6, 4   (b) 9, 5, 8   (f) 7, 12, 3

(g) 4.2, 3.1, 6.4, 1.8, 6.2   (h) $7\frac{1}{2}$, $6\frac{1}{3}$, $8\frac{3}{4}$, $6\frac{2}{3}$, $7\frac{1}{4}$ (i) 6.3, 4.7, 8.4

6. Find the median. Hint: See the section on the Special Method of Finding the Median.

(a) 2, 8, 5, 3   (b) 3, 7, 8, 1   (c) 12, 2, 4, 6, 1, 3
(d) 12, 4   (e) 4, 6   (f) 3, 4, 8, 2, 7, 9

(g) 110, 112, 100, 98   (h) 2.4, 2.8, 4.2, 6.4   (i) $7\frac{1}{2}$, $6\frac{2}{3}$, $2\frac{2}{3}$, $1\frac{3}{4}$

7. Find the mode. Hint: See the section on Mode. See Example 4d.

(**a**) 2, 3, 7, 8, 2, 9, 3, 2
(**c**) 9, 11, 6, 7, 9, 4, 9
(**e**) 4, 1, 5, 1, 6, 5, 8, 5

(**b**) 4, 1, 6, 9, 4, 2, 4, 1
(**d**) 1, 4, 6, 1, 7, 1, 2, 6, 4
(**f**) 2, 6, 9, 4, 6, 2, 6

8. Find the mode and the range. Hint: See the section on Mode and Range. See Examples **4a** and **4d**.

(**a**) 12, 14, 4, 12, 3, 1, 12, 14
(**c**) 3, 6, 9, 10, 6, 24, 4

(**e**) 2.5, 6.8, 4.1, 3, 6.8, 7.2

(**g**) $2\frac{3}{4}, 1\frac{1}{2}, 8\frac{3}{7}, 2\frac{3}{4}, 6, 2\frac{3}{4}$

(**b**) 19, 24, 6, 19, 4, 2
(**d**) 1, 4, 5, 6, 5, 13, 5

(**f**) $4\frac{1}{2}, 1\frac{7}{8}, 6\frac{4}{5}, 1\frac{7}{8}, 2$

(**h**) 1.5, 7.5, 2.5, 2.5, 1.5, 2.5, 1.5

9. The mean of 3 numbers is 2. What is the fourth number such that the mean of all the four numbers should be 5. Hint: See Example **5**.

10. The mean age of 2 girls is 4 years. What should be the age of the third girl such that the mean of all three girls should be 6 years? Hint: See Example **5**.

11. The mean of 5 numbers is 7, what should be the sixth number for the mean of all the 6 numbers to be 4? Hint: See Example **5**.

12. The mean of the ages of 3 girls is 14 years, what should be the age of the fourth girl such that the mean age of all the 4 girls should be 12 years? Hint: See Example **5**.

Challenge Questions

13. Find the average. Round off your answer to the nearest whole number.

(**a**) 2, 6, 14
(**d**) 1.6, 10.4

(**g**) $2\frac{3}{4}, 3, 4\frac{1}{2}, 2\frac{1}{4}$

(**b**) 14, 28, 31, 43
(**e**) 36, 54, 104, 64

(**h**) $10\frac{3}{4}, 11\frac{1}{4}$

(**c**) 2.4, 6.9, 1.3
(**f**) 3, 7, 8, 4, 9

(**i**) 4.4, 6.9, 3.3

14. Find the range and the mode.

(**a**) 1, 7, 6, 1, 4, 1, 9
(**d**) 8, 10, 17, 10, 34, 10

(**b**) 14, 2, 8, 1.4
(**e**) 2, 2, 4, 8, 4, 9, 4

(**c**) 2.2, 4.8, 2.2, 4
(**f**) 6, 7, 11, 14, 7

15. Find the mean.

(a) 2, 3, 4   (b) 10, 22   (c) 1.2, 4.3, 3.5

(d) $14\frac{2}{6}$, $82\frac{2}{3}$, 2   (e). 31, 3   (f). 12, 6, 12

16. Find the mean.

(a) 2, 9, 7, 1, 4   (b) 1, 6, 8, 2, 10, 3   (c) 2, 4, 1, 8

(d) 2.2, 4.2, 6.8, 1.8   (e) $1\frac{1}{4}$, $6\frac{1}{2}$, $2\frac{1}{4}$ (f) 7, 9

17. The mean of 3 numbers is 6. What should be the fourth number such that the mean of all the four numbers should be 10?

Answers to Selected Questions

1(b) $4.00   **3(a)** 3   **4(a)** 25   **9**. 14

REAL WORLD APPLICATIONS - WORD PROBLEMS

1. The average test score of 5 students is 12. If the test scores of 4 students are 10, 13, 10, and 14, what is the test score of the 5th student? Hint: See Example **3** under the chapter Average.

2. The ages of three students are 9, 10, and 11 years. Find their average age. Hint: See Example **1** under chapter Average.

Challenge Questions.

3. The average age of 6 employees is 25 years. If the ages of 4 of the employees are 20, 21, 30, and 23 years, what is the total ages of the 2 remaining employees?

4. The weekly test scores of 6 students are 90%, 78%, 89%, 98%, 86%, and 65%. What is the average test score of the students?

5. Make a line plot of the following data and using the line plot explain how you would obtain the mode, range, mean, and the median. Hint: Number the number line from 0 to 30.

       8, 12, 16, 28, 2, 18, 12, 4, 8, 12, 10, 12, 2, 2, 28.

$$\xleftarrow{\hspace{0.5cm}}\overset{\displaystyle 0 \quad 5 \quad 10 \quad 15 \quad 20 \quad 25 \quad 30}{|\text{---}|\text{---}|\text{---}|\text{---}|\text{---}|\text{---}|}\xrightarrow{\hspace{0.3cm}}$$ Number line

FRACTIONS

A fraction can be considered a "part of something." A fraction may be defined as a "part of a unit." An apple may be considered one whole or a unit and if some part of the apple is eaten, then the remaining apple is no more a unit, but a part of the whole apple, which is called a **fraction** of the whole apple.

Fraction of the apple

Whole apple = I unit ⟶   ⟵ **This part of the apple is removed**

(Note: A unit   1 whole)

A fraction consists of two numbers separated by a fraction bar as shown below. Assume that half of the apple is eaten, then it means that the apple is divided into two parts and one part of it has been eaten. This statement can be written

as half of the apple has been eaten, and the fraction half is written as: $\dfrac{1}{2}$

Numerator

Fraction bar ⟶ $\dfrac{1}{2}$ ⟵ **Denominator**

The numerator indicates how many equal parts are being considered, or how many parts are represented in the fraction. Since the apple is divided into two equal parts and one part is eaten, then we are considering one out of the two equal parts.
The denominator indicates how many equal parts the whole is divided into. The apple is divided into two equal parts.
A fraction therefore, tells us that:
(**a**) The top number (numerator) indicates how many parts are represented or considered by a fraction.
(**b**) The bottom number (denominator) indicates into how many parts the unit has been divided.

Group Exercise
The materials needed for this exercise are oranges and knives.
This exercise is to demonstrate how to divide a whole into two halves. The class

should be divided into pairs of students and with the supervision of the teacher and the parents, each pair of students should put an orange onto a plate. The teacher should give one student per group a knife to cut the orange into approximately two equal parts. These two equal parts of the whole orange are referred to as "one half of a whole orange" as shown in the diagram.

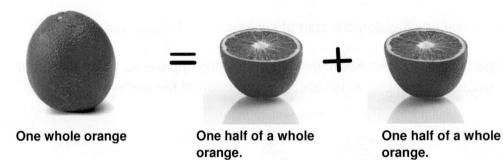

One whole orange   **One half of a whole**   **One half of a whole**
                                orange.   **orange.**

Each member of the group should be given one half of the whole orange to be eaten in order to remember one whole orange can be cut into two equal halves and the two equal halves can be shared by the two students in each group. Also, if we add the two halves of the oranges together, we should get the original whole orange.

UNDERSTANDING FRACTIONS WITH DIAGRAM

The diagrams below show an egg that is divided into two equal parts.

1 Whole part   **1 Half or**   **1 Half or**
2 Halves   **one out of 2 parts**   **one out of 2 parts**

The diagrams below show a cake that is divided into three equal parts and one part can be written in a fraction form as $\frac{1}{3}$.

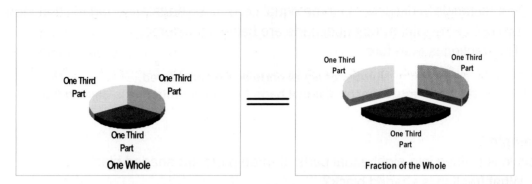

If we are considering two equal parts of the cake out of the total three equal parts, then it can be written in a fraction form as $\frac{2}{3}$.

Example 1

How many equal parts are the rectangles divided into?

(a) (b) ©

Solution

(a) The rectangle is divided into 5 equal parts.

(b) The rectangle is divided into 4 equal parts.

(c) The rectangle is divided into 3 equal parts.

Example 2

Write the shaded or colored part as a fraction of each rectangle.

(a) (b) ©

Solution

(a) The rectangle is divided into five equal parts. Two parts are shaded, and therefore, two parts are being considered out of a total of five equal parts. The fraction is therefore,

$\frac{2}{5}$ ◄——— **Number of equal parts being considered.**
◄——— **Number of equal parts the whole rectangle is divided into.**

(b) The rectangle is divided into four equal parts. Three parts are shade, and therefore, three out of the total of four equal parts are being considered. The fraction is therefore,

$\frac{3}{4}$ ◄——— **Number of equal parts being considered.**
◄——— **Number of equal parts the whole rectangle is divided into.**

(c) The rectangle is divided into three equal parts. Two parts are shaded, and therefore, two out of the total three equal parts are being considered.
The fraction is therefore,

Example 3

A circle is divided into eight equal parts. If three parts are shaded black,
(a) What fraction is shaded black?
(b) What fraction is not shaded black?

Solution

(a) The circle is divided into eight equal parts, and 3 equal parts out of the total of 8 equal parts are shaded black.
Therefore, the fraction shaded black is,

    =

The circle is divided into 8 parts.   3 out of 8 parts are shaded black.

(b) Since 3 equal parts of the circle is shaded black, the circle is divided into 8 equal parts, the number of equal parts of the circle that is not shaded black is
$$8 - 3 = 5$$
Therefore, the fraction of the circle that is not shaded black is,

    =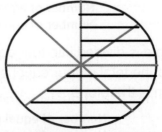

The circle is divided into 8 parts.   5 out of 8 parts are shaded black.

100

Critical Thinking

1. From the solution of Example **3**, note that the circle is divided into eight equal parts and one part is one-eighth of the circle and it is written in a fraction form as $\frac{1}{8}$.

2. In Example **3**(**a**), three-eighths of the circle is shaded black and five-eighths is not shaded black. Three-eighths is written in a fraction form as $\frac{3}{8}$, 5-eigths is written in a fraction form as $\frac{5}{8}$ and 8-eigths is written as $\frac{8}{8}$.

Using Example **3**(**b**) solution, we can then add up fractions with the same denominator as shown:

$$8\text{-eigths} = 5\text{-eigths} + 3\text{-eigths}$$
$$\updownarrow \qquad \updownarrow \qquad \updownarrow$$
$$\frac{8}{8} = \frac{5}{8} + \frac{3}{8} \qquad \text{------} [A]$$

The fractions on the right side of equation $[A]$ can be added up by just adding the numerators together putting it over the common denominator of 8. Equation $[A]$ then becomes:

$$\frac{8}{8} = \frac{5}{8} + \frac{3}{8} = \frac{5+3}{8} = \frac{8}{8}$$

Common denominator of 8.

In Example **3**(**b**), note that 8-eigths of the circle is the same as 1 whole circle and the 8-eigths can be written as $\frac{8}{8}$. Therefore, $\frac{8}{8}$ = 1 whole circle. We conclude by stating that whenever the top number of a fraction is the same as the bottom number, then the fraction = 1. Examples are: $\frac{1}{1} = 1$, $\frac{2}{2} = 1$, $\frac{3}{3} = 1$, $\frac{4}{4} = 1$, $\frac{5}{5} = 1$, $\frac{6}{6} = 1$,...

Example 4
There are 24 students in a class in a certain school. If 13 of the students are girls,
(**a**) What fraction of the students are girls?
(**b**) What fraction of the students are boys?
Solution
(**a**) Total number of students = 24

Number of girls $= 13$

The fraction of girls $= \dfrac{13}{24}$

$= \dfrac{13}{24}$ ✓ Number of parts of the whole class being considered.

✓ Number of the students in the whole class.

(b) Total number of students $= 24$
Number of girls $= 13$
Number of boys $=$ Total number of students $-$ Number of girls.
$\qquad = 24 - 13 = 11$

The fraction of boys $= \dfrac{11}{24}$

$= \dfrac{11}{24}$ ✓ Number of parts of the whole class being considered.

✓ Number of students in the whole class.

Example 5

Mary had 11 out of 12 of her mathematics test questions correct.

(a) What fraction did she have correct?

(b) What fraction did she have wrong?

Solution

(a) Total number of questions $= 12$
Number of questions correct $= 11$

Therefore, the fraction correct $= \dfrac{11}{12}$

$= \dfrac{11}{12}$ ✓ Number of questions considered to be correct.

✓ Total number of questions.

(b) Total number of questions $= 12$
Number of questions that are correct $= 11$
The number of wrong questions $=$
Total number of questions - Number of correct questions.
$\qquad = 12 - 11 = 1$

The fraction of the wrong questions $= \dfrac{1}{12}$ ✓ Number of wrong questions.

✓ Total number of questions.

Group Exercise

The class should be divided into four teams, Team A, Team B, Team C, and Team D. The class may be divided into more teams if needed. With the supervision of a teacher or a parent, each team should order a pizza which should be divided into 8 equal parts.

Team A

Team B

Team C

Team D

1. Team A should remove 5 parts of the pizza to share. What fraction of the pizza is shared and what fraction remains?
2. Team B should remove 7 parts of the pizza to share. What fraction of the pizza is shared and what fraction remains?
3. Team C should remove 6 parts of the pizza to share. What fraction of the pizza is shared and what fraction remains?
4. Team D should remove 4 parts of the pizza to share. What fraction of the pizza is shared and what fraction remains?

Each team should copy and complete Table 1.

Table 1, Team _____

Equal parts of pizza	Parts shared	Part remains	Fraction shared	Fraction Remains

Each team should post Table 1 on the blackboard, and then report their answers to the class.

The notes and the generous examples have provided me with the conceptual understanding and the computational fluency to do my homework.

Exercises

Hint: For the solutions to questions 1 - 9, see the preceding notes/information.

1. What is a fraction?
2. A fraction represents a ——————
3. The top number of a fraction is called ——————
4. The bottom number of a fraction is called ——————
5. The top number of a fraction tells us about ——————
6. The bottom number of a fraction tells us about ——————-
7. If the numerator of a fraction is the same as the denominator, the fraction is equal to ——-
8. If a whole apple is divided into seven equal parts, the bottom number of the fraction will be ————
9. If a circle is divided into five equal parts and 2 parts are removed,
   (**a**) What fraction is removed?
   (**b**) What fraction remains?
10 Write the fraction of the shaded or the colored areas. Hint: See Example **3**.

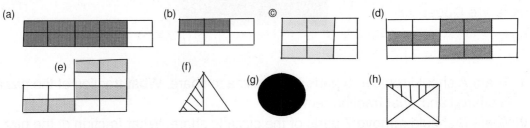

11. If a whole unit, such as a whole circle is divided into ten equal parts, the bottom number of the fraction is _____
12. Write four separate fractions which are equal to 1 or represent a whole unit. Hint: Read the section under "Critical thinking."
13. John had 7 out of 10 mathematics problems correct.
    (**a**) What fraction of the questions did John have correct?
    (**b**) What fraction of the questions did John have wrong? Hint: See Example 5.
14. There are 20 students in a class. If 3 students were absent one day,
    (**a**) what fraction were absent?
    (**b**) what fraction were present ? Hint: See Example **4**.
15. Mary bought 12 cookies and she gave away 8 of them.
    (**a**) What fraction did she give away?
    (**b**) What fraction remained? Hint: See Example **3**.
16. The school team won 5 out of the last 13 games.

(**a**) What fraction of the games did they win?

(**b**) What fraction of the games did they loose? Hint: See Example **5**.

17. If a fraction is written as $\dfrac{3}{7}$, into how many parts has the unit been divided?

Hint: See Example **2**.

18. In the picture, what part of the pizza is removed? What part of the picture remains? Hint: See Example 3.

The pizza is divided into 8 parts.

The part of the pizza that remains.

The part of the pizza that is removed.

Challenge Question

19. Mary worked 48 hours last week. If 8 hours were overtime hours, what fraction of the total hours were overtime?

Answers to Selected Questions

14(a) $\dfrac{3}{20}$ **16(a)** $\dfrac{5}{13}$

FRACTIONS AS A PART OF A SET

Quick Cumulative Review

Using the graph of blue, pink, green, and yellow rings:

1. How many pink rings are in the graph?

2. How many more blue rings are there in the graph than green rings?

3. Which colors of the rings have the same number of rings?

4. Which color has the greatest number of rings?

5. Which color has the least number of rings?

6. Which color is your favorite and why?

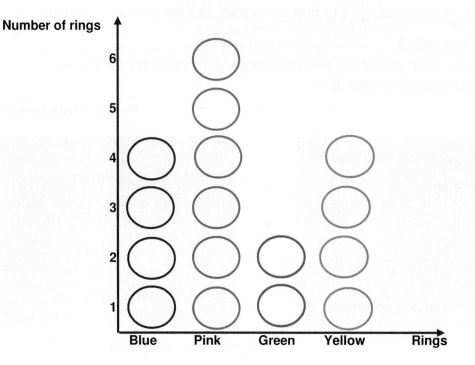

What is a Set?

Recall that we have already discussed fractions as a part of a whole. It is also possible to write fractions as a part of a set. Therefore, a fraction is a number that stands for a part of a whole or a part of a set. A set is things that belong to the same group and all the things that belong to the same group form one whole and can be considered as one. For example, the female students and the male students in grade 5 belong to the same group or belong to the same class or belong to the same set known as students. The female students form a fraction of the class or a fraction of the set or a fraction of the whole. The male students also form a fraction of the class or a fraction of the set or a fraction of the whole. The number of female students and the number of male students form the whole set. **A set is therefore, the sum or the total of things that belong to the same group or a common group**.

Example 1

There are 2 pink rings, 3 green rings, and 1 blue ring. How many rings are in the set?

Solution

The pink rings, green rings, and the blue ring belong to the same group or a common group known as rings. We have already discussed that a set is the sum of the total of things that belong to the same group or a common group.

Therefore:

The number of the rings that belong to the set

$$= \text{sum of the rings}$$
$$= 2 \text{ pink rings} + 3 \text{ green rings} + 1 \text{ blue ring}$$
$$= 6 \text{ rings}$$

Group Exercise

The class should be divided into groups of four students. Each group should put 3 blue counters, 4 yellow counters, 2 blue counters, and 1 red counter on a table. Using the explanation of a set, find the number of counters in the set on the table. Each group should record their method and answer to present to the whole class within 10 minutes.

How to Find a Fraction as a Part of a Set

A formula can be used to find a fraction as a part of a set.
The formula for finding a fraction as a part of a set is:

$$\textbf{A fraction as a part of a set} = \frac{\textbf{Number of things being considered in the set}}{\textbf{Total Number of things in the set}}$$

The formula simply means that we are considering and **comparing a certain number of things in the set to the total number of things in the set.**

Example 2

There are 3 blue balls and 1 red ball on the table.

a. What fraction of the set is blue balls?

b. What fraction of the set is red balls?

Solution

We can use the formula for finding the fraction as a part of a set to find the fraction of the blue balls as a part of a set of all the balls as shown:

a. The fraction of the blue balls as a part of a set

$$= \frac{\text{Number of things being considered in the set}}{\text{Total Number of things in the set}}$$

$$= \frac{\text{Number of blue balls in the set}}{\text{Total number of balls in the set}}$$

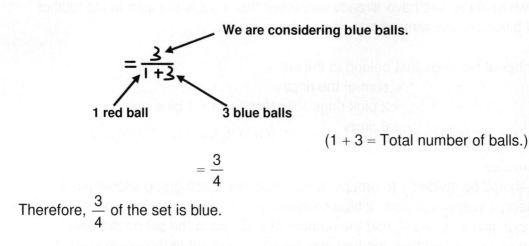

We are considering blue balls.

$= \dfrac{3}{1+3}$

1 red ball   3 blue balls

(1 + 3 = Total number of balls.)

$$= \frac{3}{4}$$

Therefore, $\dfrac{3}{4}$ of the set is blue.

b. We can use the formula for finding the fraction as a part of a set to find the fraction of the red balls as a part of a set of all the balls as shown:

The fraction of red balls as a part of a set

$$= \frac{\text{Number of things being considered in the set}}{\text{Total Number of things in the set}}$$

$$= \frac{\text{Number of red balls in the set}}{\text{Total number of balls in the set}}$$

We are considering red balls.

$= \dfrac{1}{1+3}$

1 red ball   3 blue balls

(1 + 3 = Total number of balls.)

$$= \frac{1}{4}$$

Therefore, $\dfrac{1}{4}$ of the set is red.

Example 3
The diagram represents pink, green, and blue rings.
a. What fraction of the rings is blue?
b. What fraction of the rings is pink?
c. What fraction of the rings is green?
d. What fraction of the rings is both pink and green?
e. What fraction of the rings is both pink and blue?

f. What fraction of the rings is both green and blue?

Solution

In this solution, we will practise how to use the formula to solve for the fraction as a part of a set.

a.

Number of blue rings in the set = 1.

Total number of rings in the set = 6.

The fraction of the blue rings as a part of a set of all the rings

$$= \frac{\text{Number of blue rings in the set}}{\text{Total number of rings in the set}}$$

$$= \frac{1}{6}$$

Therefore, the fraction of the blue rings as a part of a set of all the rings is $\frac{1}{6}$.

b.

Number of pink rings in the set = 2

Total number of the rings in the set = 6.

The fraction of the pink rings as a part of a set of all the rings

$$= \frac{\text{Number of pink rings in the set}}{\text{Total number of rings in the set}}$$

$$= \frac{2}{6}$$

$$= \frac{\overset{1}{\cancel{2}}}{\underset{3}{\cancel{6}}} \quad \text{Reduce to the lowest terms by dividing by 2.}$$

$$= \frac{1}{3}$$

Therefore, the fraction of the pink rings as a part of a set of all the rings is $\frac{1}{3}$.

c.

Number of green rings in the set = 3.

Total number of rings in the set = 6.
The fraction of the green rings as a part of a set of all the rings

$$= \frac{\text{Number of green rings in the set}}{\text{Total number of rings in the set}}$$

$$= \frac{3}{6}$$

$$= \frac{\overset{1}{\cancel{3}}}{\underset{2}{\cancel{6}}}$$ Reduce to the lowest terms by dividing by 3.

$$= \frac{1}{2}$$

Therefore, the fraction of the green rings as a part of a set of all the rings is $\frac{1}{2}$.

d.
Number of pink rings = 2.
Number of green rings = 3.
Number of both pink and green rings in the set

$$= \text{Number of pink rings} + \text{number of green rings.}$$
$$= 2 + 3$$
$$= 5$$

The fraction of both pink and green rings as a part of the set of all the rings

$$= \frac{\text{Number of both pink and green rings in the set}}{\text{Total number of rings in the set}}$$

$$= \frac{5}{6} \quad \overset{\nearrow \text{ Number of both pink and green rings in the set.}}{\underset{\nwarrow \text{ Total number of rings in the set.}}{}}$$

Therefore, the fraction of both pink and green rings as a part of a set of all the rings
is $\frac{5}{6}$.

e.
Number of pink rings in the set = 2.
Number of blue rings in the set = 1.

Number of both pink and blue rings in the set
$$= \text{Number of pink rings} + \text{number of blue rings.}$$
$$= 2 + 1$$
$$= 3$$

The fraction of both pink and blue rings as a part of a set of all the rings

$$= \frac{\text{Number of both pink and blue rings in the set}}{\text{Total number of rings in the set}}$$

$$= \frac{3}{6}$$

$$= \frac{\overset{1}{3}}{\underset{2}{6}} \quad \text{Reduce to the lowest terms by dividing by 3.}$$

$$= \frac{1}{2}$$

Therefore, the fraction of both pink and blue rings as a part of a set of all the rings is $\frac{1}{2}$.

f.
Number of green rings in the set $= 3$.
Number of blue rings in the set $= 1$.
Number of both green and blue rings in the set
$$= \text{Number of green rings} + \text{number of blue rings.}$$
$$= 3 + 1$$
$$= 4$$

The fraction of both green and blue rings as a part of a set of all the rings

$$= \frac{\text{Number of both green and blue rings in the set}}{\text{Total number of rings in the set}}$$

Number of both green and blue rings in the set.
$$= \frac{4}{6}$$
Total number of rings in the set.

$$= \frac{\overset{2}{\cancel{4}}}{\underset{3}{\cancel{6}}}$$ Reduce to the lowest terms by dividing by 2.

$$= \frac{2}{3}$$

Therefore, the fraction of both green and blue rings as a part of a set of all the rings is $\frac{2}{3}$.

Example 4

The Science Club of a middle school consists of 3 boys and 7 girls.

a. What fraction of the club members are boys?

b. What fraction of the club members are girls?

Solution

Both the girls and the boys belong to the Science Club.

The total number of the club members is the set of all the members of the club.

a.

Therefore, we can use the formula for finding the fraction as a part of a set to find the fraction of the boys as a part of a set of the total club members as shown:

The fraction of the boys as a part of a set of club members

$$= \frac{\text{Number of things being considered in the set}}{\text{Total number of things in the set}}$$

$$= \frac{\text{Number of boys in the club}}{\text{Total number of club members}}$$

We are considering boys in the club.

$$= \frac{3}{3 + 7}$$

3 boys ↗   ↖ 7 girls

$$= \frac{3}{10}$$

Therefore, $\frac{3}{10}$ of the club members are boys.

b.

Similar to the solution of 4a, we can use the formula for finding the fraction as a part of a set to find the fraction of the girls as a part of a set of the total club members as shown:

The fraction of the girls as a part of a set of the total club members

$$= \frac{\text{Number of things being considered in the set}}{\text{Total number of things in the set}}$$

$$= \frac{\text{Number of girls in the club}}{\text{Total number of club members}}$$

We are considering girls in the club.

$$= \frac{7}{3 + 7}$$

3 boys ↗   ↖ 7 girls

$$= \frac{7}{10}$$

Therefore, $\frac{7}{10}$ of the set or club members are girls.

The notes and the generous examples have provided me with the conceptual understanding and the computational fluency to do my homework.

Exercises
1. Explain what is meant by a set.
2. Explain what is meant by a fraction as a part of a set.
3. Give two examples of sets.
4. There is 1 red ball, 4 blue balls, and 2 green balls. What is the number of balls in the set?
   Hint: See Example 1.
5. What is the formula for finding a fraction as part of a set?
6. Use the diagram of rings to answer the questions.
   a. What is the fraction of the green rings?
   b. What is the fraction of the blue ring?
   Hint: See Example 2.

7. Use the diagram of rings to answer the questions.
   a. What is the fraction of the pink rings?
   b. What is the fraction of the blue ring?
   Hint: See Example 2

8. In each set of the diagram, find what fraction of the rings is blue and what fraction of the rings is green? Hint: See Example 2.

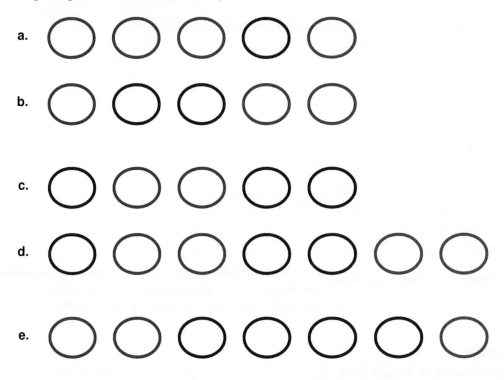

9. The diagram represents pink, green, and blue rings.
   a. What fraction of the rings is blue?
   b. What fraction of the rings is pink?
   c. What fraction of the rings is green?
   d. What fraction of the rings is both pink and green?
   e. What fraction of the rings is both pink and blue?
   f. What fraction of the rings is both green and blue?

   Hint: See Example 3.
10. The diagram represents pink, green, and blue rings.
   a. What fraction of the rings is blue?
   b. What fraction of the rings is pink?

c. What fraction of the rings is green?

d. What fraction of the rings is both pink and green?

e. What fraction of the rings is both pink and blue?

f. What fraction of the rings is both green and blue?

Hint: See Example 3.

11. The Glee Club of a school consists of 11 boys and 15 girls.

    a. What fraction of the club members are boys?

    b. What fraction of the club members are girls?

    Hint: See Example 4.

Challenge Questions

12. The diagram represents pink, green, and blue rings.

    a. What fraction of the rings is blue?

    b. What fraction of the rings is pink?

    c. What fraction of the rings is green?

    d. What fraction of the rings is both pink and green?

    e. What fraction of the rings is both pink and blue?

    f. What fraction of the rings is both green and blue?

13. In each set of the diagram, find what fraction of the rings is pink and what fraction of the rings is green? Hint: See Example 2.

    a.

    b.

c. ◯ ◯ ◯ ◯ ◯

d. ◯ ◯ ◯ ◯ ◯ ◯ ◯

e. ◯ ◯ ◯ ◯ ◯ ◯ ◯

Answers to Selected Questions

6a. $\dfrac{2}{3}$ **7a.** $\dfrac{2}{3}$ **8a.** $\dfrac{1}{5}$ is blue and $\dfrac{4}{5}$ is green   **9a.** $\dfrac{2}{5}$ **10a.** $\dfrac{2}{7}$

ADDITION OF FRACTIONS

ADDITION OF FRACTIONS THAT HAVE THE SAME DENOMINATORS

Rule: To add fractions that have the same denominators, add the numerators and put the sum or addition of the numerators over the same (common) denominator.

Example 1

Add the following:

(a) $\dfrac{1}{6} + \dfrac{2}{6} + \dfrac{1}{6}$ (b) $\dfrac{1}{7} + \dfrac{2}{7} + \dfrac{3}{7}$

Solution

(**a**) The numerators are 1, 2, and 1, and the denominator of each fraction is 6.

Step 1: Add the numerators: $1 + 2 + 1 = 4$

Step 2: Put the addition (sum) of the numerators over the same denominator as shown: $\dfrac{4}{6}$

Step 3: Therefore, $\dfrac{1}{6} + \dfrac{2}{6} + \dfrac{1}{6} = \dfrac{4}{6}$.

(**b**) The numerators are 1, 2, and 3 and the denominator is 7.

Step 1: Add the numerators: $1 + 2 + 3 = 6$

Step 2: Put the addition (sum) of the numerators over the same common denominator as shown: $\dfrac{6}{7}$

Step 3: Therefore, $\dfrac{1}{7} + \dfrac{2}{7} + \dfrac{3}{7} = \dfrac{6}{7}$

Example 2

Add the following:

(a) $\dfrac{2}{9} + \dfrac{1}{9} + \dfrac{4}{9} + \dfrac{3}{9} + \dfrac{5}{9}$ (b) $\dfrac{3}{12} + \dfrac{2}{12} + \dfrac{1}{12} + \dfrac{4}{12}$ (c) $\dfrac{3}{24} + \dfrac{2}{24} + \dfrac{4}{24} + \dfrac{5}{24}$

Solution

(**a**) The numerators are 2, 1, 4, 3, and 5, and the denominator of each fraction is 9.

Step 1: Add the numerators: $2 + 1 + 4 + 3 + 5 = 15$

Step 2: Put the addition (sum) of the numerators over the same common denominator as shown: $\dfrac{15}{9}$.

Step 3: Therefore, $\dfrac{2}{9} + \dfrac{1}{9} + \dfrac{4}{9} + \dfrac{3}{9} + \dfrac{5}{9} = \dfrac{15}{9}$

This book will later discuss how to handle fractions such as how to reduce to the lowest terms and improper fractions.

(**b**) The numerators are 3, 2, 1, and 4, and the denominator of each fraction is 12.

Step 1: Add the numerators: $3 + 2 + 1 + 4 = 10$

Step 2: Put the addition (sum) of the numerators over the same common denominator as shown: $\dfrac{10}{12}$

Step 3: Therefore, $\dfrac{3}{12} + \dfrac{2}{12} + \dfrac{1}{12} + \dfrac{4}{12} = \dfrac{10}{12}$

(**c**) The numerators are 3, 2, 4, and 5, and the denominator of each fraction is 24.

Step 1: Add the numerators: $3 + 2 + 4 + 5 = 14$

Step 2: Put the addition (sum) of the numerators over the same common denominator as shown: $\dfrac{14}{24}$

Step 3: Therefore, $\dfrac{3}{24} + \dfrac{2}{24} + \dfrac{4}{24} + \dfrac{5}{24} = \dfrac{14}{24}$

REAL WORLD APPLICATIONS - WORD PROBLEMS

Example 3

Eric needs $\dfrac{5}{12}$ foot, $\dfrac{7}{12}$ foot, $\dfrac{11}{12}$ foot, and $\dfrac{8}{12}$ foot of lumber to complete a project. How many feet of the lumber does Eric need?

Solution

The fractions of the lumber are $\dfrac{5}{12}$, $\dfrac{7}{12}$, $\dfrac{11}{12}$, and $\dfrac{8}{12}$.

Total feet of lumber needed $= \dfrac{5}{12} + \dfrac{7}{12} + \dfrac{11}{12} + \dfrac{8}{12}$

The numerators are 5, 7, 11, and 8, and the denominator of each fraction is 12.

Step 1: Add the numerators: $5 + 7 + 11 + 8 = 31$

Step 2: Put the addition (sum) of the numerators over the same common denominator as shown: $\dfrac{31}{12}$

Step 3: Therefore, the total feet of lumber needed

$$= \dfrac{5}{12} + \dfrac{7}{12} + \dfrac{11}{12} + \dfrac{8}{12} = \dfrac{31}{12} \text{ feet.}$$

Example 4

Nicholas bought the following weights of cheese: $\dfrac{6}{16}$ pound, $\dfrac{8}{16}$ pound, $\dfrac{9}{16}$ poun, and $\dfrac{11}{16}$ pound. What was the total weight of cheese that Nicholas bought?

Solution

The fractions of the cheese are:

$$\dfrac{6}{16}, \dfrac{8}{16}, \dfrac{9}{16}, \text{ and } \dfrac{11}{16}$$

The total weight of the cheese $= \dfrac{6}{16} + \dfrac{8}{16} + \dfrac{9}{16} + \dfrac{11}{16}$

The numerators are 6, 8, 9, and 11, and the denominator of each fraction is 16.

Step 1: Add the numerators: $6 + 8 + 9 + 11 = 34$

Step 2: Put the addition (sum) of the numerators over the same common denominator as shown: $\dfrac{34}{16}$

Step 3: Therefore, the total weight of the cheese $= \dfrac{6}{16} + \dfrac{8}{16} + \dfrac{9}{16} + \dfrac{11}{16}$

$$= \dfrac{34}{16} \text{ pounds}$$

Critical Thinking

To add fractions is really finding out how many parts are there in all the fractions to be added. For example, in Example **2(c)**, we are really finding out how many 24[ths] there are in all the fractions to be added.

The notes and the generous examples have provided me with the conceptual understanding and the computational fluency to do my homework.

Exercises

Add the following. Hint: See Examples 1 and 2.

(1) $\dfrac{1}{4} + \dfrac{2}{4} + \dfrac{1}{4}$

(2) $\dfrac{1}{5} + \dfrac{3}{5}$

(3) $\dfrac{1}{8} + \dfrac{3}{8} + \dfrac{4}{8}$

(4) $\dfrac{3}{11} + \dfrac{4}{11} + \dfrac{1}{11} + \dfrac{2}{11}$

(5) $\dfrac{1}{10} + \dfrac{3}{10} + \dfrac{6}{10} + \dfrac{4}{10}$

(6) $\dfrac{4}{13} + \dfrac{2}{13} + \dfrac{4}{13} + \dfrac{5}{13}$

(7) $\dfrac{3}{17} + \dfrac{2}{17} + \dfrac{1}{17} + \dfrac{6}{17}$

(8) $\dfrac{5}{15} + \dfrac{1}{15} + \dfrac{4}{15} + \dfrac{3}{15}$

(9) $\dfrac{5}{16} + \dfrac{1}{16} + \dfrac{3}{16} + \dfrac{4}{16}$

(10) $\dfrac{7}{27} + \dfrac{6}{27}$

(11) $\dfrac{2}{31} + \dfrac{5}{31} + \dfrac{7}{31}$

(12) $\dfrac{10}{41} + \dfrac{6}{41} + \dfrac{8}{41}$

(13) $\dfrac{11}{45} + \dfrac{1}{45} + \dfrac{13}{45}$

(14) $\dfrac{7}{35} + \dfrac{2}{35} + \dfrac{10}{35}$

(15) $\dfrac{9}{40} + \dfrac{6}{40} + \dfrac{13}{40}$

(16) $\dfrac{3}{28} + \dfrac{4}{28} + \dfrac{6}{28}$

(17) $\dfrac{2}{9} + \dfrac{4}{9}$

(18) $\dfrac{4}{15} + \dfrac{7}{15}$

(19) Joshua needs $\dfrac{1}{6}$ foot, $\dfrac{2}{6}$ foot, $\dfrac{3}{6}$ foot, and $\dfrac{4}{6}$ foot of wood to complete his project. How many feet of wood does Joshua need? Hint: See Example **3**.

(20) Samuel bought $\dfrac{17}{36}$ yard, $\dfrac{28}{36}$ yard, $\dfrac{25}{36}$ yard, and $\dfrac{33}{36}$ yard of fabric for his school project. How many yards did Samuel buy? Hint: See Example **3**.

(21) Mary bought the following weights of cheese: $\frac{9}{16}$ pound, $\frac{5}{16}$ pound, $\frac{7}{16}$ pound, and $\frac{13}{16}$ pound. What was the total weight of cheese that Mary bought? Hint: See Example **4**.

(22) Rose made a cake for her friend. She mixed $\frac{3}{6}$ cup of milk, $\frac{3}{6}$ cup of sugar, $\frac{3}{6}$ cup of shortening, and $\frac{3}{6}$ cup of flour. How many cups did she mix? Hint: See Example 4.

Challenge Question

(23) Karen cut off the following pieces of wood: $\frac{4}{9}$ foot, $\frac{7}{9}$ foot, $\frac{5}{9}$ foot, and $\frac{8}{9}$ foot. How many feet of wood did she cut?

Answers to Selected Questions

(1) $\frac{4}{4} = 1$, **(19)** $\frac{10}{6} = 1\frac{4}{6} = 1\frac{2}{3}$ feet

TYPES OF FRACTIONS

New Terms
Proper fraction, improper fraction, and mixed fractions

The three types of fractions are:
1. **Proper fraction**
2. **Improper fraction**
3. **Mixed fraction**

A proper fraction is a fraction where the numerator is less than the denominator. Some examples of proper fractions are: $\frac{1}{2}, \frac{3}{4}, \frac{5}{12}, \frac{99}{100}$, and $\frac{199}{200}$.

An improper fraction is a fraction where the numerator is greater than the denominator. Some examples of improper fractions are: $\frac{7}{4}, \frac{8}{3}, \frac{11}{4}, \frac{12}{7}, \frac{250}{199}$.

A mixed fraction contains both a whole number and a fractional part.

Some examples of mixed fractions are: $1\dfrac{1}{2}$, $2\dfrac{3}{4}$, $3\dfrac{4}{5}$, $4\dfrac{12}{13}$, and $5\dfrac{1}{6}$.

RAISING FRACTIONS AND LOWERING FRACTIONS.

New term
Equivalent fractions

Equivalent fractions are fractions that have the same values or fractions that represent the same part of a whole.

Group Class Exercise
Divide the class into four groups. Each group should be given three pages of 11 x 8 paper, a ruler, and a pencil.

Step 1: Each group should sketch a rectangle with dimensions of 8 inches by 4 inches.

A rectangle is a four sided figure as shown ⟶

Label the rectangle ABCD. Let AB and DC be the lengths of the rectangle. Each group should mark point E between A and B such that E should be 4 inches from A. Mark point F between D and C so that F should be 4 inches from D. With a pencil and a ruler, draw a line from E to F.

Note that rectangle EBCF is $\dfrac{1}{2}$ of rectangle ABCD.

Step 2: Measure and mark the point G between A and E such that G is 2 inches from A. Measure and mark point H between D and F so that H is 2 inches from D. Use a pencil and a ruler to draw a line from G to H. Measure and mark point I between E and B so that I is 2 inches from E. Measure and mark point J between F and C so that J is 2 inches from F. Use a pencil and a ruler to draw a line from I to J. Note that rectangle ABCD is divided into 4 equal parts and rectangle EBCF is:

$\dfrac{2}{4}$ of rectangle ABCD.

Step 3: Measure and mark point K between A and D so that point K is 2 inches from A. Measure and mark point L between B and C so that L is 2 inches from B. Use a pencil and a ruler to draw a line from K to L. Note that rectangle ABCD is divided into 8 equal parts and rectangle EBCF is:

$$\frac{4}{8} \text{ of rectangle ABCD.}$$

Summary:

Step 1: Shows that rectangle EBCF = $\frac{1}{2}$ of rectangle ABCD.

Step 2: Shows that rectangle EBCF = $\frac{2}{4}$ of rectangle ABCD.

Step 3: Shows that rectangle EBCF = $\frac{4}{8}$ of rectangle ABCD.

Conclusion: Rectangle EBCF = $\frac{1}{2} = \frac{2}{4} =$ of $\frac{4}{8}$ of rectangle ABCD, and these fractions are known as **equivalent fractions**. Equivalent fractions are fractions that represent the same part of a whole.

How are Equivalent Fractions Obtained?

Rule 1: Equivalent fractions are obtained by multiplying both the denominator and the numerator by the same number.

For example, the fraction $\frac{1}{3}$ can be changed to $\frac{2}{6}$ by multiplying both the numerator and the denominator by 2 as shown: $\frac{1}{3} = \frac{1}{3} \times \frac{2}{2} = \frac{2}{6}$

Critical Thinking

By multiplying both the numerator and the denominator by 2, we are actually multiplying $\frac{1}{3}$ by 1 because $\frac{2}{2} = 1$, and multiplying $\frac{1}{3}$ by a fraction of $\frac{2}{2}$ which is equal to 1 does not change the value of $\frac{1}{3}$, but only changes the original fraction to an equivalent fraction of $\frac{2}{6}$. When $\frac{1}{3}$ is changed to $\frac{2}{6}$ without changing the value of $\frac{1}{3}$ is called raising $\frac{1}{3}$ to $\frac{2}{6}$, and the fraction with the bigger denominator or numerator is called the higher equivalent. In this case, the higher equivalent is $\frac{2}{6}$.

Rule 2: Multiplying both the numerator and the denominator by the same number will not change the value of the fraction.

Example 1

Raise $\dfrac{1}{5}$ to a higher equivalent that has a denominator of 20.

Solution

The problem can be written as: $\dfrac{1}{5} = \dfrac{?}{20}$

Using Rule 1, which states that equivalent fractions are obtained by multiplying both the denominator and the numerator by the same number, let us find what number is multiplied by the denominator 5 to obtain 20.

$$\frac{1}{5} = \frac{?}{20}$$

The denominator of 5 is multiplied by 4 to obtain a higher equivalent denominator of 20, and the numerator of 1 should also be multiplied by the same number 4 to obtain a higher equivalent numerator of 4 as shown:

$$\text{Therefore, } \frac{1}{5} = \frac{4}{20} \leftarrow \text{Higher equivalent fraction}$$

The higher equivalent $= \dfrac{4}{20}$, and this may also be obtained by simply multiplying the numerator and the denominator by 4 as shown:

$$\frac{1}{5} \times \frac{4}{4} = \frac{4}{20} \leftarrow \text{Higher equivalent fraction}$$

Example 2

Raise $\dfrac{2}{7}$ to a higher equivalent that has a numerator of 6.

Solution

The problem can be written as: $\dfrac{2}{7} = \dfrac{6}{?}$

Using Rule 1, let us find what number is multiplied by the numerator 2 to obtain the higher equivalent numerator of 6. The numerator 2 is multiplied by 3 to obtain the higher equivalent numerator of 6, and therefore, the denominator of 7 should also be multiplied by 3 to obtain the higher equivalent denominator of 21 as shown:

$$\frac{2}{7} = \frac{6}{21} \leftarrow \text{Higher equivalent fraction}$$

The higher equivalent $= \dfrac{6}{21}$, and this may also be obtained simply by multiplying

$$\frac{3}{8} \times \frac{3}{3} = \frac{9}{24} \leftarrow \text{Equivalent fraction.}$$

$$\frac{1}{3} \times \frac{8}{8} = \frac{8}{24} \leftarrow \text{Equivalent fraction.}$$

$$\frac{1}{6} \times \frac{4}{4} = \frac{4}{24} \leftarrow \text{Equivalent fraction.}$$

Step 3: Add the numerators of the equivalent fractions and write the sum of the numerators of the equivalent fractions over the equivalent common denominator as shown:

↗Sum of the numerators of the equivalent fractions.

$$\frac{9 + 8 + 4}{24} = \frac{21}{24}$$

↖Equivalent common denominator which is the same as the LCD.

The notes and the generous examples have provided me with the conceptual understanding and the computational fluency to do my homework.

Exercises

(1) John needs the following pieces of lumber to finish a project: $\frac{5}{7}$ foot, $\frac{3}{14}$ foot, and $\frac{3}{7}$ foot. How many feet of lumber does he need? Hint: See Example **6**.

(2) Rose walked $\frac{3}{8}$ mile to the library, $\frac{3}{4}$ mile to school. How many miles did she walk? Hint: See Example **6**.

(3) Jane walked $\frac{3}{4}$ mile to school, $\frac{1}{6}$ mile to the market and $\frac{2}{3}$ mile to the football game. How many miles did she walk? Hint: See Example **7**.

(4) A class needs the following lengths of fabric for an experiment: $\frac{2}{5}$ foot, $\frac{3}{10}$ foot, and $\frac{17}{20}$ foot. How many feet of fabric are needed? Hint: see Example 7.

Challenge Questions

(5) Nick would like to bake a cake by adding $\frac{3}{5}$ cup of milk, $\frac{2}{3}$ cup of chocolate, $\frac{1}{2}$

the numerator and the denominator of $\frac{2}{7}$ by 3 as shown:

$$\frac{2}{7} \times \frac{3}{3} = \frac{6}{21} \leftarrow \text{Higher equivalent fraction}$$

Example 3

Copy and complete to make a true statement

(a) $\frac{2}{6} = \frac{10}{?}$ (b) $\frac{3}{?} = \frac{6}{8}$ (c) $\frac{?}{4} = \frac{12}{16}$

Solution

(a) Using Rule 1, let us find what number is multiplied by the numerator 2 to obtain the higher equivalent numerator of 10. The numerator 2 is multiplied by 5 to obtain the higher equivalent numerator of 10, and therefore, the denominator of 6 should also be multiplied by 5 to obtain the higher equivalent denominator of 30 as shown:

$$\frac{2}{6} = \frac{10}{30} \leftarrow \text{Higher equivalent fraction}$$

The higher equivalent fraction is $\frac{10}{30}$, and this can also be obtained simply by multiplying the denominator and the numerator by 5 as shown:

$$\frac{2}{6} \times \frac{5}{5} = \frac{10}{30} \leftarrow \text{Higher equivalent fraction}$$

(b) Let us find the number that is used to divide the numerator of 6 in order to obtain the lower equivalent numerator of 3. The numerator of 6 is divided by 2 in order to obtain the lower equivalent numerator of 3, and therefore, the denominator of 8 should also be divided by the same number 2 in order to obtain the lower equivalent denominator of 4 as shown:

$$\text{Lower equivalent fraction} \rightarrow \frac{3}{4} = \frac{6}{8}$$

The lower equivalent is $\frac{3}{4}$, and this can also be obtained by dividing the numerator

and the denominator of the higher equivalent fraction of $\frac{6}{8}$ by 2 as shown:

$$\text{Lower equivalent fraction} \rightarrow \frac{3}{4} = \frac{6 \div 2}{8 \div 2}$$

(c) Let us find the number that is used to divide the higher equivalent denominator of 16 in order to obtain a lower equivalent denominator 4. The higher equivalent denominator of 16 is divided by 4 in order to obtain the lower equivalent denominator of 4, and therefore, the numerator of 12 should also be divided by the same number 4 to obtain the lower equivalent numerator of 3 as shown:

$$\text{Lower equivalent fraction} \rightarrow \frac{3}{4} = \frac{12}{16}$$

The lower equivalent fraction $= \frac{3}{4}$, and this can also be obtained simply by dividing the numerator and the denominator of the higher equivalent of $\frac{12}{16}$ by 4 as shown:

$$\text{Lower equivalent fraction} \rightarrow \frac{3}{4} = \frac{12 \div 4}{16 \div 4}$$

Critical Thinking

1. Changing from any fraction to a higher equivalent fraction involves the multiplication of the numerator and the denominator by the same number.
2. Changing from any fraction to a lower equivalent fraction involves the division of the numerator and the denominator by the same number which is the same common factor. We will learn more about common factors later.

REAL WORLD APPLICATIONS - WORD PROBLEM
Raising Fractions and Lowering Fractions

Example 4

Mary made a pizza and she cut it into 8 slices. If she ate $\frac{1}{4}$ of the pizza, how many slices did she eat?

Solution

8 slices of pizza is the whole pizza. Therefore, the solution can be set up as shown:

$$\frac{1}{4} = \frac{?}{8}$$

Let us find the number which multiplied the lower equivalent denominator of 4 to obtain the higher equivalent denominator of 8. The lower equivalent denominator of 4 is multiplied by 2 in order to obtain the higher equivalent denominator of 8, therefore, the lower equivalent numerator of 1 should also be multiplied by the same number of 2 in order to obtain a higher equivalent numerator of 2 as shown:

$$\frac{1}{4} = \frac{2}{8} \searrow$$

This is the number of slices eaten by Mary.

Mary eats 2 slices of the pizza, and this can also be solved simply by multiplying the denominator and the numerator of the lower equivalent fraction of $\frac{1}{4}$ by 2 as shown:

$$\frac{1}{4} \times \frac{2}{2} = \frac{2}{8} \searrow$$

Mary ate 2 slices of the pizza.

The notes and the generous examples have provided me with the conceptual understanding and the computational fluency to do my homework.

Exercise

1. What is meant by equivalent fractions?
2. How are equivalent fractions obtained?
3. Write the equivalence of $\frac{1}{4}$ by raising the denominator to 24. Hint: See Example 1.
4. Write the equivalence of $\frac{3}{7}$ by raising the numerator to 12. Hint: See Example 2.
5. Copy and complete to make a true statement. Hint: See Example 3.

   (a) $\frac{2}{10} = \frac{?}{40}$ (b) $\frac{1}{8} = \frac{?}{32}$ (c) $\frac{6}{7} = \frac{36}{?}$ (d) $\frac{?}{27} = \frac{1}{3}$ (e) $\frac{5}{6} = \frac{25}{?}$

6. Raise $\frac{2}{3}$ to a higher equivalent fraction that has a denominator of 15. Hint: See Example 1.
7. Copy and complete to make true statements. Hint: See Example 3.

   (a) $\frac{1}{6} = \frac{?}{12}$ (b) $\frac{2}{8} = \frac{?}{24}$ (c) $\frac{?}{36} = \frac{2}{6}$ (d) $\frac{4}{?} = \frac{12}{2}$

   (e) $\frac{?}{14} = \frac{3}{7}$ (f) $\frac{5}{15} = \frac{1}{?}$ (g) $\frac{12}{?} = \frac{36}{9}$ (h) $\frac{?}{7} = \frac{15}{21}$

8. John made a pizza and cut it into 12 slices. If he ate $\frac{1}{4}$ of the pizza, how many slices did he eat? Hint: See Example 4.
9. In a class of 25 students, $\frac{2}{5}$ are girls. How many students are girls? Hint:

   The whole class has 25 students . Set up as follows: $\frac{2}{5} = \frac{?}{25}$, and then solve it.

Challenge Questions

10. Complete each pair of equivalent fractions.

(a) $\dfrac{1}{4} = \dfrac{?}{12}$　　　　(b) $\dfrac{2}{?} = \dfrac{12}{18}$　　　　(c) $\dfrac{3}{8} = \dfrac{?}{24}$

(d) $\dfrac{?}{21} = \dfrac{9}{7}$　　　　(e) $\dfrac{5}{35} = \dfrac{15}{?}$　　　　(f) $\dfrac{11}{77} = \dfrac{1}{?}$

(g) $\dfrac{24}{36} = \dfrac{6}{?}$　　　　(h) $\dfrac{20}{60} = \dfrac{?}{120}$　　　　(i) $\dfrac{?}{30} = \dfrac{8}{10}$

11. Write an equivalent fraction for each fraction below. You may choose to raise or lower the equivalent fraction.

(a) $\dfrac{1}{2}$　　(b) $\dfrac{1}{3}$　　(c) $\dfrac{2}{7}$　　(d) $\dfrac{2}{5}$　　(e) $\dfrac{7}{10}$

(f) $\dfrac{3}{7}$　　(g) $\dfrac{6}{12}$　　(h) $\dfrac{11}{22}$　　(i) $\dfrac{24}{25}$　　(j) $\dfrac{21}{34}$

Answers to Selected Questions

3. $\dfrac{6}{24}$　　5(a) 8　　11(a) $\dfrac{1}{2} \times \dfrac{2}{2} = \dfrac{2}{4}$

MULTIPLES, LEAST COMMON MULTIPLE, AND LEAST COMMON DENOMINATOR

1. Multiples

The multiples of a whole number are the product of that number and any other whole number except zero.

Example 1

(a) What are the multiples of 5?
(b) What are the multiples of 3?

Solution:

(a) The multiples of 5 are: $5 \times 1 = 5$, $5 \times 2 = 10$, $5 \times 3 = 15$, $5 \times 4 = 20$, $5 \times 5 = 25$, . . .

Therefore, the multiples of 5 are: 5, 10, 15, 20, 25,...

(**b**) The multiples of 3 are: 3 × 1 = 3, 3 × 2 = 6, 3 × 3 = 9, 3 × 4 = 12, 3 × 5 = 15, 3 × 6 = 18, 3 × 7 = 21, ...
Therefore the multiples of 3 are: 3, 6, 9, 12, 15, 18, 21, . . .

2. Least Common Multiples

Rule 1: The least common multiple (LCM) of two or more numbers is the least or the smallest multiple that is common to all the numbers.

Rule 2: The least common multiple (LCM) of two or more numbers can be found by listing the multiples of each number in order from the smallest to the greatest until a multiple that is common to all the numbers is obtained.

Example 2

What is the least common multiple (LCM) of 3 and 4?

Solution

The multiples of 3 are: 3 × 1 = 3
$$3 × 2 = 6$$
$$3 × 3 = 9$$
$$3 × 4 = 12 \ →\ (LCM)$$
$$3 × 5 = 15$$
$$3 × 6 = 18$$

Therefore, the multiples of 3 are: 3, 6, 9, 12, 15, 18, . . .

The multiples of 4 are: 4 × 1 = 4
$$4 × 2 = 8$$
$$4 × 3 = 12 \ →\ \text{Stop here because 12 also appears as a}$$
multiple of 3, and 12 is therefore the least common multiple of 3 and 4.

Therefore, the multiples of 4 are: 4, 8, 12, . . .
↑
LCM

The LCM = 12

Note that Rule 2 is used in solving this problem.

Example 3

What is the least common multiple of 4 and 6?

Solution

The multiples of 4 are: 4 × 1 = 4, 4 × 2 = 8, 4 × 3 = 12, 4 × 4 = 16, 4 × 5 = 20, . . .
Therefore, the multiples of 4 are: 4, 8, 12, 16, 20, . . .
The multiples of 6 are: 6 × 1 = 6, 6 × 2 = 12, . . .
↑
Stop here because 12 also appears as a multiple of 4, and therefore, 12 is the least common multiple (LCM) of 4 and 6.

The LCM = 12
Note that Rule 2 is used in solving this problem.

Example 4
Find the least common multiple (LCM) of 6 and 7.
Solution
The multiples of 6 are: $6 \times 1 = 6$, $6 \times 2 = 12$, $6 \times 3 = 18$, $6 \times 4 = 24$, $6 \times 5 = 30$,
$\qquad$ $6 \times 6 = 36$, $6 \times 7 = 42$, $6 \times 8 = 48$, . . .
The multiples of 6 are: 6, 12, 18, 24, 30, 36, 42, 48, . . .
The multiples of 7 are: $7 \times 1 = 7$, $7 \times 2 = 14$, $7 \times 3 = 21$, $7 \times 4 = 28$, $7 \times 5 = 35$,
$\qquad$ $7 \times 6 = 42$
$\qquad$ ↑

$\qquad$ Stop here because 42 also appears as a multiple
$\qquad$ of 6 and so, 42 is the least common multiple
$\qquad$ of 6 and 7.

The LCM is 42
Note that Rule 2 is used to solve this problem.

Example 5
Given that the multiples of 4 are: 4, 8, 12, 16, 20, 24, 28, 32, . . . and given that
the multiples of 6 are: 6, 12, 18, 24, 30, 36, . . ., explain why although 24 is
a common multiple of 4 and 6, 24 is not the least common multiple (LCM) of 4
and 6.
Solution
The multiples of 4 are: 4, 8, 12, 16, 20, 24, 28, 32, . . .
The multiples of 6 are: 6, 12, 18, 24, 30, 36, . . .
By observing the multiples of 4 and 6 above, 24 appears as one of the multiples of
4 and 6. It can also be observed that 12 is one of the multiples of 4 and 6, but 12 is
the smallest number that is the multiple of both 4 and 6, and therefore, 12 is the
least common multiple (LCM) of 4 and 6 and 24 is just one of the common
multiples of 4 and 6.

Example 6
Find the least common multiple of 6, 9, and 12.
Solution
The multiples of 6 are: $6 \times 1 = 6$, $6 \times 2 = 12$, $6 \times 3 = 18$, $6 \times 4 = 24$, $6 \times 5 = 30$,
$\qquad$ $6 \times 6 = 36$, $6 \times 7 = 42$, . . .
The multiples of 9 are: $9 \times 1 = 9$, $9 \times 2 = 18$, $9 \times 3 = 27$, $9 \times 4 = 36$,
$\qquad$ ↑
$\qquad$ Stop here because 36 is also one of

the multiples of 6.

The multiples of 12 are: $12 \times 1 = 12$, $12 \times 2 = 24$, $12 \times 3 = 36$,

$\uparrow$

Stop here because 36 is also one of the multiples of 6 and 9. Since 36 is the smallest multiple which is common to 6, 9, and 12, 36 is the least common multiple (LCM) of 6, 9, and 12.

The LCM is 36.

�▬▬▬▬▬▬▬ **The notes and the generous examples have provided me with the conceptual understanding and the computational fluency to do my homework.**

Exercises

1. Explain what is meant by a multiple of a number?
2. List the first eight multiples of each number. Hint: See Examples **1** and **2**.
   (**a**) 5   (**b**) 8   (**c**) 9   (**d**) 4   (**e**) 10   (**f**) 11   (**g**) 12
3. Explain what is meant by the least common multiple of two or more numbers?
4. Find the least common multiple of each set of numbers. Hint: See Examples **2, 3**, and **4**.
   (**a**) 2 and 7   (**b**) 3 and 7   (**c**) 4 and 7   (**d**) 5 and 7   (**e**) 6 and 8

   (**f**) 7 and 8   (**g**) 5 and 9   (**h**) 7 and 9   (**i**) 12 and 8   (**j**) 12 and 48

   (**k**) 10 and 7   (**l**) 11 and 4   (**m**) 13 and 4   (**n**) 7 and 4   (**o**) 5 and 7
5. Given that the multiples of 5 are: 5, 10, 15, 20, 25, 30, 35, 40, 45, 50, 55, 60, . . ., and the multiples of 6 are: 6, 12, 18, 24, 30, 36, 42, 48, 54, 60, . . . , explain why 60 cannot be the least common multiple (LCM) of 5 and 6. Hint: See Example **5**.
6. Find the least common multiple (LCM) of each set of numbers. Hint: See Example **6**.
   (**a**) 3, 4, and 6   (**b**) 4, 8, and 24   (**c**) 3, 5, and 6   (**d**) 3, 11, and 33

   (**e**) 4, 7, and 14   (**f**) 9, 4, and 6   (**g**) 6, 9, and 4   (**h**) 6, 5, and 4.
7. Explain what is the difference between the common multiples of two or more numbers and the least common multiple of two or more numbers. Hint: see Example **5**.

3. Common Denominator

A common denominator is when two or more fractions have the same denominator.

Considering the fractions $\dfrac{1}{12}$, $\dfrac{5}{12}$, $\dfrac{7}{12}$, and $\dfrac{11}{12}$, the denominator 12 is common to all

130

the fractions of $\frac{1}{12}, \frac{5}{12}, \frac{7}{12}$, and $\frac{11}{12}$, and therefore, the common denominator is 12. The usefulness of the common denominator will be discussed fully under comparing fractions.

4. Least Common Denominators

The least common denominator of two or more fractions is the least common multiple (LCM) of their denominators. Hint: Review the topic under the Least Common Multiple (LCM) to fully understand the least common multiple (LCM) of numbers.

Example 1

Find the least common denominator of $\frac{1}{3}$ and $\frac{2}{7}$.

Solution

The denominators of $\frac{1}{3}$ and $\frac{2}{7}$ are 3 and 7.

The multiples of 3 are: $3 \times 1 = 3$, $3 \times 2 = 6$, $3 \times 3 = 9$, $3 \times 4 = 12$, $3 \times 5 = 15$, $3 \times 6 = 18$,
$3 \times 7 = 21$, $3 \times 8 = 24, \ldots$

Therefore, the multiples of 3 are: 3, 6, 9, 12, 15, 18, 21, 24, . . .

The multiples of 7 are: $7 \times 1 = 7$, $7 \times 2 = 14$, $7 \times 3 = 21, \ldots$

Stop here because 21 is the smallest number which also appears as a multiple of 3. Therefore, 21 is the least common denominator of $\frac{1}{3}$ and $\frac{2}{7}$.

Example 2

Find the least common denominator of $\frac{2}{5}$ and $\frac{7}{9}$.

Solution

The denominators of $\frac{2}{5}$ and $\frac{7}{9}$ are 5 and 9.

The multiples of 5 are: $5 \times 1 = 5$, $5 \times 2 = 10$, $5 \times 3 = 15$, $5 \times 4 = 20$, $5 \times 5 = 25$,
$5 \times 6 = 30$, $5 \times 7 = 35$, $5 \times 8 = 40$, $5 \times 9 = 45$, $5 \times 10 = 50, \ldots$

Therefore, the multiples of 5 are: 5, 10, 15, 20, 25, 30, 35, 40, 45, 50, . . .

The multiples of 9 are: $9 \times 1 = 9$, $9 \times 2 = 18$, $9 \times 3 = 27$, $9 \times 4 = 36$, $9 \times 5 = 45, \ldots$

Stop here because 45 is the smallest number which also appears as a multiple of 5. Therefore, 45 is the least common denominator of $\frac{2}{5}$ and $\frac{7}{9}$.

Example 3

Find the least common denominator of $\frac{2}{3}$, $\frac{3}{4}$, and $\frac{5}{9}$.

Solution

The denominators of $\frac{2}{3}$, $\frac{3}{4}$, and $\frac{5}{9}$ are 3, 4, and 9.

The multiples of 3 are: $3 \times 1 = 3$, $3 \times 2 = 6$, $3 \times 3 = 9$, $3 \times 4 = 12$, $3 \times 5 = 15$,
$3 \times 6 = 18$, $3 \times 7 = 21$, $3 \times 8 = 24$, $3 \times 9 = 27$, $3 \times 10 = 30$,
$3 \times 11 = 33$, $3 \times 12 = 36$, $3 \times 13 = 39$, . . .
Therefore, the multiples of 3 are: 3, 6, 9, 12, 15, 18, 24, 27, 30, 33, (36), 39, . . .
The multiples of 4 are: $4 \times 1 = 4$, $4 \times 2 = 8$, $4 \times 3 = 12$, $4 \times 4 = 16$, $4 \times 5 = 20$,
$4 \times 6 = 24$, $4 \times 7 = 28$, $4 \times 8 = 32$, $4 \times 9 = 36$, . . .
↑

Stop here because 36 is the smallest number that also appears as a multiple of 3 and the third denominator which is 9 can divide 36 evenly (without a remainder). Note also that 12 and 24 appear as multiples of both 3 and 4 but we cannot choose neither 12 nor 24 as the least common multiple of 3, 4, and 9 because 9 cannot divide neither 12 nor 24 evenly (without a remainder). Note that 12 and 24 are not multiples of 9. Therefore, the least common multiple of 3, 4 and 9 is 36 and the least common denominator of $\frac{2}{3}$, $\frac{3}{4}$,

and $\frac{5}{9}$ is 36.

Note 1: The best common denominator is the LCM of the denominator.
Note 2: Knowing the multiplication tables from 1 to 12 is very helpful in detecting quickly that $9 \times 4 = 36$ or 9 can divide into 36 evenly (without a remainder).

The notes and the generous examples have provided me with the conceptual understanding and the computational fluency to do my homework.

Exercises

1. What is the best common denominator?
2. Explain why knowing the multiplication tables from 1 to 12 is very helpful in determining the LCM and the LCD.
3. List the multiplication tables that you know.

4. Explain what is meant by the least common denominator (LCD).
5. Explain what is meant by the least common multiple (LCM).
6. Find the least common multiple of the following: Hint: See Examples **1** and **2**.

(a) $\frac{1}{3}$ and $\frac{2}{5}$ 　　(b) $\frac{3}{4}$ and $\frac{5}{6}$ 　　(c) $\frac{1}{2}$ and $\frac{2}{5}$ 　　(d) $\frac{2}{3}$ and $\frac{1}{7}$

(e) $\frac{2}{7}$ and $\frac{2}{5}$ 　　(f) $\frac{1}{4}$ and $\frac{3}{7}$ 　　(g) $\frac{3}{5}$ and $\frac{3}{7}$ 　　(h) $\frac{2}{3}$ and $\frac{5}{8}$

(i) $\frac{5}{8}$ and $\frac{5}{7}$ 　　(j) $\frac{5}{6}$ and $\frac{5}{7}$ 　　(k) $\frac{5}{6}$ and $\frac{5}{9}$ 　　(l) $\frac{2}{9}$ and $\frac{5}{12}$

(m) $\frac{4}{9}$ and $\frac{1}{4}$ 　　(n) $\frac{5}{7}$ and $\frac{4}{9}$ 　　(o) $\frac{2}{11}$ and $\frac{7}{12}$ 　　(p) $\frac{2}{3}$ and $\frac{3}{8}$

7. Find the least common denominator of the following. Hint: See Examples **1, 2, and 3**.

(a) $\frac{2}{3}, \frac{1}{4}$, and $\frac{1}{2}$ 　　(b) $\frac{3}{4}, \frac{1}{5}$, and $\frac{3}{10}$ 　　(c) $\frac{1}{3}, \frac{2}{7}$, and $\frac{2}{21}$

(d) $\frac{3}{4}, \frac{5}{6}$, and $\frac{1}{2}$ 　　(e) $\frac{2}{7}, \frac{2}{9}$, and $\frac{2}{3}$ 　　(f) $\frac{5}{6}, \frac{1}{3}$, and $\frac{5}{8}$

(g) $\frac{2}{9}, \frac{1}{6}$, and $\frac{1}{4}$ 　　(h) $\frac{3}{5}, \frac{1}{2}$, and $\frac{3}{4}$ 　　(i) $\frac{7}{8}, \frac{2}{9}$, and $\frac{1}{6}$

ADDITION OF FRACTIONS THAT HAVE UNLIKE DENOMINATORS

Rule 1
In order to add fractions, follow these three steps:
Step 1: First find a common denominator.
Step 2: Change each given fraction to an equivalent fraction that has the same denominator.

Step 3: Add the numerators of the equivalent fractions and write the sum of the numerators of the equivalent fraction over the common equivalent denominator.

Note: The larger or largest denominator in the question can be used as the equivalent common denominator which is the same as the least common denominator.

Example 1

Find $\dfrac{1}{2} + \dfrac{1}{4}$

Solution

Step 1: Find the common denominator. The common denominator is 4 because the denominator of $\dfrac{1}{2}$ which is 2 can divide evenly into the denominator of $\dfrac{1}{4}$ which is 4 (without a remainder). This is an example where the larger or largest denominator in the question can at times be used as the equivalent common denominator which is the same as the least common denominator.

$$\dfrac{1}{2} = \dfrac{?}{4} \; \diagup \; \text{Equivalent common denominator}$$

$$\dfrac{1}{4} = \dfrac{1}{4} \; \diagup \text{Equivalent common denominator}$$

Step 2: Write an equivalent fraction for $\dfrac{1}{2}$ by multiplying $\dfrac{1}{2}$ by $\dfrac{2}{2}$ as shown:

$$\dfrac{1}{2} \times \dfrac{2}{2} = \dfrac{2}{4} \rightarrow \text{Equivalent fraction.}$$

$$\dfrac{1}{4} \times \dfrac{1}{1} = \dfrac{1}{4} \rightarrow \text{Equivalent fraction.}$$

We do not need to find the equivalent of $\dfrac{1}{4}$ because the denominator of 4 is already being used as the equivalent common denominator. Now, $\dfrac{2}{4}$ and $\dfrac{1}{4}$ have a common denominator of 4.

Step 3: Add the numerators of the equivalent fractions and write the sum of the numerators over the common denominator.

$$\frac{2+1}{4} = \frac{3}{4}$$ ↙Sum of the equivalent numerators

↙Common equivalent denominator (LCD).

Therefore $\frac{1}{2} + \frac{1}{4} = \frac{3}{4}$

Example 2

Find $\frac{2}{3} + \frac{1}{4}$

Solution

Step 1: Find the least common denominator. Review the section on Least Common Denominator. The denominators are 3 and 4, but in this case, 4 cannot be the common factor because 3 cannot divide into 4 evenly (without a remainder). In this case, the least common denominator (LCD) is $3 \times 4 = 12$. Note that both 3 and 4 can divide into 12 evenly (without a remainder).

$$\frac{2}{3} = \frac{?}{12}$$ ↙Least common denominator.

$$\frac{1}{4} = \frac{?}{12}$$ ↙Least common denominator.

Step 2: Write equivalent fractions. Hint: Refer to the section on Equivalent Fractions.

$$\frac{2}{3} = \frac{2}{3} \times \frac{4}{4} = \frac{8}{12} \leftarrow \text{Equivalent fraction.}$$

$$\frac{1}{4} = \frac{1}{4} \times \frac{3}{3} = \frac{3}{12} \leftarrow \text{Equivalent fraction.}$$

Now, $\frac{8}{12}$ and $\frac{3}{12}$ have a common denominator of 12.

Step 3: Add the numerators of the equivalent fractions and write the sum of the numerators over the equivalent common denominator.

↙Sum of the numerators of the equivalent fractions

$$\frac{8+3}{12} = \frac{11}{12}$$

↖Common equivalent denominator (LCD).

Therefore, $\frac{2}{3} + \frac{1}{4} = \frac{11}{12}$

Example 3

Find $\dfrac{2}{5} + \dfrac{3}{7}$

Solution

Step 1: Find the least common denominator. Refer to the Least Common Denominator section. The denominators are 5 and 7, but in this case, 5 cannot divide evenly into seven (without a remainder). In this case, the common denominator is $5 \times 7 = 35$.

Note that both 5 and 7 can divide evenly into 35 (without a remainder).

$$\dfrac{2}{5} = \dfrac{?}{35} \swarrow \text{Least common denominator.}$$

$$\dfrac{3}{7} = \dfrac{?}{35} \swarrow \text{Least common denominator.}$$

Step 2: Write equivalent fractions. Hint: Refer to the section on Equivalent Fractions.

$$\dfrac{2}{5} \times \dfrac{7}{7} = \dfrac{14}{35} \leftarrow \text{Equivalent fraction}$$

$$\dfrac{3}{7} \times \dfrac{5}{5} = \dfrac{15}{35} \leftarrow \text{Equivalent fraction}$$

Now, $\dfrac{14}{35}$ and $\dfrac{15}{35}$ have a common denominator of 35.

Step 3: Add the numerators of the equivalent fractions and write the sum of the numerators over the common denominator.

$$\swarrow \text{Sum of the numerators of the equivalent fractions}$$

$$\dfrac{14 + 15}{35} = \dfrac{29}{35}$$

$$\nwarrow \text{Common equivalent denominator (LCD)}$$

Therefore, $\dfrac{2}{5} + \dfrac{3}{7} = \dfrac{29}{35}$

Example 4

Find $\dfrac{3}{5} + \dfrac{2}{25}$

Solution

Step 1: Find the least common denominator. Review the section on Least Common

Denominators. The denominators are 5 and 25. In this case, 5 can divide into 25 evenly (without any remainder), and therefore, the least common denominator is 25. Note that both 5 and 25 can divide evenly into 25 (without any remainder).

$$\frac{3}{5} = \frac{?}{25}$$ ✓Least common denominator

$$\frac{2}{25} = \frac{?}{25}$$ ✓Least common denominator

Step 2: Write the equivalent fractions. Hint: Review the section on Equivalent Fractions.

$$\frac{3}{5} \times \frac{5}{5} = \frac{15}{25}$$ ← Equivalent fraction

$$\frac{2}{25} \times \frac{1}{1} = \frac{2}{25}$$ ← Equivalent fraction

We do not have to write an equivalent fraction for $\frac{2}{25}$ because the denominator of 25 is already the common equivalent denominator for $\frac{3}{5}$.

Now, $\frac{15}{25}$ and $\frac{2}{25}$ have a common denominator of 25.

Step 3: Add the numerators of the equivalent fractions and write the sum of the numerators of the equivalent fraction over the equivalent common denominator.

↗Sum of the numerators of equivalent fractions

$$\frac{15 + 2}{25} = \frac{17}{25}$$

↖Common equivalent denominator (LCD)

Therefore, $\frac{3}{5} + \frac{2}{25} = \frac{17}{25}$

Example 5

Find $\frac{2}{3} + \frac{2}{4} + \frac{2}{6}$

Solution

Step 1: Find the least common denominator. Review the section on the Least

137

Common Denominator. The denominators are 3, 4, and 6. Although 3 can divide into 6 evenly (without a remainder), 4 cannot divide into 6 evenly (without a remainder), and therefore, 6 cannot be the common denominator. Look for the least number that can be divided by 3, 4, and 6 evenly (without a remainder) and that number is 12. Therefore, the common denominator is 12.

$$\frac{2}{3} = \frac{?}{12} \quad \diagup \text{Least common denominator}$$

$$\frac{2}{4} = \frac{?}{12} \quad \diagup \text{Least common denominator}$$

$$\frac{2}{6} = \frac{?}{12} \quad \diagup \text{Least common denominator}$$

Step 2: Write the equivalent fractions. Hint: Review the section on Equivalent fractions.

$$\frac{2}{3} \times \frac{4}{4} = \frac{8}{12} \leftarrow \text{Equivalent fraction}$$

$$\frac{2}{4} \times \frac{3}{3} = \frac{6}{12} \leftarrow \text{Equivalent fraction}$$

$$\frac{2}{6} \times \frac{2}{2} = \frac{4}{12} \leftarrow \text{Equivalent fraction}$$

Step 3: Add the numerators of the equivalent fractions, and then write the sum of the numerators of the equivalent fractions over the equivalent common denominator.

$$\diagup \text{Sum of the numerators of the equivalent fractions.}$$

$$\frac{8+6+4}{12} = \frac{18}{12}$$

$$\diagdown \text{Common equivalent denominator (LCD).}$$

Therefore, $\frac{2}{4} + \frac{2}{6} = \frac{18}{12}$

The notes and the generous examples have provided me with the conceptual understanding and the computational fluency to do my homework.

Exercises

1. Find the sum. Hint: See Examples **1** and **4**.

    a. $\dfrac{3}{10} + \dfrac{1}{5}$ **b.** $\dfrac{1}{4} + \dfrac{5}{16}$ **c.** $\dfrac{1}{3} + \dfrac{2}{9}$ **d.** $\dfrac{2}{4} + \dfrac{1}{8}$

2. Find the sum. Hint: See Examples **2** and **3**.

    a. $\dfrac{3}{4} + \dfrac{1}{6}$ **b.** $\dfrac{2}{7} + \dfrac{1}{2}$ **c.** $\dfrac{1}{3} + \dfrac{2}{4}$ **d.** $\dfrac{2}{6} + \dfrac{3}{10}$

3. Find the sum. Hint: See Example **5**.

    a. $\dfrac{3}{5} + \dfrac{1}{3} + \dfrac{2}{15}$ **b.** $\dfrac{1}{2} + \dfrac{3}{4} + \dfrac{2}{3}$ **c.** $\dfrac{1}{4} + \dfrac{3}{5} + \dfrac{3}{10}$ **d.** $\dfrac{3}{4} + \dfrac{1}{2} + \dfrac{5}{6}$

Challenge Questions

Find the sum.

4. $\dfrac{3}{4} + \dfrac{2}{3}$ **5.** $\dfrac{3}{5} + \dfrac{4}{3} + \dfrac{7}{30}$ **6.** $\dfrac{5}{18} + \dfrac{5}{6} + \dfrac{2}{3}$ **7.** $\dfrac{2}{7} + \dfrac{2}{3} + \dfrac{1}{21}$

Answers to Selected Questions

1a. $\dfrac{5}{10}$ or $\dfrac{1}{2}$ **2a.** $\dfrac{11}{12}$

REAL WORLD APPLICATIONS - WORD PROBLEMS
Addition of Fractions that have Unlike Denominators

Example 6

Mary walked $\dfrac{3}{4}$ mile to the market and $\dfrac{1}{3}$ mile to school. How many miles did she walk?

Solution

Total miles walked = $\dfrac{3}{4} + \dfrac{1}{3}$

Step 1: Find the least common denominator. Review the section on Least Common Denominator. The denominators are 4 and 3. In this case, since 3 cannot divide into 4 evenly (without a remainder), 4 cannot be the common denominator. The least common denominator is $3 \times 4 = 12$. Note that the least number that both 4 and 3 can divide into evenly (without a remainder) is 12.

$$\frac{3}{4} = \frac{?}{12} \nearrow \text{Least common denominator}$$

$$\frac{1}{3} = \frac{?}{12} \nearrow \text{Least common denominator}$$

Step 2: Write equivalent fractions. Refer to the section under Equivalent Fractions.

$$\frac{3}{4} = \frac{3}{4} \times \frac{3}{3} = \frac{9}{12} \leftarrow \text{Equivalent fraction}$$

$$\frac{1}{3} = \frac{1}{3} \times \frac{4}{4} = \frac{4}{12} \leftarrow \text{Equivalent fraction}$$

Step 3: Add the numerators of the equivalent fractions and write the sum of the numerators of the equivalent fraction over the equivalent common denominator of 12.

$$\qquad\qquad\qquad \nearrow \text{Sum of the numerators of the equivalent fractions}$$

$$\frac{9+4}{12} = \frac{13}{12} \diagup \text{Equivalent common fraction (LCD)}$$

Example 7

John needs $\frac{3}{8}$ yard, $\frac{1}{3}$ yard, and $\frac{1}{6}$ yard of wood to do a school project. How many yards of wood is needed for the project?

Solution

Total yards needed for the project $= \frac{3}{8} + \frac{1}{3} + \frac{1}{6}$

Step 1: Find the least common denominator.

The denominators are 8, 3, and 6. The least common denominator (LCD) or the lowest number that can be divided by denominators 8, 3, and 6 evenly (without a remainder) is 24. Example: $8 \times 3 = 24$ and $6 \times 4 = 24$. Notice also that 8 is the largest denominator but 3 and 6 cannot divide into 8 evenly (without a reminder), and therefore, the LCD is 24.

$$\frac{3}{8} = \frac{?}{24} \diagup \text{least common denominator}$$

$$\frac{1}{3} = \frac{?}{24} \diagup \text{least common denominator}$$

$$\frac{1}{6} = \frac{?}{24} \diagup \text{least common denominator}$$

Step 2: Write equivalent fractions. Review the section under Equivalent Fractions.

140

cup of flour, and $\frac{1}{4}$ cup of sugar. How many cups would he need? Hint: Review how to find LCD.

Perform the following operations:

(6) $\frac{9}{16} + \frac{3}{8}$ **(7)** $\frac{15}{16} + \frac{1}{4}$ **(8)** $\frac{5}{7} + \frac{3}{14}$ **(9)** $\frac{5}{6} + \frac{1}{3}$ **(10)** $\frac{17}{21} + \frac{2}{7}$

(11) $\frac{3}{4} + \frac{2}{3}$ **(12)** $\frac{2}{3} + \frac{2}{9}$ **(13)** $\frac{2}{9} + \frac{7}{18}$ **(14)** $\frac{1}{5} + \frac{7}{15}$ **(15)** $\frac{2}{3} + \frac{1}{3}$

(16) $\frac{9}{28} + \frac{2}{7}$ **(17)** $\frac{3}{20} + \frac{2}{5}$ **(18)** $\frac{1}{5} + \frac{2}{10} + \frac{3}{20}$ **(19)** $\frac{2}{5} + \frac{3}{30} + \frac{11}{20}$

(20) $\frac{4}{5} + \frac{3}{20} + \frac{13}{20}$ **(21)** $\frac{3}{8} + \frac{3}{16} + \frac{7}{32}$ **(22)** $\frac{3}{4} + \frac{3}{8} + \frac{1}{5}$ **(23)** $\frac{3}{8} + \frac{2}{5}$

(24) $\frac{1}{3} + \frac{3}{8} + \frac{5}{12}$ **(25)** $\frac{1}{6} + \frac{2}{3} + \frac{5}{8}$ **(26)** $\frac{2}{7} + \frac{1}{4} + \frac{3}{14}$ **(27)** $\frac{5}{7} + \frac{3}{4}$

Answers to Selected Questions

1. $\frac{19}{14}$ **3.** $\frac{19}{12}$ **6.** $\frac{15}{16}$ **9.** $\frac{7}{6}$

ADDITION OF MIXED FRACTIONS

Types of fractions are:
Proper fraction
Improper fraction
Mixed fraction

A proper fraction is a fraction that has a numerator which is less than the denominator.

Examples of proper fractions are: $\frac{1}{4}, \frac{2}{4}, \frac{2}{3}$, and $\frac{14}{15}$.

An improper fraction is a fraction that has a numerator which is greater than the denominator.

Examples of improper fractions are: $\dfrac{4}{3}$, $\dfrac{12}{9}$, $\dfrac{15}{12}$, and $\dfrac{38}{25}$.

A mixed fraction is a fraction that contains both a whole number and a fraction.
Examples of mixed fractions are:

whole number$\searrow$ $\swarrow$fraction

$$1\dfrac{1}{2}, \quad 2\dfrac{2}{5}, \quad 5\dfrac{7}{9}, \quad \text{and} \quad 11\dfrac{7}{8}.$$

As stated above, a mixed fraction is a fraction that contains both a whole number and a fraction, and therefore, mixed fractions are added up in three steps as shown:

Step 1: Add the whole numbers.
Step 2: Add the fractions.
Step 3: Combine the sum (addition) of the whole numbers in step 1 and the sum (addition) of the fractions in step 2 into a final sum.

Example 1
Add: $2\dfrac{1}{3} + 1\dfrac{1}{6}$

Solution
(Notice that in Step 1, an imaginary line | separates the whole numbers from the fractions so that we can work on the whole numbers and the fractions separately.)

Step 1: Add the whole numbers first.

$$\downarrow$$

$$2|\ \dfrac{1}{3}$$
$$1|\ \dfrac{1}{6}$$
$$\overline{3}$$

$\searrow$ $\nearrow$

addition of whole numbers

Step 2: Add the fractions second.
(Review Addition of Fractions)
In order to add fractions, find the LCD.
$\swarrow$ Write equivalent fractions,
Determine LCD. and then add the fractions.

$$2|\ \dfrac{1}{3} = \dfrac{}{6}\ \swarrow\text{LCD}$$
$$1|\ \dfrac{1}{6} = \dfrac{}{6}\ \swarrow\text{LCD}$$
$$\overline{3}$$

$$\downarrow$$
$$2|\ \dfrac{1}{3} \times \dfrac{2}{2} = \dfrac{2}{6}$$
$$1|\ \dfrac{1}{6} \times \dfrac{1}{1} = \dfrac{1}{6}$$
$$\overline{3}$$
$$\dfrac{3}{6}$$

$\nearrow$

addition of fractions.

143

Step 2: Combine the sum (addition) of the whole numbers in Step 1 and the sum (addition) of the fractions in Step 2, into a final sum.

From Step 1 $\nearrow 3 + \dfrac{3}{6} = 3\dfrac{3}{6}$

$\nearrow$ $\nwarrow$ Final sum

From Step 2

Example 2

Add: $4\dfrac{2}{3} + 10\dfrac{1}{4}$

Solution

(Notice that in Step 1, an imaginary line | separates the whole numbers from the fractions so that we can work on the whole numbers and the fractions separately.)

Step 1: Add the whole number first.

↓

     $4 |\ \dfrac{2}{3}$

$10 |\ \dfrac{1}{4}$

$\overline{14}$

$\nwarrow$

Addition of whole numbers

Step 2: Add fractions second.
(Review Addition of Fractions)
In order to add fractions, find the LCD.

$\swarrow$
Determine LCD.

$4 |\ \dfrac{2}{3} = \dfrac{}{12}\ \nearrow$LCD

$10 |\ \dfrac{1}{4} = \dfrac{}{12}\ \nearrow$LCD

$\overline{14}$ $\nwarrow$LCD

$\nearrow$

Write equivalent fractions, and then add the fractions.

↓

$4 |\ \dfrac{2}{3} \times \dfrac{4}{4} = \dfrac{8}{12}$

$10 |\ \dfrac{1}{4} \times \dfrac{3}{3} = \dfrac{3}{12}$

$\overline{14}$ $\overline{}$

$\dfrac{11}{12}$

$\nearrow$

Addition of fractions

Step 3: Combine the sum (addition) of the whole numbers in Step 1 and the sum (addition) of the fractions in Step 2 into the final sum.

From Step 1 $\nearrow 14 + \dfrac{11}{12} = 14\dfrac{11}{12}\ \nearrow$Final sum

$\nwarrow$ From Step 2

Example 3

Add: $11\dfrac{3}{4} + 4\dfrac{1}{8} + 2\dfrac{1}{2}$

Solution

(Notice that in Step 1, an imaginary line | separates the whole numbers from the fractions so that we can work on the whole numbers and the fractions separately.)

Step 1: Add the whole number first.
↓

Step 2: Add the fractions second.
(Review Addition of Fraction)
In order to add fractions, find the LCD.
↙
Determine LCD.

Write equivalent fractions, and then add the fractions.
↓

$$11| \frac{3}{4}$$

$$4| \frac{1}{8}$$

$$2| \frac{1}{2}$$

$$\overline{17}$$

$$11| \frac{3}{4} = \frac{\ }{8} \diagup LCD$$

$$4| \frac{1}{8} = \frac{\ }{8} \diagup LCD$$

$$2| \frac{1}{2} = \frac{\ }{8} \diagup LCD$$

$$\overline{17}$$

$$11| \frac{3}{4} = \frac{3}{4} \times \frac{2}{2} = \frac{6}{8}$$

$$4| \frac{1}{8} = \frac{1}{8} \times \frac{1}{1} = \frac{1}{8}$$

$$2| \frac{1}{2} = \frac{1}{2} \times \frac{4}{4} = \frac{4}{8}$$

$$\overline{17} \qquad \overline{\quad} \\ \frac{11}{8}$$

↖ ↗
Addition of whole numbers

↗
Addition of fractions

Review how to change an improper fraction such as $\frac{11}{8}$ into a mixed number such as $1\frac{3}{8}$.

Step 3: Combine the sum (addition) of the whole numbers in Step 1 and the sum (addition) of the fractions in Step 2 into the final sum.

From Step 1 ↗ $17 + 1\frac{3}{8} = 18\frac{3}{8}$

↗ ↖ Final sum
From Step 2

Example 4

Add $\frac{2}{9} + 6\frac{2}{3} + 20\frac{8}{36}$

Solution

(Notice that in Step 1, an imaginary line | separates the whole numbers from the fractions so that we can work on the whole numbers and the fractions separately.)

145

Step 1: Add the whole numbers first.　　　　**Step 2**: Add the fractions second. (Review Addition of Fractions) In order to add fractions find the LCD.

Determine LCD.　　　Write equivalent fractions, and then add the fractions.

$$\frac{2}{9}$$

$$6 \mid \frac{2}{3}$$

$$20 \mid \frac{8}{36}$$

$$\overline{26}$$

$$\frac{2}{9} = \frac{}{36} \diagup LCD$$

$$6 \mid \frac{2}{3} = \frac{}{36} \diagup LCD$$

$$20 \mid \frac{8}{36} = \frac{}{36} \diagup LCD$$

$$\overline{26}$$

$$\frac{2}{9} = \frac{2}{9} \times \frac{4}{4} = \frac{8}{36}$$

$$6 \mid \frac{2}{3} = \frac{2}{3} \times \frac{12}{12} = \frac{24}{36}$$

$$20 \mid \frac{8}{36} = \frac{8}{36} \times \frac{1}{1} = \frac{8}{36}$$

$$\overline{26}$$

$$\frac{40}{36}$$

Addition of whole numbers

Fraction addition.

(Note: Review how to change improper fractions such as $\frac{40}{36}$ into a mixed fraction such as $1\frac{4}{36}$).

Example: $\frac{40}{36} = 1\frac{4}{36}$

(Note: Review how to reduce fractions, $\frac{4}{36}$ can be reduced to $\frac{1}{9}$ by dividing both numerator and denominator by 4.

Step 3: Combine the sum (addition) of the whole numbers in Step 1 and the sum (addition) of the fractions in Step 2 into the final sum.

Final sum

$$26 + 1\frac{1}{9} = 27\frac{1}{9}$$

From Step 1　　　From Step 2

The notes and the generous examples have provided me with the conceptual understanding and the computational fluency to do my homework.

Exercises

1. Add the following. Hint: See Example **1**

(a) $7\dfrac{2}{5} + 1\dfrac{3}{10}$

(b) $3\dfrac{1}{4} + 2\dfrac{3}{8}$

(c) $10\dfrac{5}{6} + 8\dfrac{2}{3}$

(d) $5\dfrac{5}{9} + 7\dfrac{2}{3}$

(e) $9\dfrac{1}{3} + 10\dfrac{2}{9}$

(f) $17\dfrac{2}{8} + 15\dfrac{2}{16}$

(g) $2\dfrac{11}{12} + 13\dfrac{1}{24}$

(h) $32\dfrac{3}{12} + 15\dfrac{1}{3}$

(i) $7\dfrac{5}{8} + 3\dfrac{1}{4}$

(j) $35\dfrac{7}{9} + 40\dfrac{5}{18}$

(k) $10\dfrac{3}{7} + 7\dfrac{3}{14}$

(l) $9\dfrac{3}{8} + 4\dfrac{7}{24}$

(m) $17\dfrac{2}{5} + 22\dfrac{16}{25}$

(n) $16\dfrac{3}{9} + 2\dfrac{5}{36}$

(o) $6\dfrac{2}{3} + 8\dfrac{5}{12}$

(p) $5\dfrac{3}{5} + 11\dfrac{2}{15}$

2. Add the following. Hint: See Examples **1** and **2**.

(a) $10\dfrac{3}{7}$
$7\dfrac{3}{14}$

(b) $17\dfrac{3}{5}$
$11\dfrac{2}{10}$

(c) $3\dfrac{3}{4}$
$27\dfrac{5}{12}$

(d) $8\dfrac{3}{9}$
$7\dfrac{4}{18}$

(e) $19\dfrac{4}{5} + 4\dfrac{2}{3}$

(f) $22\dfrac{3}{4} + 7\dfrac{1}{16}$

(g) $31\dfrac{5}{12} + 1\dfrac{3}{4}$

(h) $20\dfrac{2}{7} + 11\dfrac{2}{21}$

(i) $3\dfrac{3}{12} + 6\dfrac{2}{3}$

(j) $5\dfrac{3}{8} + 2\dfrac{2}{24}$

(k) $7\dfrac{5}{7} + \dfrac{11}{14}$

(l) $7\dfrac{5}{7} + 2\dfrac{2}{14}$

(m) $11\dfrac{9}{11} + 3\dfrac{15}{22}$

(n) $6\dfrac{7}{33} + 4\dfrac{10}{11}$

(o) $5\dfrac{3}{7} + 6\dfrac{4}{21}$

(p) $9\dfrac{3}{4} + 6\dfrac{4}{5}$

3. Add the following. Hint: See Examples **3** and **4**.

(a) $4\dfrac{2}{3} + 3\dfrac{3}{4} + 7\dfrac{5}{12}$

(b) $3\dfrac{4}{7} + 4\dfrac{4}{21} + 6\dfrac{5}{7}$

(c) $5\dfrac{3}{5} + 2\dfrac{7}{10} + 1\dfrac{7}{20}$

(d) $9\dfrac{5}{16} + 1\dfrac{7}{8} + 8\dfrac{3}{4}$

(e) $7\dfrac{2}{3} + 4\dfrac{4}{9} + 2\dfrac{5}{18}$

(f) $4\dfrac{7}{18} + 9\dfrac{5}{9} + 3\dfrac{2}{3}$

(g) $29\dfrac{1}{4} + 10\dfrac{5}{12} + 6\dfrac{3}{8}$

(h) $2\dfrac{3}{7} + 22\dfrac{11}{21} + 1\dfrac{1}{42}$

(i) $2\dfrac{3}{4} + 3\dfrac{3}{8} + 4\dfrac{1}{2}$

147

(j) $6\dfrac{2}{3} + 4\dfrac{1}{4} + 7\dfrac{5}{6}$ (k) $5\dfrac{2}{3} + 7\dfrac{1}{4} + 2\dfrac{5}{6}$ (l) $4\dfrac{5}{8} + 4\dfrac{9}{16} + 2\dfrac{27}{32}$

(m) $3\dfrac{1}{3} + 4\dfrac{5}{6} + 10\dfrac{5}{8}$ (n) $2\dfrac{11}{16} + 1\dfrac{21}{64} + 3\dfrac{3}{4}$ (o) $4\dfrac{6}{7} + \dfrac{3}{14} + 2\dfrac{5}{28}$

(p) $\dfrac{3}{5} + 7\dfrac{7}{25} + \dfrac{49}{50}$ (q) $2\dfrac{2}{5} + 2\dfrac{2}{3} + 1\dfrac{1}{5}$ (r) $1\dfrac{3}{4} + 2 + 2\dfrac{3}{5}$

4. Add the following. Hint: See Examples **3** and **4**.

(a) $3\dfrac{3}{4}$ (b) $5\dfrac{3}{4}$ (c) $9\dfrac{2}{3}$ (d) $7\dfrac{4}{5}$ (e) $5\dfrac{1}{3}$
$4\dfrac{3}{8}$ $4\dfrac{4}{5}$ $1\dfrac{1}{4}$ $5\dfrac{12}{15}$ $30\dfrac{5}{8}$
$+\ 7\dfrac{1}{2}$ $+\ 12\dfrac{1}{2}$ $+\ \dfrac{5}{6}$ $+\ 8\dfrac{5}{6}$ $+\ 7\dfrac{5}{6}$

(f) $4\dfrac{19}{28}$ (g) $7\dfrac{2}{3}$ (h) $2\dfrac{3}{4}$ (i) $24\dfrac{31}{32}$ (j) $10\dfrac{1}{2}$
$20\dfrac{5}{7}$ $8\dfrac{4}{5}$ $7\dfrac{5}{8}$ $7\dfrac{9}{16}$ $7\dfrac{3}{8}$
$+\ 3\dfrac{9}{14}$ $+\ 5\dfrac{7}{10}$ $+\ 12\dfrac{3}{5}$ $+\ 12\dfrac{3}{8}$ $+\ 5\dfrac{3}{4}$

(k) $4\dfrac{2}{3}$ (l) $7\dfrac{5}{6}$ (m) $4\dfrac{1}{3}$ (n) $22\dfrac{1}{2}$ (o) $5\dfrac{1}{7}$
$6\dfrac{3}{4}$ $8\dfrac{7}{12}$ $5\dfrac{5}{6}$ $3\dfrac{2}{3}$ $6\dfrac{3}{14}$
$+\ 7\dfrac{5}{6}$ $+\ 5\dfrac{3}{4}$ $+\ 3\dfrac{1}{4}$ $+\ 2\dfrac{5}{12}$ $+\ 4\dfrac{3}{4}$

Answers to Selected Questions

1(a) $8\dfrac{7}{10}$ **2**(a) $17\dfrac{9}{14}$ **3**(a) $15\dfrac{5}{6}$ **3**(o) $7\dfrac{7}{28} = 7\dfrac{1}{4}$ **4**(a) $14\dfrac{13}{8} = 15\dfrac{5}{8}$

REAL WORLD APPLICATIONS - WORD PROBLEMS
Addition of Mixed Fractions

Example 1

If I travelled $40\dfrac{1}{4}$ miles, $13\dfrac{1}{8}$ miles, and $15\dfrac{7}{24}$ miles in one day, what is the total number of miles that I traveled?

Solution

The total number of miles traveled $= 40\dfrac{1}{4} + 13\dfrac{1}{8} + 15\dfrac{7}{24}$

(Notice that in Step 1, an imaginary line | separates the whole numbers from the fractions so that we can work on the whole numbers and fractions separately.)

Step 1: Add the whole numbers first.

Step 2: Add the fractions second.
(Review Addition of Fractions)
In order to add fractions, find the LCD.
Determine LCD.
Write the equivalent fractions, and then add the fractions.

$$40\,|\ \dfrac{1}{4}$$

$$13\,|\ \dfrac{1}{8}$$

$$15\,|\ \dfrac{7}{24}$$

$$\overline{68}$$

$$40\,|\ \dfrac{1}{4} = \dfrac{\ }{24}\ \diagup\text{LCM}$$

$$13\,|\ \dfrac{1}{8} = \dfrac{\ }{24}\ \diagup\text{LCM}$$

$$15\,|\ \dfrac{7}{24} = \dfrac{\ }{24}\ \diagup\text{LCM}$$

$$\overline{68}$$

$$40\,|\ \dfrac{1}{4} \times \dfrac{6}{6} = \dfrac{6}{24}$$

$$13\,|\ \dfrac{1}{8} \times \dfrac{3}{3} = \dfrac{3}{24}$$

$$15\,|\ \dfrac{7}{24} \times \dfrac{1}{1} = \dfrac{7}{24}$$

$$\dfrac{16}{24}$$

Addition of whole numbers

Addition of fractions

Notice that $\dfrac{16}{24}$ can be reduced to $\dfrac{2}{3}$ by dividing the numerator and the denominator of $\dfrac{16}{24}$ by 8.

Step 3: Combine the sum (addition) of the whole numbers in Step 1 and the sum (addition) of the fractions in Step 2 into the final sum.

$$\text{From Step 1} \diagup 68 + \frac{2}{3} = 68\frac{2}{3} \text{ miles}$$

From Step 2　　　Final sum

Example 2:

Mary bought $8\frac{1}{2}$ pounds of pears, $3\frac{2}{3}$ pounds of apples, and $4\frac{5}{6}$ pounds of cherries. How many pounds of fruit did she buy?

Solution

The total number of pounds of fruit bought by Mary $= 8\frac{1}{2} + 3\frac{2}{3} + 4\frac{5}{6}$

(Notice that in Step 1, an imaginary line | separates the whole numbers from the fractions so that we can work on the whole numbers and the fractions separately.)

Step 1: Add the whole numbers first

Step 2: Add the fractions second.
(Review fraction addition)
In order to add fractions, find the LCD.
Determine the LCD.
Write the equivalent fractions, and then add the fractions.

$$
\begin{array}{l}
8| \ \dfrac{1}{2} \\[2mm]
3| \ \dfrac{2}{3} \\[2mm]
4| \ \dfrac{5}{6} \\[1mm]
\hline
15
\end{array}
\qquad
\begin{array}{l}
8| \ \dfrac{1}{2} = \dfrac{\ }{6} \ \diagup\text{LCD} \\[2mm]
3| \ \dfrac{2}{3} = \dfrac{\ }{6} \ \diagup\text{LCD} \\[2mm]
4| \ \dfrac{5}{6} = \dfrac{\ }{6} \ \diagup\text{LCD} \\[1mm]
\hline
15
\end{array}
\qquad
\begin{array}{l}
8| \ \dfrac{1}{2} \times \dfrac{3}{3} = \dfrac{3}{6} \\[2mm]
3| \ \dfrac{2}{3} \times \dfrac{2}{2} = \dfrac{4}{6} \\[2mm]
4| \ \dfrac{5}{6} \times \dfrac{1}{1} = \dfrac{5}{6} \\[1mm]
\hline
15 \qquad \dfrac{12}{6} = 2
\end{array}
$$

Addition of whole numbers.

Addition of fractions.

Step 3: Combine the sum (addition) of the whole numbers in Step 1 and the sum (addition) of the fractions in Step 2 into the final sum.

$$\diagup\text{Final sum}$$
$$15 + 2 = 17$$

From step 1.　　From step 2

Mary bought 17 pounds of fruit.

The notes and the generous examples have provided me with the conceptual understanding and the computational fluency to do my homework.

Exercises

1. A school project needs $6\frac{2}{3}$ inches, $8\frac{1}{2}$ inches and $4\frac{5}{12}$ inches of pipe. How many inches of pipe is needed? Hint: See Example **2**.

2. John needs $3\frac{2}{3}$ feet, $7\frac{1}{4}$ feet, and $2\frac{3}{4}$ feet of wood for a school project. How many feet of wood is needed by John for the total project? Hint: See Example **2**.

3. Rose walked $1\frac{1}{2}$ miles to the Post Office, $1\frac{5}{7}$ miles to the cinema, and $1\frac{3}{14}$ miles to the market. How many miles did she walk altogether? Hint: See Example **1**.

4. A baker used $3\frac{2}{3}$ dozen of eggs on Monday, $2\frac{3}{4}$ dozen on Tuesday, and $3\frac{1}{6}$ dozen on Wednesday for various mixes. How many dozen of eggs did the baker use? Hint: See Example **2**.

Challenge Questions

5. A plumber needs $8\frac{2}{3}$ inches, $6\frac{1}{6}$ inches, and $9\frac{1}{24}$ inches of pipe. What is the total length of the pipe that the plumber needs?

6. Rose bought three packages of meat weighing $6\frac{1}{5}$ pounds, 10 pounds, and $15\frac{2}{15}$ pounds. What was the total weight of the three packages of meat?

SUBTRACTION OF FRACTIONS

Rule 1: In order to subtract fractions, follow the three steps as follows:

Step 1: First find the least common denominator (LCD).

Step 2: Change each fraction to an equivalent fraction that has the same least common denominator (LCD).

Step 3: Subtract the numerators and write the difference of the numerators over the least common denominator (LCD).

Rule 2: The large or largest denominator in the question can, at times, be used as the least common denominator.

Rule 3: Knowing the multiplication tables from 1 to 12 will help to quickly identify the least common denominator (LCD).

Example 1

Subtract: $\dfrac{1}{2} - \dfrac{1}{4}$

Solution

Step 1: Find the least common denominator which is 4 because the denominator

of $\dfrac{1}{2}$ which is 2 can divide evenly (without any remainder) the denominator

of $\dfrac{1}{4}$ which is 4. Notice that Rule 2 is being used.

$$\dfrac{1}{2} = \dfrac{}{4} \quad \checkmark \text{ least common denominator (LCD)}$$

$$\dfrac{1}{4} = \dfrac{}{4} \quad \checkmark \text{ least common denominator (LCD)}$$

Step 2: Write equivalent fractions. Review the section on Equivalent Fractions.

$$\dfrac{1}{2} = \dfrac{1}{2} \times \dfrac{2}{4} = \dfrac{2}{4} \quad \leftarrow \text{ Equivalent fraction}$$

$$-\dfrac{1}{4} = -\dfrac{1}{4} \times \dfrac{1}{1} = -\dfrac{1}{4} \quad \leftarrow \text{ Equivalent fraction}$$

(Notice that $-\dfrac{1}{4}$ is from the question.)

Step 3: Subtract the numerators of the equivalent fractions and write the difference of the numerators of the equivalent fraction over the least common denominator (LCD) or over the common equivalent denominator to get the final difference.

$$\underset{\nwarrow \text{Common equivalent denominator or LCD}}{\overset{\nearrow \text{Difference of the numerators of the equivalent fraction}}{\dfrac{2-1}{4} = \dfrac{1}{4}}}$$

Example 2

Subtract: $\dfrac{3}{4} - \dfrac{2}{5}$

Solution

Step 1: Find the least common denominator. In order to find the LCD, we should find the least number that can be divided by both the denominators 4 and 5 evenly (without any remainder).

The multiples of 4 are:

$4 \times 1 = 4, 4 \times 2 = 8, 4 \times 3 = 12, 4 \times 4 = 16, 4 \times 5 = 20, 4 \times 6 = 24, \ldots$

Therefore, the multiples of 4 are: 4, 8, 12, 16, 20, 24, . . .

The multiples of 5 are:

$5 \times 1 = 5, 5 \times 2 = 10, 5 \times 3 = 15, 5 \times 4 = 20, \ldots$

↓

Stop here because 20 appears as a multiple of 4. Since 20 is the smallest number that appears as the multiple of both 4 and 5, 20 is the LCD.

$\dfrac{3}{4} = \dfrac{}{20}$ ↙LCD   Observe both sides of the equation, the denominator 4 must be multiplied by 5 in order to obtain the equivalent denominator of 20, and therefore, the numerator of 3 must also be multiplied by 5 to obtain 15 as shown in Step 2.

$-\dfrac{2}{5} = -\dfrac{}{20}$ ↙LCD   Observe both sides of the equation, the denominator 5 must be multiplied by 4 in order to obtain the equivalent denominator of 20, and therefore, the numerator of 2 must also be multiplied by 4 to obtain an equivalent numerator of 8 as shown in Step 2.

Step 2: Write equivalent fractions. Review the section on Equivalent Fractions.

$\dfrac{3}{4} = \dfrac{3}{4} \times \dfrac{5}{5} = \dfrac{15}{20}$ ← Equivalent fraction

$-\dfrac{2}{5} = -\dfrac{2}{5} \times \dfrac{4}{4} = -\dfrac{8}{20}$ ← Equivalent fraction

Step 3: Subtract the numerators of the equivalent fraction and write the difference of the numerators of the equivalent fractions over the least common denominator (LCD) or over the common equivalent denominator of 20 to get the final difference.

↙Difference of the numerators of the equivalent fractions

$\dfrac{15 - 8}{20} = \dfrac{7}{20}$

↖Denominator of the common equivalent fraction or LCD

Example 3

Subtract: $\dfrac{2}{3} - \dfrac{1}{7}$

Solution

Step 1: Find the LCD.

In order to find the LCD, we should find the least number that can be divided by both the denominators 3 and 7 evenly (without a remainder) by using multiples.

The multiples of 3 are:

$3 \times 1 = 3,\ 3 \times 2 = 6,\ 3 \times 3 = 9,\ 3 \times 4 = 12,\ 3 \times 5 = 15,\ 3 \times 6 = 18,\ 3 \times 7 = 21,$
$3 \times 8 = 24, \ldots$

Therefore, the multiples of 3 are: 3, 6, 9, 12, 15, 18, 21, 24, . . .

The multiples of 7 are:

$7 \times 1 = 7,\ 7 \times 2 = 14,\ 7 \times 3 = 21 .\ .\ .\ .\ .\ .$

Stop here because 21 also appears as a multiple of 3. Since 21 appears as the smallest number that appears as a multiple of 3 and 7, 21 is the LCD.

$$\frac{2}{3} = \frac{}{21} \quad \diagup \text{LCD}$$

Observe both sides of the equation above. The denominator 3 must be multiplied by 7 in order to obtain the equivalent denominator (LCD) of 21, and the numerator of 2 must also be multiplied by 7 to obtain 14 as shown in Step 2.

$$-\frac{1}{7} = -\frac{}{21} \quad \diagup \text{LCD}$$

Observe both sides of the equation above. The denominator of 7 must be multiplied by 3 in order to obtain the equivalent denominator (LCD) of 21, and the numerator of 1 must also be multiplied by 3 in order to obtain the equivalent numerator of 3 as shown in Step 2.

Step 2: Write equivalent fractions. Review the section on Equivalent Fractions.

$$\frac{2}{3} \times \frac{7}{7} = \frac{14}{21} \leftarrow \text{Equivalent fraction}$$

$$-\frac{1}{7} \times \frac{3}{3} = -\frac{3}{21} \leftarrow \text{Equivalent fraction}$$

Step 3: Subtract the numerators of the equivalent fractions and write the difference of the numerators of the equivalent fractions over the least common

154

equivalent denominator (LCD) to get the final difference.

$$\frac{14-3}{21} = \frac{11}{21}$$

↗ Difference of the numerators of the equivalent fractions

↗ Common equivalent denominator or the LCD

Example 4

Solve: $\dfrac{5}{6} - \dfrac{3}{8}$

Solution

Step 1: Find the LCD.

In order to find the LCD, we should find the least common number that can be divided by both 6 and 8 evenly (without a remainder) by using multiples. The multiples of 6 are:

$6 \times 1 = 6$, $6 \times 2 = 12$, $6 \times 3 = 18$, $6 \times 4 = 24$, $6 \times 5 = 30$, . . .

Therefore, the multiples of 6 are: 6, 12, 18, 24, 30, . . .

The multiples of 8 are:

$8 \times 1 = 8$, $8 \times 2 = 16$, $8 \times 3 = 24$, . . .

↓

Stop here because 24 also appears as a multiple of 6. Since 24 appears as the smallest number that appears as a multiple of both 6 and 8, 24 is the LCD.

$$\frac{5}{6} = \frac{}{24} \quad \nearrow \text{LCD}$$

Observe both sides of the equation above. The denominator 6 must be multiplied by 4 in order to obtain the equivalent denominator (LCD) of 24, and the numerator of 5 must also be multiplied by 4 to obtain 20 as shown in Step 2.

$$-\frac{3}{8} = -\frac{}{24} \quad \nearrow \text{LCD}$$

Observe both sides of the equation above. The denominator of 8 must be multiplied by 3 in order to obtain the equivalent denominator (LCD) of 24, and the numerator of 3 must also be multiplied by 3 in order to obtain the equivalent numerator of 9 as shown in Step 2.

Step 2: Write equivalent fractions. Review the topic on Equivalent Fractions.

$$\frac{5}{6} = \frac{5}{6} \times \frac{4}{4} = \frac{20}{24} \quad \leftarrow \text{Equivalent fraction.}$$

$$-\frac{3}{8} = -\frac{3}{8} \times \frac{3}{3} = -\frac{9}{24} \leftarrow \text{Equivalent fraction.}$$

Step 3: Subtract the numerators of the equivalent fractions and write the difference of the numerators of the equivalent fractions over the least common denominator (LCD) or over the common equivalent denominator to get the final difference.

Difference of the numerators of the equivalent fractions

$$\frac{20-9}{24} = \frac{11}{24}$$

Common equivalent denominator or LCD

═══════════════════ The notes and the generous examples have provided me with the conceptual understanding and the computational fluency to do my homework.

Exercises

1. State the three steps for doing subtraction.

2. What is meant by LCD?

3. Subtract the following. Hint: See Example **1**.

(a) $\dfrac{3}{4} - \dfrac{1}{8}$ (b) $\dfrac{7}{8} - \dfrac{3}{16}$ (c) $\dfrac{4}{5} - \dfrac{2}{10}$ (d) $\dfrac{5}{6} - \dfrac{3}{12}$ (e) $\dfrac{8}{9} - \dfrac{2}{3}$

4. Subtract the following. Hint: See Examples **2**, **3**, and **4**.

(a) $\dfrac{4}{5} - \dfrac{1}{4}$ (b) $\dfrac{5}{6} - \dfrac{1}{8}$ (c) $\dfrac{3}{5} - \dfrac{1}{3}$ (d) $\dfrac{4}{5} - \dfrac{3}{7}$ (e) $\dfrac{2}{3} - \dfrac{1}{7}$

(f) $\dfrac{2}{3} - \dfrac{2}{4}$ (g) $\dfrac{5}{7} - \dfrac{3}{8}$ (h) $\dfrac{4}{5} - \dfrac{2}{3}$ (i) $\dfrac{5}{6} - \dfrac{3}{8}$ (j) $\dfrac{3}{4} - \dfrac{1}{3}$

(k) $\dfrac{5}{8} - \dfrac{1}{3}$ (l) $\dfrac{2}{3} - \dfrac{1}{5}$ (m) $\dfrac{5}{6} - \dfrac{3}{4}$ (n) $\dfrac{4}{5} - \dfrac{3}{4}$ (o) $\dfrac{7}{8} - \dfrac{1}{5}$

Challenge Questions

(a) $\dfrac{10}{11} - \dfrac{2}{3}$ (b) $\dfrac{5}{7} - \dfrac{1}{6}$ (c) $\dfrac{5}{7} - \dfrac{4}{14}$ (d) $\dfrac{9}{10} - \dfrac{3}{5}$ (e) $\dfrac{1}{6} - \dfrac{3}{4}$

REAL WORLD APPLICATIONS - WORD PROBLEMS
Subtraction of Fractions

Example 1

Rose bought $\dfrac{3}{4}$ pound of sugar and she used $\dfrac{3}{16}$ pound for baking. How much sugar was left?

Solution

The amount of sugar left is $\dfrac{3}{4} - \dfrac{3}{16}$.

The subtraction is done just like the previous examples under the heading Subtraction of Fraction.

Step 1: Find the LCD.

In order to find the LCD, we should find the least common number that can be divided by both the denominators of 4 and 16 evenly (without a remainder) by using multiples.

The multiples of 4 are:

$4 \times 1 = 4$, $4 \times 2 = 8$, $4 \times 3 = 12$, $4 \times 4 = 16$, $4 \times 5 = 20$, $4 \times 6 = 24$, . . .

Therefore, the multiples of 4 are:

4, 8, 12, 16, 20, 24, . . .

The multiples of 16 are:

$16 \times 1 = 16$, . . .

$\downarrow$

Stop here because 16 also appears as a multiple of 4. Since 16 appears as the smallest number that appears as the multiple of 4 and 16, 16 is the LCD. [Shortcut: By knowing the multiplication tables, $4 \times 4 = 16$, therefore, 4 can divide into 16 evenly (without any remainder), and therefore, we can know mentally that the LCD of 4 and 16 is 16.]

157

Observe both sides of the equation above. The denominator of 4 must be multiplied by 4 in order to obtain the equivalent denominator of 16, and the numerator of 3 must also be multiplied by 4 to obtain 12 as shown in Step 2.

$$-\frac{3}{16} = -\frac{}{16}$$

↖ LCD

Observe both sides of the equation above. The denominator of 16 at the left side of the equation is the same as the denominator of 16 at the right side of the equation, and the numerator of 3 on the left hand side of the equation must be the same (3) at the right side of the equation as shown in Step 2.

Step 2: Write equivalent fractions. Review the section on Equivalent Fractions.

$$\frac{3}{4} \times \frac{4}{4} = \frac{12}{16} \leftarrow \text{Equivalent fraction.}$$

$$-\frac{3}{16} \times \frac{1}{1} = -\frac{3}{16} \leftarrow \text{Equivalent fraction.}$$

Step 3: Subtract the numerators of the equivalent fractions and write the difference of the numerators of the equivalent fractions over the least common denominator (LCD) or over the common equivalent denominator to get the final difference.

Difference of the numerators of the equivalent fraction
↙
$$\frac{12 - 3}{16} = \frac{9}{16} \text{ pound of sugar}$$
↖
Common equivalent denominator or LCD

$\frac{9}{16}$ pound of sugar was left.

Example 2

A company bought $\frac{3}{4}$ ton of drinking water and used up $\frac{1}{2}$ ton. How much of the drinking water is left. (Notice that this problem is solved without detailed explanation as in Example 1. The student may see Example 1 for the similar detailed explanation.)
Solution

The amount of the drinking water left is $\frac{3}{4} - \frac{1}{2}$.

Step 1: Find the LCD.

Since the denominator 2 can divide 4 evenly (without a remainder), 4 is the LCD of 2 and 4.

$$\frac{3}{4} = \frac{}{4} \diagup \text{LCD}$$

$$-\frac{1}{2} = -\frac{}{4} \diagup \text{LCD}$$

Step 2: Write equivalent fractions. Review the sections on Equivalent Fractions.

$$\frac{3}{4} \times \frac{1}{1} = \frac{3}{4} \leftarrow \text{Equivalent fraction}$$

$$-\frac{1}{2} \times \frac{2}{2} = -\frac{2}{4} \leftarrow \text{Equivalent fraction}$$

Step 3: Subtract the numerators of the equivalent fractions and write the difference of the numerators of the equivalent fractions over the least common denominator (LCD) to get the final difference.

Difference of the numerators of the equivalent fraction

$$\frac{3-2}{4} = \frac{1}{4} \text{ ton of drinking water}$$

LCD or the common denominator of the equivalent fractions.

Example 3

Samuel bought $\frac{3}{4}$ pound of beef and ate $\frac{3}{8}$ pound for lunch. How much of the beef is left ?

Solution

(For similar detailed explanation, see Example 1.)

The amount of beef left is $\frac{3}{4} - \frac{3}{8}$

Step 1: Find the LCD.

Since denominator of 4 can divide the denominator of 8 evenly (without any remainder), 8 is the LCD of 4 and 8.

$$\frac{3}{4} = \frac{}{8} \quad \diagup LCD$$

$$-\frac{3}{8} = -\frac{}{8} \quad \diagup LCD$$

Step 2: Write equivalent fractions. Review the sections on Equivalent Fractions.

$$\frac{3}{4} \times \frac{2}{2} = \frac{6}{8} \quad \leftarrow \text{Equivalent fractions}$$

$$-\frac{3}{8} \times \frac{1}{1} = -\frac{3}{8} \quad \leftarrow \text{Equivalent fractions}$$

Step 3: Subtract the numerators of the equivalent fractions and write the difference over the least common denominator (LCD) or over the common denominator of the equivalent fraction to get the final difference.

Difference of the numerators of the equivalent fractions

$$\frac{6-3}{8} = \frac{3}{8} \quad \text{pound of beef}$$

LCD or the common denominator of the equivalent fractions

$\frac{3}{8}$ pound of the beef is left.

Example 4

Joshua bought $\frac{7}{8}$ of a yard of material for a school project. If he only used $\frac{5}{6}$ of a yard, how much material was left?

Solution

(For similar detailed explanation, see Example 1.)

The material left is $\frac{7}{8} - \frac{5}{6}$.

Step 1: Find the LCD.

The denominators of the fractions are 8 and 6, however, 6 cannot divide 8 evenly (without any remainder), and therefore, 8 cannot be the LCD for 6 and 8.

Shortcut to find any LCD: Multiply the denominators together, then reduce the product of the denominators to the smallest number that can be divided by the denominators evenly (without any remainder), and **this**

smallest number is the LCD. To find the LCD of 8 and 6, multiply 8 and 6 which is 48, then reduce 48 to the smallest number that can be divided by both 8 and 6 evenly (without a remainder) if possible. 48 can be reduced to 24 by dividing 48 by 2, and knowing from the " Multiplication Table" that $6 \times 4 = 24$ and $8 \times 3 = 24$, 24 is the least number that can be divided evenly (without a remainder), and therefore, 24 is the LCD.

$$\frac{7}{8} = \frac{}{24} \quad \diagup \text{LCD}$$

$$-\frac{5}{6} = -\frac{}{24} \quad \diagup \text{L CD}$$

Step 2: Write equivalent fractions. Review the sections on Equivalent Fractions.

$$\frac{7}{8} \times \frac{3}{3} = \frac{21}{24} \quad \leftarrow \text{Equivalent fractions}$$

$$-\frac{5}{6} \times \frac{4}{4} = -\frac{20}{24} \quad \leftarrow \text{Equivalent fractions}$$

Step 3: Subtract the numerators of the equivalent fractions and write the difference of the numerators of the equivalent fractions over the least common denominator (LCD) or over the common equivalent denominator to get the final difference.

$$\frac{21 - 20}{24} = \frac{1}{24} \text{ of a yard of material was left.}$$

▬▬▬▬▬▬▬▬▬▬ **The notes and the generous examples have provided me with the conceptual understanding and the computational fluency to do my homework.**

Exercises

1. Samuel used $\frac{3}{4}$ cup of sugar and $\frac{1}{2}$ cup of milk to bake some cakes. How much more sugar than milk did he use? (Hint: Samuel used $\frac{3}{4} - \frac{1}{2}$ cup more of sugar than milk.) Hint: See Examples **1** to **4**.

2. John bought $\frac{6}{7}$ ton of coal and used up $\frac{1}{2}$ ton. How much coal was left?

Hint: See Examples **1** to **4**.

3. Nick bought $\frac{3}{5}$ pound of beef and ate $\frac{1}{4}$ pound for lunch. How much of the beef was left? Hint: See Examples **1** to **4**.

4. John bought $\dfrac{7}{9}$ of a yard of material for a school project. If he only used $\dfrac{1}{4}$ of a yard, how much material was left? Hint: See Examples **1** to **4**.

5. Karen is $\dfrac{9}{10}$ meter tall and Mabel is $\dfrac{4}{5}$ meter tall. How much taller is Karen? Hint: See Examples **1** to **4**.

6. A bag contained $\dfrac{9}{10}$ pound of salt. If $\dfrac{2}{8}$ pound were used, how much of the salt remained? Hint: See Examples **1** to **4**.

7. Rose had $\dfrac{5}{6}$ yard of fabric. If she used $\dfrac{3}{4}$ yard, how much fabric is left? Hint: See Examples **1** to **4**.

SUBTRACTION OF MIXED NUMBERS

Subtraction often involves the technique known as **borrowing. Borrowing** is necessary when subtracting a larger digit number from a smaller digit number. You will learn about the technique of borrowing later in this chapter.

In the subtraction of mixed numbers, subtract the fractions first, and then subtract the whole numbers, see Example **3**.

The steps for subtracting mixed numbers are:
Step 1: **Arrange the mixed numbers, one under the other and find the LCD.**
Step 2: **Write equivalent fractions.**
Step 3: **Subtract the equivalent fractions first by subtracting the numerators and put the difference over the equivalent denominator and if borrowing of a whole number is necessary, do so.**
Step 4: **Subtract the whole numbers and combine the subtraction of whole numbers and the subtraction of the equivalent fractions into the final answer.**

Example 1

Subtract: $3\dfrac{5}{8} - 2\dfrac{5}{16}$

162

Solution

(Notice that in Step 1, an imaginary line | separates the whole numbers from the fractions so that we can work on the whole numbers and the fractions separately.)

Step 1: Arrange the mixed numbers, one under the other and find the LCD. (Review the section on LCD)

$$3| \frac{5}{8} = \frac{}{16} \diagup \text{LCD}$$

$$-2| \frac{5}{16} = -\frac{}{16} \diagup \text{LCD}$$

8 can divide evenly into 16 (without any remainder) and therefore, 16 is the LCD of 8 and 16.

Step 2: Write equivalent fractions.

From Step 1, the denominator of $\frac{5}{8}$ which is 8 must have been multiplied by 2 to get the equivalent denominator of 16, and therefore, both the numerator and the denominator of $\frac{5}{8}$ in Step 2 should be multiplied by 2 as shown:

$$3| \frac{5}{8} \times \frac{2}{2} = \frac{10}{16} \leftarrow \text{Equivalent fraction}$$

From Step 1, the denominator of $\frac{5}{16}$ which is 16 must have been multiplied by 1 to get the equivalent denominator of 16, and therefore, both the numerator and the denominator of $\frac{5}{16}$ in Step 2 should be multiplied by 1 as shown:

$$2| \frac{5}{16} \times \frac{1}{1} = \frac{5}{16} \leftarrow \text{Equivalent fraction.}$$

Step 3: Subtract the equivalent fractions first by subtracting the numerators and put the difference over the equivalent denominator and if "borrowing" of a whole number is necessary, do so. (Note: "Borrowing" of a whole number is not needed in this case because $\frac{5}{16}$ is less than $\frac{10}{16}$.)

$$3| \frac{5}{8} \times \frac{2}{2} = \frac{10}{16} \leftarrow \text{Equivalent fraction}$$

$$-2|\ \frac{5}{16} \times \frac{1}{1} = -\frac{5}{16} \quad \leftarrow \text{Equivalent fraction}$$

$$\frac{10-5}{16} = \frac{5}{16} \quad \nearrow\text{Difference of the equivalent numerators}$$

$$\nwarrow\text{Equivalent denominator}$$

Step 4: Subtract the whole numbers and combine the subtraction of the whole numbers and the subtraction of the equivalent fractions into the final answer. (Notice that an imaginary line | separates the whole numbers from the fractions so that we can work on the whole numbers and fractions separately.)

$$3|\ \frac{5}{8} \times \frac{2}{2} = \frac{10}{16}$$

$$-2|\ \frac{5}{16} \times \frac{1}{1} = -\frac{5}{16}$$

$$\overline{1}$$

$$\frac{10-5}{16} = \frac{5}{16} \quad \nearrow\text{Difference of the equivalent numerators}$$

$\nearrow$

Subtraction of whole numbers. $\nwarrow$Equivalent denominator

Combine the whole number which is 1 and the fraction which is $\frac{5}{16}$ into a

final answer of $1\frac{5}{16}$.

Therefore, $3\frac{5}{8} - 2\frac{5}{16} = 1\frac{5}{16}$

Example 2

Subtract: $7\frac{3}{4} - 5\frac{1}{5}$

Solution

Step 1: Arrange the mixed numbers, one under the other and find the LCD.

$$7|\ \frac{3}{4} = \frac{}{20} \quad \nearrow\text{LCD}$$

$$-5|\ \frac{1}{5} = -\frac{}{20} \quad \nearrow\text{LCD}$$

Multiply the denominators 4 and 5 to obtain the LCD of 20. Note that 20 is the smallest number that can be divided by both 4 and 5 evenly (without any remainder).

Step 2: Write equivalent fractions.

From step 1, the denominator of 4 must have been multiplied by 5 to get the equivalent denominator of 20, and therefore, both the numerator and the denominator of $\frac{3}{4}$ in Step 2 should be multiplied by 5 as shown:

$$7\,|\ \ \frac{3}{4} \times \frac{5}{5} = \frac{15}{20} \ \leftarrow \text{Equivalent fraction}$$

From Step 1, the denominator of $\frac{1}{5}$ which is 5 must have been multiplied by 4 to get the equivalent denominator of 20, and therefore, both the numerator and the denominator of $\frac{1}{5}$ in Step 2 should be multiplied by 4 as shown:

$$-5\,|\ \ \frac{1}{5} \times \frac{4}{4} = -\frac{4}{20} \ \leftarrow \text{Equivalent fraction}$$

Step 3: Subtract the equivalent fractions first by subtracting the numerators of the equivalent fractions and put the difference over the equivalent denominator, and if "borrowing" of a whole number is necessary, do so. (Note that borrowing of a whole number is not needed in this case because $\frac{4}{20}$ is less than $\frac{15}{20}$.)

$$7\,|\ \ \frac{3}{4} \times \frac{5}{5} = \frac{15}{20} \ \leftarrow \text{Equivalent fraction}$$

$$-5\,|\ \ \frac{1}{5} \times \frac{4}{4} = -\frac{4}{20} \ \leftarrow \text{Equivalent fraction}$$

$$\frac{15-4}{20} = \frac{11}{20}$$

↗ Difference of the equivalent numerators

↘ Equivalent denominator or the denominator of the equivalent fraction

Step 4: Subtract the whole numbers and combine the subtraction of the whole numbers and the subtraction of the equivalent fractions into the final answer.

$$7 \mid \frac{3}{4} \times \frac{5}{5} = \frac{15}{20}$$

$$-5 \mid \frac{1}{5} \times \frac{4}{4} = -\frac{4}{20}$$

$$\overline{}$$
$$2$$

↗ Difference of the equivalent numerators.

$$\frac{15 - 4}{20} = \frac{11}{20}$$

Subtraction of whole numbers (7 - 5 = 2)

Combine the whole number 2 and the fraction $\frac{11}{20}$ into a final answer $2\frac{11}{20}$.

Therefore, $7\frac{3}{4} - 5\frac{1}{5} = 2\frac{11}{20}$.

Example 3

Subtract: $10\frac{2}{5} - 3\frac{5}{6}$

Solution

Step 1: Arrange the mixed numbers, one under the other and find the LCD.

$$10 \mid \frac{2}{5} = \frac{}{30} \diagup LCD$$

(Multiply the denominators 5 and 6 to obtain the LCD

of 30. Note that 30 is the smallest number that can

$$-3 \mid \frac{5}{6} = -\frac{}{30} \diagup LCD$$

be divided by both 5 and 6 evenly (without remainder.)

Step 2: Write equivalent fractions.

From Step 1, the denominator 5 must have been multiplied by 6 to get the equivalent denominator of 30, and therefore, both the numerator and the denominator of $\frac{2}{5}$ in Step 2 should be multiplied by 6 as shown:

$$10 \mid \frac{2}{5} \times \frac{6}{6} = \frac{12}{30} \leftarrow \text{Equivalent fraction}$$

From Step 1 the denominator of $\frac{5}{6}$ which is 6 must have been multiplied by 5 to get the equivalent denominator of 30, and therefore, both the numerator and the denominator of $\frac{5}{6}$ in Step 2 should be multiplied by 5 as shown:

$$-3 \mid \frac{5}{6} \times \frac{5}{5} = -\frac{25}{30} \leftarrow \text{Equivalent fraction}$$

Step 3: Subtract the equivalent fraction first by subtracting the numerators and put the difference over the equivalent denominator, and if **"borrowing"** of a

166

whole number is necessary, do so (Note that "borrowing" of a whole number from 10 is necessary because $\frac{23}{30}$ is greater than $\frac{12}{30}$.) Notice in Step 2 that the numerator of $\frac{25}{30}$ which is 25 is bigger than the numerator of $\frac{12}{30}$ which is 12. Since 25 cannot be taken from 12, borrow 1 from 10 and change 10 to 9. Put the **borrowed** 1 in front of $\frac{12}{30}$, to get the mixed number $1\frac{12}{30}$ as shown:

$$\overset{9}{10}|\ \frac{2}{5} \times \frac{6}{6} = 1\frac{12}{30} \quad \leftarrow \text{Mixed number}$$

$$-3|\ \frac{5}{6} \times \frac{5}{5} = -\frac{25}{30} \quad \leftarrow \text{Equivalent fraction}$$

Change $1\frac{12}{30}$ to an improper fraction:

Rule: To change a mixed fraction to an improper fraction, multiply the denominator by the whole number, then add the numerator and put the addition over the denominator.

To change $1\frac{12}{30}$ to an improper fraction, multiply 30 by 1, then add 12, and put the addition over 30. ($1\frac{12}{30}$ becomes $\frac{30 \times 1 + 12}{30} = \frac{42}{30}$)

Replace $1\frac{12}{30}$ in Step 3 with $\frac{42}{30}$ in the problem and subtract $\frac{25}{30}$ from $\frac{42}{30}$. Then subtract the whole numbers and combine the two results into a final answer as shown:

$$\overset{9}{10}|\ \frac{2}{5} \times \frac{6}{6} = 1\frac{12}{30} \rightarrow \frac{42}{30}$$

$$-3|\ \frac{5}{6} \times \frac{5}{5} = \quad -\frac{25}{30}$$

$$\overline{9-3} \qquad\qquad \text{———-} \quad \diagup \text{Difference of equivalent numerators}$$

$$9-3=6 \qquad\qquad \frac{42-25}{30} = \frac{17}{30}$$

$\nwarrow$
Difference of the whole numbers

Combine the whole number and the final fraction to obtain the final answer $6\frac{17}{30}$.

Therefore, $10\dfrac{2}{5} - 3\dfrac{5}{6} = 6\dfrac{17}{30}$

Special Note to the Student

The method for solving Example **3** is long, but Example **3** provides a logical detailed method of solving the problem. So that the students can understand the detail logic of the mathematics and once the detail logic is understood, the student does not need to write detailed explanations during actual problem solving in class or during test. See Example **6** for shortcut method involving "borrowing" to be used to solve problems and also Example **5** shows a shortcut method which does not involve "borrowing."

Example 4

Subtract: $10\dfrac{2}{5} - 3\dfrac{5}{6}$

Note that Example **4** is the same problem as Example **3**, however, Example **4** shows an alternate solution method to that of Example **3** where the whole number borrowed is changed to an equivalent fraction that has the common denominator as shown in Step 3.

Solution

Step 1: Find the LCD as in Step 1 of Example 3.

$$10\,|\quad \dfrac{2}{5} = \dfrac{}{30} \quad \diagup \text{LCD}$$

$$-3\,|\quad \dfrac{5}{6} = -\dfrac{}{30} \quad \diagup \text{LCD}$$

Step 2: Find the equivalent fraction as in Step 2 of Example 3.

$$10\,|\quad \dfrac{2}{5} \times \dfrac{6}{6} = \dfrac{12}{30} \quad \leftarrow \text{Equivalent fraction}$$

$$-3\,|\quad \dfrac{5}{6} \times \dfrac{5}{5} = -\dfrac{25}{30} \quad \leftarrow \text{Equivalent fraction}$$

Step 3: From Step 2, it can be seen that since $\dfrac{25}{30}$ is bigger than $\dfrac{12}{30}$, we cannot subtract the numerator of $\dfrac{25}{30}$ which is 25 from the numerator of $\dfrac{12}{30}$ which is 12. Therefore, as in Example **3**, we have to borrow 1 from the whole number of 10. The borrowed 1 should be written as an equivalent fraction that has a

168

common denominator of 30. The borrowed 1 then becomes: $1 = \dfrac{30}{30}$. (Recall that the value of any fraction which has the same number as the numerator and the denominator is 1.) Add the borrowed $\dfrac{30}{30}$ to $\dfrac{12}{30}$, and then subtract as already done in Example **3** as shown:

$$
\begin{array}{l}
\quad\quad 9 \\
10\,| \ \dfrac{2}{5} \times \dfrac{6}{6} = \dfrac{12}{30} + \dfrac{30}{30} \ \rightarrow \ \dfrac{42}{30} \quad \nearrow \text{Addition of numerators}
\end{array}
$$

$$
-\,3\,| \ \dfrac{5}{6} \times \dfrac{5}{5} = -\dfrac{25}{30} \quad \rightarrow -\dfrac{25}{30}
$$

$$
\overline{9 - 3}
$$

$9 - 3 = 6$
$\quad\quad\quad\quad\quad\quad\quad\quad \dfrac{42 - 25}{30} = \dfrac{17}{30} \ \leftarrow \text{Final fraction}$ $\nearrow$ Subtraction of numerators

$\nwarrow$ Whole number subtraction

Combine the whole number which is 6 and the final fraction which is $\dfrac{17}{30}$ to obtain the final answer $6\dfrac{17}{30}$.

Therefore, $10\dfrac{2}{5} - 3\dfrac{5}{6} = 6\dfrac{17}{30}$

Example 5

Subtract: $15\dfrac{3}{4} - 5\dfrac{5}{9}$ (See Examples **1** and **2** for sample detailed solutions.)

Solution

$$
15\,| \ \dfrac{3}{4} \times \dfrac{9}{9} = \dfrac{27}{36}
$$
$$
\quad\quad\quad\quad\quad\quad \nwarrow \text{LCD}
$$
$$
-\,5\,| \ \dfrac{5}{9} \times \dfrac{4}{4} = -\dfrac{20}{36} \ \nearrow \text{LCD}
$$
$$
\overline{10} \quad\quad\quad\quad \nearrow \text{Subtraction of the numerators}
$$
$$
\nearrow \quad\quad\quad \dfrac{27 - 20}{36} = \dfrac{7}{36} \ \leftarrow \text{Final fraction}
$$

Whole number subtraction.

Combine the final fraction and the whole number to get the final answer $10\dfrac{7}{36}$.

Therefore, $15\dfrac{3}{4} - 5\dfrac{5}{9} = 10\dfrac{7}{36}$.

Note: It is recommended that the method of solution used for Example **5** should be used in solving homework problems without the detailed explanations.

Example 6

Subtract: $13\frac{1}{2} - 8\frac{5}{8}$ (See Example **4** for sample detailed solution method.)

Solution

$$13\Big|\ \frac{1}{2} \times \frac{4}{4} = \frac{4}{8}\ \diagup\text{LCD}$$

$$-8\Big|\ \frac{5}{8} \times \frac{1}{1} = -\frac{5}{8}\ \diagup\text{LCD}$$

$\frac{5}{8}$ is bigger than $\frac{4}{8}$, so we have to borrow 1 from 13 and the 1 is added to $\frac{4}{8}$ as $\frac{8}{8}$ as shown:

$$12 \qquad\qquad\qquad\qquad \diagup\text{This is the same as 1 added to } \frac{4}{8}$$

$$\cancel{13}\Big|\ \frac{1}{2} \times \frac{4}{4} = \frac{4}{8} + \frac{8}{8} = \frac{12}{8}$$

$$-8\Big|\ \frac{5}{8} \times \frac{1}{1} \qquad\qquad = -\frac{5}{8}$$

$$\overline{12 - 8} \qquad\qquad\qquad \overline{\qquad\qquad}\ \diagup\text{Subtraction of numerators}$$

$$12 - 8 = 4 \qquad\qquad\qquad \frac{12 - 5}{8} = \frac{7}{8}\ \leftarrow \text{Final fraction}$$

$$\nwarrow$$

Whole number subtraction

Combine the whole number and the final fraction to obtain the final answer $4\frac{7}{8}$.

Therefore, $13\frac{1}{2} - 8\frac{5}{8} = 4\frac{7}{8}$

Note: **It is recommended that the method of solution of Example 6 should be used in homework and tests without the detailed explanations.**

Example 7

Subtract: $1 - \frac{2}{7}$

Solution

Step 1: Change the whole number 1 into an equivalent fraction that has the same denominator as that of $\frac{2}{7}$ which is 7. Therefore, $1 = \frac{7}{7}$. (Recall that any fraction which has the same number as both the numerator and the denominator has a value of 1.)

Therefore, $1 - \dfrac{2}{7}$ becomes $\dfrac{7}{7} - \dfrac{2}{7}$

Step 2: Subtract the numerators and put the difference over the common denominator of 7 as follows:

$$\dfrac{7}{7} - \dfrac{2}{7} = \dfrac{7-2}{7} = \dfrac{5}{7}.$$

Example 8

Subtract: $1 - \dfrac{13}{49}$

Solution

Step 1: Change the whole number 1 into an equivalent fraction that has the same denominator as that of $\dfrac{13}{49}$ which is 49. Therefore, $1 = \dfrac{49}{49}$. (Recall that any fraction which has the same number as both the denominator and the numerator has a value of 1.)

Therefore, $1 - \dfrac{13}{49}$ becomes $\dfrac{49}{49} - \dfrac{13}{49} = \dfrac{36}{49}.$

Step 2: Subtract the numerators and put the difference over the common denominator of 49 as shown:

$$\dfrac{49}{49} - \dfrac{13}{49} = \dfrac{49-13}{49} = \dfrac{36}{49}$$

═══════════════ The notes and the generous examples have provided me with the conceptual understanding and the computational fluency to do my homework.

Exercises

1. Subtract (Hint: See Examples **7** and **8**.)

(a) $1 - \dfrac{2}{5}$ (b) $1 - \dfrac{1}{4}$ (c) $1 - \dfrac{1}{10}$ (d) $1 - \dfrac{8}{9}$

(e) $1 - \dfrac{4}{7}$ (f) $1 - \dfrac{1}{6}$ (g) $1 - \dfrac{3}{11}$ (h) $1 - \dfrac{17}{18}$

(i) $1 - \dfrac{99}{100}$ **(j)** $1 - \dfrac{28}{44}$ **(k)** $1 - \dfrac{77}{78}$ **(l)** $1 - \dfrac{49}{74}$

(m) $1 - \dfrac{99}{200}$ **(n)** $1 - \dfrac{47}{64}$ **(o)** $1 - \dfrac{38}{65}$ **(p)** $1 - \dfrac{24}{37}$

2. Subtract (Hint: See Example **1**.)

(a) $3\dfrac{3}{4} - 1\dfrac{1}{8}$ **(b)** $7\dfrac{3}{4} - 5\dfrac{1}{6}$ **(c)** $5\dfrac{5}{6} - 3\dfrac{5}{12}$ **(d)** $8\dfrac{8}{9} - 2\dfrac{2}{9}$

(e) $4\dfrac{2}{3} - 2\dfrac{5}{12}$ **(f)** $10\dfrac{11}{12} - 3\dfrac{5}{6}$ **(g)** $3\dfrac{8}{9} - 1\dfrac{7}{9}$ **(h)** $6\dfrac{4}{5} - 2\dfrac{3}{10}$

(i) $8\dfrac{9}{12} - 3\dfrac{1}{3}$ **(j)** $12\dfrac{3}{4} - 7\dfrac{5}{16}$ **(k)** $6\dfrac{17}{18} - 2\dfrac{2}{9}$ **(l)** $28\dfrac{6}{7} - 2\dfrac{3}{14}$

(m) $9\dfrac{17}{21} - 3\dfrac{2}{7}$ **(n)** $13\dfrac{5}{6} - 4\dfrac{7}{18}$ **(o)** $56\dfrac{11}{15} - 6\dfrac{7}{30}$ **(p)** $10\dfrac{5}{6} - 2\dfrac{7}{24}$

(q) $110\dfrac{5}{8} - 90\dfrac{3}{64}$ **(r)** $94\dfrac{7}{9} - 64\dfrac{7}{36}$ **(s)** $32\dfrac{4}{5} - 19\dfrac{2}{15}$ **(t)** $6\dfrac{5}{6} - 2\dfrac{7}{24}$

3. Subtract (Hint: See Examples **2** and **5**.)

(a) $4\dfrac{2}{3} - 2\dfrac{1}{5}$ **(b)** $8\dfrac{4}{5} - 5\dfrac{1}{3}$ **(c)** $6\dfrac{3}{5} - 1\dfrac{1}{4}$ **(d)** $12\dfrac{1}{2} - 3\dfrac{2}{5}$

(e) $7\dfrac{2}{3} - 4\dfrac{1}{4}$ **(f)** $11\dfrac{7}{8} - 9\dfrac{1}{3}$ **(g)** $47\dfrac{4}{5} - 23\dfrac{2}{7}$ **(n)** $45\dfrac{2}{3} - 33\dfrac{3}{7}$

4. What is the rule for changing a mixed fraction into an improper fraction?

5. Subtract (Hint: See Example **1**).

(a) $10\dfrac{11}{12}$ **(b)** $4\dfrac{7}{8}$ **(c)** $12\dfrac{5}{6}$ **(d)** $9\dfrac{6}{7}$
$\underline{-\ 3\dfrac{5}{6}}$ $\underline{-\ 2\dfrac{1}{4}}$ $\underline{-\ 6\dfrac{7}{12}}$ $\underline{-\ 6\dfrac{2}{7}}$

(e) $11\dfrac{11}{12}$ **(f)** $28\dfrac{15}{16}$ **(g)** $5\dfrac{1}{2}$ **(h)** $29\dfrac{6}{7}$
$\underline{-\ 6\dfrac{1}{6}}$ $\underline{-\ 17\dfrac{3}{8}}$ $\underline{-\ 2\dfrac{1}{4}}$ $\underline{-\ 3\dfrac{10}{21}}$

6. Subtract (Hint: See Examples **2** and **5**.)

(a) $18\dfrac{2}{3}$

$-5\dfrac{1}{5}$

(b) $7\dfrac{4}{5}$

$-2\dfrac{2}{3}$

(c) $10\dfrac{11}{12}$

$-6\dfrac{3}{5}$

(d) $72\dfrac{3}{4}$

$-35\dfrac{2}{7}$

(m) $27\dfrac{4}{5}$

$-7\dfrac{1}{3}$

(n) $14\dfrac{6}{7}$

$-3\dfrac{2}{3}$

(o) $7\dfrac{7}{8}$

$-2\dfrac{4}{9}$

(f) $10\dfrac{3}{4}$

$-2\dfrac{1}{3}$

7. Subtract (Hint: See Examples **3**, **4**, and **6**.)

(a) $10\dfrac{2}{3} - 4\dfrac{4}{5}$

(b) $4\dfrac{2}{7} - 2\dfrac{15}{21}$

(c) $7\dfrac{1}{6} - 4\dfrac{2}{3}$

(d) $11\dfrac{3}{5} - 2\dfrac{9}{10}$

(e) $15\dfrac{3}{11} - 7\dfrac{15}{22}$

(f) $41\dfrac{1}{2} - 2\dfrac{7}{9}$

(g) $7\dfrac{3}{7} - 5\dfrac{4}{5}$

(h) $8\dfrac{1}{5} - 2\dfrac{2}{3}$

(i) $7\dfrac{2}{7} - 5\dfrac{2}{3}$

(j) $8\dfrac{3}{11} - 5\dfrac{2}{3}$

(k) $9\dfrac{2}{3} - 4\dfrac{7}{8}$

(l) $15\dfrac{2}{5} - 4\dfrac{2}{3}$

(m) $9\dfrac{1}{6} - 7\dfrac{3}{4}$

(n) $12\dfrac{2}{7} - 8\dfrac{16}{21}$

(o) $25\dfrac{1}{16} - 5\dfrac{7}{8}$

(p) $24\dfrac{2}{5} - 8\dfrac{14}{15}$

Challenge Questions

8. Subtract

(a) $14\dfrac{2}{9} - 2\dfrac{3}{4}$

(b) $5\dfrac{7}{12} - 3\dfrac{5}{6}$

(c) $7\dfrac{2}{3} - 2\dfrac{1}{8}$

(d) $4\dfrac{5}{18} - 1\dfrac{1}{6}$

(e) $6\dfrac{23}{24} - 2\dfrac{1}{3}$

(f) $14\dfrac{1}{4} - 6\dfrac{5}{8}$

(g) $17\dfrac{4}{5} - 1\dfrac{3}{10}$

(h) $29\dfrac{2}{9} - 9\dfrac{7}{18}$

Answers to Selected Questions

1(a) $\dfrac{3}{5}$

2(a) $2\dfrac{5}{8}$

3(a) $2\dfrac{7}{15}$

5(a) $7\dfrac{1}{12}$

7(a) $5\dfrac{13}{15}$

REAL WORLD APPLICATIONS - WORD PROBLEMS
Subtraction of Mixed Numbers

Example 1

After roasting $15\frac{1}{2}$ pounds of beef, the beef weighed $12\frac{7}{8}$ pounds. How much less did the beef weigh after roasting?

Solution

(Notice that in Step 1, an imaginary line | separates the whole numbers from the fractions so that we can work on the whole numbers and the fractions separately.)

The beef is $15\frac{1}{2} - 12\frac{7}{8}$ pounds less after roasting. (Refer to Examples **4** under the topic Subtraction of Mixed Numbers for a detailed sample solution.)

$15\frac{1}{2} - 12\frac{7}{8}$ is solved as shown:

$15 \mid \dfrac{1}{2} \times \dfrac{4}{4} = \dfrac{4}{8}$ ← Equivalent fraction

$12 \mid \dfrac{7}{8} \times \dfrac{1}{1} = \dfrac{7}{8}$ ← Equivalent fraction

$\dfrac{7}{8}$ is bigger than $\dfrac{4}{8}$, so we have to borrow 1 from 15 and add the 1 to $\dfrac{4}{8}$.

$$
\begin{array}{l}
14 \qquad\qquad\qquad\qquad\nearrow\text{This is adding the 1 borrowed from 15 here.}\\
\cancel{15} \mid \dfrac{1}{2} \times \dfrac{4}{4} = \dfrac{4}{8} + \dfrac{8}{8} \;\rightarrow\; \dfrac{12}{8}\\
-\,12 \mid \dfrac{7}{8} \times \dfrac{1}{1} = \dfrac{7}{8} \qquad\quad \rightarrow\; \dfrac{7}{8}\\
\rule{3cm}{0.4pt} \qquad\qquad \rule{2cm}{0.4pt}\quad \nearrow\text{Difference of the equivalent numerators.}\\
14 - 12 = 2 \qquad\qquad \dfrac{12-7}{8} = \dfrac{5}{8}
\end{array}
$$

$\nwarrow$
Subtraction of whole numbers

Therefore, $15\frac{1}{2} - 12\frac{7}{8} = 2\frac{5}{8}$ pounds.

Example 2

A painter had $12\frac{1}{4}$ gallons of paint. If he used $8\frac{2}{3}$ gallons of paint, how much paint is left?

Solution

The gallons of paint left $= 12\dfrac{1}{4} - 8\dfrac{2}{3}$. (Refer to Example **3**, under the topic

Subtraction of Mixed Numbers for a detailed sample solution.)

$12\dfrac{1}{4} - 8\dfrac{2}{3}$ is solved as shown:

$$12\mid \ \dfrac{1}{4} \times \dfrac{3}{3} = \dfrac{3}{12} \ \leftarrow \text{Equivalent fraction}$$

$$-8\mid \ \dfrac{2}{3} \times \dfrac{4}{4} = \dfrac{8}{12} \ \leftarrow \text{Equivalent fraction}$$

$\dfrac{8}{12}$ is larger than $\dfrac{3}{12}$, so we have to borrow 1 from 12 and add the 1 to $\dfrac{3}{12}$ as

shown:

$$\begin{matrix} & & & \text{1 which is borrowed from 12.} \\ 11 & & & \downarrow \\ 12\mid \ \dfrac{1}{4} & \times \ \dfrac{3}{3} & = 1\dfrac{3}{12} & \to \dfrac{15}{12} \ \leftarrow \text{Change mixed fraction to improper fraction.} \\ -8\mid \ \dfrac{2}{3} & \times \ \dfrac{4}{4} & = \ \dfrac{8}{12} & \to \dfrac{8}{12} \end{matrix}$$

$$11 - 8 = 3 \qquad\qquad \dfrac{15 - 8}{12} = \dfrac{7}{12} \qquad \nearrow \text{Difference in the numerators.}$$

Subtraction of whole numbers

Therefore, $12\dfrac{1}{4} - 8\dfrac{2}{3} = 3\dfrac{7}{12}$ gallons.

(Notice that an imaginary line | separates the whole numbers from the fractions so that we can work on the whole numbers and the fractions separately.)

Example 3

John had $12\dfrac{1}{3}$ cups of flour and he used $5\dfrac{4}{5}$ cups to prepare food for his friends.

How many cups of flour were left?

Solution

The cups of flour left $= 12\dfrac{1}{3} - 5\dfrac{4}{5}$. (Refer to the example under the topic Subtraction of Mixed Numbers for the detailed sample solution.)

$$12\frac{1}{3} - 5\frac{4}{5}$$ is solved as shown:

$$12| \quad \frac{1}{3} \times \frac{5}{5} = \frac{5}{15} \quad \leftarrow \text{Equivalent fractions}$$

$$-5| \quad \frac{4}{5} \times \frac{3}{3} = \frac{12}{15} \quad \leftarrow \text{Equivalent fraction}$$

$\frac{12}{15}$ is larger than $\frac{5}{15}$, so we have to borrow 1 from 12 and add the 1 to $\frac{5}{15}$ as shown:

This is the 1 added to $\frac{5}{15}$

$$11$$

$$\overset{11}{\cancel{12}}| \quad \frac{1}{3} \times \frac{5}{5} = 1\frac{5}{15} \rightarrow \frac{20}{15} \quad \leftarrow \text{Change the mixed fraction to an improper fraction.}$$

$$-5| \quad \frac{4}{5} \times \frac{3}{3} = \frac{12}{15} \rightarrow \frac{12}{15}$$

$$\underline{\qquad} \qquad \underline{\qquad\qquad} \quad \diagup \text{Difference of the numerators.}$$

$$12 - 5 = 7 \qquad\qquad \frac{20 - 12}{15} = \frac{8}{15}$$

Subtraction of whole numbers

Therefore, $12\frac{1}{3} - 5\frac{4}{5} = 7\frac{8}{15}$ cups of flour.

━━━━━━━━━━━━━━━━ **The notes and the generous examples have provided me with the conceptual understanding and the computational fluency to do my homework.**

Exercises

1. After roasting $14\frac{1}{2}$ pounds of turkey, the turkey weighed $9\frac{2}{3}$ pounds. How much less did the turkey weigh after roasting? Hint: See Example **1**.

2. If a painter had $7\frac{1}{6}$ gallons of paint and he used up $3\frac{7}{8}$ gallons of the paint. How much paint is left? Hint: See Example **2**.

3. Nick had $15\frac{3}{4}$ cups of flour and if he used $2\frac{5}{6}$ cups to prepare cakes, how many cups of flour is left? Hint: See Example **3**.

Challenge Questions

4. John weighed $260\frac{2}{5}$ pounds. After going on a diet, he lost $70\frac{1}{2}$ pounds. What was John's weight after dieting?

5. Joshua had $6\frac{1}{2}$ dozen eggs and he used $2\frac{4}{5}$ dozen. How many dozen eggs were left?

6. Mary bought $20\frac{1}{2}$ feet of board for her school project. If she cut off $5\frac{5}{8}$ feet for the, how many feet of board were left?

7. Joanna had $18\frac{2}{3}$ yards of ribbon. If she used $11\frac{7}{8}$ yards, how much ribbon did she have left?

Answers to Selected Questions

1. $4\frac{5}{6}$ pounds   **3.** $12\frac{11}{12}$ cups

SUBTRACTION OF A FRACTION FROM A WHOLE NUMBER

Example 1

Subtract: $1 - \frac{2}{3}$

Solution

Before a fraction can be subtracted from a whole number,

Step 1: Change the whole number 1 into an equivalent fraction that has the same denominator as that of $\frac{2}{3}$ which is 3. Therefore, $1 = \frac{3}{3}$. (Recall that any fraction which has the same number as both the numerator and the denominator has a value of 1.)

$$1 - \frac{2}{3} \text{ becomes } \frac{3}{3} - \frac{2}{3}$$

Step 2: Subtract the numerators and put the difference over the common denominator of 3.

$$\frac{3}{3} - \frac{2}{3} = \frac{1}{3}$$

Example 2

Subtract: $2 - \dfrac{2}{3}$

Solution

Step 1: Before a fraction can be subtracted from a whole number, 1 should be taken from the whole number and changed to an equivalent fraction that has the same denominator as the fraction which is being subtracted from the whole number. 2 can be written as $1 + 1$, and then 1 can be changed to an equivalent fraction as shown:

$$2 - \frac{2}{3} = 1 + 1 - \frac{2}{3}$$

$$= 1 + \frac{3}{3} - \frac{2}{3} \quad \text{(Note: } \frac{3}{3} = 1\text{)}$$

$$\uparrow$$

Equivalent fraction

Step 2: Subtract the numerators of the fractions and put the difference over the common denominator of 3.

$$1 + \frac{3}{3} - \frac{2}{3} = 1 + \frac{3 - 2}{3}$$

$$= 1 + \frac{1}{3}$$

$$= 1\frac{1}{3} \quad \text{Combine the whole number and the fraction.}$$

Example 3

Subtract: $6 - \dfrac{3}{4}$

Solution

Step 1: Before a fraction can be subtracted from a whole number, 1 should be taken from the whole number and changed to an equivalent fraction that has the same denominator as the fraction which is being subtracted from the whole number. 6 can be written as $5 + 1$, and then 1 can be changed to an equivalent fraction as shown:

$$6 - \frac{3}{4} = 5 + 1 - \frac{3}{4}$$

$$= 5 + \frac{4}{4} - \frac{3}{4} \quad \text{(Note: } \frac{4}{4} = 1\text{)}$$

↑
Equivalent fraction

Step 2: Subtract the numerators of the fractions and put the difference over the common denominator of 4.

$$5 + \frac{4}{4} - \frac{3}{4} = 5 + \frac{4 - 3}{4}$$

$$= 5 + \frac{1}{4}$$

$$= 5\frac{1}{4} \qquad \text{Combine the fraction and the whole number.}$$

The notes and the generous examples have provided me with the conceptual understanding and the computational fluency to do my homework.

Exercises

1. Subtract. Hint: See Example **1**.

(a) $1 - \frac{4}{8}$ **(b)** $1 - \frac{9}{10}$ **(c)** $1 - \frac{3}{6}$ **(d)** $1 - \frac{7}{8}$

(e) $1 - \frac{2}{9}$ **(f)** $1 - \frac{4}{11}$ **(g)** $1 - \frac{1}{12}$ **(h)** $1 - \frac{3}{5}$

(i) $1 - \frac{2}{19}$ **(j)** $1 - \frac{3}{4}$ **(k)** $1 - \frac{7}{12}$ **(l)** $1 - \frac{1}{99}$

(m) $1 - \frac{49}{50}$ **(n)** $1 - \frac{1}{39}$ **(o)** $1 - \frac{8}{9}$ **(p)** $1 - \frac{1}{64}$

(q) $1 - \frac{7}{49}$ **(r)** $1 - \frac{5}{16}$ **(s)** $1 - \frac{3}{25}$ **(t)** $1 - \frac{5}{6}$

(u) $1 - \frac{5}{14}$ **(v)** $1 - \frac{7}{11}$ **(w)** $1 - \frac{3}{5}$ **(x)** $1 - \frac{99}{200}$

2. Subtract. Hint: See Examples **2** and **3**.

(a) $7 - \dfrac{8}{9}$ **(b)** $2 - \dfrac{4}{11}$ **(c)** $8 - \dfrac{3}{5}$ **(d)** $10 - \dfrac{4}{9}$

(e) $12 - \dfrac{3}{7}$ **(f)** $4 - \dfrac{1}{9}$ **(g)** $9 - \dfrac{2}{7}$ **(h)** $3 - \dfrac{2}{11}$

(i) $10 - \dfrac{2}{5}$ **(j)** $5 - \dfrac{3}{8}$ **(k)** $6 - \dfrac{5}{12}$ **(l)** $10 - \dfrac{2}{5}$

(m) $90 - \dfrac{4}{5}$ **(n)** $64 - \dfrac{4}{9}$ **(o)** $3 - \dfrac{2}{9}$ **(p)** $28 - \dfrac{3}{7}$

(q) $12 - \dfrac{5}{12}$ **(r)** $15 - \dfrac{3}{5}$ **(s)** $11 - \dfrac{2}{30}$ **(t)** $9 - \dfrac{3}{16}$

(u) $8 - \dfrac{3}{7}$ **(v)** $15 - \dfrac{1}{15}$ **(w)** $12 - \dfrac{4}{9}$ **(x)** $14 - \dfrac{5}{8}$

Challenge Questions

3. Subtract:

(a) $200 - \dfrac{19}{20}$ **(b)** $4 - \dfrac{19}{100}$ **(c)** $1 - \dfrac{6}{7}$ **(d)** $1 - \dfrac{3}{8}$

Answers to Selected Questions

1(a) $\dfrac{4}{8}$ **2(a)** $6\dfrac{1}{9}$

Special Note: We will discuss how to reduce some fractions to the lowest terms under the chapter Division of Fractions. For example, $\dfrac{4}{8}$ can be reduced to $\dfrac{1}{2}$ by dividing both the numerator and the denominator by 4.

MULTIPLYING FRACTIONS

A fraction is made up of a numerator, a denominator, and a fraction bar as shown:

$\dfrac{2}{5}$

↙ numerator

← fraction bar

↘ denominator

The fraction bar is a line that separates the numerator and the denominator.

Rule 1: To multiply fractions, multiply all the numerators together and multiply all the denominators together and then put the product of the numerators over the product of the denominators and if it is possible to reduce to the lowest terms, do so.

Example 1

Multiply: $\dfrac{2}{5} \times \dfrac{3}{4}$

Solution

Step 1: Multiply all the numerators together, multiply all the denominators together, and then put the product of the numerators over the product of the denominators as shown:

$$\frac{2}{5} \times \frac{3}{4} = \frac{6}{20}$$

Step 2: Reduce $\dfrac{6}{20}$ to the lowest term by dividing both the numerator and the denominator of $\dfrac{6}{20}$ by the same number, and in this case 2 is the largest number that can divide evenly into 6 and 20 evenly without a remainder as shown:

$$\frac{\overset{3}{\cancel{6}}}{\underset{10}{\cancel{20}}} = \frac{3}{10} \qquad \text{Divide the numerator and the denominator by 2.}$$

Therefore, $\dfrac{2}{5} \times \dfrac{3}{4} = \dfrac{3}{10}$

Special Explanation

Note that Example **1** could have been solved differently by reducing $\frac{2}{5} \times \frac{3}{4}$ in

Step 1 by dividing both the numerator and the denominator by 2 because 2 can divide the numerator 2 and the denominator 4.

Rule 2: In order to simplify the multiplication of fractions, divide any numerator and any denominator by the same number, and this is called cancelling.

$$\frac{2}{5} \times \frac{3}{4} \text{ becomes } \frac{\overset{1}{2}}{5} \times \frac{3}{\underset{2}{4}} \qquad \text{Divide numerator and denominator by 2.}$$

$$\frac{1 \times 3}{5 \times 2} = \frac{3}{10} \qquad \text{This is the same answer for Example 1.}$$

Example 2

Multiply: $\frac{3}{7} \times \frac{5}{6}$

Solution

Step 1: Since 3 can divide evenly into the numerator 3 and the denominator 6 (without a remainder), divide the numerator and the denominator by 3. Rule 2 can be used here as shown:

$$\frac{3}{7} \times \frac{5}{6} = \frac{\overset{1}{3}}{7} \times \frac{5}{\underset{2}{6}} \qquad \text{Divide the numerator and the denominator by 3.}$$

$$= \frac{1 \times 5}{7 \times 2} = \frac{5}{14} \qquad \text{Multiply the numerators and multiply the denominators and put the product of the numerator over the product of the denominator which is Rule 1.}$$

Note: Since in Example 2, both the numerator and the denominator are divided by 3, and we can no more reduce $\frac{5}{14}$, Step 2 is not necessary in this case.

Recommendation

It is recommended that during the multiplication of fractions, the student should divide the numerators and the denominators by the same numbers first if possible, before multiplying all the numerators and also multiplying all the denominators. Then put the product of the numerators over the product of the denominators.

Example 3

Multiply: $\dfrac{5}{12} \times \dfrac{4}{15}$

Solution

Step 1: Since 5 is the largest number that divides the numerator 5 and the denominator 15 evenly (without a remainder) and also, 4 is the largest number that divides the numerator 4 and the denominator 12 evenly (without a remainder), Rule 2 can be used here as shown:

$$\dfrac{\overset{1}{\cancel{5}}}{\underset{3}{\cancel{12}}} \times \dfrac{\overset{1}{\cancel{4}}}{\underset{3}{\cancel{15}}}$$

Divide both numerators and denominators by 5 and 4.

$(5 \div 5 = 1,\ 15 \div 5 = 3,\ 4 \div 4 = 1,\ \text{and}\ 12 \div 4 = 3)$

$$= \dfrac{1}{3} \times \dfrac{1}{3}$$

Since we can no longer reduce $\dfrac{1}{3} \times \dfrac{1}{3}$, multiply the numerators and multiply the denominators and put the product of the numerators over the product of the denominators as shown:

$$= \dfrac{1 \times 1}{3 \times 3} = \dfrac{1}{9}$$

Example 4

Multiply: $\dfrac{5}{6} \times \dfrac{7}{9}$

Solution

Step 1: Since there is no number that can divide both the numerators and the denominators evenly (without a remainder), we can only multiply all the numerators, then multiply all the denominators, and put the product of the numerators over the denominators as shown:

$$\dfrac{5}{6} \times \dfrac{7}{9} = \dfrac{5 \times 7}{6 \times 9}$$

Rule 1 is used here.

$$= \dfrac{35}{54}$$

Example 5

Multiply: $\dfrac{12}{15} \times \dfrac{3}{8} \times \dfrac{4}{9}$

Solution

Step 1: Since the numerators and the denominators can be divided by 2, 3, and 4, the fractions should be reduced by dividing by 2, 3, and 4 before the numerators should be multiplied together and the denominators multiplied together, and then put the product of the numerators over the product of the denominators as shown:

$$\dfrac{\overset{\overset{1}{4}}{\cancel{12}}}{\underset{5}{\cancel{15}}} \times \dfrac{\overset{1}{\cancel{3}}}{\underset{2}{\cancel{8}}} \times \dfrac{\overset{\overset{2}{\cancel{4}}}{}}{\underset{\underset{1}{3}}{\cancel{9}}}$$

$(12 \div 3 = 4,\ 15 \div 3 = 5,\ 4 \div 4 = 1,\ \text{and}\ 8 \div 4 = 2)$

$(2 \div 2 = 1, 4 \div 2 = 2)$
$(3 \div 3 = 1, 9 \div 3 = 3)$
Rule 2 is being used here.

$$= \dfrac{1}{5} \times \dfrac{1}{1} \times \dfrac{2}{3}$$

$$= \dfrac{1 \times 1 \times 2}{5 \times 1 \times 3} = \dfrac{2}{15}$$

Rule 1 is used here.

The notes and the generous examples have provided me with the conceptual understanding and the computational fluency to do my homework.

Exercises

1. Multiply (Hint: See Example **2**.)

(a) $\dfrac{4}{7} \times \dfrac{5}{8}$ (b) $\dfrac{5}{7} \times \dfrac{2}{10}$ (c) $\dfrac{1}{3} \times \dfrac{3}{4}$ (d) $\dfrac{3}{5} \times \dfrac{5}{7}$

(e) $\dfrac{2}{5} \times \dfrac{1}{6}$ (f) $\dfrac{2}{3} \times \dfrac{1}{2}$ (g) $\dfrac{4}{7} \times \dfrac{14}{15}$ (h) $\dfrac{3}{4} \times \dfrac{5}{6}$

(i) $\dfrac{3}{49} \times \dfrac{7}{10}$ (j) $\dfrac{2}{9} \times \dfrac{27}{29}$ (k) $\dfrac{2}{12} \times \dfrac{7}{9}$ (l) $\dfrac{3}{11} \times \dfrac{22}{23}$

(m) $\dfrac{3}{7} \times \dfrac{77}{78}$ (n) $\dfrac{2}{3} \times \dfrac{3}{5}$ (o) $\dfrac{3}{4} \times \dfrac{4}{5}$ (p) $\dfrac{5}{6} \times \dfrac{7}{15}$

(q) $\dfrac{4}{5} \times \dfrac{7}{12}$ **(r)** $\dfrac{3}{7} \times \dfrac{4}{15}$ **(s)** $\dfrac{5}{7} \times \dfrac{21}{22}$ **(t)** $\dfrac{2}{33} \times \dfrac{11}{13}$

(u) $\dfrac{21}{22} \times \dfrac{3}{7}$ **(v)** $\dfrac{10}{18} \times \dfrac{6}{13}$ **(w)** $\dfrac{27}{30} \times \dfrac{7}{9}$ **(x)** $\dfrac{45}{46} \times \dfrac{1}{15}$

(y) $\dfrac{50}{51} \times \dfrac{7}{25}$ **(z)** $\dfrac{42}{50} \times \dfrac{3}{12}$ **(a1)** $\dfrac{7}{17} \times \dfrac{3}{14}$ **(b1)** $\dfrac{4}{9} \times \dfrac{12}{13}$

2. Multiply (Hint: See Example **3**.)

(a) $\dfrac{3}{4} \times \dfrac{2}{9}$ **(b)** $\dfrac{9}{10} \times \dfrac{2}{3}$ **(c)** $\dfrac{4}{5} \times \dfrac{5}{8}$ **(d)** $\dfrac{3}{7} \times \dfrac{14}{15}$

(e) $\dfrac{5}{6} \times \dfrac{3}{5}$ **(f)** $\dfrac{2}{5} \times \dfrac{5}{6}$ **(g)** $\dfrac{4}{7} \times \dfrac{7}{8}$ **(h)** $\dfrac{3}{8} \times \dfrac{4}{6}$

(i) $\dfrac{2}{5} \times \dfrac{10}{12}$ **(j)** $\dfrac{3}{5} \times \dfrac{10}{18}$ **(k)** $\dfrac{2}{3} \times \dfrac{24}{28}$ **(l)** $\dfrac{4}{5} \times \dfrac{15}{24}$

(m) $\dfrac{2}{9} \times \dfrac{3}{4}$ **(n)** $\dfrac{3}{16} \times \dfrac{4}{9}$ **(o)** $\dfrac{2}{5} \times \dfrac{15}{16}$ **(p)** $\dfrac{2}{5} \times \dfrac{20}{22}$

(q) $\dfrac{4}{11} \times \dfrac{22}{24}$ **(r)** $\dfrac{3}{4} \times \dfrac{8}{9}$ **(s)** $\dfrac{3}{4} \times \dfrac{12}{27}$ **(t)** $\dfrac{2}{11} \times \dfrac{33}{34}$

(u) $\dfrac{5}{7} \times \dfrac{14}{15}$ **(v)** $\dfrac{5}{6} \times \dfrac{12}{15}$ **(w)** $\dfrac{3}{8} \times \dfrac{24}{27}$ **(x)** $\dfrac{2}{9} \times \dfrac{18}{20}$

3. Multiply (Hint: See Example **4**.)

(a) $\dfrac{3}{4} \times \dfrac{3}{7}$ **(b)** $\dfrac{7}{22} \times \dfrac{5}{8}$ **(c)** $\dfrac{1}{4} \times \dfrac{5}{6}$ **(d)** $\dfrac{2}{5} \times \dfrac{3}{5}$

(e) $\dfrac{2}{7} \times \dfrac{3}{5}$ **(f)** $\dfrac{3}{7} \times \dfrac{2}{5}$ **(g)** $\dfrac{2}{9} \times \dfrac{11}{15}$ **(h)** $\dfrac{1}{8} \times \dfrac{5}{7}$

(i) $\dfrac{2}{3} \times \dfrac{3}{5}$ **(j)** $\dfrac{7}{8} \times \dfrac{9}{11}$ **(k)** $\dfrac{5}{6} \times \dfrac{5}{7}$ **(l)** $\dfrac{3}{4} \times \dfrac{5}{7}$

(m) $\dfrac{2}{5} \times \dfrac{3}{5}$ **(n)** $\dfrac{1}{7} \times \dfrac{3}{4}$ **(o)** $\dfrac{2}{11} \times \dfrac{2}{3}$ **(p)** $\dfrac{5}{6} \times \dfrac{7}{8}$

4. Multiply (Hint: See Example **5**.)

(a) $\dfrac{2}{3} \times \dfrac{6}{5} \times \dfrac{15}{18}$

(b) $\dfrac{2}{7} \times \dfrac{21}{22} \times \dfrac{11}{12}$

(c) $\dfrac{3}{4} \times \dfrac{4}{9} \times \dfrac{4}{16}$

(d) $\dfrac{5}{6} \times \dfrac{3}{15} \times \dfrac{2}{7}$

(e) $\dfrac{7}{9} \times \dfrac{18}{21} \times \dfrac{3}{4}$

(f) $\dfrac{4}{5} \times \dfrac{10}{12} \times \dfrac{3}{7}$

(g) $\dfrac{4}{5} \times \dfrac{15}{24} \times \dfrac{2}{3}$

(h) $\dfrac{1}{3} \times \dfrac{2}{3} \times \dfrac{9}{10}$

(i) $\dfrac{3}{4} \times \dfrac{16}{17} \times \dfrac{1}{6}$

(j) $\dfrac{2}{7} \times \dfrac{5}{6} \times \dfrac{14}{15}$

(k) $\dfrac{4}{7} \times \dfrac{14}{16} \times \dfrac{2}{3}$

(l) $\dfrac{4}{9} \times \dfrac{18}{19} \times \dfrac{19}{20}$

(m) $\dfrac{2}{3} \times \dfrac{4}{5} \times \dfrac{3}{8}$

(n) $\dfrac{5}{8} \times \dfrac{6}{7} \times \dfrac{14}{15}$

(o) $\dfrac{2}{3} \times \dfrac{9}{10} \times \dfrac{4}{9}$

Challenge Questions

5. Multiply:

(a) $\dfrac{3}{5} \times \dfrac{15}{16}$

(b) $\dfrac{3}{4} \times \dfrac{8}{9}$

(c) $\dfrac{1}{5} \times \dfrac{3}{5}$

(d) $\dfrac{3}{5} \times \dfrac{15}{18}$

(e) $\dfrac{4}{9} \times \dfrac{5}{8} \times \dfrac{3}{15}$

(f) $\dfrac{2}{11} \times \dfrac{3}{4} \times \dfrac{22}{24}$

(g) $\dfrac{3}{5} \times \dfrac{7}{12} \times \dfrac{5}{14}$

(h) $\dfrac{2}{7} \times \dfrac{3}{5} \times \dfrac{10}{9}$

(i) $\dfrac{4}{7} \times \dfrac{14}{15}$

(j) $\dfrac{2}{5} \times \dfrac{4}{7}$

(k) $\dfrac{2}{7} \times \dfrac{14}{15}$

(l) $\dfrac{5}{7} \times \dfrac{3}{4}$

(m) $\dfrac{2}{7} \times \dfrac{3}{7}$

(n) $\dfrac{2}{3} \times \dfrac{3}{4} \times \dfrac{4}{5}$

(o) $\dfrac{2}{5} \times \dfrac{2}{27} \times \dfrac{15}{16}$

(p) $\dfrac{3}{4} \times \dfrac{3}{4}$

Answers to Selected Questions

1(a) $\dfrac{5}{14}$ **2**(a) $\dfrac{1}{6}$ **3**(a) $\dfrac{9}{28}$ **4**(a) $\dfrac{2}{3}$

REAL WORLD APPLICATIONS - WORD PROBLEMS
Multiplying Fractions

In mathematics "**of**" means to multiply.

Example 1

Mary won $\dfrac{3}{5}$ of a million dollars in a lottery. If she pays $\dfrac{1}{3}$ of the money in federal taxes, how much of her prize:

(**a**) is paid to the federal government?

(**b**) will remain after taxes?

Solution

(**a**) $\dfrac{1}{3}$ of the money is used to pay taxes.

$\dfrac{1}{3}$ of $\dfrac{3}{5}$ of a million dollars is used to pay taxes.

In mathematics "**of**" means to multiply.

Therefore, $\dfrac{1}{3}$ of $\dfrac{3}{5} = \dfrac{1}{3} \times \dfrac{3}{5}$

$$= \dfrac{1}{\underset{1}{\cancel{3}}} \times \dfrac{\overset{1}{\cancel{3}}}{5} \qquad \text{Divide the numerator and the denominator by 3.}$$

$$= \dfrac{1 \times 1}{1 \times 5}$$

$$= \dfrac{1}{5} \text{ of a million dollars is used to pay the taxes.}$$

(**b**) The total money won $= \dfrac{3}{5}$ of a million dollars.

The money used to pay taxes $= \dfrac{1}{5}$ of a million dollars.

Therefore, the money that remains $= \dfrac{3}{5} - \dfrac{1}{5}$

(Review topics on Subtraction of Fractions.)

$$\frac{3}{5} - \frac{1}{5} = \frac{3-1}{5}$$ Since the denominators of $\frac{3}{5}$ and $\frac{1}{5}$ are the same,

subtract the numerators and put the difference over 5.

$$= \frac{2}{5}$$ of a million dollars will remain.

Example 2

A truck had a load of $\frac{11}{12}$ ton of goods. If $\frac{3}{11}$ of the goods were delivered,

(a) what part of a ton of the goods were delivered?
(b) what part of the ton of the goods remained?

Solution

(a) Total load of goods $= \frac{11}{12}$ ton

$\frac{3}{11}$ of the goods were delivered.

Therefore, $\frac{3}{11}$ of $\frac{11}{12}$ ton of goods were delivered.

In mathematics "**of**" means to multiply.

$$\frac{3}{11} \text{ of } \frac{11}{12} = \frac{3}{11} \times \frac{11}{12}$$

$$= \frac{\overset{1}{\cancel{3}}}{\underset{1}{\cancel{11}}} \times \frac{\overset{1}{\cancel{11}}}{\underset{4}{\cancel{12}}}$$ (Divide the numerators and the denominators by 3 and 11.) $(3 \div 3 = 1, 12 \div 3 = 4, \text{ and } 11 \div 11 = 1)$

$$= \frac{1 \times 1}{1 \times 4}$$

$$= \frac{1}{4} \text{ ton of the goods were delivered.}$$

(b) Total load of the goods $= \frac{11}{12}$ ton

Load of goods delivered $= \frac{1}{4}$ ton

The remaining ton of goods $= \frac{11}{12} - \frac{1}{4}$

Step 1: Find the LCD of $\dfrac{11}{12}$ and $\dfrac{1}{4}$ (Review topics on Subtraction of Fractions.)

The LCD of $\dfrac{11}{12}$ and $\dfrac{1}{4}$ is 12 because it is the least number/denominator

that both 4 and 12 can divide evenly into (without a remainder).

$$\dfrac{11}{12} = \dfrac{}{12} \quad \checkmark \text{ LCD}$$

$$-\dfrac{1}{4} = -\dfrac{}{12} \quad \checkmark \text{ LCD}$$

Step 2: Write equivalent fractions.

$$\dfrac{11}{12} \times \dfrac{1}{1} = \dfrac{11}{12} \quad \leftarrow \text{Equivalent fractions}$$

$$-\dfrac{1}{4} \times \dfrac{3}{3} = -\dfrac{3}{12} \quad \leftarrow \text{Equivalent fractions}$$

Step 3: Subtract the numerators of the equivalent fractions and write the difference of the numerators over the least common denominator (LCD) to get the final difference.

$$\dfrac{11}{12} \times \dfrac{1}{1} = \dfrac{11}{12}$$

$$-\dfrac{1}{4} \times \dfrac{3}{3} = -\dfrac{3}{12}$$

$$\overline{}$$

$$\dfrac{11-3}{12} = \dfrac{8}{12} \quad \text{ton of goods remained.}$$

Note: $\dfrac{8}{12}$ should be reduced to the lowest term by dividing both the numerator and the denominator by 4 as shown:

$$\dfrac{8}{12} = \dfrac{\overset{2}{\cancel{8}}}{\underset{3}{\cancel{12}}} = \dfrac{2}{3} \quad \text{ton of goods remained.}$$

Example 3

Mary bought $\dfrac{9}{10}$ pound of beef and she used $\dfrac{1}{2}$ of the beef.

(**a**) What fraction of a pound did she use?

(**b**) What fraction of a pound remained?

Solution

(**a**) Total weight of the beef $= \dfrac{9}{10}$ pound.

$\dfrac{1}{2}$ pound of the beef was used.

Therefore, $\dfrac{1}{2}$ of $\dfrac{9}{10}$ of the beef was used.

In mathematics "**of**" means to multiply.

$$\dfrac{1}{2} \text{ of } \dfrac{9}{10} = \dfrac{1}{2} \times \dfrac{9}{10} \qquad \text{We cannot reduce to the lowest terms.}$$

$$= \dfrac{1 \times 9}{2 \times 10}$$

(The numerators are multiplied together and the denominators are multiplied together because there is no number that can divide both the numerator and the denominator evenly (without a remainder.)

$$= \dfrac{9}{20} \text{ pound of beef was used.}$$

(**b**) Total weight of the beef $= \dfrac{9}{10}$ pound

The weight of beef used $= \dfrac{9}{20}$ pound

Therefore, the weight of beef that remains is equal to

$$\dfrac{9}{10} - \dfrac{9}{20} \qquad \text{(Review the topic on Subtraction of Fractions.)}$$

Step 1: Find the LCD.

The LCD for $\dfrac{9}{10}$ and $\dfrac{9}{20}$ is 20 because 20 is the least number that can be divided by 10 and 20 evenly (without remainder).

$$\dfrac{9}{10} = \dfrac{}{20} \qquad \diagup \text{LCD}$$

$$\frac{9}{20} = \frac{}{20} \quad \swarrow \text{LCD}$$

Step 2: Write equivalent fractions.

$$\frac{9}{10} \times \frac{2}{2} = \frac{18}{20} \quad \leftarrow \text{Equivalent fractions}$$

$$-\frac{9}{20} \times \frac{1}{1} = -\frac{9}{20} \quad \leftarrow \text{Equivalent fractions}$$

(Notice that a negative sign is put in front of $\frac{9}{20}$ because we must subtract the numerators of the equivalent fractions and write the difference of the numerators over the least common denominator (LCD) to get the final difference as stated in Step 3.)

Step 3: Subtract the numerators of the equivalent fractions and write the difference of the numerators over the least common denominator (LCD) to get the final difference.

$$\frac{9}{10} \times \frac{2}{2} = \frac{18}{20}$$

$$-\frac{9}{20} \times \frac{1}{1} = -\frac{9}{20}$$

$$\underline{\hspace{3cm}} \swarrow \text{Subtraction of numerators}$$

$$\frac{18 - 9}{20} = \frac{9}{20} \text{ pound of the beef remained}$$

Example 4

A boxer earned $\frac{8}{9}$ of a million dollars. If the agent of the boxer gets $\frac{3}{21}$ of the boxer's earnings, what fraction of a million did the agent get?

Solution

Total money earned by the boxer $= \frac{8}{9}$ of a million dollars.

$\frac{3}{21}$ of the boxer's earnings was received by the agent.

Therefore, $\frac{3}{21}$ of $\frac{8}{9}$ of a million dollars was received by the agent.

In mathematics, "**of**" means to multiply.

Therefore, $\frac{3}{21}$ of $\frac{8}{9} = \frac{3}{21} \times \frac{8}{9}$

191

$$= \frac{\overset{1}{\cancel{3}}}{21} \times \frac{8}{\underset{3}{\cancel{9}}}$$
Divide the numerator and denominator by 3.

$$(3 \div 3 = 1, 9 \div 3 = 3)$$

$$= \frac{1 \times 8}{21 \times 3}$$

$$= \frac{8}{63}$$ of a million was received by the agent.

Example 5

Rose can mow her lawn in $\frac{8}{9}$ of an hour. How long will it take two people to do the same job assuming that each of the two people works at the same rate as Rose?

Solution

Time taken by 1 person (Rose) to mow the lawn $= \frac{8}{9}$ of an hour.

Time taken by 2 people to mow the lawn $= \frac{1}{2}$ of the time taken by 1 person.

$$= \frac{1}{2}$$ of the time taken by Rose.

In mathematics, "**of**" means multiplication

$$= \frac{1}{2} \text{ of } \frac{8}{9} = \frac{1}{2} \times \frac{8}{9}$$

$$= \frac{1}{2} \times \frac{\overset{4}{\cancel{8}}}{\underset{1}{9}}$$
(Divide the numerator and the denominator by 2.)

$$= \frac{1 \times 4}{1 \times 9}$$

$$= \frac{4}{9}$$ of an hour

The notes and the generous examples have provided me with the conceptual understanding and the computational fluency to do my homework.

192

Exercises

1. John won $\dfrac{6}{7}$ of a million dollars in a lottery. If he pays $\dfrac{1}{3}$ of the money in federal taxes, how much of his prize
   (a) is paid to the federal government?
   (b) will remain?
   Hint: See Example **1**.

2. Mary won $\dfrac{5}{6}$ of a million dollars in a lottery. Assume that she paid $\dfrac{4}{15}$ of the money in federal taxes, how much of her prize
   (a) is paid to the federal government?
   (b) will remain?
   Hint: See Example **1**.

3. A truck had a load of $\dfrac{9}{10}$ ton of goods. If $\dfrac{5}{6}$ of the goods were delivered,
   (a) what part of a ton of the goods were delivered?
   (b) what part of a ton of the goods remained?
   Hint: See Example **2**.

4. A truck had a load of $\dfrac{7}{8}$ ton of sand. If $\dfrac{4}{21}$ of the sand was delivered,
   (a) what part of a ton of the sand was delivered?
   (b) what part of a ton of the sand remained?
   Hint: See Example **2**.

5. Rose bought $\dfrac{3}{4}$ pound of ham and she used $\dfrac{1}{3}$ of the ham.
   (a) What fraction of a pound did she use?
   (b) What fraction of a pound remained?
   Hint: See Example **3**.

6. Assume that a school district bought $\dfrac{3}{4}$ ton of rice for the year. If $\dfrac{1}{6}$ of the rice has been used,
   (a) what fraction of a ton was used?
   (b) what fraction of a ton remained?
   Hint: See Example **3**.

7. A coach earned $\dfrac{5}{12}$ of a million dollars. If the trainer of the team gets $\dfrac{3}{10}$ of the coach's earnings, what fraction of a million did the trainer get?
   Hint: See Example **4**

8. Frank can mow a lawn in $\dfrac{7}{9}$ of an hour. How long will it take 2 people to mow the same lawn, assuming that each of the two people works at the same rate as

193

Frank? Hint: See Example **5**.

Challenge Questions

9. Nick can rake a lawn of leaves in $\dfrac{7}{12}$ of an hour. How long will it take three people to rake the same lawn, assuming that each of the three people works at the same rate as Nick?

MULTIPLICATION OF FRACTIONS AND WHOLE NUMBERS

Rule 1: To multiply fractions and whole numbers, write the whole numbers as fractions by dividing the whole numbers by 1. (Example: The fraction form of the whole number 9 is $\dfrac{9}{1}$.)

Rule 2: Before multiplying all the numerators and also multiplying all the denominators reduce the fractions to the lowest terms by dividing the numerators, and the denominators by the same number evenly (without a remainder) if possible.

Rule 3: Multiply the numerators and then multiply the denominators.

Rule 4: Change the answer (which is an improper fraction) to a mixed number by dividing the numerator by the denominator. (For example, the improper fraction $\dfrac{12}{5}$ can be written as $2\dfrac{2}{5}$ as a mixed number.)

Example 1

Multiply: $4 \times \dfrac{3}{4}$

Solution

Step 1: Change the whole number 4 to a fraction. See Rule 1.

$$4 = \frac{4}{1}$$

Therefore, $4 \times \dfrac{3}{4} = \dfrac{4}{1} \times \dfrac{3}{4}$

Step 2: Reduce the fractions to the lowest terms by dividing the numerators and the denominators by the same number evenly (without a remainder) if possible. See Rule 2.

Therefore, $\dfrac{4}{1} \times \dfrac{3}{4} = \dfrac{\overset{1}{4}}{1} \times \dfrac{3}{\underset{1}{4}}$ $(4 \div 4 = 1)$.

Step 3: Multiply the numerators, and then multiply the denominators. See Rule 3.

From Step 2, $\dfrac{1}{1} \times \dfrac{3}{1} = \dfrac{1 \times 3}{1 \times 1} = \dfrac{3}{1} = 3$

Therefore, $4 \times \dfrac{3}{4} = 3$

Example 2

Solve the question in Example 1 without showing the detailed explanations. Use a shortcut method.

Solution

Shortcut: $4 \times \dfrac{3}{4} = \dfrac{4}{1} \times \dfrac{3}{4}$

$= \dfrac{\overset{1}{4}}{1} \times \dfrac{3}{\underset{1}{4}}$

$= \dfrac{1 \times 3}{1 \times 1} = \dfrac{3}{1} = 3$

Example 3

Multiply: $12 \times \dfrac{3}{4}$

Solution

Step 1: Change the whole number 12 to a fraction. See Rule 1.

$12 = \dfrac{12}{1}$

Therefore, $12 \times \dfrac{3}{4} = \dfrac{12}{1} \times \dfrac{3}{4}$

Step 2: Reduce the fractions to the lowest terms by dividing the numerators and the denominators by the same number evenly (without a remainder), if possible. See Rule 2.

Therefore, $\dfrac{12}{1} \times \dfrac{3}{4} = \dfrac{\overset{3}{12}}{1} \times \dfrac{3}{\underset{1}{4}}$ $\qquad (12 \div 4 = 3, \ 4 \div 4 = 1)$.

Step 3: Multiply the numerators, and then multiply the denominators. See Rule 3.

From Step 2, $\dfrac{3}{1} \times \dfrac{3}{1} = \dfrac{3 \times 3}{1 \times 1} = \dfrac{9}{1} = 9$

Therefore, $12 \times \dfrac{3}{4} = 9$

Example 4
Solve the question in Example 3 without showing any detailed explanations. Use a shortcut method.
Solution

$12 \times \dfrac{3}{4} = \dfrac{12}{1} \times \dfrac{3}{4}$

$= \dfrac{\overset{3}{12}}{1} \times \dfrac{3}{\underset{1}{4}}$

$= 9$

Example 5
Use multiplication to explain what all the shaded areas of the models represent?

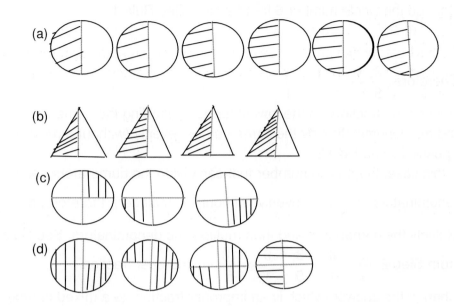

Solution

(**a**) Each shaded area shows $\dfrac{1}{2}$ of a circle.

There are 6 circles.

Therefore, the total shaded areas $= 6 \times \dfrac{1}{2}$ circles.

(**b**) Each shaded area shows $\dfrac{1}{2}$ of a triangle.

There are 4 triangles.

Therefore, the total shaded areas $= \dfrac{1}{2} \times 4$ triangles.

(**c**) Each shaded area shows $\dfrac{1}{4}$ of a circle.

There are 3 circles.

Therefore, the total shaded areas $= \dfrac{1}{4} \times 3$ circles.

(**d**) Each shaded area shows $\dfrac{3}{4}$ of a circle.

There are 4 circles.

Therefore, the total shaded areas $= 4 \times \dfrac{3}{4}$ circle.

Example 6

Multiply: $\dfrac{3}{5} \times 6$

Solution

Step 1: Change the whole number 6 to a fraction. See Rule 1.

$$6 = \frac{6}{1}$$

Therefore, $\frac{3}{5} \times 6 = \frac{3}{5} \times \frac{6}{1}$

Step 2: Reduce the fractions to the lowest terms by dividing the numerators and the denominators by the same number evenly (without a remainder) if possible. See Rule 2.

In this case, there is no number that can divide the numerators and the denominators of $\frac{3}{5} \times \frac{6}{1}$ evenly (without a remainder), therefore, go to Step 3.

Step 3: Multiply the numerators and then multiply the denominators. See Rule 3.

From Step 2, $\frac{3}{5} \times \frac{6}{1} = \frac{3 \times 6}{5 \times 1} = \frac{18}{5}$ ← Improper fraction

Step 4: Change the answer (which is an improper fraction) to a mixed number by dividing the numerator by the denominator. See Rule 4.

$$\frac{18}{5} = 3\frac{3}{5} \quad \text{(Note: } 18 \div 5 = 3 \text{ remainder 3, which is written as } 3\frac{3}{5}.\text{)}$$

Therefore, $\frac{3}{5} \times 6 = 3\frac{3}{5}$

Example 7

Solve the question in Example 6 without showing the detailed explanations. Use a shortcut method.

Solution

$$\frac{3}{5} \times 6 = \frac{3}{5} \times \frac{6}{1}$$

$$= \frac{3 \times 6}{5 \times 1}$$

$$= \frac{18}{5}$$

$$= 3\frac{3}{5}$$

Example 8

Find the product: $8 \times \frac{1}{3} \times 12 \times \frac{3}{4}$

Solution

Note: Find the product means to multiply.

Step 1: Change the whole numbers 8 and 12 to fractions. See Rule 1.

The fraction form of $8 = \dfrac{8}{1}$

The fraction form of $12 = \dfrac{12}{1}$

Therefore, $8 \times \dfrac{1}{3} \times 12 \times \dfrac{3}{4} = \dfrac{8}{1} \times \dfrac{1}{3} \times \dfrac{12}{1} \times \dfrac{3}{4}$

Step 2: Reduce the fractions to the lowest terms by dividing the numerators and the denominators by the same number evenly (without a remainder), if possible. See Rule 3.

$$\overset{2}{\underset{1}{\dfrac{\cancel{8}}{1}}} \times \dfrac{1}{\underset{1}{\cancel{3}}} \times \dfrac{12}{1} \times \overset{1}{\underset{1}{\dfrac{\cancel{3}}{\cancel{4}}}} \qquad (8 \div 4 = 2, 4 \div 4 = 1, 3 \div 3 = 1)$$

Step 3: Multiply the numerators and then multiply the denominators. See Rule 3.

From Step 2, $\dfrac{2}{1} \times \dfrac{1}{1} \times \dfrac{12}{1} \times \dfrac{1}{1} = \dfrac{2 \times 1 \times 12 \times 1}{1 \times 1 \times 1 \times 1} = \dfrac{24}{1} = 24$

Example 9

Solve the question in Example 8 without showing the detailed explanations. Use the shortcut method.

Solution

Shortcut:

$$8 \times \dfrac{1}{3} \times 12 \times \dfrac{3}{4} = \dfrac{8}{1} \times \dfrac{1}{3} \times \dfrac{12}{1} \times \dfrac{3}{4}$$

$$= \overset{2}{\underset{1}{\dfrac{\cancel{8}}{1}}} \times \dfrac{1}{\underset{1}{\cancel{3}}} \times \dfrac{12}{1} \times \overset{1}{\underset{1}{\dfrac{\cancel{3}}{\cancel{4}}}}$$

$$= 24$$

The notes and the generous examples have provided me with the conceptual understanding and the computational fluency to do my homework.

Exercises

1. Multiply the following. Hint: See Examples **1** and **3**.

(a) $12 \times \dfrac{1}{6}$

(b) $3 \times \dfrac{2}{3}$

(c) $15 \times \dfrac{2}{5}$

(d) $25 \times \dfrac{3}{5}$

(e) $14 \times \dfrac{2}{7}$

(f) $9 \times \dfrac{2}{3}$

(g) $6 \times \dfrac{2}{3}$

(h) $4 \times \dfrac{1}{4}$

(i) $16 \times \dfrac{3}{4}$

(j) $22 \times \dfrac{2}{11}$

(k) $21 \times \dfrac{3}{7}$

(l) $14 \times \dfrac{2}{7}$

(m) $18 \times \dfrac{5}{6}$

(n) $16 \times \dfrac{1}{4}$

(o) $12 \times \dfrac{1}{3}$

(p) $8 \times \dfrac{1}{4}$

(q) $18 \times \dfrac{2}{9}$

(r) $15 \times \dfrac{2}{3}$

(s) $12 \times \dfrac{3}{4}$

(t) $27 \times \dfrac{2}{3}$

(u) $36 \times \dfrac{5}{6}$

2. Solve questions **1(a)** to **1(u)** without showing detailed explanations. Use shortcut method. Hint: See Example **2** and **4**.

3. Multiply the following. Hint: See Example **6**.

(a) $\dfrac{3}{5} \times 6$

(b) $\dfrac{1}{4} \times 9$

(c) $\dfrac{3}{7} \times 3$

(d) $\dfrac{2}{3} \times 8$

(e) $\dfrac{2}{7} \times 4$

(f) $\dfrac{2}{9} \times 7$

(g) $\dfrac{1}{9} \times 14$

(h) $\dfrac{3}{7} \times 8$

(i) $\dfrac{2}{9} \times 11$

(j) $\dfrac{3}{5} \times 22$

(k) $\dfrac{3}{7} \times 5$

(l) $\dfrac{4}{5} \times 24$

(m) $\dfrac{3}{5} \times 24$

(n) $\dfrac{2}{7} \times 18$

(o) $\dfrac{3}{11} \times 30$

(p) $\dfrac{3}{4} \times 25$

4. Solve questions **3(a)** to **3(o)** without showing any detailed explanations. Use a shortcut method. Hint: See Example **7**.

5. Multiply: Hint: See Example **8**.

(a) $12 \times \dfrac{1}{4} \times 3 \times \dfrac{1}{3}$

(b) $\dfrac{2}{5} \times 15 \times \dfrac{2}{3}$

(c) $4 \times \dfrac{2}{5} \times \dfrac{5}{8}$

(d) $\dfrac{2}{7} \times 14 \times 2 \times \dfrac{3}{4}$

(e) $3 \times 4 \times \dfrac{2}{9} \times 6$

(f) $\dfrac{3}{4} \times 12 \times \dfrac{2}{5} \times 10$

(g) $\dfrac{3}{7} \times \dfrac{21}{27} \times 3 \times 2$

(h) $\dfrac{4}{5} \times \dfrac{2}{3} \times 6$

(i) $\dfrac{3}{5} \times \dfrac{2}{7} \times 35$

(j) $\dfrac{2}{9} \times 27 \times \dfrac{1}{4}$

(k) $\dfrac{2}{3} \times \dfrac{3}{4} \times \dfrac{6}{7} \times \dfrac{14}{18}$

(l) $\dfrac{3}{5} \times \dfrac{10}{12} \times \dfrac{3}{4}$

(m) $\dfrac{7}{8} \times \dfrac{3}{21} \times \dfrac{4}{9} \times 36$

(n) $\dfrac{3}{5} \times \dfrac{10}{11} \times \dfrac{22}{27}$

(p) $\dfrac{2}{7} \times \dfrac{5}{6} \times 14 \times \dfrac{2}{3}$

Challenge Questions

6. Find the product:

(a) $\dfrac{2}{3} \times 24$

(b) $24 \times \dfrac{5}{6}$

(c) $\dfrac{1}{3} \times 15$

(d) $\dfrac{2}{7} \times 5$

(e) $12 \times \dfrac{2}{3}$

(f) $14 \times \dfrac{3}{7}$

(g) $\dfrac{3}{5} \times 6$

(h) $3 \times \dfrac{7}{8}$

(i) $7 \times \dfrac{3}{21}$

(j) $\dfrac{2}{7} \times 10$

(k) $30 \times \dfrac{3}{5}$

(l) $\dfrac{3}{5} \times 20$

(m) $9 \times \dfrac{5}{8}$

(n) $\dfrac{4}{9} \times 7$

(o) $\dfrac{2}{5} \times 25$

(p) $\dfrac{4}{9} \times 27$

(q) $9 \times \dfrac{2}{3}$

(r) $16 \times \dfrac{3}{4}$

(s) $10 \times \dfrac{3}{4} \times \dfrac{2}{5} \times 6$

(t) $7 \times 3 \times \dfrac{5}{12} \times \dfrac{2}{21}$

(u) $\dfrac{2}{15} \times 8 \times \dfrac{5}{6} \times \dfrac{3}{4}$

(v) $\dfrac{2}{5} \times \dfrac{1}{3} \times \dfrac{2}{3}$

Answers to Selected Questions

1(a) 2   **3(a)** $\dfrac{18}{5}$ **5(a)** 3

REAL WORLD APPLICATIONS - WORD PROBLEMS
Multiplication of Fractions and Whole Numbers

Example 1

Given that $\dfrac{k}{3} \times 9 = 21$, find k.

Solution

Setup: Let us work on the left side of the equation which is $\dfrac{k}{3} \times 9$ to determine how 21 is obtained at the right side of the equation.

Step 1: Consider the left hand of the equation which is $\dfrac{k}{3} \times 9$ as the multiplication of a fraction by a whole number where $\dfrac{k}{3}$ is the fraction and 9 is the whole number. Recall that under the topic, Multiplication of Fractions and Whole Numbers, to multiply fractions by whole numbers, write the whole numbers as fractions by dividing the whole numbers by 1. Therefore, 9 can be written as the fraction $\dfrac{9}{1}$.

Therefore, the left side of the equation which is $\dfrac{k}{3} \times 9 = \dfrac{k}{3} \times \dfrac{9}{1}$

Step 2: Reduce the left side of the equation which is $\dfrac{k}{3} \times \dfrac{9}{1}$ to the lowest terms by dividing both the numerator and the denominator by the same number evenly (without remainder) if possible. In this case, both the numerator and the denominator can be divided by 3 as shown:

$$\dfrac{k}{3} \times \dfrac{9}{1} = \dfrac{k}{\overset{}{\underset{1}{\cancel{3}}}} \times \dfrac{\overset{3}{\cancel{9}}}{1}$$

$$= \dfrac{k}{1} \times \dfrac{3}{1}$$

Step 3: Multiply all the numerators together, and then multiply all the denominators together as shown:

$$\frac{k}{1} \times \frac{3}{1} = \frac{3k}{1}$$

$$= 3k$$

Therefore, the left side of the equation which is $\frac{k}{3} \times 9$ is simplified to become 3k.

Step 4: Compare the simplified form of the left side of the equation, which is 3k to the right side of the equation which is 21.

Therefore:

$$3k = 21$$

We have to think of a number that can be multiplied by 3 to obtain 21, and that number is 7.

Therefore, k = 7.

Check your answer

$$3k = 21$$
$$3 \times 7 = 21 \qquad \text{Substitute } k = 7$$
$$21 = 21 \qquad \text{Since the left side of the equation which is 21 is}$$

equal to the right side of the equation which is 21, then k = 7 is a correct answer.

Example 2

Solve the question in Example 1 without showing detailed explanations. Use the shortcut method.

Solution

$$\frac{k}{3} \times 9 = 21$$

$$3k = 21$$
$$3 \times 7 = 21$$

Therefore, k = 7

Critical Thinking

The shortcut method is recommended for homework, class exercises, and tests, however, the detailed explanation method is to provide the students with the necessary mathematical logic for understanding the true concepts.

Example 3

Find the value of z in the equation $\frac{1}{3} \times z = 4$

Solution

Setup: Let us work on the left side of the equation which is $\frac{1}{3} \times z$ to determine how 4 is obtained at the right side of the equation.

Step 1: Consider the left side of the equation which is $\frac{1}{3} \times z$ as a multiplication of a fraction by a whole number where $\frac{1}{3}$ is a fraction and z is the whole number.

Recall that under the topic Multiplication of Fractions and Whole Numbers, to multiply fractions by whole numbers write the whole numbers as fractions by dividing the whole numbers by 1.

Therefore, z can be written as a fraction as $\frac{z}{1}$.

Therefore, the left side of the equation which is:
$$\frac{1}{3} \times z = \frac{1}{3} \times \frac{z}{1}$$

Step 2: Reduce the left side of the equation which is $\frac{1}{3} \times \frac{z}{1}$ to the lowest terms by dividing both the numerator and the denominator by the same number evenly (without remainder) if possible.

In this case, both the numerator and the denominator cannot be divided by the same number evenly (Note: We do not know the value of z yet.) Go to Step 3.

Step 3: Multiply all the numerators together, and then multiply all the denominators together as shown:
$$\frac{1}{3} \times \frac{z}{1} = \frac{1 \times z}{3 \times 1}$$

$$= \frac{z}{3}$$

Therefore, the left side of the equation is simplified to become $\frac{z}{3}$.

Step 4: Compare the simplified form of the left side of the equation, which is $\frac{z}{3}$ to the right side of the equation, which is 4.

Therefore: $\frac{z}{3} = 4$

We have to think of a number that can be divided by 3 to obtain 4 and that number is 12. Therefore, $z = 12$.

Check your answer

$$\frac{z}{3} = 4$$

$$\frac{12}{3} = 4 \qquad \text{Substitute } z = 12$$

$$\frac{\overset{4}{\cancel{12}}}{\underset{1}{\cancel{3}}} = 4$$

$4 = 4$ Since the left side of the equation is equal to 4 and the right side of the equation is also equal to 4, then, $z = 12$ is a correct answer.

Example 4
Solve the equation in Example 3 without showing detailed explanations. Use a shortcut method.
Solution

$$\frac{1}{3} \times z = 4$$

$$\frac{1}{3} \times \frac{z}{1} = 4$$

$$\frac{z}{3} = 4$$

$$\frac{12}{3} = 4$$

Therefore, $z = 12$

Check your answer

$$\frac{z}{3} = 4$$

$$\frac{12}{3} = 4 \qquad \text{Substitute } z = 12$$

$$4 = 4$$

Example 5

Find k in the equation $\frac{2}{k} \times 9 = 6$

Solution

Setup: Let us work on the left side of the equation, which is $\frac{2}{k} \times 9$ to determine how 6 on the right of the equation is obtained.

Step 1: Consider the left side of the equation, which is $\frac{2}{k} \times 9$ as a multiplication of a fraction by a whole number, where $\frac{2}{k}$ is the fraction and 9 is the whole number.

Recall that under the topic Multiplication of Fractions and Whole Numbers, to multiply fractions by whole numbers write the whole numbers as fractions by dividing the whole numbers by 1.

So, 9 can be written as a fraction as $\frac{9}{1}$.

Therefore, the left side of the equation which is:

$$\frac{2}{k} \times 9 = \frac{2}{k} \times \frac{9}{1}$$

Step 2: Reduce the left hand side of the equation which is $\frac{2}{k} \times \frac{9}{1}$ to the lowest terms by dividing the numerators and denominators by the same number evenly (without a remainder). Since we do not know the value of k yet, we cannot divide numerators and the denominators evenly (without a remainder.) Go to Step 3.

Step 3: Multiply all the numerators together, and then multiply all the denominators together as shown:

$$\frac{2}{k} \times \frac{9}{1} = \frac{2 \times 9}{k \times 1}$$
$$= \frac{18}{k}$$

Therefore, the left side of the equation, which is $\frac{2}{k} \times \frac{9}{1}$ is simplified to become $\frac{18}{k}$.

Step 4: Compare the simplified form of the left side of the equation, which is $\frac{18}{k}$ to the right side of the equation, which is 6.

206

Therefore, $\dfrac{18}{k} = 6$

We have to think of a number that can divide 18 in order to obtain 6. The number is 3.

Therefore, k = 3.

Check your answer

$$\dfrac{18}{k} = 6$$

$$\dfrac{18}{3} = 6 \qquad \text{Substitute } k = 3$$

$$6 = 6 \qquad \text{Therefore, } k = 3 \text{ is a correct answer.}$$

Example 6

Solve the question in Example 5 without showing detailed information. Use a shortcut method.

Solution

$$\dfrac{2}{k} \times 9 = 6$$

$$\dfrac{2}{k} \times \dfrac{9}{1} = 6$$

$$\dfrac{18}{k} = 6, \qquad \dfrac{18}{3} = 6$$

Therefore, k = 3

The notes and the generous examples have provided me with the conceptual understanding and the computational fluency to do my homework.

Exercises

1. Solve for k in the following equations. (Hint: See Examples **1** and **2**.) Check your answer.

(a) $\dfrac{k}{2} \times 10 = 5$ (b) $\dfrac{k}{4} \times 12 = 9$ (c) $\dfrac{k}{5} \times 15 = 6$ (d) $\dfrac{k}{6} \times 24 = 20$

(e) $\dfrac{k}{3} \times 9 = 6$ (f) $\dfrac{k}{7} \times 21 = 12$ (g) $\dfrac{k}{8} \times 64 = 24$ (h) $\dfrac{k}{9} \times 18 = 10$

(i) $\dfrac{k}{10} \times 30 = 27$ **(j)** $\dfrac{k}{6} \times 24 = 20$ **(k)** $\dfrac{k}{5} \times 25 = 15$ **(l)** $\dfrac{k}{3} \times 24 = 16$

2. Solve for k in the following equations. (Hint: See Examples **3** and **4**.) Check your answer.

(a) $\dfrac{1}{3} \times k = 5$ **(b)** $\dfrac{2}{3} \times k = 4$ **(c)** $\dfrac{1}{4} \times k = 12$ **(d)** $\dfrac{2}{5} \times k = 4$

(e) $\dfrac{1}{5} \times k = 6$ **(f)** $\dfrac{1}{7} \times k = 6$ **(g)** $\dfrac{1}{6} \times k = 6$ **(h)** $\dfrac{1}{7} \times k = 2$

(i) $\dfrac{1}{10} \times k = 10$ **(j)** $\dfrac{1}{8} \times k = 2$ **(k)** $\dfrac{1}{6} \times k = 3$ **(l)** $\dfrac{1}{9} \times k = 9$

3. Solve for k in the following equations. (Hint: See Examples **5** and **6**.) Check your answer.

(a) $\dfrac{2}{k} \times 9 = 3$ **(b)** $\dfrac{2}{k} \times 6 = 2$ **(c)** $\dfrac{1}{k} \times 20 = 5$ **(d)** $\dfrac{1}{k} \times 28 = 4$

(e) $\dfrac{1}{k} \times 12 = 3$ **(f)** $\dfrac{1}{k} \times 12 = 4$ **(g)** $\dfrac{1}{k} \times 15 = 3$ **(h)** $\dfrac{1}{k} \times 15 = 5$

(i) $\dfrac{1}{k} \times 24 = 8$ **(j)** $\dfrac{3}{k} \times 6 = 3$ **(k)** $\dfrac{1}{k} \times 24 = 6$ **(l)** $\dfrac{1}{k} \times 24 = 4$

(m) $\dfrac{1}{k} \times 18 = 6$ **(n)** $\dfrac{1}{k} \times 18 = 3$ **(o)** $\dfrac{1}{k} \times 16 = 4$ **(p)** $\dfrac{1}{k} \times 6 = 2$

Challenge Questions

4. Solve for k in the following equations:

(a) $\dfrac{k}{5} \times 5 = 5$ **(b)** $\dfrac{2}{3} \times k = 6$ **(c)** $4 = \dfrac{2}{4} \times k$ **(d)** $\dfrac{1}{2k} \times 8 = 1$

5. Solve for w in the following equations:

(a). $w \times \dfrac{3}{4} = 9$ **(b).** $\dfrac{3}{5w} \times 15 = 27$ **(c)** $\dfrac{w}{7} = 11$ **(d)** $4w = 16$

Answers to Selected Questions.

1(a) 1   **1(d)** 5   **1(g)** 3   **2(b)** 6   **2(d)** 10   **3(a)** 6   **3(f)** 3   **3(n)** 6

Example 7

Solve for k in the equation:

$$\frac{3}{7} \times k = 3$$

Solution

Setup: Let us work on the left side of the equation, which is $\frac{3}{7} \times k$ to

determine how 3 on the right side of the equation is obtained.

Step 1: Consider the left side of the equation, which is $\frac{3}{7} \times k$ as a multiplication

of a fraction by a whole number where $\frac{3}{7}$ is the fraction and k is the whole

number.

Recall that under the topic Multiplication of Fractions and Whole Numbers, to multiply fractions by whole numbers write the whole numbers as fractions by dividing the whole numbers by 1.

Therefore, k can be written as a fraction as: $\frac{k}{1}$.

Therefore, the left side of the equation, which is:

$$\frac{3}{7} \times k = \frac{3}{7} \times \frac{k}{1}$$

Step 2: Reduce the left side of the equation, which is $\frac{3}{7} \times \frac{k}{1}$ to the lowest

terms by dividing the numerators and the denominators by the same number evenly (without a remainder.) In this case, there is no number that can divide both the numerators and the denominators evenly (without a remainder) and the value of k is not known yet. Go to Step 3.

Step 3: Multiply all the numerators together, and then multiply all the denominators together as shown:

$$\frac{3}{7} \times \frac{k}{1} = \frac{3 \times k}{7 \times 1}$$

$$= \frac{3k}{7}$$

Therefore, $\frac{3k}{7} = 3$

We have to think of a number that can be divided by 7 in order to obtain 3 on the right side of the equation. The number is 21, because $21 \div 7 = 3$. (Note: Knowing the multiplication tables is very helpful in determining that $7 \times 3 = 21$, and therefore, $21 \div 7 = 3$. So, the number that can be divided by 7 in order to obtain 3 is 21.)

We can write 3k = 21.

$$3k = 21 \text{ ——————— } [A]$$

Using equation $[A]$, the number that can be multiplied by 3 to obtain 21 is 7.
Therefore,
$$k = 7$$

Check your answer

$$\frac{3}{7} \times k = 3$$

$$\frac{3}{7} \times 7 = 3 \qquad \text{Substitute } k = 7, \text{ then the numerator 7 can divide the}$$

denominator 7 such that $3 = 3$.

$$3 = 3 \qquad \text{Therefore, the answer } k = 7 \text{ is correct.}$$

Example 8
Solve the question in Example 7 without showing detailed explanations.
Solution

$$\frac{3}{7} \times k = 3$$

$$\frac{3k}{7} = 3$$

$$\frac{3 \times 7}{7} = 3 \qquad \text{Therefore } k = 7$$

The notes and the generous examples have provided me with the conceptual understanding and the computational fluency to do my homework.

Exercises
1. Solve for k in the following equations. (Hint: See Examples **7** and **8**.) Check your answer.

(a) $\frac{4}{7} \times k = 4$ (b) $\frac{3}{9} \times k = 3$ (c) $\frac{2}{3} \times k = 6$ (d) $\frac{3}{4} \times k = 6$

(e) $\frac{3}{5} \times k = 6$ (f) $\frac{4}{7} \times k = 8$ (g) $\frac{3}{9} \times k = 6$ (h) $\frac{5}{6} \times k = 10$

Challenge Questions
2. Solve for p in the following equations.

(a) $\dfrac{3}{8} \times p = 9$ **(b)** $p \times \dfrac{3}{4} = 12$ **(c)** $21 = \dfrac{3}{7} \times p$ **(d)** $\dfrac{5}{4} \times p = 20$

Answers to Selected Questions

1(a) 7 **1(e)** 10

FINDING A NUMBER WHEN A FRACTIONAL PART OF IT IS KNOWN
REAL WORLD APPLICATIONS - WORD PROBLEMS

Explanation

Given that there are 12 students in a science class, which represent $\dfrac{1}{4}$ of the number of the students in the class. Find the total number in the class.

This means 12 students $= \dfrac{1}{4} \times$ Total number of students

$$12 \text{ students} = \dfrac{1 \times \text{Total number of students}}{4}$$

$$12 \text{ students} = \dfrac{\text{Total number of students}}{4}$$

Let us think of a number that can be divided by 4 to obtain 12. The number is 48. Therefore, the total number of students in the class is 48. Therefore, the multiplication problem involving 12 students $= \dfrac{1}{4} \times$ Total number of students can be changed to the division problem as shown:

$$12 \div \dfrac{1}{4} = ?$$

$$12 \div \dfrac{1}{4} = 12 \times \dfrac{4}{1} \quad \text{(To divide a number by a fraction, invert or flip}$$

the fraction and change the division sign to a multiplication sign. Review reciprocals.)

$$= 48 \text{ students}$$

We can therefore establish a rule to find a number when a fractional part of it is known as shown:

Rule: To find a number when a fractional part of the number is known, divide the known part by the fraction. The quotient is the unknown number.

Example 1

Given that 5 students in a class went to the zoo last week and this represents $\frac{1}{5}$ of the students in the class. Find the total number of students in the class.

Solution

Using the rule, the total number of students in the class is:

$$5 \div \frac{1}{5}$$

$$5 \div \frac{1}{5} = 5 \times \frac{5}{1}$$ (When dividing by a fraction, invert or flip the fraction and change the division sign to a multiplication sign. Review the section on reciprocals.)

$$= \frac{5 \times 5}{1}$$

$$= 25$$

There are 25 students in the class.

Example 2

Mary saves $80 of her earnings each week. If this is $\frac{3}{5}$ of her earnings, what is her weekly total earnings?

Solution

Using the rule, the total weekly earnings is:

$$80 \div \frac{3}{5}$$

$$80 \div \frac{3}{5} = 80 \times \frac{5}{3}$$ (When dividing by a fraction, invert or flip the fraction and change the division sign to a multiplication sign. Review Reciprocals.)

$$= \frac{80 \times 5}{3}$$

$$= \frac{400}{3}$$

$= 133.33$ You may use a calculator.

Therefore, the total weekly earnings is $133. 33.

Check your answer:

Savings per week $= \dfrac{3}{5} \times 133. 33 = \dfrac{400}{5}$

$= \$80$ which is given in the original question.

Therefore, the total weekly earnings of $133.33 is correct.

Example 3

If $\dfrac{3}{8}$ of a number is 24, find the number.

Solution

Using the rule, the number is:

$$24 \div \dfrac{3}{8}$$

$$24 \div \dfrac{3}{8} = 24 \times \dfrac{8}{3}$$ (When dividing by a fraction, invert or flip the

fraction and change the division sign to
a multiplication sign. Review reciprocals.)

$$= 24 \times \dfrac{\overset{8}{\cancel{3}}}{\underset{1}{\cancel{3}}}$$ Divide the numerator and the denominator by 3.

$$= 8 \times \dfrac{8}{1}$$

$$= 64$$

Therefore, the number is 64

Check your answer

$\dfrac{3}{8}$ of the unknown number $= 24$

$\dfrac{3}{8} \times 64 = 24$ Substitute 64 for the unknown number.

213

$$\frac{3}{\underset{1}{8}} \times \overset{8}{64} = 24 \qquad \text{Divide the numerator and the denominator by 8.}$$

$$\frac{3}{1} \times 8 = 24$$

$$24 = 24$$

The answer 64 is correct because the left side is equal to the right side of the equation.

Example 4

$\frac{5}{8}$ of what number is 40?

Solution

Using the Rule,

$$\text{Number} = 40 \div \frac{5}{8}$$

$$40 \div \frac{5}{8} = 40 \times \frac{8}{5} \qquad \text{Review the topic, Dividing a Number By a Fraction.}$$

$$= \overset{8}{40} \times \frac{8}{\underset{1}{5}} \qquad \text{Divide the numerator and the denominator by 5.}$$

$$= 8 \times \frac{8}{1}$$

$$= 64$$

The number is 64

Check your answer:

$$\frac{5}{8} \text{ of an unknown number} = 40$$

$$\frac{5}{8} \text{ of } 64 = 40 \qquad \text{Substitute 64 for the unknown number.}$$

$$\overset{8}{\underset{1}{\frac{5}{8}}} \times \overset{}{64} = 40$$

$$\frac{5}{1} \times 8 = 40$$

$$40 = 40$$

Since the left and the right sides of the equations are equal, the unknown number which is 64 is correct.

▬▬▬▬▬▬▬▬▬▬ **The notes and the generous examples have provided me with the conceptual understanding and the computational fluency to do my homework.**

Exercises

1. Given that 5 students of a class visited the zoo last term, which is $\frac{1}{4}$ of the class, find the total number of students in the class. (Hint: See Example **1**.) Check your answer.

2. Nancy saved $10, 000.00 a year which represents $\frac{2}{5}$ of her salary. What is her total salary? (Hint: See Example **2**.) Check your answer.

3. $\frac{4}{7}$ of a number is 28. What is the number? (Hint: See Example **3**.) Check your answer.

4. Given that in a hospital, there are 64 female nurses. If the female nurses represent $\frac{4}{7}$ of the total nurses at the hospital, what is the total number of nurses at the hospital? (Hint: See Example **1**.). Check your answer.

5. John spent $30, 000. 00 last year, which represents $\frac{3}{4}$ of his salary. What is the salary of John? (Hint: See Example **2**). Check your answer.

6. 40 is $\frac{4}{7}$ of what number? (Hint: See Example **4**.) Check your answer.

Challenge Questions

7. Mary withdrew $20.00 from the bank and if this withdrawal represents $\frac{2}{5}$ of her

total savings, how much money did she have at the bank?

8. 27 is $\frac{3}{4}$ of what number?

9. Ten members of a club went to see a football game. If the number of the club members that went to the football game represents $\frac{2}{5}$ of the total club members, what is the total number of club members?

Answers to Selected Questions.

(1) 20   (3) 49   (6) 70

MORE REAL WORLD APPLICATIONS - WORD PROBLEMS

Example 1

A stadium has 40, 000 general admission seats. Find the total number of seats if this represents $\frac{2}{3}$ of the stadium seats.

Solution

Using the rule, the total number of seats is $40,000 \div \frac{2}{3}$.

$$40,000 \div \frac{2}{3} = 40,000 \times \frac{3}{2}$$ (When dividing by a fraction, invert or flip the fraction and change division sign to a multiplication sign. Review the topic: Dividing a Number By a Fraction.)

$$= 40,000 \times \frac{3}{2}$$ Divide the numerator and denominator by 2.

$$= 20,000 \times \frac{3}{1}$$

$$= 60,000 \text{ seats.}$$

CUMULATIVE REVIEW – FRACTIONS

1. Change the following improper fractions to mixed numbers.

(a) $\dfrac{12}{3}$ (b) $\dfrac{10}{4}$ (c) $\dfrac{11}{4}$ (d) $\dfrac{28}{7}$ (e) $\dfrac{32}{5}$ (f) $\dfrac{48}{5}$

2. Change the following mixed numbers to improper fractions.

(a) $1\dfrac{3}{5}$ (b) $2\dfrac{2}{7}$ (c) $4\dfrac{1}{7}$ (d) $7\dfrac{1}{9}$ (e) $5\dfrac{3}{4}$ (f) $8\dfrac{3}{5}$

3. Arrange each set of fractions in descending order of value.

(a) $\dfrac{4}{5}, \dfrac{6}{7}$ (b) $\dfrac{2}{3}, \dfrac{2}{5}$ (c) $\dfrac{2}{7}, \dfrac{3}{8}$ (d) $\dfrac{3}{4}, \dfrac{4}{5}$

(e) $\dfrac{2}{3}, \dfrac{4}{6}, \dfrac{3}{5}$ (f) $\dfrac{1}{5}, \dfrac{2}{7}, \dfrac{5}{14}$ (g) $\dfrac{2}{5}, \dfrac{3}{6}, \dfrac{2}{3}$ (f) $\dfrac{1}{4}, \dfrac{1}{5}$

4. Divide: Reduce the answer to the lowest terms.

(a) $\dfrac{2}{3} \div \dfrac{3}{8}$ (b) $\dfrac{4}{5} \div \dfrac{3}{5}$ (c) $\dfrac{5}{7} \div \dfrac{5}{14}$ (d) $\dfrac{2}{5} \div \dfrac{3}{10}$

5. Multiply: Reduce to the lowest terms.

(a) $\dfrac{2}{5} \times \dfrac{3}{4}$ (b) $\dfrac{3}{8} \times \dfrac{4}{9}$ (c) $\dfrac{3}{5} \times \dfrac{15}{21}$ (d) $\dfrac{2}{7} \times \dfrac{49}{50}$

(e) $\dfrac{2}{3} \times \dfrac{2}{5} \times \dfrac{3}{4}$ (f) $\dfrac{1}{4} \times \dfrac{2}{7} \times \dfrac{3}{4}$ (g) $\dfrac{2}{5} \times \dfrac{1}{5} \times \dfrac{2}{3}$ (h) $\dfrac{1}{5} \times \dfrac{2}{3} \times \dfrac{3}{4}$

6. Subtract: Reduce to the lowest terms.

(a) $\dfrac{3}{4} - \dfrac{1}{3}$ (b) $\dfrac{7}{9} - \dfrac{5}{18}$ (c) $\dfrac{7}{8} - \dfrac{5}{24}$ (d) $\dfrac{2}{3} - \dfrac{5}{15}$

7. Add and change the answers to mixed numbers.

(a) $\dfrac{2}{5} + \dfrac{1}{5} + \dfrac{4}{5} + \dfrac{3}{5}$ (b) $\dfrac{5}{8} + \dfrac{7}{8} + \dfrac{3}{8} + \dfrac{1}{8}$

(c) $\dfrac{5}{7} + \dfrac{4}{5}$ (d) $\dfrac{4}{8} + \dfrac{3}{4}$ (e) $\dfrac{1}{4} + \dfrac{5}{7}$

8. Change each fraction to a higher equivalent fraction that has the given denominator.

(a) $\dfrac{3}{10} = \dfrac{}{100}$ (b) $\dfrac{5}{25} = \dfrac{}{100}$ (c) $\dfrac{5}{8} = \dfrac{}{64}$

(d) $\dfrac{4}{7} = \dfrac{}{21}$ (e) $\dfrac{8}{9} = \dfrac{}{27}$ (f) $\dfrac{3}{7} = \dfrac{}{49}$

9. Add: Reduce to the lowest terms.

(a) $\dfrac{2}{3}$
$\dfrac{4}{5}$
$\dfrac{1}{2}$

(b) $\dfrac{1}{4}$
$\dfrac{3}{4}$
$\dfrac{2}{3}$

(c) $\dfrac{2}{5}$
$\dfrac{2}{3}$
$\dfrac{7}{15}$

(d) $\dfrac{5}{12}$
$\dfrac{2}{3}$
$\dfrac{3}{4}$

10. Subtract: Reduce to the lowest terms.

(a) $21 - 17\dfrac{2}{5}$ (b) $40 - 12\dfrac{1}{4}$ (c) $14 - 10\dfrac{5}{7}$

11. Add: Reduce to the lowest terms.

(a) $2\dfrac{2}{3}$
$1\dfrac{1}{4}$
$1\dfrac{1}{4}$

(b) $3\dfrac{1}{3}$
4
$2\dfrac{3}{4}$

(c) $4\dfrac{2}{3}$
$2\dfrac{1}{4}$
8

(d) $\dfrac{2}{5}$
$\dfrac{3}{4}$
$\dfrac{2}{20}$

12. Divide: Reduce to the lowest terms.

(a) $\dfrac{3}{4} \div \dfrac{3}{4}$ (b) $6\dfrac{4}{5} \div \dfrac{2}{5}$ (c) $3\dfrac{1}{2} \div 1\dfrac{3}{4}$ (d) $\dfrac{3}{4} \div \dfrac{3}{8}$

(e) $7\dfrac{3}{6} \div 5$ (f) $10 \div 2\dfrac{2}{5}$

13. Find the unknown number.

(a) $\dfrac{2}{3}$ of what number is 90?   (b) $\dfrac{1}{4}$ of what number is 24?

(c) $\dfrac{3}{7}$ of what number is 36?   (d) $\dfrac{3}{5}$ of what number is 15?

14. Find the fractional parts.
(a) 3 is what part of 15?   (b) 4 is what part of 24?
(c) 20 is what part of 60?   (d) 5 is what part of 50?

15. Reduce the following to the lowest terms
(a) $\dfrac{4}{12}$ (b) $\dfrac{5}{45}$ (c) $\dfrac{24}{60}$ (d) $\dfrac{36}{72}$ (e) $\dfrac{18}{72}$

MULTIPLICATION OF FRACTIONS, WHOLE NUMBERS AND MIXED NUMBERS

Rule 1: To multiply whole numbers by mixed numbers or to multiply mixed numbers by whole numbers, change both the mixed numbers and the whole numbers to improper fractions.

Rule 2: To change a whole number to an improper fraction, write the whole number over the number 1 as the denominator.

Example 1
Write the following as improper fractions:

(**a**) 3   (**b**) 4   (**c**) 17   (**d**) 100

Solution

(**a**) The improper fraction of $3 = \dfrac{3}{1}$ (Use Rule 2)

(**b**) The improper fraction of $4 = \dfrac{4}{1}$ (Use Rule 2)

(**c**) The improper fraction of $17 = \dfrac{17}{1}$ (Use Rule 2)

(**d**) The improper fraction of $100 = \dfrac{100}{1}$ (Use Rule 2)

Rule 3: To change a mixed number to an improper fraction, multiply the denominator by the whole number, add the numerator to the product and then write the sum over the denominator.

Example 2
Write the following mixed numbers as improper fractions:

(**a**) $4\dfrac{3}{11}$ (**b**) $3\dfrac{3}{4}$ (**c**) $10\dfrac{4}{7}$

Solution

(**a**) Using Rule 3, multiply 11 by 4, add 3 to the product (the product of 11 and 4) and write the sum over 11.

$$\text{Therefore, } 4\dfrac{3}{11} = \dfrac{11 \times 4 + 3}{11} = \dfrac{47}{11}$$

The improper fraction of $4\dfrac{3}{11}$ is $\dfrac{47}{11}$.

(**b**) Using Rule 3, multiply 4 by 3, add 3 to the product (the product of 4 and 3) and write the sum over 4

Therefore, $3\dfrac{3}{4} = \dfrac{4 \times 3 + 3}{4} = \dfrac{15}{4}$

The improper fraction of $3\dfrac{3}{4}$ is $\dfrac{15}{4}$.

(**c**) Using Rule 3, multiply 7 by 10, add 4 to the product (the product of 7 and 10) and write the sum over 7.

Therefore, $10\dfrac{4}{7} = \dfrac{7 \times 10 + 4}{7} = \dfrac{74}{7}$

The improper fraction of $10\dfrac{4}{7}$ is $\dfrac{47}{7}$.

Example 3

Multiply: $4 \times 7\dfrac{3}{5}$

Solution

Step 1: Change both the whole number 4 and the mixed fraction $7\dfrac{3}{5}$ to improper fractions and multiply the improper fractions. (See Rule 1)

The improper fraction of $4 = \dfrac{4}{1}$ (See Rule 2)

The improper fraction of $7\dfrac{3}{5} = \dfrac{7 \times 5 + 3}{5} = \dfrac{38}{5}$ (See Rule 3)

Write the multiplication of both improper fractions as shown:

$$\dfrac{4}{1} \times \dfrac{38}{5}$$

Step 2: Reduce the improper fractions to the lowest terms by dividing both the numerators and the denominators by the same numbers if possible.

Note that in this example, $\dfrac{4}{1} \times \dfrac{38}{5}$ there are no numbers that can divide both the numerators and the denominators evenly (without a remainder), go to Step 3.

Step 3: Multiply the numerators together and multiply the denominators together and put the product of the numerators over the product of the denominators.

$$\frac{4}{1} \times \frac{38}{5} = \frac{4 \times 38}{1 \times 5}$$

$$= \frac{152}{5}$$

Step 4: Change the improper fraction $\frac{152}{5}$ in Step 3 to mixed numbers by dividing the numerator by the denominator.

$$\frac{152}{5} = 30\frac{2}{5} \qquad (152 \div 5 = 30 \text{ remainder } 2 = 30\frac{2}{5})$$

Therefore, $4 \times 7\frac{3}{5} = 30\frac{2}{5}$

Example 4

Multiply: $3 \times 4\frac{2}{3}$

Solution

Step 1: Change both the whole number 3 and the mixed fraction $4\frac{2}{3}$ to improper fractions and multiply the improper fractions. (See Rule 1)

The improper fraction of $3 = \frac{3}{1}$ (See Rule 2)

The improper fraction of $4\frac{2}{3} = \frac{4 \times 3 + 2}{3}$ (See Rule 3)

$$= \frac{14}{3}$$

Write the multiplication of both improper fractions as shown:

$$\frac{3}{1} \times \frac{14}{3}$$

Step 2: Reduce the improper fractions to the lowest terms by dividing both the numerators and the denominators by the same number or numbers if possible.

$$\frac{\overset{1}{3}}{1} \times \frac{14}{\underset{1}{3}}$$ Divide both the numerator and the denominator by 3.

Note: $3 \div 3 = 1$

Step 3: Multiply the numerators together and multiply the denominators together and put the product of the numerators over the product of the denominators.

From Step 2, $\dfrac{11}{1} \times \dfrac{1}{1} = \dfrac{11 \times 1}{1 \times 1}$

$$= \dfrac{11}{1}$$

$$= 11$$

Example 6

Multiply: $21 \times 2\dfrac{3}{14} \times 4$

Solution

Step 1: Change the whole number 21, the mixed number $2\dfrac{3}{14}$ and the whole

number 4 to improper fractions and multiply all the improper fractions.
(See Rule 1)

The improper fraction of $21 = \dfrac{21}{1}$ (See Rule 2)

The improper fraction of $2\dfrac{3}{14} = \dfrac{14 \times 2 + 3}{14}$ (See Rule 3)

$$= \dfrac{31}{14}$$

The improper fraction of $4 = \dfrac{4}{1}$ (See Rule 2)

Write the multiplication of all the improper fractions as shown:

$$\dfrac{21}{1} \times \dfrac{31}{14} \times \dfrac{4}{1}$$

Step 2: Reduce the improper fractions to the lowest terms by dividing the
numerators and the denominators by the same number or numbers if
possible.

$$\overset{3}{\underset{1}{\cancel{21}}}{\vphantom{1}} \times \dfrac{31}{\underset{2}{\cancel{14}}} \times \overset{2}{\underset{1}{\cancel{4}}} \qquad (21 \div 7 = 3,\ 14 \div 7 = 2,\ 2 \div 2 = 1,\ \text{and}\ 4 \div 2 = 2)$$

$$= \dfrac{3}{1} \times \dfrac{31}{1} \times \dfrac{2}{1}$$

Step 3: Multiply the numerators together and multiply the denominators together and put the product of the numerators over the product of the denominators.

From step 2, $\quad \dfrac{3}{1} \times \dfrac{31}{1} \times \dfrac{2}{1} = \dfrac{3 \times 31 \times 2}{1 \times 1 \times 1}$

$$= \dfrac{186}{1}$$

$$= 186$$

Example 7

Multiply: $2\dfrac{1}{2} \times 3\dfrac{1}{5}$

Solution

Step 1: Change the mixed number $2\dfrac{1}{2}$ and the mixed number $3\dfrac{1}{5}$ to improper fractions and multiply the improper fractions. (See Rule 1)

The improper fraction of $2\dfrac{1}{2} = \dfrac{2 \times 2 + 1}{2}$ (See Rule 3)

$$= \dfrac{5}{2}$$

The improper fraction of $3\dfrac{1}{5} = \dfrac{5 \times 3 + 1}{5}$ (See Rule 3)

$$= \dfrac{16}{5}$$

Write the multiplication of the improper fractions as follows:

$$\dfrac{5}{2} \times \dfrac{16}{5}$$

Step 2: Reduce the improper fractions to the lowest terms by dividing the numerators and the denominators by the same number or numbers if possible.

$$\dfrac{\overset{1}{\cancel{5}}}{\underset{1}{\cancel{2}}} \times \dfrac{\overset{8}{\cancel{16}}}{\underset{1}{\cancel{5}}} \qquad (2 \div 2 = 1,\ 16 \div 2 = 8,\ \text{and } 5 \div 5 = 1)$$

$$= \frac{1}{1} \times \frac{8}{1}$$

Step 3: Multiply the numerators together and multiply the denominators together and put the product of the numerators over the product of the denominators.

From step 2, $\dfrac{1}{1} \times \dfrac{8}{1} = \dfrac{1 \times 8}{1 \times 1}$

$$= \frac{8}{1}$$

$$= 8$$

Example 8

Multiply: $2\dfrac{3}{4} \times 3\dfrac{1}{6} \times 2\dfrac{2}{11}$

Solution

Step 1: Change the mixed numbers $2\dfrac{3}{4}$, $3\dfrac{1}{6}$, and $2\dfrac{2}{11}$ to improper fractions and multiply the improper fractions. (See Rule 1)

The improper fraction of $2\dfrac{3}{4} = \dfrac{4 \times 2 + 3}{4}$ (See Rule 3)

$$= \frac{11}{4}$$

The improper fraction of $3\dfrac{1}{6} = \dfrac{6 \times 3 + 1}{6}$ (See Rule 3)

$$= \frac{19}{6}$$

The improper fraction of $2\dfrac{2}{11} = \dfrac{11 \times 2 + 2}{11}$ (See Rule 3)

$$= \frac{24}{11}$$

Write the multiplication of the improper fractions as follows:

$$\frac{11}{4} \times \frac{19}{6} \times \frac{24}{11}$$

Step 2: Reduce the improper fractions to the lowest terms by dividing the numerators and the denominators by the same number or numbers if possible.

$$\overset{\displaystyle 1}{\underset{\displaystyle 1}{\frac{11}{4}}} \times \overset{\displaystyle 6}{\underset{\displaystyle 1}{\frac{19}{6}}} \times \overset{\displaystyle 1}{\underset{\displaystyle 1}{\frac{24}{11}}} \quad (\,11 \div 11 = 1,\ 4 \div 4 = 1,\ 24 \div 4 = 6,\ \text{and } 6 \div 6 = 1)$$

Step 3: Multiply the numerators together and multiply the denominators together and put the product of the numerators over the product of the denominators.

$$\text{From Step 2, } \frac{1}{1} \times \frac{19}{1} \times \frac{1}{1} = \frac{1 \times 19 \times 1}{1 \times 1 \times 1}$$

$$= \frac{19}{1}$$

$$= 19$$

Example 9

Multiply: $2\frac{1}{6} \times 4\frac{3}{4} \times 1\frac{1}{19} \times 3\frac{1}{5}$

Solution

Step 1: Change the mixed numbers $2\frac{1}{6}, 4\frac{3}{4}, 1\frac{1}{19}$, and $3\frac{1}{5}$ to improper fractions.

(See Rule 1)

The improper fraction of $2\frac{1}{6} = \frac{6 \times 2 + 1}{6}$ (See Rule 3)

$$= \frac{13}{6}$$

The improper fraction of $4\frac{3}{4} = \frac{4 \times 4 + 3}{4}$ (See Rule 3)

$$= \frac{19}{4}$$

The improper fraction of $1\frac{1}{19} = \frac{19 \times 1 + 1}{19}$ (See Rule 3)

$$= \frac{20}{19}$$

The improper fraction of $3\frac{1}{5} = \frac{5 \times 3 + 1}{5}$　　(See Rule 3)

$$= \frac{16}{5}$$

Write the multiplication of all the improper fractions as follows:

$$\frac{13}{6} \times \frac{19}{4} \times \frac{20}{19} \times \frac{16}{5}$$

Step 2: Reduce the improper fractions to the lowest terms by dividing the numerators and the denominators by the same numbers if possible.

$$\frac{13}{\underset{3}{6}} \times \frac{\overset{1}{19}}{\underset{1}{4}} \times \frac{\overset{\overset{2}{10}}{20}}{\underset{1}{19}} \times \frac{\overset{4}{16}}{\underset{1}{5}} \quad (19 \div 19 = 1, 6 \div 2 = 3, \text{ and } 20 \div 2 = 10,)$$

$$(5 \div 5 = 1, 10 \div 5 = 2, 4 \div 4 = 1, \text{ and } 16 \div 4 = 4)$$

$$= \frac{13}{3} \times \frac{1}{1} \times \frac{2}{1} \times \frac{4}{1}$$

Step 3: Multiply the numerators together and multiply the denominators together and put the product of the numerators over the product of the denominators.

From Step 2, $\dfrac{13}{3} \times \dfrac{1}{1} \times \dfrac{2}{1} \times \dfrac{4}{1} = \dfrac{13 \times 1 \times 2 \times 4}{3 \times 1 \times 1 \times 1}$

$$= \frac{104}{3}$$

Step 4: Change the improper fraction $\dfrac{104}{3}$ in Step 3 to mixed numbers by dividing the numerator by the denominator.

$$\frac{104}{3} = 34\frac{2}{3} \quad (104 \div 3 = 34 \text{ remainder } 2 = 34\frac{2}{3})$$

Example 10

Multiply: $3\dfrac{1}{4} \times 4 \times 2\dfrac{2}{13} \times 2$

Solution

Step 1: Change the mixed number $3\frac{1}{4}$, the whole number 4, the mixed number $2\frac{2}{13}$ and the whole number 2 to improper fractions. (See Rule 1)

The improper fraction of $3\frac{1}{4} = \dfrac{4 \times 3 + 1}{4}$ (See Rule 3)

$$= \frac{13}{4}$$

The improper fraction of $4 = \dfrac{4}{1}$ (See Rule 2)

The improper fraction of $2\frac{2}{13} = \dfrac{13 \times 2 + 2}{13}$ (See Rule 3)

$$= \frac{28}{13}$$

The improper fraction of $2 = \dfrac{2}{1}$ (See Rule 2)

Write the multiplication of the improper fractions as shown:

$$\frac{13}{4} \times \frac{4}{1} \times \frac{28}{13} \times \frac{2}{1}$$

Step 2: Reduce the improper fractions to the lowest terms by dividing the numerators and the denominators by the same number or numbers if possible.

$$\frac{\overset{1}{\cancel{13}}}{\underset{1}{\cancel{4}}} \times \frac{\overset{1}{\cancel{4}}}{1} \times \frac{28}{\underset{1}{\cancel{13}}} \times \frac{2}{1} \qquad (13 \div 13 = 1, 4 \div 4 = 1)$$

$$= \frac{1}{1} \times \frac{1}{1} \times \frac{28}{1} \times \frac{2}{1}$$

Step 3: Multiply the numerators together and multiply the denominators together and put the product of the numerators over the product of the denominators.

From Step 2, $\dfrac{1}{1} \times \dfrac{1}{1} \times \dfrac{28}{1} \times \dfrac{2}{1} = \dfrac{1 \times 1 \times 28 \times 2}{1 \times 1 \times 1 \times 1}$

$$= \frac{56}{1}$$

$$= 56$$

Recommendation

Examples 1 to 10 show the detailed methods of solving the problems in order to provide the students with the logic needed in solving similar problems. Once the students master the skills of the problem solving, the detailed solution is not needed in doing homework, class exercises, or tests. The understanding of the logic of the problem solving is very important, and then the student can use shortcuts in solving similar problems.

It is recommended that after the students master the logic of the problem solving, during homework, class exercises, or tests, the students should begin solving the problems starting from Step 2, without showing detailed solutions as shown in Example 11.

Example 11

Multiply: $4\frac{1}{5} \times 1\frac{4}{11} \times 2\frac{3}{4} \times 2$

Solution

$$\frac{\overset{3}{\cancel{21}}}{\underset{1}{\cancel{5}}} \times \frac{\overset{1}{\cancel{15}}}{\underset{1}{\cancel{11}}} \times \frac{\overset{1}{\cancel{11}}}{\underset{2}{\cancel{4}}} \times \frac{2}{1} = \frac{63}{2} = 31\frac{1}{2}$$

The notes and the generous examples have provided me with the conceptual understanding and the computational fluency to do my homework.

Exercises

1. How do you change a whole number to an improper fraction? (Hint: See Rule 2)
2. How do you change a mixed number to an improper fraction? (Hint: See Rule 3)
3. Write the following as improper fractions: (a) 2,   (b) 4,   (c) 13 ,   (d) 200.
   (Hint: See Example **1**).
4. How do you change a mixed number to an improper fraction? (Hint: See Rule 3)
5. Write the following mixed numbers as improper fractions: (Hint: See Example **2**)
   Reduce to the lowest terms.

   (a) $2\frac{1}{2}$ (b) $7\frac{3}{4}$ (c) $10\frac{3}{4}$ (d) $4\frac{5}{6}$ (e) $7\frac{1}{7}$ (f) $5\frac{3}{5}$

6. Multiply the following whole numbers and mixed numbers: (Hint See Example **3**)
Reduce to the lowest terms.

(a) $6 \times 1\frac{7}{5}$ (b) $2 \times 2\frac{2}{3}$ (c) $3 \times 3\frac{2}{5}$ (d) $5 \times 2\frac{1}{4}$

(e) $4 \times 2\frac{2}{3}$ (f) $4 \times 3\frac{1}{7}$ (g) $6 \times 2\frac{2}{7}$ (h) $2 \times 2\frac{1}{9}$

7. Multiply the following whole numbers and mixed numbers: (Hint: See Example **4**)
Reduce to the lowest terms.

(a) $4 \times 3\frac{1}{4}$ (b) $6 \times 2\frac{1}{6}$ (c) $5 \times 3\frac{2}{5}$

(d) $7 \times 2\frac{2}{7}$ (e) $3 \times 4\frac{1}{3}$ (f) $2 \times 3\frac{1}{2}$

(g) $3 \times 4\frac{2}{3}$ (h) $8 \times 2\frac{3}{8}$ (i) $5 \times 2\frac{3}{5}$

8. Multiply the following whole numbers and mixed numbers: (Hint: See Example **5**).
Reduce to the lowest terms.

(a) $3\frac{1}{3} \times 3$ (b) $2\frac{1}{2} \times 2$ (c) $3\frac{1}{4} \times 4$ (d) $2\frac{2}{5} \times 5$

(e) $4\frac{1}{2} \times 2$ (f) $3\frac{3}{4} \times 4$ (g) $5\frac{1}{5} \times 5$ (h) $2\frac{1}{6} \times 6$

9. Multiply the following whole numbers and a fraction: (Hint: See Example **6**)
Reduce to the lowest terms.

(a) $3 \times 4\frac{2}{3} \times 4$ (b) $2 \times 6\frac{1}{2} \times 3$ (c) $4 \times 2\frac{2}{3} \times 6$

(d) $4 \times 3\frac{3}{4} \times 2$ (e) $5 \times 2\frac{2}{5} \times 3$ (f) $3 \times 4\frac{1}{3} \times 2$

(g) $5 \times 3\frac{1}{5} \times 4$ (h) $7 \times 2\frac{5}{7} \times 3$ (i) $4 \times 3 \times 3\frac{3}{4}$

10. Multiply the following mixed numbers: (Hint: See Example **7**)
Reduce to the lowest terms.

(a) $3\frac{1}{3} \times 2\frac{1}{5}$ (b) $2\frac{2}{3} \times 1\frac{2}{4}$ (c) $3\frac{1}{3} \times 2\frac{2}{5}$

234

(d) $2\dfrac{1}{4} \times 2\dfrac{2}{3}$ (e) $1\dfrac{2}{5} \times 2\dfrac{1}{7}$ (f) $2\dfrac{2}{3} \times 3\dfrac{3}{4}$

(g) $4\dfrac{1}{2} \times 2\dfrac{2}{3}$ (h) $5\dfrac{3}{5} \times 4\dfrac{2}{7}$ (i) $1\dfrac{3}{4} \times 2\dfrac{2}{3}$

11. Multiply the following mixed numbers: (Hint: See Example **8**)
    Reduce to the lowest terms.

(a) $2\dfrac{1}{2} \times 4\dfrac{1}{6} \times 2\dfrac{2}{5}$ (b) $3\dfrac{2}{3} \times 2\dfrac{3}{11} \times 3\dfrac{1}{2}$

(c) $4\dfrac{2}{3} \times 2\dfrac{1}{7} \times 3\dfrac{1}{5}$ (d) $3\dfrac{1}{4} \times 2\dfrac{2}{7} \times 1\dfrac{1}{13}$

(e) $2\dfrac{1}{3} \times 4\dfrac{1}{2} \times 2\dfrac{1}{7}$ (f) $3\dfrac{1}{3} \times 1\dfrac{1}{2} \times 2\dfrac{4}{10}$

(g) $5\dfrac{3}{4} \times 2\dfrac{2}{5} \times 1\dfrac{1}{23}$ (h) $1\dfrac{3}{4} \times 2\dfrac{2}{7} \times 2\dfrac{2}{5}$

12. Multiply the following mixed numbers: (Hint: See Example **9**)
    Reduce to the lowest terms.

(a) $1\dfrac{1}{6} \times 2\dfrac{1}{5} \times 1\dfrac{1}{11} \times 2\dfrac{1}{7}$ (b) $2\dfrac{1}{7} \times 3\dfrac{1}{5} \times 4\dfrac{3}{4} \times 1\dfrac{1}{3}$

(c) $2\dfrac{1}{3} \times 6\dfrac{2}{5} \times 3\dfrac{1}{3} \times 2\dfrac{1}{2}$ (d) $4\dfrac{2}{3} \times 1\dfrac{3}{7} \times 2\dfrac{1}{6} \times 2\dfrac{2}{5}$

(e) $3\dfrac{2}{3} \times 4\dfrac{3}{4} \times 1\dfrac{1}{11} \times 2\dfrac{5}{6}$ (f) $7\dfrac{1}{7} \times 1\dfrac{4}{10} \times 3\dfrac{1}{5} \times 4\dfrac{3}{4}$

(g) $2\dfrac{2}{3} \times 3\dfrac{3}{5} \times 4\dfrac{1}{6} \times 7\dfrac{1}{3}$ (h) $4\dfrac{1}{2} \times 9\dfrac{2}{7} \times 4\dfrac{3}{5} \times 2\dfrac{3}{9}$

13. Multiply the following whole numbers and mixed numbers: (Hint: See Example **10**)
    Reduce to the lowest terms.

(a) $2\dfrac{1}{2} \times 3 \times 4\dfrac{4}{5} \times 2$ (b) $3\dfrac{1}{3} \times 3 \times 1\dfrac{1}{10} \times 4$

(c) $3\dfrac{1}{4} \times 9 \times 1\dfrac{1}{6} \times 2$ (d) $1\dfrac{3}{7} \times 14 \times 2\dfrac{2}{3} \times 3$

(e) $2 \times 4\frac{1}{3} \times 2\frac{1}{2} \times 3$

(f) $1\frac{1}{3} \times 4\frac{2}{7} \times 14 \times 2$

(g) $5 \times 2\frac{1}{2} \times 3\frac{1}{5} \times 2$

(h) $3\frac{1}{3} \times 2\frac{1}{7} \times 3 \times 2$

Challenge Questions

14. Multiply: Reduce to the lowest terms.

(a) $8 \times 3\frac{3}{4}$

(b) $1\frac{1}{3} \times 6\frac{1}{4} \times 1\frac{3}{5} \times 2\frac{1}{2}$

(c) $12 \times 5\frac{1}{6}$

(d) $4 \times 3\frac{2}{3} \times 3$

(e) $4\frac{2}{3} \times 5\frac{1}{7}$

(f) $3\frac{2}{3} \times 2\frac{1}{5} \times 2\frac{1}{7}$

(g) $2\frac{1}{2} \times 1\frac{3}{5} \times 6$

(h) $5\frac{1}{5} \times 1\frac{1}{13} \times 2 \times 2\frac{4}{7}$

(i) $3\frac{1}{3} \times 1\frac{1}{5} \times 4\frac{1}{6}$

(j) $5 \times 2\frac{2}{5} \times 2\frac{1}{4}$

Answers to Selected Questions

5(a) $\frac{5}{2}$ **6(a)** $14\frac{2}{5}$ **7(a)** 13   **8(a)** 10   **9(a)** 56

10(a) $7\frac{1}{3}$ **11(a)** 25   **12(a)** 6   **13(a)** 72

REAL WORLD APPLICATIONS - WORD PROBLEMS

MULTIPLICATION OF FRACTIONS, WHOLE NUMBERS, AND MIXED NUMBERS

Example 1

John needs $4\frac{3}{5}$ yards of material for a school project. How many yards of

material will he need for 4 projects, assuming that each project requires the same amount of material?

Solution

1 school project needs $4\frac{3}{5}$ yards of material.

4 school projects will need $4 \times 4\frac{3}{5}$ yards of material.

We need to multiply 4 by $4\frac{3}{5}$ to obtain the amount of material needed.

Step 1: Change the whole number 4 and the mixed number $4\frac{3}{5}$ to improper

fractions and multiply the improper fractions. (See Rule 1)

The improper fraction of $4 = \dfrac{4}{1}$ (See Rule 2)

The improper fraction of $4\frac{3}{5} = \dfrac{5 \times 4 + 3}{5}$ (See Rule 3)

$$= \frac{23}{5}$$

Write the multiplication of both of the improper fractions as shown:

$$\frac{4}{1} \times \frac{23}{5}$$

Step 2: Reduce the improper fractions to the lowest terms by dividing both the numerators and the denominators by the same number or numbers if possible.

Note that in this example, $\dfrac{4}{1} \times \dfrac{23}{5}$, there are no numbers that can divide both

the numerators and the denominators evenly (without a remainder.)

Step 3: Multiply the numerators together and multiply the denominators together and put the product of the numerators over the product of the denominators.

$$\frac{4}{1} \times \frac{23}{5} = \frac{4 \times 23}{1 \times 5}$$

$$= \frac{92}{5}$$

Step 4: Change the improper fraction $\dfrac{92}{5}$ in Step 3 to mixed numbers by dividing the

numerator by the denominator.

$$\frac{92}{5} = 18\frac{2}{5} \qquad (92 \div 5 = 18 \text{ remainder } 2 = 18\frac{2}{5})$$

Therefore, $18\frac{2}{5}$ yards of material will be needed for the 4 projects.

Example 2

A ground beef patty weighs $\frac{1}{3}$ pound. How many pounds will 24 ground beef patties weigh?

Solution

1 ground beef patty weighs $\frac{1}{3}$ pound.

24 ground beef patties will weigh $24 \times \frac{1}{3}$ pounds.

We have to multiply 24 by $\frac{1}{3}$ to obtain the weight of the 24 ground beef patties.

Step 1: Change the number 24 to an improper fraction and multiply the improper fraction by $\frac{1}{3}$. (See Rule 1)

The improper fraction of $24 = \frac{24}{1}$ (See Rule 2, under Multiplication of Fractions, Whole, and Mixed Numbers.)

Write the multiplication of the improper fraction $\frac{24}{1}$ and $\frac{1}{3}$ as shown:

$$\frac{24}{1} \times \frac{1}{3}$$

Step 2: Reduce the improper fraction $\frac{24}{1}$ and the proper fraction $\frac{1}{3}$ to the lowest terms by dividing the numerators and the denominators by the same number or numbers if possible.

$$\frac{\overset{8}{24}}{1} \times \frac{1}{\underset{1}{3}} \qquad (24 \div 3 = 8, 3 \div 3 = 1)$$

$$= \frac{8}{1} \times \frac{1}{1}$$

Step 3: Multiply the numerators together and multiply the denominators together and put the product of the numerators over the product of the denominators.

From Step 2, $\dfrac{8}{1} \times \dfrac{1}{1} = \dfrac{8 \times 1}{1 \times 1}$

$$= \dfrac{8}{1}$$

$$= 8$$

Therefore, 24 patties will weigh 8 pounds.

Example 3

Karen's overtime pay is $10\dfrac{1}{2}$ dollars per hour. How much overtime pay did she earn

for $8\dfrac{3}{4}$ hours. (Note: $10\dfrac{1}{2}$ dollars = \$10.50)

Solution

Overtime pay for 1 hour = $10\dfrac{1}{2}$ dollars.

Overtime pay for $8\dfrac{3}{4}$ hours = $8\dfrac{3}{4} \times 10\dfrac{1}{2}$ dollars.

We have to multiply $8\dfrac{3}{4}$ by $10\dfrac{1}{2}$ to obtain the amount of overtime pay earned

in $8\dfrac{3}{4}$ hours. (See Rule 1).

Step 1: Change the mixed numbers $8\dfrac{3}{4}$ and $10\dfrac{1}{2}$ to improper fraction and multiply

the improper fractions.

The improper fraction of $8\dfrac{3}{4} = \dfrac{4 \times 8 + 3}{4}$ (See Rule 3 under Multiplication

$$= \dfrac{35}{4}$$ of Fractions, Whole, and Mixed

Numbers.)

The improper fraction of $10\dfrac{1}{2} = \dfrac{2 \times 10 + 1}{2}$ (See Rule 3 under Multiplication

of Fractions, Whole, and Mixed

Numbers.)

$$= \dfrac{21}{2}$$

Write the multiplication of the improper fractions $\dfrac{35}{4}$ and $\dfrac{21}{2}$ as shown:

$$\dfrac{35}{4} \times \dfrac{21}{2}$$

Step 2: Reduce the improper fractions to the lowest terms by dividing the numerator

239

and the denominator by the same number or numbers if possible.

Note that in this example, $\dfrac{35}{4} \times \dfrac{21}{2}$, there are no numbers that can divide both the numerators and the denominators evenly (without a remainder.)

Step 3: Multiply the numerators together and multiply the denominators together and put the product of the numerators over the product of the denominators.

$$\frac{35}{4} \times \frac{21}{2} = \frac{35 \times 21}{4 \times 2}$$

$$= \frac{735}{8}$$

Step 4: Change the improper fraction $\dfrac{735}{8}$ in Step 3 to mixed numbers by dividing the numerator by the denominator if needed.

$$\frac{735}{8} = 91\frac{7}{8} \qquad (735 \div 8 = 91 \text{ remainder } 7 = 91\frac{7}{8})$$

Therefore, Karen earned $91\dfrac{7}{8}$ dollars for $8\dfrac{3}{4}$ hours of overtime.

Example 4

Nick needs $12\dfrac{1}{4}$ feet of lumber for his school project. How many feet of lumber does Nick need in order to complete $10\dfrac{2}{5}$ of the same project? (Hint: The solution of this example does not show the detailed solution steps. It is recommended that after the student masters the logic of the detailed solution steps, the student should use shortcuts to solve homework, class exercises, and tests as shown in this solution. It is recommended that the student should set up the solution initially, and then use Step 2 and Step 3 in solving the problem as shown in this example.

Solution

Initial setup:

1 school project requires $12\dfrac{1}{4}$ feet of lumber.

$10\dfrac{2}{5}$ school projects will require $10\dfrac{2}{5} \times 12\dfrac{1}{4}$ feet of lumber.

Shortcut step:

$10\dfrac{2}{5}$ school projects will require $10\dfrac{2}{5} \times 12\dfrac{1}{4}$ feet of lumber.

$$10\frac{2}{5} \times 12\frac{1}{4} = \frac{52}{5} \times \frac{49}{4}$$

$$= \frac{\overset{13}{\cancel{52}}}{5} \times \frac{49}{\underset{1}{\cancel{4}}} \qquad (52 \div 4 = 13,\ 4 \div 4 = 1).$$

$$= \frac{13 \times 49}{5} = \frac{637}{5} = 127\frac{2}{5}$$

Therefore, $10\frac{2}{7}$ school projects will require $127\frac{2}{5}$ feet of lumber.

Example 5

A fabric material sells at \$3. 25 per yard. How much will $2\frac{2}{13}$ yards cost? (Hint:

\$3.25 may be written as $3\frac{1}{4}$. Note that $0.25 = \frac{25}{100} = \frac{1}{4}$. $25 \div 25 = 1$,

$100 \div 25 = 4$, hence $\frac{25}{100} = \frac{1}{4}$, and therefore, $3.25 = 3\frac{1}{4}$.) Solve this problem

without showing the detailed solutions.

Solution

Initial setup:

1 yard of the fabric material sells at \$3.25.

$2\frac{2}{13}$ yards of the fabric material will cost $2\frac{2}{13} \times 3.25$ dollars.

Shortcut setup:

$2\frac{2}{13}$ yards of the fabric material will cost $2\frac{2}{13} \times 3.25$ dollars.

$$2\frac{2}{13} \times 3\frac{1}{4} = \frac{28}{13} \times \frac{13}{4}$$

$$= \frac{\overset{7}{\cancel{28}}}{\underset{1}{\cancel{13}}} \times \frac{\overset{1}{\cancel{13}}}{\underset{1}{\cancel{4}}}$$

$$= 7$$

241

Therefore, $2\dfrac{2}{13}$ yards of the fabric will cost $7.00.

=========================== The notes and the generous examples have provided
=========================== me with the conceptual understanding and the
computational fluency to do my homework.

Exercises

1. If Rose, needs $6\dfrac{2}{5}$ yards of a material for a school project, how many yards of the material will she need for 15 projects assuming that each project requires the same amount of material? (Hint: See Example **1**)

2. Given that a ground beef patty weighs $\dfrac{2}{3}$ pounds, how many pounds will 30 ground beef patties weigh? (Hint: See Example **2**)

3. John's overtime pay is $12\dfrac{2}{3}$ dollars per hour. How much overtime pay did he earn for $4\dfrac{1}{2}$ hours? (Hint: See Example **3**)

4. Karen needs $16\dfrac{1}{4}$ feet of lumber for her school project. How many feet of lumber does she need to complete $3\dfrac{1}{5}$ of the same project? (Hint: See Example **4**, use shortcut method to solve this problem.)

5. If a fabric material sells at $5.75 per yard, how much will $2\dfrac{2}{23}$ yards cost? (Hint: See Example **5**, use the shortcut method to solve this problem. $5.75 may be written as $5\dfrac{3}{4}$. Note: $0.75 = \dfrac{75}{100} = \dfrac{3}{4}$)

Answers to Selected Questions
4. 52 feet.   **5.** $12.00

DIVISION OF FRACTIONS

New words: Divisor, Quotient, and Dividend.

Quick Review

Invert: **To invert is to turn upside down.** Therefore, **to invert a fraction means that the numerator which is at the top will change to the bottom and the denominator which is at the bottom will change to the top.**

If $\frac{1}{4}$ is inverted, it becomes $\frac{4}{1}$. If $\frac{3}{5}$ is inverted, it becomes $\frac{5}{3}$.

If $\frac{99}{100}$ is inverted, it becomes $\frac{100}{99}$. If $\frac{25}{4}$ is inverted, it becomes $\frac{4}{25}$.

Reciprocal: To find the **reciprocal** of a number is the same as to **invert** the number.

Rule 1: **To divide by fractions, invert the divisor which is the second fraction and change the division sign to a multiplication sign.**

The **reciprocal** of any number or fraction is the same as to divide 1 by the number or by the fraction.

Therefore, the reciprocal of $7 = \frac{1}{7}$, _____ Case 1.

The **reciprocal** of $\frac{3}{5} = \dfrac{1}{\frac{3}{5}}$

$$= 1 \div \frac{3}{5} = 1 \times \frac{5}{3} \qquad \text{Using rule 1.}$$

$$= \frac{5}{3} \qquad \text{_____ Case 2.}$$

Considering cases 1 and 2, to invert a number or a fraction is the same as to find the reciprocal of the number.

Example 1

Divide: $\dfrac{3}{4} \div \dfrac{1}{8}$

243

denominators.

From Step 2,

$$\frac{1}{1} \times \frac{14}{1} = \frac{1 \times 14}{1 \times 1}$$

$$= \frac{14}{1}$$

$$= 14$$

Example 5

Multiply: $2\frac{2}{10} \times 5$

Solution

Step 1: Change both the fraction $2\frac{2}{10}$ and the whole number 5 to improper fractions

and multiply the improper fractions. (See Rule 1)

The improper fraction of $2\frac{2}{10} = \frac{10 \times 2 + 2}{10}$ (See Rule 3)

$$= \frac{22}{10}$$

The improper fraction of $5 = \frac{5}{1}$ (See Rule 2)

Write the multiplication of both improper fractions as shown:

$$\frac{22}{10} \times \frac{5}{1}$$

Step 2: Reduce the improper fractions to the lowest terms by dividing both the numerators and the denominators by the same number or numbers if possible.

$$\overset{\overset{11}{\cancel{22}}}{\underset{\underset{2}{\cancel{10}}}{}} \times \overset{\overset{1}{\cancel{5}}}{\underset{1}{\cancel{1}}} \quad (5 \div 5 = 1,\ 10 \div 5 = 2,\ 2 \div 2 = 1,\ \text{and } 22 \div 2 = 11)$$

$$= \frac{11}{1} \times \frac{1}{1}$$

Step 3: Multiply the numerators together and multiply the denominators together and put the product of the numerators over the product of the

226

Solution

Step 1: Use Rule 1, which states that " to divide fractions, invert the divisor which is the second fraction and change the division sign to a multiplication sign."

$\dfrac{3}{4} \div \dfrac{1}{8}$ then becomes $\dfrac{3}{4} \times \dfrac{8}{1}$ (Note that $\dfrac{1}{8}$ is inverted to become $\dfrac{8}{1}$ and the division sign changes to a multiplication sign.)

Step 2: Reduce the fractions to the lowest terms by dividing the numerators and the denominators by the same numbers if possible.

$$\dfrac{3}{4} \times \dfrac{8}{1} = \dfrac{3}{\underset{1}{4}} \times \dfrac{\overset{2}{8}}{1} \qquad (8 \div 4 = 2,\ 4 \div 4 = 1)$$

$$= \dfrac{3}{1} \times \dfrac{2}{1}$$

Step 3: Multiply the numerators together and multiply the denominators together and put the product of the numerator over the product of the denominator.

$$\text{From Step 2, } \dfrac{3}{1} \times \dfrac{2}{1} = \dfrac{3 \times 2}{1 \times 1}$$

$$= \dfrac{6}{1}$$

$$= 6$$

Example 2

Divide: $\dfrac{3}{8} \div \dfrac{3}{4}$.   Check your answer.

Solution

Step 1: Use Rule 1

$\dfrac{3}{8} \div \dfrac{3}{4}$ then becomes $\dfrac{3}{8} \times \dfrac{4}{3}$ (Note that $\dfrac{3}{4}$ is inverted to become $\dfrac{4}{3}$ and the $\div$ changes to $\times$.)

Step 2: Reduce the fractions to the lowest terms by dividing the numerators and the denominators by the same numbers if possible.

$$\frac{3}{8} \times \frac{4}{3} = \frac{\overset{1}{\cancel{3}}}{\underset{2}{\cancel{8}}} \times \frac{\overset{1}{\cancel{4}}}{\underset{1}{\cancel{3}}} \qquad (4 \div 4 = 1,\ 8 \div 4 = 2,\ 3 \div 3 = 1)$$

$$= \frac{1}{2} \times \frac{1}{1}$$

Step 3: Multiply the numerators together and multiply the denominators together and put the product of the numerators over the product of the denominators.

$$\text{From Step 2,}\ \frac{1}{2} \times \frac{1}{1} = \frac{1 \times 1}{2 \times 1}$$

$$= \frac{1}{2}$$

Check answer

From Example 2, $\dfrac{3}{8} \div \dfrac{3}{4} = \dfrac{1}{2}$

$$\overset{\text{Dividend}\searrow \qquad \swarrow \text{Divisor}}{\frac{3}{8} \div \frac{3}{4} = \frac{1}{2}}$$
$$\searrow \text{Quotient}$$

The quotient, which is the answer after the division, multiplied by the divisor should equal the dividend.

$$\textbf{Quotient} \times \textbf{Divisor} = \textbf{Dividend} \quad\text{————————}\ [\textbf{A}].$$

Substitute $\dfrac{1}{2}$ for Quotient, $\dfrac{3}{4}$ for Divisor, and $\dfrac{3}{8}$ for Dividend in equation $[\text{A}]$.

Equation $[\text{A}]$ then becomes $\dfrac{1}{2} \times \dfrac{3}{4} = \dfrac{3}{8}$

$$\frac{1 \times 3}{2 \times 4} = \frac{3}{8}$$

$$\frac{3}{8} = \frac{3}{8} \quad\text{————————}\ [\text{B}]$$

Since the left side of the equation $[\text{B}]$ is the same as the right side of equation $[\text{B}]$ which is $\dfrac{3}{8}$, the answer $\dfrac{1}{2}$ in Step 3 is correct. We can create Rule 2.

Rule 2: Quotient × Divisor = Dividend

Divisor: For example, if $\dfrac{3}{4} \div \dfrac{1}{8}$, $\dfrac{1}{8}$ is the divisor.

If $\dfrac{7}{9} \div \dfrac{2}{5}$, $\dfrac{2}{5}$ is the divisor.

If $\dfrac{11}{12} \div \dfrac{3}{8}$, $\dfrac{3}{8}$ is the divisor.

Therefore, **the divisor is the number by which a dividend is divided**.
The number to be divided is the **dividend**, as shown:

$$\dfrac{3}{4} \div \dfrac{1}{8}$$

Dividend   Divisor

Quotient is the number that results from the division of one number by another. Dividend is a quantity to be divided.

Relationship among Dividend, Divisor, and Quotient
Let us investigate the relationship among the Dividend, Divisor, and Quotient by by using the fact that $8 \div 2 = 4$ as shown:

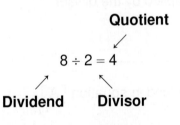

Quotient

$8 \div 2 = 4$

Dividend   **Divisor**

Therefore, (**a**) **Dividend ÷ Divisor = Quotient**
or
(**b**) **Quotient × Divisor = Dividend**. This statement will be useful in
checking some answers to some questions later.

Example 3
Divide: $\dfrac{5}{8} \div \dfrac{3}{16}$. Check the answer.
Do not show any detailed method. Although the examples are intentionally designed to provide the students with detailed explanations including mathematical logic, it is recommended that the students use shortcuts in solving homework, class exercises, and tests as much as possible as shown in Example **3**.

Solution

Shortcut:

$$\frac{5}{8} \div \frac{3}{16} = \frac{5}{8} \times \frac{16}{3}$$

$$= \frac{5}{\overset{}{\underset{1}{8}}} \times \frac{\overset{2}{16}}{3} \qquad \text{(Divide numerator and the denominator by 8.)}$$

$$= \frac{10}{3} \qquad (10 \div 3 = 3, \text{ remainder } 1, = 3\frac{1}{3})$$

$$= 3\frac{1}{3}$$

Check answer

Quotient × Divisor = Dividend

$$3\frac{1}{3} \times \frac{3}{16} = \frac{5}{8}$$

$$\frac{10}{3} \times \frac{3}{16} = \frac{5}{8} \qquad (3\frac{1}{3} = \frac{10}{3})$$

$$\frac{\overset{5}{10}}{\underset{1}{3}} \times \frac{\overset{1}{3}}{\underset{8}{16}} = \frac{5}{8} \qquad \text{(Divide the numerator and the denominator by 2 and 3).}$$

$$\frac{5}{8} = \frac{5}{8} \qquad\qquad\qquad\text{[A]}$$

Left side of equation [A] is equal to the right side of equation [A], and therefore, the answer $3\frac{1}{3}$ is correct.

The notes and the generous examples have provided me with the conceptual understanding and the computational fluency to do my homework.

Exercises

1. How are fractions divided? (Hint: See Rule 1)

2. Explain the following:

(**a**) Divisor

(**b**) Quotient

(**c**) Dividend.

(**d**). State the relationship among the Divisor, Quotient, and Dividend.

3. Divide the following fractions: (Hint: See Example **1**)

(**a**) $\dfrac{1}{4} \div \dfrac{3}{8}$ (**b**) $\dfrac{4}{5} \div \dfrac{4}{5}$ (**c**) $\dfrac{6}{7} \div \dfrac{3}{7}$ (**d**) $\dfrac{1}{3} \div \dfrac{5}{6}$

(**e**) $\dfrac{2}{5} \div \dfrac{1}{5}$ (**f**) $\dfrac{5}{12} \div \dfrac{3}{4}$ (**g**) $\dfrac{2}{3} \div \dfrac{4}{5}$ (**h**) $\dfrac{5}{6} \div \dfrac{5}{6}$

4. Divide the following fractions and check your answer. (Hint: See Examples 2 and 3)

(**a**) $\dfrac{4}{5} \div \dfrac{9}{10}$ (**b**) $\dfrac{2}{7} \div \dfrac{8}{21}$ (**c**) $\dfrac{11}{12} \div \dfrac{22}{24}$ (**d**) $\dfrac{3}{16} \div \dfrac{4}{9}$

(**e**) $\dfrac{3}{7} \div \dfrac{6}{21}$ (**f**) $\dfrac{7}{15} \div \dfrac{7}{10}$ (**g**) $\dfrac{5}{64} \div \dfrac{5}{8}$ (**h**) $\dfrac{4}{9} \div \dfrac{5}{18}$

(**i**) $\dfrac{5}{4} \div \dfrac{5}{16}$ (**j**) $\dfrac{5}{81} \div \dfrac{10}{9}$ (**k**) $\dfrac{3}{16} \div \dfrac{7}{8}$ (**l**) $\dfrac{9}{10} \div \dfrac{3}{5}$

(**m**) $\dfrac{3}{4} \div \dfrac{4}{5}$ (**n**) $\dfrac{11}{12} \div \dfrac{11}{24}$ (**o**) $\dfrac{3}{5} \div \dfrac{3}{10}$ (**p**) $\dfrac{3}{4} \div \dfrac{5}{6}$

Challenge Questions

5. (**a**) $\dfrac{1}{3} \div \dfrac{1}{24}$ (**b**) $\dfrac{11}{12} \div \dfrac{11}{24}$ (**c**) $\dfrac{4}{5} \div \dfrac{3}{10}$ (**d**) $\dfrac{6}{49} \div \dfrac{3}{7}$

(**e**) $\dfrac{5}{64} \div \dfrac{5}{8}$ (**f**) $\dfrac{16}{25} \div \dfrac{4}{15}$ (**g**) $\dfrac{3}{7} \div \dfrac{3}{14}$ (**h**) $\dfrac{2}{9} \div \dfrac{2}{3}$

Answers to Selected Questions

3(**a**) $\dfrac{2}{3}$ 4(**a**) $\dfrac{8}{9}$ 5(**a**) 8

REAL WORLD APPLICATIONS - WORD PROBLEMS
Division of Fractions

Example 1

How many $\frac{1}{8}$ yard pieces of pipe can be cut from a length of pipe measuring

$\frac{19}{24}$ yard? Check your answer.

Solution

Setup: The number of $\frac{1}{8}$ yard pieces of pipe that can be cut from a length of $\frac{19}{24}$

yard of pipe

$$= \frac{19}{24} \div \frac{1}{8}$$

Step 1: Use Rule 1, under Division of Fractions.

$$\frac{19}{24} \div \frac{1}{8} = \frac{19}{24} \times \frac{8}{1} \quad \text{(Note } \frac{1}{8} \text{ changes to } \frac{8}{1} \text{ and } \div \text{ changes to } \times.\text{)}$$

Step 2: Reduce the fractions to the lowest terms by dividing the numerators and the denominators by the same number or numbers if possible.

$$\frac{19}{24} \times \frac{8}{1} = \frac{19}{\underset{3}{24}} \times \frac{\overset{1}{8}}{1} \quad (24 \div 8 = 3, \ 8 \div 8 = 1)$$

$$= \frac{19}{3} \times \frac{1}{1}$$

Step 3: Multiply the numerators together and multiply the denominators together and put the product of the numerators over the product of the denominators.

$$\text{From Step 2, } \frac{19}{3} \times \frac{1}{1} = \frac{19 \times 1}{3 \times 1}$$

$$= \frac{19}{3}$$

Step 4: Change the improper fraction of $\frac{19}{3}$ to a mixed fraction by dividing the numerator by the denominator if needed.

$$\frac{19}{3} = 6\frac{1}{3} \qquad (19 \div 3 = 6 \text{ reminder } 1, \ = 6\frac{1}{3})$$

Therefore, $6\frac{1}{3}$ pieces of $\frac{1}{8}$ yard of pipe can be cut.

Check the answer

Quotient × Divisor = Dividend

$$6\frac{1}{3} \times \frac{1}{8} = \frac{19}{24}$$

$$\frac{19}{3} \times \frac{1}{8} = \frac{19}{24} \qquad (6\frac{1}{3} = \frac{19}{3})$$

$$\frac{19 \times 1}{3 \times 8} = \frac{19}{24}$$

$$\frac{19}{24} = \frac{19}{24} \quad\text{————————— } [A]$$

Since the left side of the equation $[A]$ is equal to the right side of the equation $[A]$, the answer $6\frac{1}{3}$ is correct.

Example 2

How many $\frac{1}{8}$ hours are there in $\frac{17}{24}$ hours? Check your answer. Use the shortcut to solve this problem.

Solution

Setup: The number of $\frac{1}{8}$ hour $= \frac{17}{24} \div \frac{1}{8}$

Shortcut: $\frac{17}{24} \div \frac{1}{8} = \frac{17}{24} \times \frac{8}{1}$

$$= \frac{17}{\underset{3}{24}} \times \frac{\overset{1}{8}}{1} \qquad (24 \div 8 = 3, \ 8 \div 8 = 1)$$

$$= \frac{17}{3}$$

$$= 5\frac{2}{3} \quad (17 \div 3 = 5 \text{ remainder } 2, = 5\frac{2}{3})$$

Therefore, there are $5\frac{2}{3}$ of $\frac{1}{8}$ hours in $\frac{17}{24}$ hours.

Check answer

Quotient × Divisor = Dividend

$$5\frac{2}{3} \times \frac{1}{8} = \frac{17}{24}$$

$$\frac{17}{3} \times \frac{1}{8} = \frac{17}{24}$$

$$\frac{17 \times 1}{3 \times 8} = \frac{17}{24}$$

$$\frac{17}{24} = \frac{17}{24} \hspace{2cm} [A]$$

Since the left side of equation $[A]$ is equal to the right side of equation $[A]$ which is $\frac{17}{24}$, the answer is correct.

Example 3

How many periods of 10 minutes are there in $\frac{3}{4}$ of an hour? Use the shortcut method in solving the problem. (Hint: 10 minutes $= \frac{10}{60}$ hour $= \frac{1}{6}$ hour.)

Note: 60 minutes = 1 hour.

Solution

Setup: The number of $\frac{1}{6}$ hour in $\frac{3}{4}$ hour

$$= \frac{3}{4} \div \frac{1}{6}$$

Shortcut:

$$\frac{3}{4} \div \frac{1}{6} = \frac{3}{4} \times \frac{6}{1}$$

$$= \frac{3}{4} \times \frac{\overset{3}{\cancel{6}}}{\underset{2}{1}} \hspace{2cm} (6 \div 2 = 3, 4 \div 2 = 2)$$

$$= \frac{9}{2}$$

$$= 4\frac{1}{2} \qquad\qquad (\, 9 \div 2 = 4 \text{ remainder } 1, = 4\frac{1}{2}\,).$$

Therefore, there are $4\frac{1}{2}$ of 10 minutes in $\frac{3}{4}$ hour.

Critical Thinking

Before any division is done, the unit of the dividend and the unit of the divisor must be the same. In Example 3 for example, we cannot divide $\frac{3}{4}$ hour by 10 minutes because we cannot divide hours by minutes, but we are able to divide $\frac{3}{4}$ hour by $\frac{1}{6}$ hour because both the unit of the dividend and the unit of the divisor are the same (hour.)

Example 4

Mary takes an average of 4 minutes to type a letter. How many similar letters can she type in $\frac{3}{4}$ hour? (Hint: Write 4 minutes as a fraction of an hour, and then reduce the fraction to the lowest terms.) Use the shortcut method to solve the problem.

Solution

Setup: First write 4 minutes as a fraction of an hour.

60 minutes = 1 hour

$$4 \text{ minutes} = \frac{4}{60} \text{ hour} \qquad (\text{Reduce } \frac{4}{60} \text{ to the lowest terms, } 4 \div 4 = 1$$

$$= \frac{1}{15} \text{ hour} \qquad 60 \div 4 = 15.)$$

In $\frac{1}{15}$ hour, 1 letter was typed.

In $\frac{3}{4}$ hour, she will type $\frac{3}{4} \div \frac{1}{15}$ letters.

Shortcut:

$$\frac{3}{4} \div \frac{1}{15} = \frac{3}{4} \times \frac{15}{1}$$

252

$$= \frac{3 \times 15}{4 \times 1}$$

$$= \frac{45}{4}$$

$$= 11\frac{1}{4}$$

Therefore, Mary will type $11\frac{1}{4}$ letters in $\frac{3}{4}$ hour.

Example 5

Anthony has $\frac{11}{12}$ gallon of drinking water. How many pint-size containers does he have? (Hint: 8 pints = 1 gallon)

Setup: Write 1 pint as a fraction of a gallon.

$$8 \text{ pints} = 1 \text{ gallon}$$

$$1 \text{ pint} = \frac{1}{8} \text{ gallon}$$

The number of pint-size containers in $\frac{11}{12}$ gallons $= \frac{11}{12} \div \frac{1}{8}$

Shortcut: $\frac{11}{12} \div \frac{1}{8} = \frac{11}{12} \times \frac{8}{1}$

$$= \frac{11}{\underset{3}{12}} \times \frac{\overset{2}{8}}{1} \qquad (8 \div 4 = 2, \ 12 \div 4 = 3)$$

$$= \frac{11 \times 2}{3 \times 1}$$

$$= \frac{22}{3}$$

$$= 7\frac{1}{3}$$

Therefore, Anthony has $7\frac{1}{3}$ pint-size containers of drinking water.

$$\overline{}$$ **The notes and the generous examples have provided me with the conceptual understanding and the computational fluency to do my homework.**

Exercises

1. How many $\frac{1}{6}$ yard pieces of wood can be cut from a length of wood measuring $\frac{5}{6}$ yard. Check your answer. (Hint: See Example **1**)

2. How many $\frac{1}{6}$ hours are there in $\frac{19}{24}$ hour? Check your answer.

(Hint: See Example **2**) Use the shortcut method to solve this problem.

3. How many periods of 15 minutes are there in $\frac{11}{12}$ of an hour? (Hint: 15 minutes $= \frac{15}{60}$ hour $= \frac{1}{4}$ hour. Note that 60 minutes = 1 hour). Use the shortcut method to solve this problem. (Hint: See Example **3**)

4. Nick takes an average of 5 minutes to type a letter. How many similar letters can he type in $\frac{7}{12}$ hour? Check your answer. (Hint: See Example **4**).

(Hint: 5 minutes $= \frac{5}{60}$ hour $= \frac{1}{12}$ hour. Note that 60 minutes = 1 hour).

Use the shortcut method to solve the problem.

5. Samuel has $\frac{7}{8}$ gallon of syrup. How many pint-size containers does he have?

(Hint: 8 pints = 1 gallon. See Example **5**) Use the shortcut method to solve the problem.

Answers Selected Questions
(**1**). 5 pieces of wood.   (**4**). 7 letters.

DIVISION BY MIXED NUMBERS

Rule 1: To divide a mixed number by another mixed number, change the mixed numbers to improper fractions, invert the divisor, and change the division sign to a multiplication sign.

Rule 2: To change a mixed number to an improper fraction, multiply the denominator by the whole number, add the numerator to the product, and then write the sum over the denominator.

Example 1

Divide: $4\dfrac{1}{3} \div 1\dfrac{1}{6}$

Solution

Step 1: Change the mixed numbers $4\dfrac{1}{3}$ and $1\dfrac{1}{6}$ to improper fractions. (See Rule 1)

The improper fraction of the mixed number

$$4\dfrac{1}{3} = \dfrac{3 \times 4 + 1}{3} = \dfrac{13}{3}$$ (See Rule 2 and also Rule 3 under Multiplication of Fractions, Whole, and Mixed Numbers.)

The improper fraction of the mixed number

$$1\dfrac{1}{6} = \dfrac{6 \times 1 + 1}{6} = \dfrac{7}{6}$$ (See Rule 2 and also Rule 3 under Multiplication of Fractions, Whole, and Mixed Numbers,)

Therefore, $4\dfrac{1}{3} \div 1\dfrac{1}{6} = \dfrac{13}{3} \div \dfrac{7}{6}$

Step 2: Invert the divisor and change the $\div$ sign to $\times$ sign. (Note: $\dfrac{7}{6}$ is the divisor)

$\dfrac{13}{3} \div \dfrac{7}{6}$ from Step 1 becomes $\dfrac{13}{3} \times \dfrac{6}{7}$ ($\dfrac{7}{6}$ is inverted to become $\dfrac{6}{7}$ and $\div$ sign is changed to $\times$ sign.)
(See Rule 1)

Step 3: Reduce the fractions to the lowest terms by dividing the numerators and the denominators by the same number or numbers if possible.

$$\dfrac{13}{3} \times \dfrac{6}{7} = \dfrac{13}{\underset{1}{3}} \times \dfrac{\overset{2}{6}}{7}$$ $(6 \div 3 = 2,\ 3 \div 3 = 1)$

Step 4: Multiply the numerators together and multiply the denominators together and put the product of the numerators over the product of the denominators.

255

$$\frac{13}{1} \times \frac{2}{7} = \frac{13 \times 2}{1 \times 7}$$

$$= \frac{26}{7} \qquad (26 \div 7 = 3 \text{ remainder } 5, = 3\frac{5}{7})$$

$$= 3\frac{5}{7}$$

Example 2

Solve the question in Example 1 without showing any detailed steps. (Hint: This is the shortcut method of problem solving. It is recommended that once the student understands the logic of the detailed solution, the students may use the shortcut method for homework, class exercises, and tests.)

Solution

Divide: $4\frac{1}{3} \div 1\frac{1}{6}$ (Question from Example **1**)

Shortcut

$$4\frac{1}{3} \div 1\frac{1}{6} = \frac{13}{\underset{1}{\cancel{3}}} \times \frac{\overset{2}{\cancel{6}}}{7}$$

$$= \frac{26}{7} = 3\frac{5}{7}$$

Example 3

Divide: $2\frac{2}{3} \div 7\frac{1}{2}$

Solution

Step 1: Change the mixed numbers $2\frac{2}{3}$ and $7\frac{1}{2}$ to improper fractions. (See Rule 1)

The improper fraction of the mixed number

$$2\frac{2}{3} = \frac{3 \times 2 + 2}{3} = \frac{8}{3}$$ (See Rule 2 and also Rule 3 under

Multiplication of Fractions, Whole, and Mixed Numbers.)

The improper fraction of the mixed number

$$7\frac{1}{2} = \frac{2 \times 7 + 1}{2} = \frac{15}{2}$$ (See Rule 2 and also Rule 3 under

Multiplication of Fractions, Whole, and

256

Therefore, $2\dfrac{2}{3} \div 7\dfrac{1}{2} = \dfrac{8}{3} \div \dfrac{15}{2}$

Step 2: Invert the divisor and change the ÷ sign to × sign. (Note: $\dfrac{15}{2}$ is the divisor)

$\dfrac{8}{3} \div \dfrac{15}{2}$ from Step 1 becomes $\dfrac{8}{3} \times \dfrac{2}{15}$ ($\dfrac{15}{2}$ is inverted to become $\dfrac{2}{15}$
and ÷ sign is changed to × sign.)
(See Rule 1)

Step 3: Reduce the fractions to the lowest terms by dividing the numerators and
the denominators by the same number or numbers if possible. In this case,
there is no number that can divide both the numerators and denominators of
$\dfrac{8}{3} \times \dfrac{2}{15}$ evenly (without a remainder.)

Step 4: Multiply the numerators together and multiply the denominators together
and put the product of the numerators over the product of the denominators
as the final answer.

$$\dfrac{8}{3} \times \dfrac{2}{15} = \dfrac{8 \times 2}{3 \times 15} = \dfrac{16}{45}$$

Example 4
Solve the question in Example **3** without showing any detailed explanations.
Solution

The question in Example **3** is to divide: $2\dfrac{2}{3} \div 7\dfrac{1}{2}$

Shortcut method:

$$2\dfrac{2}{3} \div 7\dfrac{1}{2} = \dfrac{8}{3} \times \dfrac{2}{15}$$

$$= \dfrac{16}{45}$$

Example 5
Divide: $6\dfrac{2}{3} \div 3\dfrac{1}{5}$
Solution

Step 1: Change the mixed numbers $6\dfrac{2}{3}$ and $3\dfrac{1}{5}$ to improper fractions.

(See Rule 1).

The improper fraction of the mixed number

$$6\frac{2}{3} = \frac{3 \times 6 + 2}{3} = \frac{20}{3}$$ (See Rule 2 and also Rule 3 under Multiplication of Fractions, Whole, and Mixed Numbers.)

The improper fraction of the mixed number

$$3\frac{1}{5} = \frac{5 \times 3 + 1}{5} = \frac{16}{5}$$ (See Rule 2 and also Rule 3 under Multiplication of Fractions, Whole, and Mixed Numbers.)

Therefore, $6\frac{2}{3} \div 3\frac{1}{5} = \frac{20}{3} \div \frac{16}{5}$

Step 2: Invert the divisor and change the ÷ sign to × sign. (Note: $\frac{16}{5}$ is the divisor.)

$\frac{20}{3} \div \frac{16}{5}$ from Step 1 becomes $\frac{20}{3} \times \frac{5}{16}$ ($\frac{16}{5}$ is inverted to become

$\frac{5}{16}$ and ÷ sign changes to × sign.)

(See Rule 1.)

Step 3: Reduce the fractions to the lowest terms by dividing the numerators and the denominators by the same number or numbers if possible.

$$\frac{20}{3} \times \frac{5}{16} = \frac{\overset{5}{\cancel{20}}}{3} \times \frac{5}{\underset{4}{\cancel{16}}} \qquad (20 \div 4 = 5, \ 16 \div 4 = 4)$$

Step 4: Multiply the numerators together and multiply the denominator together and put the product of the numerators over the product of the denominators.

$$\frac{5}{3} \times \frac{5}{4} = \frac{5 \times 5}{3 \times 4}$$

$$= \frac{25}{12}$$

Step 5: Change the improper fraction $\frac{25}{12}$ to mixed numbers.

$$\frac{25}{12} = 2\frac{1}{12} \qquad (25 \div 12 = 2 \text{ remainder } 1, \ = 2\frac{1}{12})$$

Example 6

Solve the question in Example **5** without showing any detailed explanations.

(Hint: Use the shortcut method.)

Solution

The question in Example **5** is Divide: $6\dfrac{2}{3} \div 3\dfrac{1}{5}$

Solution

$$6\dfrac{2}{3} \div 3\dfrac{1}{5} = \dfrac{\overset{5}{\cancel{20}}}{3} \times \dfrac{5}{\underset{4}{\cancel{16}}}$$

$$= \dfrac{25}{12}$$

$$= 2\dfrac{1}{12}$$

Critical Link

When a fraction is being divided by another fraction, once the divisor is inverted and the ÷ sign changes to × sign, the question becomes multiplication of fractions. There are many examples of solutions of multiplications of fractions under the topic Multiplication of Fractions.

The notes and the generous examples have provided me with the conceptual understanding and the computational fluency to do my homework.

Exercises

1. Divide the following: Reduce to the lowest terms. (Hint: See Example 1.)

(a) $3\dfrac{1}{2} \div 1\dfrac{3}{4}$

(b) $2\dfrac{2}{5} \div 1\dfrac{1}{5}$

(c) $7\dfrac{1}{2} \div 2\dfrac{1}{2}$

(d) $4\dfrac{2}{3} \div 1\dfrac{5}{7}$

(e) $5\dfrac{1}{3} \div 1\dfrac{1}{3}$

(f) $6\dfrac{1}{2} \div 3\dfrac{1}{4}$

(g) What is the rule or the process for dividing a mixed number by another mixed number?

2. Divide the following using the shortcut method. (Hint: See Example **2**.)
Reduce to the lowest terms.

(a) $6\dfrac{2}{3} \div 1\dfrac{2}{3}$ **(b)** $3\dfrac{1}{3} \div 1\dfrac{2}{3}$ **(c)** $4\dfrac{1}{2} \div 1\dfrac{1}{2}$

(d) $4\dfrac{2}{3} \div 2\dfrac{1}{3}$ **(e)** $4\dfrac{2}{3} \div 2\dfrac{2}{6}$ **(f)** $3\dfrac{1}{2} \div 1\dfrac{3}{4}$

3. Divide the following: Reduce to the lowest terms. (Hint: See Example **3**.)

(a) $4\dfrac{1}{3} \div 10\dfrac{1}{2}$ **(b)** $2\dfrac{2}{7} \div 3\dfrac{3}{8}$ **(c)** $1\dfrac{1}{2} \div 2\dfrac{2}{3}$

(d) $3\dfrac{1}{4} \div 9\dfrac{3}{7}$ **(e)** $5\dfrac{1}{2} \div 6\dfrac{1}{5}$ **(f)** $4\dfrac{2}{5} \div 6\dfrac{1}{3}$

4. Divide the following using shortcut method. (Hint: See Example 4.)
Reduce to the lowest terms.

(a) $2\dfrac{1}{2} \div 3\dfrac{2}{3}$ **(b)** $1\dfrac{3}{7} \div 2\dfrac{3}{8}$ **(c)** $4\dfrac{2}{3} \div 5\dfrac{4}{5}$

(d) $2\dfrac{3}{5} \div 5\dfrac{1}{3}$ **(e)** $2\dfrac{1}{5} \div 4\dfrac{1}{3}$ **(f)** $3\dfrac{2}{3} \div 5\dfrac{2}{5}$

5. Divide the following: Reduce to the lowest terms. (Hint: See Example **5**.)

(a) $4\dfrac{1}{2} \div 2\dfrac{1}{2}$ **(b)** $3\dfrac{3}{5} \div 1\dfrac{2}{3}$ **(c)** $5\dfrac{1}{3} \div 2\dfrac{2}{3}$

(d) $6\dfrac{2}{3} \div 1\dfrac{1}{4}$ **(e)** $8\dfrac{3}{4} \div 1\dfrac{2}{5}$ **(f)** $7\dfrac{1}{5} \div 2\dfrac{1}{4}$

6. Divide the following: (Hint: See Example **6**.)
Solve exercises **5(a)** to **5(f)** without showing any detailed explanations. Use the shortcut method. Reduce to the lowest terms.

Answers to Selected Questions

1(a) 2   **2(a)** 4   **3(a)** $\dfrac{26}{63}$ **3(b)** $\dfrac{128}{189}$ **3(f)** $\dfrac{66}{95}$

4(a) $\dfrac{15}{22}$ **4(c)** $\dfrac{70}{87}$ **5(a)** $1\dfrac{4}{5}$ **5(d)** $5\dfrac{1}{3}$

REAL WORLD APPLICATIONS - WORD PROBLEMS
Division by Mixed Numbers

Example 1

A rod is $8\dfrac{3}{4}$ meters long. How many pieces of rod measuring $1\dfrac{1}{4}$ meters can

the length of the $8\dfrac{3}{4}$ meters of rod be cut into?

Solution

Setup: The number of the pieces of rod measuring $1\dfrac{1}{4}$ meters that can be cut from

the $8\dfrac{3}{4}$ meters of rod $= 8\dfrac{3}{8} \div 1\dfrac{1}{4}$

(Note: We are required to find how many $1\dfrac{1}{4}$ meters are contained in $8\dfrac{3}{4}$

meters.)

Step 1: Change the mixed numbers $8\dfrac{3}{4}$ and $1\dfrac{1}{4}$ to improper fractions. (See Rule 1.)

The improper fraction of the mixed number

$$8\dfrac{3}{4} = \dfrac{4 \times 8 + 3}{4} = \dfrac{35}{4}$$ (See Rule 2 and also Rule 3 under Multiplication

of Fractions, Whole, and Mixed Numbers.)

The improper fraction of the mixed number

$$1\dfrac{1}{4} = \dfrac{4 \times 1 + 1}{4} = \dfrac{5}{4}$$ (See Rule 2 and also Rule 3 under Multiplication

of Fractions, Whole, and Mixed Numbers.)

Therefore, $8\dfrac{3}{4} \div 1\dfrac{1}{4} = \dfrac{35}{4} \div \dfrac{5}{4}$

Step 2: Invert the divisor and change the $\div$ sign to $\times$ sign (Note: $\dfrac{5}{4}$ is the divisor.)

$\dfrac{35}{4} \div \dfrac{5}{4}$ from Step 1 becomes $\dfrac{35}{4} \times \dfrac{4}{5}$ (Note: $\dfrac{5}{4}$ is inverted to become

$\dfrac{4}{5}$ and the $\div$ sign is changed to $\times$ sign.) (See Rule 1.)

Step 3: Reduce the fractions in $\dfrac{35}{4} \times \dfrac{4}{5}$ to the lowest terms by dividing the numerators and the denominators by the same number or numbers if possible.

$$\frac{35}{4} \times \frac{4}{7} = \frac{\overset{7}{\cancel{35}}}{4} \times \frac{4}{\underset{1}{\cancel{5}}} \qquad (35 \div 5 = 7,\ 5 \div 5 = 1,\ \text{and}\ 4 \div 4 = 1)$$

Step 4: Multiply the numerators together and multiply the denominators together and put the product of the numerators over the product of the denominators.

$$\frac{7}{1} \times \frac{1}{1} = \frac{7 \times 1}{1 \times 1}$$

$$= \frac{7}{1}$$

$$= 7$$

Therefore, 7 pieces of rod measuring $1\frac{1}{4}$ meters can be cut from $8\frac{3}{4}$ meters.

Example 2

Solve the question in Example **1** without showing any detailed explanations, and we refer to this as a shortcut method.

Solution

Setup: Number of $1\frac{1}{4}$ meters of rod $= 8\frac{3}{4} \div 1\frac{1}{4}$

Solve: $\dfrac{35}{4} \div \dfrac{5}{4} = \dfrac{35}{4} \times \dfrac{4}{5}$

$$= \frac{\overset{7}{\cancel{35}}}{\underset{1}{4}} \times \frac{\overset{1}{4}}{\underset{1}{\cancel{5}}}$$

$$= 7$$

Therefore, 7 pieces of rod measuring $1\frac{1}{4}$ meters can be cut from the $8\frac{3}{4}$ meters of rod.

Example 3

Given that it takes $\dfrac{2}{3}$ yard of a fabric to make a baby's shirt, how many similar shirts can be made with $10\frac{2}{3}$ yards?

Solution

Setup: The number of $\frac{2}{3}$ yard of shirts that can be made with $10\frac{2}{3}$ yards of fabric

is $10\frac{2}{3} \div \frac{2}{3}$ (Note: We are to find how many $\frac{2}{3}$ are contained in $10\frac{2}{3}$.)

Step 1: Change the mixed number $10\frac{2}{3}$ to an improper fraction. (See Rule 1.)

The improper fraction for the mixed number $10\frac{2}{3}$

$= \dfrac{3 \times 10 + 2}{3} = \dfrac{32}{3}$ (See Rule 2 and also rule 3 under Multiplication of

Fractions, Whole, and Mixed Numbers.)

Therefore, $10\frac{2}{3} \div \frac{2}{3} = \frac{32}{3} \div \frac{2}{3}$

Step 2: Invert the divisor and change the $\div$ sign to $\times$ sign. (Note: $\frac{2}{3}$ is the divisor,)

$\dfrac{32}{3} \div \dfrac{2}{3}$ from Step 1 becomes $\dfrac{32}{3} \times \dfrac{3}{2}$ (Note: $\frac{2}{3}$ is inverted to become $\frac{3}{2}$

and the $\div$ sign changes to the $\times$ sign.)
(See Rule 1.)

Step 3: Reduce the fractions in $\dfrac{32}{3} \times \dfrac{3}{2}$ to the lowest terms by dividing the

numerators and the denominators by the same number or numbers if
possible.

$$\dfrac{32}{3} \times \dfrac{3}{2} = \dfrac{\overset{16}{\cancel{32}}}{\underset{1}{\cancel{3}}} \times \dfrac{\overset{1}{\cancel{3}}}{\underset{1}{\cancel{2}}}$$ ($32 \div 2 = 16$, $2 \div 2 = 1$, and $3 \div 3 = 1$)

Step 4: Multiply the numerators together and multiply the denominators together
and put the product of the numerators over the product of the denominators.

$$\dfrac{16}{1} \times \dfrac{1}{1} = \dfrac{16 \times 1}{1 \times 1}$$

$$= \dfrac{16}{1}$$

$$= 16$$

Therefore, 16 of $\frac{2}{3}$ yard of shirts can be made from $10\frac{2}{3}$ yards of fabric.

Example 4
Solve the question in Example **3** without showing any detailed explanations.
(Note: We refer to this method of solution as the shortcut method.)

Solution

Setup: The number of $\frac{2}{3}$ yard of shirts that can be made with $10\frac{2}{3}$ yards of

fabric $= 10\frac{2}{3} \div \frac{2}{3}$

Solve:

$$10\frac{2}{3} \div \frac{2}{3} = \frac{\overset{16}{\cancel{32}}}{\underset{1}{\cancel{3}}} \times \frac{\overset{1}{\cancel{3}}}{\underset{1}{\cancel{2}}}$$

$$= \frac{16 \times 1}{1 \times 1}$$

$$= 16$$

Therefore, 16 of $\frac{2}{3}$ of shirts can be made with $10\frac{2}{3}$ yards of fabric.

_____ The notes and the generous examples have provided
me with the conceptual understanding and the
computational fluency to do my homework.

Exercise

1. A pole is $9\frac{1}{3}$ feet long. How many pieces of the pole, each measuring $2\frac{1}{3}$ feet

   can be cut from the $9\frac{1}{3}$ feet long of the pole? (Hint: See Example **1**.)

2. Solve question 1 using the shortcut method. (Hint: See Example **2**.)

3. John bought a tape, which is $12\frac{4}{5}$ yards long. If he needs 8 pieces of tape, each

   measuring $1\frac{3}{5}$ yards for his school project, is $12\frac{4}{5}$ yards of tape enough for his

   project? (Hint: Find how many $1\frac{3}{5}$ are contained in $12\frac{4}{5}$. See Example **1**.)

4. Mrs. Aggor is making matching outfits for a school band. If a matching outfit

   requires $1\frac{3}{5}$ yards of fabric, and she bought $11\frac{1}{5}$ yards of fabric, how many

   similar outfits could she make? (Hint: Find how many $1\frac{3}{5}$ are contained in $11\frac{1}{5}$.

   See Example **1**.)

5. Solve question 4 without showing any detailed explanations. (Hint: See Example **2**.)

6. Eric used $3\frac{1}{5}$ feet of wire for a school project. How many similar school projects could he make from $12\frac{4}{5}$ feet of wire? (See Example **1** or **2**.)

7. Solve question 6 without showing any detailed explanations. (Hint: See Example **2**.)

Challenge Questions

8. Given that it takes $\frac{9}{10}$ of a yard of fabric to make a baby's shirt, how many similar shirts can be made from $12\frac{3}{5}$ yards of fabric?

9. How many pieces of $2\frac{3}{4}$ meters of wire can be cut from $27\frac{1}{2}$ meters of wire?

Answer to Selected Questions

1. 4	**4.** 7	**8.** 7

DIVISION OF A WHOLE NUMBER BY A MIXED NUMBER AND DIVISION OF A MIXED NUMBER BY A WHOLE NUMBER

Rule 1: **To divide a whole number by a mixed number or to divide a mixed number by a whole number, change both the mixed number and the whole number to improper fractions, invert the divisor, and change the ÷ sign to × sign.**

Rule 2: **To change a mixed number to an improper fraction, multiply the denominator by the whole number, add the numerator to the product, and then write the sum over the denominator.**

Rule 3: **To change a whole number to an improper fraction, write the whole number over the number 1 as the denominator.**

Example 1

Divide: $8 \div 1\frac{1}{3}$

Solution

Step 1: Change 8 and $1\frac{1}{3}$ to improper fractions. (See Rule 1.)

The improper fraction of $8 = \frac{8}{1}$ (See Rule 3 and also Rule 2 under

Multiplication of Fractions, Whole, and
Mixed Numbers.)

The improper fraction of $1\frac{1}{3} = \frac{3 \times 1 + 1}{3} = \frac{4}{3}$ (See Rule 2 and also

Rule 3 under Multiplication
of Fractions, Whole, and
Mixed Numbers.)

Therefore, $8 \div 1\frac{1}{3} = \frac{8}{1} \div \frac{4}{3}$

Step 2: Invert the divisor and change the $\div$ sign to $\times$ sign. (Note: $\frac{4}{3}$ is the divisor.)

$\frac{8}{1} \div \frac{4}{3}$ from Step 1 becomes: $\frac{8}{1} \times \frac{3}{4}$ (Note: $\frac{4}{3}$ is inverted to become $\frac{3}{4}$

and $\div$ sign change to $\times$ sign.)
(See Rule 1.)

Step 3: Reduce the fractions in $\frac{8}{1} \times \frac{3}{4}$ to the lowest terms by dividing the

numerators and the denominators by the same number or numbers if possible.

$$\frac{8}{1} \times \frac{3}{4} = \frac{\overset{2}{\cancel{8}}}{1} \times \frac{3}{\underset{1}{\cancel{4}}} \quad (8 \div 4 = 2,\ 4 \div 4 = 1)$$

$$= \frac{2}{1} \times \frac{3}{1}$$

Step 4: Multiply all the numerators and multiply all the denominators and put the product of the numerators over the product of the denominators.

$$\frac{2}{1} \times \frac{3}{1} = \frac{2 \times 3}{1} = \frac{6}{1}$$

266

$$= 6$$

Therefore, $8 \div 1\frac{1}{3} = 6$

Example 2

Solve the question in Example **1** without showing any detailed solution methods. Use the shortcut method.

Solution

$$8 \div 1\frac{1}{3} = \frac{\overset{2}{\cancel{8}}}{1} \times \frac{3}{\underset{1}{\cancel{4}}}$$

$$= 6$$

Example 3

Divide: $3\frac{5}{8} \div 4$

Solution

Step 1: Change $3\frac{5}{8}$ and 4 to improper fractions. (See Rule 1.)

The improper fraction of $3\frac{5}{8} = \frac{8 \times 3 + 5}{8} = \frac{29}{8}$ (See Rule 2 and also Rule

3 under Multiplication of
Fractions, Whole, and
Mixed Numbers.)

The improper fraction of $4 = \frac{4}{1}$ (See Rule 3 and also Rule 2 under

Multiplication of Fractions, Whole, and
Mixed Numbers.)

Therefore, $3\frac{5}{8} \div 4 = \frac{29}{8} \div \frac{4}{1}$

Step 2: Invert the divisor and change the ÷ sign to × sign. (Note: $\frac{4}{1}$ is the divisor.)

$\frac{29}{8} \div \frac{4}{1}$ from Step 1 becomes $\frac{29}{8} \times \frac{1}{4}$ (Note: $\frac{4}{1}$ is inverted to become $\frac{1}{4}$

and the ÷ sign changes to × sign.)
(See Rule 1.)

Step 3: Reduce the fractions in $\frac{29}{8} \times \frac{1}{4}$ to the lowest terms by dividing the

numerators, and denominators by the same number or numbers if possible.

In this case, there is no number that can divide the numerators and the denominators evenly (without a remainder.)

Step 4: Multiply all the numerators and multiply all the denominators and put the product of the numerators over the product of the denominators.

$$\frac{29}{8} \times \frac{1}{4} = \frac{29 \times 1}{8 \times 4} = \frac{29}{32}$$

Therefore, $3\frac{5}{8} \div 4 = \frac{29}{32}$

Example 4
Solve the question in Example 3 without showing any detailed explanations.
Use the shortcut method.
Solution

$$3\frac{5}{8} \div 4 = \frac{29}{8} \times \frac{1}{4} = \frac{29}{32}$$

Example 5
Divide: $7\frac{1}{7} \div 7$

Solution

Step 1: Change $7\frac{1}{7}$ and 7 to improper fractions. (See Rule 1.)

The improper fraction of $7\frac{1}{7} = \frac{7 \times 7 + 1}{7} = \frac{50}{7}$ (See Rule 2 and also Rule 3 under Multiplication of Fractions, Whole and Mixed Numbers.)

The improper fraction of $7 = \frac{7}{1}$ (See Rule 3 and also Rule 2 under Multiplication of Fractions, Whole, and Mixed numbers.)

Therefore, $7\frac{1}{7} \div 7 = \frac{50}{7} \div \frac{7}{1}$

Step 2: Invert the divisor and change the ÷ sign to × sign.   (Note: $\frac{7}{1}$ is the divisor.)

$\frac{50}{7} \div \frac{7}{1}$ from Step 1 becomes $\frac{50}{7} \times \frac{1}{7}$ (Note: $\frac{7}{1}$ is inverted to become $\frac{1}{7}$ and ÷ sign changes to × sign.)
(See Rule 1.)

268

Step 3: Reduce the fraction in $\dfrac{50}{7} \times \dfrac{1}{7}$ to the lowest terms by dividing the

numerators and the denominators by the same number or numbers if possible. In this case, there is no number that can divide the numerators and the denominators evenly (without a remainder.)

Step 4: Multiply all the numerators and multiply all the denominators and put the product of the numerators over the product of the denominators.

$$\frac{50}{7} \times \frac{1}{7} = \frac{50 \times 1}{7 \times 7} = \frac{50}{49}$$

Step 5: Change $\dfrac{50}{49}$ to a mixed fraction, by dividing the numerator by the denominator.

$$\frac{50}{49} = 1\frac{1}{49} \qquad (50 \div 49 = 1, \text{ remainder } 1, = 1\frac{1}{49}.)$$

Therefore, $7\dfrac{1}{7} \div 7 = 1\dfrac{1}{49}$

Example 6

Solve Example **5** without showing any detailed solutions.
Use the shortcut method.

Solution

$$7\frac{1}{7} \div 7 = \frac{50}{7} \times \frac{1}{7} = \frac{50}{49} = 1\frac{1}{49} \quad \text{(See Steps 4 and 5 in Example 5.)}$$

The notes and the generous examples have provided me with the conceptual understanding and the computational fluency to do my homework.

Exercises

1. Divide the following whole numbers by the mixed numbers. (Hint: See Example **1**.)

(a) $3 \div 1\dfrac{1}{2}$ (b) $16 \div 2\dfrac{2}{3}$ (c) $12 \div 2\dfrac{2}{3}$ (d) $10 \div 2\dfrac{1}{2}$

(e) $14 \div 2\dfrac{1}{3}$ (f) $18 \div 1\dfrac{2}{4}$ (g) $24 \div 1\dfrac{1}{3}$ (h) $18 \div 4\dfrac{1}{2}$

2. Solve questions **1(a)** to **1(h)** using the shortcut method. (Hint: See Example **2**.)

3. Divide the following mixed numbers by the whole numbers. (Hint: See Examples **3** and **5**.)

(a) $4\frac{1}{2} \div 2$ (b) $9\frac{1}{3} \div 2$ (c) $4\frac{2}{3} \div 2$ (d) $10\frac{2}{3} \div 8$

(e) $5\frac{1}{3} \div 4$ (f) $12\frac{1}{2} \div 5$ (g) $3\frac{1}{2} \div 14$ (h) $4\frac{1}{2} \div 18$

4. Solve questions **3(a)** to **3(h)** using the shortcut method. (Hint: See Example **4**.)

5. Divide the following mixed numbers and whole numbers. (Hint: See Examples **1**, **3**, and **5**.)

(a) $4 \div 1\frac{1}{2}$ (b) $7\frac{1}{2} \div 5$ (c) $8 \div 3\frac{1}{3}$ (d) $64 \div 2\frac{2}{3}$

(e) $6\frac{2}{5} \div 8$ (f) $12 \div 2\frac{2}{4}$ (g) $9\frac{1}{3} \div 8$ (h) $27 \div 2\frac{1}{4}$

(i) $8\frac{1}{3} \div 5$ (j) $6 \div 1\frac{1}{3}$ (k) $3\frac{1}{3} \div 5$ (l) $4\frac{4}{5} \div 8$

6. Solve questions **5(a)** to **5(l)** using the shortcut methods. (Hint: See Examples **2**, **4**, and **6**.)

Challenge Questions

7. Divide the following mixed numbers and whole numbers.

(a) $5 \div 2\frac{1}{2}$ (b) $9\frac{1}{3} \div 7$ (c) $36 \div 2\frac{1}{2}$ (d) $17 \div 1\frac{1}{2}$

Answers to Selected Questions

1(a) 2   **1(c)** $4\frac{1}{2}$ **1(g)** 18   **2(b)** 6   **2(d)** 4

2(f) $2\frac{1}{2}$ **2(h)** $\frac{1}{4}$ **5(a)** $2\frac{2}{3}$ **5(c)** $2\frac{2}{5}$ **5(h)** 12

REAL WORLD APPLICATIONS - WORD PROBLEMS
Division of a Whole Number by a Mixed Number and
Division of a Mixed Number by a Whole Number

Example 1

A store used $3\frac{3}{4}$ yards of material to make a dress. How many dresses can be made with 60 yards of material?

Solution

Setup: The number of $3\frac{3}{4}$ yards in 60 yards = $60 \div 3\frac{3}{4}$

Step 1: Change 60 and $3\frac{3}{4}$ to improper fractions. (See Rule 1.)

The improper fraction of $60 = \frac{60}{1}$.   (See Rule 3.)

The improper fraction of $3\frac{3}{4} = \frac{4 \times 3 + 3}{4} = \frac{15}{4}$.   (See Rule 2.)

Therefore, $60 \div 3\frac{3}{4}$ becomes $\frac{60}{1} \div \frac{15}{4}$.

Step 2: Invert the divisor and change $\div$ sign to $\times$ sign. (Note: $\frac{15}{4}$ is the divisor.)

$\frac{60}{1} \div \frac{15}{4}$ from step 1 becomes: $\frac{60}{1} \times \frac{4}{15}$. (Note: $\frac{15}{4}$ is inverted to

become $\frac{4}{15}$ and the $\div$ sign changes to $\times$ sign.)   (See Rule 1.)

Step 3: Reduce the fraction in $\frac{60}{1} \times \frac{4}{15}$ to the lowest terms by dividing the numerators and the denominators by the same number or numbers if possible.

$$\frac{60}{1} \times \frac{4}{15} = \frac{\overset{4}{\cancel{60}}}{1} \times \frac{4}{\underset{1}{\underset{3}{\cancel{\cancel{15}}}}} \qquad (60 \div 5 = 12,\ 15 \div 5 = 3,\ 12 \div 3 = 4,\ \text{and}\ 3 \div 3 = 1)$$

Step 4: Multiply all the numerators together and multiply all the denominators together and put the product of the numerators over the product of the denominators.

$$\frac{4}{1} \times \frac{4}{1} = \frac{4 \times 4}{1 \times 1} = 16$$

Therefore, 16 dresses can be made from 60 yards of material.

Example 2

Solve Example **1** without showing detailed solution information. Use the shortcut method.

Solution

The number of $3\frac{3}{4}$ yards in 60 yards $= 60 \div 3\frac{3}{4}$

$$= 60 \div 3\frac{3}{4} = \frac{\overset{12}{\cancel{60}}}{1} \times \frac{\overset{4}{\cancel{4}}}{\underset{1}{\cancel{\underset{3}{\cancel{15}}}}} \quad (60 \div 5 = 12, \ 15 \div 5 = 3, \ 12 \div 3 = 4, \text{ and } 3 \div 3 = 1)$$

$$= 4 \times 4 = 16$$

Therefore, 16 dresses can be made from 60 yards of material.

Exercises

1. Mary used $1\frac{2}{3}$ ounces of honey to make a loaf of bread. How many similar loaves can she make from a 60-ounce jar of honey? (Hint: See Example **1**.)

2. The Johnson family wants to know how many pieces of fence of length $3\frac{1}{3}$ yards long is needed to fence around their garden, which has a total length of 200 yards. Is the Johnson's family correct by stating that 62 pieces of $3\frac{1}{3}$ yards are needed for the project? (Hint: See Example 1.)

COMPARISON OF FRACTIONS

New Terms: Ascending Order and Descending Order

Two or more fractions can be compared to find their magnitude in ascending or descending order. **Ascending order** of magnitude means that the fractions are arranged from the lowest to the highest. **Descending order** of magnitude means that the fractions are arranged from the highest to the lowest.

Rule 1: To compare, write fractions in ascending or descending order of magnitude of two or more fractions, change all the fractions to

equivalent fractions (with the same denominator.)

Once the equivalent fractions are written, the value of each numerator of the equivalent fraction determines how large or small each fraction is. The larger the numerator of the equivalent fraction, the larger that specific fraction and the smaller the numerator of the equivalent fraction, the smaller that specific fraction.

Critical Thinking

Two or more fractions can be compared by arranging the equivalent fractions in ascending or descending order.

Example 1

Which fraction is greater, $\dfrac{3}{5}$ or $\dfrac{3}{4}$?

Solution

Step 1: Using Rule 1, Change the fractions $\dfrac{3}{5}$ and $\dfrac{3}{4}$ to equivalent fractions. The

LCD of $\dfrac{3}{5}$ and $\dfrac{3}{4}$ is 20. Hint: See Examples under the topics Subtraction

of Fractions or Addition of Fractions. For example, $5 \times 4 = 20$ and 5 and 4 can divide evenly into 20 (without a remainder.)

$$\frac{3}{5} = \frac{}{20} \diagup \text{LCD}$$

$$\frac{3}{4} = \frac{}{20} \diagup \text{LCD}$$

Step 2: Find the equivalent fractions. Review Equivalent Fractions.

$$\frac{3}{5} = \frac{3}{5} \times \frac{4}{4} = \frac{12}{20} \leftarrow \text{Equivalent fraction}$$

$$\frac{3}{4} = \frac{3}{4} \times \frac{5}{5} = \frac{15}{20} \leftarrow \text{Equivalent fraction}$$

Step 3: Compare the equivalent fractions.

Comparing the equivalent fractions $\dfrac{12}{20}$ and $\dfrac{15}{20}$, $\dfrac{15}{20} > \dfrac{12}{20}$ because the

numerator 15 is greater than the numerator 12.

Therefore, $\dfrac{3}{4} > \dfrac{3}{5}$ The symbol > means greater than.

Example 2

Solve Example **1** without showing any detailed solutions.

Shortcut: The LCD of $\frac{3}{5}$ and $\frac{3}{4}$ is 20. Find the equivalent fractions.

$$\frac{3}{5} = \frac{3}{5} \times \frac{4}{4} = \frac{12}{20} \leftarrow \text{Equivalent fraction}$$

$$\frac{3}{4} = \frac{3}{4} \times \frac{5}{5} = \frac{15}{20} \leftarrow \text{Equivalent fraction}$$

By comparing equivalent fractions, $\frac{15}{20} > \frac{12}{20}$ because the numerator 15 is greater than the numerator 12. Therefore, $\frac{3}{4} > \frac{3}{5}$.

Example 3

Arrange the fractions in ascending and descending order of magnitude.

$$\frac{2}{3}, \frac{3}{4}, \frac{4}{5}$$

Solution

Step 1: Using Rule 1, change the fractions $\frac{2}{3}$, $\frac{3}{4}$, and $\frac{4}{5}$ to equivalent fractions.

The LCD of the fractions $\frac{2}{3}$, $\frac{3}{4}$, and $\frac{4}{5}$ is 60. (For example, $3 \times 4 \times 5 = 60$. Multiply all the denominators together to obtain the LCD.)

$$\frac{2}{3} = \frac{}{60} \diagup \text{LCD}$$

$$\frac{3}{4} = \frac{}{60} \diagup \text{LCD}$$

$$\frac{4}{5} = \frac{}{60} \diagup \text{LCD}$$

Step 2: Find the equivalent fractions. (Review topics on Equivalent Fractions.)

$$\frac{2}{3} = \frac{2}{3} \times \frac{20}{20} = \frac{40}{60} \leftarrow \text{Equivalent fraction}$$

$$\frac{3}{4} = \frac{3}{4} \times \frac{15}{15} = \frac{45}{60} \leftarrow \text{Equivalent fraction}$$

$$\frac{4}{5} = \frac{4}{5} \times \frac{12}{12} = \frac{48}{60} \quad \leftarrow \text{Equivalent fraction}$$

Step 3: Compare the equivalent fractions

$$\frac{40}{60}, \frac{45}{60}, \text{ and } \frac{48}{60}$$

$\frac{40}{60} < \frac{45}{60} < \frac{48}{60}$ because the numerator 40 is

less than the numerator 45 and the numerator 45 is less than the numerator 48.)

Therefore, the ascending (increasing) order is $\frac{40}{60}, \frac{45}{60}$, and $\frac{48}{60}$.

Therefore, the descending (decreasing) order is $\frac{48}{60}, \frac{45}{60}$, and $\frac{40}{60}$.

Example 4

Solve Example **3**, without showing any detailed explanations. Use the shortcut method.

Solution

Shortcut:

The LCD for $\frac{2}{3}, \frac{3}{4}$, and $\frac{4}{5}$ is 60.

Write equivalent fractions:

$$\frac{2}{3} = \frac{2}{3} \times \frac{20}{20} = \frac{40}{60} \quad \leftarrow \text{Equivalent fraction}$$

$$\frac{3}{4} = \frac{3}{4} \times \frac{15}{15} = \frac{45}{60} \quad \leftarrow \text{Equivalent fraction}$$

$$\frac{4}{5} = \frac{4}{5} \times \frac{12}{12} = \frac{48}{60} \quad \leftarrow \text{Equivalent fraction}$$

By comparing equivalent fractions, the ascending order is $\frac{40}{60}, \frac{45}{60}, \frac{48}{60}$ and the

descending order is $\frac{48}{60}, \frac{45}{60}, \frac{40}{60}$.

Exercise

1. Explain how fractions can be compared. (Hint: See Rule **1**.)

2. Which of the following pairs of fractions is greater? (Hint: See Example **1**)

(a) $\dfrac{3}{7}$ and $\dfrac{2}{5}$ (b) $\dfrac{1}{4}$ and $\dfrac{2}{5}$ (c) $\dfrac{2}{5}$ and $\dfrac{3}{8}$

(d) $\dfrac{3}{5}$ and $\dfrac{4}{7}$ (e) $\dfrac{2}{7}$ and $\dfrac{1}{5}$ (f) $\dfrac{4}{5}$ and $\dfrac{3}{4}$

3. Solve questions **2(a)** to **2(f)** without showing a detailed solution method. Use the shortcut method. (Hint: See Example **2**.)

4. Arrange the following fractions in ascending and descending orders.
(Hint: See Example **3**.)

(a) $\dfrac{2}{3}, \dfrac{4}{7}, \dfrac{8}{21}$ (b) $\dfrac{2}{5}, \dfrac{3}{8}, \dfrac{3}{4}$ (c) $\dfrac{4}{9}, \dfrac{1}{3}, \dfrac{1}{4}$

(d) $\dfrac{1}{5}, \dfrac{2}{7}, \dfrac{8}{35}$ (e) $\dfrac{1}{3}, \dfrac{2}{5}, \dfrac{4}{15}$ (f) $\dfrac{2}{3}, \dfrac{3}{4}, \dfrac{4}{5}$

5. Solve questions **4(a)** to **4(f)** without showing a detailed solution method. Use the shortcut method. (Hint: See Example **4**.)

Challenge Questions

6. Arrange the following fractions in ascending and descending orders.

(a) $\dfrac{1}{4}, \dfrac{2}{3}, \dfrac{5}{6}$ (b) $\dfrac{3}{5}, \dfrac{4}{7}$ (c) $\dfrac{3}{5}, \dfrac{2}{3}$ (d) $\dfrac{4}{7}, \dfrac{8}{14}, \dfrac{5}{7}$

Answers to Selected Questions

2(a) $\dfrac{3}{7}$ 4(a) Ascending order is $\dfrac{8}{21}, \dfrac{4}{7}, \dfrac{2}{3}$ Descending order is $\dfrac{2}{3}, \dfrac{4}{7}, \dfrac{8}{21}$

DECIMAL FRACTIONS

Cumulative Review

Solve:

(1). $2\dfrac{2}{3} \div 4 =$ **(2)**. $4 \times 3\dfrac{3}{4} =$ **(3)**. $6\dfrac{1}{4} \div 1\dfrac{2}{3} =$ **(4)**. $17 - 8 \div 2 \times 2 =$

New Terms

Common fractions – Common fractions are fractions with fraction bars such as

Decimal fractions – Decimal fractions are numbers to the right of the decimal point as shown below. See also fig. 1.

Decimal point – The decimal point in a number separates the whole number part from the fractional part such as shown above. See also Fig. 1.

Mixed decimals – A mixed decimal is made of a whole number and a decimal fraction such as 3.5, where 3 is the whole number and .5 is a decimal fraction.

Digits – **The numbers 0, 1, 2, 3, 4, 5, 6, 7, 8, and 9 are called digits.** The number 3.5 has a total of two digits which are 3 and 5. The number 3.56 has a total of 3 digits which are 3, 5 and 6.

Decimal place – The decimal place is the number of the digits after the decimal point. For example, 3.5 has one decimal place because 3.5 has one digit after the decimal point and the digit is 5, and 3.56 has two decimal places because 3.56 has two digits after the decimal point and these two digits are 5 and 6.

Fig.1 shows whole numbers, a decimal point, fractions such as $\dfrac{1}{10}$, and decimal fractions such as .1. Note that fig. 1 shows that the whole numbers are at the left side of the decimal point and the fractions are at the right side of the decimal point.

Fig. 1

Words	Ten thousands	Thousands	Hundreds	Tens	Units		Tenths	Hundredths	Thousandths
Numbers	10,000	1000	100	10	1	.	$\frac{1}{10}$ or .1	$\frac{1}{100}$ or .01	$\frac{1}{1000}$ or .001

Whole numbers ←———————→ Fractions or decimals

↑
Decimal point

Note: From fig.1,

    1). the names of the decimal fractions end with **–ths** such as ten**ths**, hundred**ths**, and thousand**ths**.

    2). the names of the whole numbers end in **-s** such as ten-thousand**s**, thousand**s**, hundred**s**, ten**s**, and unit**s**.

    3). it can be seen that the decimal fraction is based on 10 because as you move from left to right, each column (digit) is divided by 10, or as you move from right to left, each column (digit) is multiplied by 10. For example, as we move to the right of the decimal point, the value of the tenths is divided by 10 to get the value of the hundredths, the value of the hundredths is divided by 10 to get the value of the thousandths.

    4). It can be seen that a number can be written in words, fractional and decimal forms. For example, tenths, specifically one tenth, $\frac{1}{10}$, and .1 have the same value as shown:

$$.1 = \text{one tenth} = \frac{1}{10} \leftarrow \text{Fractional form}$$

Decimal form↗   ↖Word form

Group exercise

Using Fig. 1, complete the following statements. Hint: See the **note from Fig. 1, item 3**.

1. Starting at the ones or units place, and as you move left one place or one column, the number in the column is multiplied by _____. (Select the correct answer: 10, 20, 30, or 100.)

2. Now starting from the thousands place, and as you move right one place or one column, the number in the column is div_____ by 10.

3. Now starting from the tenths place, and as you move right one place or one column, the number in the column is divided by ___. (Select the correct answer: 10, 20, 30, or 100.)

4. Now starting from the thousandths place, and as you move left two places or two columns, the number in the final column is multip_____ by 100.

CHAPTER 8

Place Value of the Digits

Place value of the digits chart.

Place value of the digits		Ten-thousands	Thousands	Hundreds	Tens	Ones	Decimal point	Tenths	Hundredths	Thousandths	Ten-thousandths
Number		8	6	3	7	2	.	4	0	1	9

Place value of digits **is the value given to the place a digit has in a number**. By looking at the "**Place Value of the Digits**" chart, we can find out that:

a. 2 has a place value of one**s** or we can simply say **2 ones** or 2 × 1 = 2 because the first digit before the decimal point (or the first whole number just before the decimal point) has the place value of one**s**. We may say that 2 is in the ones place.

b. 7 has a place value of ten**s** or we can simply say "**7 tens**" or 7 × 10 = 70 because the second digit before the decimal point (or the second whole number before the decimal point) has the place value of ten**s**. We may say that 7 is in the tens place.

c. 3 has a place value of hundred**s** or we can simply say "**3 hundreds**" or 3 × 100 = 300 because the third digit before the decimal point (or the third whole number before the decimal point) has the place value of hundred**s**. We may say that 3 is in the hundreds place.

d. 6 has a place value of thousand**s** or we can simply say "**6 thousands**" or 6 × 1000 = 6000 because the fourth digit before the decimal point (or the fourth whole number before the decimal point) has the place value of thousand**s**. We may say that 6 is in the thousands place.

e. 8 has a place value of ten-thousand**s** or we can simply say "**8 ten-thousands**" or 8 × 10,000 = 80,000 because the fifth digit before the decimal point (or the fifth whole number before the decimal point) has a place value of ten-thousand**s**. We may say that 8 is in the ten-thousands place.

f. 4 has a place value of ten**ths** or we can simply say "**4 tenths**" or $\frac{4}{10}$ = .4 because the first digit after the decimal point has a place value of ten**ths**. We say that 4 is in the ten**ths** place.

g. 0 has a place value of hundred**ths** or we can simply say "**0 hundredths**" or $\frac{0}{100}$ = 0 because the second digit after the decimal point has a place value of hundred**ths**. We say that 0 is in the hundred**ths** place.

h. 1 has a place value of thousand**ths** or we can simply say "**1 thousandths**" or $\frac{1}{1000}$ = .001 because the third digit after the decimal point has a place value of thousand**ths**. We say that 1 is in the thousand**ths** place.

i. 9 has a place value of ten-thousand**ths** or we can simply say

"**9 ten-thousandths**" or $\dfrac{9}{10,000}$ = .0009 because the fourth digit after the decimal point has a place value of ten-thousandths. We say that 9 is in the ten-thousand**ths** place.

j. To determine the value of each digit, **look at its place in the number**.

Group Exercise or Class Exercise.

1. Explain what is meant by place value of digits.
2. Using the similar idea of the "**place value of digits**" chart, make a place value chart for (**a**) 2543.691 (**b**) 901.21 (**c**) 127.0458 (**d**) 67.9352 (**e**) 9824.375
3. What is meant by digits?
4. What is meant by a decimal point?
5. Using the similar idea of the "**place value of digits**" chart, state the value of each digit in the bold face.
   (**a**) 234.00**2** (**b**) **7**78.923 (**c**) 7.2**3**4 (**d**) 4.**5**6 (**e**) 19.20**6**

Group Exercise

Using Fig. 1, complete the following statements:

1. Starting from the place value of ones and as you move left one place, the place value is multiplied by ____. (Select the correct answer: 10, 20, 30, or 100).
2. Now starting from the place value of thousands and you move right one place, the place value is div____ by 10.
3. Now starting from the place value of tenths and you move right one place, the place value is divided by ___. (Select the correct answer: 10, 20, 30 or 100).
4. Now starting from the place value of thousandths and you move left two places, the place value is multip____ by 100

Names of Decimal Fractions

Name	Place values	Example	Number of digits to the right of the decimal point	Denominator as a power of 10
Two tenths	tenths	0.2	1 digit	10^1
Fifteen hudredths	hundredths	0.15	2 digits	10^2
One hundred eight thousandths	thousandths	0.108	3 digits	10^3
Six ten-thousandths	ten-thousands	0.0006	4 digits	10^4
Twenty-eight hundred-thousandths	hundred-thousandths	0.00028	5 digits	10^5
Two million	millionths	0.000002	6 digits	10^6

Fig. 2

DENOMINATOR OF A POWER OF 10

Compare the column ("Number of digits to the right of the decimal point ") to the column ("Denominator as a power of 10 ") in fig. 2, it can be seen that the number of the digits of the zeros corresponds to the value of the exponents. For example, 10^1 has an exponent of 1, 10^2 has 2 as the exponent, 10^4 has 4 as the exponent and so on.

In summary, recall that while a common fraction can have any number as the denominator, a decimal fraction must have a denominator which is a power of 10 such as $10^1 = 10$

$$10^2 = 10 \times 10 = 100$$
$$10^3 = 10 \times 10 \times 10 = 1,000$$
$$10^4 = 10 \times 10 \times 10 \times 10 = 10,000$$
$$10^5 = 10 \times 10 \times 10 \times 10 \times 10 = 100,000$$
$$10^6 = 10 \times 10 \times 10 \times 10 \times 10 \times 10 = 1,000,000$$

When a decimal fraction is written, the denominator is never written. The denominator is determined by the number of digits to the right side of the decimal point. For example, using the column "**Example** " in Fig. 2,

One digit

$$.2 = \frac{2}{10} \qquad \text{Denominator (with one zero)}$$

Two digits

$$.15 = \frac{15}{100} \qquad \text{Denominator (with two zeros)}$$

Three digits

$$.108 = \frac{108}{1,000} \qquad \text{Denominator (with three zeros)}$$

Four digits

$$.0006 = \frac{6}{10,000} \qquad \text{Denominator (with four zeros)}$$

Five digits

$$.00028 = \frac{28}{100,000} \qquad \text{Denominator (with five zeros)}$$

Six digits↘

$$.000002 = \frac{2}{1,000,000}$$ ↙Denominator (with six digits)

↑   ↑

Decimal   Fractions

Group Exercise

Recall that the decimal fraction .2 can be written as the common fraction $\frac{2}{10}$.

Using similar idea, write the common fractions for the following decimal fractions:

(**1**) .4   (**2**) .82   (**3**) .496   (**4**) .9   (**5**) .005

How to Read Mixed Decimal Fractions

A mixed number is made up of a whole number and a common fraction. Similarly, a mixed decimal consists of a whole number and a decimal fraction.

Mixed decimals are read by saying the name of the whole numbers, **replacing the decimal point with** "**and** " then adding the names of the decimal fractions.

Example 1

How is 8.09 read?

Solution

"**And**" is used for the decimal point. Therefore, 8.09 is read as eight and nine hundredths.

Example 2

(**a**). How is "98.64" read?

(**b**). Write the mixed decimal of 460.237 in word phrase. Hint: See the chart of Fig. 2.

(**c**). Write the mixed decimal for the word phrase two hundred forty and three hundred sixty four ten thousandths. Hint: See the chart of Fig. 2.

Solution

(**a**). "And" is used for the decimal point. Therefore, 98.64 is read as ninety-eight and sixty-four hundredths.

(**b**). Mixed decimals are read by saying the name of the whole numbers, replacing the decimal point with "and" then adding the names of the decimal fraction as shown:

     The name for the whole number 460 is four hundred sixty.

     The name for the decimal fraction .237 is two hundred thirty seven thousandths. (Note that .237 has three digits after the decimal point, and therefore, the decimal fraction of .237 must have three zeros in the denominator, and therefore, .237 has a place value of two hundred thirty seven thousandths.)

Therefore, the word phrase for 460.237 is four hundred sixty **and** two hundred thirty seven thousandths.

(**c**). The mixed decimal for the word phrase two hundred forty and three hundred sixty four ten thousandths is written as follows:

Two hundred forty is written as 240. "and" stands for a decimal point.

Three hundred sixty four ten thousandths is written as .0364. (Note that the "ten thousandths" suggests four digits after the decimal point in the "place value chart" or the "ten thousandths suggests that there are four zeros in the denominator of the decimal fraction three hundred sixty four ten thousandths, and therefore, the three hundred sixty four ten thousandths must have four digits and this is achieved by adding a zero at the front as follows, .0364.

Therefore, the mixed decimal for the word phrase two hundred forty and three hundred sixty four ten thousandths is 240.0364.

The notes and the generous examples have provided me with the conceptual understanding and the computational fluency to do my homework.

Exercises

1. How are the following decimal fractions read? Hint: See Example 1.

   a. 24.01   **b.** 5.09   **c.** 100.01   **d.** 15.07   **e.** 20.044   **f.** 4.017

2. How are the following decimal fractions read? Hint: See Example 2.

   a. 14.55   **b.** 67.94   **c.** 112.99   **d.** 23.144   **e.** 2.432   **f.** 106.4002

3. State the value of each digit in the bold face. Hint: See the topic under "Place Value of the Digits."

   a. 3**3**.84   **b.** 213.1**2**3   **c.** 74.9**5**22   **d.** 256.8**4**5   **e.** 9356.09**3**4   **f.** 321.4**5**7

4. Write the following decimal fractions and mixed decimals as word phrases. Hint: See fig. 2, Examples 1 and 2.

   a. 4.46   **b.** .9   **c** .6   **d** .064   **e.** 12.16

   f. 201.611   **g.** 2.0049   **h.** .04   **i.** .752   **j.** 475.281

   k. .0001   **l** .0401   **m.** 341.781   **n.** 75.38   **o.** 570.01

   p. 63.417   **q** .0067   **r** .777   **s.** 88.888   **t.** 250.394

5. Write the decimal fraction for each of the following word phrases. Hint: See fig. 2, Examples 1 and 2.

   a. Forty hundredths

   b. One hundred and fifty thousandths

   c. Two thousand four hundred twenty-one ten-thousandths

d. Twenty-four hundredths

e. Twenty-eight hundredths

f. Six hundred twenty-four ten-thousandths seventy-four hundredths

g. Nine tenths

h. Two and eighth thousandths

i. Ten and twenty-four ten-thousandths

j. Two and seven thousandths.

Challenge Questions

6. How are the following decimal fractions read?

    a. 99.241   **b.** 679.057   **c.** 3.001   **d.** .956   **e.** 48.039   **f.** 5431.3456

7. State the value of each digit in the bold face.

    a. 41.2**2**4   **b.** 678.**9**09   **c.** 56.000**2**   **d.** **5**43.214   **e.** 321.06**6**2   **f.** 2.1**4**

How to Convert Common Fractions to Decimal Fractions

Rule: To convert common fractions to decimal fractions, the number of the zeros in the denominator is the number of the decimal places and also the number of the digits in the decimal fraction is the number of the decimal places.

Example 3

Convert $\dfrac{3}{10}$ to a decimal fraction.

Solution

The common fraction $\dfrac{3}{10}$ has a denominator of 10. The 10 has one zero. The number of the zeros in the denominator is the number of the decimal places and also provides the number of the digits.

Therefore, $\dfrac{3}{10}$ has one decimal place and also 1 digit.

So, the decimal fraction of the common fraction $\dfrac{3}{10}$ is .3 and this is the required answer.

                          .3

Decimal point↗   ↖3 is just one number on the right hand side of the decimal point, and therefore, has one decimal place and one digit.

Note that the decimal point in .3 is located by counting from right to left one decimal place from behind the numerator of 3 as shown:

284

Count one decimal place from right to left starting from behind the numerator.

0.3

Decimal point location

One decimal place (one digit).

This example is solved showing a detailed explanations just for the students' understanding. When solving homework or doing a test, it is not necessary to show the detailed explanations. This example can easily be solved as shown:

$$\frac{3}{10} = .3$$

Example 4

What is the decimal fraction of $\frac{17}{100}$?

Solution

The common fraction $\frac{17}{100}$ has 100 as the denominator and 100 has two zeros.

The number of zeros in the denominator is the number of the decimal places and also provides the number of the digits of the decimal fraction.

Therefore, the common fraction $\frac{17}{100}$ is the decimal fraction .17.

Two decimal places (Two digits).

0.17

Second decimal place

Decimal point

First decimal place

The combination of the first decimal place and the second decimal place make the two decimal places which is determined by the two zeros of the denominator 100. Note that the decimal point in .17 is located by counting from right to left two decimal places starting from behind the numerator of 17 as shown:

Count two decimal places from right to left starting from behind the numerator.

0.17

Decimal point

Two decimal places (Two digits).

The solution to this question is simply $\frac{17}{100} = .17$

Example 5

Write $\dfrac{138}{1000}$ as a decimal fraction.

Solution

The common fraction $\dfrac{138}{1000}$ has 1000 as the denominator and

1000 has three zeros. The number of zeros in the denominator is the number of the decimal places and also provides the number of the digits of the decimal

fraction. So, the decimal fraction of the common fraction $\dfrac{138}{1000}$ is .138.

Three decimal places

Third decimal place (Third digit).

Decimal point

Second decimal place (Second digit).

First decimal place
(First digit).

The combination of the first, second and the third decimal places make the three decimals which is determined by the three zeroes of the denominator 1000.
Note that the decimal point in .138 is located by counting from right to left three decimal places from behind the numerator of 138 as shown:

Count three decimal places from right to left starting from behind the numerator 138.

Decimal point

Three decimal places (Three digits).

When doing a homework or a test, it is not necessary to give detailed explanations, but rather solve the problem directly as shown:

$$\frac{138}{1000} = .138$$

Example 6

Express $\dfrac{2748}{10,000}$ as a decimal fraction.

Solution

The decimal fraction of the common fraction

$$\frac{2748}{10,000} = .2748$$

Note that the denominator 10,000 has four zeros, and therefore, the decimal

286

fraction needs four decimal places.

Example 7

What is the decimal fraction of $\dfrac{99848}{100,000}$?

Solution

The decimal fraction of the common fraction

$$\frac{99848}{100,000} = .99848$$

Note that the denominator 100,000 has five zeros, and therefore, the decimal fraction needs five decimal places.

Example 8

Express $\dfrac{6}{10,000}$ as a decimal fraction.

Solution

The decimal fraction of the common fraction

$$\frac{6}{10,000} \text{ is } .0006$$

Note that in this case, the denominator of 10,000 has 4 zeros, and therefore, the required decimal fraction should have four decimal places, but the numerator has only the number 6. Therefore, count four decimal places from right to left starting from behind the numerator 6 as shown:

Count four decimal places from right to left starting from behind the numerator 6.

Decimal point

Numerator 6

Put zeros in the places of the decimal places which have no numbers as shown:

Four decimal places.

0.0006

Put zeros in place of the decimal places which have no numbers.

Therefore, the decimal fraction of the common fraction

$$\frac{6}{10,000} \text{ is } .0006$$

Example 9

Write the decimal fraction of $\dfrac{28}{100,000}$.

Solution

The decimal fraction of the common fraction

$$\dfrac{28}{100,000} \text{ is } .00028$$

Note that in this case, the denominator 100,000 has 5 zeros, and therefore, the required decimal fraction should have 5 decimal places, but the numerator has only the number 28. Count 5 decimal places from right to left starting from behind the numerator 28 as shown:

Count five decimal places from right to left starting from behind the numerator 28.

Put zeros in the places of the decimal places which have no numbers as shown:

Five decimal places (Five digits).

0.00028

Put zeros in places of the decimal places which have no numbers.

Therefore, the decimal fraction of the common fraction,

$$\dfrac{28}{100,000} \text{ is } .00028$$

Example 10

Write $\dfrac{2}{100}$ as a decimal fraction.

Solution

The decimal fraction of the common fraction

$$\dfrac{2}{100} \text{ is } .02$$

Note that in this case, the denominator 100 has two zeros, and therefore, the required decimal fraction should have two decimal places, but the numerator has only the number 2. Count two decimal places from right to left starting from behind the numerator 2 as shown:

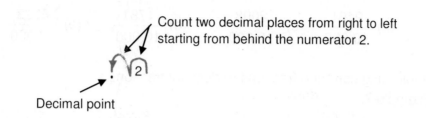

Count two decimal places from right to left starting from behind the numerator 2.

Decimal point

Put a zero in place of the decimal place which has no number as shown:

Two decimal places (Two digits).

0.02

Decimal point

Put a zero in place of the decimal place which has no numbers.

Therefore, the decimal fraction of the common fraction

$\frac{2}{100}$ is .02

The notes and the generous examples have provided me with the conceptual understanding and the computational fluency to do my homework.

Exercises

1. Change the following common fractions to decimal fractions.
Hint: See Example 3.

(a) $\frac{9}{10}$ (b) $\frac{7}{10}$ (c) $\frac{1}{10}$ (d) $\frac{5}{10}$ (e) $\frac{6}{10}$

2. Change the following common fractions to decimal fractions.
Hint: See Example 4

(a) $\frac{98}{100}$ (b) $\frac{1}{100}$ (c) $\frac{16}{100}$ d) $\frac{57}{100}$ (e) $\frac{39}{100}$

3. Change the following common fractions to decimal fractions.
Hint: See Example 5

(a) $\frac{798}{1,000}$ (b) $\frac{201}{1,000}$ (c) $\frac{157}{1,000}$ (d) $\frac{911}{1,000}$ (e) $\frac{401}{1,000}$

4. Change the following common fractions to decimal fractions.
Hint: See Example 6.

(a) $\dfrac{6749}{10,000}$ (b) $\dfrac{9461}{10,000}$ (c) $\dfrac{2008}{10,000}$ (d) $\dfrac{1781}{10,000}$ (e) $\dfrac{6223}{10,000}$

5. Change the following common fractions to decimal fractions.
   Hint: See Example 7.

(a) $\dfrac{33245}{100,000}$ (b) $\dfrac{73205}{100,000}$ (c) $\dfrac{90045}{100,000}$ (d) $\dfrac{39245}{100,000}$ (e) $\dfrac{178245}{100,000}$

6. Change the following common fractions to decimal fractions.
   Hint: See Example 8.

(a) $\dfrac{1}{10,000}$ (b) $\dfrac{9}{10,000}$ (c) $\dfrac{3}{10,000}$ (d) $\dfrac{6}{10,000}$ (e) $\dfrac{8}{10,000}$

7. Change the following common fractions to decimal fractions.
   Hint: See Example 9.

(a) $\dfrac{13}{100,000}$ (b) $\dfrac{49}{100,000}$ (c) $\dfrac{11}{100,000}$ (d) $\dfrac{13}{100,000}$ (e) $\dfrac{13}{100,000}$

8. Change the following common fractions to decimal fractions.
   Hint: See Example 10

(a) $\dfrac{9}{100}$ (b). $\dfrac{1}{100}$ (c) $\dfrac{7}{100}$ (d) $\dfrac{5}{100}$ (e) $\dfrac{8}{100}$

Challenge Questions

9. Change the following common fractions to decimal fractions.

(a) $\dfrac{17}{100}$ (b) $\dfrac{17}{10,000}$ (c) $\dfrac{967}{1,000}$ (d) $\dfrac{8}{10}$ (e) $\dfrac{1}{10,000}$

REAL WORLD APPLICATIONS - WORD PROBLEM
Decimal Fraction

Example 1
A computer selling for $1,000.00 was reduced by $100.00. Write the reduction

290

as a decimal fraction of the price.

Solution

The reduction = $100.00

Total selling price = $1,000.00

The reduction as a decimal fraction = $\dfrac{\text{Reduction}}{\text{Total Selling Price}}$

$$= \dfrac{100}{1000}$$

The denominator 1000 has three zeros, and therefore, the required decimal fraction should have three decimal places as shown:

Move three decimal places from right to left starting from behind the numerator 100.

Decimal point

The reduction as a decimal fraction is .100 or just .1 because the zeros at the end of the decimal fractions have no values.

Example 2

Mary has $10.00. If she spent $3.00, write as a decimal the part of the money she spent.

Solution

The common fraction of the amount she spent = $\dfrac{\text{Amount spent}}{\text{Total amount}}$

Amount spent = $3.00

Total amount = $10.00

The common fraction of the amount she spent = $\dfrac{3}{10}$

The decimal fraction of $\dfrac{3}{10}$ is .3 because the denominator 10 has one zero and so, the decimal fraction has one decimal place as shown:

One decimal place

0.3

One digit.

Decimal point

She spent .3 of the total money.

Example 3

John bought a house for $100,000 and made a down payment of $15,250.

Write the down payment as a decimal fraction of the cost of the house.

Solution

The common fraction of the down payment $= \dfrac{\text{Down payment}}{\text{Total Amount}}$

Down payment $= \$15,250$
Total Amount $= \$100,000$

The common fraction of $\dfrac{15,250}{100,000}$ is .15250 because the denominator 100,000 has five zeros, and therefore, the decimal fraction should have five decimal places or five digits as shown:

Five decimal places.

.15250

Decimal point

The required decimal fraction is .15250

The notes and the generous examples have provided me with the conceptual understanding and the computational fluency to do my homework.

Exercises

1. A computer selling for $1,000.00 was reduced by $108.00. Write the reduction as a decimal fraction of the price. Hint: See Example 1.

2. Eric had $10.00. If he spent $8.00, write the part of the money he spent as a decimal fraction. Hint: See Example 2.

3. Rose bought a special car for $10,000.00 and made a down payment of $1,528.00. Write the down payment as a decimal fraction of the cost of the car. Hint: See Example 3.

Challenge questions

4. A book selling for $100.00 was reduced by $32.00. Write the reduction as a decimal fraction of the price.

5. Given that a sale tax in a certain year was $0.05 for every $1.00 of purchase, write the sales tax as a decimal fraction of the purchase. (Hint: $0.05 = 5 cents and $1.00 = 100 cents).

6. Given that a salesman earns $12.00 for every $100.00 of sales, write his earnings as a decimal fraction of the sales.

7. A sweater selling for $100.00 was reduced by $8.00. Write the reduction as a decimal fraction of the price.

8. An electrical equipment which was selling at $10,000.00 was reduced by $234.00. Write the reduction as a decimal fraction of the selling price.

Compare Common Fractions and Decimal Fractions

Common fraction	Equivalent decimal fraction	Decimal fraction name	Number of digits to the right of the decimal point	Denominator
$\frac{3}{10}$	0.3	Three tenths	1 digit	10
$\frac{17}{100}$	0.17	Seventeen hundredths	2 digits	100
$\frac{138}{1000}$	0.138	One hundred thirty-eight thousandths.	3 digits	1000

Mixed Fraction and Mixed Decimals

A mixed fraction is made up of a whole number and a common fraction such as $7\frac{1}{2}$ where 7 is the whole number and $\frac{1}{2}$ is the common fraction.

A mixed decimal is made up of a whole number and a decimal fraction such as 3.68 where 3 is the whole number and .68 is the decimal fraction.

Summary of Types of Fractions

Types	Example	Comments
Common fraction	$\frac{1}{10}$	It has no whole numbers
Decimal fraction	0.1	It has no whole numbers
Mixed common fraction	$1\frac{1}{10}$	It has a whole number and a common fraction
Mixed decimal fraction	1.1	It has both a whole number and a decimal fraction.

Exercise

1. (a) Compare a mixed fraction and a mixed decimal. Hint: See the notes under "Mixed Fractions and Mixed Decimals".

(b) Given 9.48 and $9\frac{48}{100}$, state which number is a mixed fraction and which number is a mixed decimal. Give reasons for your answer. Hint: See the notes under "Mixed Fractions and Mixed Decimals".

How to Convert Decimal Fractions to Common Fractions

Rule 1: Although decimal fractions do not show their denominators, decimal fraction have denominators of powers of 10. So, simply maintain the numbers of the decimal fraction as the numerator and put this numerator over the denominator that is determined by the number of digits in the decimal fraction using the power of 10.

New phrase:

Powers of 10 means $10 \times 10 \times 10 \times \ldots = \mathbf{10^n}$ where n is the power.

For example,

(a).

$$.2 = \frac{2}{10}$$

↗ One digit   ↑ One zero   ↖ Denominator of the power of 10

(b).

↗ Numerator

$$.03 = \frac{03}{100} = \frac{3}{100}$$ Note: 03 = 3, the 0 has no value.

↗↗ Two zeros   ↖ Denominator of the power of 10 $(100 = 10 \times 10 = 10^2)$.

Similarly, for example, $.93 = \frac{93}{100}$ and the denominator has a power of 10.

(c).

↗ Numerator

$$.007 = \frac{007}{1000} = \frac{7}{1000}$$ Note: 007 = 7, 00 in front of 7 has no value.

↗↗↗ Three digits   ↑↑↑ Three zeros   ↖ Denominator of the power of 10. $(1000 = 10 \times 10 \times 10 = 10^3.)$

Similarly, for example, $.561 = \frac{561}{1000}$ and the denominator has a power of 10.

(d).

↗ Numerator

$$.0009 = \frac{0009}{10,000} = \frac{9}{10,000}$$ Note: 0009 = 9, 000 in front of 9 has no value.

↗↗↗↗ Four digits   ↑↑↑↑ Four zeros   ↖ Denominator of the power of 10 $(10,000 = 10 \times 10 \times 10 \times 10 = 10^4.)$

Similarly, for example, $.643 = \frac{643}{1000}$ and the denominator is of the power of 10.

See Rules 2 and 3 for further explanations.

Rule 2: To convert a decimal fraction to a common fraction, rewrite the decimal fraction as a fraction that has the equivalent denominator in a power of 10 and then reduce the common fraction to the lowest term.

Rule 3: The number of digits in the decimal fraction is the same as the number of zeros in the denominator.

Example 1

Change .2 to a common fraction.

Solution

Using Rule 3, the number of digits in the decimal fraction is the same as the number of zeros in the denominator. The .2 has one digit, and therefore, has one zero in the denominator as follows: (use Rules 1 and 2)

$$.2$$
$$\uparrow$$
One digit (one decimal place).

$$.2 = \frac{2}{10} \quad \text{Numerator}$$

One digit ↗   ↖ One zero in the denominator

Note that one-digit decimal fraction changes to a fraction with one zero in the denominator. Note also that the decimal fraction two tenths is rewritten as the common fraction $\frac{2}{10}$.

$.2 = \frac{2}{10}$, we can reduce $\frac{2}{10}$ to the lowest terms by dividing the numerator and

the denominator of $\frac{2}{10}$ by 2 as shown:

$$\frac{\overset{1}{2}}{\underset{5}{10}} = \frac{1}{5} . \quad \text{Therefore, } .2 = \frac{1}{5}$$

Example 2

Change .36 to a common fraction.

Solution

Using Rule 3, the number of digits in the decimal fraction is the same as the number of zeros in the denominator.

.36 has two digits, and therefore, .36 has two zeros in the denominator as follows: (use Rules 1 and 2)

$$0.36$$

Two digits(two decimal places).

Numerator

$$.36 = \frac{36}{100}$$

Two digits   Two zeros in the denominator

Note that a two-digit decimal fraction changes to a common fraction with two zeros in the denominator. Note also that the decimal fraction thirty six hundredths is

rewritten as a common fraction $\frac{36}{100}$.

$.36 = \frac{36}{100}$, we can reduce $\frac{36}{100}$ to the lowest term by dividing

both 36 and 100 by 4 as shown:

$$\frac{\overset{9}{\cancel{36}}}{\underset{25}{\cancel{100}}} = \frac{9}{25}$$

Therefore, $.36 = \frac{9}{25}$

Example 3

Convert .613 to a common fraction.

Solution

Using Rule 3, the number of digits in the decimal fraction is the same as the number of zeros in the denominator.

.613 has three digits, and therefore, has three zeros in the denominator as follows: (use Rules 1 and 2)

$$0.613$$

Three digits (three decimal places).

Numerator

$$.613 = \frac{613}{1000}$$

Three digits   Three zeros in the denominator

Note that a three-digit decimal fraction changes to a common fraction with three zeros in the denominator. Note also that the decimal fraction six hundred thirteen thousandths is rewritten as common fraction $\dfrac{613}{1000}$.

$$.613 = \dfrac{613}{1000}, \text{ and } \dfrac{613}{1000} \text{ cannot be reduced to the lowest terms}$$

because there is no number that can divide both 613 and 1000 evenly (without a remainder.)

The required answer is $.613 = \dfrac{613}{1000}$

Example 4
Convert .0891 to a common fraction
Solution
Using Rule 3, the number of digits in the decimal fraction is the same as the number of zeros in the denominator.
.0891 has four digits, and therefore, has four zeros in the denominator as follows: (use Rules 1 and 2)

Four digits (four decimal places).

$$.0891 = \dfrac{\overset{\text{Numerator has four digits.}}{0891}}{10,000} = \dfrac{891}{10,000} \quad \text{Note: } 0891 = 891 \text{ because the 0 has no value.}$$

Four digits   Four zeros in the denominator

Note that a four-digit decimal fraction changes to a common fraction with four zeros in the denominator. Note also that the decimal fraction eight hundred ninety one ten-thousandths is rewritten as a common fraction $\dfrac{891}{10,000}$.

$$.0891 = \dfrac{891}{10,000} \text{ and } \dfrac{891}{10,000} \text{ cannot be reduced to the lowest}$$

terms because there is no number that can divide both 891 and 10,000 evenly (without a remainder).

The required answer is $.0891 = \dfrac{891}{10,000}$

Example 5
Change .009 to a common fraction.

Solution

Using Rule 3, the number of digits in the decimal fraction is the same as the number of zeros in the denominator.

.009 has three digits, and therefore, has three zeros in the denominator as shown: (use Rule 1 and 2)

$$0.009$$

Three digits (three decimal places).

$$.009 = \frac{009}{1000} = \frac{9}{1000}$$ Note: 009 = 9 because the 00 has no value.

Numerator

Three digits   Three zeros in the denominator

Note that a three-digit decimal fraction changes to a common fraction with three zeros in the denominator. Note also that the decimal fraction nine thousandths is rewritten as the common fraction $\frac{9}{1000}$ and $\frac{9}{1000}$ cannot be reduced to the lowest term because there is no number that can divide both 9 and 1000 evenly (without a remainder.)

The required answer is $.009 = \frac{9}{1000}$

The notes and the generous examples have provided me with the conceptual understanding and the computational fluency to do my homework.

Exercises

1. Explain how you can change a decimal fraction to a common fraction.

2. Change the following decimal fractions to common fractions: (Hint: See Example 1.) Reduce your answers to the lowest terms.

   (a) .1   (b) .4   (c) .6   (d) .7   (e) .9

3. Change the following decimal fractions to common fractions: (Hint: See Example 2.) Reduce your answers to the lowest terms.

   (a) .12   (b) .24   (c) .99   (d) .55   (e) .79

   (f) .27   (g) . 07   (h) .06   (i) .08   (j) .09

4. Convert the following decimal fractions to common fractions: (Hint: See Example 3.) Reduce your answers to the lowest terms.

   (a) .137   (b) .322   (c) .111   (d) .222

(e) .631   (f) .412   (g) .225   (h) .362

(i) .844   (j) .255   (k) .245   (l) .842

5. Change the following decimal fractions to common fractions: (Hint: See Example 4.) Reduce your answers to the lowest terms.

(a) .0148   (b) .0946   (c) .0777   (d) .0581

(e) .0419   (f) .0762   (g) .0518   (h) .0255

(i) .0733   (j) .0650   (k) .0205   (l) .0914

6. Change the following decimal fractions to common fractions: (Hint: See Example 5.) Reduce your answers to the lowest terms.

(a) .006   (b) .007   (c) .003   (d) .001

(e) .002   (f) .004   (g) .084   (h) .002

(i) .033   (j) .096   (k) .026   (l) .071

Challenge Questions.

7. Change the following decimal fractions to common fractions. Reduce your answers to the lowest terms.

(a) .29   (b) .008   (c) .05   (d) .239

(e) .2250   (f) .0431   (g) .0001   (h) .9854

(i) .33   (j) .7   (k) .06   (l) .225

(m) .3   (n) .090   (o) .90   (p) .117

(q) .0535   (r) .72   (s) .781   (t) .060

(u) .84   (v) .9   (w) .1114   (x) .3892

Answers to Selected Questions

2(a) $\dfrac{1}{10}$ 2(b) $\dfrac{2}{5}$ 3(d) $\dfrac{11}{20}$ 4(b) $\dfrac{161}{500}$

4(g) $\dfrac{9}{40}$ 5(a) $\dfrac{37}{2500}$ 5(i) $\dfrac{733}{10,000}$ 6(a) $\dfrac{3}{500}$

REAL WORLD APPLICATIONS - WORD PROBLEMS
How to Convert Common Fractions to Decimal Fractions

Example 1

Given that John walks .28 miles to school every day, write the distance as a common fraction of a mile. Hint: See Rules 1, 2, 3, and Example 3 under the topic, "Converting Decimal Fractions to Common Fractions."

Solution

Using Rules 1, 2, and 3,

$$.28 = \frac{28}{100} \quad \text{See Rules 1, 2, and 3.}$$

Two digits   Two zeros

Reduce $\frac{28}{100}$ to the lowest term by dividing both 28 and 100 by 4 as shown:

$$\frac{\overset{7}{\cancel{28}}}{\underset{25}{\cancel{100}}} = \frac{7}{25}$$

Therefore, $.28 = \frac{7}{25}$

Example 2

Write $.97 as a common fraction of a dollar. (Hint: See Rule 1, 2, 3, and Example 1.)

Solution

Using Rules 1, 2, and 3: $\quad .97 = \frac{97}{100}$

Two digits   Two zeros

Therefore, $.97 = \frac{97}{100}$

Example 3

Given that a certain pencil has a thickness of .31 of an inch. Write the thickness as a common fraction. Hint: See Rules 1, 2, and 3 under the topic "Converting Decimal Fractions to Common Fractions."

Solution

Using Rules 1, 2, and 3:

$$.31 = \frac{31}{100}$$

Two digits   Two zeros

Therefore, $.31 = \dfrac{31}{100}$.

Example 4

The decimal fraction .75 of a mile is equal to what common fraction of a mile?
Hint: See Rules 1, 2, and 3 under the topic "Converting Decimal Fractions to Common Fractions."

Solution

Using Rules 1, 2, and 3,

$$.75 = \dfrac{75}{100}$$

Two digits   Two zeros

Reduce $\dfrac{75}{100}$ to the lowest term by dividing both 75 and 100 by 5 as shown:

$$\dfrac{\overset{15}{\cancel{75}}}{\underset{20}{\cancel{100}}} = \dfrac{15}{20}$$

Still reduce $\dfrac{15}{20}$ to the lowest term by dividing 15 and 20 by 5 as shown:

$$\dfrac{\overset{3}{\cancel{15}}}{\underset{4}{\cancel{20}}} = \dfrac{3}{4}$$

Therefore, .75 mile = $\dfrac{3}{4}$ mile.

━━━━━━━━━━━━━━━ **The notes and the generous examples have provided me with the conceptual understanding and the computational fluency to do my homework.**

Exercises

1. Given that Eric walks .95 miles to school, write the distance as a common fraction of a mile. Hint: See Example 1.
2. Write $.92 as a common fraction of a dollar. Hint: See Example 2.
3. Given that a certain pen has a thickness of .28 of an inch. Write the thickness as a common fraction of an inch. Hint: See Example 3.

Challenge Questions

4. Write $.90 as a common fraction of a dollar.

5. Eric walks .65 miles to school, write the distance as a common fraction of a mile.

6. Given that a shoe lace is .125 inches thick, write the thickness as a common fraction of an inch.

MIXED REVIEW - SIMILAR EXTERNAL TEST
Exercises

1. Write the word phrase for each decimal fraction.

(a) .1	(b) .07	(c) .002	(d) .45
(e) .0007	(f) .120	(g) .945	(h) .114
(i) .0013	(j) .725	(k) .421	(l) 3.333

2. Write the decimal fraction for each word phrase.
(a) One tenths
(b) Seventy–eight thousandths
(c) Nine ten–thousandths
(d) Forty–two hundredths
(e) Two and five hundredths

COMPARING DECIMAL FRACTIONS

Mixed Review

How are common fractions compared? Common fractions are compared by converting the denominators to a common denominator (same denominator) and then we compare the numerators. The bigger the numerator, the bigger is the common fraction and the smaller the numerator the less the common fraction. Review the topic under "Comparing Fractions."

Comparing Decimal Fractions

Rule 1: To compare decimal fractions, change all the decimal fractions to decimal fractions that have the same number of decimal places by putting zeros behind the last digit until the desired number of the decimal places is achieved, and then compare the numbers of these decimal fractions with the common number of decimal places. The bigger the common fraction with the common number of decimal places, the bigger the value of the number.

Another way to compare or order decimal fractions is by using the number line such that the decimal fractions to the right of the number line are greater than the decimal fractions to the left of the number line. Review the section on number line.

Critical Thinking

Why can decimal fractions be compared by changing the decimal fractions to decimal fractions that have the same (common) number of decimal places? The answer is, it is easier to compare decimal fractions when the decimal fractions belong to the same tenths, hundredths, thousandths, ten-thousandths, or hundred thousands. For example, it is easier to compare two tenths (.2) to five tenths (.5) than to compare two tenths (.2) to fifteen hundredths (.15).

Example 1

Compare .9 and .85, which number is bigger?

Solution

Using Rule 1, change .9 and .85 to the same or common decimal places.
.85 has the higher number of decimal places of 2, and therefore, change .9 which has 1 decimal place also to 2 decimal places by putting a zero behind .9 as shown:

.9 = .90

One decimal place   Two decimal places.

We can now compare .90 and .85 because .90 and .85 have the same (common) number of decimal places of 2 as shown:
The bigger decimal fraction is .90 (90 hundredths), followed by .85 (85 hundredths). Therefore .9 is bigger than .85 or .9 > .85

Example 2

Which number is bigger, .65 or .7?

Solution

Using Rule 1, change .65 and .7 to the same (common) number of decimal places.
.65 has the higher number of decimal places of 2, and therefore, change .7 which has one decimal place also to 2 decimal places by putting zero behind .7 as shown:

Put a zero behind .7

.7 = .70

One decimal place   Two decimal places

We can now compare .65 and .70 because both .65 and .70 have the same (common) number of decimal places of 2 as shown:
The bigger decimal fraction is .70 (70 hundredths), followed by .65 (65 hundredths). Therefore, .7 is bigger than .65 or .7 > .65

Example 3

Arrange .5, .005, .05, and .0005 in order of the (a) biggest values first, (b) smallest values first.

Solution

Using Rule 1, change .5, .005, .05, and .0005 to the same (common) number of decimal places. Note that .0005 has the highest number of decimal places of 4 and therefore change .5, .005, and .05 also to 4 decimal places by putting zero/zeros behind .5, .005, and .05 as shown:

Changing .5 to four decimal places becomes;

Put 3 zeros behind .5

.5000

Four decimal places

Changing .005 to four decimal places becomes

Put a zero behind .005

.0050

4 decimal places.

Changing .05 to four decimal places becomes

Put two zeros behind .05

.0500

Four decimal places

We can now compare .5000, .0050, .0500, and .0005 because all the decimal fractions have the same (common) number of decimal places of 4 as follows:

The biggest decimal fraction is .5000 (five thousand ten-thousandths, followed by .0500 (five hundred ten–thousandths), followed by .0050 (fifty ten–thousandths), followed by .0005 (five ten–thousandths).

(a) Therefore, the required order showing the biggest number first is .5, .05, .005, .0005 or .5 > .05 > .005 > .0005

(b) The required order showing the smallest numbers first is .0005, .005, .05, .05, .5 or .0005 < .005 < .05 < .5

_____ **The notes and the generous examples have provided me with the conceptual understanding and the computational fluency to do my homework.**

Exercises

1. Explain how you could compare two or more decimal fractions.
2. Which decimal fraction is bigger? Hint: See Examples 1 and 2.
   - (a) .3, .314
   - (b) .6, .61
   - (c) .41, .39
   - (d) .25, .35
   - (e) .07, .7
   - (f) .8, .85
3. Which decimal fraction is smaller? Hint: See Example 1 and 2.
   - (a) .21, .20
   - (b) .3, .34
   - (c) .68, .60
   - (d) .01, .10
   - (e) .9, .09
   - (f) .5 , .55

4. Arrange the following decimal fractions in order with the biggest values first. Hint: See Example 3(a).
   - (a) .606, .066, .0066
   - (b) .1, .001, .010
   - (c) .250, .205, .025
   - (d) .35, .305, .351
   - (e) .75, .705, .751
   - (f) .202, .220, .022
   - (g) .743, .734, .704, .741
   - (h) .404, .414, .441, .399
   - (i) .81, .811, .801, .081
   - (j) .371, .47, .407, .372
   - (k) .734, .704, .747, .774
   - (l) .505, .550, .005, .500
5. Arrange the decimal fractions in order with the smallest values first. Hint: See Example 3(b).
   - (a) .03, .303, .003
   - (b) .4, .4001, .404, .0404
   - (c) .489, .561, .67, .067
   - (d) .250, .025, .25
   - (e) .140, .104, .110, .141
   - (f) .871, .666, .737
   - (g) .999, .099, .909, .919
   - (h) .550, .0519, .005
6. Select the decimals that have the same value. Hint: Apply Example 3.
   - (a) .001, .100, .101, .0010
   - (b) .0040, .04, .004
   - (c) .2 , .202, .20
   - (d) .90, .9, .901
   - (e) .5, .500, .505
   - (f) .08, .008, .0800
   - (g) .7, .07, .70
   - (h) .18, .180, .0180
   - (i) .0300, .03, .003
   - (k) .101, .0110, .011

Answers to Selected Questions

2(a) .314   3(a) .20   4(a) .606, .066, .0066

5(a) .003, .03, .303   6(a) .001 and .0010

REAL WORLD APPLICATIONS – WORD PROBLEMS

Decimal Fractions

Exercises
1. John is 6.5 feet tall and Nick is 5.8 feet tall. Who is taller?
Hint: See Example 2. Compare 6.5 to 5.8.
2. Frank walks .18 miles to school and Jamal walks .2 miles to school. Who walks further? Hint: See Example 2, compare .18 to .2.
3. Robin jogs 2.8 miles every day and Diana jogs 3 miles every day. Who jogs more? Hint: See Example 2, compare 2.8 to 3.
4. Five lengths of rods are 6.58 feet, 6.56 feet, 5.68 feet, 5.98 feet, and 6.01 feet.
(a) Arrange the lengths of the rods from the longest to the shortest.
Hint: See Example 3(a).
(b) Arrange the lengths of the rods from the shortest to the longest.
Hint: See Example 3(b).

ROUNDING OFF DECIMAL FRACTIONS
Decimals are rounded in the same way that whole numbers are rounded.
When a decimal fraction is rounded off, its true value is changed to an approximate value by limiting the number of the digits such as to the nearest tenth, hundredth, or thousandth.
Rule 1:
If the digit to the right side of the required place is 5 or greater than 5,
then the digit to the right of the required place is rounded up to 1 and the 1 should be added to the digit at the required place, but if the digit to the right of the required place is less than 5 then the digit to the right side of the required place remains the same.
Rule 2:
From Rule 1, if the digit to the right of the required place is 5 or greater than 5,
then the digit to the right of the required place is rounded up to 1 and this 1 should be added to the digit at the required place, but the true value of the 1 when:
(a) we round off to the nearest tenth is .1
(b) we round off to the nearest hundredth is .01
(c) we round off to the nearest thousandth is .001
(d) we round off to the nearest ten thousandth is .0001
(e) and so on.
Rule 3:
To round off decimal fractions, omit all the digits at the right side of the required place.
Special Note:
(a) To round off to the nearest tenth, the digit in the tenths place is the digit that
1 should be added to if the digit at the right side of the tenths place is 5 or

greater than 5.

(b) To round off to the nearest hundredth, the digit in the hundredths place is the digit that 1 should be added to if the digit at the right side of the hundredths place is 5 or greater than 5.

(c) To round off to the nearest thousandth, the digit in the thousandths place is the digit that 1 should be added to if the digit at the right side of the thousandths place is 5 or greater than 5.

(d) To round off to the nearest ten-thousandth, the digit in the ten-thousandths place is the digit that 1 should be added to if the digit at the right side of the ten-thousandths place is 5 or greater than 5.

Summary of How to Round off Decimal Fractions

Step 1: Locate the position of the digit and the digit in the question such as the tenths place for the nearest tenth, the hundredths place for the nearest hundredth, the thousandths place for the nearest thousandth, or the ten-thousandths place for the nearest ten-thousandth.

Step 2: Consider the digit at the right side of the required place in step 1 to determine if this digit is 5 or greater than 5 or not, and if this digit is 5 or greater than 5, then add 1 to the digit at the required place in step 1, and if the digit at the right side of the required place is less than 5, then just round off the decimal fraction to the required place without adding 1 to the digit at the required place. See the examples for detailed explanations.

Step 3: Omit all the digits after the required place digits such as the tenths place digit, the hundredths place digit, the thousandths place digit, or the ten-thousandth place digit.

Example 1

Round off .6891 to the nearest tenth.

Solution

Step 1: The digit at the tenths place is .6 as shown:

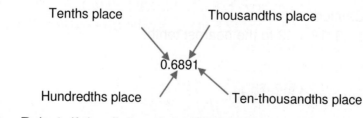

Tenths place   Thousandths place

0.6891

Hundredths place   Ten-thousandths place

Step 2: Using Rule 1, if the digit at the right side of the tenths place is 5 or greater than 5, then round up the digit to the right of the tenths place to 1 and add this 1 to the digit at the tenths place.

8 > 5, therefore, add 1 to .6

Using Rule 2, in this case $1 = $ one tenths $= \dfrac{1}{10} = .1$

Therefore,   .6
              + .1
              ‾‾‾‾
                .7

Step 3: The last three digits of .6891 which are 891 are omitted by using Rule 3 as shown:

.6891   becomes .6 + .1 = .7
↑↑↑
Omitted

Answer: .6891 = .7 to the nearest tenth.

Example 2

Round off .3418 to the nearest tenths.

Solution

Step 1: The digit at the tenths place is .3 as shown:

Tenths place   Thousandths place

0.3418

Hundredths place   Ten-thousandths place

Step 2: Using Rule 1, if the digit at the right side of tenths place is less than 5, then the digit to the right side of the tenths place is rounded down to 0 such that 0 should be added to the digit in the tenths place. Since 4 is the digit at the right side of the tenths place, and 4 is less than 5, add 0 to .3 as shown:

.3
+ 0
‾‾‾
.3

Step 3: The last three digits of .3418 which are 418 are omitted by Rule 3 as shown:

.3418 = .3 to the nearest tenth.
↑↑↑
Omitted

The required answer: .3418 = .3 to the nearest tenth.

Example 3

Round off .7643 to the nearest hundredth.

Solution

Step 1: The digit at the hundredths place is 6 as shown:

Tenths place   Thousandths place

0.7643

Hundredths place   Ten-thousandths place

308

Step 2: Using Rule 1, if the digit at the right side of the hundredths place is less than 5, then round down the digit at the right side of the hundredths place to 0 such that 0 is added to the digit at the hundredths place. Since 4 is the digit at the right side of the hundredths place, and 4 is less than 5, add 0 to .76 as shown:

$$\begin{array}{r} .76 \\ + \ \underline{0} \\ .76 \end{array}$$

Step 3: The last two digits of .7643 which are 43 are omitted by Rule 3 as shown:

.7643 = .76 to the nearest hundredth.
　　　 ↑↑
　　 Omitted

The required answer: .7643 = .76 to the nearest hundredth.

Example 4

Round off .2952 to the nearest hundredth.
Solution
Step 1: The digit at the hundredths place is 9 as shown:

Tenths place 　　　　　　　　 Thousandths place

0.2952

Hundredths place　　　　　　Ten-thousandths place

Step 2: Using Rule 1, if the digit at the right side of the hundredths place is 5 or greater than 5, then add 1 to the digit at the hundredths place. Since the digit at the right side of the hundredths place is 5 and 5 is equal to 5 add 1 to 9.

Using Rule 2, in this case, 1 = one hundredths = $\dfrac{1}{100}$ = .01.

Adding:　　　　.29
　　　　　+ $\underline{.01}$
　　　　　　.30

Step 3: The last two digits of .2952 which are 52 are omitted in the final answer by using Rule 3 as shown:

.2952 = .29 + .01 = .30 to the nearest hundredth.
　　　　↑↑
　　　Omitted

The required answer: .2952 = .29 + .01 = .30 to the nearest hundredth.

Example 5

Round off .1687 to the nearest thousandth.

Solution

Step 1: The digit at the thousandths place is 8 as shown:

Step 2: Using Rule 1, if the digit at the right side of the thousandths place is 5 or greater than 5, then add 1 to the digit at the thousandths place. Since 7 is at the right side of the thousandths place, and 7 is greater than 5, add 1 to 8. Using Rule 2, in this case, $1 =$ one thousandths $= \dfrac{1}{1000} = .001$

Adding:
$$\begin{array}{r} .168 \\ + .001 \\ \hline .169 \end{array}$$

Step 3: The last digit of .1687 which is 7 is omitted in the final answer by using Rule 3 as shown:

$$.1687 = .168 + .001 = .169 \text{ to the nearest thousandth.}$$
$$\uparrow$$
$$\text{Omitted}$$

The required answer is .1687 = .168 + .001 = .169 to the nearest thousandth.

Note: Detailed explanations in Example 1 to 5 are provided to give the student the vital understanding of the concept; however, the detailed explanations are not recommended for homework and tests.

Example 6

Round off the following to the nearest tenths without showing the detailed explanations.

(a) 2.68   (b) 3.41   (c) .761   (d) .4678   (e) .841

Solution

(a) $2.68 = 2.7$ because $8 > 5$, and therefore, 1 should be added to 6 to make 7 which is expressed in tenths as .7

(b) $3.41 = 3.4$ because $1 < 5$, and therefore, 0 is added to 4 which is expressed in tenths as .4.

(c) $.761 = .8$ because $6 > 5$, and therefore, 1 should be added to 7 to make 8 which is expressed in tenths as .8

(d) $.4678 = .5$ because $6 > 5$, and therefore, 1 should be added to 4 to make 5 which is expressed in tenths as .5

(e) .841 = .8 because 4 < 5, and therefore, 0 is added to 8 which is expressed in tenths as .8.

Example 7
Round off the following to the nearest hundredth without showing detailed explanations.

(a) 2.86514   (b) 3.640641   (c) .01841   (d) .00941   (e) .00392

Solution

(a) 2.86514 = 2.87 because 5 = 5, and therefore, 1 is added to 6 to make 7.
(b) 3.640641 = 3.64 because 0 < 5, and therefore, 0 is added to 4 to make 4.
(c) .01841 = .02 because 8 > 5, and therefore, 1 is added to 1 to make 2.
(d) .00941 = .01 because 9 > 5, and therefore. 1 is added to 0 to make 1.
(e) .00392 = .00 = 0 because 3 < 5, and therefore, 0 is added to zero to make 0.

Example 8
Round off the following to the nearest thousandth without detailed explanations.

(a) .11580   (b) .9642   (c) .0027   (d) .4119   (e) .42238

Solution

(a) .11580 = .116 because 8 > 5, and therefore, 1 is added to 5 to make 6.
(b) .9642 = .964 because 2 < 5, and therefore, 0 is added 4 to make 4.
(c) .0027 = .003 because 7 > 5, and therefore, 1 is added to 2 to make 3.
(d) .4119 = .412 because 9 > 5, and therefore, 1 is added to 1 to make 2.
(e) .42238 = .422 because 3 < 5, and therefore, 0 is added to 2 to make 2.

The notes and the generous examples have provided me with the conceptual understanding and the computational fluency to do my homework.

Exercises
1. Round off the following to the nearest tenth. Hint: See Examples 1, 2, and 6.

  (a) .17   (b) .31   (c) .55   (d) .74   (e) .774
  (f) .4893   (g) .0918   (h) .861   (k) .418   (l) .064
  (m) .731   (n) .83416   (o) .306 ·   (p) .0109   (q) .3689

2. Round off the following to the nearest hundredth. Hint: See Examples 3, 4, and 7.

  (a) .114   (b) .9165   (c) .6582   (d) .78941   (e) .74562
  (f) .41184   (g) .9678   (h) .09092   (i) .01901   (j) .94561
  (k) .84119   (l) .60918   (m) .76009   (n) .04766   (o) .57618
  (p) .8488   (q) .8422   (r) .25841   (s) .66991   (t) .88654

Answers to Selected Questions.

1(a) .2   **1(h)** .9   **2(a)** .11   **2(h)** .09

REAL WORLD APPLICATIONS - WORD PROBLEMS
(See similar Examples 1 to 8)

The notes and the generous examples have provided me with the conceptual understanding and the computational fluency to do my homework.

Exercises

1. What is the approximate weight of .834 pounds of a metal rounded off to the nearest tenth?
2. The diameter of a rod measures 2.4610. Round off the measurement to the nearest hundredth.
3. A package of beef weighs 4.8126 pounds. Round off the weight to the nearest thousandth.
4. John weighs 155.468 pounds. What is the approximate weight of John rounded to the nearest hundredth?

REVIEW — SIMILAR EXTERNAL TEST AND CHALLENGE QUESTIONS

1. Round off the following to the nearest hundredth.

    (a) .008   (b) .1096   (c) 4.236   (d) .211361

    (e) 2.0491   (f) 9.9999   (g) .289   (h) .9895

2. Round off the following to the nearest tenth.

    (a) .09   (b) .68   (c) .0995   (d) 7.894
    (e) 9.9511   (f) .2861   (g) .0095   (h) 29.097

3. Round off the following to the nearest thousandth.

    (a) .0009   (b) 1.0007   (c) .68989   (d) .41148

    (e) .4891   (f) 2.6789   (g) 4.3811   (h) 3.8971

4. Which is the greatest decimal fraction?

    (a) .090, .909, .9909, .9, .990   (b) .5, .005, .5505, .5601

    (c) .6, .0606, .606, .6606   (d) 1.1, 1.01, .1100, 11.01

312

Answers to Selected Questions.

1(a) .01   **1(c)** 4.24   **2(a)** .1   2(d) 7.9   **3(b)** 1.001   **3(g)** 4.381   **4(b)** .5601

DECIMAL PLACES

The decimal places are the positions of the digits to the right of the decimal point as shown:

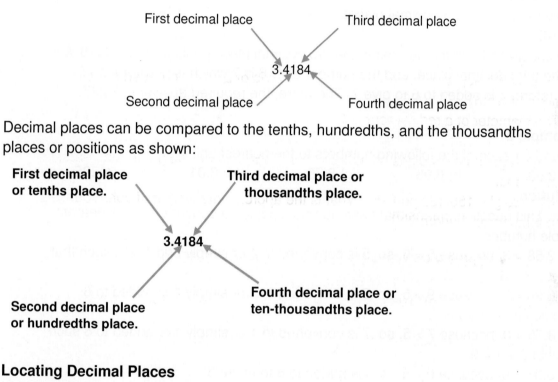

Decimal places can be compared to the tenths, hundredths, and the thousandths places or positions as shown:

First decimal place or tenths place.

Third decimal place or thousandths place.

3.4184

Second decimal place or hundredths place.

Fourth decimal place or ten-thousandths place.

Locating Decimal Places
Decimal places are located as shown:

two decimal places.
↓↓
3.4184
↑
One decimal place

three decimal places.
↓↓↓
3.4184
↑↑↑↑
four decimal places.

Note: How are decimal fractions rounded to a number of decimal places? Decimal fractions can be rounded to the nearest tenth, hundredth, and thousandth, and similarly, decimals fractions can be rounded to 1, 2, 3, 4, . . . decimal places by considering the digits to the right of the decimal point, such that if the digit to the right of the required decimal place is 5 or greater than 5, then 1 is added to the digit at the required decimal place and if the digit to the right of the required decimal place is less than 5, then 0 is added to the digit at the required decimal place.

Example 1
Convert 8.23678 to 3 decimal places.
Solution
We should first find the number in the 3rd decimal place position. In 8.23678, 6 is in the third decimal place, and the number after 6 is 7 which is greater than 5. Therefore, 1 is added to 6 to give 7. Therefore, the required answer is 8.237.

Example 2
Round off each of the following numbers to the nearest unit.
(a) 2.58   (b) 6.96   (c) 8.75   (d) 6.01   (e) .95
Solution
Hint: This question means that each number should be converted to the nearest whole number.
(a) $2.58 = 3$ because $5 = 5$, so .5 is converted to 1 or simply add 1 to 2 such that $2 + 1 = 3$.
(b) $6.96 = 7$ because $9 > 5$, so .9 is converted to 1 or simply 1 is added to 6 such that $6 + 1 = 7$.
(c) $8.75 = 9$ because $7 > 5$, so .7 is converted to 1 or simply 1 is added to 8 such that $8 + 1 = 9$.
(d) $6.01 = 6$ because $0 < 5$, so 0 is added to 6 to make 6.
(e) $.95 = 1$ because $9 > 5$, so .9 is converted to 1 or simply 1 is added to 0 such that $.95 = 0.95 = 0 + 1 = 1$

$$0 + 1 = 1$$

Example 3
Round off each of the following numbers to 1 decimal place. Hint: "to 1 decimal place" is the same as the nearest tenth.
(a) 1.46   (b) 2.894   (c) 6.63   (d).942
Solution
(a) $1.46 = 1.5$ because $6 > 5$, 1 is added to 4 to make 5.
(b) $2.894 = 2.9$ because $9 > 5$, 1 is added to 8 to make 9.
(c) $6.63 = 6.6$ because $3 < 5$, 0 is added to 6 to make 6.

(d) .942 = .9   because 4 < 5, 0 is added to 9 to make 9.

Example 4
Round each of the following numbers to 3 decimal places. Hint: "to 3 decimal places" is the same as to the nearest thousandth.
(a) 5.0847   (b) 94.14274   (c) 12.2418   (d) 3.48214   (e) .2346
Solution
(a) 5.0847 = 5.085 because 7 > 5, 1 is added to 4 to make 5.
(b) 94.14274 = 94.143 because 7 > 5, 1 is added to 2 to make 3.
(c) 12.2418 = 12.242 because 8 > 5, 1 is added to 1 to make 2.
(d) 3.48214 = 3.482 because 1 < 5, 0 is added to 2 to make 2.
(e) .2346 = .235 because 6 > 5, 1 is added to 4 to make 5.

══════════════ The notes and the generous examples have provided me with the conceptual understanding and the computational fluency to do my homework.

Exercises
1. Round off the following numbers to 3 decimal places. Hint: See Example 4.
   (a) 2.0148   (b) 4.2984   (c) .4289   (d) 12.4814

   (e) 5.6899   (f) .98718   (g) 1.4889   (h) 9.0089

2. How are decimal fractions rounded off to a number of decimal places?
3. Round off each of the following numbers to the nearest unit.
   Hint: See Example 2.
   (a) 9.01   (b) 10.82   (c) 2.11   (d) .944

   (e) 12.78   (f) 11.09   (g) 14.840   (h) .65091
4. Round off each of the following numbers to 1 decimal place.
   Hint: See Example 3.
   (a) .941   (b) .0814   (c) 2.129   (d) 6.089

   (e) 4.85   (f) 8.774   (g) .848   (h) 5.050

Challenge Question
5. Round off each of the following numbers to 2 decimal places.
   (a) .874   (b) 2.0998   (c) .908   (d) 3.145

   (e) 2.919   (f) 3.048   (g) 4.6185   (h) 4.1346

NEAREST WHOLE NUMBER.

To write a number to the nearest whole number means that the number should consist of whole numbers only. This means that the decimal part of the number should either be rounded up to 1 if the decimal is .5 or greater than .5, or if the decimal part is less than .5, the decimal part is rounded down to 0. If the decimal part is .5 or greater than .5, the decimal part is rounded up to 1 and this 1 is then added to the last digit in the whole number.

Example 1

Round off these numbers to the nearest whole number.

(a) .3   (b) .5   (c) .8   (d) 4.6

(e) 5.5   (f) 5.8   (g) 48.9   (h) 400.7

Solution

(a) .3 = 0 (to the nearest whole number because .3 < .5, so .3 is rounded down to 0.)

(b) .5 = 1 (to the nearest whole number because .5 = .5, so .5 is rounded up to 1.)

(c) .8 = 1 (to the nearest whole number because .8 > .5, so .8 is rounded up to 1.)

(d) 4.6 = 5 (to the nearest whole number because .6 > .5, so .6 is rounded up to 1 and the 1 is added to 4 to make 5; 4 + 1 = 5.)

(e) 5.5 = 6 (to the nearest whole number because .5 = .5, so .5 is rounded up to 1 and the 1 is added to 5 to make 6; 5 + 1 = 6.)

(f) 5.8 = 6 (to the nearest whole number because .8 > .5, so .8 is rounded up to 1 and the 1 is added to 5 to make 6; 5 + 1 = 6.)

(g) 48.9 = 49 (to the nearest whole number because .9 > .5, so .9 is rounded up to 1 and the 1 is added to 48 to make 49; 48 + 1 = 49.)

(h) 400.7 = 401 (to the nearest whole number because .7 > .5, so .7 is rounded up to 1 and the 1 is added to 400 to make 401; 400 + 1 = 401.)

The notes and the generous examples have provided me with the conceptual understanding and the computational fluency to do my homework.

Exercises

1. Round off the following numbers to the nearest whole number. Hint: See

Example 1 and compare how similar problems are solved.

(a) 5.14   (b) 100.2   (c) 55.8   (d) 16.5   (e) .8

(f) .01   (g) .75   (h) 1.04   (i) .005   (j) .0009

(k) 1.994   (l) 2.491   (m) .09   (n) .91   (0) 1.85

(p) 4.004   (q) 1.45   (r) 1.50   (s) 2.61   (t) 2.29

(u) .90   (v) 18.85   (w) 6.61   (x) 5.51   (y) 9.014

Challenge Questions

2. Round the following numbers to the nearest whole number.

(a) 25.09   (b). 99.9   (c) 200.61   (d) .1   (e) .69

Answers to Selected Questions.

1(a) 5   **1(h)** 1   **1(i)** 0

NEAREST TEN

Numbers may be written to the nearest ten and this means that the last digit of the number should be a zero. In this case, if the last digit of a number is 5 or greater than 5, then add 1 to the tens digit and replace the last digit of the number by 0, and if the last digit of the number is less than 5 do not add 1 to the tens digit, but replace the last digit of the number by 0.

Example 2

Round off the following numbers to the nearest ten.

(a) 2   (b) 8   (c) 23   (d) 48

(e) 81   (f) 182   (g) 103.2   (h) 108

Solution

(a) 2 = 0 (to the nearest ten because 2 < 5, so 2 is rounded down to 0.)

(b) 8 = 10 (to the nearest ten because 8 > 5, so 8 is rounded up to 10.)

(c) 23 = 20 (to the nearest ten because 3 < 5, so replace the last digit of the number by 0.)

(d) 48 = 50 (to the nearest ten because 8 > 5, so add 1 to the tens digit and replace the number at the last digit by 0.)

Further Explanation

48

／ ＼

40 + 8

↓   ↓ 8 is rounded up to 10.

40 + 10 = 50

(e) $81 = 80$ (to the nearest ten because $1 < 5$, so replace the last digit by 0.)

Further explanation

$$81$$

$$\swarrow \quad \searrow$$

$$80 \; + \quad 1$$

$$\downarrow \qquad \downarrow \; 1 \text{ is rounded down to } 0.$$

$$80 \; + \quad 0 = 80$$

(f) $182 = 180$ (to the nearest ten because $2 < 5$, so replace the last digit by 0.)

(g) $103.2 = 100$ (to the nearest ten because $3 < 5$, so replace the last digit of the whole number by 0.)

(h) $108 = 110$ (to the nearest ten because $8 > 5$, so add 1 to the tens digit and replace the last digit by 0.)

Further Explanation

$$108$$

$$\swarrow \searrow$$

$$100 \; + \; 8$$

$$\downarrow \qquad \downarrow \; 8 \text{ is rounded up to } 10.$$

$$100 \; + \; 10 \; = 110$$

The notes and the generous examples have provided me with the conceptual understanding and the computational fluency to do my homework.

Exercises

1. Round off the following numbers to the nearest ten. Hint: See Example 2(a).

(a) 3   (b) 1   (c) 4

2. Round off the following numbers to the nearest ten. Hint: See Example 2(b).

(a) 9   (b) 7   (c) 6

3. Round off the following numbers to the nearest ten. Hint; See Example 2(c) 2(e) and 2(f)..

(a) 52   (b) 14   (c) 33   (d) 201   (e) 94

4. Round the following numbers to the nearest ten. Hint: See Example 2(d) and 2(h).

(a) 78   (b). 36   (c) 69   (d) 306   (e) 155

5. Round the following numbers to the nearest ten. Hint: See Example 2(g).

(a) 44.3   (b) 167.1   (c) 94.4   (d) 29.26   (e) 208.5

Challenge Questions.

6. Round the following numbers to the nearest ten.

(a) 43.57   (b) 48   (c) 277   (d) 1   (e) 111

Answers to Selected Questions.

1(a) 0   **2(a)** 10   **3(a)** 50   **4(a)** 80   **5(e)** 210

NEAREST HUNDRED

Numbers may be written to the nearest hundred and this means that the last two digits of the number should be zeros. If the last two digits of a number are 50 or greater than 50, then this last two digits are rounded up to 100 and then added to the number. If the last two digits of the number are less than 50, then the last two digits are rounded down to zero. It may also be stated in a different way that if the last two digits of the number are 50 or greater than 50, then 1 should be added to the hundreds digit, and then replace the last two digits of the number with two zeros.

Example 3

Round off the following numbers to the nearest hundred.

(a) 10   (b) 48   (c) 51   (d) 95   (e) 154

(f) 199   (g) 201   (h) 265   (i) 762   (j) 865

Solution

(a) 10 = 0 (to the nearest hundred because the last two digits, which is 10, is less than 50, so 10 is rounded down to 0.)

(b) 48 = 0 (to the nearest hundred because the last two digits, which is 48, is less than 50, so 48 is rounded down to 0.)

(c) 51 = 100 (to the nearest hundred because the last two digits, which is 51, is greater than 50, and therefore, the 51 is rounded up to 100.)

(d) 95 = 100 (to the nearest hundred because the last two digits, which is 95, is greater than 50, and therefore, 95 is rounded up to 100.)

(e) 154 = 200 (to the nearest hundred because the last two digits, which is 54, is greater than 50, and therefore, 54 is rounded up to 100 so that 100 + 100 = 200.)

Further Explanation

154

100 + 54

↓   ↓54 is rounded up to 100.

100 + 100 = 200

319

(f) 199 = 200 (to the nearest hundred because the last two digits, which is 99,
is greater than 50, and therefore, 99 rounded up to 100, so that 100 + 100 = 200).

(g) 201 = 200 (to the nearest hundred because the last two digits, which is 01, is
less than 50, and therefore, 1 is rounded down to 0).

(h) 265 = 300 (to the nearest hundred because the last two digits, which is 65, is
greater than 50, and therefore, 65 is rounded up to 100 so that 200 + 100 = 300).

Further Explanation

(i) 762 = 800 (to the nearest hundred because the last two digits, which is 62,
is greater than 50, and therefore, 62 is rounded up to 100, so that 700 + 100 = 800).

Further Explanation

762

700 + 62

↓   ↓ 62 is rounded up to 100.

700 + 100 = 800

(j) 865 = 900 (to the nearest hundred because the last two digits, which is 65, is
greater than 50, and therefore, 65 is rounded up to 100, so that 800 + 100 = 900).

Further Explanation

The notes and the generous examples have provided
me with the conceptual understanding and the
computational fluency to do my homework.

Exercises

1. Round the following numbers to the nearest hundred. Hint: See Examples 3(a)
and 3(b).

(a) 35   (b) 49   (c) 25   (d) 1   (e) 17

2. Round the following numbers to the nearest hundred. Hint: See Examples 3(c) and 3(d).

    (a) 55   (b) 88   (c) 73   (d) 94   (e) 69

3. Round the following numbers to the nearest hundred. Hint: See Example 3(e) 3(f), 3(h) and (i).

    (a). 177   (b) 175   (c) 263   (d) 399   (e) 381

4. Round the following numbers to the nearest hundred. Hint: See Examples 3(g).

    (a) 401   (b) 125   (c) 202   (d) 738   (e) 849

Challenge Questions

5. Round the following numbers to the nearest hundred.

    (a) 94   (b) 999   (c) 25   (d) 510   (e) 678

Answers to Selected Questions.

1(a) 0   2(a) 100   3(a) 200   4(a) 400

NEAREST THOUSAND

Numbers may be written to the nearest thousand and this means that the last three digits should be zeros. If the last three digits of the number are equal to 500 or greater than 500, then the last three digits are rounded up to 1000 and the 1000 is added to the number. If the last three digits of the number are less than 500, then the last three digits are rounded down to 0. It can also be stated that when the last three digits of a number are 500 or greater than 500, then 1 is added to the thousands digit, and the last three digits of the number are replaced by zeros.

Example 4.

Round off the following numbers to the nearest thousand:

(a) 7   (b) 502   (c) 998   (d) 1,395

(e) 1,750   (f) 2,200   (g) 4,900   (h) 8,502

Solution

(a) 7 = 0 (to the nearest thousand because 7 is less than 500, so 7 is rounded down to 0.)

(b) 502 = 1000 (to the nearest thousand because the last three digits, 502, are greater than 500, so, 502 is rounded up to 1000.)

(c) 998 = 1000 (to the nearest thousand because the last three digits, 998, are greater than 500, so 998 is rounded up to 1000.)

(d) 1,395 = 1000 (to the nearest thousand because the last three digits, 395, are less than 500, so, 395 is rounded down to 0.)

(e) 1750 = 2000 (to the nearest thousand because the last three digits, 750, are greater than 500, so 750 is rounded up to 1000 so that: 1000 + 1000 = 2000.)

Further Explanation
1,750

1000 + 750
↓   ↓ 750 is rounded up to 1000.
1000 + 1000 = 2000

(f) 2,200 = 2000 (to the nearest thousand because the last three digits, 200, are than 500, and therefore, the 200 is rounded down to zero).

Further explanation
2,200

2000 + 200
↓   ↓ 200 is rounded down to zero.
2000 +   0 = 2000

(g) 4,900 = 5000 (to the nearest 1000 because the last three digits, 900, are greater than 500, so 900 is rounded up to 1000).

Further Explanation
4,900

4,000 + 900
↓   ↓ 900 is rounded up to 1,000.
4,000 + 1,000 = 5,000

(h) 8,502 = 9,000 (to the nearest 1000 because the last three digits, 502, are greater than 500, and therefore, 502 is rounded up to 1,000.

Further Explanation
8,502

8000 + 502
↓   ↓ 502 is rounded up to 1,000.
8000 + 1000 = 9000

Exercises

1. Round off the following numbers to the nearest thousand. Hint: See Example 4(a).
   (a) 90   (b) 2   (c) 479   (d) 249
2. Round off the following numbers to the nearest thousand. Hint: See Examples 4(b) and 4(c).
   (a) 570   (b) 904   (c) 744   (d). 666
3. Round off the following numbers to the nearest thousand. Hint: See Examples 4(d) and (4(f).
   (a) 1001   (b) 3,250   (c) 7073   (d) 5499

Challenge Questions

4. Round the following numbers to the nearest thousand.
   (a) 7002   (b) 1678   (c) 92   (d) 4590

Answers to Selected Questions.

   1(a) 0   2(a) 1000   3(a) 1000

ADDITION OF DECIMAL FRACTIONS

Rule 1:
Line up all the decimal points.
Rule 2:
Line up all the digits to the right and left of each decimal point according to their values such that hundredths should be under the hundredths column, the tenths should be under the tenths column and the ones should be under the ones column, and so on.

Align all decimal points

Hundreds column
Thousands column ———— Hundredths column

```
    5677.897
    1265.654
 +    78.678
```

Tens column ———— Thousandths column
Ones column ———— Tenths column

Rule 3:
Follow the procedure for adding whole numbers. (Regroup if necessary. You may review regrouping under the chapter, "Multiplication of Whole Numbers.")

Example 1
Add: 2.87 + .95
Solution
Step 1: Line up all the decimal points.

Decimal points should be lined up in a straight line.

```
   ↓
  2.87
+  .95
```

Step 2: Add the hundredths column first. Regroup if necessary.

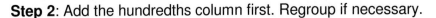

Hundredths column

```
    ₁
  2.87
+ 0.95
     2
```

Step 3: Add the tenths column second. Regroup if necessary.

Tenths column
Hundredths column

```
   ₁ ₁
  2.87
+ 0.95
    82
```

Step 4: Add the ones column third while the decimal point should be in line with the other decimal points.

Ones column — Tenths column

Hundredths column

$$
\begin{array}{r}
2.87 \\
+\ 0.95 \\
\hline
3.82
\end{array}
$$

Put the decimal point to be in line with other decimal points.

Therefore, 2.87 + .95 = 3.82

Example 2

Add: 4.78 + 9.68

Solution

Step 1: Line up all the decimal points.

Decimal points should be lined up in a straight line.

$$
\begin{array}{r}
4.78 \\
+\ 9.68 \\
\end{array}
$$

Step 2: Add the hundredths column first. Regroup if necessary.

Hundredths column

$$
\begin{array}{r}
4.78 \\
+\ 9.68 \\
\hline
6
\end{array}
$$

Step 3: Add the tenths column second. Regroup if necessary.

Tenths column — Hundredths column

$$
\begin{array}{r}
4.78 \\
+\ 9.68 \\
\hline
46
\end{array}
$$

Step 4: Add the ones column third and place the decimal point in line with the other decimal points.

Tenths column

Ones column — Hundredths column

$$
\begin{array}{r}
4.78 \\
+\ 9.68 \\
\hline
14.46
\end{array}
$$

Put the decimal point to be in line with the other decimal points.

Therefore, 4.78 + 9.68 = 14.46

Example 3

Add: 4.5 + 19.25 + .241

Step 1: Line up all the decimal points.

Decimal points should be lined up in a straight line.

```
     ↓
    4.5
   19.25
 +  .241
```

Step 2: Add the thousandths column first. Regroup if necessary.

Place a zero for each equivalent decimal

```
    4.500
   19.250
 +  .241
        1
```

Note: Zeros placed to the right of the last digit in a decimal fraction does not change its value.

Step 3: Add the hundredths column second. Regroup if necessary.

Hundredths column
↓

```
    4.500
   19.250
 +  .241
       91
```

Step 4: Add the tenths column third. Regroup if necessary.

Tenths column
↓

```
    4.500
   19.250
 +  .241
      991
```

Step 5: Add the ones column fourth, and write the decimal point. Regroup if necessary.

Ones column

```
    4.500
   19.250
 +  .241
    3.991
```

└── Put the decimal point to be in line with the other decimal points.

326

Step 6: Add the tens column fifth.

Tens column
↓

```
      4.500
     19.250
  +    .241
     23.991
```

Therefore, 4.5 + 19.25 + .241 + = 23.991

Example 4

Find the sum: 9.37 + 814.64 + 200 + 25.114

Solution

Step 1: Line up all the decimal points. Note that 200 is a whole number, so it should be written on the left side of the decimal point.

Line up all the decimal points
↓

```
     9.37
   814.64
   200.
  +  25.114
```

Step 2: Add the thousandths column first. Regroup if necessary.

Thousandths column
↓

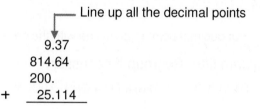

Place a zero for each equivalent decimal.

```
     9.370
   814.640
   200.000
  +  25.114
         4
```

Step 3: Add the hundredths column second. Regroup if necessary.

Hundredths column
↓

```
     9.370
   814.640
   200.000
  +  25.114
        24
```

Step 4: Add the tenths column third. Regroup if necessary.

327

Tenths column
↓

| \
9.370
814.640
200.000
+   25.114
124

Step 5: Add the ones column fourth and write the decimal point. Regroup if necessary.

Ones column
↓

||| \
9.370
814.640
200.000
+   25.114
9.124

Put decimal point to be in line with the other decimal points.

Step 6: Add the tens column fifth. Regroup if necessary.

Tens column
↓

||| \
9.370
814.640
200.000
+   25.114
49.124

Step 7: Add the hundreds column sixth.

Hundreds column

||| |
9.370
814.640
200.000
+   25.114
1049.124

The answer is 1049.124

The notes and the generous examples have provided me with the conceptual understanding and the computational fluency to do my homework.

Exercises

1. Find the sum. Hint: See Examples 1 and 2.

(a)   0.8
  + 0.7

(b)   4.5
  + 0.9

(c)   15.48
  + 6.93

(d)   14.04
  + 7.2

(d)   7.6
  + 9.3

(e)   8.36
  + 6.68

(f)   9.5
  + 2.74

(g)   3.7
  + 4.5

(h)   0.36
  + 5.38

(i)   23.04
  + 9.15

(j)   3.86
  + 4.7

(k)   7.05
  + 8.88

2. Find the sum. Hint: See Examples 3 and 4.

(a)   11.0
  13.01
  + 7.24

(b)   6.14
  2.846
  + 1.23

(c)   5.1
  12.24
  6.08
  + 1.41

(d)   51.23
  6.2
  35.321
  + 4.0

(e)   2.3
  4.2
  3.7
  + 4.4

(f)   6.34
  5.11
  + 7.7

(g)   4.45
  1.88
  + 0.22

(h)   33.56
  69.79
  + 88.45

3. Find the sum. Hint: See Examples 3 and 4.

(a) $22.4 + 7 + 478.607 =$

(b) $14.83 + 28.466 + 59.5 =$

(c) $19.93 + 44.095 + 147.2 =$

(d) $124.3 + 284.641 + 786.1482 =$

(e) $431.2 + 648.2361 + 248.69 =$

(f) $644.38 + 11 + 738.8291 =$

(g) $99.468 + 158.735 + 731 =$

(h) $539.348 + 624.84 + 2.9841 =$

(i) $8.4 + 7.5 =$

(j) $12.45 + 13.44 =$

(k) $77.32 + 15.20 + 1.7 =$

(l) $6.6 + 1.07 =$

(m) $15.22 + 13.44 =$

(n) $4.08 + 1.204 + 3.8 =$

Answers to Selected Questions

1(a) 1.5   **1(c)** 22.41   **2(a)** 31.25   **2(c)** 24.83

Challenge Questions

4. Add.

(a) $1.41 + 2.91 =$

(b) $1.39 + 6.76 =$

(c) $1.63 + 1.04 + 8 + 2.01 =$

(d) $2.9 + 3.641 + 4.09 =$

(e) $4.374 + 2.1 + 3.07 =$

(f) $7.7 + 3.001 + 14 + 25.34 =$

(g) $24.978 + 37.694 + 104.799 =$ (h) $84.39 + 78.84 + 99.189 =$

(i) 7.37
    $+\ 5.38$

(j) 43.62
    $+\ 7.15$

(k) 3.86
    $+\ 9.7$

(l) 7.05
    $+\ 4.44$

REAL WORLD APPLICATIONS – WORD PROBLEMS
Addition of Decimal Fractions

Example 1

John is a student at Peki High School in Ghana. His expenses for the week are shown in the table.

Expense Item	Monday	Tuesday	Wednesday	Thursday	Friday
Breakfast	$2.10	$1.98	$2.58	$2.25	$1.95
Lunch	$3.45	$2.95	$4.10	$3.98	$3.35
Dinner	$5.20	$4.65	$4.50	$4.30	$4.25

(a) Find his total expenses for breakfast.
(b) Find his total expenses on Thursday.

Solution

(a) Add all the money that John spent on breakfast.

$$
\begin{array}{r}
\overset{2\ 2}{\$2.10} \\
\$1.98 \\
\$2.58 \\
\$2.25 \\
+\quad \$1.95 \\
\hline
\$10.86 \quad \text{Answer}
\end{array}
$$

(b) Add all the money that John spent on Thursday.

$$
\begin{array}{r}
\overset{1\ 1}{\$2.25} \\
\$3.98 \\
+\quad \$4.30 \\
\hline
\$10.53 \quad \text{Answer}
\end{array}
$$

Example 2

Mary recorded that she traveled the following distances last December: 10.6 miles, 34.8 miles, 155.8 miles, 65.5 miles, and 25.6 miles. What is the total miles that Mary traveled?

Solution

Add all the distances traveled by Mary. Regroup if necessary.

$$
\begin{array}{r}
^{123}10.6 \\
34.8 \\
155.8 \\
65.5 \\
+\quad 25.6 \\
\hline
292.3 \quad \text{miles.} \quad \text{Answer}
\end{array}
$$

The notes and the generous examples have provided me with the conceptual understanding and the computational fluency to do my homework.

Exercises

1. Alice is a student at the Hohoe Secondary School in Ghana. Her expenses for the week are shown in the table. Hint: See Example 1.

Expense Item	Monday	Tuesday	Wednesday	Thursday	Friday
Breakfast	$1.98	$2.25	$2.24	$1.85	$1.90
Lunch	$2.95	$3.30	$3.10	$3.25	$3.15
Dinner	$4.10	$43.95	$3.85	$4.15	$3.89

(a) What is the total amount that Alice spent on dinner?

(b) What is the total amount that Alice spent on breakfast?

(c) What is the total amount that Alice spent on lunch?

(d) Using your answers for (a), (b), and (c), what is the total amount that Alice spent on food?

(e) What is the total amount spent on Wednesday?

(f) What is the total amount spent on Friday?

2. Group exercise: Make an expense account table for an average student's breakfast, lunch, and dinner for a week at your school.

3. Nick bought a shirt for $18.25, a coat for $65.95 and a pair of shoes for $55.65. How much money did he spend?

4. A man saved $505.48 and $695.37 in two different banks. What is the total amount that he saved?

Mixed Review

1. Solve the following operations using the Order of Operations:

(a) $2 + 3 \times 4 =$ (b) $4 - 4 \div 2 =$ (c) $2^3 + 4 \div 2 =$

(d) $3^2 \div 3 - 2 =$ (e) $81 \div 9 \times 3 =$ (f) $12 + 6 - 4^2 =$

2. Change the following decimal fractions to common fractions:

(a) .007   (b) .28   (c) .0421   (d) .01

3. Round off the following to 3 decimal places :

(a) .4985   (b) 2.0174   (c) 1.9096   (d) 2.8901

4. Write each fraction as a mixed number.

(a) $\dfrac{9}{2}$ (b) $\dfrac{12}{7}$ (c) $\dfrac{17}{5}$ (d) $\dfrac{15}{2}$ (e) $\dfrac{23}{7}$

5. Write the mixed numbers as a fraction.

(a) $2\dfrac{1}{4}$ (b) $3\dfrac{1}{3}$ (c) $4\dfrac{1}{2}$ (d) $4\dfrac{6}{7}$

SUBTRACTION OF DECIMAL FRACTIONS

The method for adding decimal fractions is similar to the method for subtracting decimal fractions because both methods require you to:

(a) Line up all the decimal points.

(b) Line up all the digits to the right and left of each decimal point according to their values such that hundredths should be under the hundredths column, the tenths should be under the tenths column and the ones should be under the ones column and so on. Then, follow the procedure for subtracting whole numbers.

(c) Regroup if necessary. Note that during subtraction, borrowing is the process for regrouping.

Example 1

Subtract: .94 − .68

Solution

Step 1: Line up all the decimal points.

Decimal points should be lined up in a straight line.

```
    ↓
   .94
 − .68
 ──────
```

Step 2: Regroup if necessary. Subtract the hundredths column first.

332

Hundredths column

$$\begin{array}{r} 0.94 \\ -\ 0.68 \\ \hline 6 \end{array}$$

Note: We cannot subtract 8 from 4, so we borrow 1 from 9 to be added to 4 to make 14 because of the 1 we borrowed from 9 has a value of 10, and therefore 10 + 4 = 14. We can now subtract 8 from 14 to obtain 6. (All the digits at the hundredths column have values of hundredths. For example, when we subtracted 8 from 14 to obtain 6, we actually subtracted 8 hundredths from 14 hundredths to obtain 6 hundredths.)

Step 3: Subtract the tenths column second.

Tenths column

$$\begin{array}{r} 0.94 \\ -\ 0.68 \\ \hline 0.26 \end{array}$$

Note: 8 - 6 = 2 (All digits at the tenths column have values of tenths. For example, 8 - 6 = 2 is actually 6 tenths subtracted from 8 tenths to obtain 2 tenths.)

Write the decimal point to align with the other decimal points.

Therefore, .94 − .68 = .26

Notice that the zeros before the decimal points do not change the values of the decimal fractions.

Example 2

Subtract: .632 − .346

Solution

Step 1: Line up all the decimal points.

Decimal points should be lined up in a straight line.

$$\begin{array}{r} .632 \\ -\ .346 \\ \hline \end{array}$$

Step 2: Regroup if necessary. Subtract the thousandths column first.

Thousandths column

$$\begin{array}{r} 0.632 \\ -\ 0.346 \\ \hline 6 \end{array}$$

Note: We cannot subtract 6 from 2, so we borrow 1 from 3 to be added to 2 to make 12 because the 1 we borrowed from 3 has a value of 10, and therefore, 10 + 2 = 12. We can now subtract 6 from 12 to obtain 6. When we borrowed 1 from 3, it leaves 2 and this 2 is written immediately above the 3. (All digits in the thousandths column have values of thousandths. For example, when we subtracted 6 from 12 to obtain 6, we actually subtracted 6 thousandths from 12 thousandths to obtain 6 thousandths.)

Step 3: Regroup if necessary. Subtract the hundredths column second.

Hundredths column

$$
\begin{array}{r}
\overset{12}{\cancel{5}}\overset{}{\cancel{2}} \\
0.6\cancel{3}\cancel{2} \\
-\ 0.346 \\
\hline
86
\end{array}
$$

Note: From Step 2, we borrowed 1 from 3, leaving 2, but we cannot subtract 4 from 2, and therefore, we borrow 1 from 6 and this 1 is added to 2 to make 12. The 1 we borrowed from 6 has a value of 10, and therefore, 10 + 2 = 12 and the 12 is written above the 2 in the hundredths column. We can now subtract 4 from 12 to obtain 8. (All digits in the hundredths column have values of hundredths. For example, when we subtracted 4 from 12 to obtain 8, we were actually subtracting 4 hundredths from 12 hundredths to obtain 8 hundredths.)

Step 4: Subtract the tenths column third.

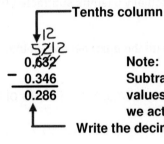

Tenths column

$$
\begin{array}{r}
\overset{12}{\cancel{5}}\overset{}{\cancel{2}} \\
0.6\cancel{3}\cancel{2} \\
-\ 0.346 \\
\hline
0.286
\end{array}
$$

Note: From Step 3, we borrowed 1 from 6, leaving 5 remaining. Subtract 3 from 5 to obtain 2. (All digits at the tenths column have values of tenths. For example, when we subtracted 3 from 5 to obtain 2, we actually subtracted 3 tenths from 5 tenths to obtain 2 tenths. Write the decimal point to align with the other decimal points.)

Therefore, .632 − .346 = 0.286

Example 3

Subtract without showing a detailed solution method:

(a) 4.4 − 1.261   (b) 58.48 − 12.8

Solution

(a)

$$
\begin{array}{r}
4.4 \\
-\ 1.261 \\
\hline
\end{array}
\quad\longrightarrow\quad
\begin{array}{r}
\overset{3\,9\,10}{4.4\cancel{0}\cancel{0}} \\
-\ 1.261 \\
\hline
3.139
\end{array}
$$

Place two zeros to help with the alignment of the digits.

(b)

$$
\begin{array}{r}
58.48 \\
-\ 12.8 \\
\hline
\end{array}
\quad\longrightarrow\quad
\begin{array}{r}
\overset{7\,14}{58.\cancel{4}8} \\
-\ 12.80 \\
\hline
45.68
\end{array}
$$

Place a zero here to help with the alignment of the digits.

The notes and the generous examples have provided me with the conceptual understanding and the computational fluency to do my homework.

Exercises

1. Subtract the following. Hint: See Examples 1 to 3, match questions with similar examples.

(a)   .9
  − .5

(b)   2.69
  − 1.79

(c)   4.84
  − .95

(d)   .948
  − .269

(e) .7 − .5 =

(f) 34.4 − 10.231 =

(g) .731 − .584 =

(h) .247 − .125 =

(i) 6.341 − 2.321 =

(j) 1.444 − .611 =

(k) 8.3 − 5.59 =

(l) 15.94 − 11.83 =

(m) 44.91 − 4.82 =

(n) 7.001 − 5.348 =

(o) 4.531 − 2.9 =

(p) 82.08 − 4.69 =

(q) 58.969 − 50.446 =

(r) 36.78 − 16.36

(s) 1.5 − .641 =

(t) $2.96 − $1.50 =

(u) $18.05 − $9.86 =

(v) 66.3 − 41.8 =

(w) 20.05 − 9.48 =

(x) 9 − .289 =

(y) 5 - 1.946 =

2. Subtract. Hint: See Examples 1 to 3, match questions with similar examples.

(a)   74.32
  − 14.44

(b)   .49
  − .28

(c)   .38
  − .09

(d)   .358
  − .147

(e)   .74
  − .52

(f)   .649
  − .438

(g)   6.891
  − 1.982

(h)   5.69
  − 1.78

(i)   37.06
  − 24.67

(j)   3.618
  − 1.729

(k)   55.7
  − 13.941

(l)   4.77
  − 2.894

(m)   .66
  − .38

(n)   .523
  − .334

(o)   29.01
  − 4.674

(p)   3.001
  − 1.982

Challenge Questions.

3. Subtract.

(a)   .56
  − .38

(b)   1.004
  − .846

(c) 57.8 − 22.976 =

(d) 18.02 − 9.866 =

(e)   6.641
  − 2.230

(f) 1.2 − .648 =

(g) .64 − .2782 =

(h) 4.6 − 2.2 =

REAL WORLD APPLICATIONS — WORD PROBLEMS
Subtraction of Decimal Fractions

Example 1
John went to the store with $100.00. If he bought a shirt for $18.95, how much money is left?

Solution

Total money that John took to the store = $100.00

Amount of money spent on the shirt   = $18.95

Amount left = Total money taken to the store – Amount spent

= $100.00 – $18.95

$$
\begin{array}{r}
\overset{\scriptstyle 9\,9\,9\,10}{100.00} \\
-\quad 18.95 \\
\hline
81.05
\end{array}
$$

Therefore, the amount left = $81.05

Example 2
Charles earns $20,000.00 per year and his brother earns $2,394.86 less, how much does his brother earn per year?

Solution

Charles' brother earns $20,000.00 – $2,394.86 which can be written as:

$$
\begin{array}{r}
\overset{\scriptstyle 1\,9\,9\,9\,9\,9\,10}{\$20,000.00} \\
-\quad 2,394.86 \\
\hline
\$17,605.14
\end{array}
$$

Therefore, Charles' brother earns $17,605.14.

Example 3
Eric took the bus to the store which is 4 miles from his house. He had a ride home which covered 3.725 miles, and he then walked the remainder of the distance home. How many miles did he walk home?

Solution

Total distance from Eric's house to the store = 4 miles.

Distance covered by the ride   = 3.725 miles.

Distance walked home =

Total distance to the store – Distance covered by the ride

= 4 – 3.725 miles.

$$\begin{array}{r} \overset{3\;9\;9\;10}{4.0\,0\,0} \\ -\;3.725 \\ \hline 0.275 \end{array}$$

Therefore, Eric walked 0.275 miles home.

Example 4

If George withdrew $245.36 from the bank, and he spent $50.30 on food, $46.01 on clothes, $18.95 on medicine and $32.58 on books, find how much money is left.

Solution

Add all the amounts that George spent and subtract the sum from the money that he withdrew from the bank in order to obtain the amount left.

Total amount spent is:

$$\begin{array}{r} {\scriptstyle |\;|\;\;|} \\ \$50.30 \\ \$46.01 \\ \$18.95 \\ +\;\$32.58 \\ \hline \$147.84 \end{array}$$

Therefore, total amount spent = $147.84

Amount of money left = Amount withdrew from bank – Total amount spent

= $245.36 – 147.84

$$\begin{array}{r} {\scriptstyle 1\;13/4\;\;13} \\ \$2\cancel{4}5.\cancel{3}6 \\ -\;\$147.84 \\ \hline \$97.52 \end{array}$$

Therefore, the amount of money left = $97.52

The notes and the generous examples have provided me with the conceptual understanding and the computational fluency to do my homework.

Exercises

1. Isabel went to the store with $200.00. She spent a total of $175.88 on food. How much is left? Hint: See Example 1.

2. Mary earns $30,000.00 per year and her brother earns $5,984.6 less, how much does her brother earn? Hint: See Example 2.

3. Sara was given 2.5 hours to play outside. If she used .2 hours to get to the play ground, .35 hours to play basket ball, .18 hours to talk to Ellen, and .58

hours to play soccer, how much of the time is left? Hint: See Example 4.

4. If Evans put a television set which cost $584.78 on a layaway plan and he made the following two payments, $64.35 and $78.98. How much does Evans still owe for the television? Hint: See Example 4.

Challenge Questions.

5. Ellen bought a computer for $945.58. If she made a down payment of $120.65 and an installment payment of $60.47, how much does she still owe?

6. A computer selling for $895.12 was reduced to $796.43. What is the amount of the reduction?

7. If Rebecca ran 150 yards in 56.48 seconds and a week later, she ran the same distance in 47.59 seconds, how much did she improve her time?

Mixed Review

1. $\begin{array}{r} 431 \\ + 679 \\ \hline \end{array}$

2. $\begin{array}{r} 911 \\ - 799 \\ \hline \end{array}$

3. $\begin{array}{r} 300 \\ - 177 \\ \hline \end{array}$

4. $\begin{array}{r} 294 \\ + 189 \\ \hline \end{array}$

5. $\dfrac{1}{2} \times \dfrac{2}{9}$

6. $\dfrac{4}{9} \div \dfrac{3}{8}$

7. $2\dfrac{3}{4} \times \dfrac{4}{11}$

8. $1\dfrac{3}{5} \div \dfrac{5}{6}$

9. $\begin{array}{r} 2.41 \\ - 1.84 \\ \hline \end{array}$

10. $\begin{array}{r} 7.348 \\ + 1.412 \\ \hline \end{array}$

11. $22 - 4 \div 2 =$

12. $14 \div 2 - 1 =$

13. $3 \times 4 \div 2 =$

14. $10 + 4 \div 2 =$

15. $10 + 4^2 \div 4 =$

16. $22 \times (12 - 2) + 1 =$

17. $2 - .584 =$

18. $14.34 - 2 =$

19. Arrange the following numbers with the smallest values first (arrange the numbers in ascending order).

   (a) .3, 3.03, .33, .303, 3.33   b) 5.55, .51, .505, 5.5, .55

20. Use the pattern to find the next two numbers:

   (a) 3, 6, 12, 24, 48, ____, ____.   (b) 18, 16, 14, 12, 10, ____, ____.

   (c) 4, 6, 8, 10, ____, ____.   (d) 1.1, 3.3, 9.9, 29.7, ____, ____.

21. Write each number as a common fraction, mixed number, and in words.

   (a) .75   (b) 6.2   (c) 37.001   (d) 181.08

   (e) .99   (f) 1.84   (g) .0001   (h) 1.1

22. Write each number as a decimal.

   (a) Nine and three tenths   (b) twenty-five and three thousandths

   (c) $\dfrac{1}{10}$ (d) $\dfrac{7}{100}$ (e) $\dfrac{31}{100}$ (f) $\dfrac{51}{1,000}$

(g) $\dfrac{731}{1,000}$ (h) $\dfrac{1}{10,000}$ (i) $\dfrac{9899}{10,000}$ (j) $2\dfrac{1}{4}$

23. Write each decimal in words.
    (a) 1.101   (b) 1.001   (c) .002   (d) .026
    (f) 5.78   (g) 12.709   (h) 628.2   (i) 628.264

24. What is the value of each bold digit?
    (a) 2.2**4**   (b) .**0**94   (c) 4.2**8**1   (d) 349.**7**8
    (e) .000**1**   (f) .00**9**   (g) .0**0**8   (h) 6**7**84.01

25. Replace each ? with <, >, or = .
    (a) 2.78 ? 2.87   (b) .75 ? .750   (c) 4.80 ? 48.08
    (d) 39.70 ? 39.700   (e) 2.99 ? 2.909   (f) 50.002 ? 50.0009

26. Write each list of numbers from the least to the greatest (write the numbers in ascending order.)
    (a) 12.728, 12.827, 12.782   (b) .2406, .2046, .2604
    (c) 2.984, 29.84, 2.998, 2.909   (d) 431.211, 43.1211, 43.099

27. Write each list of numbers from the greatest to the least (write the numbers in descending order).
    (a) 2.77, 2.707, 2.077, 2.771   (b) 14.241, 1.424, 142.4, 14.074
    (c) 38.44, 3.844, 384.44, 38.994   (d) .48, .498, 4.001, 4.9

Answers to Selected Questions.

21(g) $\dfrac{1}{10,000}$ = one ten-thousandths.

MULTIPLICATION OF DECIMALS

New Words:
1. Multiplicand — The number that is to be multiplied by another.
2. Multiplier — A number by which another number is multiplied.
3. Product — The product is the answer to a multiplication problem.

         .7   ← Multiplicand
     × .2   ← Multiplier
         ?   ← Product (the answer to the multiplication problem).

The method of multiplication of decimal fractions by whole numbers is similar to the multiplication of whole numbers by whole numbers. The only difference is to remember to insert the decimal point at the correct position in the answer. The two rules involving all types of decimal multiplications are:

Rule 1.
First follow the procedure for multiplying whole numbers.

Rule 2.
Determine the correct position of the decimal point in the product by counting the total number of the digits to the right of the decimal points in the problem (considering both the multiplier and the multiplicand), and insert the decimal point in the product by counting as many digits of the product from right to left as there are in the problem.

Note: The number of digits to the right of the decimal point is equal to the number of the decimal places.

Example 1
Multiply: $.9 \times .8 =$
Solution
Step 1: Follow the procedure for multiplying whole numbers. This is Rule 1.

$$.9 \times .8 = 72 \qquad\qquad (9 \times 8 = 72)$$

Step 2: Determine the correct position of the decimal point in the product of 72 above. This is Rule 2.

One digit after the
decimal point.   Count two digits from right to left of the product and
     ↓   ⟋⟋ insert the decimal point because the problem has a
   .9 × .8 = .72   total of 2 digits after the decimal point in the problem.
     ↑
One digit after the decimal point.

Therefore, $.9 \times .8 = .72$

Example 2
Multiply: $.2 \times 4 =$
Solution
Step 1: Follow the procedure for multiplying whole numbers. This is Rule 1.

$$.2 \times 4 = 8 \qquad\qquad (2 \times 4 = 8)$$

Step 2: Determine the correct position of the decimal point in the product of 8 above. This is Rule 2.

One digit after the
decimal point.

$\searrow$ $\swarrow$ Count one digit from right to left of the product, and then
.2 × 4 = .8   insert the decimal point because the problem has a total
↑   of one digit after the decimal point in the problem.
There is no
decimal point.

Therefore, .2 × 4 = .8

Example 3
Multiply: .842 × 2 =
Solution
Step 1: Follow the procedure of multiplying whole numbers. This is Rule 1.

$$\begin{array}{r} .842 \\ \times \quad 2 \\ \hline 1684 \end{array}$$
   (842 × 2 = 1684)

Step 2: Determine the correct position of the decimal point in the product of 1684.
This is Rule 2.

3 digits after the
decimal point.

↓↓↓
.842
× ___2 ← There is no decimal point.
1.684 ← Product
↑
Count 3 digits from right to left of the product and then insert the
decimal point because the problem has a total of 3 digits after
the decimal point.

Therefore, .842 × 2 = 1.684

Example 4
Multiply: .842 × .2 =
Solution
Step 1: Follow the procedure for multiplying whole numbers, this is rule 1.

341

```
        .842
    ×    .2                        (842 × 2 = 1684)
       1684
```

Step 2: Determine the correct position of the decimal point in the product of 1684. This is Rule 2.

```
   .842  → There are 3 digits after the decimal point.
 ×   .2  →  There is 1 digit after the decimal point.
  .1684  ← Product
  ↑
```

Count 4 digits from right to left of the product and then insert the decimal point because the problem has a total of 4 digits after the decimal points.

Example 5.

Multiply: 78.949
         ×   0.31

Solution

Step 1: Follow the procedure for multiplying whole numbers. This is Rule 1.

```
        ²|³
      78.949 ◄────── There are three digits after the decimal point.
    ×    0.31 ◄────── There are two digits after the decimal point.
       78949
    + 2368470 ◄──────   Add this zero here in order to align the numbers.
      0000000    Add the last two zeros in order to align the numbers or place value.
      2447419 ◄────────── Product
```

Step 2: Determine the correct position of the decimal point in the product 2447419. This is Rule 2.

```
        ²|³
      78.949 ◄────── There are three digits after the decimal point.
    ×    0.31 ◄────── There are two digits after the decimal point.
       78949
    + 2368470 ◄──────   Add this zero here in order to align the numbers.
      0000000    Add the last two zeros in order to align the numbers or place value.
      24.47419 ◄──────── Product
       ↑
```

Count 5 digits from right to left of the product 2447419 and then insert the decimal point in the product because the problem has a total of 5 digits after the decimal points.

Therefore, the answer is 24.47419

Example 6

Multiply: 3.74×4.83

Solution

Step 1: Follow the procedure for multiplying whole numbers. This is Rule 1.

$$
\begin{array}{r}
3.74 \\
\times \quad 4.83 \\
\hline
1122 \\
+ \quad 29920 \\
149600 \\
\hline
180642
\end{array}
$$

29920 ←——— Add one zero here to align the numbers or the place value.

149600 ←——— Add two zeros here to align the numbers or the place values.

180642 ←——— Product

Step 2: Determine the correct position of the decimal point in the product 180642.
This is Rule 2.

3.74 ←——— There are two digits after the decimal point.

$\times$ 4.83 ←——— There are two digits after the decimal point.

1122

+ 29920 ←——— Add one zero here to align the numbers or the place value.

149600 ←——— Add two zeros here to align the numbers or the place values.

18.0642 ←——— Product

Count 4 digits from right to left of the product 180642 and then insert the decimal point because the problem has a total of 4 digits after the decimal points.

The answer is 18.0642

The notes and the generous examples have provided me with the conceptual understanding and the computational fluency to do my homework.

Exercises

1. What two major steps or rules should you follow when doing multiplication involving decimals?

2. Multiply. Hint: See Example 1.

(a) $.4 \times .4 =$ (b) $.3 \times .5 =$ (c) $.7 \times .7 =$

(d) $.9 \times .2 =$ (e) $.10 \times .4 =$ (f) $.9 \times .5 =$

(g) $.6 \times .7 =$ (h) $.7 \times .6 =$ (i) $.5 \times .5 =$

(j) $.12 \times .1 =$ (k) $.3 \times .4 =$ (l) $.16 \times .4 =$

3. Multiply. Hint: See Examples 2 and 3.

(a) $.421 \times 3 =$ (b) $764 \times .3 =$ (c) $.148 \times 2 =$

(d) .52 × 4 =   (e) .981 × 5 =   (f) 8 × .431 =

(g) .641 × 6 =   (h) .251 × 2 =   (i) 734 × .2 =

(j) 841 × .4 =   (k) 232 × .9 =   (l) .24 × 3 =

(m) 4.06 × 16 =   (n) 631 × .016 =   (o) .07 × 9 =

(p) .013 × 4 =   (q) .72 × 7 =   (r) 2.11 × 6 =

4. Solve. Hint: See Example 4.

(a) .93 × .5 =   (b) .416 × .9 =   (c) .627 × .8 =

5. Solve. Hint: See Example 5.

(a)	24.41	(b)	3.64	(c)	5.04	(d)	2.982
	× .22		× .2		× .01		× .44

(e)	4.21	(f)	71.4	(g)	48.08	(h)	.05
	× .61		× .23		× .91		× .27

6. Solve. See Example 6.

(a)	4.37	(b)	4.9	(c)	34.71	(d)	73.2
	× 2.08		× 2.9		× 3.2		× 3.7

(e)	9.48	(f)	2.6	(g)	9.19	(h)	34.62
	× 2.41		× 5.7		× 8.12		× 2.03

Challenge Questions.

7. Solve.

(a) 28.041 × .08 =   (b) .8 × .9 =   (c) 946 × .7 =

(d) 7.04 × 3.41 =   (e) .7 × 6 =   (f) .741 × .24 =

(g) .4 × 3 =   (h) .009 × .45 =   (i) 30.64 × .09 =

(j) .07 × 1.09 =   (k) 7.04 × 1.08 =   (l) 36.6 × 29 =

Answers to Selected Questions.

2(a) .16   **3(a)** 1.263   **4(a)** .465   **5(a)** 5.3702   **6(a)** 9.0896

Special Cases.

Example 1

Solve: .4 × .1 =

Solution

Step 1: Follow the procedure for multiplying whole numbers, this is rule 1.

344

$$.4$$
$$\times \ \underline{.1}$$
$$4 \leftarrow \text{ Product} \qquad\qquad (4 \times 1 = 4)$$

Step 2: Determine the correct position of the decimal point in the product of 4. This is Rule 2.

$$.4 \leftarrow \text{ There is 1 digit after the decimal point.}$$
$$\times \ \underline{.1} \leftarrow \text{ There is 1 digit after the decimal point.}$$
$$4 \ \leftarrow \text{ Product}$$

There are a total of 2 digits after the decimal points in the problem, but the product has only one digit of 4.
We have to count two digits from right to left in the product and then insert the decimal point, but the product has one digit of 4 after the decimal point and therefore, we have to put 0 in front of 4 to make 04 before inserting the decimal point as shown:

$$.4$$
$$\times \ \underline{.1}$$
$$.04 \leftarrow \text{ The product has 2 decimal places or 2 digits after the}$$
$$\uparrow \qquad \text{decimal point.}$$
Add zero in order to make 2 digits after the decimal point.

Therefore, $.4 \times .1 = .04$

Example 2
Multiply: $.44 \times .2 =$
Solution
Step 1: Follow the procedure for multiplying whole numbers. This is Rule 1.

$$.44$$
$$\times \ \underline{.2}$$
$$88 \qquad\qquad (44 \times 2 = 88)$$

Step 2: Determine the correct position of the decimal point in the product of 88. This is Rule 2.

$$.44 \leftarrow \text{ There are 2 digits after the decimal point.}$$
$$\times \ \underline{.2} \ \leftarrow \text{ There is 1 digit after the decimal point.}$$
$$88 \ \leftarrow \text{ Product.}$$

There are a total of 3 digits after the decimal points in the problem, but the

345

product has only 2 digits of 88. We have to count 3 digits from right to left at the product, but the product has only two digits of 88, and therefore, place 0 in front of 88 to make 088. This makes the 3 digits in the product. Insert the decimal point after the 3 digits (after counting 3 digits from right to left) as shown:

$$
\begin{array}{r}
.44 \\
\times \quad .2 \\
\hline
.088
\end{array}
$$
← The product has 3 digits after the decimal point.

↑

Attach a zero in order to make 3 digits after the decimal point.

Therefore, .44 × .2 = .088

The notes and the generous examples have provided me with the conceptual understanding and the computational fluency to do my homework.

Exercises

1. Multiply. Hint: See Examples 1 and 2.

(a) .11 × .1 =   (b) .62 × .1 =   (c) .42 × .2 =

(d) .222 × .2 =   (e) .414 × .2 =   (f) .3 × .3 =

(g) .411 × .2 =   (h) .3211 × .2 =   (i) .243 × .3 =

Challenge Questions

2. Multiply: (a) .99 × .1   (b) .24 × .21   (c) 24.34 × .102

(d) .021 × .04   (e) 2.03 × 1.041   (f) .421 × 2.41

Answers to Selected Questions

1(a) .011   **1(h)** .06422

(Are you having fun with mathematics?)

346

REAL WORLD APPLICATIONS — WORD PROBLEMS
Multiplication of Decimals

Example 1

Eric bought a box of pencils for $3.48. If John wants to buy 5 boxes of the same pencils that Eric bought, how much will John pay for the 5 boxes of the pencils?

Solution

Setup:

Cost of 1 box of pencils = $3.48
Cost of 5 boxes of pencils = $3.48 × 5

Step 1: Follow the procedure for multiplying whole numbers, this is rule 1.

$$
\begin{array}{r}
^{2\ 4} \\
\$3.48 \\
\times \qquad 5 \\
\hline
\$1,740
\end{array}
$$
— Product

Step 2: Determine the correct position of the decimal point in the product of 1740. This is Rule 2.

$$
\begin{array}{r}
^{2\ 4} \\
\$3.48 \\
\times \qquad 5 \\
\hline
\$17.40
\end{array}
$$

$3.48 ◄——— There are 2 digits after the decimal point.
5 ◄——— There is no decimal point.
$17.40 ◄——— Product

Count 2 digits from right to left of the product and then insert the decimal point because the problem has a total of 2 digits after the decimal point.

Therefore, John paid $17.40 for 5 boxes of the pencils.

Example 2

How much will 112 erasers cost at $.28 each?

Solution

Setup: Cost of 1 eraser = $.28
Cost of 112 erasers = $.28 × 112

Step 1: Follow the procedure for multiplying whole numbers. This is Rule 1.

Ignore this zero

$$
\begin{array}{r}
\$0.28 \\
\times \qquad 112 \\
\hline
56 \\
280 \\
+ \quad 2800 \\
\hline
\$3,136
\end{array}
$$

56
280 ◄——— Inser a zero here to align the numbers or place values.
+ 2800 ◄——— Insert two zeros here to align the numbers or the place values.
$3,136 ◄——— Product

347

Step 2: Determine the correct position of the decimal point in the product 3136. This is Rule 2.

Ignore this zero

$0.28
× 112
─────
56
280 ◄──── Insert a zero here to align the numbers or place values.
+ 2800 ◄──── Insert two zeros here to align the numbers or the place values.
─────
$31.36 ◄──── Product

Count 2 digits from right to left of the product 3136, and then insert the decimal point because the problem has a total of 2 digits after the decimal point.

Therefore, 112 erasers costs $31.36

Example 3

Given that a box of tile weighs 24.68 pounds, how much would 4 boxes of the tile weigh?

Solution

Setup: Weight of 1 box of tile   = 24.68 pounds

Weight of 4 boxes of tile   = 24.68 × 4 pounds

Step 1: Follow the procedure for multiplying whole numbers. This is Rule 1.

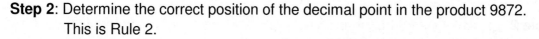

1 2 3
24.68
× 4
─────
9872 ◄──── Product

Step 2: Determine the correct position of the decimal point in the product 9872. This is Rule 2.

1 2 3
24.68 ◄──── There are 2 digits after the decimal point
× 4 ◄──── There is no decimal.
─────
98.72 ◄──── Product

Count 2 digits from right to left of the product 9872 and then insert the decimal point because the problem has a total of 2 digits after the decimal point.

Example 4:

Nick bought a computer set by paying 7 installment payments of $75.68 each. What is the total cost of the computer set?

Solution

Setup: 1 installment payment = $75.68

7 installment payments = $75.68 × 7

Step 1: Follow the procedure for multiplying whole numbers. This is Rule 1.

$$\begin{array}{r} \overset{3\;4\;5}{\$75.68} \\ \times \qquad 7 \\ \hline \$52,976 \end{array}$$ ⟵ Product

Step 2: Determine the correct position of the decimal point in the product of 52976. This is Rule 2.

$\overset{3\;4\;5}{\$75.68}$ ⟵ There are 2 digits after the decimal point.

$\times \qquad 7$ ⟵ There is no decimal point.

$\$529.76$ ⟵ Product

Count 2 digits from right to left of the product 52976 and then insert the decimal point because the problem has a total of 2 digits after the decimal point.

Therefore, the total cost of the computer set is $529.76

The notes and the generous examples have provided me with the conceptual understanding and the computational fluency to do my homework.

Exercises

1. A box of pens costs $4.98. If Jones bought 4 boxes of the same type of the pens, how much did he pay for them? Hint: See Example 1.
2. One eraser costs $.38, how much will 98 erasers cost? Hint: See Example 2.
3. A science book costs $75.59. How much will 35 of the same science books cost? Hint: See Example 2.
4. A box of nails weighs 24.94 pounds. How much will 9 boxes of the same type of nails cost? Hint: See Example 3.
5. Given that a car can be bought by paying 39 equal installments of $125.97, how much does the car cost? Hint: See Example 4.

Challenge Questions

6. If a mathematics book weighs 2.48 pounds, what is the weight of 27 of the same mathematics books?
7. If Beatrice can pay her school fees by making 9 equal installments of $48.79, how much is the total cost of her school fees?
8. Insert the decimal point in each product. Hint: Count the total number of digits after the decimal point in the problems.
   (a) $.8 \times .75 = 600$ (b) $24.84 \times .23 = 57132$

   (c) $.001 \times .075 = 000075$ (d) $4.09 \times .15 = 6135$

DIVIDING DECIMALS

New Terms/Review
Dividend — A number to be divided
Divisor   — The number by which a dividend is divided.
Quotient — The number obtained by dividing one number by another.

Dividend, divisor, and quotient are shown as shown:

Quotient

Dividend

Divisor

or

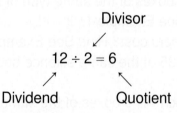

Divisor

$12 \div 2 = 6$

Dividend   Quotient

Dividing When the Dividend is a Decimal
In order to perform division involving decimals, follow the procedure for the
division of whole numbers, but you should be careful to know where to insert
the decimal point in the answer.

Rule 1
Use the long division symbol and insert a decimal point directly above the decimal
point in the dividend.

⌐ ← This is the long division symbol.

Rule 2
Then follow the procedure for the division of whole numbers.

Example 1

Divide: $4.2 \div 2$

Solution

Step 1: Follow Rule 1 by using the long division symbol and inserting a decimal point directly above the decimal point in the dividend as shown:

Insert a decimal point directly above the decimal point in the dividend

$2\overline{)4.2}$ ◄——Dividend

Step 2: Follow Rule 2 by following the procedure for the division of whole numbers.

$$
\begin{array}{r}
2.1 \\
2\overline{)4.2} \\
-\underline{4} \\
0\ 2 \\
-\underline{2} \\
0
\end{array}
$$

Therefore, $4.2 \div 2 = 2.1$

Example 2

Divide: $.42 \div 2$

Solution

Step 1: Follow Rule 1 by inserting a decimal point directly above the decimal point in the dividend.

Insert a decimal point directly above the decimal point in the dividend.

$2\overline{)0.42}$ ◄——— Dividend

Step 2: Follow Rule 2 by following the procedure for the division of whole numbers.

$$
\begin{array}{r}
.21 \\
2\overline{)0.42} \\
-\underline{4} \\
0\ 2 \\
-\underline{2} \\
0
\end{array}
$$

Therefore, $.42 \div 2 = .21$

Example 3

Divide: $.425 \div 5$

Solution

Step 1: Follow Rule 1 by inserting a decimal point directly above the decimal point in the dividend.

Insert a decimal point directly above the decimal point in the dividend.

5)0.425 ◄──────── Dividend

Step 2: Follow Rule 2 by following the procedure for the division of whole numbers.

Write 0 here because 4 < 5, and therefore, 5 cannot divide 4 easily.

```
      .085
5) 0.425
  - 40
    025
  -  25
     00
```

Therefore, .425 ÷ 5 = .085

Example 4
Divide: .0425 ÷ 5
Solution
Step 1: Follow Rule 1 by inserting a decimal point directly above the decimal point in the dividend.

Insert a decimal point directly above the decimal point in the dividend.

5)0.0425 ◄──────── Dividend

Step 2: Follow Rule 2 by following the procedure for the division of whole numbers.

Write 0 here because the 0 after the decimal point is < 5, which is the divisor.
Write 0 here because 4 < 5, which is the divisor.

```
       .0085
5) 0.0425
  - 040
    00 25
  -    25
       00
```

Therefore, .0425 ÷ 5 = .0085

Example 5
Divide: 2.52 ÷ 6
Solution
Step 1: Follow Rule 1 by inserting a decimal point directly above the decimal point in the dividend.

Insert a decimal point directly above the decimal point in the dividend.

6 ⟌ 2.52 ◄——— Dividend

Step 2: Follow Rule 2 by following the procedure for the division of whole numbers.

$$
\begin{array}{r}
.42 \\
6 \, \overline{)\, 2.52} \\
-\underline{24} \downarrow \\
12 \\
-\underline{12} \\
00
\end{array}
$$

Therefore, 2.52 ÷ 6 = .42

Example 6
Divide:

42 ⟌ 136.78   Give your answer to 2 decimal places.

Solution

Step 1: Follow Rule 1 by inserting a decimal point directly above the decimal point in the dividend.

Insert a decimal point directly above the decimal point in the dividend.

42 ⟌ 136.78 ◄——— Dividend

Step 2: Follow Rule 1 by following the procedure for the division of whole numbers.

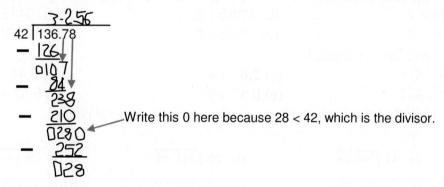

Write this 0 here because 28 < 42, which is the divisor.

Note: It is required in the problem to give the answer to 2 decimal places, but we have to work to three decimal places and then round up the second digit to the right of the decimal point, if the third digit is > 5, then 1 is added to the second digit to the right of the decimal point, but if the third digit is < 5, then 1 will not be added to the second digit to the right of the decimal point. In this particular case, the answer is 3.256 to three decimal places, and since the third digit to the right of the decimal point is 6 and 6 > 5, 1 is added to the second digit to the right of the decimal point as shown:

$$
\begin{array}{r}
3.25 \\
+1 \\
\hline
3.26
\end{array}
$$

Therefore, the answer is 3.26 to 2 decimal places.

━━━━━━━━━━━━━━━ **The notes and the generous examples have provided me with the conceptual understanding and the computational fluency to do my homework.**

Exercises

1. Divide. Hint: See Example 1.

(a) $9.3 \div 3$ (b) $2.2 \div 2$ (c) $8.2 \div 2$

(d) $5.5 \div 5$ (e) $6.2 \div 2$ (f) $4.8 \div 4$

(g) $8.4 \div 4$ (h) $2.8 \div 2$ (i) $6.3 \div 3$

2. Divide. Hint: See Example 2.

(a) $.93 \div 3$ (b) $.82 \div 2$ (c) $.42 \div 2$

(d) $.62 \div 2$ (e) $.48 \div 4$ (f) $.84 \div 4$

3. Divide. Hint: See Example 3.

(a) $.435 \div 5$ (b) $.246 \div 6$ (c) $.324 \div 4$

(d) $.332 \div 4$ (e) $.656 \div 8$ (f) $.365 \div 5$

4. Divide. Hint: See Example 4.

(a) $.0324 \div 4$ (b) $.0365 \div 5$ (c) $.0435 \div 5$

(d) $.0246 \div 6$ (e) $.0656 \div 8$ (f) $.0332 \div 4$

5. Divide. Hint: See Example 5.

(a) $3.55 \div 5$ (b) $2.64 \div 4$ (c) $6.44 \div 7$

(d) $7.44 \div 8$ (e) $8.37 \div 9$ (f) $5.52 \div 6$

6. Divide. Hint: See Example 6. Give your answer to 2 decimal places.

(a) $44\overline{)144.38}$ (b) $36\overline{)241.58}$ © $26\overline{)48.42}$

(d) $46\overline{)228.64}$ (e) $24\overline{)138.84}$ (f) $27\overline{)46.23}$

Answers to Selected Questions

1(h) 1.4   **2(a)** .31   **3(b)** .041

4(a) .0081   **5(a)** .71   **6(d)** 4.970

Challenge Questions
Divide.

(a) .64 ÷ 4

(b) .048 ÷ 12

(c) 6. 64 ÷ 8

(d) .00081 ÷ 3

(e) 9.2 ÷ 4

(f) 12.84 ÷ 32

REAL WORLD APPLICATIONS — WORD PROBLEMS
Dividing When the Dividend is a Decimal

Example 1
In a week, Nick spent $13.45 for his lunch at school. If he goes to school 5 days in a week, how much does he spend on his lunch daily. Assume that he spent an equal amount of money for his lunch every day.

Solution
Setup: In 5 days, Nick spent $13.45

In 1 day, Nick spent $ 13.45 ÷ 5

Step 1: Follow Rule 1 by inserting a decimal point directly above the decimal point in the dividend.

Insert a decimal point directly above the decimal point in the dividend.

5 ⟌ 13.45 ←——— Dividend

Step 2: Follow Rule 1 by following the procedure for the division of whole numbers.

$$
\begin{array}{r}
2.69 \\
5\,\overline{)\,13.45} \\
-10 \\
\hline
34 \\
-30 \\
\hline
45 \\
-45 \\
\hline
00
\end{array}
$$

Therefore, Nick spent $2.69 daily on lunch.

The notes and the generous examples have provided me with the conceptual understanding and the computational fluency to do my homework.

Exercises
1. Edward spent $14.75 weekly on his lunch at school. If he went to school five days in a week and he spent an equal amount of money daily on his lunch, how

much did he spend daily on his lunch? Hint: See Example 1.

2. The Aggor's family paid $4,806.6 for rent last year. What was the monthly rent? Hint:1 year = 12 months. Hint: See Example 1.

3. A man bought 5 boxes of the same type of tile for $61.65. How much did he pay for a box of tile? Hint: See Example 1.

Challenge Question

4. A lady paid $135.96 for 11 of the same type of shirts. How much did she pay for one shirt?

Answer to Selected Questions
(3) $12.33

DIVISION WHEN THE DIVISOR HAS A DECIMAL POINT

Rule 1
The divisor must always be a whole number before dividing.

How to Change a Decimal Divisor to a Whole Number.
The decimal point in the divisor must be removed before dividing. The decimal point in the divisor is removed by moving the decimal point towards the right of the decimal point such that the number of the movements of the decimal point should be equal to the number of digits after the decimal point. Since the decimal point in the divisor is moved towards the right of the decimal point so that the number of the movements of the decimal point is equal to the number of digits after the decimal point, the decimal point in the dividend should also be moved the same number of digits or places to the right. Each time a decimal point is moved one place to the right, it is the same as multiplying by 10. Review the section on "Place Values."

How to Divide With a Decimal Point in the Divisor.
After changing the decimal divisor to a whole number, follow the procedure for dividing whole numbers.

Example 1
Divide. 4.2 ÷ .2 =   Check your answer.
Solution
Step 1: Make the divisor a whole number, and this is Rule 1.

The divisor .2 has one digit after the decimal point, and therefore, the

356

decimal point should be moved one unit or one place to the right such that .2 becomes 2 which is a whole number as shown:

One unit movement to the right.

Step 2: Since the decimal point in the divisor is moved one unit or one place to the right, the decimal point in the dividend should also be moved one unit or one place to the right as shown:

One unit movement to the right.

Step 3: Follow the procedure for dividing whole numbers.

$$
\begin{array}{r}
21 \\
2\,\overline{)42} \\
-\,4 \\
\hline
2 \\
-\,2 \\
\hline
0
\end{array}
$$

Therefore, $4.2 \div 2 = 21$ Answer

Check your answer: Quotient × Initial Divisor = Initial Dividend

Quotient = 21, initial divisor = .2, and the initial dividend = 4.2

$$
\begin{array}{r}
21 \\
\times\ .2 \\
\hline
4.2
\end{array}
$$
← This is the initial dividend, and therefore, the answer is correct.

Example 2
Divide. $34.1 \div .11$ Check your answer.
Solution
Step 1: Make the divisor a whole number.

The divisor .11 has two digits after the decimal point, and therefore, the decimal point should be moved two units or two places to the right such that .11 becomes 11 which is a whole number as shown:

Decimal fraction   Whole number

.11 $\overline{)34.1}$ becomes   11 $\overline{)34.1}$

Two units of movements to the right.

Step 2: Since the decimal point in the divisor is moved two units to the right, the decimal point in the dividend should also be moved two units to the right as shown:

Write 0 here to obtain 2 units of the movement of the decimal point.

11 $\overline{)34.1}$ becomes   11 $\overline{)3410}$

Two units of movements to the right.

Step 3: Follow the procedure for dividing whole numbers.

$$
\begin{array}{r}
310 \\
11\overline{)3410} \\
-33 \\
\hline
11 \\
-11 \\
\hline
0 \\
-0 \\
\hline
0
\end{array}
$$

Therefore, 34.1 ÷ .11 = 310   Answer

Check your answer: Quotient × Initial Divisor = Initial Dividend

Quotient = 310, Initial Divisor = .11, and the Initial Dividend = 34.1.

$$310 \times .11 = ?$$

$$
\begin{array}{r}
310 \\
\times\ \ .11 \\
\hline
310 \\
3100 \\
\hline
34.10
\end{array}
$$

310 — Write this zero to align the numbers or place values.

34.10 ← This is the initial dividend, and therefore, the answer is correct.

Note that 34.10 is the same as 34.1.

Example 3

Divide. 24.36 ÷ 1.2   Check your answer,

Solution

Step 1: Make the divisor a whole number.

The divisor 1.2 has one digit after the decimal point, and therefore, the decimal point should be moved one unit to the right such that 1.2 becomes 12 which is a whole number as shown:

Decimal fraction

Whole number

$1.2 \overline{)24.36}$ becomes $12 \overline{)24.36}$

Move the decimal point one unit to the right.

Step 2: Since the decimal point in the divisor is moved one unit to the right, the dividend should also be moved one unit to the right as shown:

$12 \overline{)24.36}$ becomes $12 \overline{)243.6}$

Move the decimal point one unit to the right.

Step 3: Follow the procedure for dividing whole numbers.

Write this 0 here because the 3 in the quotient is < 12, and 12 is the divisor.

```
        20.3
   12 |243.6
      -24
         36
       - 36
          00
```

This 3 is < 12.

Check your answer: Quotient × Initial Divisor = Initial Dividend

Quotient = 20.3, Initial Divisor = 1.2, and the Initial Dividend = 24.36

$20.3 \times 1.2 = ?$

```
      20.3
   ×   1.2
      406
     2030   ← Write this 0 to align the numbers or place values.
    24.36   ← This is the initial dividend, and therefore, the answer
               is correct.
```

Example 4

Divide. $0.3042 \div .13 =$ Check your answer.

Solution

Step 1: Make the divisor a whole number.

The divisor .13 has two digits after the decimal point, and therefore, the

decimal point should be moved two units to the right such that .13
becomes 13, which is a whole number as shown:

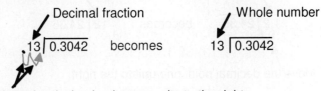

Move the decimal point two units to the right.

Step 2: Since the decimal point in the divisor .13 has been moved two units to the
right, the decimal point in the dividend should also be moved two units to
the right.

Move the decimal point two places to the right.

Step 3: Follow the procedure for dividing whole numbers.

$$\begin{array}{r} 2.34 \\ 13\overline{)30.42} \\ -26 \\ \hline 44 \\ -39 \\ \hline 52 \\ -52 \\ \hline 00 \end{array}$$

Therefore, $0.3042 \div .13 = 2.34$ Answer.

Check your answer: Quotient × Initial Divisor = Initial Dividend

Quotient = 2.34, Initial Divisor = .13 and Initial Dividend = 0.3042

$$2.34 \times .13 = ?$$

$$\begin{array}{r} 2.34 \\ \times\quad .13 \\ \hline 702 \\ +\quad 2340 \\ \hline .3042 \end{array}$$ ← Write a zero here as a place holder.

← This is the initial dividend, therefore, the answer is correct.

Note that .3042 is the same as 0.3042.

 The notes and the generous examples have provided
me with the conceptual understanding and the
computational fluency to do my homework.

Exercises

1. Divide. Check your answer. Hint: See Example 1.

(a) 9.3 ÷ .3 =   (b) 8.2 ÷ .2 =   (c) 6.2 ÷ .2 =

(d) 4.4 ÷ .4 =   (e) 7.7 ÷ .7 =   (f) 5.5 ÷ .5 =

(g) 6.3 ÷ .3 =   (h) 3.3 ÷ .3 =   (i) 8.8 ÷ .4 =

2. Divide. Hint: See Example 2. Check your answer.

(a) 25.2 ÷ .12 =   (b) 89.1 ÷ .11 =   (c) 27.3 ÷ .13 =

(d) 15.4 ÷ .14 =   (e) 13.2 ÷ .12 =   (f) 16.5 ÷ .15 =

(g) 33.6 ÷ .16 =   (h) 29.4 ÷ 14 =   (i) 45.1 ÷ .11 =

3. Divide. Hint: See Example 3. Check your answer.

(a) 24.24 ÷ 1.2 =   (b) 26.13 ÷ 1.3 =   (c) 36.12 ÷ 1.2 =

(d) 11.11 ÷ 1.1 =   (e) 28.14 ÷ 1.4 =   (f) 30.30 ÷ 1.5 =

(g) 15.15 ÷ 1.5 =   (h) 13.13 ÷ 1.3 =   (i) 32.32 ÷ 1.6 =

4. Divide. Hint: See Example 4. Check your answer.

(a) $.12\overline{)0.4092}$ (b) $.14\overline{)0.2982}$ © $.13\overline{)0.2769}$

(d) $.9\overline{)0.4068}$ (e) $.11\overline{)0.6204}$ (f) $.8\overline{)0.2736}$

(g) $.12\overline{)0.3216}$ (h) $.9\overline{)0.3078}$ (i) $.14\overline{)0.3402}$

Challenge Questions

5. Divide. Check your answer.

(a) 2.1 ÷ .3 =   (b) 3.6 ÷ .4 =   (c) 2.55 ÷ .5 =   (d) 1.44 ÷ 1.2 =

(f) 15.075 ÷ 2.5 =   (g) 38.4 ÷ 1.2 =   (h) .605 ÷ .5 =   (i) 38.4 ÷ .6 =

Answer to Selected Questions.

1(a) 31   **2**(a) 210   **3**(a) 20.2   **4**(a) 3.41

REAL WORLD APPLICATIONS — WORD PROBLEMS
Division When the Divisor has a Decimal Point

Example 1

If a pen costs $.23, how many pens of the same type can be bought with $3.45?

Solution

Setup: $.23 can buy one pen.

　　　　$3.45 can buy $3.45 ÷ .23 pens.

Step 1: Make the divisor a whole number.

　　　　The divisor .23 has two digits after the decimal point, and therefore, the decimal point should be moved two units to the right such that .23

361

becomes 23 which is a whole number as shown:

Move the decimal point two units to the right.

Step 2: Since the decimal point in the divisor is moved two units to the right, the decimal point in the dividend 3.45 should also be moved two units to the right as shown:

Move the decimal point two units to the right.

Step 3: Follow the procedure for dividing whole numbers.

Therefore, 15 pens can be bought with $3.45.

Example 2

Eric drove 25.2 miles in 1.2 hours. What is his speed per hour?
(Hint: Speed per hour = Distance traveled ÷ Time taken to travel).

Solution

Setup: Speed per hour = Distance traveled ÷ Time taken to travel the distance.
$$= 25.2 \div 1.2$$

Step 1: Make the divisor a whole number.

The divisor 1.2 has one digit after the decimal point, and therefore, the decimal point should be moved one unit to the right such that 1.2 becomes 12 which is a whole number as shown:

Move the decimal point one unit to the right.

Step 2: Since the decimal point in the divisor has been moved one unit to the right, the decimal point in the dividend should also be moved one unit to the right. Move the decimal point in the dividend also one unit to the right as shown:

$$12\overline{)25.2}$$ becomes $$12\overline{)252}$$

Move the decimal point one unit to the right.

Step 3: Follow the procedure for dividing whole numbers.

$$
\begin{array}{r}
21 \\
12\overline{)252} \\
-24 \\
\hline
12 \\
-12 \\
\hline
00
\end{array}
$$

Therefore, the speed per hour = 21 miles per hour.

Example 3

Alice bought a computer set on an installment plan for \$413.76. If her monthly payment is \$34.48, how many months will she be making the payment?

Solution

Setup: \$34.48 is the payment for 1 month.

\$413.76 is the payment for \$413.76 ÷ \$34.48 months.

Step 1: Make the divisor a whole number.

The divisor 34.48 has two digits after the decimal point, and therefore, the decimal point should be moved two units to the right such that 34.48 becomes 3448 which is a whole number as shown:

Decimal fraction   Whole number

$$34.48\overline{)413.76}$$ becomes $$3448\overline{)413.76}$$

Move the decimal point two units to the right.

Step 2: Since the decimal point in the divisor is moved two units to the right, the decimal point in the dividend should also be moved two units to the right as shown:

$$3448\overline{)413.76}$$ becomes $$3448\overline{)41376}$$

Move the decimal point two units to the right.

Step 3: Follow the procedure for dividing whole numbers.

$$3448 \overline{) 41376}$$

Therefore, Alice will use 12 months in making the payments.

The notes and the generous examples have provided me with the conceptual understanding and the computational fluency to do my homework.

Exercises

1. If an eraser costs $.61, how many similar erasers can be bought with $6.71? Hint: See Example 1.

2. Grace traveled 18.2 miles in 1.4 hours on her bicycle. What is her speed per hour? Hint: See Example 2.

3. George bought a camera for $19.36 on an installment plan. If he paid $1.21 monthly, how many months did he take to finish paying for the camera? Hint: See Example 3.

Challenge Questions

4. If a special pen costs $.27, how many similar pens can be bought for $3.24?

5. Alice bought a telephone for $47.79 on an installment plan. If she paid $5.31 monthly, how many months did she take to finish paying for the telephone?

6. Nick traveled 36.3 miles in 1.1 hour. What is his speed per hour?

Mixed Questions — Review

(1) $2.46 \div 6$ **(2)** $2.46 \div .6$ **(3)** $\dfrac{3}{4} \div \dfrac{3}{5} =$ **(4)** $\dfrac{4}{25} \times \dfrac{5}{16} =$

(5) $11.24 + .46 + 1.4 + 2 =$ **(6)** $\dfrac{1}{4} + \dfrac{2}{3}$ **(7)** $\dfrac{3}{4} - \dfrac{1}{3}$ **(8)** $4^2 - 10 =$

Dividing a Smaller Whole Number by a Bigger Whole Number

If one apple is shared by two students, each student will receive a fraction of the apple and similarly, after dividing a smaller whole number by a bigger whole number, the answer (quotient) will be a common fraction or a decimal fraction.

Rule 1: In order to divide a smaller number by a bigger number, put a decimal point and a zero behind the smaller number (dividend), and then put another decimal point directly above the decimal point in the dividend, and then divide as in whole numbers.

Rule 2: While dividing, continue to put zeros behind the dividend until the answer with the required number of the decimal places or digits after the decimal point such as the nearest tenths, nearest hundredths, nearest thousandths, or nearest ten-thousandths is obtained.

Example 1

Divide: $2 \div 3$, give your answer to the nearest tenth.

Solution

Step 1: Follow Rule 1, which is to put a decimal point and a zero behind the smaller number (dividend), and then put another decimal point directly above the decimal point in the dividend. Then, divide as in whole numbers.

Put a decimal point directly above the decimal point in the dividend.

$$3\overline{)2.0}$$
Note that 2 is the dividend.

Put a decimal point and a zero behind the dividend.

Step 2: Follow Rule 2, which is to continue to put zeros behind the dividend during division until the answer with the required number of the decimal places or the number of the digits after the decimal point such as the nearest tenths, hundredths, thousandths, or ten-thousandths is obtained.

Write this zero in order to continue the division.

Note: To work to the nearest tenths, we have to work to the nearest hundredths and if the hundredths position digit is 5 or greater than 5, then 1 is added to the tenths digit (we round up the tenths digit), and if the hundredths digit is less than 5, nothing is added to the tenths digit.

Since the quotient is .66, the 6 in the hundredths position is greater than 5, and therefore, 1 is added to the 6 at the tenths position to become 7 (we round up 6 to become 7.)

0.66

Hundredths

Tenths

Therefore, the final answer is .7 to the nearest tenths.

How many digits after the decimal point are required to round to the

nearest tenths, hundredths, thousandths, or ten-thousandths?

After reviewing the section on place values, the following table can be made.

To the nearest position	Number of digits after the decimal point
Nearest tenths	1
Nearest hundredths	2
Nearest thousandths	3
Nearest ten-thousandths	4

Example 2

Divide: $3 \div 8$, round off your answer to the nearest hundredths.

Solution

Step 1: Follow Rule 1, which is to put a decimal point and a zero behind the smaller number (dividend), and then put another decimal point directly above the decimal point in the dividend. Then, divide as in whole numbers.

Put a decimal point directly above the decimal point in the dividend.

Put a decimal point and a zero behind the dividend.

Step 2: Follow Rule 2, which states that, during division, is continue to put zeros behind the dividend until the answer with the required number of the decimal places or the number of the digits after the decimal point, such as the nearest tenths, hundredths, thousandths, or ten-thousandths is obtained.

Write this zero in order to continue the division.

Write this zero in order to continue the division.

Note: To work to the nearest hundredths, we have to work to the nearest thousandths and if the thousandths position digit is 5 or greater than 5, 1 is added to the digit at the hundredths position, but if the digit at the thousandths position is less than 5, nothing is added to the hundredths position. Since the quotient is .375, the digit at the thousandths position is 5, and therefore, 1 is added to 7 to make 8.

Hundredths

.375

Tenths

Thousandths

Therefore, the final answer is .38 to the nearest hundredths.

Example 3
Divide: 1 ÷ 12. Round off your answer to the nearest thousandths.
Solution
Step 1: Follow Rule 1, which is to put a decimal point and a zero behind the smaller number (dividend), and then put another decimal point directly above the decimal point in the dividend. Then, divide as in whole numbers.

Put a decimal point directly above the decimal point in the dividend.

$$12\overline{)1.0}$$

Put a decimal point and a zero behind the dividend.

Step 2: Follow Rule 2, which during division, is continue to put zeros behind the dividend until the answer with the required number of the decimal places or the number of the digits after the decimal point such as the nearest tenths, hundredths, thousandths, or ten-thousandths is obtained.

$$12\overline{)1.0}$$

Critical Thinking: From Step 2 above, 1.0 which is read as ten cannot be divided by 12, and therefore, a 0 is written after the decimal point in the quotient, and another zero is added to the dividend of 1.0 to make 1.00. (1.00 is read as one hundred). Note carefully that whenever two zeros are placed in the dividend before a division can take place, then a zero is placed in the quotient as a place holder as shown:

Place a 0 in the quotient as a place holder when the second 0 is placed in the dividend.

$$12\overline{)1.00}$$

Place the second 0 in the dividend.

Continue the division.

```
        .0833
12 | 1.00
    - 96
       40  ←——— Place a 0 here in order to continue the division.
     - 36
        40 ←——— Place a 0 here in order to continue the division.
      - 36
         4
```

Note: To work to the nearest thousandths, we have to work to the nearest ten-thousandths, and then if the ten-thousandths position digit is 5 or greater than 5, 1 is added to the digit at the thousandths position, but if the digit at the ten-thousandth position is less than 5, nothing is added to the thousandths position digit. Since the quotient is .0833, the 3 at the ten-thousandths position is less than 5, and therefore, nothing is added to the thousandths position digit.
Therefore, the final answer is .083 to the nearest thousandths.

The notes and the generous examples have provided me with the conceptual understanding and the computational fluency to do my homework.

Exercises

1. Divide and round your answer to the nearest tenths. Hint: See Example 1.

(a) $2 \div 6 =$ (b) $2 \div 7 =$ (c) $3 \div 4 =$ (d) $3 \div 7 =$ (e) $4 \div 6 =$

(f) $7 \overline{)5}$ (g) $8 \overline{)5}$ (h) $11 \overline{)8}$ (i) $12 \overline{)9}$ (j) $13 \overline{)2}$

(k) $9 \overline{)8}$ (l) $9 \overline{)2}$ (m) $7 \overline{)6}$ (n) $13 \overline{)4}$ (o) $12 \overline{)10}$

2. Divide and round your answer to the nearest hundredths. Hint: See Example 2.

(a) $8 \overline{)3}$ (b) $6 \overline{)1}$ (c) $12 \overline{)3}$ (d) $11 \overline{)2}$ (e) $9 \overline{)4}$

(f) $14 \overline{)7}$ (g) $13 \overline{)9}$ (h) $12 \overline{)3}$ (i) $15 \overline{)2}$ (j) $8 \overline{)7}$

(k) $3 \div 5 =$ (l) $3 \div 7 =$ (m) $2 \div 12 =$ (n) $9 \div 11 =$ (o) $5 \div 12 =$

3. Divide and round your answer to the nearest thousandths.
Hint: See Example 3.

(a) $1 \div 11$ (b) $2 \div 21$ (c) $1 \div 14$ (d) $2 \div 22$ (e) $2 \div 25$

(f) $15 \overline{)1}$ (g) $31 \overline{)3}$ (h) $16 \overline{)1}$ (i) $20 \overline{)1}$ (j) $25 \overline{)2}$

Challenge Questions

4. Divide, $1 \div 13$, round your answer to the nearest hundredths.

5. Solve, round your answer to the nearest thousandths.

(a) 8 ⟌16   (b) 24 ⟌2   (c) 9 ⟌2   di) 30 ⟌1   (j) 22 ⟌2

REAL WORLD APPLICATIONS — WORD PROBLEMS
Dividing a Smaller Whole Number by a Bigger Whole Number

Example 1

If 3 oranges sell for $2, what is the cost of 1 orange? Solve the problem without showing a detailed explanation.

Solution

Setup: 3 oranges cost $2

  1 orange cost $2 ÷ 3

Solve the problem without showing a detailed explanation.

1 orange will cost $.67

Example 2

If a package of 5 pencils sells for $2, what is the cost of 1 pencil? Solve the problem without showing a detailed explanation.

Solution

Setup: 5 pencils cost $2

  1 pencil costs $2 ÷ 5

Solve the problem without showing a detailed explanations.

1 pencil costs $.40

369

Example 3

A mechanic took 4 hours to repair 9 cars. Given that it takes the same amount of time to repair each car, find the time needed to repair 1 car. The answer should be in decimal fraction of an hour. Do not show a detailed solution method.

Solution

Setup: 9 cars were repaired in 4 hours.

1 car will be repaired in 4 ÷ 9 hours.

Solve the problem without showing a detailed solution method.

$$
\begin{array}{r}
.444 \\
9\overline{)4.0} \\
-36 \\
\hline
40 \\
-36 \\
\hline
40 \\
-36 \\
\hline
4
\end{array}
$$

The time needed to repair 1 car is .44 hours.

The notes and the generous examples have provided me with the conceptual understanding and the computational fluency to do my homework.

Exercises

1. If 7 oranges cost $3, what is the price of 1 orange? Hint: See Example 1.

2. A package of 12 pencils sells for $3. What is the cost of 1 pencil? Hint: See Example 2.

3. A technician can assemble 12 toys in 5 hours. How long does it take the technician to assemble 1 toy? Hint: See Example 3.

Challenge Questions

1. A man can assemble 15 similar toys in 7 hours. How long does it take the man to assemble 1 toy? Round your answer to the nearest hundredth of an hour.

Cumulative Review

(1) $4.348 - 1.2 =$

(2) $7.689 - 2 =$

(3) $\dfrac{3}{4} \div \dfrac{3}{2} =$

(4) $\dfrac{6}{7} \div \dfrac{14}{24} =$

(5) $1 \div 8 =$

(6) $22 - 17\dfrac{2}{5} =$

(7) $41 - 13\dfrac{1}{4} =$

(8) $2\dfrac{4}{5}$
$1\dfrac{1}{4}$
$+ \ 2\dfrac{3}{4}$

(9) $2\dfrac{1}{3}$
6
$+ \ 2\dfrac{3}{4}$

(10) $9^2 - 2^4 =$

(11) $12 - 8 \div 2 \times 3 =$

(12) $.041 \times 2.64 =$

(13) $2.67 \times .102 =$

(14) Given that $\dfrac{k}{3} \times 9 = 21$, find the value of k.

(15) Find each quotient and write each answer in the lowest terms.

(a) $6\dfrac{3}{4} \div 6 =$

(b) $9 \div 5\dfrac{3}{4} =$

(c) $4 \div \dfrac{2}{3} =$

(d) $\dfrac{6}{16} \div \dfrac{3}{8} =$

(e) $1 \div \dfrac{1}{9} =$

(f) $2 \div \dfrac{5}{8} =$

(g) $14 \div \dfrac{7}{11} =$

(h) $4\dfrac{1}{4} \div \dfrac{1}{2} =$

(16) Find each sum and write each sum in the lowest terms.

(a) $\dfrac{3}{7} + \dfrac{6}{7} =$

(b) $\dfrac{3}{5} + \dfrac{2}{3} =$

(c) $4\dfrac{3}{4} + 2\dfrac{1}{4} =$

(d) $3\dfrac{1}{5} + \dfrac{14}{8} =$

(e) $1\dfrac{1}{2} + 2\dfrac{1}{3} + 6\dfrac{1}{4} =$

(f) $\dfrac{1}{4} + \dfrac{5}{8} + \dfrac{1}{2} + \dfrac{3}{8} =$

(17) A lady paid $120.25 for 13 shirts. How much did 1 shirt cost?

Change Common Fractions to Decimal Fractions

To change common fractions to decimal fractions is the same as dividing a smaller whole number, by a bigger whole number, which was discussed in the preceding section.

Rule 1

In order to change a common fraction to a decimal fraction divide the numerator by the denominator.

Example 1

Change $\dfrac{3}{4}$ to a decimal fraction.

Solution

Follow Rule 1 and Rule 2 under the topic "Dividing a Smaller Number by a Bigger Whole Number."

The decimal fraction of $\dfrac{3}{4}$ is .75

> The notes and the generous examples have provided me with the conceptual understanding and the computational fluency to do my homework.

Exercises

Change the following common fractions to decimal fractions and round your answers to the nearest hundredths. Hint: See Example 1.

(a) $\dfrac{1}{4}$ (b) $\dfrac{2}{3}$ (c) $\dfrac{3}{5}$ (d) $\dfrac{7}{20}$ (e) $\dfrac{4}{17}$ (f) $\dfrac{1}{12}$

(g) $\dfrac{2}{9}$ (h) $\dfrac{4}{11}$ (i) $\dfrac{9}{15}$ (j) $\dfrac{13}{17}$ (k) $\dfrac{23}{28}$ (l) $\dfrac{49}{50}$

(m) $\dfrac{14}{40}$ (n) $\dfrac{23}{30}$ (o) $\dfrac{3}{13}$ (p) $\dfrac{4}{14}$ (q) $\dfrac{2}{17}$ (r) $\dfrac{5}{12}$

Answers to Selected Questions.

(a) .25   (k) .82

PERCENT

Percent Concept

The word **percent** means per one hundred. Percent may also be explained as a certain number out of 100. For example, 40 out of 100 students went to the zoo, means 40 percent went to the zoo and the 40 percent can be written as 40%. The 40% or 40 out of 100 can also be expressed as the fraction $\dfrac{40}{100}$.

The word percent is replaced by the symbol %. Note also that any common fraction that has a denominator of 100 can be expressed as a percent as shown:

(a) $\dfrac{12}{100} = 12\%$

(b) $\dfrac{8}{100} = 8\%$

(c) $\dfrac{99.9}{100} = 99.9\%$

(d) $\dfrac{300}{100} = 300\%$

(e) $\dfrac{100}{100} = 100\%$

(f) $\dfrac{2\frac{1}{2}}{100} = 2\frac{1}{2}\%$

(g) $\dfrac{\frac{1}{2}}{100} = \frac{1}{2}\%$

(h). $\dfrac{.8}{100} = .8\%$

(i) $\dfrac{1}{100} = 1\%$

Let us use the grid that has 100 squares to explain the concept of percent.

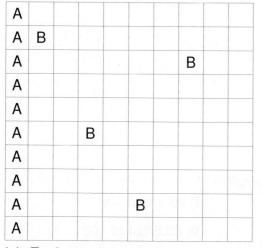

(**a**). Each square represents 1 out of 100 squares of the grid which can be expressed as one percent or 1%.

(**b**). There are 10 squares that contain the letter A, out of the 100 squares of the grid, and this can be expressed as 10 percent (10%) of the squares of the grid contain the letter A.

(**c**). There are 4 squares that contain the letter B, out of the 100 squares of the grid. This can be expressed as 4 percent (4%) of the squares of the grid contain the letter B.

Team Exercise

The class should be divided into four groups. Each group should use the grid to answer the following questions, and then report the answers to the class. The grid has a total of 100 squares.

What percent of the squares contain:

(**a**). Q   (**b**). P   (**c**). X   (**d**). M   (**e**). K

K		Q	X	K	P			P	
	M						M		
P		Q					Q		
P			K						
			P						
	K	K					Q		
P									
P		X	P		M		Q		

Example 1

70 out of 100 is what percent?

Solution

Step 1: Express 70 out of 100 as a percent.

$$70 \text{ out of } 100 = \frac{70}{100} = 70\%$$

Therefore, 70 out of 100 is 70%.

Exercises

Express the following as a percent. Hint: See Example 1.

(**1**) 2 out of 100   (**2**) 28 out of 100   (**3**) 23 out of 100

(**4**) 100 out of 100   (**5**) $78\frac{1}{2}$ out of 100   (**9**) 48.5 out of 100

Answers to Selected Exercises

(**1**) 2%   (**2**) 28%

$$= \frac{31}{1000} \times \frac{1}{25}$$

$$= \frac{31}{2500} \qquad 25 \times 100 = 2500$$

The required fraction is $\frac{31}{2500}$.

The notes and the generous examples have provided me with the conceptual understanding and the computational fluency to do my homework.

Exercises

1. Express the following percents as fractions and reduce the answers to the lowest terms if possible. Hint: See Examples 1, 2, and 3.
   (a) 27%   (b) 20%   (c) 135%   (d) 90%   (e) 110%

2. Express the following percents as fractions and reduce the answers to the lowest terms if possible. Hint: See Example 4.
   (a) $32\frac{1}{2}\%$ (b) $4\frac{2}{3}\%$ (c) $6\frac{3}{4}\%$ (d) $17\frac{1}{3}\%$ (e) $1\frac{1}{9}\%$

3. Express the following percents as fractions and reduce the answers to the lowest terms if possible. Hint: See Example 5.
   (a) .2%   (b) .7%   (c) .5%   (d) .3%   (e) .8%

4. Express the following percents as fractions and reduce the answers to the lowest terms if possible. Hint: See Example 6.
   (a) .14%   (b) .11%   (c) .15%   (d) .31%   (e) .70%

5. Express the following percents as fractions and reduce the answers to the lowest terms if possible. Hint: See Example 7.
   (a) .114%   (b) .133%   (c) .115%   (d) .131%   (e) .105%

Challenge Exercises

6. Express the following percents as fractions and reduce the answers to the lowest terms if possible.

   (a) .6%   (b) 75%   (c) $7\frac{3}{5}\%$ (d) .215%   (e) 135%

   (f) 10%   (g) 6%   (h) .12%   (i) $6\frac{1}{2}\%$ (j) 110%

1(a) $\dfrac{27}{100}$ 1(b) $\dfrac{1}{5}$ 2(a) $\dfrac{13}{40}$ 2(b) $\dfrac{7}{150}$

3(a) $\dfrac{1}{500}$ 3(b) $\dfrac{7}{1000}$ 4(a) $\dfrac{7}{5000}$ 4(b) $\dfrac{11}{10,000}$

5(a) $\dfrac{57}{50,000}$ 5(b) $\dfrac{133}{100,000,}$

REAL WORLD APPLICATIONS - WORD PROBLEMS
Express Percent as Fraction

Example 1

Yesterday, 2% of the students in a school were absent. What fraction of the students were absent?

Solution

Using the rule to express a percent as a fraction, write the percent number as the numerator over 100 and then reduce to the lowest terms if possible.

$$2\% = \frac{2}{100}$$

$$= \frac{\overset{1}{\cancel{2}}}{\underset{50}{\cancel{100}}} \qquad \text{Reduce to the lowest terms by dividing by 2.}$$

$$= \frac{1}{50}$$

The fraction of the students that were absent was $\dfrac{1}{50}$.

Example 2

A television set was reduced by 15%. What fraction of the price is the reduction?

Solution

Using the rule to express a percent as a fraction, write the percent number as the numerator over 100, and then reduce the fraction to the lowest terms if possible.

$$15\% = \frac{15}{100}$$

$$= \frac{\overset{3}{\cancel{15}}}{\underset{20}{\cancel{100}}} \qquad \text{Reduce to the lowest terms by dividing by 5.}$$

$$= \frac{3}{20}$$

The fraction of the price that was the reduction is $\dfrac{3}{20}$

Example 3

In a school, 65% of the students like soccer, what fraction of the students like soccer?

Solution

Using the rule to express a percent as a fraction, write the percent number as the numerator over 100, and then reduce the fraction to the lowest terms if possible.

$$65\% = \frac{65}{100}$$

$$= \frac{\overset{13}{\cancel{65}}}{\underset{20}{\cancel{100}}} \qquad \text{Reduce to the lowest terms by dividing by 5.}$$

$$= \frac{13}{20}$$

The fraction of the students that like soccer is $\dfrac{13}{20}$.

Example 4

A computer system was on sale at 10% off the regular price. What fraction of the regular price was the reduction?

Solution

Using the rule to express a percent as a fraction, write the percent number as the numerator over 100, and then reduce to the lowest terms if possible.

$$10\% = \frac{10}{100} \qquad \text{The reduction was 10\%.}$$

$$= \frac{\overset{1}{\cancel{10}}}{\underset{10}{\cancel{100}}} \qquad \text{Reduce to the lowest terms by dividing by 10.}$$

$$= \frac{1}{10}$$

The fraction of the regular price that was on sale is $\frac{1}{10}$.

> The notes and the generous examples have provided me with the conceptual understanding and the computational fluency to do my homework.

Exercises

1. 25% of the students in a class went to the zoo. What fraction of the students went to the zoo? Hint: See Example 1.
2. A television set was reduced by 10%. What fraction of the price is the reduction? Hint: See Example 2.
3. 75% of the students in a class like science. What fraction of the students like science? Hint: See Example 3.
4. A car is on sale at 6% off the regular price. What fraction of the regular price is the the reduction? Hint: See Example 4.
5. A house was sold at 8% off the original selling price. What is the fraction of the reduction of the price of the house? Hint: See Example 4.
6. 16% of the students in a class went to medical schools. What is the fraction of the students that went to medical schools? Hint: See Example 3.

Challenge Questions

7. 55% of the students at the Peki Secondary School are girls. What is the fraction of the girls in the school?
8. A printer was sold at 25% off the original price. What is the fraction of the reduction of the price of the computer?

Answers to Selected Exercises

1. $\frac{1}{5}$ 2. $\frac{1}{10}$ 3. $\frac{3}{4}$

Express Fractions as Percents

Recall that we already discussed the grid at the beginning of this chapter (Percent). One square out of the 100 squares in the grid can be written as 1% and this can be expressed as $\frac{1}{100}$. This means that if we have a fraction such as $\frac{1}{100}$ and we want to change the fraction which is $\frac{1}{100}$ to a percent, we have to multiply the fraction by 100, and then attach the % sign.

$$\frac{1}{100} \times 100$$

$$= \frac{1}{\underset{1}{\cancel{100}}} \times \overset{1}{\cancel{100}} \qquad \text{Do the division.}$$

$$= 1\%$$

Rule: To express a fraction as a percent multiply the fraction by 100, and then attach the % sign to the answer.

Example 1

Express $\dfrac{1}{10}$ as a percent.

Solution

Using the rule express the fraction as a percent by multiplying the fraction by 100, and then attach the % sign to the answer.

$$\frac{1}{10} \text{ as a percent} = \frac{1}{10} \times 100$$

$$= \frac{\overset{10}{\cancel{100}}}{\underset{1}{\cancel{10}}} \qquad \text{Reduce to the lowest terms by dividing by 10.}$$

$$= 10\%$$

Example 2

Change $\dfrac{2}{15}$ to a percent.

Solution

Using the rule express the fraction as a percent by multiplying the fraction by 100, and then attach the % sign to the answer.

$$\frac{2}{15} \text{ as percent} = \frac{2}{15} \times 100$$

$$= \frac{2}{\underset{3}{\cancel{15}}} \times \overset{20}{\cancel{100}} \qquad \text{Reduce to the lowest terms by dividing by 5.}$$

$$= \frac{40}{3} = 13\frac{1}{3}\%$$ Review the section on mixed numbers.

Example 3

Change $\frac{3}{7}$ to a percent.

Solution

Using the rule express the fraction as a percent by multiplying the fraction by 100, and then attach the % sign to the answer.

$$\frac{3}{7} \text{ as a percent} = \frac{3}{7} \times 100$$

$$= \frac{300}{7}$$

$$= 42\frac{6}{7}$$ Review the section on mixed numbers.

$$\frac{3}{7} \text{ as a percent} = 42\frac{6}{7}\%.$$

The notes and the generous examples have provided me with the conceptual understanding and the computational fluency to do my homework.

Exercises

1. Express the following fractions as percents. Hint: See Example 1.

   a) $\frac{1}{2}$ **b)** $\frac{1}{4}$ **c)** $\frac{1}{5}$ **d)** $\frac{1}{15}$ **e)** $\frac{1}{25}$ **f)** $\frac{1}{50}$

2. Express the following fractions as percents. Hint: See Example 2.

   a) $\frac{2}{5}$ **b)** $\frac{3}{10}$ **c)** $\frac{4}{5}$ **d)** $\frac{4}{15}$ **e)** $\frac{1}{25}$ **f)** $\frac{7}{25}$

3. Change the following fractions to percents. Hint: See Example 3.

   a). $\frac{2}{3}$ **b).** $\frac{2}{7}$ **c).** $\frac{2}{9}$ **d).** $\frac{3}{8}$ **e).** $\frac{3}{11}$ **f).** $\frac{5}{12}$

Challenge Questions

4. Change the following fractions to percents.

a) $\dfrac{4}{15}$ b). $\dfrac{1}{3}$ c). $\dfrac{1}{20}$ d). $\dfrac{7}{30}$ e). $\dfrac{7}{8}$ f). $\dfrac{4}{9}$

Answers to Selected Exercises

1(a) 50%   **1(b)** 25%   **2(a)** 40%   **2(b)** 30%

3(a) $66\dfrac{2}{3}\%$ **3(b)** $28\dfrac{4}{7}\%$

REAL WORLD APPLICATIONS – WORD PROBLEMS
Express Fractions as Percents (More Examples)

Example 1

Given that $\dfrac{4}{5}$ of the students in a high school like soccer. What percent of

the students like soccer?

Solution

Using the rule express the fraction as a percent by multiplying the fraction by 100, and then attach the % sign to the answer.

Percent of the student population $= 100\%$

Percent of $\dfrac{4}{5}$ of the students like soccer $= \dfrac{4}{5}$ of 100%

$$= \dfrac{4}{5} \times 100\% \quad \text{"of" becomes a}$$

multiplication sign.

$$= \dfrac{4}{\underset{1}{\cancel{5}}} \times \overset{20\%}{\cancel{100\%}} \quad \text{Divide by 5.}$$

$$= 4 \times 20\% = 80\%$$

Therefore, 80% of the students like soccer.

Example 2

A television set was reduced by $\dfrac{1}{5}$ off the regular price. What was the percent

of reduction in the price?

Solution

Using the rule express the fraction as a percent by multiplying the fraction by 100, and then attach the % sign to the answer.

The percent of the original price of the television set = 100%

The percent of $\frac{1}{5}$ off the original price $= \frac{1}{5}$ of 100%

$$\downarrow \quad \downarrow \quad \downarrow$$

$$= \frac{1}{5} \times 100\% \quad \text{"of" becomes a multiplication sign.}$$

$$= \frac{1}{\cancel{5}} \times \overset{20}{\cancel{100}}\% \quad \begin{array}{l}\text{Reduce to the lowest terms by}\\ \text{dividing by 5.}\end{array}$$

$$= 20\%$$

The percent of reduction in the price = 20%

━━━━━━━━━━━━━━━━ **The notes and the generous examples have provided me with the conceptual understanding and the computational fluency to do my homework.**

Exercises

1. Given that $\frac{1}{25}$ of the workers in a plant are engineers, what percent of the workers are engineers? Hint: See Example 1.

2. A computer set was reduced by $\frac{1}{15}$ off the regular price. What was the percentage of reduction in price? Hint: See Example 2.

Challenge Questions

3. In 1990, the population of the Peki High School was 950 students. In 1991, the students population increased by $\frac{1}{10}$.

   a. What is the increase of the population of the students in 1991?

   Hint: The increase of the population of the students $= \frac{1}{10} \times 950$

   b. What is the percent increase of the population of the students?
   c. What is the population of the students in 1991?
   Hint: Population of the students in 1991
   $\qquad\qquad$ = Population in 1990 + Increase in population.

4. A television set was increased by $\frac{3}{50}$ of the regular price. What was the percent increase in price?

Express Percents as Decimals

Recall that we already discussed the grid at the beginning of this chapter (percent). One square out of the 100 squares in the grid can be written as 1% and this can be expressed as $\dfrac{1}{100}$. Recall from the chapter on decimal fractions that the fraction $\dfrac{1}{100}$ can be changed to a decimal by dividing 1 by 100 as shown:

$$100\overline{)1} = 100\overline{)\overset{.01}{100}}$$
$$\underline{-\ 100}$$
$$000$$

Therefore, $1\% = \dfrac{1}{100} = .01$. Note that 1% is changed to the decimal fraction .01 by dividing 1 by 100 or simply moving the decimal point in the percent number two places or two digits to the left.

Decimal point

Write 0 here to hold the place value.

$$1\% = \,.01 = .01$$

Move the imaginary decimal point behind 1 two places or two digits to the left.

Note: There is an imaginary decimal point behind the last digit of all whole numbers. (Review the chapter on decimal fractions.)

Rule: To express a percent as a decimal fraction, move the decimal point in the percent number two places or two digits to the left of the decimal point, and ignore the percent sign.

Example 1
Express 25.5% as a decimal fraction.
Solution
Using the rule, to express a percent as a decimal fraction, move the decimal point in the percent number two places or two digits to the left of the decimal point, and ignore the percent sign as shown:

$$25.5\% = 25.5 = .255$$

Move the decimal point two places or two digits to the left.

Therefore, 25.5% = .255

Example 2
Express 25% as a decimal fraction.
Solution
Using the rule, to express a percent as a decimal fraction, move the decimal point in the percent number two places or two digits to the left of the decimal point, and ignore the percent sign as shown:

$$25\% = .25 = .25$$

Move the imaginary decimal point behind 25 two places or two digits to the left.

Therefore, 25% = .25
Note: There is an imaginary decimal point behind the last digit of every whole number.

Example 3
Express 2.55% as a decimal fraction.
Solution
Using the rule, to express a percent as a decimal fraction, move the decimal point in the percent number two places or two digits to the left of the decimal point, and ignore the percent sign.

Write a 0 here to hold the place value.

$$2.55\% = 2.55 = .0255$$

Move the decimal point two places or two digits to the left.

Therefore, 2.55% = .0255

Example 4
Express .255% as a decimal fraction.
Solution
Using the rule, to express a percent as a decimal fraction, move the decimal point in the percent number two places or two digits to the left of the decimal point, and ignore the percent sign.

Write two 0 here to hold the place values

$$.255\% = .255 = .00255$$

Move the decimal point two places or two digits to the left.

Therefore, .255% = .00255

Exercises

1. Express the following percents as decimals. Hint: See Example 1.

(**a**) 28.1%   (**b**) 95.5%   (**c**) 64.9%   (**d**) 75.5%   (**e**) 95.3%

(**f**) 12.4%   (**g**) 17.7%   (**h**) 55.6%   (**i**) 49.9%   (**j**) 99.9%

(**k**) 39.8%   (**l**) 16.6%   (**m**) 11.1%   (**n**) 36.7%   (**o**) 57.8%

2. Express the following percents as decimals. Hint: See Example 2.

(**a**) 26%   (**b**) 27%   (**c**) 99%   (**d**) 35%   (**e**) 64%

(**f**) 75%   (**g**) 38%   (**h**) 45%   (**i**) 17%   (**j**) 19%

(**k**) 11%   (**l**) 34%   (**m**) 17%   (**n**) 88%   (**o**) 96%

3. Express the following percents as decimals. Hint: See Example 3.

(**a**) 3.22%   (**b**) 4.45%   (**c**) 7.1%   (**d**) 9.61   (**e**) 1.1%

(**f**) 2.1%   (**g**) 9.9%   (**h**) 8.5%   (**i**) 6.25%   (**j**) 7.9%

4. Express the following percents as decimals. Hint: See Example 4.

(**a**) .234%   (**b**) .641%   (**c**) .111%   (**d**) .2%   (**e**) .12%

(**f**) .75%   (**g**) .35%   (**h**) .99%   (**i**) .1%   (**j**) .4%

Challenge Questions

5. Express the following percents as decimal fractions.

(**a**) 72%   (**b**) 33.4%   (**c**) .01%   (**d**) 1.71%   (**e**) .09%

(**f**) .3%   (**g**) 4.2%   (**h**) 13.1%   (**i**) 95%   (**j**) .88%

Answers to Selected Questions.

(**1**)(**a**) .281   **2**(**a**) .26   **3**(**a**) .0322   **4**(**a**) .00234

REAL WORLD APPLICATIONS – WORD PROBLEMS
Percents to Decimal Fractions

Example 1

Given that 12.32% of the items in a store are on sale, what decimal fraction of the items is on sale?

Solution

Using the rule to express a percent as a decimal fraction, move the decimal point in the percent number two places or two digits to the left of the decimal point, and ignore the percent sign.

$$12.32\% = 12.32 = .1232$$

Move the decimal point two places or
two digits to the left.

The decimal fraction of the items on sale = .1232

Example 2

There are 7% of the boys at the Peki High School who work at the Peki Super Market.
What is the decimal fraction of the boys that work at the Peki Super Market?

Solution

Using the rule to express a percent as a decimal fraction, move the decimal point in
the percent number two places or two digits to the left of the decimal point, and ignore
the percent sign.

Write a 0 here to hold the place value.

$$7\% = 7 = .07$$

Move the imaginary decimal point behind 7
to two places or two digits to the left.

Therefore, .07 is the decimal fraction of the boys.

Example 3

.64% of a certain concentration of orange drink is water. What is the decimal fraction
of the concentration made of water?

Solution

Hint: Orange drink is made by mixing pure orange juice with water.

Using the rule to express a percent as a decimal fraction, move the decimal point in
the percent number two places or two digits to the left of the decimal point, and ignore
the percent sign.

Write two 0 here to hold the place value.

$$.64\% = .64 = .0064$$

Move the decimal point two places or
two digits to the left.

The decimal fraction of the concentration of the orange drink is .0064.

The notes and the generous examples have provided me with the conceptual understanding and the computational fluency to do my homework.

Exercises
1. Given that 17.2% of the computers in a certain store are on sale, what decimal fraction of the computers are on sale? Hint: See Example 1.
2. In a certain elementary school, 3% of the girls like soccer. What is the decimal fraction of the girls that like soccer? Hint: See Example 2.
3. The concentration of a certain orange drink is made up of .95% water. What is the decimal fraction of the concentration of water in the orange drink? Hint: See Example 3.

Challenge Questions
4. Given that the concentration of a certain drink is .5% water, what is the decimal fraction of the concentration of the water in the drink?
5. If 1% of the employees in a certain company prefer to take their vacation in the summer, what is the decimal fraction of the employees that prefer to take their vacation in the summer?
6. Mrs. Aggor went to the store to buy a shirt because 46.8% of the shirts were on sale. What is the decimal fraction of the shirts that are on sale?

Express Decimal Fractions as Percents

Note that expressing decimal fractions as percents is the opposite of expressing percents as decimal fractions, and therefore, the method of expressing decimal fractions as percents is the opposite of the method of expressing the percents as decimal fractions. Review the rule for expressing percents as decimal fractions in the preceding rule.

Rule: To express decimal fractions as percent, move the decimal point two places or two digits to the right, and then attach the % sign.

Example 1
Express .92 as a percent.
Solution
Using the rule to express decimal fractions as percents, move the decimal point two places or two digits to the right, and then attach the % sign.

Attach the % sign.

$$.92 = .92 = 92\%$$

Move the decimal point two places or two digits to the right.

Therefore, .92 = 92%

Example 2

Change the following decimal fractions to percents:

(**a**) 1.87   (**b**) 1.8

Solution

(**a**). Using the rule to express decimal fractions as percents, move the decimal point two places or two digits to the right, and then attach the % sign:

Attach the % sign.

$$1.87 = 1.87 = 187\%$$

Move the decimal point two places or two digits to the right.

Therefore, 1.87 = 187%

(**b**). Using the rule to express decimal fractions as percents, move the decimal point two places or two digits to the right, and then attach the % sign.

Write a 0 here to hold the place value.

$$1.8 = 1.8 = 180\% \longleftarrow \text{Attach the \% sign.}$$

Move the decimal point two places or
two digits to the right.

Example 3

Change the following decimal fractions to percents.

(**a**) .001   (**b**) .275   (**c**) 1.00

Solution

(**a**). Using the rule to express decimal fractions as percents, move the decimal point two places or two digits to the right, and then attach the % sign.

Attach the % sign.

$.001 = .001 = .1\%$

Move the decimal point two places or two digits to the right.

Therefore, $.001 = .1\%$

(**b**). Using the rule to express decimal fractions as percents, move the decimal point two places or two digits to the right, and then attach the % sign.

Attach the % sign.

$.275 = .275 = 27.5\%$

Move the decimal point two places or two digits to the right.

Therefore, $.275 = 27.5\%$

(**c**). Using the rule to express decimal fractions as percents, move the decimal point two places or two digits to the right, and then attach the % sign.

Attach the % sign.

$1.00 = 1.00 = 100\%$

Move the decimal point two places or two digits to the right.

Therefore, $1.00 = 100\%$

The notes and the generous examples have provided me with the conceptual understanding and the computational fluency to do my homework.

Exercises
1. Change the following decimal fractions to percents. Hint: See Example **1**.
   (**a**) .79   (**b**) .34   (**c**) .07   (**d**) .12   (**e**) .11
2. Change the following decimal fractions to percents. Hint: See Example **2(a)**.
   (**a**) 2.94   (**b**) 9.99   (**c**) 3.40   (**d**) 7.75   (**e**) 1.25
3. Change the following decimal fractions to percents. Hint: See Example **3(a)**.
   (**a**) 3.9   (**b**) 9.9   (**c**) 28.1   (**d**) 44.6   (**e**) 7.8
4. Change the following decimal fractions to percents. Hint : See Example **3(a)**.
   (**a**) .002   (**b**) .009   (**c**) .004   (**d**) 2.001   (**e**) 10.002
5. Change the following decimal fractions to percents. Hint: See Example **3(b)**.
   (**a**) .298   (**b**) .444   (**c**) .891   (**d**) .658   (**e**) .481

6. Change the following decimal fractions to percents. Hint: See Example 3(**c**).

    (**a**) 9.00   (**b**) 6.00   (**c**) 4.00   (**d**) 8.00   (**e**) 2.00

Challenge Questions

7. Express the following decimal fractions as percents.

    (**a**) .3   (**b**) 4.2   (**c**) 13.1   (**d**) 95   (**e**) .88

8. Express the following decimal fractions as percents.

    (**a**) 1.1   (**b**) .001   (**c**) 1.78   (**d**) 7.0   (**e**) .09

    (**f**) .90   (**g**) 3.0   (**h**) 1   (**i**) .21   (**j**) .01

Answers to Selected Exercises

1(a) 79%   **2(a)** 294%   **3(a)** 390%

4(a) 0.2%   **5(a)** 29.8%   **6(a)** 900%

REAL WORLD APPLICATIONS – WORD PROBLEMS
Express Decimal Fractions as Percents

Example 1

Given that .65 of the students in a certain school are girls, what percent of the students are girls?

Solution

Using the rule to express decimal fractions as percents, move the decimal point two places or two digits to the right, and then attach the % sign.

Attach the % sign.

$$.65 = .65 = 65\%$$

Move the decimal point two places or two digits to the right.

The percent of the girls $= 65\%$.

Example 2

John will make 1.9 profit in his investment.

Express his profit as a percent.

Solution

Using the rule to express decimal fractions as percents, move the decimal point two places or two digits to the right, and then attach the % sign.

Write a 0 here to hold the place value.

$$1.9 = 1.9 = 190\%$$ ← Attach the % sign.

Move the decimal point two places or two digits to the right.

The percent profit = 190%.

Example 3

Given that .268 of the computers in a certain store were sold at a discount. What percent of the computers were sold at a discount ?

Solution

Using the rule to express decimal fractions as percents, move the decimal point two places or two digits to the right, and then attach the % sign:

Attach the % sign.

$$.268 = .268 = 26.8\%$$

Move the decimal point two places or two digits to the right.

The percent of the computers sold at a discount was 26.8%

Example 4

Given that .022 of the students in a certain class study history, what is the percent of the students that study history?

Solution

Using the rule, to express decimal fractions as percents, move the decimal point two places or two digits to the right, and then attach the % sign.

Attach the % sign.

$$.022 = .022 = 2.2\%$$

Move the decimal point two places or two digits to the right.

The percent of the students that study history is 2.2%

The notes and the generous examples have provided me with the conceptual understanding and the computational fluency to do my homework.

Exercises

1. Given that .75 of the students in a certain class are boys, what percent of the students are boys? Hint: See Example 1.

2. Eric made .078 profit on his investment. What is his percent profit? Hint: See Example 2.

3. Given that .289 of the people who go to the zoo are children, what percent of the people who go to the zoo are children? Hint: See Example 3.

4. Given that .501 of the students in a certain class study chemistry, what percent of the students study chemistry? Hint: See Example 4.

Challenge Questions

5. Given that .018 of the animals in a certain zoo are lions, what percent of the animals are lions?

6. Given that .684 of the books in a certain library involve science, what is the percent of the books that involve science?

Key Facts - Summary

a. To change a percent to a common fraction, put the percent number over 100 as a denominator, and then reduce to the lowest terms if possible.

b. To change a common fraction to decimal fraction, move the decimal point in the numerator two places or two digits to the left if the denominator is 100, otherwise, just divide the numerator by the denominator.

c. To change a decimal fraction to a common fraction, count the number of the decimal places or the number of digits after the decimal point and this number of decimal places or the number of digits after the decimal point is equal to the number of zeros which form the denominator of the common fraction, and the actual number of the decimal fraction becomes the numerator as follows:

(1) .5 has one decimal place or one digit after the decimal point, so the denominator has one zero and the denominator is 10 and the numerator is 5 and the common fraction is $\dfrac{5}{10}$.

(2) .05 has two decimal places or two digits after the decimal point, so the denominator has two zeros and the denominator is 100 and the numerator is 5 and the common fraction is $\dfrac{5}{100}$.

(3) .005 has three decimal places or three digits after the decimal point, so the denominator has three zeros and the denominator is 1000, and the numerator is 5 and the common fraction is $\dfrac{5}{1000}$.

(4) .523 has three decimal places or three digits after the decimal point, therefore the denominator has three zeros and the denominator is 1000 and the numerator is 523 and the common fraction is $\dfrac{523}{1000}$.

The table below summarizes how to change decimal fractions to common fractions.

Decimal Fraction	No. of decimal places	No. of zeros in denominator	Common fraction
.5	1	1	$\dfrac{5}{10}$
.05	2	2	$\dfrac{5}{100}$
.005	3	3	$\dfrac{5}{1,000}$
.523	3	3	$\dfrac{523}{1,000}$
.0931	4	4	$\dfrac{931}{10,000}$
.74895	5	5	$\dfrac{74895}{100,000}$

d. To change a common fraction to a percent, multiply the common fraction by 100, and then attach the % sign. For example,

$\dfrac{5}{100}$ is:

$$\dfrac{5}{100} \times 100$$

$$\dfrac{5}{\cancelto{1}{100}} \times \cancelto{1}{100} = 5\%$$

e. To change a percent to a decimal fraction, move the decimal point in the percent to two decimal places or two digits to the left, or just express the percent as a common fraction with 100 as the denominator and divide.

 The notes and the generous examples have provided me with the conceptual understanding and the computational fluency to do my homework.

Exercises

1. Complete the table by filling in the columns for percents, fractions, and decimal fractions. Hint: See examples in the sections under percents, fractions, and decimals. See also the example in the second row of the table in this question.

Percents (%)	Fractions	Decimals or Decimal Fractions
5%	$\frac{5}{100}$	.05
65%		
16%		
	$\frac{17}{100}$	
	$\frac{73}{100}$	
		.008
		.08
		.8
2.1%		
.33%		

2. Complete the table by filling in the columns for decimal fractions, percents, and fractions. Hint: See examples under the sections in decimal fractions, percents, common fractions, and also see the two examples in the second and the third rows of the table in this question.

Decimal fractions	Percent (%)	Common fractions
.8	$\dfrac{8}{10} \times 100 = 80\%$	$\dfrac{8}{10} = \dfrac{4}{5}$
.004	$\dfrac{4}{1000} \times 100 = .4\%$	$\dfrac{4}{1000} = \dfrac{1}{250}$
2.67		
85.8		
.561		
.018		
.o8		
.7		
9.49		
72.004		
.47		
.15		
$\dfrac{35}{100} = .35$	35%	$\dfrac{35}{100} = \dfrac{7}{20}$
	60%	
	160%	
	74.5%	
	9.8%	
	2%	
	13.11%	
12.5% = .125	$\dfrac{1}{8} \times 100 = 12.5\%$	$\dfrac{1}{8}$
		$\dfrac{272}{100}$
		$\dfrac{6}{12}$
		$\dfrac{9.7}{100}$
		$\dfrac{24\frac{1}{3}}{60}$
		$\dfrac{100}{100}$

3. Copy and complete the table by filling in the columns for common fractions,

399

decimal fractions, and percents. Hint: See separate examples under the sections on Decimal Fractions, Percents and Common Fractions.

Common fraction	Decimal fraction	%
$\frac{57}{100}$		
$\frac{8}{24}$		
$\frac{7}{9}$		
$\frac{9.7}{100}$		
$\frac{5645}{100}$		
$\frac{18}{65}$		
	.358	
	.019	
	75.45	
	38.01	
	3.2	
	.6	
		2.5%
		275%
		1%
		60%
		4700.8%
		26.15%

Understanding 100%

(**1**) 100% means $\frac{100}{100} = \frac{1}{1} = 1$. 100% therefore means one whole of anything or the total of anything.

(**2**) If 100% of the employees at a certain company are women, it means that no men work at the company.

(**3**). If 100% of the students in grade 5B are boys, it means that all the students in grade 5B are boys.

(**4**) If 100% of the students visited the zoo yesterday, it means that all the students visited the zoo.

Understanding Percent

(**1**) If 70% of the students in a certain school are girls, it means that
100% − 70% = 30% are boys since the whole student population should be 100%.
(**2**) If 55% of the doctors in a certain hospital are women, then the percent of the male doctors is 100% − 55% = 45% since the whole doctor population in the hospital should be 100%.
(**3**) If 5% of a class is absent, it means that 100% − 5% = 95% of the students are present since the whole class should be 100%.

REAL WORLD APPLICATIONS − WORD PROBLEMS
Understanding Percent

Example 1
There are 48% of boys in a school. What is the percent of the girls?
Solution
The percent of the girls = 100% − 48% = 52%

Example 2
An advance school consists of students studying chemistry, physics, and biology. A student may study only one subject. Given that 25% of the students study chemistry and 30% of the students study biology, what is the percent of the students that study physics?
Solution
Total student population = 100%
Percent of students that study chemistry and biology = 25% + 30% = 55%.
Percent of students that study physics = 100% − 55% = 45%.

Example 3
A school has 800 students. If 55% of the student population are boys,
(**a**) what is the percent of girls in the school?
(**b**) how many girls are in the school?
Solution
(**a**) Total student population = 100%
   Percent of the boys = 55%
   Percent of the girls = 100% - 55% = 45%

(b) From solution (a), the percent of the girls = 45%

The number of the girls in the school = 45% of 800

$$= \frac{45}{100} \times 800 \qquad \text{Note: } 45\% = \frac{45}{100}, \text{ "of" is } \times.$$

$$= \frac{45}{\underset{1}{100}} \times \overset{8}{800} \qquad \text{Divide by 100.}$$

$$= 45 \times 8$$
$$= 360 \text{ girls}$$

Therefore, the number of the girls in the school is 360.

Example 4

A school has a population of 1,200 students. If 5 percent of the students are absent,
(a) what is the percent of the students present?
(b) what is the number of the students present?
(c) what is the number of the students absent?

Solution

(a) The percent of the whole student population = 100%
   The percent of the students that are absent = 5%
   The percent of the students that are present = 100% - 5% = 95%

(b) From the solution of **(a)**, the percent of the students that are present = 95%
   Student population of the school = 1,200
   The number of the students present = 95% of the student population.

$$= 95\% \text{ of } 1,200$$

$$= \frac{95}{100} \times 1,200 \qquad \text{Note: } 95\% = \frac{95}{100}, \text{ "of" is } \times.$$

$$= \frac{95}{\underset{1}{100}} \times \overset{12}{1,200} \qquad \text{Divide by 100.}$$

$$= 95 \times 12$$
$$= 1140 \text{ students.}$$

Therefore, 1140 students were present.

(c) The number of students absent
$$= \text{Student population} - \text{Number of students present.}$$
$$= 1,200 - 1140$$
$$= 60 \text{ students.}$$
Therefore, 60 students were absent.

Fractional Parts of Percents

The fractional part of a percent such as $\frac{1}{5}\%$ means $\frac{1}{5}$ out of 100. Recall that, for

example, 2% means 2 out of 100. Recall that $2\% = \frac{2}{100}$, and therefore, $\frac{1}{5}\% = \frac{\frac{1}{5}}{100}$.

Rule: To express a fraction of a percent as a decimal fraction, write the fraction over 100, and then divide, ignoring the % sign.

Example 1

Express $\frac{1}{5}\%$ as a decimal fraction

Solution

Using the rule to express a fraction of a percent as a decimal fraction, write the fraction over 100, and then divide, ignoring the % sign.

$$\frac{1}{5}\% = \frac{\frac{1}{5}}{100}$$

$$= \frac{\frac{1}{5}}{\frac{100}{1}} \quad \text{Change 100 to a fraction by writing 100 as } \frac{100}{1} = 100.$$

$$= \frac{1}{5} \times \frac{1}{100} \quad \text{Recall that to divide a fraction by another fraction, the}$$

top fraction $(\frac{1}{5})$ is multiplied by the inverted bottom

fraction $(\frac{1}{100})$. The inverted bottom fraction is called the

reciprocal.

$$= \frac{1 \times 1}{5 \times 100} = \frac{1}{500}$$

403

$$500\overline{)1} = 500\overline{)1.000}$$

with quotient $.002$ shown and subtraction 1000, remainder 0000.

(Review the chapter on Dividing a Smaller Number by a Bigger Number).

Therefore, $\dfrac{1}{5}\% = .002$

Example 2

Change $\dfrac{6}{8}\%$ to a decimal fraction.

Solution

Using the rule to express a fraction of a percent as a decimal fraction, write the fraction over 100, and then divide, ignoring the % sign.

$$\dfrac{6}{8}\% = \dfrac{\dfrac{6}{8}}{100}$$

$$= \dfrac{\dfrac{6}{8}}{\dfrac{100}{1}} \qquad \text{Change 100 to a fraction by writing 100 as } \dfrac{100}{1} = 100.$$

$$= \dfrac{6}{8} \times \dfrac{1}{100} \qquad \text{Recall that to divide a fraction by another fraction, the top}$$

fraction ($\dfrac{6}{8}$) is multiplied by the inverted bottom

fraction ($\dfrac{1}{100}$). The inverted bottom fraction is called the

reciprocal.

$$= \dfrac{\overset{3}{\cancel{6}}}{\underset{4}{\cancel{8}}} \times \dfrac{1}{100} \qquad \text{Divide the numerator and the denominator by 2.}$$

$$= \dfrac{3}{4} \times \dfrac{1}{100} = \dfrac{3 \times 1}{4 \times 100} = \dfrac{3}{400}$$

$$400\overline{)3} = 400\overline{)3.0000} \quad \begin{array}{r} .0075 \\ \hline \end{array}$$

$$\begin{array}{r} 2800\downarrow \\ \hline 2000 \\ 2000 \\ \hline 0000 \end{array}$$

(Review the chapter on Dividing a Smaller Number by a Bigger Number).

Therefore, $\dfrac{6}{8}\% = .0075$

Example 3

Change $2\dfrac{1}{2}\%$ to decimal fraction.

Solution

Using the rule to express a fraction of a percent as a decimal fraction, write the fraction over 100, and then divide, ignoring the % sign.

$$2\dfrac{1}{2}\% = \dfrac{2\dfrac{1}{2}}{100}$$

$$= \dfrac{\dfrac{5}{2}}{100} \qquad \text{Change } 2\dfrac{1}{2} \text{ to an improper fraction of } \dfrac{5}{2}.$$

$$= \dfrac{\dfrac{5}{2}}{\dfrac{100}{1}} \qquad \text{Change 100 to a fraction by writing 100 as } \dfrac{100}{1} = 100.$$

$$= \dfrac{5}{2} \times \dfrac{1}{100} \qquad \text{Recall that to divide a fraction by another fraction,}$$

$$\text{the top fraction } (\dfrac{5}{2}) \text{ is multiplied by the inverted}$$

$$\text{bottom fraction } (\dfrac{1}{100}), \text{ which is the reciprocal.}$$

$$= \dfrac{\overset{1}{5}}{2} \times \dfrac{1}{\underset{20}{100}} \qquad \text{Divide numerator and denominator by 5.}$$

$$= \frac{1}{2} \times \frac{1}{20} = \frac{1 \times 1}{2 \times 20} = \frac{1}{40}$$

$$40\overline{)1} = 40\overline{)1.000}$$

(Review the chapter on Dividing a Smaller Number by a Bigger Number.)

Therefore, $2\frac{1}{2}\% = .025$

The notes and the generous examples have provided me with the conceptual understanding and the computational fluency to do my homework.

Exercises

1. Express the following fractions of percents as decimal. Round your answer to 3 decimal places. Hint: See Example 1.

(a) $\frac{1}{2}\%$ (b) $\frac{1}{4}\%$ (c) $\frac{1}{3}\%$ (d) $\frac{1}{10}\%$ (e) $\frac{1}{12}\%$

(f) $\frac{1}{7}\%$ (g) $\frac{1}{9}\%$ (h) $\frac{1}{15}\%$ (i) $\frac{1}{11}\%$ (j) $\frac{1}{20}\%$

2. Change the following fractions of percents to decimals. Round your answer to 3 decimal places. Hint: See Example 2.

(a) $\frac{2}{10}\%$ (b) $\frac{2}{5}\%$ (c) $\frac{3}{7}\%$ (d) $\frac{2}{7}\%$ (e) $\frac{3}{5}\%$

(f) $\frac{3}{5}\%$ (g) $\frac{3}{11}\%$ (h) $\frac{4}{15}\%$ (i) $\frac{5}{8}\%$ (j) $\frac{9}{10}\%$

3. Change the following mixed numbers of percents to decimals. Round your answer to 3 decimal places, Hint: See Example 3.

(a) $2\frac{1}{4}\%$ (b) $1\frac{1}{2}\%$ (c) $2\frac{2}{5}\%$ (d) $1\frac{3}{5}\%$ (e) $4\frac{3}{4}\%$

(f) $5\frac{2}{5}\%$ (g) $6\frac{5}{6}\%$ (h) $10\frac{2}{3}\%$ (i) $8\frac{2}{5}\%$ (j) $3\frac{3}{4}\%$

Challenge Questions

4. Change the following mixed numbers and fractions from percents to decimals.

(a) $2\frac{3}{4}\%$ (b) $\frac{1}{6}\%$ (c) $\frac{2}{9}\%$ (d) $2\frac{3}{5}\%$ (e) $\frac{1}{10}\%$

(f) $\frac{3}{8}\%$ (g) $5\frac{5}{6}\%$ (h) $\frac{1}{8}\%$ (i) $7\frac{1}{7}\%$ (j) $\frac{5}{7}\%$

Answers to Selected Questions
1(a) 0.005 **2(a)** 0.002 **3(a)** 0.023

REAL WORLD APPLICATIONS - WORD PROBLEMS
Express Fractions of Percents as Decimals

Example 1
Given that $\frac{3}{4}\%$ of the goods in a certain store are on sale, what is the decimal fraction of the goods that are on sale?

Solution
Using the rule, to express a fraction of a percent as a decimal fraction, write the fraction over 100, and then divide, ignoring the % sign.

$$\frac{3}{4}\% = \frac{\frac{3}{4}}{100}$$

$$= \frac{\frac{3}{4}}{\frac{100}{1}}$$ Change 100 to a fraction by writing 100 as $\frac{100}{1} = 100$.

$$= \frac{3}{4} \times \frac{1}{100}$$ Recall that to divide a fraction by another fraction, the top fraction ($\frac{3}{4}$) is multiplied by the inverted bottom fraction ($\frac{1}{100}$). The inverted bottom fraction is called the reciprocal.

$$= \frac{3 \times 1}{4 \times 100} = \frac{3}{400}$$

$$400\overline{)3} = 400\overline{)3.0000} \quad \begin{array}{r} .0075 \\ \hline \end{array}$$
$$\begin{array}{r} -2800\downarrow \\ \hline 2000 \\ -2000 \\ \hline 0000 \end{array}$$

(Review the chapter on Dividing a Smaller Number by a Bigger Number).

Therefore, $\frac{3}{4}\% = .0075$.

Example 2

Agbeko Fish Pond has a lot of fish. Mr. Johnson owns $22\frac{1}{2}\%$ of the fish in the pond. What is the decimal fraction of the fish that is owned by Mr. Johnson?

Solution

Using the rule, to express a fraction of a percent as a decimal fraction, write the fraction over 100, and then divide, ignoring the % sign.

$$22\frac{1}{2}\% = \frac{22\frac{1}{2}}{100}$$

$$= \frac{\frac{45}{2}}{100} \qquad \text{Change } 22\frac{1}{2} \text{ to an improper fraction } (\frac{45}{2}).$$

$$= \frac{\frac{45}{2}}{\frac{100}{1}} \qquad \text{Change 100 to fraction by writing 100 as } \frac{100}{1} = 100.$$

$$= \frac{45}{2} \div \frac{100}{1} \qquad \text{Review Division of Fractions.}$$

$$= \frac{45}{2} \times \frac{1}{100} \qquad \text{Recall that to divide a fraction by another fraction,}$$

the top fraction is multiplied by the inverted

bottom fraction ($\frac{1}{100}$). The inverted bottom fraction is

called the reciprocal.

408

$$= \frac{\overset{9}{\cancel{45}}}{2} \times \frac{1}{\underset{20}{\cancel{100}}}$$ Divide the numerator and the denominator by 5.

$$= \frac{9 \times 1}{2 \times 20} = \frac{9}{40}$$

$$40\overline{\smash{)}9} \quad = \quad 40\overline{\smash{)}9.000}$$

(Review the chapter on Dividing a Smaller Number by a Bigger Number).

Therefore, $22\frac{1}{2}\% = .225$.

The notes and the generous examples have provided me with the conceptual understanding and the computational fluency to do my homework.

Exercises

1. A bank rate was increased by $\frac{3}{10}\%$, what is the decimal fraction of the increase? Hint: See Example 1.

2. The population of a certain country increased by $8\frac{1}{3}\%$ last year. What is the decimal fraction of the increase? Hint: See Example 2.

Challenge Questions.

3. Eric's academic performance has improved by $5\frac{1}{3}\%$. What is the decimal fraction of his improvement?

4. The number of books at the library has been reduced by $\frac{7}{10}\%$. What is the decimal fraction of the reduction of the books?

FRACTIONAL PARTS OF PERCENTS - Alternative Method

The preceding sections show how to change the fractional parts of percents to decimals. This section shows an alternative method of changing the fractional parts of percent to decimals.

Rule: **To express a fraction of a percent as a decimal, change the common fraction to a decimal fraction by dividing the numerator by the denominator, then dividing the result by 100 by moving the decimal point two places or digits to the left, and then ignore the % sign.**

Example 1

Express $\frac{2}{5}$% as a decimal.

Solution

Use the rule which states, to express a fraction of a percent as a decimal, change the common fraction to a decimal fraction by dividing the numerator by the denominator, and then divide the result by 100 by moving the decimal point two places or two digits to the left, and then ignore the % sign.

Step 1: Change the common fraction to a decimal fraction by dividing the numerator by the denominator.

$$\frac{2}{5} = 5\overline{\smash{)}2.0} \quad \frac{.4}{\underset{00}{-20}}$$

$$\frac{2}{5}\% = .4\%$$

Step 2: Divide the result in Step 1 by 100 by moving the decimal point two places or two digits to the left.

Write two 0s here to hold the place value.

$$.4\% = \frac{.4}{100} = .4 = .004$$

Move the decimal point two places or two digits to the left.

Therefore, $\frac{2}{5}\% = .004$

The notes and the generous examples have provided me with the conceptual understanding and the computational fluency to do my homework.

Exercise

Use the preceding alternative method in Example 1 for "changing a fractional part of a percent to a decimal" to solve the exercises under the section, "Fractional Parts of Percent."

How to Find the Percent of a Number

Rule 1: To find the percent of a number, multiply the given percent by the given number.

Example 1

Find 5% of 80

Solution

Using the rule to find the percent of a number, multiply the given percent by the given number.

$$5\% \text{ of } 80 = 5\% \times 80 \qquad \text{Note: "of" means to multiply.}$$

$$= \frac{5}{100} \times 80 \qquad \text{Note: } 5\% = \frac{5}{100}.$$

$$= \frac{\overset{1}{\cancel{5}}}{\underset{20}{\cancel{100}}} \times 80 \qquad \text{Divide by 5.}$$

$$= \frac{1}{\cancel{20}} \times \overset{4}{\cancel{80}} \qquad \text{Divide by 20.}$$

$$= \frac{4}{1} = 4$$

Therefore, 5% of 80 = 4

Rule 2: To find the percent of a number, change the percent to a decimal fraction, and then multiply the decimal fraction equivalent of the percent by the number.

411

Note: Rule 2 is an alternative method of finding the percent of a number.

Example 2

Find 5% of 80. Hint: Use Rule 2 in solving this problem. (This problem is the same as Example 1.)

Solution

Using Rule 2 to find the percent of a number, change the percent to a decimal fraction, and then multiply the decimal fraction equivalent of the percent by the number as shown:

Step 1: Change the percent to a decimal fraction.

Write a 0 here as a place holder.

$$5\% = \frac{5}{100} = .05 = .05$$

Move the imaginary decimal point behind 5 two places or two digits to the left.

Note: There is an imaginary decimal point behind the last digit of any whole number. (Review the chapter on Decimals.)

Step 2: Multiply the decimal fraction equivalent of the percent by the number as shown:

```
      80
  ×  .05     Review Decimal Multiplication.
     400
+  000  ←  Write this 0 as a place holder.
    4.00
```

Therefore, 5% of 80 is 4.

Note that the methods used in Example 1 and 2 give the same answer of 4.

Example 3

What is 1.7% of $50?

Solution

Using Rule 2 to find the percent of a number, change the percent to a decimal fraction, and then multiply the decimal fraction equivalent of the percent by the number as shown:

Step 1: Change the percent to a decimal fraction.

Write a 0 here as a place holder.

$$1.7\% = \frac{1.7}{100} = .017$$

Move the decimal point two places to the left.

Step 2: Multiply the decimal fraction equivalent of the percent by the number ($50) as shown:

$$
\begin{array}{r}
\$50 \\
\times\ .017 \\
\hline
350 \\
500 \quad\leftarrow \\
+\ 0000 \quad\leftarrow \\
\hline
0.850
\end{array}
$$

350

$500 \leftarrow$ Write a 0 here as a place holder.

$+ 0000 \leftarrow$ Write two 0s here as a place holder

0.850

Move the decimal point three decimal places or 3 digits to the left. Review Decimal Multiplication.

Therefore, 1.7% of $50 is $.85

Example 4

Find $6\frac{1}{4}$% of $28.14.

Solution

Using Rule 2 to find the percent of a number, change the percent to a decimal fraction, and then multiply the decimal fraction equivalent of the percent by the number as shown:

Step 1: Change the percent to a decimal fraction.

$$\frac{1}{4} = 4\overline{)1} = 4\overline{)1.00}$$

$$
\begin{array}{r}
.25 \\
4\overline{)1.00} \\
-8\downarrow \\
\hline
20 \\
-20 \\
\hline
00
\end{array}
$$

Write a 0 here as a place holder.

$$6\frac{1}{4}\% = \frac{6\frac{1}{4}}{100} = \frac{6.25}{100} = .\ 6.25 = .0625 \qquad \text{Note: } 6\frac{1}{4} = 6.25$$

Move the decimal point two decimal places

413

or two digits to the left.

Step 2: Multiply the decimal fraction equivalent of the percent by the number ($28.14) as shown:

$$
\begin{array}{r}
\$28.14 \\
\times\ .0625 \\
\hline
14070 \\
56280 \\
+\ 1688400 \\
\hline
1.758750
\end{array}
$$

← Write a 0 here as a place holder.

← Write two 0s here as place holders.

Move the decimal point 6 decimal places or 6 digits to the left.

Therefore, $6\frac{1}{4}$ of $28.14 is $1.76 to the nearest hundredths or cent.

_____ The notes and the generous examples have provided me with the conceptual understanding and the computational fluency to do my homework.

Exercises

1. Find 7% of the following numbers. Hint: See Example 1. Give your answer to three decimal places.
   (a) 160   (b) 16.4   (c) 58.2   (d) 142.1

2. Find 15% of the following numbers. Hint: See Example 2. Give your answer to 3 decimal places.
   (a) 35   (b) 46.2   (c) 10   (d) 242

3. Find 26% of the following numbers. Hint See Example 2. Give your answer to 3 decimal places.
   (a) 24   (b) 78.51   (c) .01   (d) .8

4. Find 3.8% of the following amounts. Hint: See Example 3.
   (a) $70   (b) $75   (c) $115   (d) $275

5. Find 35.8% of the following amounts. Hint: See Example 3.
   (a) $48   (b) $12   (c) 28   (d) $36

6. Find $8\frac{1}{2}$% of the following amounts. Hint: See Example 4.
   (a) $50.25   (b) $12.78   (c) $78.17   (d) 124.48

7. Find $16\frac{1}{4}$% of the following amounts. Hint: See Example 4.
   (a) $24.25   (b) 47.34   (c) $66.48   (d) $164.28

8. Find $12\frac{1}{5}$% of the following numbers. Hint: See Example 4. Give your answer to 3 decimal places.

(**a**) 72   (**b**) 36.3   (**c**) 46.32   (**d**) 147.18

Challenge Questions

9. Find $\frac{1}{4}$% of 100. Hint : Review the section on "Fractional Parts of Percent." Give your answer to 3 decimal places.

10. Find .8% of 64.12. Hint: Review the section on "Fractional Parts of Percent." Round your answer to 3 decimal places.

11. Find 7.8% of $36.87.

12. Find 8% of 1348. Round your answer to 3 decimal places.

13. Find $\frac{4}{5}$% of 125. Hint: Review the section on "Fractional Parts of Percent." Round your answer to 3 decimal places.

14. Find $24\frac{1}{4}$% of $78.36

Answers to Selected Questions

1(a) 11.200   **4(a)** $2.66   **6(a)** $4.27

REAL WORLD APPLICATIONS – WORD PROBLEMS
How To Find the Percent of a Number.

Example 1

There are 20 students in a class. If 45% of the students are boys, how many boys are in the class?

Solution

Using Rule 2 to find the percent of a number, change the percent to a decimal fraction, and then multiply the decimal fraction equivalent of the percent by the number as shown:

Step 1: Change the percent to a decimal fraction

$$45\% = \frac{45}{100} = .45 = .45$$

$\uparrow$

Move the imaginary decimal point
2 decimal places to the left.

415

Step 2: Multiply the decimal fraction equivalent of the percent by the number (20) as shown:

$$
\begin{array}{r}
20 \\
\times\ .45 \\
\hline
100 \\
+\ 800 \\
\hline
9.00
\end{array}
$$

← Write a 0 here as a place holder.

↑

Move the decimal point two decimal or
two digits to the left. Review the section on Decimal Multiplication.
The number of boys in the class is 9.

Example 2

An employee earns $9\frac{1}{2}$% commission. What is the commission earned on a sale of $3,580.28?

Solution

Using Rule 2 to find the percent of a number, change the percent to a decimal fraction, and then multiply the decimal fraction equivalent of the percent by the number as shown:

Step 1: Change the percent to a decimal fraction.

Need to fill this digit position with
a zero as a place holder.

↓

$$
9\frac{1}{2}\% = 9.5\% = \frac{9.5}{100} = 9.5 = .095
$$

↑↑

Move the decimal point two decimal places or two digits
to the left.

Step 2: Multiply the decimal fraction equivalent of the percent by the
number (3,580.28) as shown:

$$
\begin{array}{r}
\$3,580.28 \\
\times\ \ \ \ \ .095 \\
\hline
1790140 \\
32222520 \\
+\ 00000000 \\
\hline
\$340.12660
\end{array}
$$

← Write a 0 here as a place holder.
← Write two 0s here as a place holder.

↑

Move the decimal point 5 places to the left.
Review the section on Decimal Multiplication.

Therefore, $9\frac{1}{2}$% of \$3,580.28 is \$340.13 to the nearest cent.

Example 3

George's salary was \$45,200. If his salary is increased by 12%,

(**a**) what is the increase in his salary?

(**b**) what is his new salary?

Solution

Using Rule 2 to find the percent of a number, change the percent to a decimal fraction, and then multiply the decimal fraction equivalent of the percent by the number as shown:

(**a**) **Step 1**: Change the percent to a decimal fraction.

$$12\% = \frac{12}{100} = .12 = .12$$

⇑⇑

Move the decimal point two decimal or two digits to the left.

Step 2: Multiply the decimal fraction equivalent of the percent by the number (45,200) as shown:

$$
\begin{array}{r}
\$45,200 \\
\times\quad .12 \\
\hline
90400 \\
+\ 452000 \\
\hline
\$5424.00
\end{array}
$$

← Write a 0 here as a place holder.

⇑⇑

Move the decimal point two places or digits to the left.

Therefore, the increase in George's salary is \$5424.00

(**b**) George's new salary = current salary + Increase in salary

$$= \$45,200.00 + \$5,424.00$$
$$= \$50,624.00$$

Example 4

Mr. Benson needs a 15% down payment on a new house. If the new house costs \$200,000, how much of a down payment does Mr. Benson need?

Solution

Using Rule 2 to find the percent of a number, change the percent to a decimal fraction, and then multiply the decimal fraction equivalent of the percent by the number.

Step 1: Change the percent to a decimal fraction.

$$15\% = \frac{15}{100} = .15 = .15$$

⇈

Move the decimal point two decimal
places or two digits to the left.

Step 2: Multiply the decimal fraction equivalent of the percent by the
number (200,000).

$$
\begin{array}{r}
\$200,000 \\
\times \quad .15 \\
\hline
1000000 \\
+ \quad 2000000 \\
\hline
\$30,000.00
\end{array}
$$
← Write a 0 here as a place holder.

⇈

Move two decimal places or
two digits to the left.

Therefore, the down payment is $30,000.00.

The notes and the generous examples have provided
me with the conceptual understanding and the
computational fluency to do my homework.

Exercises

1. In a school, 55% of the students are boys. If there are 500 students in the school,
   (a) how many boys are in the school?
   (b) how many girls are in the school? Hint: See Example 1.

2. An employee earns $13\frac{1}{4}$% commission. What is the commission earned on a sale
   of $6,258? Hint: See Example 2.

3. Ama's salary was $55,436.19. If her salary is increased by 5%,
   (a) what is the increase in her salary?
   (b) what is her new salary?
   Hint: See Example 3.

4. Seth bought a new house for $175,000. If he paid 8% down payment on the new
   house, how much did he pay for the new house? Hint: See Example 4.

Challenge Questions

1. Mr. Albert has to pay 14% down payment on a new house. If the new house
   cost $225,000, what is the down payment of Mr. Albert?

2. Elizabeth's current salary is increased by $12\frac{1}{2}$% . If her current salary is

$55,200.78, what is the increment in her salary?

3. An employee earns $8\frac{1}{2}$% commission. What is the commission earned on a sale of $3,648.37?

4. The population of a school is 650 students. If 40% of the students are girls,
   (**a**) how many girls are in the school?
   (**b**) how many boys are in the school?

Percent of One Number Compared to Another Number

In mathematics, it is possible to find what percent a number is of another number, and this is really a ratio expressed in percent.

Rule: To find what percent a number is of another number, divide the first number by the second number, and then move the decimal point two places or two digits to the right in the quotient, and then attach the % sign.

Special note: Some students who may find it difficult in setting up the solution of the percent problems can use the "is of" ($\frac{is}{of}$) method. The facts in the rule can be stated as "a number is what percent of another number?", and this can be expressed generally as:

$$\frac{is}{of} = \frac{a\ number}{another\ number}$$

Example 1

Express 3 as a percent of 5.

Solution

The facts in the question can be stated as: "3 **is** what percent **of** 5?" and this can be expressed as:

$$\frac{is}{of} = \frac{3}{5}$$

Using the rule to find what percent of a number is of another number, divide 3 by 5, and then move the decimal point two places or two digits to the right in the quotient, and then attach the % sign.

Step 1: Divide the first number by the second number as shown:

$$\frac{3}{5} = 5\overline{)3} = 5\overline{)3.0}\ \ \overset{.6}{}$$
$$-\underline{30}$$
$$00$$

Step 2: Change the .6 to a percent by moving the decimal point two places or two digits to the right, and then adding the percent sign, which is the same as multiplying

419

.6 by 100.

Write a 0 here as a place holder.
↓
.6 = .6 = 60%
⇑⇑
Move the decimal point two places or two digits to the right.

(Review the chapter on Decimal Fraction and Percent.)
Therefore, 3 is 60% of 5.

Example 2

Express the ratio 2 out of 10 as a percent to the nearest whole number.

Solution

The facts in the question can be stated as: "2 **is** what percent **of** 10?" and this can be expressed as:

$$\frac{is}{of} = \frac{2}{10}$$

Using the rule to find what percent a number is of another number, divide 2 by 10, and then move the decimal point two places or two digits to the right in the quotient, and then attach the % sign.

Step 1: " 2 out of 10 " is $\frac{2}{10}$ or simply divide 2 by 10.

$$\frac{2}{10} = 10\overline{)2} = 10\overline{)2.0} \quad \begin{array}{r} .2 \\ \underline{-2\ 0} \\ 0\ 0 \end{array}$$

Step 2: Change .2 to a percent by moving the decimal point two places or two digits to the right, and then attach the percent sign.

Write a 0 here as a place holder.

.2 = .2 = 20%

Move the decimal point two places or two digits to the right.

Therefore, 2 is 20% of 10.

The notes and the generous examples have provided me with the conceptual understanding and the computational fluency to do my homework.

420

Exercises. Round all answers to the nearest whole number.

1. Express the following ratios as percents. Hint: See Example 2.

   (**a**) 1 out of 5　　　　　　(**b**) 3 out of 10　　　　　(**c**) 3 out of 20

   (**d**) 4 out of 12　　　　　 (**e**) 3 out of 9　　　　　　(**f**) 2 out of 8

   (**g**) 2 out of 20　　　　　 (**h**) 4 out of 100　　　　 (**i**) 20 out of 50

   (**j**) 12 out of 60　　　　　(**k**) 3 out of 15　　　　　(**l**) 8 out of 64

2. Express 2 as a percent of 8. Hint: See Example 1.

3. Express 10 as a percent of 100. Hint: See Example 1.

4. Express 5 as a percent of 25. Hint: See Example 1.

5. Express 6 as a percent of 24. Hint: See Example 1.

6. Express 40 as a percent of 90. Hint: See Example 1.

7. 15 is what percent of 125? Hint: See Example 1.

Challenge Questions

8. Express the following ratios as percents. Round your answers to the nearest whole number.

   (a) 25 out of 75　　　　　　(b) 5 out of 65　　　　　　(c) 6 out of 36

   (d) 35 out of 100　　　　　 (e) 15 out of 100　　　　　(f) 50 out of 150

9. 25 is what percent of 125? Round your answer to the nearest whole number.

10. Express 4 as a percent of 48. Round your answer to the nearest whole number.

REAL WORLD APPLICATIONS – WORD PROBLEMS
Percent of One Number Compared to Another Number

Example 1

There are 8 girls and 12 boys in a class. What percent of the class is boys?

Solution

Total number of the students = 8 + 12 = 20 students.

The facts in the question can be stated as: "12 **is** what percent **of** 20?" and this can be expressed as:

$$\frac{is}{of} = \frac{12}{20}$$

Using the rule to find what percent a number is of another number, divide the number of boys by the total number of the students, and then move the decimal point two places or two digits to the right in the quotient, and then attach the % sign.

Step 1: Divide the number of boys by the total number of students as shown:

$$\frac{\text{Number of boys}}{\text{Total number of students}} = \frac{12}{20}$$

$$= \frac{12}{20}$$ Reduce to the lowest terms by dividing by 4.

$$\begin{array}{c} 5 \\ \end{array}$$

$$= \frac{3}{5}$$

$$\frac{3}{5} = 5\overline{)3} = 5\overline{)3.0} \atop \begin{array}{r} .6 \\ -30 \\ \hline 0 \end{array}$$

Step 2: Change .6 to a percent by moving the decimal point 2 places to the right, and then attach the percent sign which is the same as multiplying by 100.

Write a 0 here as a place holder.

.6 = .6 = 60%

Move the decimal point two places or two digits to the right.

Therefore, 60% of the class are boys.

Example 2

In a class of 24 students, 8 students like biology. What is the percent of the students that like biology?

Solution

The facts in the question can be stated as: "8 **is** what percent **of** 24?" and this can be expressed as:

$$\frac{is}{of} = \frac{8}{24}$$

Using the rule to find what percent a number is of another number, divide the number of students that like biology by the total number of the students, and then move the decimal point two places or two digits to the right in the quotient, and then attach the % sign.

Step1: Divide the number of students who like biology by the total number of students as shown:

$$\frac{\text{Number of students that like biology}}{\text{Total number of students}} = \frac{8}{24}$$

$$= \frac{\overset{1}{\cancel{8}}}{\underset{3}{\cancel{24}}}$$ Reduce to the lowest term by dividing by 8.

422

$$= \frac{1}{3}$$

Step 2: Change .333 to a percent by moving the decimal point 2 places to the right, and then attach the percent sign as follows:

$$.333 = .333 = 33.3\%$$

Move the decimal point two places or two digits to the right.

Therefore, 33.3% of the students like biology.

Example 3

Judith earned $10.25 for baby-sitting. If she spent $2.50, what percent of the money did she spend?

Solution

The facts in the question can be stated as: "$2.50 **is** what percent **of** $10.25?" and this can be expressed as:

$$\frac{\text{is}}{\text{of}} = \frac{\$2.50}{\$10.25}$$

Using the rule to find what percent a number is of another number, divide the amount spent by the total amount earned, and then move the decimal point two places or two digits to the right in the quotient, and then attach the % sign.

Step 1: Divide the amount that she spent by the total amount that she earned.

$$\frac{\text{Amount spent}}{\text{Total amount earned}} = \frac{\$2.50}{\$10.25}$$

$$= .244 \quad \text{You may use a calculator to divide.}$$

Step 2: Change .244 to a percent by moving the decimal point two places to the right, and then adding the percent sign.

$$.244 = .244 = 24.4\%$$

Move the decimal point two places or two digits to the right.

Therefore, Judith spent 24.4% of her money.

Example 4

Helen earned $25,600 last year. If she saved $5,000, what percent of her income did she save?

Solution

The facts in the question can be stated as: "$5,000 **is** what percent **of** $25,600?" and this can be expressed as:

$$\frac{\text{is}}{\text{of}} = \frac{\$5,000}{\$25,600}$$

Using the rule to find what percent a number is of another number, divide the amount saved by the total amount earned, and then move the decimal point two places or two digits to the right in the quotient, and then attach the % sign.

Step 1: Divide the amount saved by the total amount earned.

$$\frac{\text{Amount saved}}{\text{Total Amount earned}} = \frac{\$5,000}{25,600}$$

$$= .195 \quad \text{You may use a calculator to divide.}$$

Step 2: Change .195 to a percent by moving the decimal point two places to the right, and then attach the % sign.

$$.195 = .195 = 19.5\%$$

Move the decimal point two places or two digits to the right.

Therefore, Helen saved 19.5% of what she earned last year.

The notes and the generous examples have provided me with the conceptual understanding and the computational fluency to do my homework.

Exercises

1. There are 10 boys and 15 girls in a certain class. What is the percent of the girls in the class? Hint: See Example 1.
2. In a class of 30 students, 5 of them like Chemistry. What is the percent of the students that like chemistry? Hint: See Example 2.
3. George earned $15 for baby-sitting. If he spent $5, what is the percent of the money that he spent? Hint: See Example 3.
4. If Hope made a down payment of $12 on a television set that cost $224, what is the percent of her down payment? Hint: See Example 4.

Challenge Questions

5. If Grace earned $8 for baby-sitting and she spent $2.50 of it, what is the percent of the money that she spent?
6. Robert made a down payment of $20 on a computer that cost $350. What is the percent of his down payment?
7. There are 26 students in a class. If 10 of the students like history, what is the percent of the students that like history?
8. A certain class consists of 6 girls and 14 boys. What percent of the class is boys?

Cumulative Review

1. Find: (Round your answer to 2 decimal places).
   (**a**) 2 out of 125   (**b**) 5% of 100   (**c**) 15% of 52.50
2. Change each percent to a decimal. Round the answer to 2 decimal places.
   (**a**) 1%   (**b**) $8\frac{1}{2}\%$ (**c**) 120%

   (**d**) 15%   (**e**) 12%   (**f**) 45%
3. Write the following ratios as percents. Round your answer to 2 decimal places.
   (**a**) 2 out of 5   (**b**) 9 out of 10   (**c**) 8 out of 20
   (**d**) 7 out of 49   (**e**) 15 out of 125   (**f**) 3 out of 12
4. Change each decimal to a percent. Round your answer to 2 decimal places.
   (**a**) .5   (**b**) .48   (**c**) .34
   (**d**) 4.98   (**e**) .08   (**f**) .002

(**g**) .7   (**h**) 1.25   (**i**) .041

5. Change the following to decimal fractions. Round off each answer to the nearest hundredths.

(**a**) $\dfrac{1}{5}$ (**b**) $\dfrac{9}{10}$ (**c**) $\dfrac{4}{7}$ (**d**) $\dfrac{3}{8}$ (**e**) $\dfrac{5}{12}$

(**f**) $\dfrac{4}{9}$ (**g**) $\dfrac{5}{14}$ (**h**) $\dfrac{5}{9}$ (**i**) $\dfrac{2}{7}$ (**j**) $\dfrac{13}{15}$

6. $120 \div .24 =$ **7.** $5.04 \times .09 =$ **8.** $.91 + 784.1 =$

9. $91 - 7.989 =$ **10.** $45.381 - 2.492 =$ **11.** $.41 \times .98 =$

12. $\dfrac{1}{2} \div \dfrac{1}{2} =$ **13.** $\dfrac{3}{4} \div \dfrac{3}{8} =$ **14.** $\dfrac{5}{7} \times \dfrac{14}{2} =$

15. $.4 \div 10 =$ **16.** $18.7 \times 100 =$ **17.** $78 \times 10 =$

18. $\$24.64 \times .23 =$ **19.** $36.93 \div 3 =$ **20.** $56 \div 1,000 =$

21. $2\dfrac{1}{2} \div 3\dfrac{1}{3} =$ **22.** $3\dfrac{2}{4} \div 4\dfrac{2}{3} =$ **23.** $4\dfrac{3}{4} \times 2\dfrac{1}{2} =$

24. Change each percent to a decimal.

(**a**) 12%   (**b**) 15.5%   (**c**) $4\dfrac{1}{2}\%$ (**d**) 9%

25. Change each decimal to a percent.
(**a**) .002   (**b**) .7   (**c**) .95   (**d**) 4.12

26. Write each decimal as a word phrase:
(**a**) 4.44   (**b**) 5.09   (**c**) .038   (**d**) 2.009

27. Write each word phrase as a decimal:
(**a**) Nine tenths.   (**b**) Fourteen thousandths.
(**c**) Eight and three hundred fifteen ten–thousandths.
(**d**) Twelve thousandths.

28. (**a**) $8 \div \dfrac{1}{4} =$ (**b**) $\dfrac{3}{4} \div 12 =$ (**c**) $\dfrac{7}{8} \div \dfrac{21}{24} =$

CHAPTER 10

INEQUALITY

The statement that uses > and < to show that two quantities are not equal is an **inequality**. The symbols for inequalities, their meanings, examples and their solutions are shown in the table below:

Table 1

Symbols	Meaning	Examples	Solutions
<	is less than.	x < 10 means x is less than 10.	Every number less than 10 is a solution.
>	is greater than	x > -3 means x is greater than -3.	Every number greater than -3 is a solution.
≤	is less than or equal to.	x ≤ 6 means x is less than or equal to 6.	Every number less than 6 or equal to 6 is a solution.
≥	is greater than or equal to.	y ≥ -2 means y is greater or equal to -2.	Every number greater than -2 or equal to -2 is a solution.

Conclusions From Table 1

1. Notice that the information under the column "Solutions" shows that:
  a. An inequality may have **more than one solution**.
  b. Values that make **the inequality true** are solutions of the inequality.
2. Notice that the information under the column "Examples" shows that:
  a. An inequality may contain a variable, as in the inequality x < 10. In this inequality, x is the variable.
  b. An inequality may not contain a variable, as in the inequality 3 > -3.

Example 1

a. Is the number 2 one of the solutions of x < 8?

b. Are -9, 0, and $9\frac{1}{2}$ also solutions of x < 10?

Solution

a. Yes, the number 2 is one of the solutions of x < 8, because 2 < 8 is true. Hint: The meaning of the symbol < in Table 1 is used in deciding the solution.

b. Yes, -9, 0, and $9\frac{1}{2}$ are also solutions of x < 10 because -9, 0, and $9\frac{1}{2}$ are less than 10. Hint: The meaning of the symbol < in Table 1 is used in deciding the solution.

Example 2

Are $-2\frac{1}{2}$, 0, and 100 also solutions of $x > -3$?

Solution

Yes, $-2\frac{1}{2}$, 0, and 100 are also solutions of $x > -3$ because $-2\frac{1}{2}$, 0, and 100 are greater than -3. Hint: The meaning of the symbol $>$ in Table 1 is used in deciding the solution.

Example 3

Are -99, 0, and $\frac{1}{4}$ also solutions of $x \le \frac{1}{3}$?

Solution

Yes, -99, 0 and $\frac{1}{4}$ are also solutions of $x \le \frac{1}{3}$ because -99, 0, and $\frac{1}{4}$ are less than $\frac{1}{3}$. Hint: The meaning of the symbol $\le$ in Table 1 is used in deciding the solution.

Example 4

a. Are $\frac{1}{8}$, 0, and 50 also solutions of $y \ge -\frac{1}{4}$?

b. Are -10, −1, and $-\frac{3}{4}$ also solutions of $y \ge -\frac{1}{4}$?

Solution

a. Yes, $\frac{1}{8}$, 0, and 50 are also solutions of $y \ge -\frac{1}{4}$ because $\frac{1}{8}$, 0, and 50 are greater than $-\frac{1}{4}$. Hint: The meaning of the symbol $\ge$ in Table 1 is used in deciding the solution.

b. No, -10, −1, and $-\frac{3}{4}$ are not also solutions of $y \ge -\frac{1}{4}$ because -10, −1, and $-\frac{3}{4}$ are less than $-\frac{1}{4}$. Hint: The meaning of the symbol $\ge$ in Table 1 is used in deciding the solution, additionally, the graphical solution of inequalities on a number line (which is the next section) may help more in the understanding of the solution of Example 4b.

How to Graph the Solutions of Inequalities on the Number Line

There are three main steps in graphing all the solutions of inequalities as follows:

Step 1: Draw a number line as shown:

Step 2: Find the solutions of the inequality and use:

    a. a hollow dot to show that a specific number is not a solution as shown:

The hollow dot shows that 4 is not a solution.

    b. a solid dot to show that a specific number is also a solution as shown:

The solid dot shows that 4 is a solution.

Step 3: Start at the:

    a. hollow dot and color over the solutions you have found as shown:

The hollow dot shows that 4 is also a solution.

Color over the solutions that you have found.
For example, the red color is the solution for x > 4.

    b. solid dot and color over the solutions you have found as shown:

The solid dot shows that 4 is also a solution

Color over the solutions that you have found.
For example, the red color is the solution for x ≥ 4.

Note: **1**. You may combine Step 1, Step 2, and Step 3 in solving problems.
     2. The red color arrow on the number line shows that the solutions go on forever.

Example 5

Graph the solution of x < 6 on a number line.
Solution
Every number less than 6 is a solution of x < 6. Let us graph the solution as shown:

The hollow dot shows that 6 is not a solution

Example 6

Graph the solution of x > 3 on a number line.

Solution

Every number greater than 3 is a solution to x > 3. Let us graph the solution as shown:

The hollow dot shows that 3 is not a solution

Example 7

Graph the solution of $x \leq \dfrac{1}{3}$ on a number line.

Solution

Every number less than $\dfrac{1}{3}$ or equal to $\dfrac{1}{3}$ is a solution to $x \leq \dfrac{1}{3}$. Let us graph the

solution as shown:

The solid dot shows that $\dfrac{1}{3}$ is also a solution.

Example 8

Graph the solution of $y \geq -\dfrac{1}{4}$ on a number line.

Solution

Every number that is greater than or equal to $-\dfrac{1}{4}$ are solutions to $y \geq -\dfrac{1}{4}$. Let us

graph the solution as shown:

The solid dot shows that $-\dfrac{1}{4}$ is also a solution.

Exercises or Group Exercises

1. List the four symbols of inequality and state what each symbol means.
Hint: See the Table 1.

2. If $x < 6$, is 5 a solution? Explain. Hint: See Example 1.

3. If $x < 3$, are -11 and 0 also solutions? Hint: See Example 1.

4. If $x < 8$, is 10 a solution? Explain. Hint: See Example 1.

5. If $x > 2$, is 10 a solution? Explain. Hint: See Example 2.

6. If $x > 2$, is 0 a solution? Explain. Hint: See Example 2.

7. If $y > 14$, is 13 a solution? Explain. Hint: See Example 4b.

8. Are -50, 0 and $\dfrac{1}{4}$ also solutions to $x \le \dfrac{1}{2}$? Explain. Hint: See Example 3.

9. Are -1, 0, and $\dfrac{1}{8}$ also solutions to $x \le \dfrac{2}{3}$? Explain. Hint: See Example 3.

10. Are 0, 1 and 20 also solutions to $y \ge -1$? Explain. Hint: See Example 4a.

11. Are -2, 0, 1 and 100 also solutions to $y \ge -3$? Explain. Hint: See Example 4a.

12. Graph the solutions of the following inequalities on a number line.
Hint: See Example 5.
   a. $x < 4$ **b.** $x < 7$ **c.** $y < 2$ **d.** $x < -3$

13. Graph the solutions of the following inequalities on a number line.
Hint: See Example 6.
   a. $x > 2$ **b.** $x > 5$ **c.** $x > -2$ **d.** $y > 0$

14. Graph the solutions of the following inequalities on a number line.
Hint: See Example 7.
   a. $x \le \dfrac{1}{2}$ **b.** $x \le 4$ **c.** $y \le -2$ **d.** $x \le 5$

15. Graph the solutions of the following inequalities on a number line.
Hint: See Example 8.
   a. $y \ge -\dfrac{1}{2}$ **b.** $y \ge 3$ **c.** $x \ge -2$ **d.** $y \ge 1$

Challenge Questions

16. Graph the solutions of the following inequalities on a number line.
   a. $x \ge 0$ **b.** $x \le 0$ **c.** $x \ge -1$ **d.** $x < -2$
   e. $y \le -5$ **f.** $y < -6$ **g.** $y > 6$ **h.** $x > -4$

17. Explain why -2 is one of the solutions of $x \ge -3$

18. Explain why -4 is not a solution of $x \ge -3$

How to Solve Inequalities

How to solve inequalities is much the same as how to solve equations, but the **only difference is that when both sides of an inequality are multiplied or divided by a negative number, the inequality symbol must be reversed. Regard this as Rule 1**.

Example 1
Solve for x.

$x + 7 \leq 3$

Solution

$x + 7 \leq 3$

$x + 7 - 7 \leq 3 - 7$ Subtract 7 from both sides of the equation in order to eliminate the 7 at the left side of the equation so that x alone will remain at the left side of the equation. $7 - 7 = 0$ and $3 - 7 = -4$.

$x + 0 \leq -4$

$x \leq -4$

Example 2
Solve for x.

$x - 5 \leq -6$

Solution

$x - 5 \leq -6$

$x - 5 + 5 \leq -6 + 5$ Add 5 to both sides of the equation in order to eliminate the -5 from the left side of the equation so that only x remains at the left side of the equation. $-5 + 5 = 0$ and $-6 + 5 = -1$.

$x + 0 \leq -1$

$x \leq -1$

Example 3
Solve for n

$n + 6 \geq -4$

Solution

$n + 6 \geq -4$

$n + 6 - 6 \geq -4 - 6$ Subtract 6 from both sides of the inequality so that only n remains at the left side of the inequality. $6 - 6 = 0$ and $-4 - 6 = -10$

$n + 0 \geq -10$

$n \geq -10$

Example 4
Solve for t.

$\dfrac{t}{4} \geq -8$

Solution

$$\frac{t}{4} \geq -8$$

$$\frac{t}{4} \times 4 \geq -8 \times 4$$

Multiply both sides of the inequality by 4 in order to eliminate the denominator of 4 from the left side of the inequality so that only t should remain at the left side of the inequality.

$$\frac{t}{\underset{1}{4}} \times \overset{1}{4} \geq -32$$

Divide by 4 and also $-8 \times 4 = -32$

$$t \geq -32$$

Example 5

Solve for y. $-2y \leq -5$

Solution

$-2y \leq -5$

$$\frac{-2y}{-2} \geq \frac{-5}{-2}$$

↑

(Reverse the symbol).

Divide both sides of the inequality by -2 and **reverse** the inequality symbol so that only y should remain at the left side of the equation. **See Rule 1.**

$$\frac{\cancel{-2}y}{\underset{1}{\cancel{-2}}} \overset{y}{\geq} \frac{\cancel{-5}}{\cancel{-2}}$$

Note: The negative symbols attached to the numerators and the denominators cancel out each other.

$$y \geq \frac{5}{2}$$

$$\geq 2\frac{1}{2}$$

Example 6

Solve for k.

$$\frac{k}{-3} > 6$$

Solution

$$\frac{k}{-3} > 6$$

433

$\dfrac{k}{-3} \times (-3) < 6 \times (-3)$

$\uparrow$
(Reverse the symbol).

Multiply both sides of the inequality by -3 in order to eliminate the denominator on the left side of the inequality so that only k remains at the left side of the inequality. **See Rule 1**.

$\dfrac{k}{\cancel{-3}} \times (\cancel{-3}) < -18$

1

Note: The negative symbols at the left side of the inequality cancel out and also $6 \times (-3) = -18$.

$k < -18$

Example 7
Solve for p.
$-4p \geq 12$
Solution
$-4p \geq 12$

$\dfrac{-4p}{-4} \leq \dfrac{12}{-4}$

$\uparrow$
(Reverse the symbol).

Divide both sides of the inequality by -4 in order to eliminate the -4 from the left side of the inequality so that only p should remain at the left side of the inequality, and then **reverse** the inequality symbol. **See Rule 1**.

$\dfrac{\cancel{-4}p}{\cancel{-4}} \leq -3$

1

Note: The negative symbols that are attached to the inequality cancel out to give positive p which is simply written as p, also $4p \div 4 = p$ and $12 \div (-4) = -3$.

$p \leq -3$

The notes and the generous examples have provided me with the conceptual understanding and the computational fluency to do my homework.

Exercises
1. Judith said that when both sides of an inequality are multiplied or divided by a negative number, the symbol of the inequality is reversed.
   Is her statement true or false?
2. Solve for x, n, and k. Hint: See Example 1, 2, and 3.
   a. $x + 10 \leq 12$ **b.** $n + 2 \geq 3$ **c.** $k - 4 \leq -3$

d. $n + 11 \geq -3$ **e.** $x - 3 \leq 4$ **f.** $k + 3 < -5$

3. Solve for x, n, and k. Hint: See Example 4.

   a. $\dfrac{k}{6} \geq -2$ **b.** $\dfrac{n}{4} \leq 3$ **c.** $\dfrac{x}{2} > 4$

   d. $\dfrac{n}{3} < -6$ **e.** $\dfrac{k}{3} > -4$ **f.** $\dfrac{x}{5} \leq 4$

4. Solve for x, y, n, and k. Hint: See Examples 5 and 7.

   a. $-2y < -8$ **b.** $-3n < 12$ **c.** $-4k \geq 16$
   d. $-3x \geq -2$ **e.** $-5y > 25$ **f.** $-6k \leq 36$
   g. $-4k \geq 8$ **h.** $-2n \leq -24$ **i.** $-7x > -21$

5. Solve for x, n, and k. Hint: See Example 6.

   a. $\dfrac{k}{-4} < 2$ **b.** $\dfrac{n}{-3} \geq 3$ **c.** $\dfrac{n}{-5} \leq -2$

   d. $\dfrac{n}{-5} > -3$ **e.** $\dfrac{x}{-4} < -12$ **f.** $\dfrac{n}{-2} > 0$

Challenge Questions

6. Solve for x, n, and k.

   a. $\dfrac{x}{3} > 5$ **b.** $\dfrac{k}{-2} \leq -1$ **c.** $\dfrac{n}{-5} \geq -2$

   d. $k + 4 \geq -7$ **e.** $n - 6 < 3$ **f.** $x - 8 \leq -4$

Answers to Selected Questions

2a. $y < 2$ **3a.** $k \geq -12$ **4a.** $x > 4$ **5a.** $k > -8$

Cumulative Review

1. $2 - \dfrac{7}{8}$ **2.** $\dfrac{6}{7} \div \dfrac{6}{7}$ **3.** $2.34 \times 5 =$ **4.** $32.8 \times 4 =$

5. 10% of 100 =   **6.** 25% of 200 =   **7.** $4 \times 4 \times 4 =$ **8.** $10 + 7 + 3 =$

9. $\dfrac{3}{8} \div \dfrac{9}{16} =$ **10.** $\dfrac{2}{5} \times \dfrac{15}{16} =$ **12.** $\dfrac{2}{5} + \dfrac{1}{4} =$ **11.** $\dfrac{3}{5} - \dfrac{1}{4} =$

(Are you having fun with the mathematics?)

METRIC AND CUSTOMARY SYSTEMS

Understanding Measures
When the early humans changed from hunters to farmers, they needed to measure the size of their farms. The first units of length were based on the human body parts such as the length of the palm and the length of a finger. For example, the people of Ghana in West Africa use the distance from the tip of the left middle finger to the tip of the right middle finger of an adult as approximately 6 feet or 2 yards.
(3 feet = 1 yard). People do not have the same body size, and therefore each of the measures using body parts differed considerably. In order **to avoid confusion, measures were made standard** so that everybody would use the same standards.

The **National Bureau of Standards in Washington D.C**. determines the units on rulers or measuring tapes. When you measure something with a ruler or a tape measure, you are actually comparing it with these standard units.

The two main systems of measurements are the Customary and the Metric systems. The Customary system is also known as the English system. The metric system is used in most countries and the metric system is also known as SI which stands for **System International**.

METRIC SYSTEM

Metric Length
The metric unit is named after the unit of length, the meter, because the metric units of length are based on the meter. The diagram shows a part of the metric length of a ruler in centimeters. The distance between any small division = 1 millimeter (mm) and 10 millimeters (mm) = 1 centimeter (cm). Note carefully that when you take a ruler, the type of the units at any edge of the ruler is indicated such as centimeter (cm) or inch (in.).

Let us measure the length of an eraser as shown in the diagram.

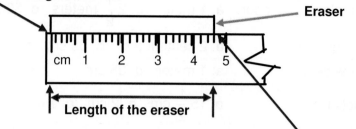

The end of the eraser coincides with the first marking on the ruler

Eraser

Length of the eraser

The end of the eraser coincides with a marking on the ruler

The length of the ruler is **4 centimeters and 6 millimeters**.

To measure the length of an eraser or any object, one of the edges of the eraser or the object should coincide with the first marking on the ruler and then read the marking on the ruler that coincides with the other edge of the eraser or the object. This method of measuring the length of any object is very useful in solving many exercises later.

Benchmark

A benchmark is an object whose measure is already known and we can then use the object to estimate the lengths of other objects. For example, if we know the length of your mathematics textbook, we can then use the textbook as a benchmark to measure the length of the top of your desk at school. We should then record the length of your desk in "mathematics textbook lengths."

Team Exercise

1. Use a ruler to measure the length of your mathematics textbook to the nearest millimeter (for example, the measurement could be 10 centimeters and 4 millimeters.)
2. Now use the length of the mathematics textbook to estimate the length of the top of your desk.
3. Record the length of the top of your desk in "mathematics textbook lengths."

   For example, your record could be $3\frac{1}{3}$ mathematics textbook lengths.

4. Now use a ruler to measure the length of the top of your desk.
5. Which unit is more convenient to use in measuring the length of the top of your desk? (Length of the mathematics textbook or using a ruler.) Explain your answer.

Team Exercise

Each team should measure the following objects and then select the most appropriate measure. (Hint: It is more convenient to use a measuring tape to measure longer distances or objects.)

Object to be measured.	Measurements
1. The length of your classroom door.	**a.** 1 meter **b.** $2\frac{1}{2}$ meters **c.** 50 meters
2. The thickness of a quarter.	**a.** 2 centimeters **b.** 35 cm **c.** 1 millimeters
3. The length of a new pencil.	**a.** 1 meter **b.** 35 cm **c.** 19 cm
4. The length of a dollar bill.	**a.** $15\frac{1}{2}$ cm **b.** 2 cm **c.** 1 m
5. The width of a dollar bill.	**a.** $2\frac{1}{2}$ m **b.** $6\frac{1}{2}$ cm **c.** 12 cm

6. Track events are measured in meters. Each team should record two track events in meters.

7. Each team should use a measuring tape to measure the length and width of the classroom. What unit would be the most appropriate for measuring the length and the width of the classroom? (a) meters (b) centimeters (c) millimeters.
   Hint: The largest feasible unit is the correct answer.

8. What unit would be the most appropriate for measuring the length of a postage stamp?
   (a) meters (b) centimeters (c) millimeters. Hint: The largest feasible unit is the correct answer.

9. Explain why the length of the chalkboard should be expressed in meters instead of millimeters?

10. Select the correct answer
    a. Your classroom door is about 92 cm, 92 m, or 92 km wide.
    b. The thickness of a dime is about 1 kg, 1 cm, or 1 mm.
    c. The width of an index fingernail is about 1 mm, 1 cm, or 1 km.
    d. The height of a kitchen counter is about 90 km, 90 m, or 90 cm.
    e. The width of a quarter is about 1 mm, 1 cm, or 1 m

Each team should report their answers to the whole class.

The notes and the generous worked examples have provided me with conceptual understanding and computational fluency to do my homework.

Group Exercises/Exercises
Use the method of measuring the length of the eraser to measure the length of each line with a ruler. Record your answers in centimeters and millimeters.
(Group Exercises: 1 - 4, Exercises: 5 - 10)

1 ———————————————— = ? cm and ? mm

2 ———————————— = ? cm and ? mm

3 ————————————————————— = ? cm and ? mm

4 —— = ? cm and ? mm

5 ——— = ? cm and ? mm

6 ————————————— = ? cm and ? mm

7 ——————————————————— = ? cm ? mm

8 ——————————————————————— = ? cm and ? mm

9 ————————————————————— = ? cm and ? mm

10 ————————————————— = ? cm and ? mm

Metric Units of Length
10 millimeters (mm) = 1 centimeter (cm)
100 centimeters (cm) = 1 meter (m)
1,000 meters (m) = 1 kilometer (km)

Look at the metric equations involving millimeters, centimeters, meters, and kilometers. Note that the metric system is easy to use because the units of measurements are related by the powers of 10. For example, to change different size units you just divide or multiply by 10, 100, or 1,000. The prefixes **milli**-, **centi**-, **deci**-, **deka**-, **hecto**-, and **Kilo**- shows how the measures are related to the basic unit which is the meter. For example;

a. milli - means "thousandth," and therefore, 1 **milli**meter is .001 or $\frac{1}{1000}$ of a meter.

b. Centi - means "hundredth," and therefore, 1 **centi**meter is .01 or $\frac{1}{100}$ of a meter.

c. Kilo - means "one thousand," and therefore, 1 Kilometer means 1000 meters.

(Mathematics is the easiest subject if you understand the concepts.)

439

Table of Metric Prefixes - Based on the Meter

Prefix	Meaning
milli-	one thousandth or .001 or $\dfrac{1}{1000}$
centi-	one hundredth or .01 or $\dfrac{1}{100}$
deci-	one tenth or .1 or $\dfrac{1}{10}$
basic unit (meter)	1
deka	ten or 10
hecto-	one hundred or 100
kilo-	one thousand or 1000

The prefixes that are in the bold type are most commonly used units of measurement.

Table of Metric Units

Unit	Abbreviation	Equivalent
millimeter	**mm**	**.001 m**, .01 dm, **.1 cm**
centimeter	**cm**	**.01 m**, .1 dm, **10 mm**
decimeter	dm	.1m, 10 cm, 100 mm
meter	**m**	10 dm, **100 cm**, **1,000 mm**, .1 dam, .01 hm, .001 km
dekameter	dam	10 m, .1 hm, .01 km
hectometer	hm	100 m, 10 dam, .1 km
kilometer	**km**	**1,000 m**, 100 dam, 10 hm

The prefixes that are in the bold type are most commonly used units of measurement.

Converting between the Metric Units

There are two ways to convert between the metric units as follows:

(a). by multiplying by .001, .01, .1, 10, 100, or 1,000 as applicable.

(b). by multiplying or dividing by 10, 100, or 1000 as applicable.

Rule 1: To change a smaller unit to a larger unit follow the following two steps:

Step 1: Find how many smaller units are contained in one unit of the larger unit.

Step 2: **Divide** the given number of smaller units by the number you have determined in Step 1.

Rule 2: To change a larger unit to a smaller unit follow the following two steps:

Step 1: Find how many smaller units are **contained** in one unit of the larger unit.

Step 2: **Multiply** the given number of larger units by the number you have determined in Step 1.

Example 1

How many centimeters are there in 200 millimeters?

Solution

We are converting from millimeters to centimeters, and therefore, we are converting from a smaller unit to a larger unit. Therefore, we can use **Rule 1** as shown:

Step 1: 10 mm = 1 cm

Step 2: Therefore, 200 mm = 200 mm ÷ 10 mm = $\dfrac{200}{10}$ = $\dfrac{\overset{20}{200}}{\underset{1}{10}}$ = 20 cm.

Example 2

Solve: 25 cm = ? mm

Solution

We are converting from centimeters to millimeters, and therefore, we are converting from a larger unit to a smaller unit. Therefore, we can use **Rule 2** as shown:

Step 1: l cm = 10 mm

Step 2: Therefore, 25 cm = 25 × 10 mm = 250 mm.

Example 3

Solve: 15 m = ? cm.

Solution

We are converting from meters to centimeters, and therefore, we are converting from a larger unit to a smaller unit. Therefore, we can use **Rule 2** as shown:

Step 1: 1 m = 100 cm.

Step 2: Therefore, 15 m = 15 × 100 cm = 1500 cm.

Example 4

Solve: ? m = 250 cm.

Solution

We are converting from centimeters to meters, and therefore, we are converting from a smaller unit to a larger unit. Therefore, we can use **Rule 1** as shown:

Step 1: 1m = 100 cm

Step 2: Therefore $\dfrac{250}{100}$ m = 250 cm.

$$\frac{250}{100} \text{ m} = 250 \text{ cm.}$$

$$\frac{250}{100} \text{ m} = 250 \text{ cm.}$$

$$2.5\text{m} = 250 \text{ cm.} \qquad \frac{250}{100} = 2.5 \text{ by moving the decimal}$$

point two places to the left.

Example 5

Solve: 8 km = ? m.

Solution

We are converting from kilometers to meters, and therefore, we are converting from a larger unit to a smaller unit. Therefore, we can use **Rule 2** as shown:

Step 1: 1 km = 1000 m.

Step 2: Therefore, 8 km = 8 × 1000 m = 8,000 m.

Example 6

Solve: 300 m = ? km.

Solution

We are converting from meters to kilometers, and therefore, we are converting from a smaller unit to a larger unit. Therefore, we can use **Rule 1** as shown:

Step 1: 1 km = 1000 m.

Step 2: Therefore, 300 m = $\dfrac{300}{1000}$ km.

$$= \frac{300}{1000} \text{ km.}$$

$$= \frac{3}{10} \text{ km.} \qquad (\frac{300}{1000} = \frac{3}{10} \text{ by dividing by 100})$$

$$= .3 \text{ km.}$$

Example 7

Solve: 5 km = ? cm.

Solution

We are converting kilometers to centimeters, and therefore, we are converting from a larger unit to a smaller unit. Therefore, we can use **Rule 2** as shown:

Step 1: 1 km = 100,000 cm.

Step 2: Therefore, 5 km = 5 × 100,000 cm = 500,000 cm.

Example 8

Solve: 250,000 cm = ? km.

Solution

We are converting centimeters to kilometers, and therefore we are converting from a smaller unit to a larger unit. Therefore, we can use **Rule 1** as shown:

Step 1: 1 km = 100,000 cm.

Step 2: Therefore, 250,000 cm = $\dfrac{250,000}{100,000}$ km.

$$= \frac{25}{10} \text{ km.} \qquad (\frac{250,000}{100,000} = \frac{25}{10} \text{ by dividing by 10,000.})$$

$$= 2.5 \text{ km.} \qquad (\frac{25}{10} = 2.5 \text{ by moving the decimal point one place to the left.})$$

Summary

1. In order to convert a smaller unit to a larger unit, **divide** by moving the decimal point to the **left** as needed.

2. In order to convert a larger unit to a smaller unit, **multiply** by moving the decimal point to the **right** as needed.

The notes and the generous examples have provided me with the conceptual understanding and the computational fluency to do my homework.

Exercises

1. How many centimeters are there in 300 millimeters? Hint: See Example 1.
2. How many centimeters are there in the following? Hint: See Example 1.
   a. 150 mm   b. 500 mm   c. 520 mm   d. 80 mm
3. Solve the following: Hint: See Example 2.
   a. 100 cm = ? mm   b. 60 cm. = ? mm   c. 15 cm. = ? mm
   d. 5 cm. = ? mm   e. 8 cm = ? mm   f. 18 cm = ? mm
4. Solve the following: Hint :See Example 3.
   a. 10 m = ? cm   b. 13 m = ? cm   c. 18 m = ? mm
   d. 5 m. = ? cm   e. 17 m. = ? cm   f. 22 m = ? mm
5. Solve the following: Hint: See Example 4.
   a. ? m = 270 cm   b. ? m = 300 cm   c. ? m = 150 cm
   d. ? m = 200 cm   e. ? m = 90 cm   f. ? m = 180 cm
6. Solve the following: Hint: See Example 5.
   a. 10 km = ? m   b. 5 km = ? m   c. 20 km = ? m

d. 6 km = ? m   **e.** 2 km = ? m   **f.** 11 km = ? m

7. Solve the following: Hint: See Example 6.

    a. 200 m = ? km   **b.** 2500 m = ? km   **c.** 20 km = ? km

    d. 900 m = ? km   **e.** 2 km = ? m   **f.** 560 m = ? km

8. Solve the following: Hint: See Example 7.

    a. 6 km = ? cm   **b.** 12 km = ? cm   **c.** 16 km = ? cm

    d. 2 km = ? cm   **e.** 8 km = ? cm   **f.** 3 km = ? cm

9. Solve the following: Hint: See Example 8.

    a. 150,000 cm = ? km   **b.** 200,000 cm = ? km   **c.** 100,000 cm = ? km

Challenge Questions

10. Solve the following:

    a. 9 m = ? cm   **b.** 3 km = ? m   **c.** 95 cm = ? mm

    d. 450 mm = ? cm   **e** 1500 m = ? km   **f.** 160,000 cm = ? km

Answers to Selected Questions

1. 30 cm   **2a.** 15 cm   **3a.** 1000 mm   **4a.** 1000 cm

REAL WORLD APPLICATIONS - WORD PROBLEMS
Converting Between the Metric Units

Example 1

John runs 4.2 kilometers every day. How many meters does he run in a week?

Solution

Setup: There are 7 days in a week, therefore, multiply 4.2 kilometes by 7 to obtain the total number of kilometers that John runs in a week. Then, change the total number of kilometers that John runs in a week to meters.

Step 1: Find the total number of kilometers that John runs every week as shown:

    In 1 day John runs 4.2 km.

    In 7 days (1 week) John will run 7 × 4.2 km = 29.4 km.

Step 2: Change the 29.4 km into meters as shown:

    1 km = 1000 m (See the section on "Metric units of Length,")

    therefore, 29.4 km = 29.4 × 1000 m = 29,400 m.   (Review decimal multiplication.)

    Therefore, John runs 29,400 m. in a week.

Example 2

How many meters are in $\frac{4}{5}$ kilometer?

Solution

Setup: Change the common fraction $\frac{4}{5}$ to a decimal fraction. Then find the number of meters that are contained in the decimal fraction of the kilometer.

Step 1: Change the common fraction $\frac{4}{5}$ to a decimal fraction as shown:

$$\frac{4}{5} = 5 \overline{\smash)\begin{array}{c} 0.8 \\ 40 \end{array}} = .8$$
$$\begin{array}{c} -\ 40 \\ \hline 00 \end{array}$$

Step 2: Find the number of meters that are contained in .8 km as shown:
1 km = 1000 m (See the section on "Metric units of Length")
Therefore, .8 × 1000 m = 800 m.   (Review decimal multiplication).

Example 3

Mary has a wire that measures .8 meters long. If her school project requires many lengths of a wire measuring 20 millimeters, how many lengths can she cut from the .8 meter long wire?

Solution

Setup: Change the .8 meters to millimeters, and then **divide** by 20 millimeters.

Step 1: Change the .8 meters to millimeters as shown:
1 m = 1000 mm (See the section on "Metric units of Length.")
Therefore, .8 m = .8 × 1000 mm = 800 mm. (Review decimal multiplication.)

Step 2: Find the number of 20 mm that are contained in 800 mm as shown:
Divide 800 mm by 20 mm to obtain the number of 20 mm that are contained in 800 mm as shown:

$$800 \div 20 = \frac{800}{20}$$

$$= \frac{800}{20} \qquad \text{Cancel out the zero by dividing by 10.}$$

$$= \frac{\overset{40}{\cancel{80}}}{\underset{1}{\cancel{2}}} \qquad \text{Divide by 2.}$$

$$= 40$$

Therefore, 40 lengths of 20 mm can be cut from the .8 m of the wire.

Example 4

Given that the scale on a map is 10 mm = 78 km, how many kilometers are represented by 5.5 cm?

Solution

Setup: Change 5.5 cm to millimeters, and then find how many 10 mm
(10 mm = 1 cm) are contained in 5.5 cm. Finally, multiply 78 km by the
number of 10 mm in 5.5 cm.

Step 1: Change the 5.5 cm to millimeters as shown:
1 cm = 10 mm (See the section on "Metric units of Length.")
Therefore, 5.5 cm = 5.5 × 10 mm = 55 mm. (Review decimal multiplication.)

Step 2: Find the number of 10 mm that are contained in the 55 mm shown:
Divide 55 mm by 10 = 55 ÷ 10 = $\frac{55}{10}$ = 5.5

Step 3: Find the kilometers represented by 5.5 cm on the map as shown:
Multiply 78 km by 55 = 78 km × 55 = 429 km.

Therefore, 5.5 cm on the map represents 429 km.

━━━━━━━━━━━━━━━━━━━━ The notes and the generous examples have provided
━━━━━━━━━━━━━━━━━━━━ me with the conceptual understanding and the
computational fluency to do my homework.

Exercises

1. Eric runs 3.8 kilometers every day. How many meters does he run in a week?
   Hint: See Example 1.

2. How many meters are contained in $\frac{3}{5}$ kilometers? Hint: See Example 2.

3. Susan has a wire that measures .95 meters long. If her school project requires many
   lengths of the wire measuring 30 millimeters, how many lengths can she cut from
   the .95 meter long wire. Hint: See Example 3.

4. Given that the scale on a certain map is 5 mm = 74 km, how many kilometers are
   represented by 7.2 cm? Hint: See Example 3.

Challenge Question

5. How many meters are contained in $\frac{2}{5}$ km?

Add and Subtract Measurements

Example 1

Copy and complete.

2 m + 150 cm = ? cm

Solution

Change the 2 m to centimeters by multiplying 2 m by 100 because 1 m = 100 cm
(See the section on "Metric Units of Length") and then add as follows:

2 m × 100 + 150 cm = ? cm

200 cm + 150 cm = 350 cm

Example 2

Copy and complete.

3 m + 400 cm = ? m

Solution

Change the 400 cm to meters by dividing 400 cm by 100 because 1 m = 100 cm
(See the section on "Metric Units of Length") and then add as shown:

$$3 \text{ m} + \frac{400}{100} \text{ m} = ? \text{ m}$$

$$3 \text{ m} + \frac{\overset{4}{\cancel{400}}}{\underset{1}{\cancel{100}}} \text{ m} = ? \text{ m}$$

3 m + 4 m = 7 m

Example 3

Copy and complete.

2 cm + 8 mm + 7 mm + 1 cm =

Solution

Step 1: Add the like units together as shown:

     2 cm + 1 cm + 8 mm + 7 mm =

     3 cm + 15 mm =

Step 2: Change 15 mm to centimeters and millimeters by dividing 15 mm by 10
because 1 cm = 10 mm (See the section on "Metric Units of Length,") such
that 15 mm ÷ 10 = 1 remainder 5 and the 1 has a unit of cm and the 5 has
a unit of mm as shown:

     3 cm + 1 cm + 5 mm = 4 cm + 5 mm

Example 4

Solve: 10 km   600 m

       - 2 km   900 m

Solution

Step 1: We cannot subtract 900 m from 600 m, and therefore, we have to borrow
1 km from the 10 km. The borrowed 1 km = 1000 m (See the section on "Metric
Units of Length") and add the 1000 m to the 600 m to obtain 1600 m as

shown:

$$
\begin{array}{cc}
9 & 1600 \\
10\text{ km} & 600\text{ m} \\
-\ 2\text{ km} & 900\text{ m}
\end{array}
$$

Step 2: Do the subtraction now as shown:

$$
\begin{array}{cc}
9 & 1600 \\
10\text{ km} & 600\text{ m} \\
-\ 2\text{ km} & 900\text{ m} \\
\hline
7\text{ km} & 700\text{ m}
\end{array}
$$

Example 5

Solve: 6 cm 3 mm - 2 cm 8 mm =

Solution

Step 1: Rewrite the question as shown:

$$
\begin{array}{cc}
6\text{ cm} & 3\text{ mm} \\
-\ 2\text{ cm} & 8\text{ mm}
\end{array}
$$

Step 2: We cannot subtract 8 mm from 3 mm and therefore we have to borrow 1 cm from 6 cm and then change the 1 cm to millimeters, 1 cm = 10 mm (See the section on "Metric Units of Length,") then add the 10 mm to the 3 mm to obtain 13 mm as shown:

$$
\begin{array}{cc}
5 & 13 \\
6\text{ cm} & 3\text{ mm} \\
-\ 2\text{ cm} & 8\text{ mm}
\end{array}
$$

Step 3: Do the subtraction now as shown:

$$
\begin{array}{cc}
5 & 13 \\
6\text{ cm} & 3\text{ mm} \\
-\ 2\text{ cm} & 8\text{ mm} \\
\hline
3\text{ cm} & 5\text{ mm}
\end{array}
$$

Example 6

Solve:
$$
\begin{array}{cc}
12\text{ m} & 9\text{ cm} \\
-\ 8\text{ m} & 5\text{ cm}
\end{array}
$$

Solution

Do the subtraction as shown:

$$
\begin{array}{r}
12\text{ m}\quad 9\text{ cm} \\
-\ 8\text{ m}\quad 5\text{ cm} \\
\hline
4\text{ m}\quad 4\text{ cm}
\end{array}
$$

═══════════════ The notes and the generous examples have provided me with the conceptual understanding and the computational fluency to do my homework.

Exercises

1. Copy and complete. Hint: See Example 1.

   a. 4 m + 125 cm =? cm   **b.** 1 m + 85 cm = ? cm

   c. 6 m + 201 cm = ? cm   **d.** 3 m + 111 cm = ? cm

2. Copy and complete. Hint: See Example 2.

   a. 4 m + 300 cm = ? m   **b.** 1 m + 100 cm = ? m

   c. 2 m + 500 cm = ? m   **d.** 3 m + 200 cm = ? m

3. Copy and complete. Hint: See Example 3.

   a. 3 cm + 4 mm + 12 mm + 2 cm =

   b. 7 mm + 1 cm + 3 mm + 4 cm =

   c. 10 cm + 6 mm + 4 cm + 12 mm =

   d. 12 mm + 5 cm + 5 mm + 2 cm =

4. Solve: See Example 4.

   a.
$$
\begin{array}{r}
4\text{ km}\quad 200\text{ m} \\
-1\text{ km}\quad 400\text{ m} \\
\hline
\end{array}
$$
   b.
$$
\begin{array}{r}
3\text{ km}\quad 700\text{ m} \\
-\ 2\text{ km}\quad 800\text{ m} \\
\hline
\end{array}
$$
   c.
$$
\begin{array}{r}
5\text{ km}\quad 98\text{ m} \\
-\ 3\text{ km}\quad 100\text{ m} \\
\hline
\end{array}
$$

5. Solve: Hint: See Example 5.

   a. 3 cm 4 mm - 1 cm 6 mm =

   b. 2 cm 5 mm - 1 cm 7 mm =

   c. 6 cm 8 mm - 2 cm 9 mm =

   d. 12 cm 6 mm - 9 cm 7 mm =

6. Solve: Hint: See Example 6.

   a.
$$
\begin{array}{r}
10\text{ m}\quad 8\text{ cm} \\
-\ 5\text{ m}\quad 3\text{ cm} \\
\hline
\end{array}
$$
   b.
$$
\begin{array}{r}
2\text{ m}\quad 5\text{ cm} \\
-\ 1\text{ m}\quad 2\text{ cm} \\
\hline
\end{array}
$$
   c.
$$
\begin{array}{r}
4\text{ m}\quad 7\text{ cm} \\
-\ 2\text{ m}\quad 5\text{ cm} \\
\hline
\end{array}
$$

Challenge Questions

7. Copy and complete.

   a. 9 cm + 4 mm + 2 cm + 8 mm =

   b. 4 cm 3 mm - 2 cm 9 mm =

   c. 6 cm 7 mm - 5 cm 5 mm =

d. 3 m + 600 cm = ? m

e. 10 m + 150 cm = ? cm

8. Solve:

a.	12 km 700 m	**b.**	2 cm 9 mm
	- 2 km 800 m		+ 5 cm 5 mm

c.   6 m + 700 cm = ? m

Answers to Selected Questions

1a. 525 cm   **2a.** 7 m   **3a.** 6 cm 6 mm   **4a.** 2 km 800 m

CUSTOMARY UNITS OF LENGTH

The Customary unit of length are the inch, foot, yard, and mile.

12 inches (in.) = 1 foot (ft)
3 feet (ft) = 1 yard (yd)
5,280 feet (ft) = 1 mile (mi)
1,760 yards = 1 mile

Detailed Customary Units of Length table

Unit	Abbreviation	Equivalence
inch	in.	12 in. = 1 foot
foot	ft	1 ft = 12 in., 3 ft = 1 yard, 5,280 ft = 1 mile
yard	yd	1 yd = 3 ft, 1 yd = 36 in., 1,760 yd = 1 mile

Example 1

How many inches are in 5 feet?

Solution

We are to find 5 feet = how many inches.

Note: **To change from a larger unit (for example feet) to a smaller unit, (for example inches), multiply as follows**:

Number of feet × Number of inches in 1 foot = Number of inches.

450

Number of feet × Number of inches in 1 foot = Number of inches

$$5 \quad \times \quad 12 \quad = \quad 60 \text{ inches.}$$

There are 60 inches in 5 feet.

Example 2

How many feet are in 48 inches?

Solution

We are to find 48 inches = how many feet.

Note: To change from a smaller unit (such as inches) to a larger unit (such as feet), divide.

Number of inches ÷ Number of inches in 1 foot = Number of feet.

Number of inches ÷ Number of inches in 1 foot = Number of feet.

$$48 \quad \div \quad 12 \quad = \quad 4 \text{ feet}$$

There are 4 feet in 48 inches.

Example 3

An electric wire is 72 yards long. How many feet does the wire contain?

Solution

We are to find 72 yards = how many feet.

Note: To change from a larger unit (yard) to a smaller unit (feet), multiply.

Number of yards × Number of feet in 1 yard = Number of feet.

Number of yards × Number of feet in 1 yard = Number of feet.

$$72 \quad \times \quad 3 \quad = \quad 216 \text{ feet}$$

There are 216 feet in 72 yards.

Example 4

One of the school's hallways is 99 feet long. How long is the hallway in yards?

Solution

We are to find 99 feet = how many yards.

Note: To change from a smaller unit (feet) to a larger unit (yard), divide.

Number of feet ÷ Number of feet in 1 yard = Number of yards.

451

Number of feet ÷ Number of feet in 1 yard = Number of yards.

$$99 \quad \div \quad 3 \quad = \quad 33 \text{ yards}$$

There are 33 yards in 99 feet.

Example 5

Find 3 ft 5 in + 6ft 11 in.

Solution

Step 1: Rewrite the question and add the like units as shown:

```
      3 ft   5 in.
   + 6 ft   11 in.
      9 ft   16 in.
```

Step 2: Change 16 in. into feet and inches as shown:

16 in. is more than 1 foot because 12 in. = 1 ft, therefore, rename 16 in. as
1 ft + 4 in (16 in. ÷ 12 =1 ft remainder 4 in.).
(Note that from the customary unit of length, 12 inches = 1 foot).
Therefore, the 9 ft 16 in. = 9 ft + (1 ft + 4 in.).

Step 3: Combine the like units as shown:

9 ft + (1 ft + 4 in.) = 9 ft + 1 ft + 4 in.
= 10 ft 4 in.

Example 6

Solve:
```
     8 yd   1 ft
   - 3 yd   2 ft
```

Solution

Step 1: 2 ft cannot be subtracted from 1 ft because 2 ft is greater than 1 ft, and
therefore, we have to borrow 1 yd from 8 yd and this 1 yd = 3 ft (See
customary unit of length.) Add the 3 ft to 1 ft to become 4 ft and rewrite
the question as shown:

```
     7       4
     8 yd   1 ft
   - 3 yd   2 ft
```

Step 2: Do the subtraction as shown:
```
     7       4
     8 yd   1 ft
   - 3 yd   2 ft
     4 yd   2 ft
```

Example 7

Solve: 5 yd   2 ft
          - 2 yd   1 ft

Solution

Do the subtraction as shown:

     5 yd   2 ft
   - 2 yd   1 ft
     3 yd   1 ft

The notes and the generous examples have provided me with the conceptual understanding and the computational fluency to do my homework.

Exercises

1. What are the customary units of length?
2. How many inches are in the following lengths? Hint: See Example 1.
   a. 10 ft   **b.** 4 ft   **c.** 8 ft   **d.** 2 ft
3. How many feet are in the following lengths? Hint See Example 2.
   a. 24 in.   **b.** 60 in.   **c.** 36 in.   **d.** 72 in.
4. A fence is 144 yards long. How long is the fence in feet?
   Hint: See Example 3.
5. A swimming pool is 39 ft long. How long is the swimming pool in yards?
   Hint: See Example 4.
6. Solve: Hint: See Example 5.
   a. 4 ft 8 in. + 7 ft 6 in. =   **b.** 2 ft 7 in. + 3 ft 8 in. =
   c. 12 ft 5 in. + 2 ft 8 in. =   **c.** 1 f 9 in. + 8 ft 6 in. =
7. Solve: Hint: See Example 6.
   a. 6 yd 1 ft   **b.** 9 yd 1 ft   **c.** 5 yd 0 ft
        - 4 yd 2 ft   - 6 yd 2 ft   - 3 yd 1 ft

Challenge Questions

8. Copy and complete
   a. 72 in. = ? ft   **b.** 6 yd = ? ft   **c.** 9 ft = ? in.
   d. 36 ft = ? yd   **e.** 15 yd = ? ft   **f.** 9ft = ? yd

Answers to Selected Questions

2a. 120 in.   **3a.** 2 ft   **6a.** 12 ft 2 in.

CUSTOMARY UNITS OF SQUARE MEASURE

The basic customary units of square measures are square inches, square foot, square yard, acre, and square miles. These basic customary units of square measure are shown in the table.

Table

Unit	Equivalence	Abbreviation
Square inch (in.²)	144 in.² = 1 ft² 1,296 in.² = 1 yd²	in.²
Square foot (ft²)	1 ft² = 144 in.² 9 ft² = 1 yd²	ft²
Square yard (yd²)	1 yd² = 9 ft² 1 yd² = 1,296 in² 4,840 yd² = 1 A.	yd²
Acre	1 A. = 43,560 ft² 1 A. = 4,840 yd² 640 A. = 1 mi.²	A.
Square mile (mi.²)	1 mi.² = 640 A.	mi.²

Although the basic customary units of the square measure are given in the table, we will only discuss two most important ones as shown:

$$1 \text{ ft}^2 = 144 \text{ in.}^2$$
$$1 \text{ yd}^2 = 9 \text{ ft}^2$$

It is important to know that the rules for changing units of square measurement are the same as the rules for the linear measurements as shown:

First, **find how many smaller units are contained in one unit of the bigger unit and then**;

1. **To change a smaller unit to a bigger unit, divide by the number that you have found.**
2. **To change a bigger unit to a smaller unit, multiply by the number that you have found.**

Example 1

Change 288 in.² to square feet.

Solution

When we compare inches to feet, the smaller unit is inches. Using the rule, to change from smaller unit to bigger unit, we must divide.

144 in.^{2} = 1 ft^2 See the table.

Therefore, 288 in.^{2} = 288 in.^{2} ÷ 144 in.^{2} = 2 ft^2 Using the rule, we must divide.

Example 2

Change 2 ft^2 to square inches.

Solution

When we compare feet to inches, the feet is a bigger unit. Using the rule, to change a bigger unit to a smaller unit, we must multiply.

1 ft^2 = 144 in.^{2} See table

Therefore, 2 ft^2 = 2 × 144   Using the rule, we must multiply.

= 288 in.^{2}

Example 3

Change 4 yd^2 to square feet.

Solution

When we compare yards to feet, the yard is a bigger unit. Using the rule, to charge a bigger unit to a smaller unit, we must multiply.

1 yd^2 = 9 ft^2 See the table.

Therefore, 4 yd^2 = 4 × 9   Using the rule, we must multiply.

= 36 ft^2

Example 4

Change $5\frac{2}{3}$ yd^2 to square feet

Solution

When we compare yards to feet, the yard is a bigger unit. Using the rule, to change a bigger unit to a smaller unit, we must multiply.

1 yd^2 = 9 ft^2 See the table.

Therefore, $5\frac{2}{3}$ yd^2 = $5\frac{2}{3}$ × 9 ft^2 Using the rule, must multiply.

= $\frac{17}{3}$ × 9 ft^2 Review fractions.

$$= \frac{\overset{3}{\cancel{17}}}{\underset{1}{\cancel{3}}} \times 9 \text{ ft}^2 \qquad \text{Divide by 3.}$$

$$= 17 \times 3 \text{ ft}^2$$
$$= 51 \text{ ft}^2$$

Example 5

Change 63 square feet to square yards.

Solution

When we compare feet and yard, feet is the smaller unit. Using the rule, changing from the smaller unit to the bigger unit, we must divide.

$$9 \text{ ft}^2 = 1 \text{ yd}^2 \qquad \text{See the table.}$$
Therefore, $63 \text{ ft}^2 = 63 \div 9 \qquad$ Using the rule, we must divide.
$$= 7 \text{ yd}^2$$

━━━━━━━━━━━━━━ The notes and the generous examples have provided me with the conceptual understanding and the computational fluency to do my homework.

Exercises

1. Change the following square inches to square feet. Hint: See Example 1.
   a. 432 in.^{2} **b**. 720 in.^{2}

2. Change the following square feet to square inches. Hint: See Example 2.
   a. 3 ft^2 **b**. 8 ft^2 **c**. 10 ft^2 **d**. 12 ft^2

3. Change the following square yards to square feet. Hint: See Example 3.
   a. 3 yd^2 **b**. 7 yd^2 **c**. 10 yd^2 **d**. 6 yd^2

4. Change the following square yards to square feet. Hint: See Example 4.
   a. $4\frac{1}{3}$ yd^2 **b**. $6\frac{2}{3}$ yd^2 **c**. $7\frac{1}{3}$ yd^2 **d**. $3\frac{2}{3}$ yd^2

5. Change the following square feet to square yards. Hint: See Example 5.
   a. 18 ft^2 **b**. 90 ft^2 **c**. 45 ft^2 **d**. 72 ft^2

Challenge Questions

5. Change the following square yards to square feet
   a. $2\frac{2}{3}$ yd^2 **b**. 1 yd^2 **c**. 11 yd^2

6. Change the following square inches to square feet.
   a. 144 in^2 **b**. 576 in^2

7. Change the following square feet to square inches.

    a. 4 ft²   **b.** 7 ft²   **c.** 8 ft²

8. Change the following square feet to square yards.

    a. 27 ft²   **b.** 36 ft²   **c.** 45 ft²   **d.** 9 ft²

Answers to Selected Questions.

    1a. 3 ft²   **2a.** 432 in²   **3a.** 27 ft²

REAL WORLD APPLICATIONS - WORD PROBLEMS
Customary Units of Square Measure

Example 1

A room has 99 square feet of floor space. How many square yards of tiles is needed for the floor assuming that there will be no waste of the tiles.

Solution

When we compare feet to yard, the yard is a bigger unit. Using the rule, to change from smaller unit to bigger unit, we must divide.

          9 ft² = 1 yd²   See the table.

Therefore, 99 ft² = 99 ÷ 9   Using the rule, we must divide.

          = 11 yd²

Exercise

A room has 72 square feet of floor space. How many square yards of tiles is needed for the floor assuming that there will be no waste of the tiles.
Hint: See Example 1.

Cumulative Review

1. Explain average, median, and mode.

2. Find the average of each of the following test scores:

    a. 80%, 90%, and 40%.

    b. 100% and 90%.

    c. 60%, 85%, 95%, and 40%.

3. Find the median and the mode of each set of numbers.

    a. 3, 8, 5, 12, and 4

    b. 12, 10, 8, and 4.

CHAPTER 13

METRIC MASS AND CUSTOMARY WEIGHT

Metric Mass

Recall that the units of the metric length are based on the meter, similarly the units of the metric mass are based on the gram. A benchmark for 1 gram is the mass of a large paper clip.

Team Work

Each team should do a research at a super market and list the names and the weights of 4 different packages of cookies in grams. The weights are already written on the packages. Can you compare the mass of a large paper clip, which is 1 gram to the mass of each package of cookie?

Metric Prefixes

Prefix	Meaning	Abbreviations
milli-	one thousandth, 0.001, or $\dfrac{1}{1000}$	mg for milligram
kilo-	one thousand, (1,000)	kg for kilogram

The prefix for gram is g.

Metric Mass Units

1 milligram (mg) = .001 g or $\dfrac{1}{1000}$ g

1 gram (g) = 1,000 mg, .001 kg, or $\dfrac{1}{1000}$ kg

1 kilogram (kg) = 1,000, .001 metric ton, or $\dfrac{1}{1000}$ metric tons.

1 metric ton (t) = 1,000 kg, 1,000,000 g.

Rule 1: To change smaller units to larger units **divide**.
Rule 2: To change larger units to smaller units **multiply**.

Example 1

How many grams are there in 5 kilograms?
Solution

The question may be rewritten as follows:

5 kilograms = ? grams.

To change larger units to smaller units multiply.

Number of kilograms × Number of grams in 1 kilogram = Number of grams.

| 5 | × | 1,000 | = | 5,000 gram. |

There are 5,000 grams in 5 kilograms.

Example 2

If glucophage 1000 mg tablet is one of the medications that Nick takes daily, what is the mass of 1 tablet of the glucophage in grams?

Solution

The question may be rewritten as follows:

1000 mg = ? g

To change from smaller units (for example mg) to larger units (for example g) divide as shown:

Number of mg ÷ Number of mg in 1 g = Number of grams.

| 1,000 | ÷ | 1,000 | = | 1 gram |

Therefore, the mass of 1 tablet of glucophage is 1 gram.

Example 3

Replace ? with the number that makes the statement true.

6 g = ? mg

Solution

To change from larger units (for example g) to smaller units (for example mg) multiply as shown:

Number of grams × Number of milligrams in 1 gram = Number of milligrams.

| 6 | × | 1,000 | = | 6,000 milligrams |

Therefore, 6 g = 6,000 mg.

Example 4

Solve: 3.6 kg = ? g.

Solution

To change from larger units (for example kg) to smaller units (for example g) multiply as shown:

Number of kilograms × Number of grams in 1 kilogram = Number of grams.

$$3.6 \qquad × \qquad 1,000 \qquad = \qquad 3,600$$

Therefore, 3.6 kg = 3, 600 grams.   (Review decimal multiplication).

Example 5

Solve: 7500 kg = ? metric ton

Solution

To change from smaller units (for example kg) to larger units (for example metric tons) divide as shown:

Number of kilograms ÷ Number of kilograms in 1 metric ton = Number of metric tons.

$$7,500 \qquad ÷ \qquad 1,000 \qquad = \qquad \frac{7500}{1000}$$

$$= \qquad \frac{75\cancel{0}\cancel{0}}{10\cancel{0}\cancel{0}}$$

$$= \qquad 7.5$$

Therefore, 7,500 kg = 7.5 metric tons

Example 6

Compare and write =, <, or > for ?

3 metric tons ? 2,500,000 g

Solution

Setup: The first step in comparing numbers is to change the numbers to the same units before comparing.

Step 1: Change 3 metric tons to grams. To change from larger units (for example metric tons) to smaller units (for example grams) multiply as shown:

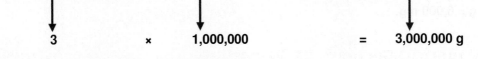

Number of metric tons × Number of grams in 1 metric tons = Number of grams.

$$3 \qquad × \qquad 1,000,000 \qquad = \qquad 3,000,000 \text{ g}$$

Therefore, 3 metric tons = 3,000,000 g.

But 3,000,000 g is greater than 2,500,000 g. Therefore, 3 metric tons > 2,500,000 g.

The notes and the generous examples have provided me with the conceptual understanding and the computational fluency to do my homework.

Exercises

1. Select the correct answer. The metric mass is based on:
   a. inches   **b.** meter   **c.** gram   **d.** kilogram

2. How many grams are there in the following? Hint: See Example 1.
   a. 6 kg   **b.** 2 kg   **c.** 1.5 kg   **d.** 3 kg

3. If the mass of 1 tablet of a medication is 500 mg, what is the weight of the tablet in grams? Hint: See Example 2.

4. Replace ? with the number that makes the statement true. Hint: See Example 3.
   a. 2 g = ? mg   **b.** 4 g = ? mg   **c.** 3 g = ? mg

5. Solve the following: Hint: See Example 4.
   a. 4.2 kg = ? g   **b.** 2.3 kg = ? g   **c.** 1.5 kg = ? g

6. Solve: Hint: See Example 5.
   a. 2,500 kg = ? metric tons   **b.** 3,300 kg = ? metric tons
   c. 1,100 kg = ? metric tons   **d.** 6,200 kg = ? metric tons

7. Compare and write =, <, or > for ? Hint: See Example 6.
   a. 2 metric tons ? 2,000,000 g   **b.** 4 metric tons ? 3,900,000 g
   c. 3 metric tons ? 3,100,000 g   **d.** 5 kg ? 4,900 g

Challenge Questions

8. Solve:
   a. 4 metric tons = ? kg   **b.** 8 g = ? mg   **c.** 5000 g = ? kg.
   d. 3,000,000g = ? metric tons   **e.** 4,500 mg = ? g.

CUSTOMARY UNITS OF WEIGHT

The basic unit of mass in the Customary System is the pound.
16 ounces (oz) = 1 pound (lb)
2,000 pounds = 1 ton (T)

461

Example 1

Solve: 40 oz = ? lb

To change from smaller units (for example, ounces) to larger units (for example pound), divide as shown:

Number of ounces ÷ Number of ounces in 1 pound = Number of pounds.

$$40 \quad ÷ \quad 16 \quad = \quad \frac{40}{16}$$

$$= \quad \frac{\overset{5}{\cancel{40}}}{\underset{2}{\cancel{16}}}$$

$$= \quad \frac{5}{2}$$

Therefore, 40 oz = $2\frac{1}{2}$ lb.

Example 2

Solve: 4lb = ? oz.

Solution

To change from larger units (for example, pounds) to smaller units (for example ounces), multiply as shown:

Number of pounds × Number of ounces in 1 pound = Number of ounces.

4   16   64 ounces.

Therefore, 4 lb = 64 oz.

Example 3

Solve: 6,000 lb = ? T

Solution

To change from smaller units (for example, pounds) to larger units (for example tons), divide as shown:

Number of pounds ÷ Number of pounds in 1 ton = Number of tons.

$$6{,}000 \quad ÷ \quad 2{,}000 \quad = \quad \frac{6{,}000}{2{,}000} \text{ tons.}$$

$$= \frac{6{,}\cancel{000}}{2{,}\cancel{000}} \text{ tons.} \quad \text{Divide by 1,000}$$

$$= \frac{6}{2} \text{ tons} = 3 \text{ T.}$$

Therefore, 6,000 lb = 3 T

Example 4

Solve: 4 T = ? lb

Solution

To change from larger units (for example, tons) to smaller units (for example pounds), multiply as shown:

Number of tons × Number of pounds in 1 ton = Number of pounds.

$$4 \quad × \quad 2{,}000 \quad = \quad 8{,}000 \text{ pounds}$$

Therefore, 4 T = 8,000 lb.

REAL WORLD APPLICATION - WORD PROBLEMS
Customary Units of Weight

Example 5

How many 100-pound bags of potatoes can be obtained from a ton of potatoes?

Solution

Setup: Change a ton of potatoes to pounds of potatoes and then divide by 100 pounds.
To change from larger units (for example, tons) to smaller units (for example pounds), multiply as shown:

Number of tons × Number of pounds in 1 ton = Number of pounds.

$$1 \quad × \quad 2{,}000 \quad = \quad 2{,}000 \text{ pounds.}$$

Therefore, there are 2000 lb in 1 ton.
To find how many 100-pound bags of potatoes are contained in the 2000 lb of potatoes, divide 2000 lb by 100 lb as shown:

$$\frac{2{,}000 \text{ lb}}{100 \text{ lb}} = \frac{2{,}000 \text{ lb}}{100 \text{ lb}}$$ Divide by 100.

$$= 20$$

Therefore, there are 20-pound bags of potatoes in a ton of the potatoes.

Example 6

How much would 48 ounces of candy cost at $4.00 per pound?

Solution

Setup: Let us find how many pounds are there in 48 ounces, and then multiply the number of pounds in 48 ounces by $4.00 to obtain the cost of 48 ounces of the candy as shown:

To change from smaller units (for example, ounces) to larger units (for example pounds), divide as shown:

Number of ounces ÷ Number of ounces in 1 pound = Number of pounds.

$$48 \qquad \div \qquad 16 \qquad = \qquad \frac{48}{16} \text{ pounds}$$

$$= \frac{\overset{3}{\cancel{12}}\,\cancel{48}}{\underset{1}{\underset{\cancel{4}}{\cancel{16}}}}$$

$$= 3 \text{ (Divide by 4 and by 4 again).}$$

Therefore, there are 3 pounds in 48 ounces.

If 1 lb of the candy costs $4.00, then 3 lb of the candy will cost 3 × $4.00 = $12.00.

▬▬▬▬▬▬▬▬▬ **The notes and the generous examples have provided me with the conceptual understanding and the computational fluency to do my homework.**

Exercises

1. The basic unit of mass in the Customary System is the_____.
2. Solve: (Hint: See Example 1).
   a. 32 oz = ? lb **b.** 24 oz = ? lb **c.** 8 oz = ? lb **d.** 48 oz = ? lb
3. Solve: (Hint: See Example 2).
   a. 2 lb = ? oz **b.** 5 lb = ? oz **c.**10 lb = ? oz **d.** 7 lb = ? oz
4. Solve: (Hint: See Example 3).

a. 2000 lb = ? T   **b.** 1000 lb = ? T   **c.** 4000lb = ? T   **d.** 8000 lb = ? T

5. Solve: (Hint: See Example 6).

   a. 2 T = ? lb   **b.** 6 T = ? lb   **c.** 3 T = ? lb   **d.** 5 T = ? lb

6. Solve: (Hint: See Example 5).

How many 50-pound bags of rice can be obtained from 2 tons of rice?

7. Solve: (Hint: See Example 6).

How much would 32 ounces of candy cost at $3.00 per pound?

Challenge Questions

8. Solve: **a.** 6 lb = ? oz   **b.** 40 oz = ? lb   **c.** 10 T = ? lb   **d.** 5000 lb = ? t

Answers to Selected Questions

2a. 2 lb   **3a.** 32 oz   **4a.** 1 T   **5a.** 4000 lb

Cumulative Review

1. $4 \times \dfrac{3}{8} =$ 2. $5\dfrac{3}{4} - \dfrac{1}{8}$ 3. $.23 \times 4 =$

4. Explain how to change a decimal fraction into a percent.

5. Explain how to change a percent to a decimal fraction.

6. Explain how to change a percent into a fraction.

7. Solve for x:

      $8x \geq 24$

8. Solve for x:

      $-8x \geq 24$

9. Solve for k:

      $3k < 12$

10. Solve for k:

      $-3k < 12$

11. Solve for p:

      $-4p > -16$

12. Solve for f:

      $-2f \leq -20$

13 $\dfrac{6}{7} \div \dfrac{3}{14} =$ 14. $\dfrac{6}{7} \times \dfrac{3}{14} =$ 15. $4\dfrac{2}{3} - 2\dfrac{3}{4} =$

CHAPTER 14

METRIC CAPACITY AND CUSTOMARY CAPACITY

METRIC CAPACITY

The basic unit in measuring liquid is the liter. The metric units of capacity are:

1,000 milliliter (mL) = 1 liter (L)
250 milliliters = 1 metric cup
4 metric cups = 1 liter
1,000 liters = 1 kiloliter (kL)

Team Project

The class should be divided into four teams. (Each team should bring the big, bigger, and the biggest empty containers of milk, orange juice and soda drink from the super market to the class.) Each team should sketch and complete the chart using the labels on the containers.

Table 1

Product Name	Big size/Sketch	Bigger size/Sketch	Biggest size/Sketch
Milk containers	Capacity = ?	Capacity = ?	capacity = 3.78 L
Orange juice container	Sketch = ? Capacity = ?	Sketch = ? Capacity = ?	Sketch = ? Capacity = ?
Soda drink container	Sketch = ? Capacity = ?	Sketch = ? Capacity = ?	Sketch = ? Capacity = ?

a. What size and what capacity of milk is used most in each team member's family?

b. What size and what capacity of orange juice is used the least in each member's family?

c. What size and what capacity of the soda drink is used the most in each team member's family?

Example 1

Explain when you will multiply or divide in order to change one unit to another unit.

Solution

In order **to change from lower units** such as milliliters to higher units such as liters, we should **divide** because the final answer we are looking for should be less than the number of the lower unit. For example, 1,000 milliliters = 1 liter. Therefore, to change 1,000 milliliters to liters, we have to **divide** 1,000 milliliters by 1,000 to obtain the number of liters that are contained in 1,000 milliliters.

In order **to change from higher units** such as liters to metric cups, we should **multiply** because the final answer that we are looking for should be more than the number of the higher units. For example, 4 metric cups = 1 liter and to change 1 liter to metric cups we have to **multiply** the 1 liter by 4.

Example 2

Solve: 8 metric cups = ? liters.

Solution

To change smaller units (metric cups) to bigger units (liters) we **divide** as follows:

Number of metric cups ÷ Number of metric cup in 1 liter = Number of liters.

$$8 \div 4 = 2$$

There are 2 liters in 8 metric cups.

Example 3

a. Change 22 liters to milliliters.

b. Change 164 milliliters to liters.

Solution

a. **To change from larger units** (such as liters) to smaller units (such as milliliters), we should **multiply** as **shown**:

Number of liters × Number of milliliters in 1 liter = Number of milliliters.

$$22 \times 1,000 = 22,000 \text{ milliliters.}$$

Therefore, there are 22,000 milliliters in 22 liters.

b. **To change from smaller units** (such as milliliters) to larger units (such as liters), we should **divide** as shown:

467

Number of milliliters ÷ Number of milliliters in 1 liter = Number of liters.

164   ÷   1,000   = $\dfrac{164}{1,000}$

=   .164

We are dividing by 1,000 which has three zeros, and therefore, we have to move the decimal point three places or three digits to the left.

Therefore, there are .164 liters in 164 milliliters.

Example 4

Solve: ? milliliters = 10 metric cups

Solution

To change from larger units (such as metric cups) to smaller units (such as milliliters) we multiply as shown:

Number of metric cups × Number of milliliters in 1 mtric cup = Number of milliliters.

10   ×   250   =   2,500 milliliters

Therefore, there are 2500 milliliters in 10 metric cups.

Example 5

Compare. Write <, >, or = for ? in the question.

a. 4,000 L ? 3 kL

b. 2 L ? 9 metric cups

Solution

a. In order to compare two quantities, we must change both quantities to the **same units** first before comparing. In this case, let us change kL to L first as follows:

To change from larger units (such as kL) to smaller units (such as L), multiply as shown:

Number of kL × Number of liters in 1 kL = Number of L.

3   ×   1000   =   3,000

Therefore, there are 3,000 liters in 3 kL.

We can now compare the 4,000 L and the 3,000 L because 3,000 L and 4,000 L have the same units. Since 4,000 L is greater than 3,000 L, we can write:

4,000 L > 3,000 L, and therefore, 4,000 L > 3 kL.

(Note: We have already showed that 3kL = 3,000 L.)

b. In order to compare two quantities, we must change both quantities to the same

468

units first before comparing them. In this case, let us change 2L to metric cups first as shown:

To change from larger units (such as liters) to smaller units (such as metric cups) we multiply as shown:

Number of liters × Number of metric cups in 1 liter = Number of metric cups.

2 × 4 = 8 metric cups.

Therefore, there are 8 metric cups in 2 L.

Now, we can compare the 8 metric cups and the 9 metric cups because the 8 metric cups and the 9 metric cups have the same units. Since 8 metric cups is less than 9 metric cups we can write:

8 metric cups < 9 metric cups. Therefore, we can write:

2 L < 9 metric cups (Note: We have already showed that 2 L = 8 metric cups).

REAL WORLD APPLICATIONS - WORD PROBLEMS
Metric Capacity

Example 6

How many bottles each holding 150 milliliters of orange juice can be filled from a plastic container that holds 4.5 liters of the orange juice?

Solution

Change the 150 milliliters and 4.5 liters to the same unit, and then divide 4.5 liters by 150 milliliters. Let us change 4.5 liters to milliliters as shown:

Number of liters × Number of milliliters in 1 liter = Number of milliliters.

4.5 × 1,000 = 4500.0 milliliters.

Therefore, there are 4,500 milliliters in 4.5 liters.

Let us find how many 150 milliliters are contained in 4,500 milliliters by dividing 4,500 milliliters by 150 milliliters as shown:

$$\frac{4,500}{150} = \frac{4,500}{150}$$ Divide the numerator and the denominator by 10.

$$= \frac{\overset{90}{\cancel{450}}}{\underset{3}{\cancel{15}}}$$ Divide the numerator and the denominator by 5.

$$= \frac{\overset{30}{\cancel{90}}}{\underset{1}{\cancel{3}}}$$

Divide the numerator and the denominator by 3.

$$= 30$$

Therefore, 30 bottles each holding 150 milliliters of orange juice can be filled from a plastic container that holds 4.5 liters of orange juice.

Example 7

Five engineers drank a total of 4 L of water. If each engineer drank an equal amount of water, how many milliliters did each engineer drink?

Solution

Step 1: Change 4 L to milliliters as follows:

To change from larger units (such as liters) to smaller units (such as milliliters) we should multiply as shown:

Number of liters × Number of milliliters in 1 liter = Number of milliliters.

$$4 \quad \times \quad 1,000 \quad = \quad \textbf{4000 milliliters.}$$

Therefore, there are 4000 milliliters in 4 liters.

Step 2: To find the amount of water that each engineer drank, find the average amount of water that each engineer drank by dividing 4000 milliliters by 5 engineers as shown:

$$\frac{4,000}{5} = \frac{\overset{800}{\cancel{4,000}}}{\underset{1}{\cancel{5}}}$$

$$= 800 \text{ milliliters of water.}$$

Therefore, each engineer drank 800 milliliters of water.

─────────────────── The notes and the generous examples have provided me with the conceptual understanding and the computational fluency to do my homework.

Exercises

1. When do we divide and when do we multiply if we want to convert one unit to

470

another? Hint: See Example 1.

2. Solve: (Hint: See Example 2).

    a. 12 metric cups = ? liters   **b**. 4 metric cups = ? liters

    c. 16 metric cups = ? liters   **d**. 2 metric cups = ? liters

3a. Change 8 liters to milliliters. Hint: See Example **3a**.

3b. Change 158 milliliters to liters. Hint: See Example **3b**.

4. Solve: (Hint: See Example 4).

    a. ? milliliters = 8 metric cups.   **b**. ? milliliters = 5 metric cups.

    c. ? milliliters = 3 metric cups.   **d**. ? milliliters = 4 metric cups

5. Compare. Write <, >, or = for ? in the questions. Hint: See Example **5a**.

    a. 2000 L ? 4 kL   **b**. 2500 L ? 2 kL   **c**. 3000 L ? 3 kL   **d**. 5000 L ? 4 kL

6. Compare. Write <, >, or = for ? in the questions. Hint: See Example **5b**.

    a. 2 L ? 8 metric cups   **b**. 3L ? 12 metric cups

    c. 16 metric cups ? 4 L   **d**. 8 metric cups ? 3 L

7. How many bottles each holding 100 milliliters can be filled from a plastic container that holds:

    a. 1 liter?   **b**. 2 liters?   **c**. 3 liters?   (Hint: See Example **6**.)

8. How many bottles each holding 250 milliliters of apple juice can be filled from a plastic container that holds:

    a. 1 liter of the apple juice?   **b**. 2 liters of the apple juice?

    c. 3 liters of the apple juice?

    Hint: See Example 6.

9. Four nurses drank a total of 2 L of water. If each nurse drank an equal amount of water, how many milliliters did each nurse drink? Hint: See Example **7**.

Challenge Questions

10. Solve: **a**. ? milliliters = 6 metric cups   **b**. ? milliliters = 7 metric cups

11. Solve: **a**. 6 metric cups = ? liters   **b**. 10 metric cups = ? liters

12. How many bottles each holding 200 milliliters can be filled from a plastic container that holds:

    a. 1 liter?   **b**. 4 liters?

14. Compare. Write <, >, or = for ? in the questions.

    a. 3 L ? 12 metric cups   **b**. 5000 L ? 4 kL

Answers to Selected Questions

2a. 3 L   **3a**. 8,000 ml   **4a**. 2 L   **5a**. <

CUSTOMARY CAPACITY

The basic unit in measuring liquids in the Customary system is the gallon.

The Customary units of capacity are as shown:

$$8 \text{ fluid ounces (fl oz)} = 1 \text{ cup (c)}$$
$$2 \text{ cups} = 1 \text{ pint (pt)}$$
$$2 \text{ pints} = 1 \text{ quart (qt)}$$
$$4 \text{ cups} = 1 \text{ quart (qt)}$$
$$4 \text{ quarts} = 1 \text{ gallon (gal)}$$

Group Exercise

The class should be divided into four groups.

a. Each group should list four liquid products that can be seen at the supermarket with their corresponding measurements involving capacity. For example, a container of milk at the supermarket may have a capacity of one gallon or half a gallon.

b. Sketch the container of each product.

c. Compare the lists with the corresponding capacities from the other groups and list the products in increasing order of their capacity.

Example 1

In the Customary system the basic unit in measuring liquids is the gallon, true or false? Hint: See notes.

Solution

The student is to find the answer to Example 1 by reading the notes/text in this book.

Example 2

Solve: 12 quarts = ? pints

Solution

To change larger units (such as quarts) to smaller units (such as pints) **multiply** as shown:

Number of quarts × Number of pints in 1 quart = Number of pints.

12   ×   2   =   24 pints

Example 3

Solve: 20 quarts = ? gal

Solution

To change smaller units (such as quarts) to larger units (such as gallons) **divide** as shown:

Number of quarts ÷ Number of quarts in 1 gallon = Number of gallons.

20   ÷   4   =   5 gallons.

Example 4

Solve: 16 c = ? qt

Solution

To change smaller units (such as cups) to larger units (such as quarts) **divide** as shown:

Number of cups ÷ Number of cups in 1 quart = Number of quarts.

16   ÷   4   =   4 quarts

Example 5

Solve: 6 gal = ? c

Solution

Setup: This is a two step solution.

Step 1: Change the gallons to quarts.

To change from larger units (such as gallons) to smaller units (such as quarts), **multiply** as shown:

Number of gallons × Number of quarts in 1 gallon = Number of quarts.

6   ×   4   =   24 quarts

Step 2: Change the 24 quarts to cups.

To change from larger units (such as quarts) to smaller units (such as cups), **multiply** as shown:

Number of quarts × Number of cups in 1 quart = Number of cups.

24   ×   4   =   48 cups.

Example 6

Solve: 7 c = ? ft oz

To change larger units (such as cups) to smaller units (such as fluid ounces) **multiply** as shown:

Number of cups × Number of fluid ounces in 1 cup = Number of fluid ounces.

7   ×   8   =   56 fluid ounces.

Therefore, there are 56 fluid ounces in 7 cups.

REAL WORLD APPLICATIONS - WORD PROBLEMS
Customary Capacity

Example 7

Given that 1 gallon of a certain ice cream is on sale for $3.95 and two 1-quart containers of the same ice cream are on sale for $2.25. If Mary needs 1 gallon of ice cream for her birthday party, which is a better buy?

Solution

Setup: The better buy will be the least expensive buy. One choice is to buy the 1 gallon ice cream for $3.95 and the other choice is to buy four 1-quart containers of the same ice cream because 4 quarts makes 1 gallon.

Step 1: Find the cost of four 1-quart containers of the same ice cream.

Two 1–quart containers of ice cream = $2.25

Four 1–quart containers of ice cream = 2.25 × 2 = $4.50.

Step 2: Decide which size of the ice cream is a better buy.

Since $3.95 < $4.50, the 1 gallon of ice cream which is on sale for $3.95 is a better buy.

━━━━━━━━━━━━━━━━ **The notes and the generous examples have provided me with the conceptual understanding and the computational fluency to do my homework.**

Exercises

1. In the customary system the basic unit for measuring liquid is _____
   Hint: See Example 1

2. Solve: (See Example 2).
   a. 10 quarts = ? pints   **b.** 4 quarts = ? pints
   c. 2 quarts = ? pints   **d.** 12 quarts = ? pints

3. Solve: (See Example 3).
   a. 12 quarts = ? gal   **b.** 8 quarts = ? gal
   c. 16 quarts = ? gal   **d.** 4 quarts = ? gal

4. Solve: (See Example 4).
   a. 4 c = ? qt   **b.** 12 c = ? qt
   c. 20 c = ? qt   **d.** 10 c = ? qt

5. Solve: (See Example 5).
   a. 4 gal = ? c   **b.** 10 gal = ? c
   c. 8 gal = ? c   **d.** 3 gal = ? c

6. Solve: (See Example 6).
   a. 6 c = ? ft oz   **b.** 3 c = ? ft oz
   c. 2 c = ? ft oz   **d.** 5 c = ? ft oz

7. If 1 gallon of type A ice cream costs $2.85 and 4 cups of type B ice cream costs $.50, which type of the ice cream is cheaper? Hint: See Example 7.

Challenge Questions
8. Solve:

a. 7 gal = ? c   **b.** 16 c = ? qt   **c.** 24 c = ? qt

d. 10 quarts = ? gal   **e.** 6 qt = ? qt   **f.** 4 gal = ? c

Cumulative Review

1. $15 \div (-3) =$ **2.** $-15 \div (-3) =$ **3.** $-24 \div 6 =$ **4.** $\dfrac{3}{4} \div \dfrac{3}{8} =$

5. 9% of 50 =   **6.** 45% of 80 =   **7.** 2% of 100 =   **8.** .5% of 50 =

9. $4.34 \times 5 =$ **10.** $3.67 \times 2.3 =$ **11.** $7.22 \times .5 =$ **12.** $10.6 - 7.4 =$

13. $12 \div 4 =$ **14.** $12 \div .4 =$ **15.** $.12 \div .4 =$ **16.** $23 + 132 =$

17. Find the range of each of the following sets of numbers:

    a. 2, 12, 1, 33, 32, 6

    b. 45, 6, 9, 35, 3, 8, 15

    c. 4, 7, 8, 4, 3, 17

18. Find the mean, mode, and median of each of the following sets of numbers:

    a. 12, 8, 4

    b. 2, 4, 3, 3

    c. 8, 1, 5, 8, 3

19. $2 \times 3 \times 4 =$ **20.** $15 + 25 =$ **21.** $18 - 6 =$ **22.** $36 \div 3 =$

23. $8 \times 9 =$ **24.** $7 \times 8 =$ **25.** $19 - 13 =$ **26.** $8.3 \times 5 =$

(Are you having fun with the mathematics?)

CHAPTER 15

TIME

Review of How to Tell the Time

The time is 12: 20

The time is 9:55

Measuring time is measuring the interval of time between two separate events. An example of two separate events is when John started to eat and when John finished eating. We should be able to determine the length of the interval between two given times. There are 24 hours that make up a day and this 24 hours is divided into two periods, the A.M. (which is before noon) hours from 12 o'clock midnight to 12 o'clock noon and the P.M. (which is after noon) hours from 12 o'clock noon to 12 o'clock midnight.

Rule 1: To find the length of the time interval between two given times that are both A.M. or both P.M., subtract the hours and the minutes of the earlier time from the later time.

Rule 2: To find the length of the time interval between two given times when one is A.M. and the other is P.M., use the fact that 12:00 o'clock is the time that separates A.M. from P.M. hours, and therefore, we first find how far each of the given times is from 12:00 o'clock and secondly, we add the two results.

Table 1

The units of time are as follows:	
60 seconds (sec) = 1 minute (min)	
60 minutes	= 1 hour (hr)
24 hours	= 1 day (da)
7 days	= 1 week (wk)
4 weeks	= 1 month (mo)
52 weeks	= 1 year (yr)
365 days	= 1 year (yr)
366 days	= 1 leap year
10 years	= 1 decade
100 years	= 1 century
1,000 years	= 1 millennium

Example 1

What is the length of time between 7:15 A.M. and 10:50 A.M.?

Solution

Use Rule 1 to solve the question as shown:

```
  10 hr    50 min
-  7 hr    15 min
   3 hr    35 min
```

Therefore, the length of time between 7:15 A.M. and 10:50 A.M. is 3 hr and 35 minutes.

Example 2

Find the length of time between 2:50 P.M. and 10:23 P.M.

Solution

Use Rule 1 to solve the question as follows:

```
  10 hr    23 min
-  2 hr    50 min
```

We cannot subtract 50 minutes from 23 minutes, and therefore, we have to borrow 1 hr from 10 hr and this 1 hr becomes 60 minutes (see Table 1), and we then add the 60 minutes to the 23 minutes to obtain 83 minutes, and the 10 hours is therefore reduced to 9 hours, and then subtract as shown:

```
   9        83
  10 hr    23 min
-  2 hr    50 min
   7 hr    33 min
```

Therefore, the length of the time between 2:50 P.M. and 10:23 P.M. is 7 hr 33 min.

Example 3

The school day of the Accra Middle School starts at 8:10 A.M and ends at 2:51 P.M. How long is the school day?

Solution

Use Rule 2 to solve the question as shown:

Step 1: Subtract to find the length of the time from 8:10 A.M. to 12:00 noon.

```
  12 hr    00 min
-  8 hr    10 min
```

We cannot subtract 10 minutes from 00 minutes, and therefore, we have to borrow 1 hour from 12 hours, and this 1 hr is 60 minutes (see Table 1), and we then add the 60 minutes to the 00 minutes to become 60 minutes and the 12 hours is therefore, reduced to 11 hours, and then we subtract as shown:

$$
\begin{array}{rr}
11 & 60 \\
\cancel{12}\ \text{hr} & \cancel{00}\ \text{min} \\
-\ 8\ \text{hr} & 10\ \text{min} \\
\hline
3\ \text{hr} & 50\ \text{min}
\end{array}
$$

Step 2: 2:51 P.M. is 2 hours and 51 minutes after 12:00 noon.

Step 3: Add the two intervals found in Steps 1 and 2 as shown:

$$
\begin{array}{rr}
3\ \text{hr} & 50\ \text{min} \\
+\ 2\ \text{hr} & 51\ \text{min} \\
\hline
5\ \text{hr} & 101\ \text{min}
\end{array}
$$

Note that 101 minutes is more than 60 minutes and 60 minutes is equal to one hour. Divide 101 minutes by 60 to obtain the hours and minutes that are contained in 101 minutes as shown:

Therefore, 5 hr 101 min can be written as:

$$
\begin{array}{rr}
5\ \text{hr} & \\
+\ 1\ \text{hr} & 41\ \text{min} \\
\hline
6\ \text{hr} & 41\ \text{min}
\end{array}
$$

Therefore, the school day is 6 hours and 41 minutes.

Example 4
Find the length of the interval between 9:45 P.M and 4:10 A.M.
Solution
Use Rule 2 to solve the question as shown:
Step 1: Subtract to find the length of the time from 9:45 P.M to 12:00 midnight.

$$
\begin{array}{rr}
12\ \text{hr} & 00\ \text{min} \\
-\ 9\ \text{hr} & 45\ \text{min} \\
\hline
\end{array}
$$

We cannot subtract 45 minutes from 00 minutes, and therefore, we borrow 1 hour from 12 hours and this 1 hour is 60 minutes and we add the 60 minutes to 00 minutes to obtain 60 minutes and the 12 hours is reduced to 11 hours and we then subtract as shown:

$$
\begin{array}{ll}
11 & 60 \\
12\ \text{hr} & 00\ \text{min} \\
-\ 9\ \text{hr} & 45\ \text{min} \\
\hline
2\ \text{hr} & 15\ \text{min}
\end{array}
$$

Step 2: 4:10 A.M. is 4 hours and 10 minutes after 12 midnight.

Step 3: Add the two intervals found in steps 1 and 2 as shown:

$$
\begin{array}{ll}
2\ \text{hr} & 15\ \text{min} \\
+\ 4\ \text{hr} & 10\ \text{min} \\
\hline
6\ \text{hr} & 25\ \text{min}
\end{array}
$$

Therefore, the interval between 9:45 P.M and 4:10 A.M is 6 hr 25 min.

Example 5

How many hours are in 3 days?

Solution

To change from larger units such as days to smaller units such as hours, multiply as shown:

Number of days × Number of hours in 1 day = Number of hours.

↓	↓	↓
3 ×	24 =	72 hours

Therefore, there are 72 hours in 3 days.

Example 6

How many weeks are in 28 days?

Solution

To change from smaller units such as days to larger units such as weeks, divide as shown:

Number of days ÷ Number of days in 1 week = Number of weeks.

↓	↓	↓
28 ÷	7 =	4 weeks

Therefore, there are 4 weeks in 28 days.

The notes and the generous examples have provided me with the conceptual understanding and the computational fluency to do my homework.

Exercises

1. State the rule that is used in finding the length of the time interval between two given times that are both A.M. or both P.M. Hint:See Rule 1.

2. State the rule that is used in finding the length of the time interval between two given times when one is A.M. and the other is P.M. Hint:See Rule 2.

3. Find the length of the interval between the two given times. Hint: See Example 1.
   a. 7:30 A.M. to 11:46 A.M.   **b.** 6:14 A.M. to 10:34 A.M.
   c. 9:47 A.M. to 10:59 A.M.   **d.** 10:01 A.M. to 11:09 A.M.

4. Find the length of the interval between the two given times. Hint: See Example 2.
   a. 6:30 P.M. to 9:40 P.M   **b.** 4:10 P.M. to 8:30 P.M.
   c. 7:20 A.M. to 10:45 A.M   **d.** 8:15 A.M. to 11:35 A.M

5. Find the length of the interval between the two given times. Hint: See Example 3.
   a. 10:30 A.M to 3:15 P.M   **b.** 9:00 A.M. to 2:30 P.M.
   c. 7:40 A.M. to 2:45 P.M.   **d.** 8:07 A.M. to 5:45 P.M.

6. Find the length of the interval between the two given times. Hint: See Example 4.
   a. 10:30 P.M to 2:30 A.M   **b.** 7:00 P.M. to 4:00 A.M
   c. 8:18 P.M. to 8:19 A.M   **d.** 11:20 P.M. to 1:40 A.M

7. Solve: (Hint: See Example 5).
   a. How many hours are in 6 days?   **b.** How many hours are in 2 days?

8. Solve: (Hint: See Example 6).
   a. How many weeks are in 21 days?   **b.** How many weeks are in 35 days?

Challenge Questions

9. Find the length of the interval between the two given times.
   a. 11:15 P.M. to 3:00 A.M.   **b.** 5:20 A.M. to 10:30 A.M.
   c. 7:48 A.M. to 11:57 A.M.   **d.** 1:31 P.M. to 9:20 P.M.
   e. 7:25 A.M. to 4:15 P.M.   **f.** 9:00 A.M. to 11:30 A.M.
   g. 6:18 A.M. to 11:30 A.M.   **h.** 2:40 P.M. to 3:15 A.M.

Answers to Selected Questions

3a. 4 hr 16 min   **4a.** 3 hr 10 min   **5a.** 4 hr 45 min.   **6a.** 4 hr 0 min

(How do you find the Math Teaching Series?)

PROBABILITY

Cumulative Review

1. 8 + 9 =   **2.** 12 + 9 =   **3.** 11 - 8 =   **4.** 7 × 2 =

5. 12 ÷ 3 =   **6.** 23 - 14 =   **7.** 24 ÷ 6 =   **8.** 13 - 7 =

9. 11
    × 2

10.   26
    + 25

11.   31
    - 13

12.   8
    × 4

13. 18 ÷ 6 =   **14.** 24 ÷ 3 =   **15.** 12 + 8 =   **16.** 19 - 12 =

17. 27
    × 3

18.   17
    + 18

19.   39
    - 13

20. 18
    × 4

21. 48 ÷ 3 =   **22.** 24 ÷ 8 =   **23.** 12 + 38 =   **24.** 36 - 17 =

25. 14
    × 5

26.   23
    + 27

27. 19
    - 15

28. 12
    × 3

29. 48 - 17 =   **30.** 20 ÷ 4 =   **31.** 16 + 38 =   **32.** 28 - 16 =

New Terms: probability, outcome, experiment

Probability is sometimes used in decision making. For example, if two friends want to go to either a movie or a football game together, but they are not sure if they should go to the movie first or the football game, then they may use coin flipping for decision making. There must be established rules before the coin is flipped, such as, if a head appears, they should go to the movie first and if a tail appears, they should go to the football game first.

Class Exercise

1. Give reasons why you think that coin flipping for decision making is not fair.

2. Give reasons why you think that coin flipping for decision making is fair
.

Group Exercise

In a soccer game, a coin toss is used to decide which team gets to select on which direction of the field it wants to play towards on the first play of the game.

Let us divide the class into two soccer teams of Team A and Team B. Each team should toss a coin 10 times and record the results using the tally table as shown:

Team A and Team B Sample Chart

Trials	Heads tally	Tails tally
1st trial		
2nd trial		
3rd trial		
4th trial		
5th trial		
6th trial		
7th trial		
8th trial		
9th trial		
10th trial		
Total trials		
Fraction	$\dfrac{\text{Number of Heads}}{\text{Sum of total trials of heads and tails}} = \dfrac{?}{10}$	

Add up the results for the heads and tails. Find the fraction of the heads by using the formula :

$$\text{Fraction of the heads} = \frac{\text{Number of heads}}{\text{Number of trials}} = \frac{?}{10}$$

Find the fraction of the tails by using the formula:

$$\text{Fraction of the tails} = \frac{\text{Number of tails}}{\text{Number of trials}} = \frac{?}{10}$$

Conclusions of the Group Exercise

1. The group exercise is an example of an **experiment**. Therefore, the toss of a coin is an experiment.
2. The result of the experiment is the **outcome**. Therefore, the results of the number of heads and tails during the toss of the coin is the outcome.
3. The fraction of heads is actually the chances of obtaining a head when the coin is tossed 10 times, and this is known as the **probability** of obtaining a head.

4. The fraction of tails is actually the chances of obtaining a tail when the coin is tossed 10 times, and this is known as the **probability** of obtaining a tail.
5. From the group exercise, what is the fraction of heads? What is the probability of obtaining a head?
6. From the group exercise, what is the fraction of tails? What is the probability of obtaining a tail?
7. The outcomes of Team A and Team B should not necessarily be the same.
8. Note that the probability that Team A and Team B have found are fractions, for example, $\frac{?}{10}$. However, the probability can be expressed in **decimal** and **percent** also. Each group should change the fractional probability to decimal and percent probability (review the section on Decimal and Percent.)
9. When a coin was tossed, it was equally likely for either a head or a tail to occur. When outcomes have the same chance of occurring, they are said to be **equally likely**.
10. In the group exercise, we tossed the coin 10 times. It is possible to toss the coin more than 10 times, such as 20, 40, 100, or 200 times. Note that **the more we repeat the experiment, the closer we are to the true value of the probability**.

Experimental Probability
Experimental probability can be found by repeating an experiment many times and observing the results, as we did with the group exercise.
The formula for finding the experimental probability is given as shown:

$$\text{Experimental probability (outcome)} = \frac{\text{number of outcomes}}{\text{number of times the experiment was repeated}}$$

The experimental probability is sometimes called the **relative frequency**.

Example 1
A coin was tossed 45 times and 25 heads occurred.
(a) What is the experimental probability of obtaining heads? Express your answer as a fraction, a decimal, and a percent. Round your answer to the nearest hundredth.
(b) What is the experimental probability of obtaining tails? Express your answer as a fraction, a decimal and a percent. Round your answer to two decimal places.
Solution
The number of times the coin was tossed = 45
The number of times the heads occurred = 25

$$\text{Experimental probability of heads} = \frac{\text{number of times heads occurred}}{\text{number of times the coin was tossed}}$$

$$= \frac{25}{45} \qquad \text{This is the fractional form.}$$

$$= \frac{\overset{5}{\cancel{25}}}{\underset{9}{\cancel{45}}} \qquad \text{Reduce to the lowest terms by dividing by 5.}$$

$$= \frac{5}{9} \qquad \text{This is the probability in the fractional form,}$$

reduced to the lowest terms.

To change the probability of $\frac{5}{9}$ to decimal, divide 5 by 9 as shown:

$$
\begin{array}{r}
.555 \\
9\,\overline{)\,50} \\
-45 \\ \hline
050 \\
-45 \\ \hline
050 \\
-\;45 \\ \hline
05
\end{array}
$$

The decimal probability is .56 to the nearest hundredth. (Review the section on Decimal Fractions.)

The decimal probability of .56 can be changed to a percent form by moving the decimal point in .56 two decimal places or two digits to the right which is the same as multiplying .56 by 100 as shown:

$$.56 = .56 = 56\%$$

Move the decimal point two decimal places to the right.

Decimal
↓

Therefore, the probability of $\frac{5}{9}$ = .56 = 56%.

↑   ↑

Fraction   Percent

(b) The coin was tossed 45 times and the outcome in each toss was either a head or a tail. Since the heads occurred 25 times, then the number of tails is 45 − 25 = 20.

Experimental probability of tails $= \dfrac{\text{Number of times tails occurred}}{\text{Number of times the coin was tossed.}}$

$= \dfrac{20}{45}$ This is the fractional form.

$= \dfrac{\overset{4}{\cancel{20}}}{\underset{9}{\cancel{45}}}$ Reducing to the lowest terms by dividing by 5.

$= \dfrac{4}{9}$ This is the probability in the fractional form,

reduced to the lowest terms.

To change the probability of $\dfrac{4}{9}$ to a decimal form, divide 4 by 9 as shown:

$$
\begin{array}{r}
.444 \\
9\overline{)40} \\
-36 \\
\overline{40} \\
-36 \\
\overline{40} \\
-36 \\
\overline{4}
\end{array}
$$

The decimal probability = .44 to the nearest hundredth.
The decimal probability of .44 can be changed to a percent by moving the decimal point in .44 two decimal places or two digits to the right which is the same as multiplying .44 by 100 as shown:

$.44 = .44 = 44\%$

Move the decimal point two places to the right.

Decimal
$\downarrow$

Therefore, the probability of $\dfrac{4}{9} = .44 = 44\%$

$\uparrow$ $\uparrow$
Fraction   Percent

Example 2

What is the probability of getting a tail when a coin is tossed?

Solution

We can use the tree diagram to solve the problem as follows with H representing a head and T representing a tail when a coin is tossed once.

There is one successful outcome of a tail or a T out of two possible outcomes of H or T as shown in the diagram. There are two possible outcomes, which are a head or a tail when a coin is tossed.

The probability of getting a tail when a coin is tossed

$$= \frac{\text{Number of successful outcomes}}{\text{Number of possible outcomes}} = \frac{1}{2}$$

Special Note: The probability of getting a tail is $\frac{1}{2}$ and this can also be expressed in a decimal form as .5 and in percent form as 50%. This means that the probability of getting a head $=100\% - 50\% = 50\%$ (The total probability $= 100\%$ or 1). We can then say that there is a **fifty-fifty chance** of getting a head or a tail when a coin is tossed.

Example 3

(a) Using T_1 and T_2 for tails and H_1 and H_2 for heads, show all the possible outcomes of tossing a coin twice by drawing a tree diagram.
(b) How is the tree diagram read? Write the possible outcomes.
(c) Explain the possible outcomes in terms of probability.

Solution

(a) The tree diagram is shown as shown:

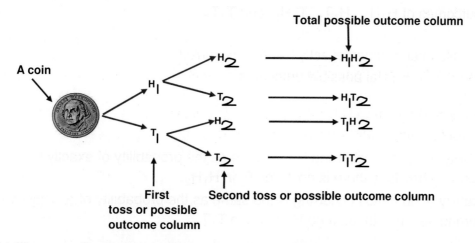

Total possible outcome column

A coin

H_1

H_2 ⟶ H_1H_2

T_2 ⟶ H_1T_2

T_1

H_2 ⟶ T_1H_2

T_2 ⟶ T_1T_2

First toss or possible outcome column

Second toss or possible outcome column

(b) The tree diagram is read by following each branch from left to right. Using this idea and starting from the top of the tree diagram, the possible outcomes are: H_1H_2, H_1T_2, T_1H_2, and T_1T_2.

(c) There are 4 possible outcomes which are H_1H_2, H_1T_2, T_1H_2, and T_1T_2. Exactly two heads or H_1H_2 occurred one time out of the 4 outcomes, and therefore, the probability of obtaining exactly two heads

$$= \frac{\text{Number of times } H_1H_2 \text{ occurred}}{\text{Total possible outcomes}}$$

$$= \frac{1}{4}$$

The probability that at least one head occurred is 3 times in H_1H_2, H_1T_2, and T_1H_2 out of 4 possible outcomes of H_1H_2, H_1T_2, T_1H_2, and T_1T_2 is:

$$= \frac{\text{Number of times that at least one head occurred}}{\text{Total possible outcomes}}$$

$$= \frac{3}{4} \quad \text{(At least one head occurred 3 times in } H_1H_2, H_1T_2, \text{ and } T_1H_2\text{).}$$

The probability that at least one tail occurred 3 times in H_1T_2, T_1H_2, and T_1T_2 out of 4 possible outcomes of H_1H_2, H_1T_2, T_1H_2, and T_1T_2

$$= \frac{\text{Number of times at least one tail occurred}}{\text{Total possible outcomes}}$$

$$= \frac{3}{4}$$

The probability of exactly two tails or T_1T_2 occurred one time out of the 4 possible outcomes of H_1H_2 , H_1T_2, T_1H_2, and T_1T_2

$$= \frac{\text{Number of times exactly two tails occurred}}{\text{Total possible outcomes}}$$

$$= \frac{1}{4}$$

The probability of no tails occurring is the same as the probability of exactly two heads occurring because there is no T_1 or T_2 in H_1H_2.

The probability of no heads occurring is the same as the probability of exactly two tails occurring because there is no H_1 or H_2 in T_1T_2.

Special Note: Tossing two coins once is the same as tossing one coin twice.

Group Exercise

Recall that experimental probability is sometimes called relative frequency. Let us find out how we can use relative frequency to find the probability. The class should select one person as the recorder to record the month in which every student in the class was born on a frequency table as shown:

Months	Jan	Feb	Mar	Apr	May	June	July	Aug	Sept	Oct	Nov	Dec
Frequency												

Frequency here means how many students are born in each month.
Sum of the frequencies = Total number of students in the class.
Let us answer a few questions.
(a) What is the fraction of the students who were born in January?

The fraction of the students who were born in January $= \dfrac{\text{Frequency for January}}{\text{Sum of the frequencies}}$

$$= \frac{\text{No. of students born in January}}{\text{Total number of students}}$$

Using your frequency table, find the fraction of the students who were born in January. How do you think that we can interpret this fraction? We can interpret this fraction by stating that the probability of selecting a student at random from the class that was born in January.

(b) Similarly, we can find the probability of selecting a student at random that was born in August as shown:
Probability of selecting a student at random that was born in August =

$$\frac{\text{Frequency of students born in August}}{\text{Sum of the frequencies}} = \frac{\text{No. of students born in August}}{\text{Total number of students in the class}}$$

Using your frequency table, find the probability that if a student is selected at random from the class, that student was born in August.

(c) Similarly using your frequency table, find the probability that if a student is selected at random, the student was born in: (1) June, (2) December, (3) April, or (4) October.

Note: **Random** selection means that the selection is from a population without being biased. Population means a group, such as a group of students in a class or the total number of students is a population of students.

━━━━━━━━━━━━ The notes and the generous examples have provided me with the conceptual understanding and the computational fluency to do my homework.

Exercises

1. Explain what is meant by probability.
2. Explain what is meant by an experiment and an outcome of an experiment.
3. Explain what is meant by the probability of obtaining a head.
4. Explain what is meant by "an outcome is equally likely."
5. The more we repeat the experiment, the closer we are to the true value of the probability. True or False?
6. What is the formula for finding experimental probability?.
7. The experimental probability is sometimes called relative frequency. True or False?
8. A coin was tossed 10 times and 3 heads occurred.
   (a) What is the experimental probability of obtaining a head. Express your answer in a fraction, a decimal, and a percent. Hint: See Example **1**.
   (b) What is the experimental probability of obtaining a tail? Express your answer in a fraction, a decimal, and a percent. Hint: See Example 1.
9. A coin was tossed 15 times and 5 tails occurred.
   (a) What is the probability of obtaining a tail? Express your answer in a fraction, a decimal, and a percent. Hint: See Example **1**.
   (b) What is the probability of obtaining a head? Express your answer in a fraction, a decimal,l and a percent. Hint: See Example **1**.
10. Explain why a coin is tossed, there is a fifty-fifty chance of obtaining a head or a tail? Hint: See Example **2**.
11. Draw a tree diagram when a coin is tossed twice.
    (a) From your diagram, what are the possible outcomes?
    (b) What is the probability of obtaining exactly 2 tails?
    (c) What is the probability of obtaining exactly 2 heads?

Hint: See Example **3**.

THEORETICAL PROBABILITY

Theoretical probability is when the probability of an event is found without doing an experiment.

A set of outcomes for a particular experiment is known as an **event**.

$$\text{Theoretical probability of an event} = \frac{\text{Number of outcomes in the event}}{\text{Total number of possible outcomes}}$$

Example 1

What is the theoretical probability that in the spinner below, the pointer will:

(a) land on 2?   (b) land on an even number?

(c) land on an odd number?   (d) land on a prime number?

Solution

(a) There is one outcome of 2 out of a total of 4 possible outcomes of 1, 2, 3, and 4 when the pointer lands on 2. Therefore, the theoretical probability that the spinner

will land on 2 $= \dfrac{\text{Number of the number 2 outcomes}}{\text{Total number of possible outcomes}}$

$$= \frac{1}{4}$$

(b) The even numbers on the spinner are 2 and 4, and that means, there will be two outcomes of even numbers out of a possible of 4 outcomes of 1, 2, 3, and 4. Therefore, the theoretical probability that the spinner will land on an even number

$$= \frac{\text{Number of even number outcomes}}{\text{Total number of possible outcomes}}$$

$$= \frac{2}{4}$$

$= \dfrac{\frac{1}{2}}{\frac{4}{2}}$ Reduce to the lowest terms by dividing by 2.

$= \dfrac{1}{2}$

(c) The odd numbers on the spinner are 1 and 3, that means, there will be two outcomes of odd numbers out of a total of 4 possible outcomes of 1, 2, 3, and 4. Therefore, the theoretical probability that the spinner will land on an odd number

$= \dfrac{\text{Number of odd number outcomes}}{\text{Total number of possible outcomes}}$

$= \dfrac{2}{4}$

$= \dfrac{\frac{1}{2}}{\frac{4}{2}}$ Reduce to the lowest terms by dividing by 2.

$= \dfrac{1}{2}$

(d) A prime number is a number that has exactly two factors, which are 1 and the number itself. Out of the numbers 1, 2, 3, and 4 on the spinner, only 2 and 3 are prime numbers. Therefore, two out of four numbers are prime numbers. Therefore, there will be two outcomes of prime numbers out of the possible 4 outcomes of 1, 2, 3, and 4.

Theoretical probability of a prime number $= \dfrac{\text{Number of prime number outcomes}}{\text{Total number of possible outcomes}}$

$= \dfrac{2}{4}$

$= \dfrac{\frac{1}{2}}{\frac{4}{2}}$ Reduce to the lowest terms by dividing by 2

$= \dfrac{1}{2}$

Example 2

Find the theoretical probability of each event .

(a) The spinner stops on C.

(b) The spinner stops on a vowel.

Solution

(a) There is one letter which is C out of a possible 8 letters.

The theoretical probability of event C $= \dfrac{\text{Number of outcomes of C}}{\text{Total number of possible outcomes}}$

$$= \frac{1}{8}$$

(b) All the vowels in the English language are a, e, i, o, and u. The vowels on the spinner are A, O, and U, therefore, there are 3 vowels out of the 8 possible letters on the spinner.

The theoretical probability that the spinner stops on a vowel

$$= \frac{\text{Number of outcomes of a vowel}}{\text{Total number of possible outcomes}}$$

$$= \frac{3}{8}$$

0 and 1 Probability Values

A probability of 0 is an event that cannot happen, and it is therefore, an **impossible event**. A probability of 1 is an event that must happen, and it is therefore, a **certain event**. Some events are either impossible or certain. For example, if a bag contains only 10 green apples, the probability of drawing a green apple is $\dfrac{10}{10}$ which is 1.

The event of drawing a green apple is certain to occur because no other types of apples are in the bag, and therefore, no other result is possible. An event which is certain to occur has a probability of 1.

Using the same bag of green apples, the event of drawing a red apple is impossible because the bag contains no red apples. Therefore, the probability of drawing a red apple is $\dfrac{0}{10} = 0$. An **impossible event has a probability of 0**.

Some more examples of impossible events are:

(a) obtaining an outcome of 7 from a single roll of a die because the maximum number on a die is 6, and so the outcome of a 7 will never occur. The number of outcomes of a 7 is 0 out of the possible outcomes of 6. Therefore, the probability of obtaining a 7 is $\frac{0}{6} = 0$. Obtaining an outcome of a 7 is impossible.

(b) A spinner has the numbers 1, 2, 3, 4, and 5. The probability of obtaining an outcome of a 9 out of 5 possible outcomes is 0 because there is no 9 on the spinner. Obtaining an outcome of a 9 is impossible.

Group Exercise

Decide if the following events are impossible or certain:

(a) A spinner has the numbers 1, 2, 3, 4, 5, 6, 7, and 8. What is the probability of the pointer stopping on 10?

(b) A bag has 6 black pens. What is the probability of drawing a red pen? What is the probability of drawing a black pen?

(c) The probability of obtaining a 10 from the roll of a single die.

Extreme Values of Probability

The extreme values of probability are 0 and 1 where an impossible event is 0 and an event certain to happen is 1. The probability of all other events is between 0 and 1. The extreme values of probability means the minimum and the maximum values of probability.

Example 3

Plot the probability of an impossible event, certain event, a 50-50 chance event, an equally likely event, 0% chance of an event and 100% chance of an event.

Solution

Since the extreme values of probability are 0 and 1, probabilities can be plotted on the part of a number line between 0 and 1 as shown:

493

Comparing the Values of Probability

Since an event which is certain to happen has a probability of 1 and an impossible event has a probability of 0, an event which has a probability value close to 1 has a better chance of occurring than an event that has a probability value that is close to 0.

Rule: Given the probability values of many events, the event that has the highest probability value has the best chance of occurring and the event that has the lowest probability value has the least chance of occurring.

If the value of **an event is close to 0**, it is likely that the **event will not occur**.
If the value of **an event** is **close to 1**, it is likely that the **event will occur**.

Group Exercise

1. Using the rule, select the event which has the best chance of occurring and the least chance of occurring and explain your choices.

(a) Event A has the probability of .4 of occurring, event B has the probability of .2 of occurring, and event C has the probability of .9 of occurring.

(b) Event A has the probability of $\frac{3}{4}$ of occurring, event B has the probability of $\frac{1}{4}$ of occurring, and event C has the probability of $\frac{4}{4}$ of occurring.

(c) Event A has the probability of $\frac{1}{2}$ of occurring, event B has the probability of $\frac{1}{4}$ of occurring, and event C has the probability of $\frac{1}{3}$ of occurring. Hint: Change all the fractions of the probabilities to have the **same** least common denominator (LCD), and then you will be able to compare the fractions (numerators). (Hint: Refer to the sections/chapter on Fractions.) You may also change all the fractions to decimals and then compare the decimals. (Hint: Refer to the section/chapter on Decimals.)

(d) Event A has an 80% chance of occurring, event B has a 20% chance of occurring, and event C has a 100% chance of occurring.

2. Discuss five examples of impossible events and five examples of certain events in everyday life. The class should be divided into 8 groups for the discussion and each group should record their five examples and report them to the class.

Example 4

A spinner is divided into 8 sections. If the pointer is spun, find the theoretical probability that it will land on:

(a) a number 3   (b) an even number   (c) an odd number
(d) a prime number   (e) a number 9   (f) a number greater than 8
(g) a number which is not a 6   (h) a number less than 5
(i) a number greater than 3

Indicate the probabilities of the events on a number line.

Solution

These solutions may be considered by some students to be long, but this example is designed to show the students various ways to solve the problem and also to enable the students to logically compare many solution methods.

(a) There is only one number 3 out of the total number of 8. Therefore, the probability of landing on the number 3 out of 8 numbers can be represented as shown:

$$\text{The the theoretical probability of landing on 3} = \frac{\text{Number of outcomes of 3}}{\text{Total number of possible outcomes}}$$

$$= \frac{1}{8}$$

(b) An even number is a number that can be divided by 2. The spinner has 4 even numbers which are 2, 4, 6, and 8 out of a total of 8 numbers on the spinner. Therefore, the probability of landing on an even number can be represented as shown:

The theoretical probability of landing on an even number

$$= \frac{\text{Number of even number outcomes}}{\text{Total number of possible outcomes}}$$

$$= \frac{4}{8}$$

$$= \frac{\overset{1}{\cancel{4}}}{\underset{2}{\cancel{8}}} \quad \text{Reduce to the lowest terms by dividing by 4}$$

$$= \frac{1}{2}$$

(c) An odd number is a number that cannot be divided by 2. The spinner has 4 odd numbers which are 1, 3, 5, and 7 out of a total of 8 numbers on the spinner. Therefore, the probability of landing on an odd number can be represented as shown:

The theoretical probability of landing on an odd number

$$= \frac{\text{Number of odd number outcomes}}{\text{Total number of possible outcomes}}$$

$$= \frac{4}{8}$$

$$= \frac{\overset{1}{\cancel{4}}}{\underset{2}{\cancel{8}}} \quad \text{Reducing to lowest terms by dividing by 4.}$$

$$= \frac{1}{2}$$

(d) A prime number is a number that has exactly two factors, which are 1 and the number itself. There are four prime numbers on the spinner, which are 2, 3, 5, and 7 out of the total of 8 numbers on the spinner. Therefore, the probability of landing on a prime number can be represented as follows:

Theoretical probability of landing on a prime number

$$= \frac{\text{Number of outcomes of a prime number}}{\text{Total number of possible outcomes}}$$

$$= \frac{4}{8}$$

$$= \frac{\overset{1}{\cancel{4}}}{\underset{2}{\cancel{8}}} \quad \text{Reduce to the lowest terms by dividing by 4.}$$

$$= \frac{1}{2}$$

(e) There is no number 9 on the spinner, so it is impossible for the pointer to land on number 9. The impossible events have the probability of 0.

(f) There is no number greater than 8, so it is impossible for the pointer to land on a number greater than 8. The impossible events have the probability of 0.

(g) The total number of numbers on the spinner is 8. If the pointer will not land on 6, then the pointer will land on the other 7 remaining numbers of 1, 2, 3, 4, 5, 7, and 8 out of the total number of 8 on the spinner. The probability that the pointer will not land on the number 6 can be represented as:

$$\text{Theoretical probability of not landing on 6} = \frac{\text{Number of outcomes of not landing on 6}}{\text{Total possible outcomes}}$$

$$= \frac{7}{8}$$

(h) The numbers on the spinner which are less than 5 are 1, 2, 3, and 4. Therefore, there are 4 numbers that are less than 5 out of the total number of 8 numbers on the spinner. The probability that the pointer will land on a number less than 5 can be represented as:

Theoretical probability of landing on a number less than 5

$$= \frac{\text{Number of outcomes that are less than 5}}{\text{Total possible outcomes}}$$

$$= \frac{4}{8}$$

$$= \frac{\overset{1}{\cancel{4}}}{\underset{2}{\cancel{8}}} \quad \text{Reduce to the lowest terms by dividing by 4.}$$

$$= \frac{1}{2}$$

(i) The numbers on the spinner which are greater than 3 are 4, 5, 6, 7, and 8. There are a total of five numbers that are greater than 3 out of the total number of 8 on the spinner.

Theoretical probability of landing on a number which is greater than 3

$$= \frac{\text{Number of outcomes} > 3}{\text{Total possible outcomes}}$$

$$= \frac{5}{8}$$

The probabilities of the events are indicated on the number line using assigned solution numbers.

Example 5

(a) Find the theoretical probability of the outcome of B. Give your answer in a
    fraction, a decimal, and a percent form.
(b) Find the experimental probability of the outcome of B.
(c) Find the experimental probability of the outcome of A.
(d) Find the experimental probability of the outcome of C.
(e) Find the experimental probability of the outcome of D.

This diagram is used to find the theoretical
probability because the data on the spinner
is obtained without conducting any
experiment.

Outcome	Number of spins
A	8
B	2
C	7
D	3
Total	20

This diagram is used to find the
experimental probability because
the data in the diagram is got from
conducting the experiment.

Solution

(a) The spinner is divided into 4 equal sections labelled A, B, C, and D. Section B is 1
out of the 4 equal parts of the spinner.

$$\text{Theoretical probability of outcome of B} = \frac{\text{Number of outcomes of B}}{\text{Total number of possible outcomes}}$$

$$= \frac{1}{4} \quad \text{(Fraction form of the probability).}$$

The decimal form of the theoretical probability of $\frac{1}{4}$ can be obtained by dividing 1

by 4 as shown:

$$
\begin{array}{r}
.25 \\
4\overline{)10} \\
-8 \\
\hline
20 \\
-20 \\
\hline
00
\end{array}
$$

The decimal form of the theoretical probability of $\frac{1}{4} = .25$

The decimal form of the theoretical probability of .25 can be changed to a percent by
moving the decimal point 2 places or two digits to the right, and attaching the
percent sign (%), which is the same as multiplying by 100 as shown:

$$.25 = .25. = 25\%$$

Therefore, the theoretical probability of $\dfrac{1}{4}$ = .25 = 25%

(b) The number of spins that give the outcomes of B are 2 out of the total of 20 spins.

Experimental probability of outcome of B = $\dfrac{\text{Number of spins that give outcomes of B}}{\text{Total number of possible spins}}$

$$= \dfrac{2}{20}$$

$$= \dfrac{\overset{1}{\cancel{2}}}{\underset{10}{\cancel{20}}} \quad \text{Reduce to the lowest terms by dividing by 2.}$$

$$= \dfrac{1}{10}$$

(c) The number of spins that give the outcomes of A are 8 out of the total of 20 spins.

Experimental probability of outcome of A = $\dfrac{\text{Number of spins that give outcomes of A}}{\text{Total number of possible spins}}$

$$= \dfrac{8}{20}$$

$$= \dfrac{\overset{2}{\cancel{8}}}{\underset{5}{\cancel{20}}} \quad \text{Reduce to the lowest terms by dividing by 4.}$$

$$= \dfrac{2}{5}$$

(d) The number of spins that give the outcomes of C are 7 out of the total of 20 spins.

Experimental probability of outcome of C = $\dfrac{\text{Number of spins that give outcomes of C}}{\text{Total number of possible spins}}$

$$= \dfrac{7}{20}$$

(e) The number of spins that give the outcomes of D are 3 out of the total of 20 spins.

Experimental probability of outcome of D = $\dfrac{\text{Number of spins that give outcomes of D}}{\text{Total number of possible spins}}$

$$= \dfrac{3}{20}$$

Example 6
A die is a small solid cube marked on each face from one to six spots or dots.

This is a die.

A die was rolled 10 times. On 2 of the rolls, the outcome was three dots on the die.
(a) What is the experimental probability of rolling a three?
    Give your answer as a fraction, a decimal, and a percent.
(b) How many rolls was the outcome not showing the side with three dots? What is the experimental probability of not rolling the side with three dots?
(c) Based on the experimental probabilities that you have found, and suppose the die is rolled 100 times, about how many times do you expect to roll a side:
    (i) with three dots?
    (ii) without three dots?

Solution
Note that this is an experimental probability because the event was repeated, for example, it was repeated 10 times.
(a) The outcome of the three dots on the die is 2 out of 10 total possible rolls.
    Experimental probability of the outcome of rolling a three

$$= \dfrac{\text{Number of outcomes of rolling a three on a side}}{\text{Total number of possible rolls or outcomes}}$$

$$= \dfrac{2}{10}$$

$$= \dfrac{\overset{1}{\cancel{2}}}{\underset{5}{\cancel{10}}} \qquad \text{Reduce to the lowest terms by dividing by 2.}$$

$$= \dfrac{1}{5}$$

The experimental probability of $\dfrac{1}{5}$ can be expressed as a decimal by dividing 1 by 5 as shown:

500

$$\begin{array}{r} .2 \\ 5\overline{)10} \\ -\underline{10} \\ 00 \end{array}$$

Therefore, the decimal form of the experimental probability of $\dfrac{1}{5} = .2$

The decimal form of the experimental probability of .2 can be expressed as a percent by moving the decimal point two places or two digits to the right and attaching the percent sign (%) which is the same as multiplying by 100 as shown:

Write a zero here as a place holder.

$$.2 = .20 = 20\%$$

Therefore, the experimental probability of $\dfrac{1}{5} = .2 = 20\%$

(b) The die was rolled 10 times. The outcome of the side with three dots was 2 and therefore, the number of rolls that the outcomes were not the side with three dots
= 10 rolls - 2 rolls
= 8 rolls
Experimental probability of not rolling the side with three dots

$$= \dfrac{\text{Number of outcomes with not rolling a three}}{\text{Total number of possible rolls or outcomes}}$$

$$= \dfrac{8}{10}$$

$$= \dfrac{\overset{4}{\cancel{8}}}{\underset{5}{\cancel{10}}} \qquad \text{Reduce to the lowest terms by dividing by 2.}$$

$$= \dfrac{4}{5}$$

(c)(i) From Example 6(c), the number of possible rolls = 100.
Let the number of outcomes with three dots when the die is rolled 100 times = x. The experimental probability of the outcomes with the three dots when the die is rolled 100 times

$$= \dfrac{\text{Number of outcomes with a three when the die is rolled 100 times}}{\text{Number of possible rolls}}$$

$$= \frac{x}{100} \qquad\qquad\qquad\qquad\qquad\qquad\qquad\qquad\qquad [A]$$

From the solution of Example 6(a), the experimental probability of the outcome

of the side with the three dots $= \frac{1}{5}$ $\qquad\qquad\qquad\qquad\qquad\qquad [B]$

Equation $[A]$ and equation $[B]$ are equal because $\frac{x}{100}$ and $\frac{1}{5}$ are equivalent

fractions or equivalent ratios, therefore,

$$\frac{x}{100} = \frac{1}{5} \qquad\qquad\qquad\qquad\qquad\qquad\qquad\qquad [C]$$

(Review the section on Equivalent Fractions or Equivalent Ratios).
The cross products of equivalent fractions or ratios are equal, so

$$\frac{x}{100} \diagdown\diagup \frac{1}{5}$$

Therefore, $5 \times x = 100 \times 1$

$$5x = 100 \qquad\qquad\qquad\qquad\qquad\qquad\qquad\qquad [D]$$

Divide each side of equation $[D]$ by 5 in order to obtain the value of x as shown:

$$\frac{\cancel{5}x}{\cancel{5}}_1 = \frac{\overset{20}{\cancel{100}}}{\cancel{5}}_1$$

$x = 20$ outcomes of three dots.

(ii) From Example 6(c), the number of possible rolls $= 100$.
   Let $y =$ "the number of times of outcomes with no side with three dots out of 100 possible rolls."

The experimental probability of not rolling the side with three dots out of 100 possible outcomes

$= \dfrac{\text{Number of outcomes with no three dots when the die is rolled 100 times}}{\text{Total number of possible rolls}}$

$$= \frac{y}{100} \qquad\qquad\qquad\qquad\qquad\qquad\qquad\qquad [E]$$

From solution of Example 6(b), the experimental probability of not rolling the side

with three dots $= \frac{4}{5}$ $\qquad\qquad\qquad\qquad\qquad\qquad\qquad [F]$

Equation $[E]$ and equation $[F]$ are equal because $\dfrac{y}{100}$ and $\dfrac{4}{5}$ are equivalent fractions or ratios, and therefore,

$$\frac{y}{100} = \frac{4}{5}$$

(Review the section on Equivalent Fractions and Equivalent Ratios).
The cross products of equivalent fractions or ratios are equal, so

Therefore, $= 5 \times y = 4 \times 100$

$$5y = 400 \rule{6cm}{0.4pt} [G]$$

Divide each side of equation $[G]$ by 5 in order to obtain the value of y as shown:

$$\frac{5y}{5} = \frac{400}{5}$$

$$\frac{\overset{y}{\cancel{5y}}}{\underset{1}{\cancel{5}}} = \frac{\overset{80}{\cancel{400}}}{\underset{1}{\cancel{5}}} \quad \text{Divide each side of the equation by 5.}$$

$y = 80$ outcomes of not rolling a side with three dots.

Example 7

(Example 7 is intentionally designed to be long to provide the student with critical and logical methods of solving diverse problems.)
A die was thrown once.
(a) List the possible outcomes.
   From your possible outcomes in (a), what is the theoretical probability of rolling:
(b) an even number.   (c) an odd number.   (d) a number greater than 2.
(e) a number between 2 and 5. (f) a multiple of 3.   (g) not a multiple of 3.
(h) a prime number.   (i) not a prime number.

Solution

(a) A die has six sides and the sides are numbered from 1 to 6. When the die is thrown, any of the six sides can show up, so there are six possible outcomes, which are 1, 2, 3, 4, 5, and 6.
(b) The even numbers out of the total possible outcomes of 1, 2, 3, 4, 5, and 6 are 2, 4, and 6. There are three even numbers out of the total of 6 possible outcomes. The theoretical probability of obtaining an even number

$$= \frac{\text{Number of outcomes of an even number}}{\text{Total number of possible outcomes}}$$

$$= \frac{3}{6}$$

$$= \frac{\overset{1}{\cancel{3}}}{\underset{2}{\cancel{6}}} \qquad \text{Reduce to the lowest terms by dividing by 3.}$$

$$= \frac{1}{2}$$

(c) The odd numbers out of the total possible outcomes of 1, 2, 3, 4, 5, and 6 are 1, 3, and 5. Therefore, there are three odd numbers out of the total of 6 possible outcomes.

The theoretical probability of obtaining an odd number

$$= \frac{\text{Number of outcomes of an odd number}}{\text{Total number of possible outcomes}}$$

$$= \frac{3}{6}$$

$$= \frac{\overset{1}{\cancel{3}}}{\underset{3}{\cancel{6}}} \qquad \text{Reduce to the lowest terms by dividing by 3.}$$

$$= \frac{1}{2}$$

(d) The outcome of the numbers that are greater than 2 out of the total possible outcomes of 1, 2, 3, 4, 5, and 6 are 3, 4, 5, and 6. There are four numbers, which are greater than 2 out of the total possible outcome of 6 numbers.
The theoretical probability of obtaining a number greater than 2

$$= \frac{\text{Number of outcomes greater than 2}}{\text{Total number of possible outcomes}}$$

$$= \frac{4}{6}$$

$$= \frac{\overset{2}{\cancel{4}}}{\underset{3}{\cancel{6}}}$$ Reduce to the lowest terms by dividing by 2.

$$= \frac{2}{3}$$

(e) The numbers between 2 and 5 are 3 and 4 out of the total possible outcomes of 1, 2, 3, 4, 5, and 6. There are two numbers between 2 and 5 out of the total possible outcome of 6 numbers.

The theoretical probability of obtaining a number between 2 and 5

$$= \frac{\text{Number of outcomes of a number between 2 and 5}}{\text{Total number of possible outcomes}}$$

$$= \frac{2}{6}$$

$$= \frac{\overset{1}{\cancel{2}}}{\underset{3}{\cancel{6}}}$$ Reduce to the lowest terms by dividing by 2.

$$= \frac{1}{3}$$

(f) The multiples of 3 out of the total numbers of possible outcomes of 1, 2, 3, 4, 5, and 6 are 3 and 6. There are two numbers (3 and 6) that are multiples of 3 out of the total of the 6 possible outcomes of 1, 2, 3, 4, 5, and 6.

The theoretical probability of obtaining a multiple of 3

$$= \frac{\text{Number of outcomes of a multiple of 3}}{\text{Total number of possible outcomes}}$$

$$= \frac{2}{6}$$

$$= \frac{\overset{1}{\cancel{2}}}{\underset{3}{\cancel{6}}}$$ Reduce to the lowest terms by dividing by 2..

$$= \frac{1}{3}$$

(g) The numbers that are not multiples of 3 out of the total outcomes of 1, 2, 3, 4, 5,

505

and 6 are 1, 2, 4, and 5. There are 4 numbers (1, 2, 4, and 5) that are not multiples of 3 out of a total of 6 possible outcomes.

The theoretical probability of obtaining a number that is not a multiple of 3

$$= \frac{\text{Number of outcomes that are not multiples of 3}}{\text{Total number of possible outcomes}}$$

$$= \frac{4}{6}$$

$$= \frac{\overset{2}{\cancel{4}}}{\underset{3}{\cancel{6}}} \qquad \text{Reduce to the lowest terms by dividing by 2}$$

$$= \frac{2}{3}$$

(h) A prime number has exactly two factors which are 1 and the number itself. The prime numbers out of the total possible outcomes of 1, 2, 3, 4, 5, and 6 are 2, 3, and 5. There are 3 prime numbers (2, 3, and 5) out of the total possible outcomes of 6 numbers.

The theoretical probability of obtaining a prime number

$$= \frac{\text{Number of outcomes of a prime number}}{\text{Total number of possible outcomes}}$$

$$= \frac{3}{6}$$

$$= \frac{\overset{1}{\cancel{3}}}{\underset{2}{\cancel{6}}} \qquad \text{Reduce to the lowest terms by dividing by 3.}$$

$$= \frac{1}{2}$$

(i) The numbers which are not prime numbers out of the total possible outcome of 1, 2, 3, 4, 5, and 6 are 1, 4, and 6. There are 3 numbers (1, 4, and 6), which are not prime numbers out of a total possible outcomes of 6 numbers.

The theoretical probability of not getting a prime number

$$= \frac{\text{Number of outcomes which are not a prime number}}{\text{Total number of possible outcomes}}$$

$$= \frac{3}{6}$$

$$= \frac{\overset{1}{\cancel{3}}}{\underset{2}{\cancel{6}}} \quad \text{Reduce to the lowest terms by dividing by 3.}$$

$$= \frac{1}{2}$$

The notes and the generous examples have provided me with the conceptual understanding and the computational fluency to do my homework.

Exercises
1. Explain what is meant by (a) theoretical probability, (b) an event.
2. How do you find the theoretical probability of an event?
3. What is the theoretical probability that if you spin the spinner:

    (a). The pointer will land on 3?
    (b). The pointer will land on an even number?
    (c). The pointer will land on an odd number?
    (d). The pointer will land on a prime number?
    Hint: See example 1.

4. Find the theoretical probability of each event:

    (a). The spinner will stop on E.
    (b). The spinnerwill stop on a vowel.
    Hint: See example 2.

5. Explain (a) an impossible event, (b) equally likely event, (c) certain event.
    Hint: See Example 3.
6. The probability of an event A occurring is .6, B occurring is .9, C occurring is .5, and D occurring is .2. By comparing the probability values, which event is most likely to occur and which event is least likely to occur? Hint: See the section under "Comparing the Values of Probability."
7. Find the theoretical probability that the pointer will land on:

(a). a number 10.
(b). a number 0.
(c). an odd number.
(d). an even number.
(e). a number less than 3.
(f). a prime number.

Indicate the probabilities on a number line.
Hint: See example 4.

8. (a) Find the theoretical probability of outcome of Y.
    Give your answer as a fraction, a decimal, and a percent.
  (b) Find the experimental probability of the outcome of W.
  (c) Find the experimental probability of the outcome of Z.
  (d) Find the experimental probability of the outcome of Y.
  (e) Find the experimental probability of the outcome of X.
    Hint: See Example **5**.

Outcome	Number of spins
W	3
X	6
Y	8
X	4

9. A die was rolled 20 times. On 4 of the rolls the outcome was a 2.
  (a) What is the experimental probability of rolling a 2?
    Give your answer as a fraction, a decimal, and a percent.
  (b) How many rolls was the outcome not showing a 2? What is the experimental
    probability of not rolling a 2?
  (c) Based on the experimental probabilities that you have found and suppose the
    die is rolled 100 times, about how many times do you expect to roll a side:
      (i) with a 2?
      (ii) without a 2?
    Hint: See Example **6**.

10. A die was thrown once.
  (a) List the possible outcomes.
    From your possible outcomes in (a), what is the theoretical probability of
    obtaining:
  (b) an odd number?   (c) an even number?
  (d) a number greater than 4?   (e) a number between 3 and 6?
  (f) a multiple of 2?   (g) not a multiple of 2?
  (h) a prime number?   (i) not a prime number?
    Hint: See Example **7**.

Challenge Questions

11. Using the spinner, what is the probability in fractions, decimals, and percent of:

    (a). Obtaining a number less than 30.
    (b). Obtaining a number between 15 and 35.
    (c). Obtaining an even number?
    (d). Obtaining an odd number?
    (e). Obtaining a number greater than 60.

12. A bag contains 3 green balls and 7 yellow balls. If a ball is selected at random, what is the probability that the ball is: (a) green, (b) yellow, (c) not green, (d) not yellow?

Answers to Selected Questions

3a. $\dfrac{1}{3}$ **4a.** $\dfrac{1}{4}$ **7a.** 0

(How do you rate the Math Teaching Series?)

(Do you find the generous examples in the Math Teaching Series helpful?)

CHAPTER 17

GRAPHS

Cumulative Review

1. $13 + 8 =$ **2.** $12 \div 4 =$ **3.** $16 - 8 =$ **4.** $8 \times 3 =$

5. $25 \div 5 =$ **6.** $21 - 12 =$ **7.** $30 \div 6 =$ **8.** $17 - 8 =$

9. $\begin{array}{r} 24 \\ \times\ \ 3 \\ \hline \end{array}$ **10.** $\begin{array}{r} 14 \\ +\ 19 \\ \hline \end{array}$ **11.** $\begin{array}{r} 35 \\ -\ 13 \\ \hline \end{array}$ **12.** $\begin{array}{r} 19 \\ \times\ 4 \\ \hline \end{array}$

13. $48 \div 3 =$ **14.** $24 \div 8 =$ **15.** $12 + 38 =$ **16.** $36 - 17 =$

17. $2.9 + 3.7 =$ **18.** $5.6 \times 4 =$ **19.** $2.5 \times 3.4 =$ **20.** $24.7 - 1.6 =$

21. $\dfrac{2}{3} \times \dfrac{1}{5} =$ **22.** $\dfrac{2}{3} \div \dfrac{2}{5} =$ **23.** $\dfrac{3}{4} - \dfrac{1}{5} =$ **24.** $2\dfrac{1}{3} + 3\dfrac{3}{4} =$

New Terms: frequency table, at least, at most, fewer than, relative frequency

Interpreting Data

Frequency Table

A **frequency table** is a table that shows the number of times each event occurs.

> Note that in the tally column in example 1, the 5th time of an event is indicated by crossing the previous 4 events as follows: ̄TTHL .

Example 1

The frequency table shows the number of subjects studied by students in grade 11 at the Peki Secondary school in Ghana.

Number of subjects studied by students		
Number of subjects studied	Number of students. Tally	Number of students. Frequency
9	1111	4
8	̄TTHL ̄TTHL 11	12
7	̄TTHL 1	6
6	111	3
5	11	2

a. How many students studied 8 subjects?

b. How many students studied at least 7 subjects?

c. How many students studied 6 or more subjects?

d. How many students studied at most 7 subjects?

510

e. How many students were in the survey?

f. What percent of the students studied 6 subjects?

g. What percent of the students studied fewer than 6 subjects?

h. What percent of the students studied at least 7 subjects?

i. What percent of the students studied at most 7 subjects?

j. What is the relative frequency of the students that studied 5 subjects?

k. If a student is selected at random, what is the probability that the student studied 9 subjects?

Solution

a. The frequency column shows that 12 students studied 8 subjects.

b. "**At least 7 subjects**" means 7 or more subjects. Therefore, the number of students that studied at least 7 subjects is the sum of the frequencies of the students that studied 7, 8, and 9 subjects which = 6 + 12 + 4 = 22 students.

c. The number of students that studied 6 or more subjects is the sum of the frequencies of the students that studied 6, 7, 8, and 9 subjects which = 3 + 6 + 12 + 4 = 25 students.

d. "**At most 7 subjects**" means 7 or less subjects. Therefore, the number of students that studied at most 7 subjects is the sum of the frequencies of the students that studied 7, 6, and 5 subjects which = 6 + 3 + 2 = 11 students.

e. The number of the students in the survey is the sum of the total frequency which = 4 + 12 + 6 + 3 + 2 = 27 students.

f. Percent of students that studied 6 subjects

$$= \frac{\text{Number that studied 6 subjects}}{\text{Total number of students}} \times 100 \quad \text{(Hint: Review the section on percent.)}$$

$$= \frac{3}{27} \times 100 \qquad\qquad (\frac{\text{Part}}{\text{Total}} \times 100 = \text{Percent of the total.})$$

$$= \frac{\overset{1}{\cancel{3}}}{\underset{9}{\cancel{27}}} \times 100 \qquad\qquad \text{Divide by 3.}$$

$$= \frac{100}{9} = 11\frac{1}{9}\% \qquad\qquad \text{Divide by 9.}$$

g. Those who studied **fewer than** 6 subjects means those who studied 5 subjects. The number of students that studied 5 subjects = 2

h. Percent of the students that studied **at least** 7 subjects

511

$$= \frac{\text{Number that studied at least 7 subjects}}{\text{Total number of students}} \times 100 \quad \text{(Review the section on percent).}$$

$$= \frac{22}{27} \times 100 \qquad \text{(From solution (b) 22 students studied at least 7 subjects)}$$

$$\left(\frac{\text{part}}{\text{Total}} \times 100 = \text{percent of total}\right).$$

$$= 81.48\% \qquad \text{You many use a calender.}$$

i. Percent of students that studied **at most** 7 subjects

$$= \frac{\text{Number of students that studied at most 7 subjects}}{\text{Total number of students}} \times 100$$

Review the section on Percent.

$$= \frac{11}{27} \times 100 \qquad \left(\frac{\text{Part}}{\text{Total}} \times 100 = \text{Percent of the total}\right).$$

(From solution **d**, the number of the students that studied at most 7 subjects is 11).

$$= 40.74\% \qquad \text{You may use a calculator.}$$

j. The relative frequency of an event

$$= \frac{\text{Frequency of the event.}}{\text{Total frequencies}}, \text{ therefore,}$$

the **relative frequency** of the students that studied 5 subjects

$$= \frac{\text{Frequency of the students that studied 5 subjects}}{\text{Total frequencies}}$$

$$= \frac{2}{27}$$

k. Probability that a student selected studied 9 subjects

$$= \frac{\text{Number of students that studied 9 subjects}}{\text{Total number of students}}$$

(Review the section on probability).

$$= \frac{4}{27}$$

Bar Graph
A bar graph is a graph in which the height of the vertical bars represent the

512

frequencies or values assigned to each activity. The bars are spaced evenly and they may be drawn vertically or horizontally. A bar graph is drawn from a frequency table.

Example 2
Use the bar graph to answer the following question:

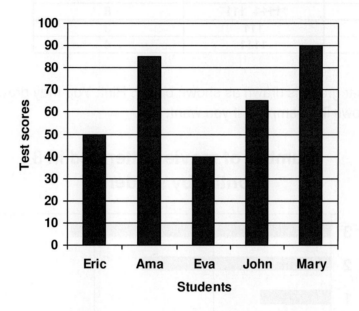

Students' test scores in percent.

a. Who did the best in the test?
b. Who did the poorest in the test?
c. How many more marks did Mary have than Erica?
d. Who scored 10% more marks than Eva?
e. What is the range of the scores?

Solution
a. Mary had the highest score of 90%, and therefore, Mary did the best in the test.
b. Eva had the lowest score of 40%, and therefore Eva did poorest in the test.
c. Mary's score was 90%, and Eric's score was 50%, and therefore, Mary has 40% or (90% - 50%) more marks than Eric.
d. Eric scored 50%, and Eva scored 40%, and therefore, Eric scored 10% or (50% - 40%) more marks than Eva.
e. The range of the scores:

$$= \text{Greatest score - Least score}$$
$$= 90\% - 40\%$$
$$= 50\%$$

Example 3

Use the frequency table to draw a bar graph on graph paper. Hint: Recall that the bar graph is spaced evenly and may be drawn vertically or horizontally.

Number of movies attended in 3 months by students		
Number of movies	Number of students. Tally	Number of students. Frequency
3	~~1111~~ ~~1111~~ 1	11
2	~~1111~~ 111	8
1	111	3
0	1111	4

Solution

The horizontal bar graph is drawn as shown below. Hint: You may draw the vertical bar graph as shown in Example **2** if you want.

Number of movies attended in 3 months by students.

Hint: It is best to draw graphs on a graph or grid paper.

Multiple Bar Graph

A multiple bar graph consists of two or more component bar columns or graphs which are evenly spaced and the heights of the component bars represent the frequencies or values assigned to each activity. Like a bar graph, the multiple bar graph can be vertical or horizontal.

Test scores of two schools in percent		
Year	School A	School B
2000	95	80
2001	85	90
2002	95	95

a. Which school had the better score in 2000?

b. In which year were the performance of schools A and B the same?

Solution

Test scores of two schools in percent.

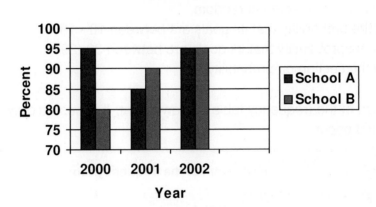

The graph shows a vertical multiple bar graph. The component bar column or graph are evenly spaced and the heights of the component bar columns represent the frequencies or values assigned to each activity.

a. School A had a better score than school B because school A had a higher score of 95% in 2000 whereas school B has a score of 80%.

b. The performance of the schools A and B were the same in 2002 because both schools had the same score of 95%. Hint: It is best to draw graphs on graph paper or grid paper.

Histogram

A histogram is a bar graph which does not have any space between the bars. Like the bar graph, a histogram can be vertical or horizontal.

Example 5

Some school districts in Ghana were surveyed to find the number of goals scored by the soccer teams during the year. A frequency table is made with intervals of 10 goals.

515

Goals	Frequency of the school district
0 - 9	3
10 - 19	4
20 - 29	2
30 - 39	0
40 - 49	1
50 - 59	3

a. Draw a histogram of the frequency table.

b. From the survey, how many school districts scored the highest number of goals?

c. How many school districts took part in the survey?

d. How many school districts scored the least number of goals?

e. If a school district is selected at random,

      (i) what is the probability that its goals are between 10 - 19?

      (ii) what is the probability that its goals are between 30 -39?

   Hint: Review the section on probability.

Solution

a. The histogram of the frequency table is drawn. Hint: It is best to draw a graph on a paper or grid paper.

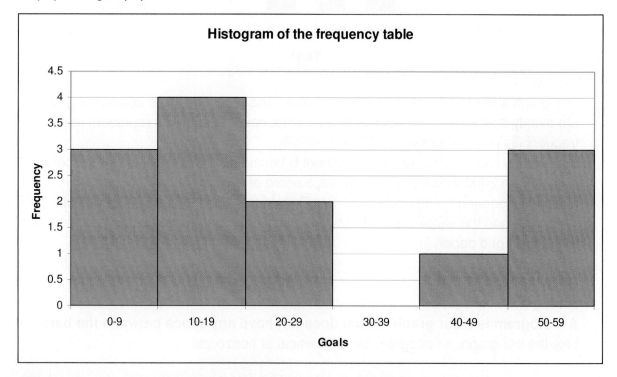

b. Three schools scored the highest number of goals between 50 - 59 goals.

c. The number of the school districts that took part in the survey

$$= \text{sum of the frequencies}$$
$$= 3 + 4 + 2 + 0 + 1 + 3$$
$$= 13 \text{ school districts.}$$

516

d. Three schools scored the least goals in the interval of 0 - 9 goals.

e(i). The number of school districts that have goals between 10 - 19 is 4. The total number of school districts that took part in the survey is the sum of the frequencies which is $(3 + 4 + 2 + 0 + 1 + 3 = 13)$.

The probability of selecting a school district that has goals between 10 - 19

$$= \frac{\text{Number of school districts that have goals between 10 - 19}}{\text{Total number of schools}}.$$

$$= \frac{4}{13}$$

e(ii). The number of school districts that have goals between 30 - 39 is 0. The total number of school districts that took part in the survey is the sum of the frequencies which is $(3 + 4 + 2 + 0 + 1 + 3 = 13)$. Therefore, the number of school districts that has goals between 30 - 39

$$= \frac{\text{Number of school districts that have goals between 30 - 39}}{\text{Total number of school districts}}$$

$$= \frac{0}{13} = 0$$

Example 6

Use the frequency table to draw a histogram.

Students	Joe	Mary	Eric	Ben	Eli
Ages in years	6	7	10	9	8

Solution

The histogram of the frequency table is drawn. Hint: It is best to draw graphs on graph paper or grid paper.

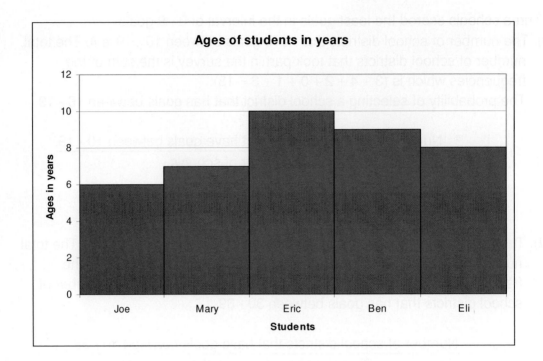

Line Graphs

Line graphs are ordered pairs from a data in a table and the ordered pairs are plotted on a grid or graph paper and the points of the plotted ordered pairs are connected with lines. What is the line graph used for? **The line graph is used to find or estimate one of the ordered pairs if the other ordered pair is known**.

Example 7

Make a line graph of the given data.

Months	1	2	3	4	5	6	7
Savings in dollars	10	15	10	8	5	20	30

Solution

Use the ordered pairs of the data to plot each point, for example, the first set of the data is the savings in the first month which is $10 which may be written as a pair of data as (months, dollars) or (1,10) where 1 is the first month's savings and 10 is $10 saved in the first month. Similarly, the other sets of data or ordered pairs of data are (2, 15), (3, 10), (4, 8), (5, 5), (6, 20), and (7, 30). To plot the points using the ordered pairs of data, first draw the axis for the savings for the months horizontally and draw the axis for the savings vertically and then for the first ordered pair of data (1,10), locate 1 which represents the first month on the horizontal axis and locate the 10 which represent the $10 on the vertical axis. Where (1,10) meet is the required point to be plotted. Similarly, you can plot the points of the remaining ordered pairs of data. (Hint: See how to plot points under the chapter on "Coordinate Geometry.") Connect the points with lines to form a line

518

graph as shown.

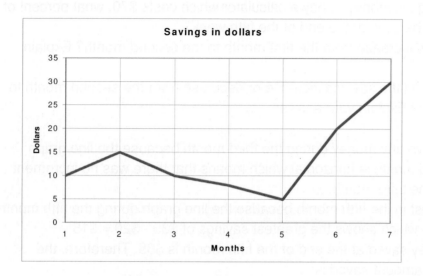

When a line in a line graph goes up from left to right, it shows that there is **an increase in the data**. When a line in a line graph goes down from left to right, it shows that there is **a decrease in the data**. When a line in a line graph is horizontal (for example between two points,) it shows that there is **no change in the data**. The **trend** in the data is the increase or decrease in the data.

Example 8
Use the line graph to answer each question (**a** to **d**.)

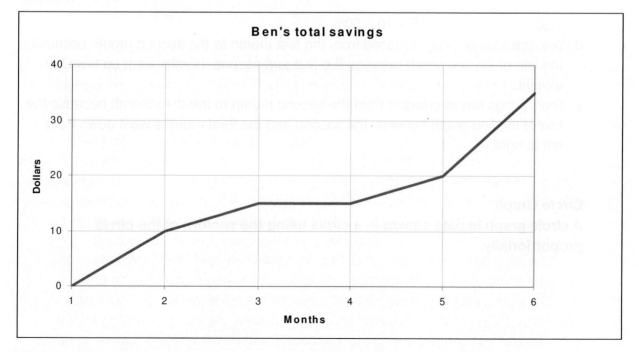

a. During which month did Ben not save any money? Explain your answer.

b. During which month did Ben save most? Give reasons for your answer.

c. If Ben is saving his money to buy a calculator which costs $70, what percent of the money did he save at the end of the fifth week?

d. Did the savings increase from the first month to the second month? Explain your answer.

e. In Example 7, did the savings increase or decrease from the second month to the third month? Explain your answer.

Solution

a. Ben did not save any money during the third month because the line graph during the third month is horizontal which means that there was no increment of savings in the third month.

b. Ben saved most in the fifth month because the line graph during the fifth month is the steepest which shows the greatest savings of $35 - $20 = $15.

c. The total money saved at the end of the fifth month is $35. Therefore, the percent of the amount saved is:

$$= \frac{35}{70} \times 100 \qquad (\frac{\text{Part}}{\text{Total}} \times 100 = \text{Percent of the total}).$$

$$= \frac{\overset{5}{\cancel{\underset{7}{\cancel{\frac{35}{70}}}}}}{1} \times 100 \qquad \text{Divide by 10 and 7.}$$

$$= 5 \times 10 = 50\%$$

d. Yes, the savings has increased from the first month to the second month because, the line of the line graph between the first and second months went up from left to right.

e. The savings has decreased from the second month to the third month because the line of the line graph between the second and the third months went down from left to right.

Circle Graph
A circle graph is data shown in a circle using the sectors of the circle proportionally.

In this circle graph, the area 1, 2, 3 and 4 represent sectors. For example, the sector ABC is represented by area 1.

Example 9

If Mary spends her monthly income according to the circle graph, find:

a. How much she spends on rent?

b. How much she spends on food?

c. How much more does she spend on the rent than food monthly?

d. On which item does she spend the least amount of money?

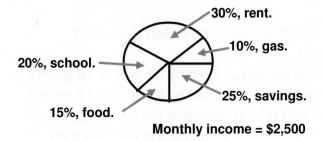

30%, rent.

10%, gas.

20%, school.

25%, savings.

15%, food.

Monthly income = $2,500

Solution

a. She spent 30% of $2,500 on rent,

$$= \frac{30}{100} \times \$2,500$$ (Express 30% as $\frac{30}{100}$ and "of" is the same as

multiplication). Hint: Review the section on percent.

$$= \frac{30}{\cancel{100}} \times \$2,\cancel{500}^{25}$$ Divide by 100 by canceling the two zeros.

$$= 30 \times \$25$$
$$= \$750.$$

b. She spends 15% of $2,500 on food,

$$= \frac{15}{100} \times \$2,500$$ (Express 15% as $\frac{15}{100}$ and "of" is the same as

multiplication.) Hint: Review the section on percent.

$$= \frac{15}{\cancel{100}} \times \$2,\cancel{500}$$ Divide by 100 by canceling the zeros

521

$= 15 \times \$25 = \$375$

c. From the solution of **a**, she spends $750 on rent, from the solution of **b**, she spends $375 on food, and therefore, she spends

$$\$750 - \$375 \text{ more on rent than food.}$$
$$= \$375$$

d. She spends the least amount of money on gas because the percent of gas is the lowest percent among the items that she spends money on.

The notes and the generous examples have provided me with the conceptual understanding and the computational fluency to do my homework.

Exercises

1. Answer the questions by using the frequency table. Hint: See Example 1.

   a. How many students were surveyed?

   b. How many students had their driving lessons at least by the age of 18 years?

   c. How many students had their driving lessons at most by the age of 17 years?

   d. What percent of the students had their driving license at the age of 18 years?

   e. What percent of the students had their driving license at the age less than 18 years?

   f. What percent of the students had their driving license at the age of at least 17 least?

   g. What is the relative frequency of the students who had their driving license at the age of 19 years.

   h. If a student is selected at random, what is the probability that the student is 16 years old?

Student's age of obtaining a license.		
Age	Tally	Frequency
16	~~HHH~~ ~~HHH~~ 11	12
17	~~HHH~~ 111	8
18	~~HHH~~	5
19	111	3

2. Describe a bar graph.

3. Use the bar graph to answer the following questions:

   a. Who did the best in the test?

   b. Who did the poorest on the test?

   c. How many more marks did student D have than student A?

   d. Which student had 25% more marks than student A?

   e. What is the range of scores?

   Hint: See Example **2**.

Test scores of students A, B, C, and D in percent.

4. Use the frequency table to draw a bar graph on a graph paper.
   Hint: See Example **3**.

Number of movies attended in 3 months by students		
Number of movies.	Number of students. Tally	Number of students. Frequency
4	~~1111~~ 11	7
3	1111	4
2	~~1111~~ 111	8
1	~~1111~~	5
0	11	2

5. Describe a multiple bar graph.
6. Use the table to draw a multiple bar graph.

	Test scores of two schools A and B in percent.	
Year	School A	School B
2002	88	92
2003	79	80
2004	95	95
2005	98	97

(**a**) Which school had the better score in 2004?
(**b**) In which year were the scores of schools A and B the same?
Hint: See Example **4**.

7. Describe a histogram.
8. Use the data in the table to draw a histogram.

Goals (soccer)	Frequency of schools.
0 - 9	2
10 - 19	5
20 - 29	3
30 - 39	0
40 - 49	4
50 - 59	7
60 - 69	1

a. How many schools scored the highest number of goals?

b. How many schools took part in the survey?

c. How many schools scored the least number of goals?

d. If a school is selected at random, what is the probability that the school's goals were between 50 - 59?

e. If a school is selected at random, what is the probability that the school's goals were between 20 - 29?

f. If a school is selected at random, what is the probability that the school's goals were between 30 - 39?

Hint: See Example **5**.

9. Use the frequency table to draw a histogram.

Students	Nick	Rose	Josh	Sam	Eric
Ages in years.	12	14	10	15	8

Hint: See Example **6**.

10. Describe a line graph. What is a **trend** in a line graph?

11. Make a line graph of the given data.

Weeks	1	2	3	4	5	6
Savings in dollars.	12	8	13	9	10	11

Hint: See Example **7**.

12. Use the line graph to answer each question.

The line graph is on the next page.

524

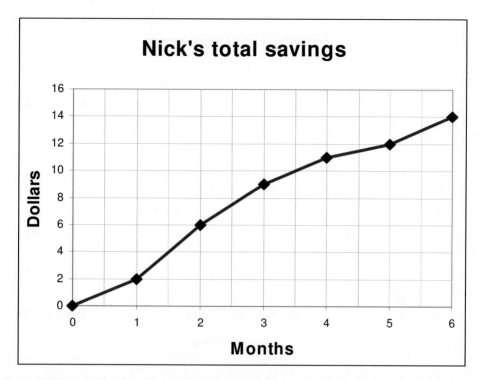

Nick's total savings

(y-axis: Dollars, 0 to 16; x-axis: Months, 0 to 6)

a. During which month did Nick not save any money? Explain your answer.

b. During which month did Nick save the most?
Explain you answer.

c. If Nick is saving his money to buy a calculator which costs $21, what percent of the money did he save by the end of the sixth month?
Hint: See Example **8**.

13. Describe a circle graph.

14. If Nick spends his monthly income according to the circle graph, find:
   a. How much he spent on insurance?
   b. How much he spent on school?
   c. How much more does he spend on school than on insurance monthly?
   d. On which item does he spend the least amount of money?
   Hint: See Example **9**.

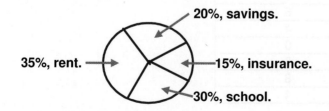

20%, savings.

35%, rent. ——— ←——15%, insurance.

30%, school.

Challenge Questions

15. Use the line graph to answer each question.

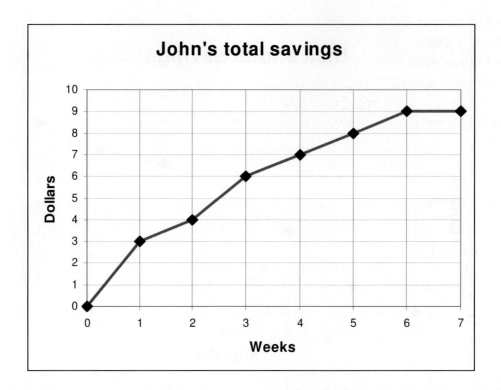

John's total savings

(**a**) If John is saving his money to buy a toy that costs $12.00, what percent of the money did he save by the end of the seventh week?

(**b**) During which week did he save most?
Explain your answer.

(**c**) During which week did he not save any money? Explain your answer?

16. Make a line graph of the given data.

Weeks	1	2	3	4	5	6	7
Savings in dollars.	5	8	4	10	9	7	5

17. Use the data in the table to draw a histogram.

Goals (soccer)	Frequency of schools.
0 - 9	7
10 - 19	5
20 - 29	6
30 - 39	4
40 - 49	0
50 - 59	3
60 - 69	8
70 - 79	4

a. If a school is selected at random, what is the probability that the school scored between 50 - 59 goals?

b. How many schools scored the most goals?

c. If a school is selected at random, what is the probability that the school scored between 40 - 49 goals?

18. If the circle graph shows how a bookstore spent $2000 on books for specific subjects, find:

   a. the amount spent on math books.

   b. the amount spent on history books.

   c. the greatest amount spent on history books.

   d. which subject is the least money spent on?

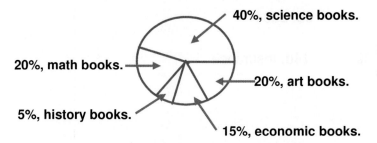

40%, science books.

20%, math books.

20%, art books.

5%, history books.

15%, economic books.

19. Use the bar graph to answer the following questions.

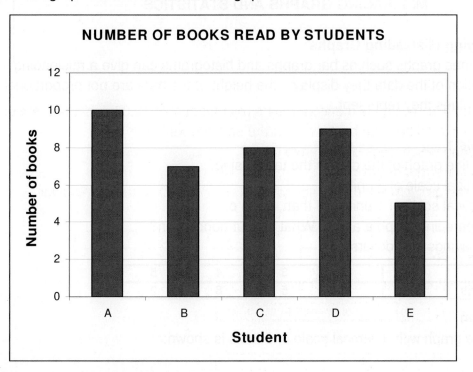

NUMBER OF BOOKS READ BY STUDENTS

   a. Which student read the most books?

   b. What is the range of the number of books read?

   c. How many more books did student A read than student E?

   d. What fraction of the total books in the survey was read by student D?

Hint: Fraction of books read by student D = $\dfrac{\text{Number of books read by student D}}{\text{Total number of books}}$

   e. What percent of the books was read by student D?

Hint: Percent of books read by student D $= \dfrac{\text{Number of books read by student D}}{\text{Total number of books.}} \times 100$

Answers to Selected Questions.

1a. 28 students   **1h**. $\dfrac{3}{7}$ **6b**. 2004

8f. 0   **12c**. $66\dfrac{2}{3}\%$ **14d**. Insurance

MISLEADING GRAPHS AND STATISTICS

Identifying Misleading Graphs

Sometimes graphs such as bar graphs and histograms can give a misleading impression of the data they display if the height of the bars are not proportional to the values they represent.

Example 1

Draw a line graph of the data in the table using:

a. a vertical scale of 5 units.

b. a vertical scale of 1 unit, and then, go to **c**.

c. compare line graph **a** and **b**. What is your conclusion?
   The savings is in dollars.

Week	1	2	3	4	5
Savings	2	3	5	8	9

Solution

a. A line graph with a vertical scale of 5 units is shown:

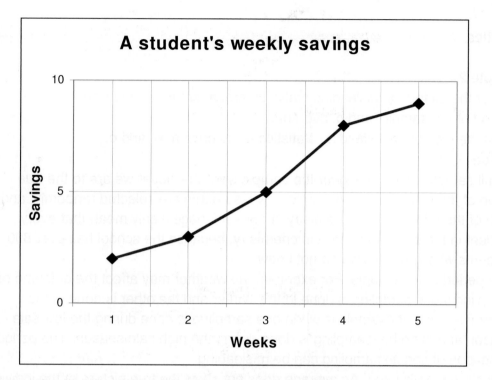

b. A line graph with a vertical scale of i unit is shown below.

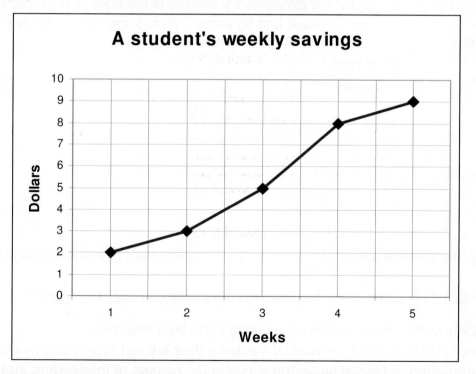

c. By changing the vertical scale of the line graph from 5 units as in **a**, to 1 unit as in **b**, the data values seem large in **b**. It can be concluded that the vertical scale of a line graph can be changed or adjusted to make the data values seem larger or smaller.

Statistics

Example 2
Some of the factors of misleading statistics are: **a**. small sample size,
b. period of the sample, and **c**. average.
Explain the factors of misleading statistics as listed in **a**, **b**, and **c**.

Solution

a. Small sample size: The bigger the sample size, the closer we are to the true value of the statistics. For example, if two students are selected randomly, and both of them had an A in chemistry, it does not necessarily mean that every student in the school had an A in chemistry, because the school has over 800 students whose grades we do not know.

b. The period of the sample: For example, the weather may affect the outcome of a sampling if one sampling is done in the Winter and the other is done in the Summer. Another example is when one sampling is done during the low sale season and the other sampling is done during the high sale season. The period or season of certain sampling can be misleading.

c. When average is used: An average does not show the true picture of the individual data that form the sample. For example, the sample of the ages of 5 people are 10 years,12 years,11 years,10 years, and 95 years. The average age of the five people is

$$= \frac{\text{Sum of ages}}{\text{Total ages}}$$

$$= \frac{10 + 12 + 11 + 10 + 95}{5}$$

$$= \frac{138}{5} = 27\frac{3}{5} \text{ years.}$$

Although the average age is $27\frac{3}{5}$ years, only one person out of five whose age is greater than $27\frac{2}{5}$ years. Note that although the average is high, the age of the majority of the people is rather low and this can be misleading.

The samples in **a**, **b**, and **c** are **biased because they are not representative of each population**. A **biased sampling** is one of the **causes of misleading statistics**.

Example 3
A business had 6 employees with the following salaries: $14,000, $15,000, $13,000, $14,000, $120,000 (owner), $10,000. "Employment available, average salary

$31,000" was the owner's ad. It is therefore, not likely that the salary of a new employee would be $31,000. The ad is misleading noting that only the owner had a huge salary of $120, 000.

Example 4

If the total revenue of market A during the three months in the summer was $400,000 and the total revenue of market B in the winter was $800,000,
a. Will it be misleading to compare the revenues of markets A and B?
b. What is the correct method of comparing the revenues of markets A and B?
Solution
a. Yes, it is misleading to compare the revenues of markets A and B because the revenues were measured at two different seasons of the year which are winter and summer and that during the busy shopping season of winter, the revenue of market B is greater than revenue of market A in the summer.
b. The correct method of comparing the revenues of markets A and B is to measure the revenue for both markets at the same season.

Example 5

a. If a car dealership claims that out of a survey of 10 customers, 5 of them are satisfied with their cars, and the dealership's ad states: "5 out of 10 customers are satisfied with their cars", is this ad misleading?
b. What is the correct way of doing the survey?
Solution
a. Yes, the ad is misleading because the sample size of 10 customers is too small. The sample size of 10 customers is not representative of the population of the customers who bought cars from the dealership. The dealership has many more customers than 10.
b. The correct method of doing the survey is to include all the customers who bought vehicles from the dealership in the survey and that will enable the dealership to know the total number of people who are satisfied with their vehicles.

The notes and the generous examples have provided me with the conceptual understanding and the computational fluency to do my homework.

Exercises

1. It can be concluded that the vertical scale of a line graph can be changed or adjusted to make changes in the data values seem larger or smaller. True or false? Explain. Hint: See Example 1.
2. "Five out of seven students scored 90% in the math test".
   a. How many students are in the sample?

b. Can you say that the number of students in the sample is representative of the student population?

c. Is the statement misleading? Hint: See Examples **2a** and **5**.

3. A school newspaper is comparing the total revenue of two stores, P-mart and J-Mart. If the total revenue of P-Mart from May 1st to August 1st is compared to the total revenue for J-Mart from October 1st to January 1st, do you think that the comparison is misleading? Explain your answer. Hint: See Examples 2b and 4.

Challenge Questions

4. A biased sampling is one of the causes of misleading statistics. True or False? Explain.

5. Comparing the total summer revenue of one super market to the total winter revenue of another super market is misleading statistics. True or false? Explain.

6. Explain how the average revenue for twelve months of a supermarket could be misleading statistics.

7. Explain how a vertical scale of a line graph can be adjusted to make changes in a data value seem larger or smaller.

TWO OR THREE LINE GRAPHS ON THE SAME AXES

Examples of "Two or Three Line Graphs on the Same Axes" are shown to provide the logic in solving similar problems. "Two or Three Line Graphs on the Same Axes" are used to compare two or three events, such as the populations of two or three cities.

Example 1

The graph shows the basketball scores of schools A and B.

The games were played six times (2000, 2001, 2002, 2003, 2004, and 2005.)

a. How many times did schools A and B have a tie? Explain your answer.

b. What is the highest point scored by school B? Explain your answer.

c. Between what two years did school A score the same points? Explain your answer.

d. What were the scores in 2002 for both school?

e. What was the difference in scores in 2002 between schools A and B?

Basketball scores

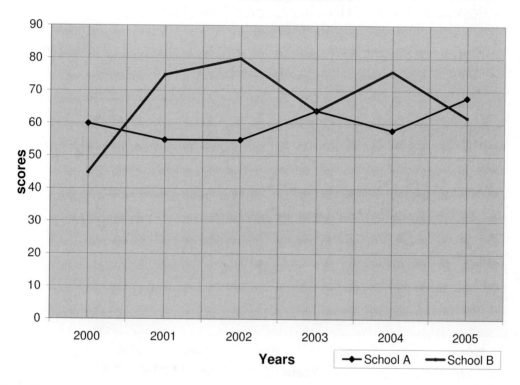

Solution

a. Schools A and B had a draw once, because the line graphs of schools A and B intersect or cross each other at one point (in 2003) where there was a game. (Notice that the scores of both teams are the same at the point of intersection where there was a game.) Hint: We have to determine in which year there was a draw.

b. The highest points scored by school B is 80 because 80 is the highest point on the graph for school B.

c. School A scored the same points in 2001 and 2002 because the line graph for school A was horizontal between 2001 and 2002. A horizontal line graph shows that there has been no increase or decrease in the scores between 2001 and 2002. So, the scores in 2001 and 2002 must be the same.

d. From the graph, school A scored 55 points and school B scored 80 points in 2002.

e. From the solution **d**, school A scored 55 points and school B scored 80 points in 2002. So, the difference in scores in 2002 is 80 - 55 = 25.

Example 2

The graph shows the math test scores for Kent School and Rosa School.
The tests were given six times (2001, 2002, 2003, 2004, 2005, and 2006.)
a. What was the test score in 2001 of Kent School?
b. What was the difference in scores in 2001 between the two schools?

c. In which year did the Kent School and Rosa School have the same math test scores? Explain your answer.

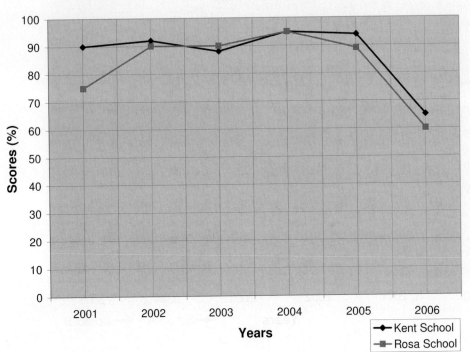

Math Test Scores

SOLUTION

a. In 2001, Kent School scored 90% and Rosa School scored 75%. (Notice that the scores can be read at the point on the graph where each line graph crosses or intersects the year 2001 line.)

b. From solution **a**, Kent School scored 90% and Rosa School scored 75%. So, the difference in scores in 2001 is 90% - 75% = 15%.

c. Kent School and Rosa School had the same math test scores in 2004 because the line graphs of the test scores of both schools intersect in 2004. (Notice that at the point of intersection, where there were actual tests, both line graphs (test scores) have the same value.) Hint: We have to determine in which year the scores were the same.

Example 3
The two line graphs show the basketball scores of James School and Rox Schools from 2002 to 2006. Five games were played (2002, 2003, 2004, 2005, and 2006.)

a. In which year did James School have the highest score? Explain your answer.

b. What were the highest and the lowest scores of James school? Explain your answer?

c. What is the range of the scores of James School? Explain your answer.

d. How many times did James School and Rox School have a tie?

Basketball Scores

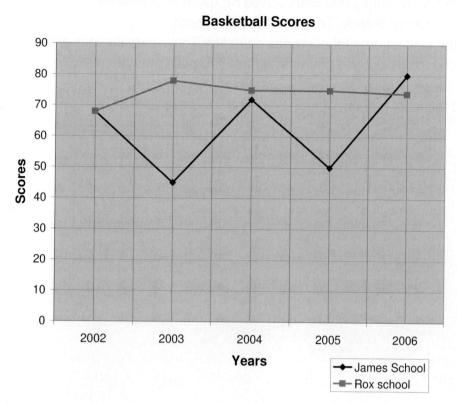

Solution

a. James School scored the highest goals in 2006 because 2006 indicates the highest point on the graph for James School.

b. The highest score of the James School was 80 because 80 was the highest point on the graph for James School. The lowest score of the James School was 45, because 45 was the lowest point on the graph.

c. The range is the difference between the greatest score and the least score. (Hint: Review the chapter on "Median, Mode, and Range.) From the solution of **b**, the highest score was 80 and the lowest score was 45. So, the range of the scores was:

$$\text{Range} = \text{Highest score} - \text{Lowest score}$$
$$= 80 - 45$$
$$= 35$$

d. James School and Rox School had a draw once because the line graphs of the James School and the Rox School intersect or cross each other at one point (2002) where there was a game. Hint: We should find the year the tie occurred. Notice that the scores at the point of each intersection where actual games took place are the same.

Example 4

The line graph shows the savings of Nick, Tom, and Mary.

a. In which month did Mary save the most money? Explain your answer.

535

b. What was the most money that Mary saved? Explain your answer.

c. Describe the savings of Nick, Tom, and Mary in March.

d. What was the highest amount of money saved by Tom? Explain your answer.

e. In which month did Nick save the most money? Explain your answer.

f. What is the range of Mary's savings? Explain your answer.

g. Who saved the least amount of money in May? Explain your answer.

Students' Savings

Solution

a. Mary saved the most money in January because the line graph of her savings indicates the highest point in January.

b. The most money that Mary saved was $20.00 because the highest point on the line graph for Mary indicates $20.00.

c. Nick, Tom, and Mary saved the same amount of money ($10.00) in March, because the three line graphs for Nick, Tom, and Mary intersect at a point that indicates or corresponds to $10.00.

d. The highest amount of money saved by Tom was $15.00, because the highest point on Tom's line graph indicates or corresponds to $15.00.

e. Nick saved the highest money in April because the highest point of Nick's line graph occurs in April.

f. The highest amount of money saved by Mary was $20.00, because the $20.00 corresponds to the highest point on Mary's line graph. The least amount of money saved by Mary corresponds to the amount that corresponds to the lowest point on Mary's line graph. This lowest point corresponds to about $7.50. The range of the money saved by Mary is the difference between the most money saved and the least money saved. So:

Range = Most money saved - Least money saved
= $20.00 - $7.50
= $12.50

g. Tom saved the least amount of money in May because Tom's line graph shows the lowest point in May compared to that of Nick's and Mary's.

━━━━━━━━━━━━━━━━ **The notes and the generous examples have provided me with the conceptual understanding and the computational fluency to do my homework.**

Exercises

1. The graph shows the basketball scores of Peki School and Mawul School.

a. What was the highest score of Peki School? Explain your answer.

b. What is the highest point scored by the Peki School? Explain your answer.

c. Between what two months are the scores of the two schools the same? Explain your answer.

d. What were the scores in January for both schools?

e. What was the difference in scores in January?

f. Explain why there was not a tie between the two schools. (Hint: Did the lines of the line graph intersect or cross each other during a game? The games occur at the locations where the points are plotted on the line graph.)
Hint: See Examples 1 and 3.

Basketball Scores

2. The graph shows the basketball scores of Team A and Team B.

a. What were the scores in April of both teams? Explain your answer.

b. What was the difference in the scores in April between the two teams? Explain your answer.

c. What was the highest score of Team B? Explain your answer.

537

Hint: See Examples 1 and 3.

Basketball Scores

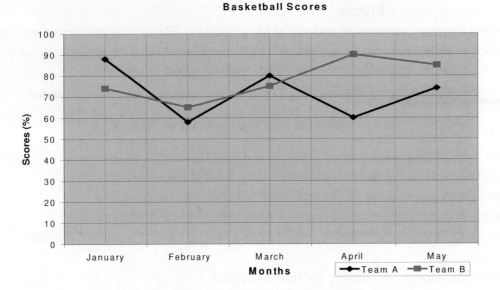

3. The graph shows the test scores of Rose and Amanda.
   a. What was the highest score of Amanda? Explain your answer.
   b. How many times did they score the same points? (Hint: "To score the same points is similar to a draw.") Explain your answer.
   c. What were the scores in June for both girls? Explain your answer.
   d. What were the scores in January for both girls?
   e. What was the difference in scores in January between Rose and Amanda?
   Hint: See Example 2.

Test Scores

4. The line graph shows the savings of three students.

a. In which month did all the students save the same amount of money? Explain your answer.

b. What was the highest amount of money saved? Explain your answer.

c. What was the lowest amount of money saved in April? Explain your answer.

d. What was the lowest amount of money saved in January? Explain your answer.

e. Who saved the most money in May? Explain your answer.

f. Who saved the least money in April? Explain your answer.

g. What is the range of the savings of Mary? Explain your answer.

h. What is the difference between the savings of Nick and Tom in January?

Hint: See Example 4.

Students' Savings

Challenge Questions

5. The graph shows Sam's and Josh's science test scores.

   a. In which months did Sam and Josh have the same score?

   b. Who had the lowest test score?

   c. What is the difference between Sam's and Josh's test scores in February?

   d. What is the difference between Sam's and Josh's test scores in May?

Science Test Scores

6. The graph shows the savings of Nick, John, and Mark.

   a. In which two months were their savings the same? How much did they save?

   b. What is the range of the savings of Nick?

   c. What is the range of the savings of John?

   d. What is the range of the savings of Mike?

Savings

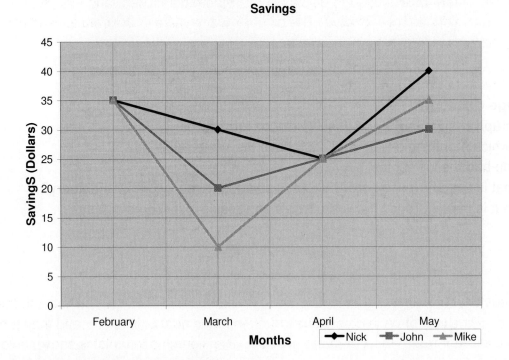

Answers to Selected Questions

5c. 90% - 85% = 5%   **6b.** $40 - $25 = $15

540

CHAPTER 18

STEM-AND-LEAF PLOT

Cumulative Review

1. $18 + 9 =$　　　　**2.** $12 \div 4 =$　　　**3.** $12 - 7 =$　　　**4.** $8 \times 2 =$

5. $15 \div 3 =$　　　　**6.** $13 - 9 =$　　　**7.** $18 \div 6 =$　　　**8.** $14 - 7 =$

9. $\begin{array}{r} 13 \\ \times\ 2 \\ \hline \end{array}$　　　**10.** $\begin{array}{r} 12 \\ +\ 25 \\ \hline \end{array}$　　　**11.** $\begin{array}{r} 22 \\ -\ 13 \\ \hline \end{array}$　　　**12.** $\begin{array}{r} 9 \\ \times\ 3 \\ \hline \end{array}$

13. $16 \div 4 =$　　　**14.** $28 \div 2 =$　　　**15.** $10 + 7 =$　　　**16.** $17 - 12 =$

17. $8.6 \div 2 =$　　　**18.** $2.7 \times 2 =$　　　**19.** $3.8 \times 8 =$　　　**20.** $9.1 - 1.9 =$

New Term: stem-and-leaf plot

The stem-and-leaf plot is a table that shows groups of data arranged by place value. The **stem-and-leaf plot** is used to display and compare data. Stem-and-leaf plot is also used to condense a set of data. The greatest place value of the data is used for the stem and the next greatest place value forms the leaves.

How to Make a Stem-and-Leaf Plot.

Example 1

Using the data values, (a) make a stem-and-leaf plot.

　　　　　　　　(b) explain how the stem-and-leaf plot is made.

　　Ages of people in a club.

　　Data values

28	34	16	50	12	13
34	14	7	16	25	19
16	9	28	50	55	19
74	36	8			

Solution

a). The tens digit of each number is its stem. The **stems** are listed from the least to the greatest. The **leaf** of each data value is written to the right of its stem, and they are written in order from the least to the greatest. The stem and leaf plot is shown below:

```
            Stem │Leaf
                0│7 8 9
                1│2 3 4 6 6 6 6 9 9
                2│5 8 8
                3│4 4 6
                4│
                5│0 0 5
                6│
                7│4
```

The tens digit of each number is its stem.

The ones digit of each number is the leaf.

Key
5│5 represents 55 years.

This vertical line separates the stems from the leaves.

b). **The stem and leaf plot is made from data values using the four items listed below:**

1. Under the stems column, list the tens digit of every data in order from the least to the greatest and these tens digits become the stems. The data values contain one-digit numbers which are ones, and therefore, the stem column begins with zero because the ones has no place value for tens. The highest data is 74, and therefore, the tens digit under the stem column range from 0 to 7, and therefore, choose 0 to 7 as stems also.

2. Under the leaves column and beside each ten digit, write the ones digits of each data in order from least to greatest, and these ones digits become the leaves. For example, the data values for the stem and leaf plot:

$$2│5\ 8\ 8 \quad \text{are 25, 28, and 28.}$$

tens   ones

3. The ones digits are written under the leaf to the right of its stem, and they are written from the least to the greatest.

4. The "key" helps us to confirm the place values of the stem and leaf columns. For example, the key "5│5" means 55 years" and it confirms that the stem column is tens and the leaf column is ones.

Example 2

List the data values in the stem-and-leaf plot.

```
     Stem │Leaf
         0│1 7 9
         1│4 4 8
         2│0 1 6                    Key
         3│0 0 9              1│4   means 14
         4│4 5 6 8 9
         5│1 4
```

Solution

Using the information in Example 1, regarding the fact that the stem column is the tens

542

column and the leaf column is the ones column and the key shows "1|4 means 14", which confirms that the stem column is tens and the leaf column is ones, the data values are: 1, 7, 9, 14, 14, 18, 20, 21, 26, 30, 30, 39, 44, 45, 46, 48, 49, 51, and 54.

Example 3

a. Use the given data to make a stem-and-leaf plot.
b. How many teams have scores beyond 65?
c. How many leaves are in the stem-and-leaf plot?
d. Using the stem-and-leaf plot, what is the median?
e. Using the stem-and-leaf plot, what is the mode?
f. What is the range?

Teams	A	B	C	D	E	F	G	H	I	J	K	L	M	N
Scores per year	24	30	30	48	56	29	70	72	27	32	30	44	50	48

Solution

a. The scores range from 24 to 72 and therefore the stems are from 2 to 7, and the ones digits are written under the leaf column to the right of the stems, and they are written from the least to the greatest as shown:

```
Stem  | Leaf
    2 | 4 7 9
    3 | 0 0 0 2
    4 | 4 8 8
    5 | 0 6
    6 |
    7 | 0 2
```
key
7|0 means 70.

b. There are two teams which have scores beyond 65 and the scores are:

7|0 2 which are 70 and 72.

c. There are 14 leaves in the stem-and-leaf plot. The number of leaves is the same as the number of the scores.

d. The middle score is the median, however, since there are 14 scores, the middle score is the average of the 7th and the 8th scores.
The 7th score = 32 and the 8th score = 44.
Therefore, the average of the 7th and 8th scores

$$= \frac{\text{7th score} + \text{8th score}}{2}$$

$$= \frac{32 + 44}{2} = \frac{76}{2} = 38 \text{ scores.}$$

In order to find the median, the data needs to be arranged in order from the least to the greatest. Note that the stem-and-leaf plot already arranges the numbers in

543

order.

e. The score that occurs the most is the mode. From the stem-and-leaf plot, the
   mode is:

$$3 \mid 0\ 0\ 0 \quad \text{which is 30, 30 and 30 because 30 occurs the most.}$$

f. The **range is the greatest score minus the least score** which is 72 - 24 = 48

Example 4

a. Use the data to make a stem-and-leaf plot. The weights are given to the nearest
   whole number.
b. Explain what

$$7 \mid 0\ 8 \quad \text{means.}$$

c. What does

$$1\ 2 \mid 0\ 0 \quad \text{mean?}$$

d. What is the mean?

People	A	B	C	D	E	F	G	H	I	J	K	L	M
Weight in lbs.	145	85	94	142	100	68	140	120	85	100	70	78	120

Solution

a. The numbers range from 68 to 145 and therefore, the stem should range from 6 to
   14, and from the key the numbers under the leaf column are ones. The stem and
   leaf plot is shown as shown:

```
Stem | Leaf
   6 | 8
   7 | 0 8
   8 | 5 5
   9 | 4
  10 | 0 0
  11 |
  12 | 0 0          key
  13 |              14|0  means 140 lbs.
  14 | 0 2 5
```

   b. $7 \mid 0\ 8$ means 70 lbs. and 78 lbs. (See similar explanation in Examples 1 and 2).
   c. $1\ 2 \mid 0\ 0$ means 120 lbs. and 120 lbs. (See similar explanation in Examples 1 and 2).

   d. The mean is the same as the average.

$$\text{Mean} = \frac{\text{Sum of all the numbers}}{\text{Total number of the numbers}}$$

544

$$= \frac{68 + 70 + 78 + 85 + 85 + 94 + 100 + 100 + 120 + 120 + 140 + 142 + 145}{13}$$

$$= \frac{1347}{13}$$

= 103.6 lbs. You may use a calculator to obtain the answer.

The notes and the generous examples have provided me with the conceptual understanding and the computational fluency to do my homework.

Exercises

1. What is a stem-and-leaf plot?

2. What is the stem-and-leaf plot used for?

3. Use the data values to:

(**a**) make a stem-and-leaf plot. Hint: See Example **1**.

(**b**) explain how the stem-and-leaf plot is made. Hint: See Example **1**

Ages of people in a club (ages in years).

15	17	34
22	38	34
34	45	62
40	60	28
15	65	29

4. Use the data values to make a stem-and-leaf plot.

(**a**). Weight of people in lbs.

25	44	55	20
68	37	34	16
34	62	47	20
16	20	59	37
77	32	25	32

(**b**). Number of books per shelf

44	69	30
19	30	20
36	40	40
30	62	36
27	31	44

Hint: See Example **1**.

5. List the data values in the following stem-and-leaf plots. Hint: See Example **2**.

(a)
```
0 2 8 9
1 3
2 5 8 9
3 0 0 0 5 8
4 0 1 8 9
```
key: 4|0   means 40

(b)
```
0 1 4 8 9
1 7 8 9
2 0 0 3 8
3 4 9
4 0 3 7 9
5 0 0 9
```
key: 1|7   means 17

©
```
0 0 3 5
1 0 0 4
2 3
3 4 8
4 0 0 0 1
5 1 3 6 8
```
key: 3|4   means 34.

6a. Use the given data in tables 1 and 2 to make two separate stem-and-leaf plots.

Hint: See Example **3**.

Table 1	Teams	A	B	C	D	E	F	G	H	I	J
	Scores per year	16	10	25	16	16	34	48	25	40	37

Table 2	Teams	A	B	C	D	E	F	G	H	I	J	K	L
	Scores per year	9	27	17	35	27	17	30	34	27	35	42	30

6b. From each stem-and-leaf plot, how many teams have scores above 40?
Hint: See Example **3**.

6c. How many leaves are there in each stem-and-leaf plot? Hint: See example **3**.

6d. Find the median from each stem-and-leaf plot. Hint: See Example **3**.

6e. Find the mode and the range of each stem-and-leaf plot. Hint: See Example **3**.

7a. Use the data to make a stem-and-leaf plot. The weights are given to the nearest whole number in lbs. Hint: See Example **4**.

7b. Explain the meaning of 3|007. Hint: See Example **4**.

7c. Explain the meaning of 4|88. Hint: See Example **4**.

7d. What is the mean of the data? Hint: See Example **4**.

Animals	A	B	C	D	E	F	G	H	I	J	K	L
Weight in lbs.	77	30	29	37	30	48	44	56	70	54	61	48

Challenge Questions

8. List the data values in the following stem-and-leaf plots.

(a)
```
0 |2 3 4
1 |0 0 1
2 |8 9
3 |
4 |4 8 9
5 |0 0 0 2
```
key: 2 |8 means 28.

(b)
```
1 |0 0 0
2 |4 8 9
3 |2
4 |7 8
5 |0 5 8
6 |1 1 14
```
key: 4 |7 means 47.

©
```
1 |7 9
2 |0 0 4
3 |4
4 |
5 |1 3 8 9
6 |4 7
```
key: 6 |4 means 6.4

9. Use the data values to make stem-and-leaf plots.

a. Age of people in years.

17	25	23
25	17	23
18	19	18
20	23	17
24	24	19
38	39	42

b. Weight of people in lbs.

65	60	50
72	78	63
78	84	78
50	80	71
55	50	55

c. From the stem-and-leaf plot of **a** and **b**, find the median, mode, and range.

d. What does 1|99 mean?

e. What does 5|000 mean?

COORDINATE SYSTEM

INTRODUCTION
New Terms: **coordinate system, coordinate plane, x-axis, y-axis, origin, quadrants,ordered pair, x-coordinate, y-coordinate**

The **coordinate system** or the **coordinate plane** is formed by two perpendicular and intersecting number lines called the x-axis and the y-axis. The horizontal number line is called the x-axis and the vertical number line is called the y-axis. The point where the two number lines intersect is called the **origin** and the origin has a coordinate of (**0, 0**). The coordinate of a point is an **ordered pair of numbers** such that the first number is related to a point on the x-axis and the second number is related to a point on the y-axis. The x-axis, y-axis, and the origin are shown in the diagram.

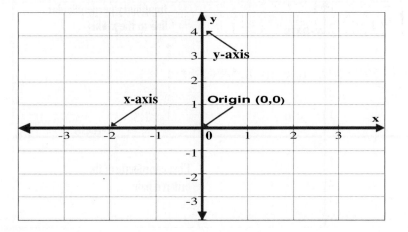

Example 1
Describe how to find the coordinates of the ordered pair of point A.

Solution

Step 1: Find the x-coordinate first. From point A, imagine a perpendicular line on the x-axis and this imaginary perpendicular line meets the x-axis at point 3, and therefore, the first coordinate of the ordered pair is 3.

Step 2: Find the y-coordinate second. From point A, imagine a perpendicular line on the y-axis and this imaginary perpendicular line meets the y-axis at point 4, and therefore, the second coordinate of the ordered pair is point 4.

Step 3: Combine the first coordinate of the ordered pair which is 3 with the second coordinate of the ordered pair which is 4 to form the **coordinates of the ordered pair of the point A as (3, 4)**.

Special Notes
1. In general, the coordinates of the ordered pair of any point may be written as (x, y) where x, which is always the first pair refers to a number on the x-axis and y which is always the second pair refers to a number on the y-axis.
2. How can the coordinates of a point be read? The coordinates of a point can be read by moving along the x-axis to read the first coordinate and then moving along the y-axis to read the second coordinate.

The notes and the generous examples have provided me with the conceptual understanding and the computational fluency to do my homework.

Exercises
1. Find the coordinates of the ordered pair of point B in the diagram.
   Hint: See Example **1**.

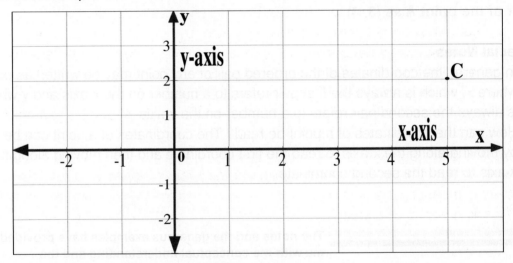

2. Find the coordinates of the ordered pair of the point C in the diagram.
   Hint: See Example 1.

3. Using the diagram, copy and complete the sentences.
   Hint: See Example **1**, Step **3**.

a. (2, 6) are the coordinates of the ordered pair of the point _____.

b. (-2, 6) are the coordinates of the ordered pair of the point _____.
Hint: The negative x-coordinates are at the left side of the origin.

c. (_, _) are the coordinates of the ordered pair of point C.

d. The coordinates of the ordered pair of the point E is (5, -5) and (_, _) are the coordinates of the ordered pair of the point D.
Hint: The negative y-coordinates are below the origin.

e. The coordinates of the ordered pair of the point G is (-2, -4) and (_, _) are the coordinates of the ordered pair of the point F.

f. (1, 1) are the coordinates of the ordered pair of point B.

4. What is meant by the coordinate system or the coordinate plane?

5. What is meant by the origin?

6. What is meant by the coordinate plane.

Answers to Selected Questions

1. (2, 3)   **3b.** point H

Critical Thinking: What is the importance of the coordinates of a point? The coordinates of a point show how far and in which direction to move horizontally along the x-axis, and then vertically along the y-axis on the coordinate plane.

Graphing on the Coordinate Plane

We can graph the coordinates of the ordered pair of any point by moving along the x-axis until we are at the x-coordinate of the required ordered pair. Then we continue by moving perpendicularly to the x-axis until we meet the imaginary perpendicular line from the y-coordinate of the ordered pair which is on the y-axis. The point where the imaginary perpendicular line from the x-coordinate of the ordered pair meets the imaginary perpendicular line from the y-coordinate of the ordered pair is the point or the graph of the point.

Example 1
Graph the point (3, 5).

Solution
Move along the x-axis from the origin (0, 0) until you are at the coordinate of the first required ordered pair which is 3, then you move perpendicular to the x-axis (imaginary) until you meet the imaginary perpendicular line from point 5 on the y-axis. Where the imaginary perpendicular line from the x-axis coincide with the imaginary perpendicular line from the y-axis is the point (3, 5).

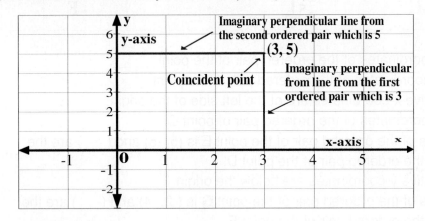

Importance of the Sign of the Coordinates
1. If the first coordinate is negative, then move along the x-axis is toward the left side of the origin (0, 0), but if the sign is positive, then the move is towards the right of the origin (0, 0).
2. If the second coordinate is negative, then move along the y-axis is below the origin (0, 0)

Example 2
Graph the point (-3, 4).

Solution
Move along the x-axis from the origin (0, 0) until you are at the x-coordinate of -3, and then move perpendicularly to the x-axis until you coincide with the imaginary perpendicular line from the point 4 on the y-axis. Where the imaginary perpendicular lines from the x-coordinate of -3 and the y-coordinate of 4 meet is the coordinate of the ordered pair of the point (-3, 4) or the graph of the point.

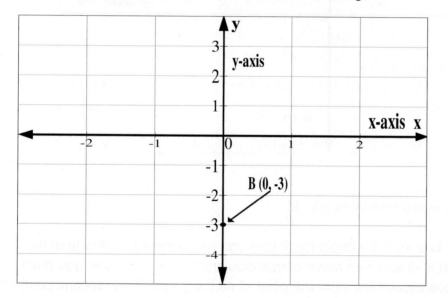

Example 3

a. Graph the points B and C with the coordinates (0, -3) and (2, 0) respectively on the same diagram.

b. Draw a line through points B and C.

Solution

a. To graph the point B(0, -3), from the x-coordinate of 0 on the x-axis, move perpendicularly to the x-axis until you come to the y-coordinate of -3 and this point will have the coordinates of (0, -3) as shown in the diagram.

To graph the point C(2, 0), move along the x-axis from the origin (0, 0) until you are at the x-coordinates of 2 but y = 0 on the x-axis and this means that the y-coordinate of 0 is on the x-axis therefore, the point (2, 0) is the graph of point C as shown in the diagram.

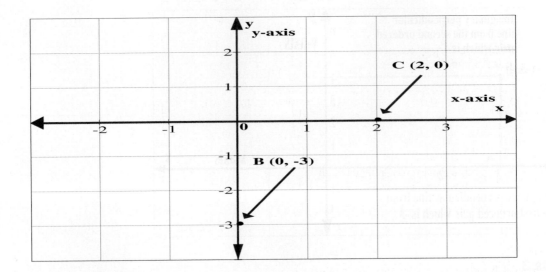

b. Draw a line through the points B(0, -3) and C(2, 0).

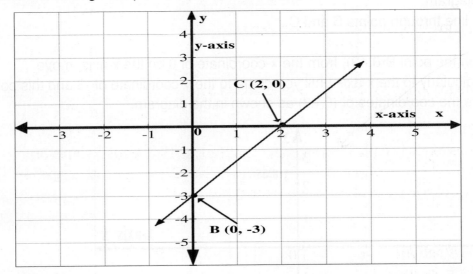

Example 4

Graph the point A with coordinates (-3, -2).

Solution

Move along the x-axis from the origin (0, 0) until you are at the x-coordinate of the ordered pair which is -3 and then move perpendicularly to the x-axis until you meet the imaginary perpendicular line from the point -2 on the y-axis. This meeting point are the coordinates of the ordered pair (-3,-2) or the graph of the point (-3, -2).

Exercises

1. Graph the following points. Hint: See Example **1**.
   a. A(2, 1)   **b.** B(3, 1)   **c.** C(4, 1)   **d.** D(2, 1)
   e. E(2, 2)   **f.** F(-1, 1)   **g.** G(4, 4)   **h.** H(2, 4)
2. Graph the following points. Hint: See Example **2**.
   a. A(-2, 1)   **b.** B(-3, 4)   **c.** C(-1, 2)   **d.** D(-4, 1)
   e. E(-2, 2)   **f.** F(-1, 1)   **g.** G(-2, 3)   **h.** H(-3, 1)
3. Graph the following points. Hint: See Example **3a**.
   a. A(0, -2)   **b.** B(0, -1)   **c.** C(0, -4)   **d.** D(0, -5)
   e. E(1, 0)   **f.** F(3, 0)   **g.** G(5, 0)   **h.** H(6, 0)
4. Using question 3, join the following points with a line. Hint: See Example **3b**.
   a. A and E   **b.** B and F   **c.** C and G   **d.** D and H
5. Graph the following points. Hint: See Example **4**.
   a. A(-1, -1)   **b.** B(-3, -2)   **c.** C(-2, -3)   **d.** D(-1, -4)

Challenge Questions

6. Graph the following points.
   a. A(0, 4)   **b.** B(1, 4)   **c.** C(0, -6)   **d.** D(-3, -3)
7. Graph the three points (1, 2), (3, 1), and (1, 3).
   Join the three points to form a triangle.

Quadrants

Quadrants are the four areas that the x-axis and the y-axis divide the coordinate system into as shown in Figure 1.

555

Figure 1

Critical Thinking

Using Figure 1:

1. The coordinates of the point A are (5, 2) which are positive and the point A is located in the quadrant 1, and therefore, any point that has both positive x-coordinate and y-coordinates is in quadrant 1.

2. The coordinates of the point B are (-2, 3) which shows that the x-coordinate is negative and the y-coordinate is positive and the point B is located in the quadrant 2. Therefore, any point that has a negative x-coordinate and a positive y-coordinate is located in the quadrant 2.

3. The coordinates of the point C are (-3, -4) which shows that both the x-coordinate and the y-coordinate are negative and the point C is located in the quadrant 3. Therefore, any point that has a negative x-coordinate and a negative y-coordinate is located in the quadrant 3.

4. The coordinates of the point D are (3, -2) which shows that the x-coordinate is positive and the y-coordinate is negative and the point D is located in the quadrant 4. Therefore, any point that has a positive x-coordinate and a negative y-coordinate is located in the quadrant 4.

Team Exercises

Using the notes under "Critical Thinking,"

1. in which quadrant is the graph of the following ordered pairs located?
   a. (-1, -3) **b.** (3, -1) **c.** (-2, 3) **d.** (4, 3).

2. in which quadrant is a graph of the ordered pair located when both coordinates are negative?

3. in which quadrant is a graph of the ordered pair located when both coordinates are positive?

Cumulative Review

1. Draw a number line and use dots to locate the integers on it. Then list the integers

from the greatest to the smallest.
10, 2, -3, -8, 6, 0, and -1

2. Solve:

a. $\dfrac{2}{3} \div \dfrac{1}{6} =$

b. $2\dfrac{1}{4} - 1\dfrac{1}{2} =$

c. $\dfrac{7}{9} \times \dfrac{12}{4} =$

d. $\dfrac{3}{4} + \dfrac{2}{3} =$

REAL WORLD APPLICATIONS - WORD PROBLEMS
Coordinate System

Example 1

Mary started walking from the origin (0, 0). If she went 4 units to the right on the x-axis, and then went 3 units down what are the coordinates of the final location of Mary?

Solution

Mary walked 4 units from the origin (0, 0) to the right on the x-axis and therefore her location is 4 units to the right. She then went 3 units down and her position on the y-axis is -3. The coordinates of her location are (4, -3) as shown in the diagram.

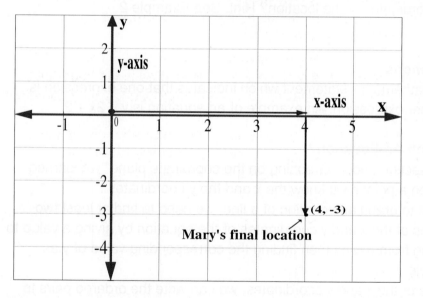

Example 2

John started walking from the origin. If he moved 6 units to the left and then 5 units up what are the coordinates of John?

Solution

John moved 6 units to the left from the origin, and therefore the x-coordinate of his location is -6. He then moved 5 units up, and therefore, his y-coordinate is 5. The coordinates of his location are (-6, 5) as shown in the diagram.

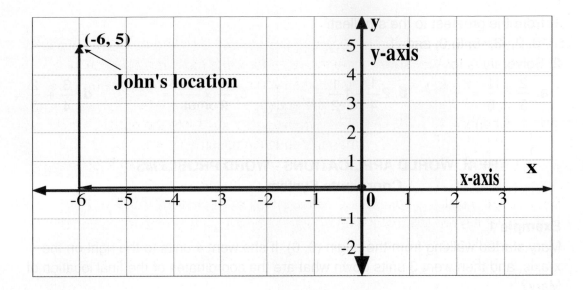

Exercises

1. Eric started at the origin, moved 5 units to the right, and then 5 units down. What are the coordinates of Eric? Hint: See Example 1.

2. Start at the origin, move 1 unit to the left, and then 4 units up. What are the coordinates of the location? Hint: See Example 2.

Graphing of Equations

An equation is a mathematics statement which indicates that one expression is equivalent to another expression. An example of an equation is $y = 2x + 2$.

How Can We Graph An Equation?

1. In the previous section under "Graphing on the coordinate plane" we learned that we can graph a point if we know the x and the y coordinates.

2. Similarly in order to graph an equation of a line, we need to find at least two sets of the values of the x and y coordinates of the equation by giving a value to x (usually starting from 0) and then finding the corresponding value of y as shown in Example 1.

3. Using the values of the x and y coordinates, we can write the ordered pairs to be graphed.

4. Make the graph by:
   a. Plotting each ordered pair on a coordinate plane
   b. Connect all the points by using a straight line
   c. Put arrows at both ends of the line to show that the line continues in both directions.

Example 1

Graph the equation $y = x$ on a coordinate plane.

Solution

Step 1: Pick values for x (usually starting from 0) and then find the corresponding values for y by substituting the value for x into the given equation y = x.

when x = 0, y = 0   Note, when you put x = 0 into the equation y = x, then the equation becomes y = 0.

when x = 1, y = 1   Note, when you put x = 1 into the equation y = x, then the equation becomes y = 1.

when x = 2, y = 2   Note, when you put x = 2 into the equation y= x, then the equation becomes y = 2.

Therefore, the ordered pairs of the coordinates are (0, 0), (1, 1), and (2, 2).

Step 2: Plot the ordered pairs of the coordinates on a coordinate plane and draw a line through the points.

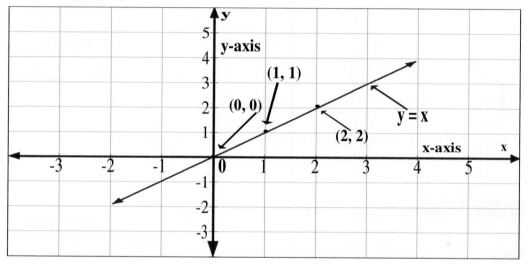

The graph shows the equation y = x.

Example 2

Graph the equation y = x +1 on a coordinate plane.

Solution

Step 1: Pick values for x (usually starting from 0) and then find the corresponding values for y by substituting the values for x in the given equation y = x + 1.

When x = 0, y = 0 + 1 = 1.   Note, when you put x = 0 into the equation y = x + 1, the equation becomes y = 0 + 1 = 1. Therefore, when x = 0, y = 1.

When x = 1, y = 1 + 1 = 2   Note, when you put x = 1 into the equation y = x + 1, the equation becomes y = 1 + 1 = 2. Therefore, when x = 1, y = 2.

When x = 2, y = 2 + 1 = 3   Note, when you put x = 2 into the equation y = x + 1, the equation becomes y = 2 + 1 = 3. Therefore, when x = 1, y = 3.

Therefore, the ordered pairs of the coordinates are (0, 1), (1, 2), and (2, 3).

Step 2: Plot the ordered pairs on a coordinate plane, and draw a line through the points.

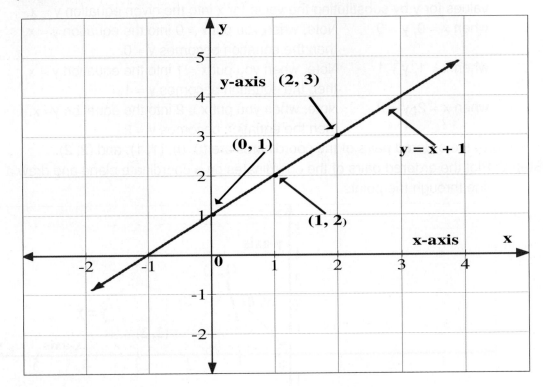

The graph shows the equation y = x + 1.

Example 3

Graph the equation y = 2x + 3.

Solution

Step 1: Pick values for x (usually starting from 0), and then find the corresponding values for y.

When x = 0, y = 2 × 0 + 3 = 3   Note, when you put x = 0 into the equation
y = 2x + 3, the equation becomes
y = 2 × 0 + 3 = 3. Therefore, when x = 0, y = 3.

When x = 1, y = 2 × 1 + 3 = 5   Note, when you put x = 1 into the equation
y = 2x + 3, the equation becomes
y = 2 × 1 + 3 = 5. So, when x = 1, y = 5.

When x = 2, y = 2 × 2 + 3 = 7   Note, when you put x = 2 into the equation
y = 2x + 3, the equation becomes
y = 2 × 2 + 3 = 7. Therefore, when x = 2, y = 7.

Therefore, the ordered pair of the coordinates are (0, 3), (1, 5), and (2, 7).

Step 2: Plot the ordered pairs of the coordinates on a coordinate plane and draw a line through the points.

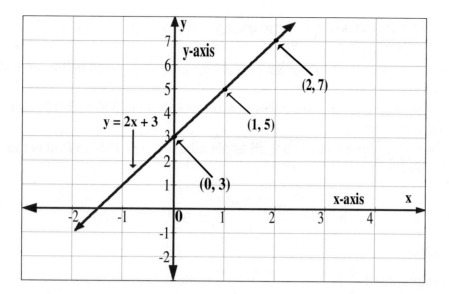

The graph shows the equation y = 2x + 3

The notes and the generous examples have provided me with the conceptual understanding and the computational fluency to do my homework.

Exercises

1 Graph the following equations Hint: See Example **1**.

   a. y = 2x   **b.** y = 3x   **c.** y = 4x   **d.** y = 5x

2. Graph the following equations. Hint: See Example **2**.

   a. y = x + 2   **b.** y = x + 3   **c.** y = x + 5   **d.** y = x + 4

3. Graph the following equations. Hint: See Example **3**.

   a. y = 2x + 2   **b.** y = 3x + 1   **c.** y = 4x + 1   **d.** y = 2x - 1

Challenge Questions

4. Graph the following equations.

   a. y = 3x - 1   **b.** y = 2x + 3   **c.** y = 3x + 2   **d.** y = 2x - 2

5. A real world application of the ordered pair of numbers may be the temperature corresponding to each day as shown in the table.

Day	1	2	3	4	5	6
Temperature (°F)	4	-2	6	0	-3	2

Let the day be on the x-coordinate and the temperature be on the y-coordinate and graph each ordered point. Hint: the first coordinate may be written as (1, 4).

Mixed Review

1. The sum of the measures of two angles of a triangle is 101^0. What is the measure of the third angle?

2. The sum of the measures of three angles of a quadrilateral is 300^0. What is the measure of the fourth angle?

3. The sum of the angles on a line except an angle labelled A is 155^0. What is the measure of angle A?

4. Solve for x:

   a. $5x - 3 = 3x + 7$ **b.** $\dfrac{3x}{8} = \dfrac{3}{4}$ **c.** $90^0 + 3x = 180^0$

5. Find 20% of $200

6. What is the reciprocal of $\dfrac{2}{5}$?

7. A square swimming pool has an area of 100 m². Find the perimeter of the swimming pool.

8. Simplify:

   a. $\dfrac{4}{5} \div \dfrac{3}{20}$ **b.** $\dfrac{5 \times 3 \times 4 \times 2}{3 \times 20 \times 2 \times 3}$ **c.** $20 \div 4 - 2$ **d.** $20 - 4 \div 2$

SLOPE OF A LINE

The slope of a line is the ratio: $\dfrac{\text{Vertical change}}{\text{Horizontal change}} = \dfrac{\text{Change in y distance}}{\text{Change in x distance}} = \dfrac{\text{rise}}{\text{run}}$

where the "rise" is the number of units moved up or down, and the "run" is the number of units moved to the left or right.

Types of Slopes

The four types of slopes are positive, zero, negative, and undefined slopes.
The four types of slopes may be described as follows:
The four types of slopes are:

a. An upward slope (↗) has a positive slope.
b. A horizontal slope (→) has a zero slope.
c. A downward slope (↘) has a negative slope.
d. A vertical slope (↓) has an undefined slope.

Students may be able to remember the four types of slopes if they can recall the slopes sketch below. Let us call this slopes sketch the "Aggor slopes sketch."

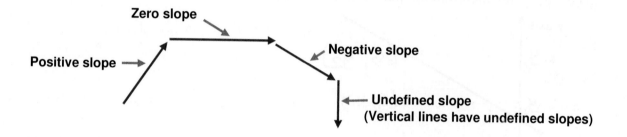

Hint: Example 1 explained positive, zero, negative, and undefined slopes.

Example 1

a. Name the four types of slopes.
b. Sketch the four types of slopes on a coordinate plane.
c. Describe a line with a positive slope.
d. Describe a line with a negative slope.
e. Describe a line with a zero slope.
f. Describe a line with an undefined slope.

Solution

a. The four types of slopes are positive slope, zero slope, negative slope, and undefined slope.
b. The four types of slopes on the coordinate plane are as shown:

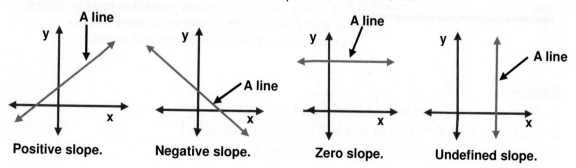

563

c. A line with a positive slope goes up in the direction from left to right. Hint: See the positive slope diagram in the solution **b**.

d. A line with a negative slope goes down from the direction of left to right. Hint: See the negative slope diagram in the solution **b**.

e. A line with a zero slope is parallel to the horizontal or the x axis. Hint: See the diagram of the line with a zero slope in the solution **b**.

f. A line with an undefined slope is parallel to the y axis or it is vertical. Hint: See the diagram of the line with the undefined slope in the solution **b**.

Example 2

What is the slope of the line that passes through the points $(x_1, y_1,)$ and (x_2, y_2).

Solution

The line is sketched with the points as shown below.

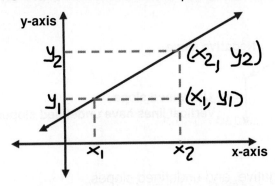

The slope of a line is the ratio: $\dfrac{\text{Vertical change}}{\text{Horizontal change}} = \dfrac{\text{change in y-distance}}{\text{change in x-distance}}$

$$= \dfrac{\text{rise}}{\text{run}} = \dfrac{y_2 - y_1}{x_2 - x_1}$$

Note: The formula for finding the slope of a line is:

$$\textbf{Slope} = \dfrac{\textbf{Vertical change}}{\textbf{Horizontal change}} = \dfrac{\textbf{change in y-distance}}{\textbf{change in x-distance}} = \dfrac{\textbf{rise}}{\textbf{run}} = \dfrac{y_2 - y_1}{x_2 - x_1}$$

===============

The notes and the generous examples have provided me with the conceptual understanding and the computational fluency to do my homework.

Exercises

1. What is the slope of a line? Hint: See the notes.
2. What are the four types of slopes? Hint: See Example **1**.
3a. Sketch the four types of slopes. Hint: See Example **1**.

3b. Label each slope of the line as undefined, zero, positive, and negative. Hint: See the notes.

4. The slope of a line $= \dfrac{y_2 - y_1}{x_2 - x_1}$. Is this true or false? Hint: See Example **2**.

5. a. Vertical change = change in y distance = rise. True or false?
   b. Horizontal change = change in x distance = run. True or false?
   c. Rise is the number of units moved up or d_____.
   d. Run is the number of units moved to the left or r_____.
   e The slope of a line is the ratio:

$$\frac{\text{Vertical change}}{\text{horizontal change}} = \frac{\text{Change in y distance}}{\text{Change in x distance}} = \frac{\text{rise}}{\text{run}}, \text{true or false?}$$

Hint: See the notes.

6. Describe the slope of the line x at the top of the mountain and the slopes of the two lines Y and Z at the sides of the mountain. Hint: See the notes.

Mountain

7. Do the following slopes appear to be zero, positive, negative, or undefined? Hint: See Example **1**.

a.   b.   c.   d.

CHAPTER 20

AREA AND PERIMETER OF RECTANGLES AND RECTANGULAR FIGURES

Cumulative Review

1. $14 + 17 =$ 2. $15 \div 3 =$ 3. $25 - 8 =$ 4. $7 \times 7 =$
5. $45 \div 5 =$ 6. $31 - 12 =$ 7. $36 \div 6 =$ 8. $33 - 8 =$

9. $\begin{array}{r} 28 \\ \times\ 4 \\ \hline \end{array}$ 10. $\begin{array}{r} 35 \\ +\ 19 \\ \hline \end{array}$ 11. $\begin{array}{r} 34 \\ -\ 19 \\ \hline \end{array}$ 12. $\begin{array}{r} 27 \\ \times\ 6 \\ \hline \end{array}$

13. $42 \div 6 =$ 14. $45 \div 9 =$ 15. $14 + 37 =$ 16. $31 - 17 =$
17. $2.5 + 3.9 =$ 18. $5.7 \times 5 =$ 19. $3.6 \times 3.5 =$ 20. $21.7 - 1.4 =$

21. $\dfrac{2}{3} \times \dfrac{2}{5} =$ 22. $\dfrac{2}{3} \div \dfrac{4}{3} =$ 23. $\dfrac{3}{4} - \dfrac{2}{3} =$ 24. $1\dfrac{1}{3} + 4\dfrac{3}{4} =$

Area
Rectangle and Square

The area of a figure is the number of the square units that covers it. For example, in the diagram, the area colored yellow is 8 square units because 8 units are colored yellow.

Example 1

What is the area of the region colored yellow in the diagram? Give a reason to justify your answer.

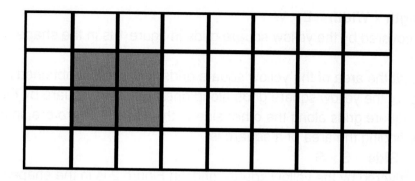

Solution

The area of the region colored yellow is 4 units because there are 4 squares that are colored yellow.

Team Work

1. Each team should draw a rectangle which consists of 10 squares by 6 squares and color the squares as shown in Figure 1. Count the number of the colored grid squares.

2. Each team should draw a square which consists of 6 squares by 6 squares and shade the squares as shown in Figure 2.

Figure 1   **Figure 2**

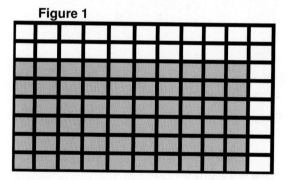

3. Observe the yellow square grids in the Figures 1 and 2 and complete the chart.

Activities	Figure 1	Figure 2
(a). Count the number of the yellow grids which is the area of the yellow grids.	60 yellow square grids.	36 yellow square grids.
(b). Multiply the number of the yellow square grids along the length of the yellow area by the number of the yellow square grids along the width of the yellow area.	10 × 6 = 60 yellow square grids.	6 × 6 = 36 yellow square grids.

4. Comparing 3(a) and 3(b), Figure 1 shows that if we multiply the number of the yellow square grids along the length of the yellow grid area by the number of the yellow square grids along the width of the yellow grid area will give the area of the yellow square grids. Therefore, in general, the formula for finding the area of a rectangular Figure is:

Length × Width = L × W

(The area covered by the yellow square grids in figure 1 is in the shape of a rectangle.)

5. Observe that the area of the yellow square grids in figure 2 is obtained by multiplying the number of the yellow square grids along one side of the square by the number of the yellow square grids along the other side of the square. Therefore, in general, the formula for finding the area of a square is:

Side × Side = S × S

(The area covered by the yellow square grids in Figure 2 is in the shape of a square.)

Observe that the area is a measurement of two dimensions (such as length × width or side × side), and therefore, it is expressed in square units such as centimeter square or cm × cm = cm².

Example 2

The length of a rectangle is 4 cm and the width is 3 cm. Find the area of the rectangle.

4 cm

3 cm

Solution

The formula for finding the area of a rectangle is:

$$Area = Length \times Width$$
$$= L \times W$$
$$= 4 \text{ cm} \times 3 \text{ cm}$$
$$= 12 \text{ square cm}$$
$$= 12 \text{ cm}^2$$

Example 3

The side of a square is 5 ft. What is the area of the square?

5 ft

5 ft

Solution

$$Area \text{ of a square} = Side \times Side$$
$$= S \times S$$
$$= 5 \text{ ft} \times 5 \text{ ft}$$
$$= 25 \text{ square ft}$$
$$= 25 \text{ ft}^2$$

Example 4

Find the area of the figure.

Solution

Step 1: Divide the polygon into two parts.

The area of some polygons can be found by dividing them into two or more different polygons. Divide the figure/polygon into two rectangles B and C by the broken line as shown:

Broken line.

Step 2: Find the areas of the rectangles B and C.

Considering area B;	Considering area C;
L = 4 cm, W = 3 cm	L = 2 cm, W = 1 cm
Area = L × W	Area = L × W
= 4 cm × 3 cm	= 2 cm × 1 cm
= 12 cm²	= 2 cm²

Step 3: Combine the areas of the rectangles B and C.

Total area = Area of rectangle B + Area of rectangle C.

$$= 12 \text{ cm}^2 + 2 \text{ cm}^2$$
$$= 14 \text{ cm}^2$$

Example 5

Find the area of the figure.

Solution

Step 1: Divide the polygon into two rectangles X and Y by the dotted lines.

Broken line.

Step 2: Find the areas of the rectangles X and Y.

Considering rectangles X .. Considering area Y.

L = 5 cm, W = 4 cm

Area = L × W

= 5 cm × 4 cm

= 20 cm²

$L = \overline{GC} + \overline{CD}$

= 4 cm + 20 cm = 24 cm

$W = \overline{GF} = \overline{AF} - \overline{AG}$

= 10 cm - 5 cm

= 5 cm

Note that $\overline{AG} = \overline{BC}$ = 5 cm because ABCG is a rectangle and the opposite sides of a rectangle are equal.

Area = L × w

= 24 cm × 5 cm (L = 24 cm, W = 5 cm).

= 120 cm²

Step 3: Combine the areas of rectangles X and Y.

Total area = Area of rectangle X + Area of rectangle Y.

= 20 cm² + 120 cm²

= 140 cm²

Example 6

Find the area of the figure given that AFGH forms a rectangle, and also BCDE forms a rectangle.

$\overline{AB}$ = 4 yd
$\overline{ED}$ = 5 yd
$\overline{CD}$ = 1 yd

Solution

Step 1: Divide the figure into 3 rectangles X, Y, and Z by the broken lines.

$\overline{AB}$ = 4 yd
$\overline{ED}$ = 5 yd
$\overline{CD}$ = 1 yd

Step 2: Find the areas of the rectangles X, Y, and Z.

Considering the area of rectangle X.

L = $\overline{BC}$ = 5 yd because $\overline{BC}$ and $\overline{ED}$ have the same lengths.

W = $\overline{AB}$ = 4 yd.

Therefore, the area of the rectangle X = L × W

$$= 5 \text{ yd} \times 4 \text{ yd.}$$
$$= 20 \text{ yd}^2$$

Considering the area of the rectangle Y

L = $\overline{AH}$ - $\overline{AI}$ and $\overline{AI}$ has the same length as $\overline{BC}$ because the $\overline{AI}$ and the $\overline{BC}$ are the opposite sides of the rectangle ABCI and the opposite sides of a rectangle are congruent (equal).

L = $\overline{AH}$ - $\overline{AI}$

$$= 12 \text{ yd} - 5 \text{ yd}$$
$$= 7 \text{ yd}$$

W = $\overline{HG}$ = 6 yd

Area of rectangle Y = L × W

$$= 7 \text{ yd} \times 6 \text{ yd}$$
$$= 42 \text{ yd}^2$$

Considering the area of the rectangle Z

L = $\overline{DE}$ = 5 yd.

W = $\overline{HG}$ - $\overline{AB}$ - $\overline{CD}$ because $\overline{HG}$ = $\overline{AF}$ (AFGH is a rectangle, and the opposite sides of a rectangle are equal).

W = 6 yd - 4 yd - 1 yd.

$$= 6 \text{ yd} - 5 \text{ yd}$$
$$= 1 \text{ yd}$$

Area of rectangle Z = L × W

$$= 5 \text{ yd} \times 1 \text{ yd}$$
$$= 5 \text{ yd}^2$$

Step 3: Combine the areas of the rectangles X, Y, and Z.

Total area = Area of rectangle X + Area of rectangle Y + Area of rectangle Z.

$$= 20 \text{ yd}^2 + 42 \text{ yd}^2 + 5 \text{ yd}^2$$
$$= 67 \text{ yd}^2$$

Example 7

The area of a rectangle is 24 ft². If the length is 6 ft, find the width of the rectangle.

Solution

Step 1: Setup using the formula for finding the area of a rectangle.

Using the formula for finding the area of a rectangle:

$$A = L \times W \qquad\qquad A = \text{Area, } L = \text{Length, and } W = \text{Width.}$$

From the question, $A = 24$ ft² and $L = 6$ ft.

Substitute $A = 24$ ft² and $L = 6$ ft into the equation $A = L \times W$ as follows:

$$A = L \times W$$
$$24 \text{ ft}^2 = 6 \text{ ft} \times W$$

Step 2: Find the width of the rectangle.

Divide both sides of the equation (24 ft² $= 6$ ft $\times$ W) by 6 ft in order to obtain the value for W as shown:

$$\frac{24 \text{ ft}^2}{6 \text{ ft}} = \frac{6 \text{ ft} \times W}{6 \text{ ft}}$$

$$\frac{\overset{4 \text{ ft}}{\cancel{24 \text{ ft}^2}}}{\underset{1}{\cancel{6 \text{ ft}}}} = \frac{\overset{1}{\cancel{6 \text{ ft}}} \times W}{\underset{1}{\cancel{6 \text{ ft}}}}$$

$$4 \text{ ft} = W$$

Therefore, the width of the rectangle is 4 ft.

Example 8 - Application

The area of a special rectangular classroom is 200 yd². If the width of the classroom is 10 yd, how long is the classroom?

Solution

Step 1: Setup using the formula for finding the area of a rectangle.

Using the formula for finding the area of a rectangle;

$$A = L \times W \qquad\qquad A = \text{Area, } L = \text{Length, and } W = \text{Width.}$$

From the question, $A = 200$ yd² and $W = 10$ yd.

Substitute $A = 200$ ft² and $W = 10$ ft into the equation $A = L \times W$ as shown:

$$A = L \times W$$
$$200 \text{ yd}^2 = L \times 10 \text{ yd}$$

Step 2: Find the length of the rectangle (classroom)

Divide both sides of the equation (200 yd² $= L \times 10$ yd) by 10 yd in order to obtain the value for L as shown:

$$\frac{200 \text{ yd}^2}{10 \text{ yd}} = \frac{L \times 10 \text{ yd}}{10 \text{ yd}}$$

$$\frac{\overset{1}{\cancel{200 \text{ yd}^2}}}{\underset{1}{\cancel{10 \text{ yd}}}} = \frac{L \times \overset{1}{\cancel{10 \text{ yd}}}}{\underset{1}{\cancel{10 \text{ yd}}}}$$

20 yd = L

Therefore, the length of the rectangle (classroom) is 20 yd.

Perimeter

Example 9

a. What is the perimeter of an object?

b. Find the perimeter of the following figures:

c. One side of a square is 3 ft. What is the area and the perimeter of the square?

Solution

a. The perimeter of an object is the distance around the object.

b. The figure in Figure 1 is a rectangle and recall from the "Geometric Figures" that the opposite sides of a rectangle are equal. Therefore, the dimensions of Figure 1 are shown in the diagram as shown:

The perimeter of Figure 1 is:

$$5 \text{ cm} + 3 \text{ cm} + 5 \text{ cm} + 3 \text{ cm} = 16 \text{ cm}.$$

Alternative solution

The formula for finding the perimeter of a rectangle can also be used to find the perimeter of figure 1 as shown:

Perimeter = 2L + 2W   (where L = length and W = width).

$= 2 \cdot 5 \text{ cm} + 2 \cdot 3 \text{ cm}$ (where L = 5 cm and W = 3 cm).

$= 10 \text{ cm} + 6 \text{ cm}$

$= 16 \text{ cm}.$

573

The perimeter of figure 2 is the distance around figure 2 as shown:

$$\text{Perimeter} = \overline{AB} + \overline{BC} + \overline{CD} + \overline{DE} + \overline{EF} + \overline{FA}$$
$$= 3\text{ cm} + 3\text{ cm} + 3\text{ cm} + 6\text{ cm} + 6\text{ cm} + 3\text{ cm}$$
$$= 24\text{ cm}$$

c. It is given that one side of a square is 3 ft, and therefore, all the other sides of the square are also 3 ft because all the sides of a square are equal. The perimeter of the square is:

$$\text{Perimeter} = S + S + S + S \qquad (S = \text{dimension of a side of the square}).$$
$$= 3\text{ ft} + 3\text{ ft} + 3\text{ ft} + 3\text{ ft}$$
$$= 12\text{ ft}.$$

The formula for finding the area of a square is $S \times S$.

$$\text{Area of a square} = S \times S \qquad (S = \text{dimension of a side of the square}).$$
$$= 3\text{ ft} \times 3\text{ ft}$$
$$= 9\text{ ft}^2$$

Example 10

Given that the perimeter of a rectangle is 24 ft and the length is 8 ft,

a. find the width.

b. find the area.

Solution

a. The formula for finding the perimeter of a rectangle is:

$$\text{Perimeter} = 2L + 2W \qquad \qquad \qquad [A]$$

Substitute perimeter = 24ft and L = 8ft into equation $[A]$ as shown:

$$24\text{ ft} = 2 \cdot 8\text{ ft} + 2W$$
$$24\text{ ft} = 16\text{ ft} + 2W \qquad \qquad [B]$$

Subtract 16 ft from both sides of the equation $[B]$ in order to obtain 2W only on the right side of the equation $[B]$ as shown:

$$24\text{ ft - } 16\text{ ft} = 16\text{ ft - } 16\text{ ft} + 2W$$
$$8\text{ ft} = 0 + 2W$$
$$8\text{ ft} = 2W \qquad \qquad [C]$$

Divide both sides of equation $[C]$ by 2 to obtain the value for W as shown:

$$\frac{8\text{ ft}}{2} = \frac{2W}{2}$$

$$\frac{\overset{4\text{ ft}}{\cancel{8\text{ ft}}}}{\underset{1}{\cancel{2}}} = \frac{\overset{W}{\cancel{2W}}}{\underset{1}{\cancel{2}}}$$

$$4\text{ ft} = W$$

Therefore, the width of the rectangle is 4 ft.

b. The formula for the area of the rectangle is:

Area $= L \times W$

$= 8\ ft \times 4\ ft$

$= 32\ ft^2$

Therefore, the area is 32 ft.

The notes and the generous examples have provided me with the conceptual understanding and the computational fluency to do my homework.

Exercises

1. Explain what is meant by the area of a figure? Hint: See notes in this book.

2. What is the formula for finding the area of a rectangle? Hint: See the notes in this chapter.

3. What is the formula for finding the area of a square? Hint: See the notes in this chapter.

4. What is the area of the yellow square grid/s in the diagrams. Hint: See Example **1**.

5. Find the area of each rectangle. Hint: See Example **2**.

a. L = 2ft W = 1 ft	**b**. L = 4 in. W = 3 in.	**c**. L = 6 cm W = 3 cm
d. L = 4.2 yd W = 3 yd	**e**. L = 5 cm W = 4 cm	**f**. L = $5\frac{1}{2}$ W = 3 ft

6. Find the area of each square figure with the following sides. Hint: See Example **3**.

  a. 6 cm   **b**. 10 ft   **c**. 7 in   **d**. 5 cm   **e**. 8 m

7. Find the area of the following figures. Hint: See Example **4**.

8. Find the area of the following figures. Hint: See Example **5**.

a. 18 cm, 5 cm, 3 cm, 3 cm

b. 6 ft, 14 ft, 11 ft, 2 ft

9. Find the area of each figure. Hint: See Example **6**.

a. 4 m, A, 2 m, B, 7 m, 8 m, $\overline{AB}$ = 2 m

b. 10 yd, A, 8 yd, C, 2 yd, B, $\overline{AB}$ = 4 yd, $\overline{BC}$ = 3 yd

10. Find the missing measurement of each rectangle. Hint: See Example **7**.

    a. A = 16 cm²   **b.** A = 20 ft²   **c.** A = 36 m²
       L = 8 cm   L = 5 ft   L = 9 m
       W = ?   W = ?   W = ?

11. Find the missing measurement of each rectangle. Hint: See Example **8**.

    a. A = 100 in.²   **b.** A = 48 cm²   **c.** A = 27 m²
       W = 5 in   W = 6 cm   W = 3 m
       L = ?   L = ?   L = ?

12a. Find the perimeter of the following figures. Hint: See Example **9b**.

Figure 1: 7 cm, 4 cm

Figure 2: C, 5 cm, D, 5 cm, A, 5 cm, 7 cm, B, 5 cm, F, 7 cm, E

12b. Find the area and the perimeter of a square given that one side of the square
    is 6 m long. Hint: See Example **9b**.

13. The perimeter of a rectangle is 26 m and the length is 9 m.
    a. Find the width of the rectangle.
    b. Find the area of the rectangle .
    Hint: See Example **10**.

14. Find the missing measurements of the rectangles. Hint: See Example **10**.

576

a. Perimeter = 12 cm
L = 4 cm
W = ?
A = ?

b. Perimeter = 36 m
W = 4 m
L = ?
A = ?

Challenge Questions

15. Find the missing measurement of each rectangle.

a. $A = 18 \text{ m}^2$
L = 6 m
W = ?
Perimeter =?

b. L = 5 ft
W = 3 ft
A = ?
Perimeter = ?

c. $A = 28 \text{ cm}^2$
W = 4 cm
L = ?
Perimeter = ?

d. L = 7 ft
W = 3 ft
A = ?
Perimeter = ?

e. Perimeter = 36 cm
L = 12 cm
W = ?
A = ?

f. Perimeter = 16 ft
W = 2 ft
L = ?
A = ?

16. The area of a square is 100 cm^2. Find the measure of the sides of the square.
Hint: The formula for the area of the square is **Side** × **Side** therefore, find a number that can be multiplied by itself to obtain 100.

Answer to Selected Questions

4a 1 square unit.

5a. 2 ft^2

6a. 36 cm^2

7a. 34 cm^2

10a. 2 cm

11a 20 in.

(**Are the generous examples helpful**?)

(**Are you having fun with the mathematics**?)

CHAPTER 21

AREA AND PERIMETER OF TRIANGLES

New Terms: **base**, **height**

Area of a Triangle

Example 1
Show that the area of a triangle is half the area of a rectangle and also show that the area of a triangle $= \dfrac{1}{2}$base × height.

Solution
Step 1: Sketch a rectangle ABCD with the length 10 cm and the width 6 cm.

Step 2: Find the area of the rectangle ABCD.
        Length of the rectangle ABCD = 10 cm.
        Width of the rectangle ABCD = 6 cm.
        The formula for finding the area of a rectangle is **Length × Width**.
        Area of rectangle ABCD = 10 cm × 6 cm
                           = 60 cm²

Step 3: Let us divide the rectangle ABCD into two equal halves by drawing a line from B to D.

Step 4: Notice that the area of triangle BCD is half the area of the rectangle ABCD and this can be written as shown:

        Area of triangle ABC $= \dfrac{1}{2}$ × (Area of rectangle ABCD)

                   $= \dfrac{1}{2}$ × Length × Width   (Note: Area of a rectangle = **L × W**)

$$= \frac{1}{2} \times L \times W$$

Step 5: In the triangle BCD we can replace the length BC by "height" and the width DC by "base" and therefore, the area of the triangle BCD

$$= \frac{1}{2} \times \text{base} \times \text{height}$$

$$= \frac{1}{2} \times b \times h \qquad\qquad b = \text{base and } h = \text{height.}$$

$$= \frac{1}{2} \times 6 \text{ cm.} \times 10 \text{ cm} \qquad\qquad b = 6 \text{ cm and } h = 10 \text{ cm}$$

$$= \frac{1}{2} \times \overset{3}{\underset{1}{6}} \text{ cm} \times 10 \text{ cm} \qquad\qquad \text{Divide by 2}$$

$$= 3 \text{ cm} \times 10 \text{ cm} = 30 \text{ cm}^2$$

The **height** of a triangle is the perpendicular segment to the base of the triangle. The **base** of the triangle is the perpendicular segment to the height of the triangle.

Team Project
The class may be divided into four teams.
1. Sketch the rectangle ABCD in Example 1, Step 1 on a grid paper where each unit of length is 1 cm.
2. Do step 3 in Example 1.
3. Use a pair of scissors to cut out the rectangle ABCD.
4. Use a pair of scissors to cut along the segment BD.
5. Place the triangle BCD over the triangle DAB.

6. Could you say that triangle BCD has the same area as triangle DAB? Why?

7. Could you say that the area of a triangle is half the area of a rectangle? Why?

Example 2

Find the area of the following triangles:

a.   4 cm   2 cm

b.   7 cm   3 cm

Solution

a. The height of the triangle = 4 cm

The base of the triangle = 2 cm

The formula for finding the area of a triangle $= \frac{1}{2} \times b \times h$

Therefore, the area of the triangle $= \frac{1}{2} \times 2 \text{ cm} \times 4 \text{ cm}$

$$= \frac{1}{\overset{1}{2}} \times \overset{1}{2} \text{ cm} \times 4 \text{ cm} \qquad \text{Divide by 2.}$$

$$= 4 \text{ cm}^2$$

b. The height of the triangle = 7 cm.

The base of the triangle = 3 cm.

The formula for finding the area of a triangle $= \frac{1}{2} \times b \times h$

Therefore, the area of the triangle $= \frac{1}{2} \times 3 \text{ cm} \times 7 \text{ cm} =$

$$= \frac{21}{2} \text{ cm}^2 = 10\frac{1}{2} \text{ cm}^2$$

Note: Some triangles are not right triangles and in order to find the height of such triangles, draw a perpendicular line from a vertex of the triangle to the base of the triangle as shown:

580

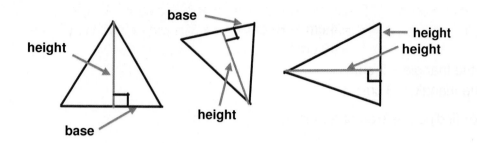

Example 3

Find the area of the following triangle:

a. 6 cm, 5 cm

b. 8 cm, 10 cm

c. 6 cm, 7 cm

Solution

a. The height of the triangle = 6 cm.

The base of the triangle = 5 cm.

The formula for finding the area of a triangle is $\frac{1}{2} \times b \times h$

Therefore, the area of the triangle $= \frac{1}{2} \times 5 \text{ cm} \times 6 \text{ cm}$

$$= \frac{1}{\underset{1}{2}} \times 5 \text{ cm} \times \overset{3}{6} \text{ cm}$$

$$= 5 \text{ cm} \times 3 \text{ cm}$$
$$= 15 \text{ cm}^2$$

b. The height of the triangle = 10 cm.

The base of the triangle = 8 cm.

The formula for finding the area of a triangle is $\frac{1}{2} \times b \times h$

Therefore, the area of the triangle $= \frac{1}{2} \times 8 \text{ cm} \times 10 \text{ cm}$

$$= \frac{1}{\underset{1}{2}} \times \overset{4}{8} \text{ cm} \times 10 \text{ cm}$$

$$= 4 \text{ cm} \times 10 \text{ cm}$$
$$= 40 \text{ cm}^2$$

c. The height of the triangle = 7 cm

The base of the triangle = 6 cm

The formula for finding the area of a triangle is $\frac{1}{2} \times b \times h$

Therefore, the area of a triangle $= \frac{1}{2} \times 6 \text{ cm} \times 7 \text{ cm}$

$$= \frac{1}{\underset{1}{2}} \times \overset{3}{6} \text{ cm} \times 7 \text{ cm}$$

$$= 3 \text{ cm} \times 7 \text{ cm}$$
$$= 21 \text{ cm}^2$$

Example 4

A triangle has an area of 50 cm^2 and if the base of the triangle is 5 cm, find the height of the triangle.

Solution

The area of the triangle = 50 cm^2.

The base of the triangle = 5 cm.

Let the height of the triangle = h.

The formula for finding the area of a triangle is $\frac{1}{2} \times b \times h$.

Therefore, $50 \text{ cm}^2 = \frac{1}{2} \times 5 \text{ cm} \times h$

$$50 \text{ cm}^2 = \frac{5h}{2} \text{ cm} \underline{\hspace{6cm}}[A]$$

Multiply both sides of the equation [A] by 2 in order to eliminate the 2 at the right side of the equation as a denominator as follows:

$$50 \text{ cm}^2 \times 2 = \frac{5h}{2} \times 2 \text{ cm}$$

$$100 \text{ cm}^2 = \frac{5h}{\underset{1}{2}} \times \overset{1}{2} \text{ cm}$$

$$100 \text{ cm}^2 = 5h \text{ cm} \underline{\hspace{6cm}}[B]$$

Divide both sides of the equation [B] by 5 cm in order to obtain the value of h as shown:

$$\frac{\overset{20}{\cancel{100}}}{\underset{1}{\cancel{5}\ cm}}\ cm^2 = \frac{\overset{h}{\cancel{5h}}}{\underset{1}{\cancel{5}\ cm}}\ cm$$

$$20\ cm = h \qquad \text{(Note: } cm^2 \div cm = cm, \text{ and } cm \div cm = 1)$$

Therefore, the height of the triangle = 20 cm.

Example 5

Find the length of the base of each triangle.

a.

16 cm

C   B

Area = 24 cm²

b.

B

9 cm

A

C

Area = 36 cm²

c.

X

Y

8 cm

Z

Area = 18 cm²

Solution

a. The area of the triangle = 24 cm².

The height of the triangle = 16 cm.

Let the length of the base of the triangle = b. The base is $\overline{BC}$.

The formula for finding the area of a triangle is:

$$\text{Area} = \frac{1}{2} \times b \times h$$

Therefore, $24\ cm^2 = \frac{1}{2} \times b \times 16\ cm$ (Substitute 24 cm² = area, and 16 cm = h.)

$$= \frac{1}{2} \times b \times \overset{8}{\cancel{16}}\ cm \qquad \text{(Dividing by 2)}$$

$$= 8b\ cm \underline{\hspace{6cm}}[A]$$

Divide both sides of the equation [A] by 8 cm in order to eliminate the 8 at the right side of equation [A], and then obtain the value of b as shown:

$$\frac{24}{8}\ cm^2 = \frac{8b}{8}\ cm$$

$$\frac{\overset{3}{\cancel{24}}\ cm^2}{\underset{1}{\cancel{8\ cm}}} = \frac{\overset{b}{\cancel{8b}}\ \cancel{cm}}{\underset{1}{\cancel{8\ cm}}}$$

$3\ cm = b.$ (Note: $cm^2 \div cm = cm$, and $cm \div cm = 1$)

The base is 3 cm.

b. The area of the triangle $= 36\ cm^2$

The height of the triangle $= 9\ cm$

Let the length of the base $= b$. The base is $\overline{AC}$.

The formula for finding the area of a triangle is:

$$Area = \frac{1}{2} \times b \times h$$

Therefore, $36\ cm^2 = \frac{1}{2} \times b \times 9\ cm$ (Substitute area $= 36\ cm^2$, and $h = 9\ cm$)

$$36\ cm^2 = \frac{9b}{2}\ cm \underline{\hspace{10cm}}[B]$$

Multiply both sides of the equation $[B]$ by 2 in order to eliminate the 2 at the right side of the equation $[B]$ as shown:

$$36 cm^2 \times 2 = \frac{9b}{\underset{1}{\cancel{2}}}\ cm \times \cancel{2}$$

$$36\ cm^2 \times 2 = \frac{9b}{\underset{1}{\cancel{2}}}\ cm \times \cancel{2}$$

$$72\ cm^2 = 9b\ cm \underline{\hspace{9cm}}[C]$$

Divide each side of equation $[C]$ by 9 cm in order to obtain the value of b as shown:

$$\frac{72\ cm^2}{9\ cm} = \frac{9b\ cm}{9\ cm}$$

$$\frac{\overset{8\ cm}{\cancel{72\ cm^2}}}{\underset{1}{\cancel{9\ cm}}} = \frac{\overset{b}{\cancel{9b}}\ \cancel{cm}}{\underset{1}{\cancel{9\ cm}}}$$ (Note: $cm^2 \div cm = cm$, and $cm \div cm = 1$)

584

$$8 \text{ cm} = b.$$

The length of the base $= 8$ cm

c. The area of the triangle $= 18 \text{ cm}^2$

The height of the triangle $= 8$ cm

Let the length of the base $= b$. The base is $\overline{XY}$.

The formula for finding the area of a triangle is:

$$\text{Area} = \frac{1}{2} \times b \times h$$

Therefore, $18 \text{ cm}^2 = \dfrac{1}{2} \times b \times 8 \text{ cm}$ (Substitute $18 \text{ cm}^2 = $ area, and 8 cm $= h$)

$$= \frac{1}{\underset{1}{2}} \times b \times \overset{4}{8} \text{ cm} \qquad \text{(Dividing by 2)}$$

$$18 \text{ cm}^2 = 4b \text{ cm} \underline{\hspace{6cm}} [\text{D}]$$

Divide both sides of equation $[\text{D}]$ by 4 cm in order to eliminate the 4 at the right side of equation $[\text{D}]$, and then to obtain the value of b as shown:

$$\frac{18 \text{ cm}^2}{4 \text{ cm}} = \frac{4b \text{ cm}}{4 \text{ cm}}$$

$$\frac{18 \text{ cm}^2}{4 \text{ cm}} = \frac{\overset{1}{4b} \cancel{\text{cm}}}{\underset{1}{4} \cancel{\text{cm}}}$$

$$4\frac{2}{4} \text{ cm} = b \qquad\qquad 18 \div 4 = 4\frac{2}{4}, \text{ cm}^2 \div \text{cm} = \text{cm, and cm} \div \text{cm} = 1$$

$$4\frac{\overset{1}{2}}{\underset{2}{4}} \text{ cm} = b \qquad\qquad \text{Reduce to the lowest terms by dividing by 2}$$

$$4\frac{1}{2} \text{ cm} = b.$$

585

The base of the triangle is $4\frac{1}{2}$ cm.

━━━━━━━━ **The notes and the generous examples have provided me with the conceptual understanding and the computational fluency to do my homework.**

Exercises

1. The area of a triangle is half the area of a rec_____. Hint: See the notes in Example **1.**

2. Find the area of the following triangles. Hint: See Example **2.**

a. 5 cm 2 cm
b. 6 ft 4 ft
c. 8 cm 6 cm
d. 6 cm 3 cm

3. Find the area of each triangle. Hint: See Example **3.**

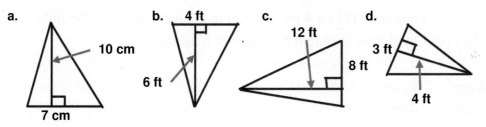

a. 10 cm 7 cm
b. 4 ft 6 ft
c. 12 ft 8 ft
d. 3 ft 4 ft

4. Find the height of each triangle. Hint: See Example **4.**
  a. Area = 12 cm^2 **b.** Area = 16 ft^2 **c.** Area = 24 cm^2
    Base = 4 cm   Base = 3 ft   Base = 3 cm

5. Find the base of each triangle. Hint: See Example **5.**
  a. Area = 16ft^2 **b.** Area = 9 cm^2 **c.** Area =18 cm^2
    Height = 4ft   Height = 2 cm   Height = 6 cm

Challenge Questions

6. Find the missing measurement for each triangle.
  a. Base = 3 cm   **b.** Base = ?   **c.** Base = 5 cm
    Height = 5 cm   Height = 6ft   Height = ?
      Area = ?   Area =28ft^2 Area = 25 cm^2

7. Find the area of each triangle.

a. 11 cm
    8 cm

b. 12 cm
    7 cm

c. 5 cm
    3 cm

8. Find the base of each triangle.

a. 5 cm
    Area = 10 cm²

b. 9 cm
    Area = 36 cm²

c. 10 ft
    Area = 25 ft²

9. Find the height of each triangle.

a. 3 ft
    Area = 18 ft²

b. 4 cm
    Area = 28 cm²

c. 6 cm
    Area = 24 cm²

Answers to Selected Questions

2a. 5 cm²   **3a.** 35 cm²   **4a.** 6 cm   **5a.** 8 ft

Cumulative Review

1. Solve:

a. $\dfrac{5}{12} \div \dfrac{2}{3}$ b. $\dfrac{4}{7} \div 8$ c. $1\dfrac{3}{4} \div \dfrac{3}{4}$ d. $\dfrac{2}{5} \times \dfrac{15}{16}$

e. $\dfrac{3}{4} - \dfrac{1}{2}$ f. $1\dfrac{1}{2} - \dfrac{3}{4}$ g. $3 \div \dfrac{3}{4}$ h. $1\dfrac{3}{4} + \dfrac{1}{2}$

2. What is the reciprocal of each of the following:

a. 5   b. $\dfrac{1}{7}$ c. $\dfrac{9}{10}$ d. $2\dfrac{1}{2}$

Perimeter of a Triangle

The perimeter of any object is the distance around the object, and therefore, the perimeter of a triangle is the distance around the triangle. The formula for finding the perimeter of a triangle is:

Perimeter = Side + Side + Side

$$= S_1 + S_2 + S_3 \quad (S_1, S_2, \text{ and } S_3 \text{ represent the lengths of the sides of the triangle})$$

Example 1

The measure of the sides of a triangle are 2 cm, 5 cm, and 6 cm. Find the perimeter of the triangle.

Solution

The formula for finding the perimeter of a triangle is:

Perimeter = Side + Side + Side

$$= S_1 + S_2 + S_3 \underline{\hspace{8cm}}[A]$$

Therefore, substitute $S_1 = 2$ cm, $S_2 = 5$ cm, and $S_3 = 6$ cm into equation $[A]$.

Equation $[A]$ then becomes:

Perimeter = 2 cm + 5 cm + 6 cm

$$= 13 \text{ cm}$$

Example 2

The perimeter of a triangle is 25 cm. If the sum of the two sides of the triangle is 15, what is the measure of the third side of the triangle?

Solution

The formula for finding the perimeter of a triangle is:

$$\text{Perimeter} = S_1 + S_2 + S_3 \underline{\hspace{7cm}}[B].$$

Since the perimeter of the triangle = 25 cm and the sum of the two sides = 15 cm, let $S_1 + S_2 = 15$ cm. Substitute perimeter = 25 cm and the sum of the two sides of the triangle = 15 cm into equation $[B]$ as shown:

$$25 \text{ cm} = 15 + S_3 \underline{\hspace{7cm}}[C]$$

Subtract 15 from both sides of equation $[C]$ in order to eliminate the 15 at the right side of equation $[C]$, and then isolate S_3 as shown:

$$25 \text{ cm} - 15 \text{ cm} = 15 \text{ cm} - 15 \text{ cm} + S_3$$

$$10 \text{ cm} = S_3$$

The third side of the triangle is 10 cm.

Example 3

One side of an equilateral triangle is 8 ft. Find the perimeter of the triangle.

Recall that an equilateral triangle is a triangle which has all the three sides equal, and therefore, each side of the triangle is 8 ft. The formula for finding the perimeter of a triangle is:

$$\textbf{Perimeter} = S_1 + S_2 + S_3 \underline{\hspace{7cm}}[D]$$

Substitute $S_1 = 8$ ft, $S_2 = 8$ ft and $S_3 = 8$ ft into equation $[D]$ in order to find the perimeter of the triangle as shown:

Perimeter = 8 ft + 8 ft + 8ft

= 24 ft

Therefore, the perimeter of the triangle is 24 ft.

Example 4

The area of a triangle is 12 cm^2 and the height of the triangle is $3\frac{1}{2}$ cm.

a. Find the base of the triangle.

b. Assume that the triangle is an equilateral triangle, find the perimeter of the triangle.

Solution

a. The formula for finding the area of a triangle is:

$$\textbf{Area} = \frac{1}{2}\,\textbf{base} \times \textbf{height} \hspace{3cm} [E]$$

Substitute the area = 12 cm^2 and the height of the triangle $= 3\frac{1}{2}$ cm into equation $[E]$ as shown:

$$12 \text{ cm}^2 = \frac{1}{2}\,\text{base} \times 3\frac{1}{2} \text{ cm} \hspace{3cm} [F].$$

Multiply both sides of the equation $[F]$ by 2 in order to eliminate the $\frac{1}{2}$ at the right side of equation $[F]$ as shown:

$$12 \text{ cm}^2 \times 2 = \frac{1}{2} \times 2 \times \text{base} \times 3\frac{1}{2} \text{ cm}$$

$$24 \text{ cm}^2 = \frac{\overset{1}{\cancel{1}}}{\underset{1}{\cancel{2}}} \times \cancel{2} \times \text{base} \times 3\frac{1}{2} \text{ cm}$$

$$24 \text{ cm}^2 = \text{base} \times 3\frac{1}{2} \text{ cm} \hspace{3cm} [G].$$

Divide both sides of the equation $[G]$ by $3\frac{1}{2}$ cm in order to eliminate the $3\frac{1}{2}$ cm from the right side of equation and so that we can obtain the value of the base as shown:

$$\frac{24 \text{ cm}^2}{3\frac{1}{2} \text{ cm}} = \frac{\text{base} \times 3\frac{1}{2} \text{ cm}}{3\frac{1}{2} \text{ cm}}$$

589

$$\frac{24 \text{ cm}}{3\frac{1}{2}} = \text{base}$$

$$3\frac{1}{2} \text{ cm} \div 3\frac{1}{2} \text{ cm} = 1 \text{ and cm}^2 \div \text{cm} = \text{cm}$$

$$\frac{24 \text{ cm}}{\frac{7}{2}} = \text{base}$$

$$3\frac{1}{2} = \frac{7}{2} \text{ (review improper fractions).}$$

$$24 \text{ cm} \times \frac{2}{7} = \text{base}$$

To divide by a fraction is the same as to multiply by the reciprocal of the fraction.

$$\frac{48}{7} \text{ cm} = \text{base}$$

$$6.86 \text{ cm} = \text{base}$$

You may use a calculator and round your answer to two decimal places.

Therefore, the base of the triangle is 6.86 cm.

b. If we assume that the triangle is an equilateral triangle, then the all the side s are equal. The formula for finding the perimeter of a triangle is:

Perimeter = $\mathbf{S_1 + S_2 + S_3}$ _____[H]

Substitute $S_1 = 6.86$ cm, $S_2 = 6.86$ cm, and $S_3 = 6.86$ cm into equation [H] as shown:

$$\text{Perimeter} = 6.86 \text{ cm} + 6.86 \text{ cm} + 6.86 \text{ cm}$$
$$= 20.58 \text{ cm}$$

You may use a calculator.

The notes and the generous examples have provided me with the conceptual understanding and the computational fluency to do my homework.

Exercises

1. The measure of the three sides of each triangle is given. Find the perimeter of each triangle. Hint: See Example **1**.

   a. 3 m, 8 m, and 7 m **b**. 9 ft, 2 ft, and 6 ft **c**. 5 in., 8 in., and 11 in.

   d. 9 cm, 12 cm, and 5 cm **e**. 6 m, 17 m, and 4 m **f**. 7 ft, 4 ft, and 9 ft

   g. 8 m, 12 m, and 10 m **h**. 7 ft, 13 ft, and 5 ft **i**. 10 cm, 5 cm, and 9 cm

2. The perimeter and the sum of the two sides of each triangle are given. Find the measure of the third side of the triangle. Hint: See Example **2**.

   a. Perimeter = 28 cm and the sum of the two sides = 17 cm.

b. Perimeter = 15 ft and the sum of the two sides = 9 ft.

c. Perimeter = 30 in. and the sum of the two sides = 19 in.

d. Perimeter = 25 cm and the sum of the two sides = 19 cm.

3. One side of each equilateral triangle is given. Find the perimeter of each equilateral triangle. Hint: See Example **3**.

    a. 10 cm   **b**. 5 ft   **c**. 8 in.   **d**. 7 m   **e**. 4 cm

    f. 11 m   **g**. 9 cm   **h**. 6 m   **i**. 12 in.   **j**. 3 ft

4. The area of a triangle is 7 m² and the height of the triangle is $3\frac{1}{2}$ m.

    a. Find the measure of the base triangle.

    b. Find the perimeter of the triangle given that the triangle is an equilateral triangle. Hint: See Example **4**.

Challenge Questions

5. The sum of the measure of the two sides of a triangle is 19 cm. If the perimeter of the triangle is 27 cm, find the measure of the third side of the triangle.

6. The measure of the sides of a triangle are 8 ft, 6 ft, and 5 ft. Find the perimeter of the triangle.

7. The measure of one side of an equilateral triangle is 12 cm. Find the perimeter of the triangle.

Answers to Selected Questions

1a. 18 m   **2a**. 11 cm   **3a**. 30 cm

(Do not forget to use the generous examples as guides.)

CHAPTER 22

AREA AND PERIMETER OF PARALLELOGRAMS

What is a parallelogram? Recall that the parallelogram is a quadrilateral which has parallel and congruent opposite sides. The height and the base of a parallelogram is shown below.

$$\overline{AE} = \overline{FC} = \textbf{Height}$$
$$\overline{DC} = \textbf{Base}$$

The height of a parallelogram is the perpendicular segment to the base of the parallelogram. The base of a parallelogram is a side of the parallelogram that the height of the parallelogram is perpendicular to.

Example 1
Show that the area of a parallelogram is equal to the area of a rectangle that has the same base (length) and height (width).

Solution

Step 1: Sketch the parallelogram ABCD on a grid paper with height $\overline{AE}$.

Step 2: Cut out the left triangle AED, and then paste the left triangle AED at the right side of the parallelogram to form a rectangle ABEE as shown:

Step 3: Conclude that the same area that forms the parallelogram ABCD also forms the rectangle ABEE as shown:

Team Project

1. The class should be divided into four teams and each team should do steps 1, 2, and 3 of Example 1.
2. From your project, do you agree with the question in Example 1? Explain.

Formula for Finding the Area of a Parallelogram

Since the area of a parallelogram is equal to the area of a rectangle that has the same base (length) and height (width), the formula for finding the area of a parallelogram is similar to the formula for finding the area of a rectangle as follows:

Area of a rectangle = **Length** × **Width**
Area of a parallelogram = **Base** × **Height**

Example 2

Find the area of each parallelogram.

a.

2 cm
3 cm

b.

A   B
4 cm
D   6 cm   C

c.

4 ft
10 ft

Solution

a. Height of the parallelogram = 2 cm
Base of the parallelogram = 3 cm
The formula for finding the area of a parallelogram is:

Area = Base × Height.

Therefore, the area of the parallelogram is:

Area = 3 cm × 2 cm
= 6 cm^2

b. Height of the parallelogram = 4 cm.

Base of the parallelogram = $\overline{AB}$

But $\overline{AB} = \overline{DC}$ because the opposite sides of a parallelogram are equal.
Therefore, the base of the parallelogram = 6 cm.
The formula for finding the area of a parallelogram is

Area = **Base** × **Height**.

593

Therefore, the area of the parallelogram = 6 cm × 4 cm = 24 cm²

c. Height of the parallelogram = 4 ft

Base of the parallelogram = 10 ft

The formula for finding the area of a parallelogram = Base × Height.

Therefore, the area of the parallelogram = 10 ft × 4 ft = 40 ft²

Example 3

Find the missing dimension for each parallelogram.

a. Base = 6 cm   b. Base = ?

   Height = ?   Height = 8 cm

   Area = 32 cm²   Area = 24 cm²

Solution

a. Let the height of the parallelogram = H

The formula for finding the area of a parallelogram is:

$$\text{Area} = \text{Base} \times \text{Height}.$$

Therefore, the area of the parallelogram is:

$$32 \text{ cm}^2 = 6 \text{ cm} \times H \underline{\hspace{5cm}}[A]$$

Divide both sides of equation [A] by 6 cm in order to eliminate the 6 cm from the right side of the equation, and then to obtain the value of H as shown:

$$\frac{32 \text{ cm}^2}{6 \text{ cm}} = \frac{6 \text{ cm}}{6 \text{ cm}} \times H$$

$$\frac{32 \text{ cm}^2}{6 \text{ cm}} = \frac{\overset{1}{\cancel{6 \text{ cm}}}}{\underset{1}{\cancel{6 \text{ cm}}}} \times H$$

$$5\frac{2}{6} = H \qquad\qquad 32 \div 6 = 5 \text{ remainder 2 or } 5\frac{2}{6}.$$

$$5\frac{1}{3} = H \qquad\qquad \text{Reduce } \frac{2}{6} \text{ to the lowest terms by dividing}$$

the numerator and the denominator by 2.

b. Let the base of the parallelogram = B

The formula for finding the area of the parallelogram is:

$$\text{Area} = \textbf{Base} \times \textbf{Height}.$$

Therefore, the area of the parallelogram is:

$$24 \text{ cm}^2 = B \times 8 \text{ cm} \underline{\hspace{5cm}}[Y]$$

Divide both sides of equation [Y] by 8 cm in order to eliminate the 8 cm at the right side of equation [Y] and then to obtain the value of B as shown:

$$\frac{24 \text{ cm}^2}{8 \text{ cm}} = B \times \frac{8 \text{ cm}}{8 \text{ cm}}$$

$$\frac{\overset{3}{\cancel{24 \text{ cm}^2}}}{\underset{1}{\cancel{8 \text{ cm}}}} = B \times \frac{\overset{1}{\cancel{8 \text{ cm}}}}{\underset{1}{\cancel{8 \text{ cm}}}}$$

3 cm = B   **Note**: cm² ÷ cm = cm, and cm ÷ cm = 1.

The base of the parallelogram is 3 cm.

Exercises

1. What is the formula for finding the area of a parallelogram? Hint: See Example **1**.

2. Find the area of each of the parallelogram. Hint: See Example **2**.

a. 7 cm 2 cm

b. 5 cm 10 cm

c. 8 ft 5 ft

3. Find the missing dimension for each parallelogram. Hint: See Example **3**.

    a. Base = 5 cm   **b.** Base = ?   **c.** Base = 7 ft   **d.** Base = ?

       Height = ?   Height = 9 cm   Height = ?   Height = 4 in.

       Area = 30 cm²   Area = 36 cm²   Area = 63 ft²   Area = 32 in²

Challenge Questions

4. Find the missing dimension for each parallelogram.

    a. Base = 6 cm   **b.** Base = ?   **c.** Base = 5 ft   **d.** Base = ?

       Height = 8 cm   Height = 2 m   Height = ?   Height = 3 m

       Area = ?   Area = 24 m²   Area = 35 ft²   Area = 30 m²

5. Find the area of each parallelogram.

a. 5 cm 7 cm

b. 11 ft 3 ft

c. 6 cm 2 cm

Answers to Selected Questions
2a. 14 cm²   **3a**. 6 m

Perimeter of a Parallelogram

Recall that a parallelogram is a quadrilateral that has parallel and congruent opposite sides. Since the opposite sides of a parallelogram are congruent, the opposite sides of a parallelogram are equal. The perimeter of the parallelogram is the distance around the parallelogram. Therefore, the perimeter of the parallelogram in figure 1 is:

    Perimeter = L + L + W + W   (L represents length and W represents width)
            = 2L + 2W

Therefore, the formula for finding the perimeter of a parallelogram is:

    Perimeter = 2L + 2W

figure 1

Example 1

The length of a parallelogram is 7 cm and the width is 4 cm. Find the perimeter of the parallelogram.

Solution

The formula for finding the perimeter of a parallelogram is:

    Perimeter = 2L + 2W   ————————————————————[B]

Substitute L = 7 cm and W = 4 cm into equation [B] as follows:

    Perimeter = 2 · 7 cm + 2 · 4 cm
              = 14 cm + 8 cm
              = 22 cm

Therefore, the perimeter of the triangle is 22 cm.

Example 2

The perimeter of a parallelogram is 24 cm. If the width of the parallelogram is 3 cm, find the length of the parallelogram.

Solution

The formula for finding the perimeter of a parallelogram is:

    Perimeter = 2L + 2W   ————————————————————[C].

Substitute the perimeter = 24 cm and W = 3 cm into equation [C] as follows:

    24 cm = 2L + 2·3 cm
    24 cm = 2L + 6 cm   ————————————————————[D]

Subtract 6 cm from both sides of the equation [D] in order to eliminate the 6 cm at the right side of the equation [D], and then to isolate the 2L as follows:

    24 cm - 6 cm = 2L + 6 cm - 6 cm

$$18 \text{ cm} = 2L \underline{\hspace{6cm}} [E]$$

Note: 6 cm - 6 cm = 0

Divide both sides of the equation $[E]$ by 2 in order to eliminate the 2 at the right side of the equation $[E]$, and then to isolate L as shown:

$$\frac{18}{2} \text{ cm} = \frac{2L}{2}$$

$$\frac{\overset{9}{\cancel{18}}}{\cancel{2}} \text{ cm} = \frac{\overset{L}{\cancel{2L}}}{\cancel{2}}$$

$$9 \text{ cm} = L$$

Therefore, the length of the perimeter is 9 cm.

Note: The method for the solution of example 2 can also be used to find the width of the parallelogram when the length and the perimeter of the parallelogram are given.

The notes and the generous examples have provided me with the conceptual understanding and the computational fluency to do my homework.

Exercises

1. Find the perimeter of each of the parallelograms with the given length and width. Hint: See Example **1**.
   a. L = 10 m and W = 4 m
   b. L = 6 ft and W = 2 ft
   c. L = 12 cm and W = 6 cm
   d. L = 6 cm and W = 3 cm
2. The perimeter of a parallelogram is 36 cm and the width is 4 cm. Find the length of the parallelogram. Hint: See Example **2**
3. The length of a side of a parallelogram is 14 cm and the perimeter is 48 cm. Find the width of the parallelogram. Hint: See Example **2**.

Challenge Questions

4. Find the missing dimension in each of the parallelograms.
   a. Perimeter = 16 cm, L = ?, and W = 2 cm.
   b. Perimeter = ?, L = 9 m, and W = 3 m.
   c. Perimeter = 26 ft, L = 9 ft, and W = ?
   d. Perimeter = 33 m, L = 10 m, and W = ?
   e. Perimeter = 29 cm, L = ?, and W = 4 cm.

Summary of Perimeter and Area

Shape	Sketch	Perimeter	Area
Square		Perimeter = S + S + S + S Perimeter = 4S	Area = S × S Area = S²
Rectangle		Perimeter = L + W + L + W Perimeter = 2L + 2W Perimeter = 2(L + W)	Area = L × W
Parallelogram		Perimeter = b + s + b + s Perimeter = 2b + 2s Perimeter = 2(b + s)	Area = b × h
Triangle		Perimeter = a + b + c	Area = $\frac{1}{2}$b × h

Cumulative Review

1. What is an equilateral triangle.

2. Explain what is meant by parallel lines.

3. Solve for n:

    a. 3n + 1 = 10   **b.** 4n = 16   **c.** 8 = 2 + 3n

CHAPTER 23

NETS FOR SOLID FIGURES

New Terms: net, polyhedron

What is a **net**? A net is **a two-dimensional pattern** that can be folded into a **three-dimensional object** or polyhedron.

A **Polyhedron** is a solid formed by plane faces that are polygons.

Table showing the sketches of nets.

Name	Nets	Number of faces	Three-dimensional polyhedron
Rectangular prism	base top	6	
Square prism	top bottom	6	
Rectangular pyramid	bottom	5	
Square pyramid	base	5	
Triangular pyramid	base	4	
Pentagonal prism	base	6	
Hexagonal prism	top bottom	8	

Team Project

1. Each team should sketch the nets in the table containing nets.
2. Cut out the nets.
3. Fold and tape each net to form the object.
4. Confirm the number of faces that each object has.

Exercises

Match each solid figure with its net by writing a, b, c, d, e, or f. Hint: See the table of nets.

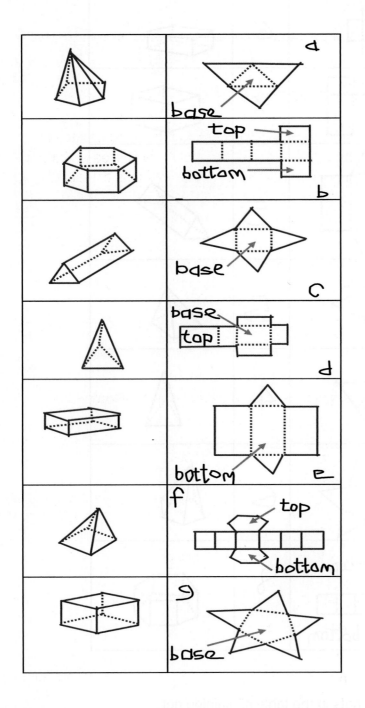

CHAPTER 24

SURFACE AREA OF SOLID FIGURES

The **surface area** of a solid figure is the **sum of the areas of the faces of the solid figure**.

How to Find the Surface Area of a Solid Figure.

To find the surface area of a solid figure, use the net of each solid figure to determine the number of faces that is contained in each solid figure, find the area of each face, and then add up the areas of all the faces to obtain the total surface area of the solid figure. Refer to the chapter on Nets to determine the number of faces contained in each solid figure.

Example 1

Find the surface area of the rectangular prism.

Solution

Step 1: Sketch the net of the rectangular prism with dimensions as shown:

Step 2: Find the area of each face as follows:

Face	Length (L)	Width (W)	Area = L × W
A	6 cm	3 cm	18 cm²
B	2 cm	3 cm	6 cm²
C	6 cm	2 cm	12 cm²
D	6 cm	3 cm	18 cm²
E	6 cm	2 cm	12 cm²
F	2 cm	3 cm	6 cm²

Step 3: Add the area of each face together in order to obtain the surface area as shown:

$$\text{Surface Area} = 18 \text{ cm}^2 + 6 \text{ cm}^2 + 12 \text{ cm}^2 + 18 \text{ cm}^2 + 12 \text{ cm}^2 + 6 \text{ cm}^2$$
$$= 72 \text{ cm}^2$$

Alternative Method

Example 1 can be solved by noting that the opposite faces of a rectangular prism are congruent, and therefore, the opposite areas of a rectangular prism are congruent. (Note: Congruent simply means "is equal to".)

Therefore: Face A is congruent to face D.

　　　　　Face B is congruent to face F.

　　　　　Face C is congruent to face E

Therefore, we can find the surface area by multiplying the sum of the areas of faces A, B, and C by 2 as shown:

From step 2:

The area of face A = 18 cm^2

The area of face B = 6 cm^2

The area of face C = 12 cm^2

The sum of the surface area of the faces A, B, and C

$$= 18 \text{ cm}^2 + 6 \text{ cm}^2 + 12 \text{ cm}^2 = 36 \text{ cm}^2$$

(Area of faces A, B, and C) $\times$ 2 = 36 cm^2 $\times$ 2 = 72 cm^2

Therefore, the surface area = 72 cm^2

Or from Step 2:

The area of face D = 18 cm^2

The area of face E = 6 cm^2

The area of face F = 12 cm^2

The sum of the surface area of faces D, F, and E = 18 cm^2 + 6 cm^2 + 12 cm^2 = 36 cm^2

(Area of faces A, B, and C) $\times$ 2 = 36 cm^2 $\times$ 2 = 72 cm^2

Therefore, the surface area = 72 cm^2

Special Note:

It is not always necessary to sketch the nets before solving the surface area problems of solid figures. However, the knowledge of nets will help the student to determine the number of faces and the associated dimensions mentally.

Example 2

Find the surface area of the square pyramid.

$\overline{EF}$ = 3 cm

Solution

Setup:

From the chapter on nets, we know that a square pyramid has 5 faces consisting of four congruent triangles and one square base as shown:

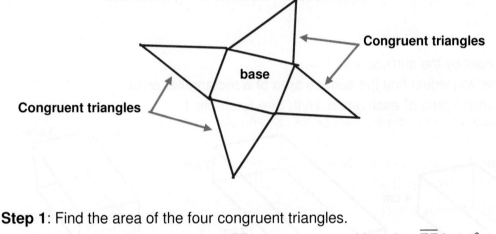

Congruent triangles

base

Congruent triangles

Step 1: Find the area of the four congruent triangles.

The height of the triangle = EF = 3 cm.   Note that $\overline{EF}$ is 90⁰ to $\overline{AB}$

The base of each triangle = 4 cm.

The formula for finding the area of a triangle = $\frac{1}{2}$ base × height.

Therefore, the area of each triangle = $\frac{1}{2}$ × 4 cm × 3 cm

$$= \frac{\overset{2}{1}}{\underset{1}{2}} \times 4\ cm \times 3\ cm \qquad \text{Divide by 2.}$$

$$= 2\ cm \times 3\ cm$$
$$= 6\ cm^2$$

Therefore, the area of the 4 congruent triangles = 6 cm² × 4

= 24 cm²

Step 2: Find the area of the square base. The length of the side of the

square base = 4 cm

The formula for finding the area of the square base = **Side** × **Side**.

Therefore, the area of the square base = 4 cm × 4 cm

$$= 16 \text{ cm}^2$$

Step 3: Find the surface area of the square pyramid.

The surface area of the pyramid

= Area of the 4 congruent triangles + Area of the square base.

$$= 24 \text{ cm}^2 + 16 \text{ cm}^2$$

$$= 40 \text{ cm}^2$$

The notes and the generous examples have provided me with the conceptual understanding and the computational fluency to do my homework.

Exercises

1. What is meant by the surface area?

2. Explain how you would find the surface area of a rectangular prism.

3. Find the surface area of each prism. Hint: See Example **1**.

a. 4 cm, 10 cm, 3 cm

b. 3 cm, 12 cm, 5 cm

c. 3 cm, 2 cm, 8 cm

4. Find the surface area of each square pyramid. Hint: See Example **2**.

a. 6 cm, 2 cm

b. 8 cm, 3 cm

c. 8 cm, 6 cm

Example 3

What is the surface area of a box 4 cm long, 2 cm wide and 3 cm high?

Solution

Step 1: Sketch the box with the associated dimensions.

The area of the opposite sides or opposite faces of the box are congruent.

Step 2: Find the area of each face as shown:

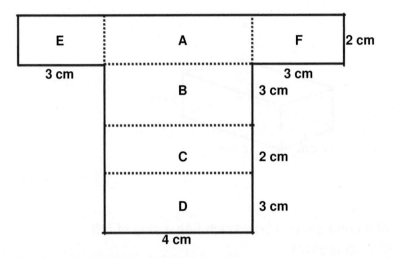

Step 3: Find the surface area of each face as follows:

Face	Length	Width	Area = L × W
A	4 cm	2 cm	4 cm × 2 cm = 8 cm^2
B	4 cm	3 cm	4 cm × 3 cm = 12 cm^2
C	4 cm	2 cm	4 cm × 2 cm = 8 cm^2
D	4 cm	3 cm	4 cm × 3 cm = 12 cm^2
E	3 cm	2 cm	3 cm × 2 cm = 6 cm^2
F	3 cm	2 cm	3 cm × 2 cm = 6 cm^2

The surface area = The sum of the areas of all the faces of the box.

The surface area = 8 cm^2 + 12 cm^2 + 8 cm^2 + 12 cm^2 + 6 cm^2 + 6 cm^2 = 52 cm^2

The notes and the generous examples have provided me with the conceptual understanding and the computational fluency to do my homework.

Exercises

1. What is the surface area of a rectangular box which is 10 cm long, 9 cm wide, and 4 cm high. Hint: See Example **3**.

2. Find the surface area of a rectangular block which is 8 ft long, 6 ft wide, and 5ft high. Hint: See Example **3**.

Challenge Questions

3. Find the surface area of each solid figure.

a.

10 cm

6 cm

Square pyramid

b.

5 cm

6 cm   10 cm

4. What is the surface area of a cube-shaped box which has a side of 5 ft.
   Hint: A cube-shaped box has equal sides.

Cumulative Review

1. What is the reciprocal of 10?

2. $\dfrac{3}{5} \div \dfrac{3}{10} =$

3. $\dfrac{3}{5} \times \dfrac{3}{10} =$

4. $\dfrac{3}{5} - \dfrac{3}{10} =$

5. $\dfrac{3}{5} + \dfrac{3}{10} =$

6. $6\dfrac{2}{5} + 1\dfrac{3}{4} =$

7. $4\dfrac{2}{3} - 2\dfrac{3}{4} =$

8. 25% of 20 =

9. $2\dfrac{2}{3} \times 1\dfrac{3}{4} =$

10. $\dfrac{1}{3} \times \dfrac{12}{13} =$

CHAPTER 25

VOLUME

What is volume? **Volume** is the amount of space occupied by any object. Volume is measured in cubic units because the volume is a measurement of three dimensions (such as Length × Width × Height), and therefore, it is expressed in cubic units such as centimeter cube or cm × cm × cm = cm^3. Note: cm^3 is called centimeter cube. We can therefore, estimate or find the volume of a rectangular prism by visualizing how many cubes will fill it.

Volume of Rectangular Prisms

Team Project
Goal of the project: Whether we can use cubes to estimate or find the volume of a rectangular prism?
Material: 1 transparent rectangular prism or container and 60 plastic cubes of the same size.
Method:
Step 1
Make a row of 5 cubes along the length of the container.

Step 2: Make 3 rows of 5 cubes along the width to make 1 layer.

Step 3: Make 4 layers of 15 cubes to fill the container or to complete the rectangular prism.

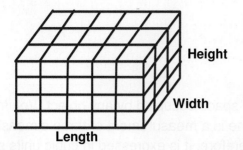

Height

Width

Length

Step 4: Count the total number of the cubes that fill up the container or that makes the prism = 60 cubes or 5 × 3 × 4 = 60 cubes

Step 5: The space occupied by the total number of the cubes is the volume of the container occupied by the cubes.

Since the cubes are placed closely together so that there is no gap between the cubes, the total space occupied by the cubes is the space contained in the container and this space is known as the volume. The number of cubes that occupy the space/container is obtained by multiplying the Length by Width by Height to obtain 60 cubes as shown:

Number of the cubes that occupy the space/container.

   = Length × Width × Height

   = 5 × 3 × 4

   = 60

Therefore, the volume of the container/prism.

   = 60 cubes

   = Length × Width × Height

Special Note: Some schools may not have the exact size of the plastic cubes and the transparent container for this experiment, however, any size of the cubes and the container may be used. The logic of the project will be the same.

Formula for Finding the Volume of a Rectangular Prism

From the team project, we know that we can find the volume of a rectangular prism or containers by counting cubes. However, instead of counting cubes, we can use a formula to find the volume of a rectangular prism as shown:

1. Volume = Length × Width × Height

   = L × W × H

2. Volume = Area × Height   (Note: L × W = Area. Review the topic on area).

   = A × H   (A = Area and H = Height).

Example 1

The length of a rectangular prism is 6 cm, the width is 5 cm, and the height is 2 cm. What is the volume of the rectangular prism?

Solution

L = 6 cm, W = 5 cm, and H = 2 cm.

608

The formula for finding the volume of a rectangular prism is:

$V = L \times W \times H$ _____ [A]

$\quad = 6 \text{ cm} \times 5 \text{ cm} \times 2 \text{ cm}$ $\qquad$ (Substitute L = 6 cm, W = 5 cm
$\qquad\qquad\qquad\qquad\qquad\qquad$ and H = 2 cm into equation [A].)

$\quad = 60 \text{ cm}^3$

Example 2

A rectangular tank has all the sides equal. If one side of the tank is 5 cm, what is the volume of the tank?

Solution

Since all the sides of the rectangular tank are equal,
L = 5 m, W = 5 m, and H = 5 m.
The formula for finding the volume of a rectangular tank or object is:

$V = L \times W \times H$ _____ [B]

$\quad = 5 \text{ m} \times 5 \text{ m} \times 5 \text{ m}$ (Substitute L = 5 cm, W = 5 cm, and H = 5 cm into equation [B]).

$\quad = 125 \text{ m}^3$

Example 3

The volume of a water tank is 36 m³. If the length of the water tank is 6 m, the width is 3 m, what is the height of the water tank?

Solution

$V = 36 \text{ m}^3$, L = 6m, W = 3 m, and H = ?
The formula for finding the volume of a water tank is:

$V = L \times W \times H$ _____ [C]

Substitute V = 36 m³, L = 6 m, and W = 3 m into equation [C] as shown:

$\qquad 36 \text{ m}^3 = 6 \text{ m} \times 3 \text{ m} \times H$

$\qquad 36 \text{ m}^3 = 18 \text{ m}^2 \times H$ _____ [D]

$\qquad\qquad\qquad$ (6 m × 3 m = 18 m² because m × m = m².)

Divide both sides of the equation [D] by 18 m² in order to isolate and to obtain the value of H as shown:

$$\frac{36 \text{ m}^3}{18 \text{ m}^2} = \frac{18 \text{ m}^2}{18 \text{ m}^2} \times H$$

$$\frac{\overset{2\ m}{\cancel{36}\ \text{m}^3}}{\underset{1}{\cancel{18}\ \text{m}^2}} = \frac{\overset{1}{\cancel{18}\ \text{m}^2}}{\underset{1}{\cancel{18}\ \text{m}^2}} \times H$$

(**Note:** $\dfrac{\text{m}^3}{\text{m}^2} = \dfrac{\overset{1}{\cancel{\text{m}}} \times \overset{1}{\cancel{\text{m}}} \times \text{m}}{\underset{1}{\cancel{\text{m}}} \times \underset{1}{\cancel{\text{m}}}} = \text{m}$)

$$2\ m = H$$

Therefore, the height of the water tank is 2 m.

Example 4

A gasoline tank is 10 m long and 3 m high. If the volume of the gasoline tank is 90 m^3, how wide is the gasoline tank?

Solution

$V = 90$ m^3, $L = 10$ m, $H = 3$ m, and $W = ?$

The formula for finding the volume of the tank is:

$V = L \times W \times H$ _____[E]

Substitute $V = 90$ m^3, $L = 10$ m, and $H = 3$ m, into equation [E] as shown:

$$90\ \text{m}^3 = 10\ \text{m} \times W \times 3\ \text{m}$$
$$90\ \text{m}^3 = 30\ \text{m}^2 \times W \qquad\qquad\text{_____[F]}$$

(Note: 10 m × 3 m = 30 m^2 because m × m = m^2).

Divide both sides of the equation [F] in order to isolate and to obtain the value of W as shown:

$$\frac{90\ \text{m}^3}{30\ \text{m}^2} = \frac{30\ \text{m}^2}{30\ \text{m}^2} \times W$$

$$\frac{\overset{3\ m}{\cancel{90}\ \text{m}^3}}{\underset{1}{\cancel{30}\ \text{m}^2}} = \frac{\overset{1}{\cancel{30}\ \text{m}^2}}{\underset{1}{\cancel{30}\ \text{m}^2}} \times W$$

(**Note:** $\dfrac{\text{m}^3}{\text{m}^2} = \dfrac{\overset{1}{\cancel{\text{m}}} \times \overset{1}{\cancel{\text{m}}} \times \text{m}}{\underset{1}{\cancel{\text{m}}} \times \underset{1}{\cancel{\text{m}}}} = \text{m}$).

$$3\ m = W$$

Therefore, the width of the gasoline tank is 3 m.

Example 5

A new milk tank is installed in a chocolate factory. If the tank is 3 yd wide, 4 yd high and has a volume of 60 yd^3, what is the length of the milk tank?

Solution

$V = 60$ yd^3, $L = ?$, $W = 3$ yd, and $H = 4$ yd

The formula for finding the volume of the milk tank is:

$$V = L \times W \times H \hspace{4cm} [G]$$

Substitute V = 60 yd^3, W = 3 yd, and H = 4 yd into equation [G] as shown:

$$60 \text{ yd}^3 = L \times 3 \text{ yd} \times 4 \text{ yd}$$
$$60 \text{ yd}^3 = 12 \text{ yd}^2 \times L \hspace{4cm} [H]$$

(Note: 3 yd × 4 yd = 12 yd^2 because yd × yd = yd^2).

Divide both sides of equation [H] by 12 yd^2 in order to isolate and obtain the value of H as shown:

$$\frac{60 \text{ yd}^3}{12 \text{ yd}^2} = \frac{12 \text{ yd}^2}{12 \text{ yd}^2} \times L$$

$$\frac{\overset{5 \text{ yd}}{\cancel{60 \text{ yd}^3}}}{\underset{1}{\cancel{12 \text{ yd}^2}}} = \frac{\overset{1}{\cancel{12 \text{ yd}^2}}}{\underset{1}{\cancel{12 \text{ yd}^2}}} \times L \qquad \left(\text{Note: } \frac{\text{yd}^3}{\text{yd}^2} = \frac{\overset{1}{\cancel{\text{yd}}} \times \overset{1}{\cancel{\text{yd}}} \times \text{yd}}{\underset{1}{\cancel{\text{yd}}} \times \underset{1}{\cancel{\text{yd}}}} = \text{yd}\right).$$

$$5 \text{ yd} = L$$

Therefore, the length of the milk tank = 5 yd.

━━━━━━━━━━━━━━ **The notes and the generous examples have provided me with the conceptual understanding and the computational fluency to do my homework.**

Exercises

1. Explain what is meant by volume?
2. Which of the following is a correct unit of volume?
   a. cm   **b.** cm^2 **c.** cm^3
3. What is the formula for finding the volume of a rectangular prism?
4. Find the volume of each rectangular prism. Hint: See Example 1.

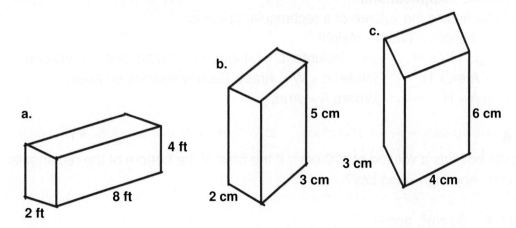

a. 2 ft, 8 ft, 4 ft

b. 2 cm, 3 cm, 5 cm

c. 4 cm, 3 cm, 6 cm

5. Find the height of each rectangular prism. Hint: See Example **3**.

a. $V = 24$ cm^3 **b.** $V = 36$ ft^3 **c.** $V = 48$ in^3 **d.** $V = 28$ cm^3
    L $= 6$ cm   L $= 9$ ft   L $= 6$ in   L $= 7$ cm
    W $= 2$ cm   W $= 2$ ft   W $= 4$ in   W $= 2$ cm
    H $= ?$ H $= ?$ H $= ?$ H $= ?$

6. Find the width of each rectangular prism. Hint: See Example **4**.

a. $V = 36$ cm^3 **b.** $V = 40$ yd^3 **c.** $V = 45$ cm^3 **d.** $V = 16$ cm^3
    L $= 4$ cm   L $= 5$ yd   L $= 5$ cm   L $= 4$ cm
    W $= ?$ W $= ?$ W $= ?$ W $= ?$
    H $= 3$ cm   H $= 4$ yd   H $= 3$ cm   H $= 2$ cm

7. Find the length of each rectangular object. Hint: See Example **5**.

a. $V = 24$ ft^3 **b.** $V = 16$ yd^3 **c.** $V = 45$ m^3 **d.** $V = 18$ m^3
    L $= ?$ L $= ?$ L $= ?$ L $= ?$
    W $= 3$ ft   W $= 2$ yd   W $= 5$ m   W $= 1$ m
    H $= 2$ ft   H $= 2$ yd   H $= 1$ m   H $= 2$ m

Challenge Questions

8. Find the unknown measure in each rectangular block.

a. L $= 3$ ft   **b.** $V = 15$ m^3 **c.** $V = 50$ ft^3 **d.** $V = 60$ m^3
    W $= 2$ ft   L $= 5$ m   L $= ?$ L $= 5$ m^3
    H $= 1$ft   W $= 1$ m   W $= 2$ ft   W $= ?$
    V $= ?$ H $= ?$ H $= 1$ ft   H $= 4$ m

9. Mary is using construction paper to cover a box 4 ft long, 3 ft wide, and 1 ft high. What is the volume of the construction paper? Hint: This question is the same as asking for the volume of the box.

Answers to the Selected Questions

    4a. 64 ft   **5a.** 2 cm   **6a.** 3 cm   **7a.** 4 ft

More on Volume - Applications

The formula for finding the volume of a rectangular prism is:

    Volume = Length $\times$ Width $\times$ Height

      $V = L \times W \times H$ (V = Volume, L = Length, W = Width, and H = Height)

        $= $ Area $\times$ H   (**Note**: L $\times$ W = Area). Review lessons on Area.

        $= A \times H$ Where A = Area

Example 6

A rectangular box has a volume of 120 cm^3. If the area of the bottom of the rectangular box is 30 cm^2, how high is the box?

Solution

$V = 60$ cm^3, A $= 30$ cm^2, and H $= ?$

The formula for finding the volume of a rectangular prism or box is:

$$V = L \times W \times H$$
$$V = \text{Area} \times H \qquad \textbf{Note: } \text{Area} = L \times W$$
$$V = A \times H \underline{\hspace{5cm}} [A]$$

Substitute $V = 120 \text{ cm}^3$ and $A = 30 \text{ cm}^2$ into equation $[A]$ as shown:

$$120 \text{ cm}^3 = 30 \text{ cm}^2 \times H \underline{\hspace{5cm}} [B]$$

Divide both sides of the equation $[B]$ by 30 cm^2 in order to isolate H in order to obtain the value of H as shown:

$$\frac{120 \text{ cm}^3}{30 \text{ cm}^2} = \frac{30 \text{ cm}^2}{30 \text{ cm}^2} \times H$$

$$\frac{\overset{4 \text{ cm}}{\cancel{120 \text{ cm}^3}}}{\underset{1}{\cancel{30 \text{ cm}^2}}} = \frac{\overset{1}{\cancel{30 \text{ cm}^2}}}{\underset{1}{\cancel{30 \text{ cm}^2}}} \times H \qquad (\textbf{Note: } \frac{\text{cm}^3}{\text{cm}^2} = \frac{\overset{1}{\cancel{\text{cm}}} \times \overset{1}{\cancel{\text{cm}}} \times \text{cm}}{\underset{1}{\cancel{\text{cm}}} \times \underset{1}{\cancel{\text{cm}}}} = \text{cm}).$$

$$4 \text{ cm} = H$$

Therefore, the box is 4 cm high.

Example 7

A rectangular swimming pool is 6 ft deep and the volume of the water in the pool is 240 ft^3. What is the area of the bottom of the swimming pool? Hint: 6 ft deep is the same as 6 ft high which is the same as the height of the pool.

Solution

The formula for finding the volume of a rectangular object is:

$$V = L \times W \times H$$
$$V = \text{Area} \times H \qquad \text{Note: } \text{Area} = L \times W$$
$$V = A \times H \underline{\hspace{5cm}} [A]$$

Substitute $V = 240 \text{ ft}^3$ and $H = 6 \text{ ft}$ into equation $[A]$ as shown:

$$240 \text{ ft} = A \times 6 \text{ ft} \underline{\hspace{5cm}} [B]$$

Divide both sides of the equation $[B]$ by 6 ft in order to isolate A which is the area and also to obtain the value of A as shown:

$$\frac{240 \text{ ft}^3}{6 \text{ ft}} = A \times \frac{6 \text{ ft}}{6 \text{ ft}}$$

$$\frac{\overset{40 \text{ ft}^2}{\cancel{240 \text{ ft}^3}}}{\underset{1}{\cancel{6 \text{ ft}}}} = A \times \frac{\overset{1}{\cancel{6 \text{ ft}}}}{\underset{1}{\cancel{6 \text{ ft}}}} \qquad (\text{Note: } \frac{\text{ft}^3}{\text{ft}} = \frac{\text{ft} \times \text{ft} \times \text{ft}}{\underset{1}{\cancel{\text{ft}}}} = \text{ft} \times \text{ft} = \text{ft}^2).$$

$40 \text{ ft}^2 = A$

Therefore, the area of the bottom of the swimming pool is 40 ft^2

Example 8

The bottom area of a rectangular swimming pool is 180 yd^2. If the swimming pool is 4 yd deep what is the volume of the water that the swimming pool can hold?
Hint: 4 yd deep is the same as 4 yd high which is the same as the height of the swimming pool.

Solution

$A = 180 \text{ yd}^2$, $H = 4$ yd, and $V = ?$

The formula for finding the volume of any rectangular object is.

$V = L \times W \times H$

$V = \text{Area} \times H$ **Note**: Area $= L \times W$

$V = A \times H$ _____$[L]$

Substitute $A = 180 \text{ yd}^2$ and $h = 4$ yd into the equation $[L]$ as shown:

$V = 180 \text{ yd}^2 \times 4$ yd

$V = 720 \text{ yd}^3$ (**Note**: $\text{yd}^2 \times \text{yd} = \text{yd} \times \text{yd} \times \text{yd} = \text{yd}^3$). Review the power of numbers.

Therefore, the volume of the water that the swimming pool can hold is 720 yd^3.

 The notes and the generous examples have provided me with the conceptual understanding and the computational fluency to do my homework.

Exercises

1. What is the formula for finding the volume of a rectangular object if only the bottom area and the height of the object is known?

2. A rectangular swimming pool has a volume of 360 ft^3 and if the bottom of the swimming pool has an area of 40 ft^2 how deep is the swimming pool? Hint: See Example **6**. Hint: How deep is the pool is the same as how high is the pool and it is also the same as what is the height of the swimming pool?

3. A rectangular swimming pool is 3 yd deep and the volume of the water in the swimming pool is 180 yd^3. What is the area of the bottom of the swimming pool? Hint: See Example **7**.

4. If the bottom area of a rectangular block is 9 in^2 and the block is 10 in high. What is the volume of the block? Hint: See Example **8**.

Challenge Questions

5. Find the unknown measure in each rectangular object.

   a. $V = 24 \text{ m}^3$ **b.** $V = 16 \text{ ft}^3$ **c.** $V = ?$ **d.** $V = 45 \text{ cm}^3$

      $A = 8 \text{ m}^2$ $A = ?$ $A = 5 \text{ cm}^2$ $A = 15 \text{ cm}^2$

      $H = ?$ $H = 4$ ft $H = 4$ cm $H = ?$

6. A rectangular object has a volume of 36 cm² and if the area of the bottom of the object is 9 cm² how high is the object?
7. If the bottom area of a rectangular fish tank is 12 ft² and the tank is 10 ft high, what is the volume of the tank?
8. The volume of water in a swimming pool is 160 yd³. If the swimming pool is 2 yd deep what is the area of the bottom of the swimming pool?

Cumulative Review
1. What is the formula for finding the area of a triangle?
2. What is meant by perpendicular lines?
3. 5 m = ? cm   4. $4^2 \div 2 =$ 5. $\dfrac{3}{4} \div \dfrac{3}{4} =$ 6. $1\dfrac{1}{2} \times 2\dfrac{1}{4} =$ 7. 2 yd = ? ft
8. An equilateral triangle is a____.   9. Parallel lines are____.   10. A trapezoid is a____.

VOLUME OF A CUBE
New Term: **cube**
What is a cube? **A cube is a rectangular prism that has all sides equal**.
We can use the method of the team project under the chapter on the "Volume of Rectangular Prisms" to find or estimate the volume of a cube by using cubes (Hint: See the team project under the chapter "Volume of Rectangular Prisms.")

The formula for finding the volume of a rectangular prism is:

$V = L \times W \times H$, but since the length of the sides of a cube are all equal, the **formula for finding the volume of a cube is**:

$V = S \times S \times S$, where S is the length of a side of the cube.
The **formula for finding the volume of a cube can also be represented as**:
$V = S^3$, since $S \times S \times S = S^3$.

Example 1
Find the volume of the cube.

2 cm

615

Solution

Length of a side of the cube = 2 cm.

Formula for the volume of a cube is:

$V = S \times S \times S$, where S is the length of a side of the cube.

$V = 2$ cm $\times 2$ cm $\times 2$ cm. All the sides of a cube are equal.

$V = 8$ cm^3

Therefore, the volume of the cube is 8 cm^3.

Example 2

The length of a side of a cube is 5 ft. What is the volume of the cube?

Solution

Length of a side of the cube = 5 ft.

Formula for the volume of a cube is:

$V = S \times S \times S$, where S is the length of a side of the cube.

$V = 5$ ft $\times 5$ ft $\times 5$ ft. All the sides of a cube are equal.

$V = 125$ ft^3

Example 3

The volume of a cube is 8 cm^3. What is the length of a side of the cube?

Solution

The formula for finding the volume of a cube is

$V = S \times S \times S$, where S is the length of a side of the cube.

The side of the cube is multiplied by itself 3 times to obtain the volume of the cube. Therefore, let us find a number that can be multiplied by itself 3 times to obtain 8 cm^3 which is the volume. If we select the dimension 4 cm as the length of a side of the cube and we multiply the 4 cm by itself 3 times, we obtain 64 cm^3 as shown:

4 cm $\times 4$ cm $\times 4$ cm $= 64$ cm^3

But 64 cm^3 is greater than the volume of the cube which is 8 cm^3. Let us try 3 cm which is a less dimension than 4 cm as the length of the side of the cube by multiplying 3 cm by itself for 3 times to see if the result will be 8 cm^3 as shown:

3 cm $\times 3$ cm $\times 3$ cm $= 27$ cm^3

But 27 cm^3 is greater than the volume of the cube which is 8 cm^3. Let us try 2 cm which is a less dimension than 3 cm as the length of the side of the cube by multiplying 2 cm by itself for 3 times to see if the result will be 8 cm^3 as shown:

2 cm $\times 2$ cm $\times 2$ cm $= 8$ cm^3

Since 2 cm $\times 2$ cm $\times 2$ cm $= 8$ cm^3 and 8 cm^3 is the volume of the cube, **then 2 cm is the correct dimension of the cube**.

Note: You can find the dimension of the side of the cube to be 2 cm directly, if you know that 2 cm $\times 2$ cm $\times 2$ cm $= 8$ cm^3 without trying 4 cm and 3 cm first.

Exercises

1. What is a cube?

2. What is the formula for finding the volume of a cube?

3. Find the volume of each cube. Hint: See Example 1.

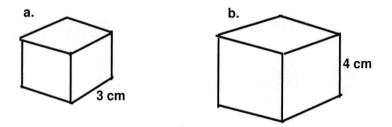

a. 3 cm

b. 4 cm

4. The length of a side of each cube is given. What is the volume of each cube? Hint: See Example 2, and also **the unit of a volume can be cm^3, m^3, in^3, ft^3, or yd^3**.

    a. 1 m   **b**. 3 ft   **c**. 4 yd   **d**. 5 cm

5. The volume of each cube is given. What is the length of a side of each cube? Hint: See Example 3.

    a. 27 cm^3 **b**. 125 ft^3 **c**. 64 in^3 **d**. 216 m^2

Review - Comparing the Dimensions of Perimeter, Area, and Volume.

Let us compare the dimension of the measures of perimeter, area, and volume. Geometric figures are measured in one, two, or three dimensions. The units of perimeter, area, and volume depends upon the number of the dimensions being used.

Perimeter: What is a perimeter? A perimeter is the distance around any figure. For example the distance around a rectangular block is the perimeter. Since the perimeter is measured in **one dimension** which is the **length** the unit of measure is **linear** such as ft, yd, cm, or m.

Area: What is an area? An area of a figure is the number of the square units needed to cover the figure. For example, the number of the square units needed to cover a football field is the area of the football field. Since an area is measured in two dimensions which are **length** and **width**, the unit of measure is **square units** such as in^2, ft^2, yd^2, cm^2, or m^2.

Volume: What is meant by volume? The volume is the amount of space occupied by a solid figure. For example, the number of cubic units that can fill a space or a container is the volume of that space or container. Since volume is measured in three dimensions which are **length**, **width**, and **height**, the unit of measure is cubic such as cm^3, m^3, in^3, ft^3, and yd^3.

Cumulative Review
1. Explain a regular polygon.
2. About 52 weeks = ? year/s.
3. -7 + 2 =   **4**. -8 - 3 =   **5**. The factors of 36 are: _____

CHAPTER 26

SCALE DRAWINGS

New Terms: **scale drawing, reduction, enlargement**

What is a **scale drawing**? A **scale drawing** shows a real distance smaller than or longer than the real distance. When a scale drawing shows a real distance that is smaller than the real distance, is called a **reduction**. When a scale drawing shows a real distance that is longer than the real distance, is called an **enlargement**. A **map scale** is the ratio that compares the distance on a map to the actual distance.

Team Project 1
Goal of the project: To use a scale drawing and a map scale to find the actual distance between Peki and Hoe by using equivalent ratios.
Method

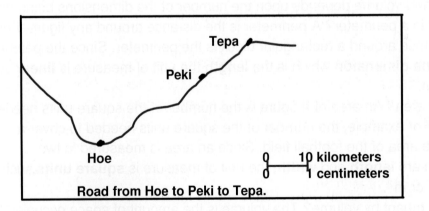

Road from Hoe to Peki to Tepa.

Step 1: **Read the map scale**.

The map shows the scale of 1 cm = 10 km, or $\dfrac{1\ cm}{10\ km}$.

Step 2: **Use a string to measure the distance from Peki to Hoe on the map**.
The distance between Peki and Hoe is marked on the string.

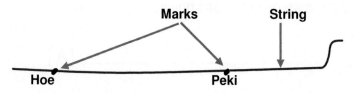

(Note: The distance from Hoe to Peki on the string is an approximate distance.)

Step 3: **Use a centimeter ruler to measure the distance between the two marks on the string as shown**.

The distance between the two marks on the string is about 5.2 cm.

Step 4: **Use equivalent ratios to find the actual distance as follows**:

$$\frac{1}{10} = \frac{5.2}{k}$$

k is the actual distance in kilometers.

Hint: Review the chapter/section on equivalent ratios.

$1 \times k = 10 \times 5.2$ Cross multiply.

$k = 52$ km

Therefore, the distance from Peki to Hoe is 52 km.

Team Project 2

Goal of the project: To use the scale drawing and the map scale to find the actual distance between Peki and Tepa by using equivalent ratios. Use the map provided under Team Project 1. Use the same method as in Team Project 1 to find the distance between Peki and Tepa.

Example 1

Complete the map scale ratio table.

Map distance (cm)	1	?	5	?
Actual distance (km)	15	30	?	105

Solution

To find the map distance when the actual distance is 30 km.

Step 1: From the table, the map scale is 1 cm = 15 km or $\frac{1 \text{ cm}}{15 \text{ km}}$.

Step 2: When the actual distance is 30 km, let the map distance be k.

Step 3: Use equivalent ratios to find the map distance as shown:

$$\frac{1\ cm}{15\ km} = \frac{k}{30\ km} \hspace{3cm} [A]$$

Step 4: Cross multiply equation $[A]$ because **cross products of equivalent ratios are equal** as shown:

$$\frac{1\ cm}{15\ km} \diagdown\diagup \frac{k}{30\ km}$$

$$15\ km \times k = 1\ cm \times 30\ km \hspace{2.5cm} [B]$$

Divide both sides of the equation $[B]$ by 15 km in order to isolate k and also to obtain the value of k as shown:

$$\frac{15\ km \times k}{15\ km} = \frac{1\ cm \times 30\ km}{15\ km}$$

$$\frac{\overset{1}{\cancel{15\ km}} \times k}{\underset{1}{\cancel{15\ km}}} = \frac{1\ cm \times \overset{2}{\cancel{30\ km}}}{\underset{1}{\cancel{15\ km}}}$$

$$k = 1\ cm \times 2$$
$$k = 2\ cm$$

Therefore, when the actual distance = 30 km, the map distance = 2 cm.

To find the actual distance when the map distance is 5 cm.

Step 1: From the table, the map scale is 1 cm = 15 km or $\frac{1\ cm}{15\ km}$.

Step 2: When the map distance is 5 cm, let the actual distance be n.
Step 3: Use equivalent ratios to find the actual distance as shown:

$$\frac{1\ cm}{15\ km} = \frac{5\ cm}{n} \hspace{3cm} [C]$$

Step 4: Cross multiply equation [C] because cross products of equivalent ratios are equal as shown:

$$\frac{1\ cm}{15\ km} \diagdown\diagup \frac{5\ cm}{n}$$

$$1\ cm \times n = 15\ km \times 5\ cm. \hspace{2.5cm} [D]$$

Divide both sides of equation [D] by 1 cm in order to obtain the value for n as shown:

$$\frac{1\ cm \times n}{1\ cm} = \frac{15\ km \times 5\ cm}{1\ cm}$$

$$\frac{1\ \cancel{cm} \times n}{\underset{1}{\cancel{1\ cm}}} = \frac{15\ km \times \overset{5}{\cancel{5\ cm}}}{\underset{1}{\cancel{1\ cm}}}$$

$$n = 15\ km \times 5$$
$$n = 75\ km$$

Therefore, when the map distance is 5 cm, the actual distance is 75 km.

To Find the Map Distance When the Actual Distance is 105 km

Step 1: From the table, the map scale is 1 cm =15 km or $\frac{1\ cm}{15\ km}$.

Step 2: When the map distance is 105 km, let the map distance be w.

Step 3: Use equivalent ratios to find the actual distance as shown:

$$\frac{1\ cm}{15\ km} = \frac{w}{105\ km} \hspace{3cm} [E]$$

Step 4: Cross multiply equation [E] because cross products of equivalent ratios are equal as shown:

$$1\ cm \times 105\ km = 15\ km \times w \hspace{2cm} [F]$$

Divide both sides of equation [F] by 15 km in order to isolate w and also to obtain the value of w as shown:

$$\frac{1\ cm \times 105\ km}{15\ km} = \frac{15\ km \times w}{15\ km}$$

$$\frac{1\ cm \times \overset{7}{\cancel{105\ km}}}{\underset{1}{\cancel{15\ km}}} = \frac{\overset{1}{\cancel{15\ km}} \times w}{\underset{1}{\cancel{15\ km}}}$$

$$1\ cm \times 7 = w$$

$$7 \text{ cm} = w$$

Therefore, when the actual distance is 105 km, the map distance is 7 cm.
Therefore, the completed table is:

Map Distance (cm)	1	2	5	7
Actual distance (km)	15	30	75	105

Example 2

Using the map, an inch ruler, and the map scale, find the distance from Peki to Jawa to the nearest mile. Hint: Assume that the distance between any two cities is a straight line, and therefore, the distance can be measured directly with a ruler to the nearest inch.

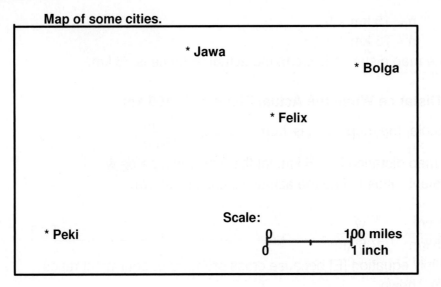

Map of some cities.

* Jawa

* Bolga

* Felix

Scale:

* Peki

0   100 miles
0   1 inch

Solution

Step 1: Read the map scale.

The map shows a scale of 1 inch = 100 miles or $\dfrac{1 \text{ inch}}{100 \text{ miles}}$.

Step 2: Use an inch ruler to measure the distance from Peki to Jawa on the map. The distance from Peki to Jawa on the map is approximately 2 inches to the nearest inch.

Step 3: When the map distance from Peki to Jawa is 2 inches, let the actual distance from Peki to Jawa be n.

Step 4: Use equivalent ratios to find the actual distance as shown:

$$\frac{1 \text{ inch}}{100 \text{ miles}} = \frac{2 \text{ inches}}{n} \hspace{3cm} \text{[A]}$$

Step 5: Cross multiply equation [A] because cross products of equivalent ratios are equal as shown:

$$\begin{array}{c} \underset{\text{100 mi}}{\text{1 in.}} \quad \underset{\text{n}}{\text{2 in.}} \end{array}$$

1 in. × n = 100 miles × 2 in.   [B]

Step 6: Divide both sides of the equation [B] by 1 in. in order to isolate n and also to obtain the value of n as shown:

$$\frac{1 \text{ in.} \times n}{1 \text{ in.}} = \frac{100 \text{ miles} \times 2 \text{ in.}}{1 \text{ in.}}$$

$$\frac{1 \cancel{\text{in.}} \times n}{1 \cancel{\text{in.}}} = \frac{100 \text{ miles} \times 2 \cancel{\text{in.}}}{1 \cancel{\text{in.}}}$$

$$n = 100 \text{ miles} \times 2$$
$$= 200 \text{ miles}$$

Therefore, the distance from Peki to Jawa is 200 miles.

The notes and the generous examples have provided me with the conceptual understanding and the computational fluency to do my homework.

Exercises

1. Explain what is meant by a scale drawing.
2. Explain what is meant by a map scale.
3. Copy and complete each ratio table. Hint: See Example 1.

a.

Scale length (cm)	1	2	?	4
Actual length (km)	4	?	12	?

b.

Scale length (cm)	1	3	4	?
Actual length (km)	20	?	80	100

c.

Scale length (in.)	1	2	?	4
Actual length (ft)	5	?	15	?

4. Using the map in Example 2, find the:
   a. distance from Peki to Bolga.
   b. distance from Jawa to Bolga.
   Hint: See Example 2. The map distance should be to the nearest whole number. Assume that the road between any two cities is straight, and therefore, a ruler could be used to measure the map distance.

Challenge Questions

5. Copy and complete the ratio tables.

6. Explain how to find the actual distance between two cities on a map.

CHAPTER 27

LINES AND ANGLES

New Terms
1. Plane.
2. Parallel lines.
3. Intersecting lines.
4. Perpendicular lines.

Quick Review
1. The unit of measure for an angle is called d——— and the symbol is ^{0} .
2. An angle is formed by two r—— that ——— .
3. A ray is ————————— .
4. A point is ————————— .
5. A line is ————————— .
6. A segment is ————————— .

A **plane** is a continuous flat surface. Three points that are not on a line are used to name a plane such as "plane ABC." The diagram of plane ABC is shown below.

The diagram shows plane ABC.

The arrows in the diagram indicate that **the plane continues in all directions**.

Line Relationships
The three kinds of line relationships are:
(a) **parallel lines**
(b) **intersecting lines**
(c) **perpendicular lines**

Table of line relationships

Line type	Description	Diagram
Parallel lines	Pararallel lines are lines in a plane that never intersect.	Line AB is parallel to line CD.
Intersecting lines	Intersecting lines are lines that cross each other at a point.	Line AB intersects line CD at point E.
Perpendicular lines	Perpendicular lines are lines that intersect at a point to form four right angles.	Line W X is perpendicular to line YZ at point P. ∟ is the symbol for perpendicular lines, 90º or right angle.

Symbols and Concepts
The symbol ∥ means "is parallel to".

Example 1
Use symbols to write that the line AB is parallel to the line CD.
Solution
Line AB is written with a symbol as $\overleftrightarrow{AB}$.

Line CD is written with a symbol as $\overleftrightarrow{CD}$.

The symbol for "is parallel to" is ∥.

Therefore, use symbols to write that line AB is parallel to line CD as shown:

$$\overleftrightarrow{AB} \parallel \overleftrightarrow{CD}$$

Example 2
Use symbols to write that the segment AB is parallel to the segment CD.
Solution
Segment AB is written with a symbol as $\overline{AB}$.

Segment CD is written with a symbol as $\overline{CD}$.

The symbol for "is parallel to" is ∥.

Therefore, to use symbol to write that the segment AB is parallel to the segment CD is as shown:

$$\overline{AB} \parallel \overline{CD}$$

The symbol ⊥ means "is perpendicular to". Note that perpendicular lines form 90^0 angles or right angles.

Example 3
(**a**). Use symbols to write that the segment WX is perpendicular to the segment YZ.
(**b**). Show in two ways how a segment WX can be perpendicular to the segment YZ in a diagram.
(**c**). Use symbols to write that segment PK is perpendicular to a line RC.
   Use symbols to write that segment PK is parallel to a line RC.
   Show in a diagram that segment PK is perpendicular to a line RC.
   Show in a diagram that segment PK is parallel to a line RC.

Solution
(**a**). Segment WX is written with a symbol as $\overline{WX}$.

Segment YZ is written with a symbol as $\overline{YZ}$.
The symbol for "is perpendicular to" is ⊥.
Therefore, to use a symbol to write that the segment WX is perpendicular to the segment YZ is as shown:

$$\overline{WX} \perp \overline{YZ}$$

(b)   (b)

(**c**). Segment PK is written with a symbol as $\overline{PK}$.

Line RC is written with a symbol as $\overleftrightarrow{RC}$.
The symbol for "is perpendicular to" is ⊥.
Therefore, segment PK is perpendicular to the line RC is written with a symbol as shown:

$$\overline{PK} \perp \overleftrightarrow{RC}$$

The symbol for "is parallel to" is ∥.
Therefore, segment PK is parallel to the line RC is written with a symbol as shown:

$$\overline{PK} \parallel \overleftrightarrow{RC}$$

Segment PK is perpendicular
to the line RC.

Segment PK is parallel to the line RC.

Key facts

1. The angle formed by two perpendicular lines or two segments or a line and a segment is a right angle and the measure of a right angle is 90^0.
2. The understanding of two perpendicular segments is very important because it helps us later to understand that the angles of a rectangle or a square are formed by two perpendicular segments and that is why each angle of a rectangle or a square is 90^0.
3. The arrowheads at the ends of the symbol of a line show that the line continues at both directions or that a line is endless.

Critical Geometric Points

The solution to Example **4** is long, but it is designed to provide the students with useful geometric points.

Group Exercise - Example 4

Using a diagram drawn on a square grid paper or a paper, explain the geometric condition for any two lines or any two segments or any line and any segment to be parallel.

Solution

The solution to this question is long, however, the solution is intentionally designed to provide the students with important geometric concepts. (**If Example 4 were to be a class test, the key answer would be just the last paragraph of this solution**).

The class should be divided into four teams, Team A, Team B, Team C and team D.

Each team should use a pencil, $8\frac{1}{2}$ inches ×11 inches square grid paper, and a ruler

to draw figure 1 by using Step **1** to Step **4**.

Figure 1

Step 1: Pick one of the horizontal grid lines on the grid paper and draw the line CD which should be 6 inches long by placing one of the edges of the ruler along the horizontal grid line that you have selected. Mark a point C, which should correspond to the 0 mark on the ruler, and then mark a point D on the same horizontal grid paper which should correspond to the 6 inches marking on the ruler. With the edge of the ruler still on the same horizontal grid line, draw a line through the points C and D.

Step 2: Pick another horizontal grid line which should be about 2 inches from the line CD that you have drawn in Step 1. Place the edge of the ruler on this horizontal grid and mark point A approximately above point C, also mark point B approximately above point D and then draw a line through point A and point B.

Step 3: Pick 3 vertical grid segments and label them EF, KL, and MN such that segment EF should be close to point A and point C, and the segment MN should be close to point B and point D as shown in figure 1. Place one edge of a ruler on point E and point F and draw the segment EF. Place one edge of the ruler on point K and point L and draw the segment KL. Place one of the edges of the ruler on point M and point N and draw the segment MN.

Step 4: Measure segments EF, KL, and MN as shown:

Place the edge of the ruler on segment EF such that point E should be on the 0 mark of the ruler and then read the number of the mark on the ruler that corresponds to point F, and this number is the length of segment EF. Record the length of the segment EF.

Place the edge of the ruler on segment KL such that point K should be on the 0 mark of the ruler, and then read the number of the mark on the ruler that corresponds to point L. This number is the length of segment KL. Record the length of the segment KL. Place the edge of the ruler on segment MN such that point M should be on the 0 mark of the ruler, and then read the number of the mark on the ruler that corresponds to point N. This number is the length of segment MN. Record the length of the segment MN.

Step 5: Analysis and conclusion

(a). From the measurements of the segment EF, segment KL, and segment MN, it should be found that:

length of segment EF = length of segment KL = length of segment MN

(b). Line AB or segment AB is parallel to line CD or segment CD because horizontal grid lines are parallel. Note that line AB can become segment AB without the two

628

arrowheads at the ends of the diagram of the line AB.

(c). The segments EF, KL, and MN form 90⁰ angle with the lines AB and CD because the horizontal grid lines and the vertical grid lines form 90⁰ and therefore the segments EF, KL, and MN are called the **perpendicular distances** between lines AB and CD.

The geometric condition for any two lines or any two segments or any line and any segment to be parallel is that the **perpendicular distance** at any point between the two lines or the two segments or the line and the segment must be the same. Also, recall that in the "table of line relationships," parallel lines are described as "lines in a plane that never intersect."

Group Exercise

Bricklayers use the idea of parallel lines to lay bricks when they are building brick walls as shown in the picture.

The class should be divided into four groups. Each group should write about how the idea of parallel lines are used to:

1. make roads
2. make the floor of stairways
3. make your math textbook.

The notes and the generous examples have provided me with the conceptual understanding and the computational fluency to do my homework.

Exercises

1. What symbol means "is parallel to?"

2. A right angle has the same angle measure as a 90⁰ angle. True or false?

3. A plane is a cont_____ flat surf_____. Complete the statement.

4. Select the correct answer. How many points are used to name a plane?
   Answer: (a) 1   (b) 4   (c) 3

5. What symbol means "is perpendicular to?"

6. The arrowheads at the ends of a line indicate that the line is endl_____

7. What are parallel lines?

8. What are intersecting lines?

9. What are perpendicular lines?

10. Use symbols to write that line WX is parallel to line YZ. Hint: See Example **1**.

11. Use symbols to write that segment AD is parallel to segment EF. Hint: See
    Example **2**.

12. Use symbols to write that segment PK is perpendicular to segment LM.
    Hint: See Example **3**.

13. Use symbols to write that segment GK is parallel to line AB.
    Hint: See Example **3**.

Challenge Questions

14. What is meant by the perpendicular distance of a segment?

15. What is the geometric condition for two segments to be parallel?

Group Exercises

1. The class should be divided into four teams and each team should draw the following
   diagrams and write all the segments that appear to be parallel using the symbol ∥
   and also write all the segments that appear to be perpendicular using the symbol ⊥.
   Explain why the segment KH and the segment JI appear not to be parallel.

2. Each team should classify the following angles as acute, obtuse, or right angle.
   Explain your answer.

   (a) ∠AFE   **(b)** ∠AFG   **(c)** ∠ HAL   **(d)** ∠HAB

   (e) ∠ABE   **(f)** ∠IBA   **(g)** ∠BED   **(h)** ∠FEJ

   (i) Explain why $\overline{FA}$ does not appear to be parallel to $\overline{EB}$.

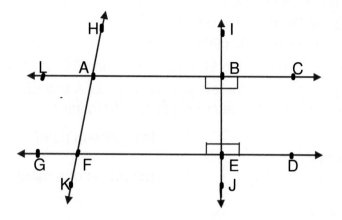

Solutions to the "Group Exercises."

The solution to the "Group exercises" is provided so as to provide the students with more understanding of the problem solving methods.

1. (a) $\overline{AB} \parallel \overline{DC}$, $\overline{AD} \parallel \overline{BC}$

There are no perpendicular segments because none of the angles are 90^0.

(b) $\overline{DE} \parallel \overline{GF}$, $\overline{DG} \parallel \overline{EF}$

$\overline{DE} \perp \overline{EF}$ because $\overline{DE}$ forms 90^0 angle with $\overline{EF}$.

$\overline{EF} \perp \overline{FG}$ because $\overline{EF}$ forms 90^0 angle with $\overline{FG}$.

$\overline{FG} \perp \overline{GD}$ because $\overline{FG}$ forms 90^0 angle with $\overline{GD}$.

$\overline{GD} \perp \overline{DE}$ because $\overline{GD}$ forms 90^0 angle with $\overline{DE}$.

(c) $\overline{HI} \parallel \overline{KJ}$, $\overline{KH}$ does not appear to be parallel to $\overline{JI}$ because $\overline{KH}$ and $\overline{JI}$ do not appear to be going in the same direction, and therefore, if we extend $\overline{KH}$ and $\overline{JI}$, they will intersect at a point, but parallel lines are not supposed to intersect as explain with a diagram as shown:

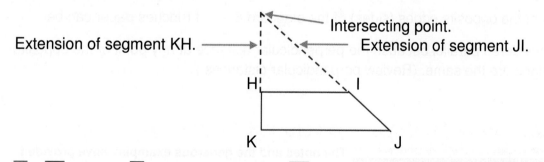

$\overline{IH} \perp \overline{HK}$ because $\overline{IH}$ forms 90^0 angle with $\overline{HK}$.

$\overline{HK} \perp \overline{KJ}$ because $\overline{HK}$ forms 90^0 angle with $\overline{KJ}$.

2. (a) $\angle AFE$ is an acute angle because it is less than 90^0.

(b) $\angle AFG$ is an obtuse angle because it is greater than 90^0.

(c) $\angle HAL$ is an obtuse angle because it is greater than 90^0.

(d) $\angle HAB$ is an acute angle because it is less than 90^0.

(e) $\angle ABE$ is a right angle because it is 90^0.

(f) ∠IBA is a right angle because it is 90⁰.

(g) ∠BED is a right angle because it is 90⁰.

(h) ∠FEJ is a right angle because it is 90⁰.

(i) $\overline{FA}$ does not appear to be parallel to $\overline{EB}$ because $\overline{FA}$ and $\overline{EB}$ do not appear to be going in the same direction, and therefore, if we extend $\overline{FA}$ and $\overline{EB}$, they will intersect at a point, but parallel lines are not supposed to intersect as shown:

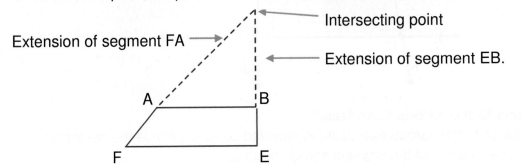

Example 1

What is the difference between parallel lines and perpendicular lines?

Solution

Parallel lines will never intersect or meet each other, but perpendicular lines intersect or meet each other at a point.

Example 2

Can the opposite edges (sides) of the standard $8\frac{1}{2}$ × 11 inches paper be considered parallel? Explain your answer.

Solution

Yes, the opposite edges (sides) of the standard $8\frac{1}{2}$ × 11 inches paper can be considered parallel because the perpendicular distance at any point of the opposite edges are the same. (Review perpendicular distances.)

The notes and the generous examples have provided me with the conceptual understanding and the computational fluency to do my homework.

Exercises

1. Draw (a) parallel lines AB and XY, (b) intersecting lines PQ and KL, and (c) perpendicular lines JK and XY.

2.

Using the diagram, name two examples of each term or statement.
Hint: Review this chapter.

(**a**) plane   (**b**) perpendicular lines   (**c**) Intersecting lines
(**d**) right angles   (**e**) parallel lines   (**f**) line segments
(**g**) rays   (**h**) acute angles   (**i**) obtuse angles
(**j**) points   (**k**) straight angles   (**l**) intersecting point.

Sum of the Measure of the Angles on a Straight Line

A straight angle measures 180^0 and this means that the sum of the measure of the angles on a straight line is 180^0 as shown below.

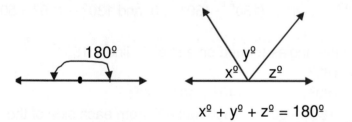

$$x^0 + y^0 + z^0 = 180^0 \qquad n^0 + m^0 = 180^0$$

Example 1

Find the value of the angle measure of x^0 in the diagram.

Solution

The sum of the measure of the angles on a straight line $= 180^0$.
Therefore, $x^0 + 75 = 180^0$

$\qquad x^0 + 75^0 - 75^0 = 180^0 - 75^0$ (Subtract 75^0 from each side of the equation
$\qquad\qquad\qquad\qquad\qquad\qquad\qquad$ in order to eliminate 75^0 from the left side

of the equation.)

$$x^0 + 0 = 105^0$$
$$x^0 = 105^0$$

Example 2

Find the value of x^0 in the diagrams.

(a)   (b)

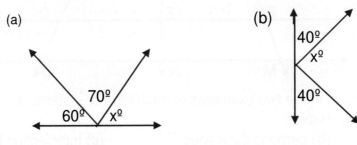

Solution

(**a**) The sum of the measure of the angles formed on a straight line = 180^0.

Therefore, $60^0 + 70^0 + x^0 = 180^0$

$$130^0 + x^0 = 180^0 \qquad (70^0 + 60^0 = 130^0)$$
$$x^0 + 130^0 - 130^0 = 180^0 - 130^0 \qquad \text{(Subtract } 130^0 \text{ from each side of the}$$
equation in order to eliminate the 130^0
from the left side of the equation.)

$$x^0 + 130^0 - 130^0 = 180^0 - 130^0$$
$$x^0 + 0 \qquad\qquad = 50^0 \qquad (130^0 - 130^0 = 0, \text{ and } 180^0 - 130^0 = 50^0)$$
$$x^0 = 50^0$$

(**b**) The sum of the measure of the angles formed on a straight line = 180^0.

Therefore, $40^0 + x^0 + 40^0 = 180^0$

$$x^0 + 80^0 = 180^0 \qquad (40^0 + 40^0 = 80^0)$$
$$x^0 + 80^0 - 80^0 = 180^0 - 80^0 \qquad \text{(Subtract } 80^0 \text{ from each side of the}$$
equation in order to eliminate the 80^0
at the left side of the equation.)

$$x^0 + 80^0 - 80^0 = 180^0 - 80^0$$
$$x^0 + 0 \qquad\qquad = 100^0 \qquad (80^0 - 80^0 = 0, \text{ and } 180^0 - 80^0 = 100^0)$$
$$x^0 \qquad\qquad = 100^0$$

Example 3

Find the value of x^0 in the diagram.

634

Solution

Consider the diagram as angles formed on a straight line but the diagram is inverted
The sum of the measure of the angles on a straight line = 180^0.

Therefore, $20^0 + x^0 + x^0 + 2x^0 = 180^0$

$$20^0 + 4x^0 \qquad\qquad = 180^0 \qquad (x^0 + x^0\ 2x^0 = 4x^0)$$

$$20^0 - 20^0 + 4x^0\ = 180^0 - 20^0 \qquad \text{(Subtract } 20^0 \text{ from each side of the}$$
equation in order to eliminate 20^0
from the left side of the equation.)

$$20^0 - 20^0 + 4x^0 = 160^0 \qquad\qquad (180^0 - 20^0 = 160^0)$$

$$0 + 4x^0 = 160^0 \qquad\qquad (20^0 - 20^0 = 0)$$

$$4x^0 = 160^0 \ \text{————————————} [A]$$

Divide each side of equation $[A]$ by 4 in order to obtain the value of x^0 as shown:

$$\frac{4x^0}{4} = \frac{160^0}{4}$$

$$\frac{\overset{x^0}{\cancel{4x^0}}}{\underset{1}{4}} = \frac{\overset{40^0}{\cancel{160^0}}}{\underset{1}{4}}$$

$$x^0 = 40^0$$

Example 4

Find the value of x^0

Solution

The sum of the measure of the angles on a straight line is = 180^0.

Therefore, $3x^0 + x^0 + x^0 = 180^0$

$$5x^0 = 180^0 \qquad\qquad (3x^0 + x^0 + x^0 = 5x^0).$$

$$5x^0 = 180^0 \ \text{————————————} [B]$$

Divide each side of equation $[B]$ by 5 in order to obtain the value of x^0 as shown:

$$\frac{5x^0}{5} = \frac{180^0}{5}$$

$$x^0 \qquad 36^0$$

$$\frac{5x^0}{5} = \frac{180^0}{5}$$

$$1 \qquad 1$$

$$x^0 = 36^0$$

▰▰▰▰▰▰▰ **The notes and the generous examples have provided me with the conceptual understanding and the computational fluency to do my homework.**

Exercises

1. Find the value of x^0 in the following diagrams Hint: See Example **1**.

(a)   (b)   ©

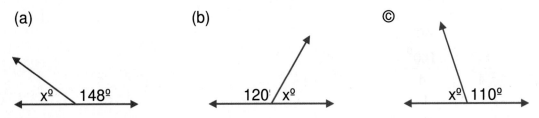

2. Find the value of x^0 in the following diagrams. Hint: See Example **2**.

(a)   (b)   ©

3. Find the value of x^0 in the diagrams. Hint: See Example **3**.

(a)   (b)   ©

(d)   (e)   (f)

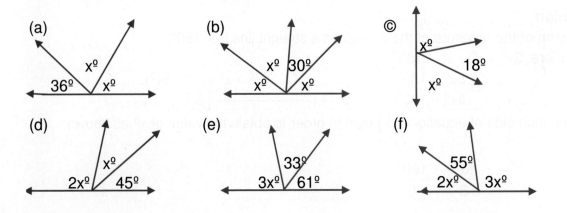

4. Find the value of x^0 in the diagrams. Hint: See Example 4.

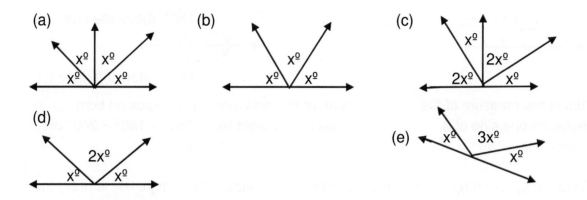

(a)

(b)

(c)

(d)

(e)

Challenge Questions

5. Find the value of x and the measure of the angle ABC in the diagrams. Hint: Note that the measure of the angle ABC is a multiple of x.

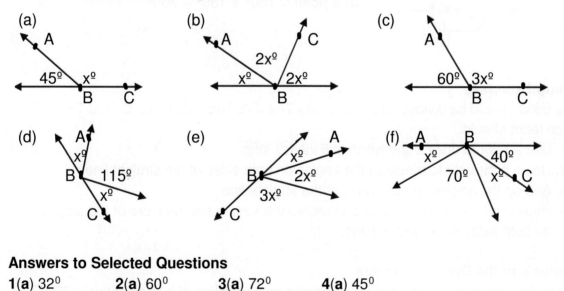

(a)

(b)

(c)

(d)

(e)

(f)

Answers to Selected Questions
1(a) 32^0 **2(a)** 60^0 **3(a)** 72^0 **4(a)** 45^0

Sum of the Measure of the Angles at a Point
Recall that a straight angle measures 180^0 and this means that the sum of the angles on a straight line is 180^0. When we say that a straight angle measures 180^0, we only consider one side of the straight line. If we consider both sides of the straight line, we can say that the sum of the angle measures on both sides of a straight line.

$$= 2 \times 180^0$$
$$= 360^0$$

One side of the straight line.

180º

Sum of the measure of the angles on one side of a straight line = 180⁰.

180º above the line

180º below the line.

Sum of the measure of the angles on both sides of a straight line = 180⁰ + 180⁰ = 360⁰ or 2 × 180⁰ = 360⁰.

Since the sum of the measure of the angles on both sides of a straight line is really the same as the sum of the angles at a point, we can conclude that the sum of the angles at a point = 360⁰ as shown:

180º

Sum of the measure of the angles at a point = 180º + 180º = 360º

180º

Group Exercises

The class should be divided into four teams, Team A, Team B, Team C, and Team D. Each team should:

1. Use a ruler to draw a line which is 6 inches long.
2. Use a protractor to measure the angles on both sides of the straight line.
3. Add up the angles on both sides of the straight line.
4. Repeat this project five times and record the sum of the measure of the angles on both sides of the straight line.

Analysis of the Group Exercises

1. Are the sum of the measures of the angles on both sides of a straight line = 360⁰?
2. Can we conclude that the sum of the measures of the angles at a point = 360⁰.

Let us examine the following examples to see what types of questions could be asked regarding the sum of angles at a point and how they can be solved.

Example 1

Find the value of x^0 in the diagram.

(a) (b)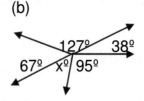

Solution

(a) The sum of the measure of the angles at a point $= 360^0$.

Therefore,

$$x^0 + 65^0 + 130^0 + 110^0 = 360^0$$
$$x^0 + 305^0 = 360^0 \qquad (65^0 + 130^0 + 110^0 = 305^0)$$
$$x^0 + 305^0 - 305^0 = 360^0 - 305^0 \qquad \text{(Subtract } 305^0 \text{ from each side of}$$
the equation in order to eliminate
the 305^0 at the left side of the
equation.)
$$x^0 + 0 = 55^0 \qquad (305^0 - 305^0 = 0, \text{ and } 360^0 - 305^0 = 55^0)$$
$$x^0 = 55^0$$

(b) The sum of the measure of the angles at a point $= 360^0$.

Therefore,

$$x^0 + 67^0 + 127^0 + 38^0 + 95^0 = 360^0$$
$$x^0 + 327^0 = 360^0 \qquad (67^0 + 127^0 + 38^0 + 95^0 = 327^0)$$
$$x^0 + 327^0 - 327^0 = 360^0 - 327^0 \qquad \text{(Subtract } 327^0 \text{ from each side of}$$
the equation in order to eliminate
the 327^0 at the left side of the
equation.)
$$x^0 + 0 = 33^0 \qquad (327^0 - 327^0 = 0, \text{ and } 360^0 - 325^0 = 33^0)$$
$$x^0 = 33^0$$

Example 2

Find the angle measure for x^0 in the diagrams. Find the measure of $\angle ABC$. The angles are formed at point B which is not shown in the diagram.

(a)   (b)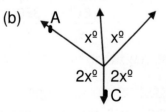

Solution

(a) The sum of the measure of the angles at a point $= 360^0$

Therefore,

$$x^0 + 110^0 + 3x^0 + 30^0 + 80^0 = 360^0$$
$$x^0 + 3x^0 + 110^0 + 30^0 + 80^0 = 360^0 \qquad \text{(Group all the } x^0 \text{ together.)}$$
$$4x^0 + 220^0 = 360^0 \qquad (x^0 + 3x^0 = 4x^0, 110^0 + 30^0 + 80^0 = 220^0)$$

$$4x^0 + 220^0 - 220^0 = 360^0 - 220^0$$

(Subtract 220^0 from each side of the equation in order to eliminate the 220^0 at the left side of the equation.)

$$4x^0 + 0 = 140^0$$

$$(220^0 - 220^0 = 0 , 360^0 - 220^0 = 140^0)$$

$$4x^0 = 140^0 \text{ ————————————— } [A]$$

Divide each side of the equation $[A]$ by 4 in order to obtain the value of x^0 as shown:

$$\frac{4x^0}{4} = \frac{140}{4}$$

$$\frac{\overset{x^0}{\cancel{4x^0}}}{\underset{1}{\cancel{4}}} = \frac{\overset{35^0}{\cancel{140}}}{\underset{1}{\cancel{4}}}$$

$$x^0 = 35^0$$

$\angle ABC = 3x^0$, so, the measure of
$\angle ABC = 3 \times 35^0 = 105^0$

(b) The sum of the measure of the angles at a point $= 360^0$.

Therefore,

$$x^0 + x^0 + 2x^0 + 2x^0 = 360^0$$
$$6x^0 = 360^0$$

$$(x^0 + x^0 + 2x^0 + 2x^0 = 6x^0)$$

$$6x^0 = 360^0 \text{ ——————————— } [B]$$

Divide each side of equation $[B]$ by 6 in order to obtain the value of x^0 as shown:

$$\frac{6x^0}{6} = \frac{360^0}{6}$$

$$\frac{\overset{x^0}{\cancel{6x^0}}}{\underset{1}{\cancel{6}}} = \frac{\overset{60^0}{\cancel{360}}}{\underset{1}{\cancel{6}}}$$

$$x = 60^0$$

$\angle ABC = 2x^0$, therefore, the measure of
$\angle ABC = 2 \times 60^0 = 120^0$.

The notes and the generous examples have provided me with the conceptual understanding and the computational fluency to do my homework.

Exercises

1. What is the sum of the measures of the angles formed at a point?

2. Find the value of x^0 in the diagram. Hint: See Example 1.

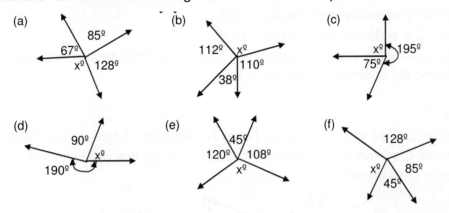

(a)
85º
67º
x^0 128º

(b)
112º x^0
110º
38º

(c)
x^0 195º
75º

(d)
90º
x^0
190º

(e)
45º
120º 108º
x^0

(f)
128º
x^0 85º
45º

3. Find the angle measure for x^0 in the diagrams. Find the measure of $\angle ABC$ given that B is the point where the angles are formed. Hint: See Example 2.

(a)
A 2x⁰ C
x^0
108º
93º

(b)
37º
2x⁰ 63º
2x⁰
A C

(c)
C
A 3x⁰ 2x⁰
2x⁰ 2x⁰

Challenge Questions

4. Find the angle measure for x^0 in the diagrams.

(a)
3x⁰ x^0
2x⁰

(b)
x^0 x^0
x^0
x^0
x^0 x^0

(c)
x^0
x^0 2x⁰
2x⁰ x^0
x^0

Answers to Selected Questions

2(a) 80^0 **2(d)** 80^0 **2(f)** 102^0 **3(c)** $x^0 = 45^0$, $\angle ABC = 135^0$

VERTICAL ANGLES

New Terms: **vertical angle**
Vertical angles are formed when two lines intersect as shown:

In the figure, ∠AOD is vertically opposite to ∠COB
∠AOC is vertically opposite to ∠DOB
The measure of the vertically opposite angles are congruent. This means that the measure of the vertically opposite angles are equal.

Group Exercise
The class should be divided into four teams, Team A , Team B , Team C, and Team D.
1. Each team should draw two intersecting lines AB and CD so that the two lines intersect at point O as shown:

2. Each team should put the center of a protractor at the intersection point, which is O, and measure ∠AOD and ∠COB. Is the measure of ∠AOD the same as the measure of ∠COB? Can we say that the measures of the opposite angles are equal?
3. With the center of the protractor at the intersecting point , which is O again, measure ∠AOC and ∠DOB. Is the measure of ∠AOC and ∠DOB the same? Can we say that the opposite angles are equal?

Example 1
Find the value of x^0 in each figure.

Solution
(a) ∠AOD is vertically opposite to ∠COB, and therefore, the measures of their angles are congruent. Therefore,

642

$$m\angle AOD = m\angle COB$$
$$\text{Therefore, } 40^0 = x^0 \qquad (m\angle AOD = 40^0, \text{ and } m\angle COB = x^0)$$

(b) $\angle AOD$ is vertically opposite to $\angle BOC$ and therefore, the measure of their angles are congruent. Therefore,
$$m\angle AOD = m\angle BOC$$
$$\text{Therefore, } 30^0 = x^0 \qquad (m\angle AOD = 30^0, \text{ and } m\angle BOC = x^0)$$

Example 2

Find the value of x^0 in each of the figure.

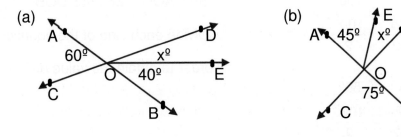

(a)

(b)

Solution

(a) $\angle AOC$ is vertically opposite to $\angle DOB$

Since vertically opposite angles are congruent,

$$m\angle AOC = m\angle DOB$$
$$60^0 = x^0 + 40^0 \qquad (m\angle AOC = 60^0, \text{ and } m\angle DOB = x^0 + 40^0)$$
$$60^0 - 40^0 = x^0 + 40^0 - 40^0 \qquad \text{(Subtract } 40^0 \text{ from each side of the equation in order to obtain the value of } x^0.)$$
$$20^0 = x^0 + 0 \qquad (60^0 - 40^0 = 20^0, \text{ and } 40^0 - 40^0 = 0)$$
$$20^0 = x^0$$

(b) $\angle AOD$ is vertically opposite to $\angle COB$.

Since vertically opposite angles are congruent,

$$m\angle AOD = m\angle COB$$
$$45^0 + x^0 = 75^0 \qquad (m\angle AOD = 45^0 + x^0, \text{ and } m\angle COB = 75^0)$$
$$45^0 - 45^0 + x^0 = 75^0 - 45^0 \qquad \text{(Subtract } 45^0 \text{ from each side of the equation in order to obtain the value of } x^0.)$$
$$0 + x^0 = 30^0 \qquad (45^0 - 45^0 = 0^0, \text{ and } 75^0 - 45^0 = 30^0)$$
$$x^0 = 30^0$$

Example 3

Find the value of x^0 in each figure.

Solution

(a) ∠AOC is vertically opposite to ∠DOB.

Since vertically opposite angles are congruent,

m∠AOC = m∠DOB

Therefore, $2x^0 = 100^0$ (m∠AOC = $2x^0$, m∠DOB = 100^0)

$$\frac{2x}{2} = \frac{100^0}{2}$$ Divide each side of the equation by 2 in

order to obtain the value of x^0.)

$$\frac{\overset{x^0}{\cancel{2x}}}{\underset{1}{2}} = \frac{\overset{50^0}{\cancel{100^0}}}{\underset{1}{2}}$$

$$x^0 = 50^0$$

(b) ∠AOD is vertically opposite to ∠COB.

Since vertically opposite angles are congruent,

m∠AOD = m∠COB

Therefore, $54^0 = 3x^0$ (m∠AOD = 54^0, m∠COB = $3x^0$).

$$\frac{54^0}{3} = \frac{3x^0}{3}$$ (Divide each side of the equation by 3 in

order to obtain the value of x^0.)

$$\frac{\overset{18^0}{\cancel{54^0}}}{\underset{1}{3}} = \frac{\overset{x^0}{\cancel{3x^0}}}{\underset{1}{3}}$$

$$18^0 = x^0$$

The notes and the generous examples have provided me with the conceptual understanding and the computational fluency to do my homework.

Exercises

1. Vertically opposite angles are —————————.

2. The measure of the vertically opposite angles are ————————.

3. Find the value of x^0 in each figure. Hint: See Example **1**.

(a) x^0 58°

(b) 27° x^0

© 10° x^0

4. Find the value of x^0 in each figure. Hint: See Example **2**.

(a)   A   E   D 85° x^0 O 110° C   B

(b)   A   D 60° O 84° E x^0 C   B

5. Find the value of x^0 in each figure. Hint: See Example **3**.

(a)   A   D $2x^0$ O 64° B   C

(b)   A   D   O 81° $3x^0$ C   B

Challenge Questions

6. List all the vertically opposite angles in each figure.

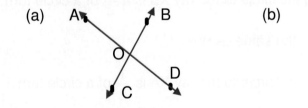

(a)   A   B   O   D   C

(b)   X   Y   O   W   Z

7. Find the value of x^0 in each figure, given that the lines join at point O.

(a)   P   Z x^0 W 110° 140° X   Y

(b)   A   C   W 47° 60° x^0 D   B

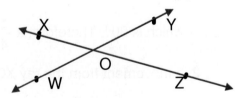

Draw each of the following diagrams.

1. Two parallel lines | **2**. A right angle | **3**. A segment
4. An isosceles triangle | **5**. Two perpendicular lines | **6**. A point
7. An acute angle | **8**. An obtuse angle | **9**. A ray
10. 180^0 angle | **11**. An equilateral triangle | **12**. A line

ASSOCIATE AN ANGLE WITH A CERTAIN AMOUNT OF TURNING

How to find $\frac{1}{4}, \frac{1}{2}, \frac{3}{4}$, and full turns

Recall that an angle is formed by the intersection of two rays and that a ray is a line that has a beginning point but no an end point. **Angular measure** is obtained by dividing a circle into 360 equal parts and each part is called **one degree**.

If a circle is divided into two halves, then each half contains $\frac{360^0}{2} = 180^0$ as shown in figure 1. Figure 1 shows that the angular measure of a straight angle or a straight line is 180^0. Figure 2 shows that if the circle is divided into four equal parts, then each part will contain 90°. Assume that the line AC intersects the line BD at the point X in figure 2 (X is not shown in the diagram), then:

1. a movement from the ray XC along the circle to the ray XB is a $\frac{1}{4}$ of a circle turn which is 90°. Therefore, a $\frac{1}{4}$ turn is the same as 90°.

2. a movement from the ray XC along the circle to the ray XA is $\frac{1}{2}$ of a circle turn which is 180°. Therefore, $\frac{1}{2}$ turn is the same as 90° + 90° which is 180°.

3. a movement from the ray XC along the circle in anti-clockwise direction to the ray XD is $\frac{3}{4}$ of a circle turn, which is 90° + 90° + 90° which is 270°. Therefore, $\frac{3}{4}$ turn is the same as 270°.

4. a movement from the ray XC along the circle in the anti-clockwise direction to the ray XC again is a full circle turn which is 90° + 90° + 90° + 90° which is 360°. Therefore, a full turn is the same as 360°

Figure 1   **Figure 2.**

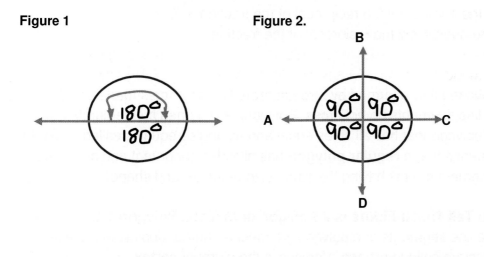

━━━━━━━━━━━━━━ The notes and the generous examples have provided me with the conceptual understanding and the computational fluency to do my homework.

Exercises

1. A full turn is 360^0. How many degrees is a half turn?
2. A quarter turn is $90°$. How many turns is 270^0?
3. Which is greater, $\frac{3}{4}$ turn or full turn? Explain your answer.

CHAPTER 28

POLYGONS AND ANGLES

Quick Review

1. What is the difference between a ray and a line?
2. What is the difference between a segment and a ray?
3. Solve: (a) $\frac{2}{3} \div \frac{1}{2}$ (b) $\frac{3}{4} \times \frac{2}{3}$ (c) $\frac{4}{7} + \frac{5}{14}$ (d) 25% of 120

4. Find the reciprocal of: (a) $\frac{3}{4}$ (b) 2   (c) 1

5. Find n in the equations;

  (a) $\frac{n}{3} = \frac{6}{9}$ (b) $\frac{3}{5} = \frac{6}{n}$ (c) $4n = 24$

6. What is the difference between a right angle and a 90^0 angle?
7. What is the difference between an obtuse angle and an acute angle?
8. Choose the correct answer. In order to divide a number by a fraction,

(**a**) multiply the number by the reciprocal of the fraction.

(**b**) divide the number by the reciprocal of the fraction.

Polygons

A **polygon** is a closed figure formed by three or more line segments made on a flat surface and the line segments do not cross. Polygons are named by the number of their sides. Any polygon that has all sides equal and all angles equal is called a **regular polygon**. This means that a **regular polygon** has all sides congruent and all angles **congruent**. Congruent means having the same size or length and shape.

How Could You Tell That a Figure is a Polygon or is Not a Polygon?

The sides or the line segments of a polygon intersect at their endpoints and these intersection points are called **vertices**. Vertices is the plural of **vertex**.

(**a**). For example, the triangle in (a) shows a closed figure or the sides of the figure intersect at their endpoints and the sides of the figure is made up of line segments, and therefore, the triangle in (a) is a polygon.

(**b**). The figure in (b) shows a figure that is not closed and that means that all the sides of the figure do not intersect at their endpoints, and therefore, the figure in (b) is not a polygon.

(**c**). The figure in (c) is not a polygon because although the figure is a closed figure, a part of the figure is formed by a curve or an arc instead of line segments.

(**d**). The figure in (d) is not a polygon because the line segments of a polygon intersect only at the endpoints. Also, the description of the polygon states that the segments of the polygon do not cross but the figure (d) shows that two segments cross.

The Sum of the Interior Angles of a Polygon

The formula for finding the sum of the interior angles of a polygon is:

$$(n - 2) \times 180^0 \text{ where n is the number of sides of the polygon.}$$

Some examples of polygons are listed in Figure 1.

Figure 1

Regular polygons	Polygons that are not regular	Name	Number of sides	Sum of the interior angles =(n - 2) × 180º
		Triangle	3	(3 - 2) × 180º = 180º
		Quadrilateral	4	(4 - 2) × 180º = 360º
		Pentagon	5	(5 - 2) × 180º = 540º
		Hexagon	6	(6 - 2) × 180º = 720º
?		Heptagon	7	(7 - 2) × 180º = 900º
	?	Octagon	8	(8 - 2) × 180º = 1080º
?	?	Nonagon	9	(9 - 2) × 180º = 1260º
?	?	Decagon	10	(10 - 2) × 180º = 1440º

Group Exercises

1. The class should be divided into four teams, Team A, Team B, Team C, and team D.

2. Each team should use the model of the other regular polygons in figure 1 to sketch regular heptagon, nonagon, and decagon. Hint: Do not use a ruler to measure the lengths of the sides of the polygons, but you should draw each length of the sides of the polygon to be approximately equal visually. If you could draw the sides of the polygons to be approximately equal visually, then each angle of the polygon will appear to be approximately equal visually.

3. Each team should use the model of the other polygons that are not regular in Figure 1 to sketch irregular octagon, nonagon, and decagon.
4. List the problems you have in sketching the polygons.
5. Could your sketches replace the missing polygons in Figure 1?

Sum of the Measures of the Angles in a Triangles
Group Exercise

It is possible to show that the sum of the angles in a triangle appear to be the same as the sum of the angles on a straight line or a straight angle which is 180^0 by using the following steps:

Step 1: Draw a straight line AB and with a protractor measure the straight angle which should be 180^0 as shown.

Step 2: Draw an equilateral triangle XYZ with sides 3 inches and angles 60^0 as shown:

(**a**) With a pencil and a ruler, draw a line segment XY which is 3 inches long.

(**b**) Place the center of the protractor on the endpoint X, measure and draw the 60^0 angle as shown. Hint: See the chapter/section on how to use a protractor to draw angles.

(**c**) Place the center of the protractor at the endpoint Y and measure and draw 120^0. Label the endpoint where the line from endpoint Y intersects the line segment from the endpoint X as Z.

650

Sum of the Measures of the Angles of a Quadrilateral

We can use the sum of the measures of the angles of a quadrilateral $= 360^0$ to solve many problems.

Example 1

Find the angle measure of x^0.

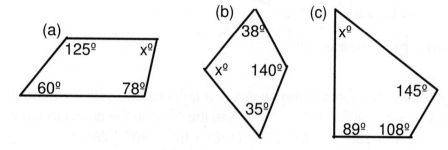

(a)

125º x⁰

60º 78º

(b)

38º

x⁰ 140º

35º

(c)

x⁰

145º

89º 108º

Solution

(a) The sum of the measures of the angles of a quadrilateral $= 360^0$, therefore,

$$x^0 + 78^0 + 60^0 + 125^0 = 360^0$$
$$x^0 + 263^0 = 360^0 \qquad (78^0 + 60^0 + 125^0 = 263^0)$$
$$x^0 + 263^0 - 263^0 = 360^0 - 263 \qquad \text{(Subtract } 263^0 \text{ from each side of the equation in order to obtain the value of } x^0.)$$
$$x^0 + 0 = 97^0 \qquad (263^0 - 263^0 = 0^0, \text{ and } 360^0 - 263^0 = 97^0)$$
$$x^0 = 97^0$$

(b) The sum of the measures of the angles of a quadrilateral $= 360^0$, therefore,

$$x^0 + 38^0 + 140^0 + 35^0 = 360^0$$
$$x^0 + 213 = 360^0 \qquad (38^0 + 140^0 + 35^0 = 213^0)$$
$$x^0 + 213^0 - 213^0 = 360^0 - 213^0 \qquad \text{(Subtract } 213^0 \text{ from each side of the equation in order to obtain the value of } x^0.)$$
$$x^0 + 0 = 147^0 \qquad (213^0 - 213^0 = 0 \text{ and } 360^0 - 213^0 = 147^0)$$
$$x^0 = 147^0$$

(c) The sum of the measures of the angles of a quadrilateral $= 360^0$, therefore,

$$x^0 + 145^0 + 108^0 + 89^0 = 360^0$$
$$x^0 + 342^0 = 360^0 \qquad (145^0 + 108^0 + 89^0 = 342^0)$$
$$x^0 + 342^0 - 342^0 = 360^0 - 342^0 \qquad \text{(Subtract } 342^0 \text{ from each side of the equation in order to obtain the value of } x^0.)$$
$$x^0 + 0 = 18^0 \qquad (342^0 - 342^0 = 0^0, \text{ and } 360^0 - 342^0 = 18)$$
$$x^0 = 18^0$$

Example 2

Find the value of x^0.

(a) x^0 128^0 62^0

(b) 60^0 x^0

(c) x^0 45^0

Hint: ⌐ means 90^0

Solution

(**a**) The sum of the measures of the angles of a quadrilateral $= 360^0$, therefore,

$$x^0 + 128^0 + 62^0 + 90^0 = 360^0 \qquad \text{(See the "hint" in the question regarding } 90^0.)$$
$$x^0 + 280^0 = 360^0 \qquad (128^0 + 62^0 + 90^0 = 280^0)$$
$$x^0 + 280^0 - 280^0 = 360^0 - 280^0 \quad \text{(Subtract } 280^0 \text{ from each side of the}$$
equation in order to obtain the value of x^0.)
$$x^0 + 0 = 80^0 \qquad (280^0 - 280^0 = 0, \text{ and } 360^0 - 280^0 = 80^0)$$
$$x^0 = 80^0$$

(**b**) The sum of the measures of the angles of a quadrilateral $= 360^0$, therefore,

$$x^0 + 60^0 + 90^0 + 90^0 = 360^0 \qquad \text{(See the "hint" in the question regarding } 90^0.)$$
$$x^0 + 240^0 = 360^0 \qquad (60^0 + 90^0 + 90^0 = 240^0)$$
$$x^0 + 240^0 - 240^0 = 360^0 - 240^0 \quad \text{(Subtract } 240^0 \text{ from each side of the}$$
equation in order to obtain the value
of x^0.)
$$x^0 + 0 = 120^0 \qquad (240^0 - 240^0 = 0, \text{ and } 360^0 - 240^0 = 120^0)$$
$$x^0 = 120^0$$

(**c**) The sum of the measures of the angles of a quadrilateral $= 360^0$, so that,

$$x^0 + 90^0 + 90^0 + 45^0 = 360^0 \qquad \text{(See the "hint" in the question regarding } 90^0.)$$
$$x^0 + 225^0 = 360^0 \qquad (90^0 + 90^0 + 45^0 = 225^0)$$
$$x^0 + 225^0 - 225^0 = 360^0 - 225^0 \quad \text{(Subtract } 225^0 \text{ from each side of the}$$
equation in order to obtain the value of x^0.)
$$x^0 + 0 = 135^0 \qquad (225^0 - 225^0 = 0^0, \text{ and } 360^0 - 225^0 = 135^0)$$
$$x^0 = 135^0$$

═══════════════ The notes and the generous examples have provided
me with the conceptual understanding and the
computational fluency to do my homework.

Exercises

1. Find the value of x^0. Hint: See Example **1**.

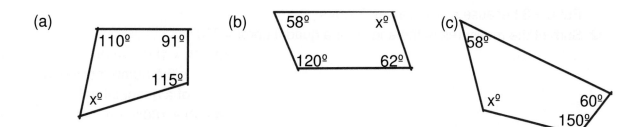

(a) 110° 91° 115° x°

(b) 58° x° 120° 62°

(c) 58° x° 60° 150°

2. Find the value of x^0. Hint: See Example **2**.

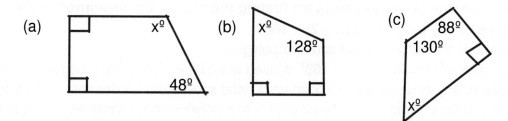

(a) x° 48°

(b) x° 128°

(c) 88° 130° x°

Challenge Questions
3. Find the value of x^0.

(a) x°

(b) x° 120° 109°

(c) 93° 112° x° 85°

Review
1. Draw: (**a**) a hexagon, (**b**) an octagon, and (**c**) a pentagon.
2. State whether the measure of the angle is an acute, an obtuse, or a right angle.
   (**a**) 90^0 (**b**) 25^0 (**c**) 101^0

Sum of the Measures of the Angles of a Polygon
The sum of the measures of the angles of a triangle $= 180^0$
The sum of the measures of the angles of a quadrilateral $= 360^0$. Let us find a general formula for finding the sum of the measure of the angles of a polygon as follows:
1. Sum of measures of the angles of a triangle $= 180^0$
$$= (n - 2) \times 180^0, \text{ where n} = \text{number}$$
$$\text{of sides of a triangle.}$$
$$= (3 - 2) \times 180^0, \quad (n = 3)$$
$$= 1 \times 180^0$$
$$= 180^0$$

Put n = 3 because a triangle has 3 sides.

2. Sum of the measures of the angles of a quadrilateral $= 360^0$

$$= (n - 2) \times 180^0, \text{ where n}$$
is the number of sides
of a quadrilateral.
$$= (4 - 2) \times 180^0, \ (n = 4)$$
$$= 2 \times 180^0$$
$$= 360^0$$

Put n = 4 because a quadrilateral has 4 sides.

3. Therefore, **the general formula for finding the sum of the measures of the angles of any polygon is (n − 2) × 180^0**.
   where n is the number of sides of the polygon.

4. The general formula **(n − 2) × 180^0** is used to find the sum of the measures of the angles of any polygon, but this formula is used specifically for the sum of the interior angles of the polygon. The interior angles of a polygon is the same as the angles inside the polygon as shown:

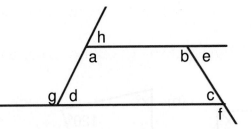

The angle measures of a, b, c, and d are inside the polygon and they are called **interior angles**. The angle measures of e, f, g, and h are outside the polygon and they are called **exterior angles**.

Some important formulas and facts about a polygon are as shown:

1. The sum of the measures of the interior angles of a polygon $= (n - 2) \times 180^0$, where n is the number of sides of the polygon.

2. The interior angle of a regular polygon $= \dfrac{(n - 2) \times 180^0}{n}$,

   where n is the number of sides of the polygon.

3. The sum of the measures of the exterior angles of a polygon is 360^0.

4. All the exterior angles of a regular polygon are equal.

5. An exterior angle of a regular polygon $= \dfrac{360^0}{n}$,

   where n is the number of the sides.

Example 1

Find the sum of the measures of the interior angles of:

(**a**) a pentagon.

(**b**) a heptagon.

Solution

(**a**) The number of sides of a pentagon = 5.

The sum of the measures of the interior angles of a polygon = $(n - 2) \times 180^0$ where n is the number of the sides.

Therefore, the sum of the measures of the interior angles of the pentagon

$$= (n - 2) \times 180^0$$
$$= (5 - 2) \times 180^0 \quad \text{(Substitute n = 5, because a pentagon has 5 sides.)}$$
$$= 3 \times 180^0$$
$$= 540^0$$

(**b**) The number of sides of a heptagon = 7.

The sum of the measures of the interior angles of a polygon = $(n - 2) \times 180^0$, where n is the number of the sides.

Therefore, the sum of the measures of the interior angles of the heptagon

$$= (n - 2) \times 180^0$$
$$= (7 - 2) \times 180^0 \quad \text{(Substitute n = 7, because a heptagon has 7 sides.)}$$
$$= 5 \times 180^0$$
$$= 900^0$$

Example 2

A polygon has 12 sides. Find the sum of the of the measures of the interior angles.

Solution

The sum of the measures of the interior angles of a polygon = $(n - 2) \times 180^0$ where n is the number of sides of the polygon.

Therefore, the sum of the measures of the angles of the 12 sided polygon

$$= (n - 2) \times 180^0$$
$$= (12 - 2) \times 180^0 \quad \text{(Substitute n = 12, because the polygon has 12 sides.)}$$
$$= 10 \times 180^0$$
$$= 1800^0$$

Example 3

The sum of the measures of the interior angles of a polygon is 540^0.

(**a**) Find the number of sides of the polygon.

(**b**) What is the name of the polygon in (a)?

Solution

(**a**) The sum of the measures of the interior angles of a polygon = $(n - 2) \times 180^0$, where n is the number of the sides of the polygon.

From the question, the sum of the measures of the interior angles of the polygon

$$= 540^0.$$

Therefore, $(n-2) \times 180^0 = 540^0$

$180^0 \times n - 2 \times 180^0 = 540^0$ Multiply $(n-2)$ by 180^0.

$180n^0 - 360^0 = 540^0$ $(180^0 \times n = 180n^0$, and $2 \times 180^0 = 360^0)$

$180n^0 - 360 + 360^0 = 540^0 + 360^0$ (Add 360^0 to each side of the equation in order to eliminate -360^0 from the left side of the equation.)

$180n^0 = 900^0$ $(-360^0 + 360^0 = 0$, and $540^0 + 360^0 = 900^0)$

$$\frac{180n^0}{180^0} = \frac{900^0}{180^0}$$ (Divide each side of the equation by 180^0 in order to obtain the value of n.)

$$\frac{180n^0}{180^0}\overset{n^0}{\underset{1}{}} = \frac{900^0}{180^0}\overset{5}{\underset{1}{}}$$

$n = 5$ sides.

(b) From solution (a), $n = 5$ sides, and therefore, the polygon is a pentagon.

━━━━━━━━━━━━━━━ **The notes and the generous examples have provided me with the conceptual understanding and the computational fluency to do my homework.**

Exercises

1. Identify the figure as a triangle, a quadrilateral, a pentagon, a hexagon, or a heptagon, and give reasons for your answer.

(a)   (b)   ©   (d)   (e)

2. Find the sum of the measure of the interior angles of (a) a hexagon, (b) an octagon. Hint: See Example 1.

3. A polygon has 7 sides, find the sum of the measure of the interior angles. Hint: See Example 2.

4. The sum of the measure of the interior angles of a polygon is 720^0.

     (a) Find the number of sides of the polygon.

     (b) What is the name of the polygon?

Hint: See Example **3**.

5. Given the measure of the 3 exterior angles of each polygon (convex polygon), find the measure of the fourth exterior angle of each polygon (convex polygon).
   Hint: See Example 4 and also note that the sum of the exterior angles of a polygon (convex polygon) is 360^0.

   a. 126^0, 75^0, and 54^0 **b.** 106^0, 75^0, and 94^0 **b.** 56^0, 88^0, and 132^0
   d. 66^0, 59^0, and 129^0 **e.** 101^0, 85^0, and 94^0 **f.** 50^0, 83^0, and 123^0

6. Find the missing measure of angle in each polygon (convex polygon). Hint: See Example 4.

   a. $m\angle a = 112^0$ **b.** $m\angle e = 135^0$
   $m\angle b = ?$ $m\angle f = 73^0$
   $m\angle c = 110^0$ $m\angle g = ?$
   $m\angle d = 68^0$ $m\angle h = 58^0$

   c. $m\angle i = ?$ **d.** $m\angle m = 90^0$
   $m\angle j = 118^0$ $m\angle n = 90^0$
   $m\angle k = 67^0$ $m\angle o = ?$
   $m\angle l = 68^0$ $m\angle p = 90^0$

7. Find the missing measure of angle in each polygon (convex polygon). Hint: See Example 5.

   (a). $m\angle a = 140^0$ **(b).** $m\angle d = 79^0$
   $m\angle b = ?$ $m\angle e = 142^0$
   $m\angle c = 85^0$ $m\angle f = ?$

   (c). $m\angle g = 130^0$ **(d).** $m\angle j = ?$
   $m\angle h = ?$ $m\angle k = 128^0$
   $m\angle i = 90^0$ $m\angle l = 95^0$

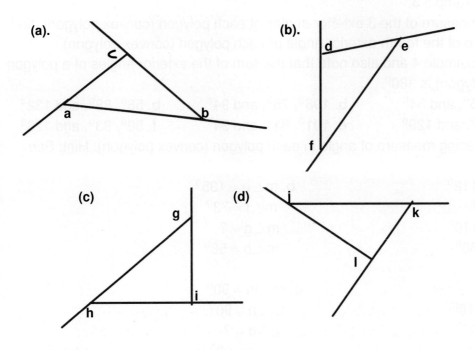

(a).

(b).

(c)

(d)

Challenge Questions

8. What is the name given to a polygon with the following number of sides:

    (a) 8 sides   (b) 6 sides   (c) 9 sides.

9. Find the sum of the measure of the interior angles of an octagon.

10. A polygon has 10 sides, find the sum of the measure of the interior angles.

11. Find the missing measure of angle in each polygon (convex polygon).

    (a). $m\angle a = 144^0$ **(b).** $m\angle d = 84^0$

          $m\angle b = ?$ $m\angle e = 140^0$

          $m\angle c = 83^0$ $m\angle f = ?$

    (c). $m\angle g = 133^0$ **(d).** $m\angle j = ?$

          $m\angle h = ?$ $m\angle k = 129^0$

          $m\angle i = 89^0$ $m\angle l = 92^0$

(a).

(b).

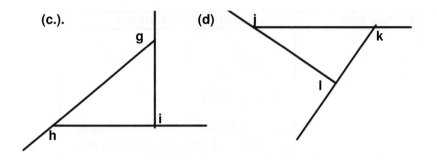

(c.).   (d)

Answers to Selected Questions
5a. 105^0 **6a.** 70^0 **7a.** 135^0

Critical Geometrical Facts
1. **The sum of the measures of the interior angles of a triangle $= 180^0$**
2. **The sum of the measures of the exterior angles of a triangle $= 360^0$**
3. **The sum of the measures of the exterior angles of a polygon including triangles and quadrilaterals $= 360^0$**
4. **The sum of the interior angles of any quadrilateral $= 360^0$**

Classification of Triangles Using the Sides and the Angles of the Triangle.
You may read more information on the classification of triangles under the chapter "Geometric Figures."
The sides and the angles of a triangle can be used to classify triangles as:
    Equilateral triangle.
    Isosceles triangle.
    Scalene triangle.
    Right-angle triangle.
An equilateral triangle has all sides and all angles equal.
An isosceles triangle has two or more sides equal and two or more angles equal.
A scalene triangle has no sides equal and no angles equal .
A right angle triangle has one 90^0 angle and the sides may or may not be equal.
The classification of the triangles is summarized in the table.

Triangle type	Sample diagram	Description
Equilateral triangle	✗ indicates the sides that are equal.	All sides are equal and all angles are equal.
Isosceles triangle	✗ indicates the sides that are equal	Two or more sides are equal and two or more angles are equal.
Scalene triangle		No sides are equal and no angles are equal.
Right-angle triangle	⌐ indicates 90º	There is one angle which is 90º

Exercises

Classify the following triangles as an equilateral, an isosceles, a scalene, or a right-angle triangle. Give reasons for your classifications. Hint: See the preceding section or the table and also match each figure with the description of each classification of the triangles to determine the classification of each figure.

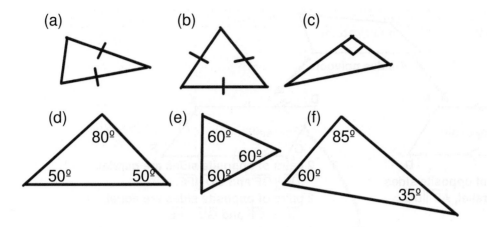

(a)　　(b)　　(c)

(d) 80º 50º 50º　(e) 60º 60º 60º　(f) 85º 60º 35º

Cumulative Review
1. 2.33 × 4 =　　　2. 2.33 × 4.2　　　3. 2.33 × 5.4 =
4. 84 × 22 =　　　5. 1.6 ÷ 4 =　　　6. 2.7 + 9.45 =
7. A side of a square is 4.9 cm. Find the perimeter and the area of the square.
8. The length of a rectangle is $6\frac{1}{2}$ ft and the width is $3\frac{1}{2}$ ft. Find the perimeter and the area of the rectangle.
9. The base of a rectangle is 8 m and the height is 6 m. Find the area of the rectangle.
10. The sum of the measures of the two angles of a triangle is 100^0. What is the measure of the third angle of the triangle?
11. Find the mean and the mode of each set of numbers.
    a. 3, 8, 5, 8　　　**b**. 9, 6, 6, 5, 3, 1　　　**c**. 3, 3, 4, 12, 3
12. Find the median and the mode of each set of numbers.
    a. 7, 7, 2, 4, 2, 2　　**b**. 4, 8, 1, 2,1　　　**c**. 5, 4, 3, 1, 2
13. The sum of the measure of the angles of a quadrilateral is _____
14. The sum of the measure of the angles of a triangle is _____

(Are you having fun with the mathematics?)

Classification of Quadrilaterals
Quadrilaterals can be classified by the number of parallel sides, length of sides and the measure of the angles as shown in Figure 2.

Figure 2

quadrilateral

4-sides polygon

trapezoid

1 pair of opposite sides are parallel, $\overline{AB}\parallel\overline{DC}$.

paralellogram

2 pairs of opposite sides are paralel, $\overline{DE}\parallel\overline{GF}$ and $\overline{GD}\parallel\overline{FE}$.

2 pairs of opposite sides are equal, $\overline{DE}=\overline{GF}$ and $\overline{GD}=\overline{FE}$.

2 pairs of opposite angles are equal, $m\angle D = m\angle F$ and $m\angle G = m\angle E$.

rectangle

Parallelogram with:
4 right angles,
   $m\angle K = m\angle H = m\angle I = m\angle J = 90^{\circ}$
2 pairs of opposite sides are parallel, $\overline{HI}\parallel\overline{KJ}$, $\overline{KH}\parallel\overline{JI}$.
2 pairs of opposite sides are equal, $\overline{HI}=\overline{KJ}$, $\overline{KH}=\overline{JI}$.

rhombus

Parallelogram with:
4 equal sides, $\overline{PQ}=\overline{SR}=\overline{SP}=\overline{RQ}$.
2 pairs of opposite sides are parallel, $\overline{PQ}\parallel\overline{SR}$, $\overline{SP}\parallel\overline{RQ}$.
2 pairs of opposite angles are equal, $m\angle S = m\angle Q$, $m\angle P = m\angle R$.

square

A square is both a rhombus and a rectangle.

A parallelogram with:
4 right angles, $m\angle L = m\angle M = m\angle N = m\angle O = 90^{\circ}$.
4 sides equal, $\overline{LM}=\overline{MN}=\overline{NO}=\overline{OL}$.
2 pairs of opposite sides are parallel, $\overline{LM}\parallel\overline{ON}$, $\overline{OL}\parallel\overline{NM}$.

The explanation of the symbols in figure 2 are:

means a group of segments that are parallel.
means a second group of segments that are parallel.
means a group of segments that are equal in length.
means a second group of segments that are equal in length.
means a right angle or a 90º angle.

Exercises

1. Select the correct word to complete each statement. Hint: See the preceding notes and Figure 2.

(**a**) A quadrilateral is a 4-sided **polygon** or a 4-sided (opened, closed) figure.

(**b**) A quadrilateral that has two pairs of opposite sides parallel is called a (trapezoid, parallelogram).

(**c**) A quadrilateral that has exactly one pair of opposite sides parallel is called a (parallelogram, trapezoid.)

(**d**) A quadrilateral or a parallelogram that has all sides the same length with the angles not right angles is called a (rhombus. square.)

(**e**) A quadrilateral or a parallelogram that has all sides the same length with the angles being right angles is called a (rhombus, square.)

(**f**) A quadrilateral or a parallelogram that has 2 pairs of opposite sides equal and all the measures of the angles are right angles is called a (trapezoid, rectangle, square.)

(**g**) A square is both a rhombus and a rectangle. True or false?

(**h**) What is the difference between a square and a rhombus? (All sides are equal, the angles of the rhombus are not 90^0 but the angles of the square are 90^0.)

2. Classify each figure as a rectangle, a square, a trapezoid, a parallelogram, or a rhombus. Give detailed reasons for your classification. Hint: See Figure 2.

3. A regular polygon has equal sides and equal measure of angles. Does each figure appear to be a regular polygon? Explain your answer. Hint: See figure 1 at the beginning of this chapter.

(a) (b) (c) (d) (e)

4. Sketch an example of each polygon. Hint: See figure 1 at the beginning of this chapter and figure 2.
(**a**) equilateral triangle (**b**) rectangle (**c**) regular pentagon (**d**) quadrilateral.

CHAPTER 29

GEOMETRIC FIGURES

Cumulative Review

1. $17 + 43 =$ **2.** $50 \div 10 =$ **3.** $32 - 18 =$ **4.** $9 \times 4 =$

5. $44 \div 4 =$ **6.** $28 - 12 =$ **7.** $60 \div 6 =$ **8.** $33 - 8 =$

9.
$$\begin{array}{r} 240 \\ \times\ \ 4 \\ \hline \end{array}$$

10.
$$\begin{array}{r} 144 \\ +\ 195 \\ \hline \end{array}$$

11.
$$\begin{array}{r} 29 \\ -\ 14 \\ \hline \end{array}$$

12.
$$\begin{array}{r} 33 \\ \times\ \ 4 \\ \hline \end{array}$$

13. $36 \div 3 =$ **14.** $28 \div 7 =$ **15.** $13 + 35 =$ **16.** $4^2 - 8 =$

17. $5.9 + 3.8 =$ **18.** $5.7 \times 3 =$ **19.** $2.9 \times 3.6 =$ **20.** $27.7 - 1.8 =$

21. $\dfrac{2}{3} \times \dfrac{2}{5} =$ **22.** $\dfrac{2}{3} \div \dfrac{7}{3} =$ **23.** $\dfrac{3}{4} - \dfrac{2}{3} =$ **24.** $2\dfrac{2}{3} + 2\dfrac{3}{4} =$

Geometric Figures

There are four basic geometric figures, which are:

1. A point
2. A ray
3. A line
4. A segment

The four basic geometric figures can be represented in a table as shown:

Diagram (figure)	Name	Symbol	Description
• X	Point X	X	A point is the smallest specific location in space.
X → Y	Ray XY	$\overrightarrow{XY}$	A ray is a part of a line that starts at a point and continuous in one direction.
← X → Y	Line XY or line YX	$\overleftrightarrow{XY}$ or $\overleftrightarrow{YX}$	A line is a straight continuous arrangement of points in opposite directions.
X —— Y	Segment XY or segment YX	$\overline{XY}$ or $\overline{YX}$	A segment is a part of a line that starts at a point and ends at another point.

Group Exercises

1. Every student should take a 11 × 8 inches of paper and divide it into four sections.
2. Each student should draw one of the four basic geometric figures on one of each section of the paper. Cut out the four sections of the paper and put the individual sections into a container.
3. The class should be divided into four groups, such as group A, B, C, and D. "Group A" should compete against "group D" and "group B" should compete against "group C." A student in "group A" should pick one of the sections of the paper in the container and change the statement on the paper into a question for "group B" to answer. For example, if the section of the paper shows the diagram of line XY, then the "group A" student should ask "group B" students, "what is meant by a line XY and draw the line XY on the blackboard.
4. Record each correct answer on the tally table as shown. Each group should ask at least 20 questions.

Group	A	B	C	D
Tally	///	////	//	////

Outcome of the Group Exercises

1. Which group understands the concept of the four basic geometric figures best?
2. Which figure do many students have problems with?
3. Which figure do many students have no problems with?

Example 1

Match the letters A, B, and C with the correct basic geometric figure.

(a)		A.	Point
(b)		B.	Ray
(c)		C.	Line
(d)		D.	Segment

Solution

The letters are matched with the correct basic geometric figures as shown:

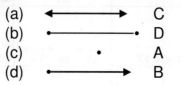

(a)		C
(b)		D
(c)		A
(d)		B

Example 2

By referring to the diagrams /figures of a ray, a segment and a line:

(**a**) What is the difference among a ray, a segment and a line?

(**b**) Are a ray, a segment and a line alike?

(**c**) What is the difference between a line and a ray?

(**d**) What is the difference between a line and a segment?

(**e**) What is the difference between a segment and a ray?

Solution

(**a**) A ray, a segment and a line are different because by referring to the diagram/figure of a ray, a segment and a line, the one arrow head in the diagram of a ray shows that the **ray is continuous in one direction**. The diagram of a segment does not show any arrow head, therefore **a segment is not continuous**. The diagram of a line shows two arrows in opposite directions. Therefore, **a line continues in opposite directions**.

(**b**) A ray, a segment, and a line are alike in the sense that all of them are made up of points in a close and straight arrangements as shown:

Close and straight arrangements of points.

(**c**) The two arrow heads of the diagram of a line show that **a line is continuous in opposite directions** but a ray which has one arrow head shows that **a ray is continuous just in one direction**.

(**d**) The two arrow heads of the diagram of a line shows that **a line is continuous in opposite directions** but a diagram of a segment has no arrow heads, and therefore, **a segment continuous in neither direction**.

(**e**) There are no arrow heads in the diagram of a segment and therefore **a segment continuous in neither directions** but the diagram of a ray has one arrow head, and therefore, a ray is continuous in one direction.

Group Exercises

The class should be divided into four groups, A, B, C, and D. Each group should use the table for the four basic geometric figures to complete the following statements:

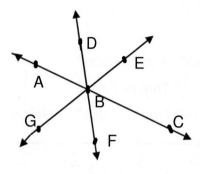

1. $\overline{GB}$ is s_____ GB. The answer to Exercise 1 as example is: $\overline{GB}$ is segment GB.

2. $\overline{GE}$ is s_____ GE.

3. $\overleftrightarrow{GE}$ is l_____ GE.

4. $\overrightarrow{GE}$ is r_____ GE.

5. B is p_____ B.

6. C is p_____ C.

7. $\overleftrightarrow{AC}$ is l_____ AC.

8. $\overrightarrow{AC}$ is r_____ AC.

9. $\overline{AC}$ is s_____ AC.

10. $\overrightarrow{FD}$ is r_____ FD.

11. $\overrightarrow{DF}$ is r_____ DF.

12. D is p_____ D.

13. $\overleftrightarrow{DF}$ is l_____ DF.

16. $\overleftrightarrow{FD}$ is l_____ FD.

15. $\overrightarrow{BF}$ is r_____ BF.

17. The symbol for ray FB is ———-

18. The symbol for ray DF is ———

19. The symbol for point E is ———-

20. The symbol for point A is ———-

21. The symbol for segment CA is ———

22. The symbol for segment EG is ———

23. The symbol for line GE is ———

24. The symbol for line FD is ———

25. The symbol for ray GE is ———

26. The symbol for ray EG is ———

Group A should check group B's answers, group B should check group A's answers, group C should check group D's answers, and group D should check group C's answers.

Analysis of the Group Exercises

1. Which group did best?
2. Which answers did all the groups get wrong?
3. How many answers did each group get correct?
4. How many answers did each group get wrong? Review the table of geometric figures to correct the wrong answers.

Example 3

(**a**) $\overline{AB}$ is the same figure as $\overline{AB}$? True or False?

(**b**) $\overleftrightarrow{BD}$ is the same figure as $\overleftrightarrow{BD}$? True or False?

(**c**) $\overrightarrow{AC}$ is the same figure as $\overrightarrow{CA}$? True or False? Explain your answer.

(**d**) Name all the rays in the diagram.

Solution

(**a**) True   (**b**) True

(**c**) False, because the direction of the ray AC is opposite to the direction of the ray CA.

(**d**) The rays in the diagram are $\overrightarrow{XZ}$, $\overrightarrow{XY}$, and $\overrightarrow{YZ}$.

Exercises

1. Sketch: (**a**) a ray   (**b**) a line   (**c**) a segment. Hint: See Example **1**.
2. Use symbols to write the following: See the table under the section Geometric Figures. (**a**) a line PK   (**b**) a ray PK   (**c**) a segment PK   (**d**) a point P.
3. List all the possible rays in the diagram. Hint: See Example **3(d)**.

Challenge Questions

4. John's house is 200 feet from his school. Can the distance from John's house to the school be considered as a ray, a segment, or a line? Explain. Hint: The distance starts from John's house and then ends at the school. How many endpoints are involved with the distance from John's house to his school? **Note also that from the geometric diagram, a ray has one end point, a segment has two end points, and a line has no end points**.
5. Is the light from a flashlight a segment, a ray or a line? Hint: The ray from a flashlight has a start point, and then it continues.
6. Explain what is meant by a line.
7. Name all the lines, rays, points and segments in the diagram.

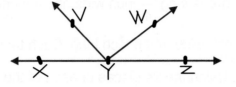

CLASSIFICATION OF TRIANGLES BY USING THE LENGTH OF THE SIDES

A triangle is a three sided figure.
The three types of a triangle according to the length of its sides are:
1. **equilateral triangle**
2. **isosceles triangle**
3. **scalene triangle**

Equilateral triangles are triangles that have all the three sides of equal length.
Isosceles triangles are triangles that have two or more sides of equal length.
Scalene triangles are triangles that have no sides of equal length.
Summary of triangle types

Triangle Types	Description	Diagrams	Examples
Equilateral triangle	An equilateral triangle is a triangle that has all the three sides of equal lengh.		6cm 6cm 6cm
Isosceles triangle	An isosceles triangle is a triangle that has two or more sides of equal length.		6cm 6cm 6cm / 8cm 8cm 5cm
Scalene triangle	A scalene triangle has no sides of equal length.		3cm 12cm 10cm

Group Exercises — Construction
The class should be divided into four teams. The teams should be named Team A, Team B, Team C, and Team D. Every team should use a pair of scissors to cut

675

strips of colored paper measuring $\frac{1}{4}$ inch wide and 4 inches long, $\frac{1}{4}$ inch wide and

5 inches long, and $\frac{1}{4}$ inch wide and 6 inch long. Each team should cut 24 pieces

of each measurement. Using the 24 pieces of each of the three types of the measurements of the paper strips, each team should:

(**a**) Join the strips at the ends to form 3 types of equilateral triangles. Sketch each type of the equilateral triangle that you have formed with the strips showing the measurements.

(**b**) Join the strips at the ends to form 3 types of isosceles triangles. Sketch each type of the isosceles triangle that you have formed with the strips showing the measurements.

(**c**) Join the strips at the ends to form 3 types of scalene triangles. Sketch each type of the scalene triangle that you have formed with the strip showing the measurements.

(**d**) All the teams should compare their sketches with the measurements.

(**e**) How many teams got all the exercises correct? Which exercises are wrong? Review the table on geometric figures to form the strips according to how an equilateral triangle, an isosceles triangle and a scalene triangle are described.

(f) Can you identify an equilateral triangle, an isosceles triangle, and a scalene triangle. Can you describe an equilateral triangle, an isosceles triangle, and a scalene triangle after these exercises?

Triangle Inequality
Test of the requirements of the length of the sides of a triangle to form a triangle

Group Exercises
The class should be divided into Team A and Team B. Each team should:

(**a**) Cut a strip of colored paper which should be $\frac{1}{4}$ in wide with the following lengths:

   (**i**) 4 in., 6 in., 5 in.   (**ii**) 7 in., 4 in., 5 in.

(**b**) Each team should form a triangle with each set of dimension in (a)(i) and (a)(ii), by joining the ends of the paper strips.

(**c**) Is it possible to form the triangle in (**a**)(**i**) and (**a**)(**ii**) ? Explain your answer. Hint: See the rule that follows:

   Rule: The sum of the lengths of the shortest two sides of a triangle must be greater than the longest side in order to form the triangle.

Example 3
Using the rule above write an inequality regarding the lengths of the following triangles:

Note that this inequality is the condition that the side lengths of a triangle can form a triangle.

Solution

The rule contains the words "greater than," and therefore, we can use the greater than sign (>) to write the inequality as shown:

(i) $a + b > c$ (The sum of the shortest lengths "a " and " b" is greater than the longest length c.)

(ii) 5 m. + 4 m. > 6 m.   (The sum of the shortest lengths, 5 m. and 4 m. is greater than the longest length of 6 m.)

$\qquad$ 9 m. > 6 m.

The notes and the generous examples have provided me with the conceptual understanding and the computational fluency to do my homework.

Exercises

1. Explain if each combination of side lengths can or cannot form a triangle. Hint: See Example **3**.

   (**a**) 3 ft, 6 ft, 5 ft   (**b**) 2 ft, 3 ft, 8ft   (**c**) 12 in., 5 in., 9 in.   (**d**) 6 yd, 10 yd, 8 yd

Challenge Question

2. Considering the description of an isosceles triangle and an equilateral triangle, can we say that the equilateral triangle is also an isosceles triangle? Explain.

CHAPTER 30

TYPES OF ANGLES

New Terms: acute angle, right angle, obtuse angle, and straight angle

The types of angles are as shown:

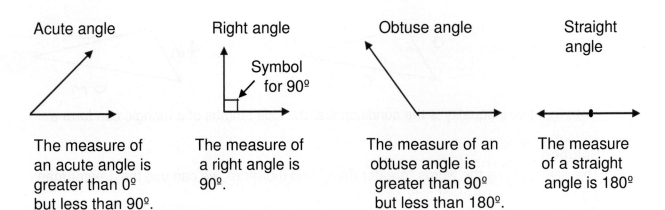

Acute angle	Right angle	Obtuse angle	Straight angle
The measure of an acute angle is greater than 0º but less than 90º.	The measure of a right angle is 90º.	The measure of an obtuse angle is greater than 90º but less than 180º.	The measure of a straight angle is 180º

By observing the diagrams of the types of angles:

(1) We can write that "m∠acute < m∠right < m∠obtuse < m∠straight,
where "m" stands for "measure of."

∠ is the symbol for angle.

< is the symbol for "is less than"

"m∠acute" stands for "measure of an acute angle."

"m∠right" stands for "measure of a right angle."

"m∠obtuse" stands for "measure of an obtuse angle."

"m∠straight" stands for "measure of a straight angle."

(2) It can be concluded that **an angle is formed by two rays that have a common endpoint.**

This common endpoint is called the vertex as shown in the diagram.

Vertex (common point).

(3) A right angle is the same as an angle which has a measure of 90^0.
Also, if two lines or two rays intersect or meet at a point such that the two lines or the two rays form a 90^0 angle, then the two lines or the two rays are said to be perpendicular to each other.

(4) A straight angle is the same as an angle which has a measure of 180^0.

Review:

1. Is it true that an angle is formed by two rays that have a common endpoint? True or False? Explain.

2. Can we say that angles are classified by comparing them to 90^0? True or False? Explain.

The notes and the generous examples have provided me with the conceptual understanding and the computational fluency to do my homework.

Exercises

1. Sketch an acute angle, an obtuse angle, a right angle, and a straight angle.
Hint: See section under "Types of Angles."

2. Classify the angles as an acute, an obtuse, a right, or a straight angle.
Hint: See the section on "Types of Angles."

3. Write a connection involving the symbol $<$, straight angle, acute angle, obtuse angle, and right angle. Hint: See the section on "Types of Angles."

Measuring Angles

Angles are measured in units called degrees and the degrees are represented by the symbol ^{0}. For example, 90 degrees can be written using the symbol for degrees (^{0}) as 90^0. **Angles can be measured with a protractor**. Figure 1 shows the protractor with the features.

Figure 1

There are several shapes of the protractor. However, the base line of a protractor is always the segment joining the 0^0 and the 180^0. The point at the middle of the segment joining the 0^0 and the 180^0 is the center of the protractor.

Example 1

Measure angle ABC as shown in Step 1 with a protractor.

Solution

Step 1: Place the protractor on the angle to be measured so that the straight line of 0^0 and 180^0 (base line) on the protractor should be on one of the rays (the rays are BC and BA) that form the angle. The point at the middle of the 0^0 and 180^0 segment on the protractor should be on the vertex of the angle to be measured as shown in the diagram.

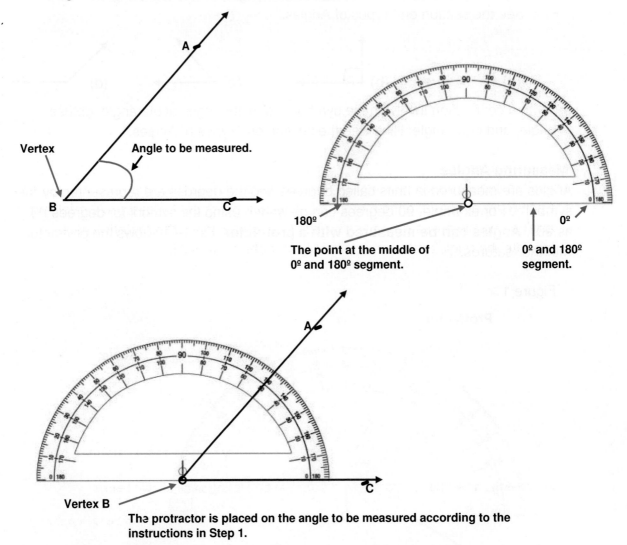

The protractor is placed on the angle to be measured according to the instructions in Step 1.

Step 2: Read the measure of the marking on the protractor that coincides with the ray BA as the measure of the angle ABC ($m\angle ABC$). Since the ray BA coincides with the measure of 50^0 on the protractor, the measure of angle ABC is 50^0 as shown:

Read the measure of the protractor that coincides with the ray BA which is 50º.

Vertex B

Group Exercises
The class should be divided into four teams, Team A, Team B, Team C, and Team D.
1. Each team should use the method of "measuring angles" to measure the following angles and the measurements should be recorded. From the recorded data, indicate the angles that are acute, obtuse, right, or straight.

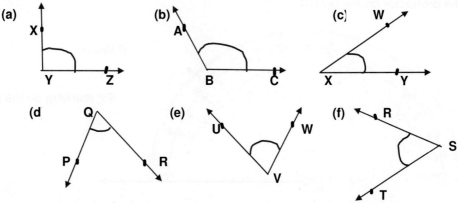

Note that the arcs specify the required angles to be measured as shown below.

Arc (required angle to be measured)

Hint: One of the rays of each of the triangles (a), (b), and (c) are horizontal as in Example 1 which makes it convenient to align and place the protractor on the angle ABC. However, triangles (d), (e), and (f) do not have one of their rays at the horizontal position, but still the angles can be measured by placing the middle of the segment joining the 0^0 and the 180^0 on the protractor on the vertex of angle ABC so that the segment (base line of the protractor) should be placed on one of the rays that forms the angle, and then follow step 2 of Example **1**.

How to Draw Angles Using a Protractor

Example 2
Use a protractor to draw an angle ABC which measures 45^0.
Solution
Step 1: Draw the ray BC of the triangle ABC horizontally.

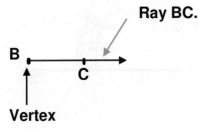

Ray BC.

B
C

Vertex

Step 2: Take a protractor and place it on the ray BC such that the point at the middle of the protractor from 0^0 to 180^0 marking coincides with the vertex (point B) and that the segment from the 0^0 to 180^0 marking on the protractor should be on the ray BC.

Take a pencil and make a dot at the location where the 45^0 marking on the protractor coincides with the paper, and label this dot as point A.

Place the protractor on the ray BC.

Point A

45º marking on the protractor.

C

180º

0º

The point at the middle of 0º and 180º segment (Center of the protractor) is on point B.

0º and 180º segment of the protractor (base line of the protractor) is on the ray BC.

Step 3: Remove the protractor from the ray BC and set it aside. Take a pencil and a ruler. Place the edge of the ruler on point A and on the vertex B. Draw a line through point A to the vertex B. Angle ABC is the required angle which should be 45^0.

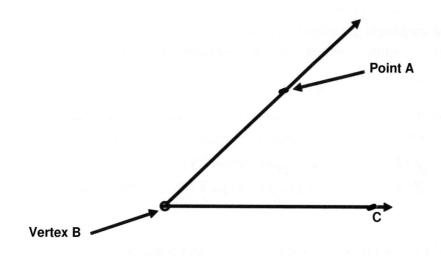

Point A

C

Vertex B

Group exercises.

The class should be divided into four teams. Each team should use a protractor to draw the following angle measures:

(**a**) 30^0 (**b**) 42^0 (**c**) 68^0 (**d**) 90^0 (**e**) 151^0

Hint: See Example **2**.

The notes and the generous examples have provided me with the conceptual understanding and the computational fluency to do my homework.

Exercises

1. Use the protractor to measure the following angles. Hint: See Example **1**.

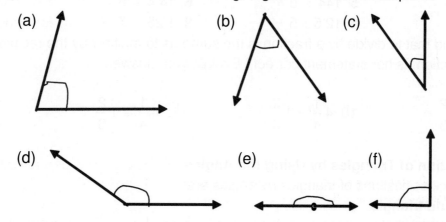

(a)   (b)   (c)

(d)   (e)   (f)

2. Use a protractor to draw $15^0, 25^0$, 28^0, 51^0, and 145^0. Hint: See Example **2**.

How to Name Angles and Measure of Angles.

The symbol that represents an angle is $\angle$. The symbol that represents the measure of

an angle is "m∠."
The tables show how the angle and the measure of the angle of angle Y, angle XYZ, and angle ZYX can be named in words and using symbols as shown:

Table A

Name in words	Name in symbols
Angle Y	∠Y
Angle XYZ	∠XYZ
Angle ZYX	∠ZYX

Table B

Name in words	Name in symbols
Measure of angle Y	m∠Y
Measure of angle XYZ	m∠XYZ
Measure of angle ZYX	m∠ZYX

Exercises
Using the fact that angle XYZ and angle ZYX represent the same angle:
1. How many possible ways can an angle be named? (one way, two ways, three ways).
2. The position of the vertex in naming an angle is at the middle, or we can say that the vertex is the middle alphabet when the angle is named using symbols. True or False? Hint: See the diagrams in Example **1** or Example **2**.
3. Use the symbols to write the following:
   (**a**) Angle A   (**b**) Angle C   (**c**) Angle ABC   (**d**) Angle BCD
   Hint: See Table A.
4. Use the symbols to write the following:
   (**a**) measure of angle A   (**b**) measure of angle ABC   (**c**) measure of angle BCD
   Hint: See Table B.

Cumulative Review
1. $144 \div 6 =$ 2. $144 \times 6 =$ 3. $144 - 6 =$
4. $14.4 \div 6 =$ 5. $144 \div .6 =$ 6. $14.4 \div .6 =$
7. $125 \div 5 =$ 8. $12.5 \div 5 =$ 9. $1.25 \div .5 =$
8. Mary said that to divide by a fraction is the same as to multiply by the reciprocal of the fraction. Is her statement correct? Explain your answer.

9. $4\frac{1}{4} - 1\frac{2}{3} =$ 10. $4\frac{1}{4} \times 1\frac{2}{3} =$ 11. $4\frac{1}{4} \div 1\frac{2}{3} =$

Classification of Triangles by Using the Angles
The three classifications of triangles by angles are:
     1. **Acute triangle.**
     2. **Right triangle.**
     3. **Obtuse triangle.**

$$x \qquad 36^0$$
$$\frac{\cancel{5}x}{\cancel{5}} = \frac{\cancel{180^0}}{\cancel{5}}$$
$$1 \qquad 1$$

$$x = 36^0$$

To Solve for the Unknown Angle of a Triangle by Using the Property of One of the Measures of a Right Angle of a Triangle is 90^0

Example 2
Write and solve an equation to find x.

a. 30° **b.**   **c.** $(x + 10)^\circ$

$2x$ $2x$ x

Solution

Special Note: A right angle may be written as 90º.

This is the symbol for a right angle which is 90º.

a. The triangle is a right triangle, and therefore, one of the angles is 90^0.
Therefore, an equation can be written to solve for x as shown:

$2x + 30^0 + 90^0 = 180^0$ 　　　Because the sum of the measures of the
　　　　　　　　　　　　　　angles of any triangle is 180^0.

$2x + 30^0 - 30^0 + 90^0 - 90^0 = 180^0 - 30^0 - 90^0$
　　　　　　　　　　　Move similar or like terms to one side of the
　　　　　　　　　　　equation by subtracting 30^0 and 90^0 from
　　　　　　　　　　　both sides of the equation.

$2x = 180^0 - 120^0$ 　　　　　$- 30^0 - 90^0 = -120^0$
$2x = 60^0$ 　　　　　　　　$180^0 - 120^0 = 60^0$

$$\frac{2x}{2} = \frac{60^0}{2}$$ 　　Divide both sides of the equation by 2 in order to

obtain the value of x.

$$\frac{2\overset{x}{\cancel{x}}}{\underset{1}{\cancel{2}}} = \frac{\overset{30^0}{\cancel{60^0}}}{\underset{1}{\cancel{2}}}$$ Do the division.

$$x = 30^0$$

b. The triangle is a right triangle, and therefore, one of the angles is 90^0.
Therefore, an equation can be written to solve for x as shown:

$2x + x + 90^0 = 180^0$ Because the sum of the measures of the angles of any triangle is 180^0.

$2x + x + 90^0 - 90^0 = 180^0 - 90^0$ Move similar or like terms to one side of the equation by subtracting 90^0 from both sides of the equation.

$2x + x = 180^0 - 90^0$ Now we have like terms on both sides of the equation. $90^0 - 90^0 = 0$

$3x = 90^0$ $2x + x = 3x$ and $180^0 - 90^0 = 90^0$

$$\frac{3x}{3} = \frac{90^0}{3}$$ Divide both sides of the equation by 3 in order to obtain the value of x.

$$\frac{3\overset{x}{\cancel{x}}}{\underset{1}{\cancel{3}}} = \frac{\overset{30^0}{\cancel{90^0}}}{\underset{1}{\cancel{3}}}$$ Do the division.

$$x = 30^0$$

c. The triangle is a right triangle, and therefore, one of the angles is 90^0.
Therefore, an equation can be written to solve for x as shown:

$x + (x + 10)^0 + 90^0 = 180^0$ Because the sum of the measures of the angles of any triangle is 180^0.

$x + x^0 + 10^0 + 90^0 = 180^0$ $(x + 10)^0 = x^0 + 10^0$

$x + x + 10^0 + 90^0 = 180^0$ Let x^0 be x.

$x + x + 10^0 - 10^0 + 90^0 - 90^0 = 180^0 - 10^0 - 90^0$

Move similar or like terms to one side of the equation by subtracting 10^0 and 90^0 from both sides of the equation.

$x + x = 180^0 - 10^0 - 90^0$ Now we have similar or like terms on each side of the equation. $10^0 - 10^0 = 0$ and $90^0 - 90^0 = 0$.

$2x = 180^0 - 100^0$ Simplify, $x + x = 2x$ and $- 10^0 - 90^0 = -100^0$.

In the parallelogram ABCD, **∠A is opposite to ∠**C **and**
∠B **is opposite to ∠D.**
Therefore, m∠A = m∠C and m∠B = m∠D,
or **a = c and b = d.**
3. The consecutive angles of a parallelogram are supplementary.
Two angles are supplementary if the sum of their measures is 180^0.

In the parallelogram ABCD, the consecutive angles are:
∠A and ∠B, ∠B and ∠C, ∠C and ∠D, ∠D and ∠A.
Therefore, **m∠A + m∠B = 180^0, or a + b = 180^0.**
m∠B + m∠C = 180^0, or b + c = 180^0.
m∠C + m∠D = 180^0, or c + d = 180^0.
m∠D + m∠A = 180^0, or d + a = 180^0.

To solve for the unknown angle of a parallelogram by using the property of the sum of the measures of the angles in any quadrilateral, including the parallelogram is 360^0. A rectangle is also a parallelogram.

Example 1
Find the measure of angle C and also find the value of n in each parallelogram.

a.

Parallellogram

b.

Rectangle

Solution
a. $70^0 + 110^0 + m\angle C + 110^0 = 360^0$ Because the sum of the measures of the
angles in any parallelogram is 360^0.

$70^0 - 70^0 + 110^0 - 110^0 + m\angle C + 110^0 - 110^0 = 360^0 - 70^0 - 100^0 - 110^0$.
Move similar or like terms to one side of the

$m\angle C = 360^0 - 70^0 - 100^0 - 110^0$.

equation by subtracting 70^0, 110^0, and 110^0 from both sides of the equation.

Now we have similar or like terms on each side of the equation. $70^0 - 70^0 = 0$ and $110^0 - 110^0 = 0$.

$m\angle C = 360^0 - 270^0$

Simplify, $- 70^0 - 100^0 - 110^0 = -270^0$.

$m\angle C = 90^0$

Simplify, $360^0 - 270^0 = 90^0$.

b. $n + 90^0 + 90^0 + 90^0 = 360^0$

Because the sum of the measures of the angles in any parallelogram is 360^0.

$n + 90^0 - 90^0 + 90^0 - 90^0 + 90^0 - 90^0 = 360^0 - 90^0 - 90^0 - 90^0$

Move similar or like terms to one side of the equation by subtracting 70^0, 110^0, and 110^0 from both sides of the equation.

$n = 360^0 - 90^0 - 90^0 - 90^0$

Now we have similar or like terms on each side of the equation. $90^0 - 90^0 = 0$.

$n = 360^0 - 270^0$

Simplify, $- 90^0 - 90^0 - 90^0 = -270^0$

$n = 90^0$

Simplify, $360^0 - 270^0 = 90^0$

To solve for the unknown angle of a parallelogram by using the property of the the measure of the opposite angles of any parallelogram are equal.

Example 2

Find the measure of the angles represented by b and x.

a. $\angle B$ is opposite to $\angle D$ and since the measure of the opposite angles of a parallelogram are equal, the $m\angle B$ is equal to the $m\angle D$.
Therefore, $m\angle D = m\angle B = b = 115^0$

b. Using similar reasoning as in Example 2a, $x = 88^0$.

To solve for the unknown angle of a parallelogram by using the property of the consecutive angles of a parallelogram are supplementary.

Two angles are **supplementary** if the sum of their measures is 180^0.

Example 3

Find the angle measure represented by n and x in the parallelogram.

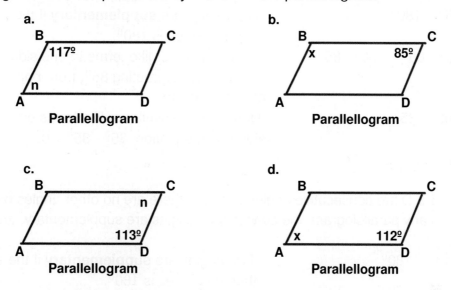

a.

B   117º   C

n

A   D

Parallellogram

b.

B   x   85º   C

A   D

Parallellogram

c.

B   C

n

113º

A   D

Parallellogram

d.

B   C

x   112º

A   D

Parallellogram

Solution

a. $\angle A$ and $\angle B$ are consecutive angles because there are no other angles between them. In any parallelogram, the consecutive angles are supplementary, and therefore:

$n + 117^0 = 180^0$	Two angles are **supplementary** if the sum of their measures is 180^0.
$n + 117^0 - 117^0 = 180^0 - 117^0$	Move similar or like terms to one side of the equation by subtracting 117^0, from both sides of the equation.
$n = 180^0 - 117^0$	Now we have similar or like terms on each side of the equation. $117^0 - 117^0 = 0$.
$n = 63^0$.	

b. $\angle B$ and $\angle C$ are consecutive angles because there are no other angles between them. In any parallelogram, the consecutive angles are **supplementary**, and therefore:

$x + 85^0 = 180^0$	Two angles are **supplementary** if the sum of their measures is 180^0.
$x + 85^0 - 85^0 = 180^0 - 85^0$	Move similar or like terms to one side of the equation by subtracting 85^0, from both sides of the equation.
$x = 180^0 - 85^0$	Now we have similar or like terms on each side of the equation. $85^0 - 85^0 = 0$.
$x = 95^0$.	

c. $\angle$B and $\angle$C are consecutive angles because there are no other angles between them. In any parallelogram, the consecutive angles are **supplementary**, and therefore:

$x + 85^0 = 180^0$ Two angles are **supplementary** if the sum of their measures is 180^0.

$x + 85^0 - 85^0 = 180^0 - 85^0$ Move similar or like terms to one side of the equation by subtracting 85^0, from both sides of the equation.

$x = 180^0 - 85^0$ Now we have similar or like terms on each side of the equation. $85^0 - 85^0 = 0$.

$x = 95^0$.

c. $\angle$C and $\angle$D are consecutive angles because there are no other angles between them. In any parallelogram, the consecutive angles are supplementary, and therefore:

$n + 113^0 = 180^0$ Two angles are **supplementary** if the sum of their measures is 180^0.

$n + 113^0 - 113^0 = 180^0 - 113^0$ Move similar or like terms to one side of the equation by subtracting 113^0, from both sides of the equation.

$n = 180^0 - 113^0$ Now we have similar or like terms on each side of the equation. $113^0 - 113^0 = 0$.

$n = 67^0$.

d. $\angle$A and $\angle$D are consecutive angles because there are no other angles between them. In any parallelogram, the consecutive angles are supplementary, and therefore:

$x + 112^0 = 180^0$ Two angles are **supplementary** if the sum of their measures is 180^0.

$x + 112^0 - 112^0 = 180^0 - 112^0$ Move similar or like terms to one side of the equation by subtracting 112^0, from both sides of the equation.

$x = 180^0 - 112^0$ Now we have similar or like terms on each side of the equation. $112^0 - 112^0 = 0$.

$x = 68^0$.

===============================

The notes and the generous examples have provided me with the conceptual understanding and the computational fluency to do my homework.

Exercises

1. Write all the three properties of the parallelogram that are used to find the unknown angles of a parallelogram.

2. Explain what is meant by the consecutive angles of a parallelogram.
   Hint: See Example **3a**.

3. The measure of the opposite angles of a parallelogram are equal. True or false?
   Hint: See Example **2**.

4. The sum of the measure of the supplementary angles is 180^0. True or false?
   Hint: See Example **3**.

5. The measure of any consecutive angles of a parallelogram is supplementary.
   True or false? Hint: See Example **3**.

6. Find the measure of the unknown angle in each parallelogram. Hint: See Example **1**.

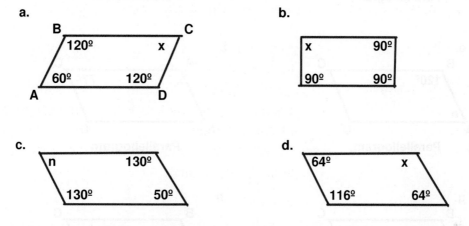

a.

b.

c.

d.

7. Find the measure of the angles represented by b and x. Hint: See Example **2**.

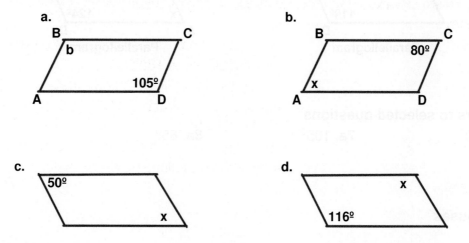

a.

b.

c.

d.

8. Find the angle measure represented by n and x in the parallelogram.
   Hint: See Example **3**.

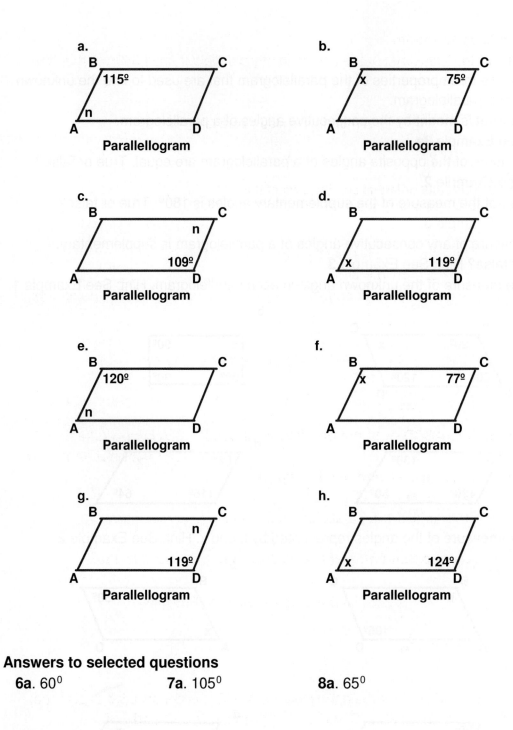

a.
B — 115º — C
A — n — D
Parallellogram

b.
B — x — 75º — C
A — D
Parallellogram

c.
B — C — n
A — 109º — D
Parallellogram

d.
B — C
A — x — 119º — D
Parallellogram

e.
B — 120º — C
A — n — D
Parallellogram

f.
B — x — 77º — C
A — D
Parallellogram

g.
B — C — n
A — 119º — D
Parallellogram

h.
B — C
A — x — 124º — D
Parallellogram

Answers to selected questions

6a. 60⁰   **7a.** 105⁰   **8a.** 65⁰

Rhombuses

To solve for the unknown angle in rhombuses, the following properties of the rhombuses are used:

A rhombus is an equilateral quadrilateral and all rhombuses are parallelograms. Since all rhombuses are parallelograms, the three preceding properties of the parallelograms that are listed under the section "Parallelograms" is also true for the rhombuses as shown:

1. The sum of the measures of the angles in any parallelogram is 360^0. A rhombus is also a parallelogram.

A rhombus is also a parallelogram.

Rhombus ABCD is a quadrilateral and the sum of the measures of the angles of any quadrilalteral is 360°.

Therefore, $m\angle A + m\angle B + m\angle C + m\angle D = 360^0$,
or $a + b + c + d = 360^0$.

2. The measures of the opposite angles of any parallelogram, including the rhombus are equal.

A rhombus is also a parallelogram.

In the rhombus ABCD or In the parallelogram ABCD, $\angle A$ is opposite to $\angle C$,
$\angle B$ is opposite to $\angle D$.

Therefore, $m\angle A = m\angle C$ and $m\angle B = m\angle D$,
or $a = c$ and $b = d$.

3. The consecutive angles of a parallelogram, including a rhombus are supplementary.

Two angles are **supplementary if the sum of their measures is 180^0.**

A rhombus is also a parallelogram.

In the rhombus ABCD or in the parallelogram ABCD, the consecutive angles are:
$\angle A$ and $\angle B$, $\angle B$ and $\angle C$, $\angle C$ and $\angle D$, $\angle D$ and $\angle A$.
Therefore, $m\angle A + m\angle B = 180^0$, or $a + b = 180^0$.
$m\angle B + m\angle C = 180^0$, or $b + c = 180^0$.
$m\angle C + m\angle D = 180^0$, or $c + d = 180^0$.
$m\angle D + m\angle A = 180^0$, or $d + a = 180^0$.

Note that two angles form **consecutive angles** if there is no other angle between them.

To solve for the unknown angle of a rhombus by using the properties of the

rhombus, see the worked examples under the section "Parallelograms" because rhombuses are also parallelograms. Also, the exercises under the section "Parallelograms" apply to the rhombuses.

Trapezoids

To solve for the unknown angle in a trapezoid, the following properties of the trapezoid are used:

1. The trapezoid, including the isosceles trapezoid is a quadrilateral that has one pair of parallel sides and the sum of the measures of the angles in any quadrilateral is 360^0.

Segment BC and segment AD are the parallel sides of the trapezoid ABCD.

Trapezoid ABCD is a quadrilateral and the sum of the measures of the angles of any quadrilalteral is 360º.

$$\text{Therefore, } m\angle A + m\angle B + m\angle C + m\angle D = 360^0,$$
$$\text{or } a + b + c + d = 360^0.$$

2. The **isosceles trapezoid** is a trapezoid that has **a pair of equal legs and the measure of each pair of base angles are equal**.

Segment BC and segment AD are the parallel sides of the trapezoid ABCD. The parallel sides of a trapezoid are called the bases and the nonparallelel sides are called the legs. The pairs of the angles that include each base are called the base angles. In trapeziod ABCD, the two pairs of the base angles are:

$\angle$ B and $\angle$ C
$\angle$ A and $\angle$ D

The measure of the base angles of a trapezoid do not have any special relationship unless the legs of the trapezoid are equal. In the trapezoid ABCD, the length of the leg AB is equal to the length of the leg CD. Therefore, the correct name of the trapezoid ABCD is isosceles trapezoid. Therefore, an isosceles trapezoid is a trapezoid that has equal legs.

In an **isosceles trapezoid**, each **pair of the base angles are equal**.

Therefore, in the isosceles trapezoid ABCD:
$$m\angle B = m\angle C \text{ and,}$$
$$m\angle A = m\angle D$$

To solve for the unknown angle of a trapezoid by using the property of the trapezoid, that states that the measures of the angles in any quadrilateral is 360°, see the worked examples under the section "Parallelograms" because trapezoids and parallelograms are quadrilaterals. Also, the exercises under the section "Parallelograms" apply to the trapezoids.

To solve for the unknown angle of a trapezoid by using the property of the trapezoid, that states, the isosceles trapezoid is a trapezoid that has a pair of equal legs, and the measure of each pair of base angles are equal.

Example 1
Find the value of n in each isosceles trapezoid.

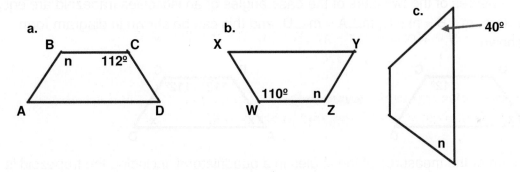

Solution
a. n = 112⁰ because the measures of the two pairs of the base angles of an isosceles trapezoid are equal. The two pairs of the equal measures of the base angles are as follows:
$$m\angle B = m\angle C \text{ and}$$
$$m\angle A = m\angle D$$

b. n = 110⁰ because the measures of the two pairs of the base angles of an isosceles trapezoid are equal. The two pairs of the equal measures of the base angles are as shown:
$$m\angle X = m\angle Y \text{ and}$$
$$m\angle W = m\angle Z$$

c. n = 40⁰ because the measures of the two pairs of the base angles of an isosceles trapezoid are equal.

Example 2

Find the value of x in each isosceles trapezoid. Hint: Use the combination of two properties of the isosceles trapezoid to find x. The two isosceles trapezoid properties are the measures of the two pairs of the base angles of an isosceles trapezoid are equal and the sum of the measures of the angles in a quadrilateral, including the trapezoid is 360^0.

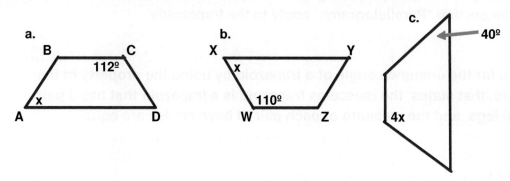

Solution

a. The measures of the two pairs of the base angles of an isosceles trapezoid are equal. Therefore, $m\angle B = m\angle C$, $m\angle A = m\angle D$, and this can be shown in diagram form as shown:

The sum of the measures of the angles in a quadrilateral, including the trapezoid is 360^0, and therefore:

$112^0 + 112^0 + x + x = 360^0$

$\qquad\qquad 224^0 + 2x = 360^0$ Simplify, $112^0 + 112^0 = 224^0$ and $x + x = 2x$.

$\qquad 224^0 - 224^0 + 2x = 360^0 - 224^0$ Subtract 224^0 from both sides of the equation in order to isolate 2x.

$\qquad\qquad\qquad\quad 2x = 360^0 - 224^0$ Now, we have isolated 2x, $224^0 - 224^0 = 0$.

$\qquad\qquad\qquad\quad 2x = 136^0$ $360^0 - 224^0 = 136^0$

$$\frac{2x}{2} = \frac{136^0}{2}$$ Divide both sides of the equation $2x = 136^0$ by 2 to obtain the value of x.

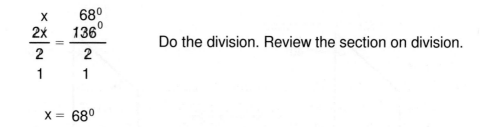

Do the division. Review the section on division.

$$x = 68^0$$

b. The measures of the two pairs of the base angles of an isosceles trapezoid are equal. Therefore, $m\angle X = m\angle Y$, $m\angle W = m\angle Z$, and this can be shown in diagram form as shown:

The sum of the measures of the angles in a quadrilateral, including the trapezoid is 360^0, and therefore:

$$x + x + 110^0 + 110^0 = 360^0$$
$$2x + 220^0 = 360^0 \qquad \text{Simplify, } x + x = 2x \text{ and } 110^0 + 110^0 = 220^0.$$
$$2x + 220^0 - 220^0 = 360^0 - 220^0 \qquad \text{Subtract } 220^0 \text{ from both sides of the equation } 2x + 220^0 = 360^0 \text{ in order to isolate } 2x.$$
$$2x = 360^0 - 220^0 \qquad \text{Now, we have isolated } 2x, 220^0 - 220^0 = 0.$$
$$2x = 140^0 \qquad 360^0 - 220^0.$$

$$\frac{2x}{2} = \frac{140^0}{2} \qquad \text{Divide both sides of the equation } 2x = 140^0 \text{ by}$$

2 in order to obtain the value of x.

$$\frac{2x}{2} = \frac{140^0}{2} \qquad \text{Do the division.}$$

$$x = 70^0$$

c. The measures of the two pairs of the base angles of an isosceles trapezoid are equal. Therefore, this can be shown in diagram form as shown:

705

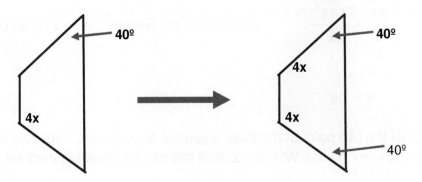

The sum of the measures of the angles in a quadrilateral, including the trapezoid is 360^0, and therefore:

$4x + 4x + 40^0 + 40^0 = 360^0$

$\qquad\qquad 8x + 80^0 = 360^0$ Simplify, $4x + 4x = 8x$ and $40^0 + 40^0 = 80^0$.

$\qquad 8x + 80^0 - 80^0 = 360^0 - 80^0$ Subtract 80^0 from both sides of the equation

$\qquad\qquad\qquad\qquad\qquad\qquad$ $8x + 80^0 = 360^0$ in order to isolate $8x$.

$\qquad\qquad\qquad 8x = 360^0 - 80^0$ Now, we have isolated $8x$, $80^0 - 80^0 = 0$.

$\qquad\qquad\qquad 8x = 280^0$ $360^0 - 80^0 = 280^0$

$$\frac{8x}{8} = \frac{280^0}{8}$$

Divide both sides of the equation $8x = 280^0$ by

8 in order to obtain the value of x.

$$\frac{\overset{x}{\cancel{8}x}}{\underset{1}{\cancel{8}}} = \frac{\overset{35^0}{\cancel{280}^0}}{\underset{1}{\cancel{8}}}$$

Do the division. Review the chapter on division.

$$x = 35^0$$

═══════════════ The notes and the generous examples have provided me with the conceptual understanding and the computational fluency to do my homework.

Exercises

1. A trapezoid is a quadrilateral. True or False?
2. What is an isosceles trapezoid?
3. The sum of the measures of the angles of a trapezoid is 360^0. True or False?
4. Explain what is meant by the bases of a trapezoid?
5. Explain what is meant by the base angles of a trapezoid.
6. The pairs of base angles of an isosceles trapezoid are equal. True or False?

7. Find the value of x in each isosceles trapezoid. Hint: See Example **1**.

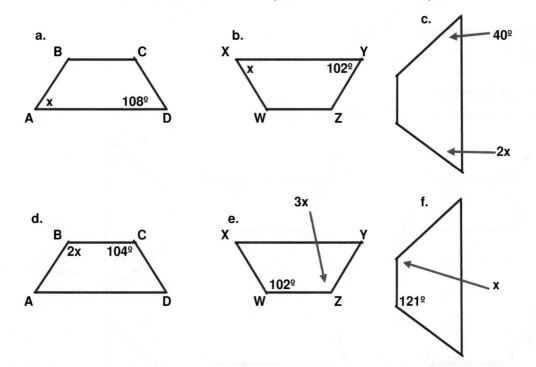

8. Find the value of x in each isosceles trapezoid. Hint: Use the combination of two properties of the isosceles trapezoid to find x. The two isosceles trapezoid properties are the measures of the two pairs of the base angles of an isosceles trapezoid are equal and the sum of the measures of the angles in a quadrilateral, including the trapezoid is 360°. Hint: See Example 2.

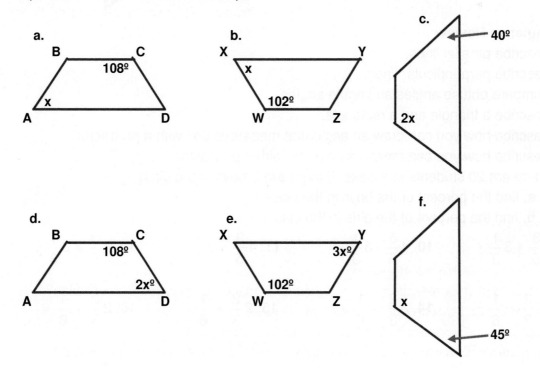

Answers to selected questions

7a. 108^0 **8a.** 72^0

Challenge Questions

9. Find the value of x in each isosceles trapezoid.

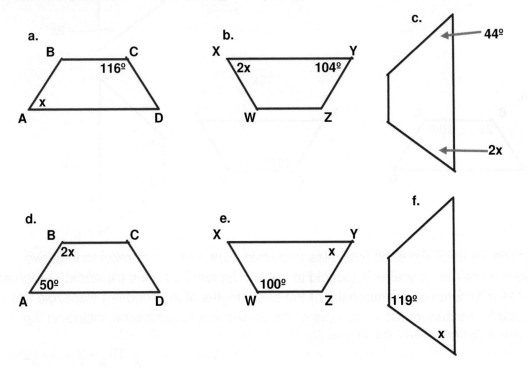

Cumulative Review

1. Describe parallel lines.

2. Describe perpendicular lines.

3. Compare obtuse angles and acute angles.

4. Describe a triangle and a rectangle.

5. Describe how you can draw an angle that measures 65^0 with a protractor.

7. Describe how you can measure an angle with a protractor.

8. There are 20 students in a class. If there are 5 boys in the class:

    a. find the percent of the boys in the class.

    b. find the percent of the girls in the class.

9. $4\dfrac{3}{5} + 3\dfrac{1}{3} =$ **10.** $4\dfrac{3}{5} - 3\dfrac{1}{3} =$ **11.** $4\dfrac{3}{5} \times 3\dfrac{1}{3}$ **12.** $4\dfrac{3}{5} \div 3\dfrac{1}{3} =$

13. $2\dfrac{2}{3} \div \dfrac{1}{6} =$ **14.** $2\dfrac{2}{3} \times \dfrac{1}{6} =$ **15.** $2\dfrac{2}{3} + \dfrac{1}{6} =$ **16.** $2\dfrac{2}{3} + \dfrac{1}{6} =$

708

CHAPTER 31

CIRCLES

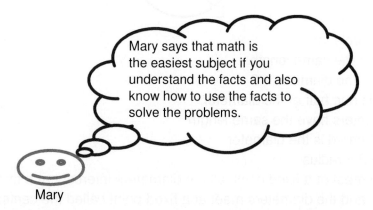

Mary says that math is the easiest subject if you understand the facts and also know how to use the facts to solve the problems.

Mary

A **circle** is a closed plane figure such that all the points on it are the same distance from the center. A **radius** (plural of radius is radii) is the distance from the center of a circle to any point on the circle. Therefore, we can also say that the radius of a circle is the line segment with one endpoint on the circle and the other endpoint at the center of the circle.

Could you give two examples of objects that are in the form of a circle?

An example of an object in the form of a circle is the bicycle wheel. The spokes of the wheel represent the radii of the circle and the spokes join at a fixed point called the center of the wheel or hub, as shown in the picture.

bicycle wheel (the wheel is like a circle).

spokes (the spokes are similar to the radius of a circle).

hub (center of the wheel, which is similar to the center of the circle).

The **chord** of a circle is the line segment that connects two points on a circle.
The **diameter** of a circle is the chord that passes through the center of the circle.
In the diagram,

      (1) The fixed point O is the center of the circle.

      (2) $\overline{AB}$ is the diameter.

      (3) $\overline{AO}$ is a radius.

      (4) $\overline{OB}$ is a radius.

(5) $\overline{EO}$ is the radius.

(6) $\overline{CD}$ is the chord.

(7) $\overline{AB}$ and $\overline{CD}$ are chords.

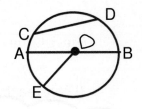

In any specific circle,

1. all radii have the same length
2. any radius = the diameter ÷ 2
3. the radius is one half of the diameter
4. all the diameters have the same length
5. the longest chord is the diameter
6. diameter = 2 × radius
7. all the radii meet at a fixed point, all the diameters intercept at a fixed point and all the radii and the diameters meet at a fixed point called the center.

Example 1

In the diagram, O is the center of the circle.

(a) $\overline{AB}$ is a diameter?

(b) $\overline{AO}$, $\overline{OG}$, and $\overline{OB}$ are radii?

(c) $\overline{CD}$, $\overline{CE}$, $\overline{DE}$, $\overline{EF}$, and $\overline{DF}$ are chords?

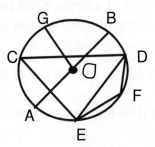

Solution

(a) $\overline{AB}$ is a diameter because $\overline{AB}$ passes through the center of the circle at point O, and $\overline{AB}$ is a chord. (Note that a chord is a line segment that connects two points on a circle and the chord that passes through the center of the circle is the radius.)

(b) $\overline{AO}$, $\overline{OG}$, and $\overline{OB}$ are radii because they are line segments with one endpoint at the center of the circle, which is point O, and the other endpoints on the circle at points A, G, and B.

(c) $\overline{CD}$, $\overline{CE}$, $\overline{DE}$, $\overline{EF}$, and $\overline{DF}$ are chords because they are line segments that connect two points on the circle and they do not pass through the center of the circle.

Example 2
(**a**) The diameter of a circle is 4 inches. How long is the radius?
(**b**) The radius of a circle is 9 inches. How long is the diameter?
Solution
(**a**) Diameter = 4 inches
    Diameter = 2 × radius   (Review the preceding notes.)

$$\frac{\text{Diameter}}{2} = \frac{2 \times \text{radius}}{2}$$
(Divide each side of the equation in

order to obtain the value of the radius.)

$$\frac{\text{Diameter}}{2} = \frac{\overset{1}{2} \times \text{radius}}{\underset{1}{2}}$$

$$\frac{\text{Diameter}}{2} = \text{radius} \quad\text{————————————————————————}[A]$$

$$\frac{4 \text{ inches}}{2} = \text{radius}$$
(Substitute diameter = 4 inches Into

equation $[A]$.)

$$\frac{\overset{2}{4 \text{ inches}}}{\underset{1}{2}} = \text{radius}$$

2 inches = radius
(**b**) Radius   = 9 inches
    Diameter = 2 × radius   ————————————————————$[B]$
    Diameter = 2 × 9 inches   (Substitute radius = 9 inches into equation $[B]$.)
    Diameter = 18 inches.

The notes and the generous examples have provided me with the conceptual understanding and the computational fluency to do my homework.

Exercises
1. In the diagram, the center of the circle is point O.
  (**a**) List two line segments that passe through the center of the circle.
  (**b**) List all the diameters, radii and chords. Hint : See Example **1**.

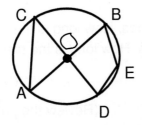

2. In the diagram, classify the line segments as radius, diameter or chord. Give reasons for your answer. The center of the circle is point O. Hint: See Example **1**.

(a) $\overline{DE}$
(b) $\overline{AO}$
© $\overline{AE}$
(d) $\overline{AB}$

(e) $\overline{CO}$
(f) $\overline{BD}$
(g) $\overline{OB}$

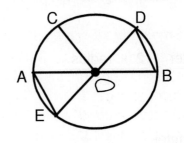

3. (**a**) The diameter of a circle is 10 inches. How long is the radius? Hint: See Example 2.
   (**b**) The radius of a circle is 7 cm. How long is the diameter? Hint: See Example 2.

How to Draw a Circle
Group Exercise
Objective: To draw a circle which has a radius of 3 centimeters.
Materials that are needed in order to construct a circle are a ruler, a pencil and a compass.
A compass is a device for drawing circles.

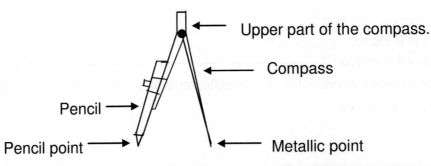

Step 1: Take a pencil and mark a point P which will be the center of the circle.

Point P ⟶ • P

Step 2: Take a compass and a ruler. Put the ruler on the table with the centimeter scale showing upwards. Put the metallic point of the compass on the zero mark of the centimeter scale of the ruler and then open the compass such that the pencil point should be on the 3 centimeter mark on the ruler. (Note that how much the compass is opened determines the length of the radius.)

Upper part of the compass.

Centimeter symbol.

cm

0 1 2 3 4 5 6 7 8 9 10

(The smaller markings on the centimeter scale have been omitted.)

Step 3: (Caution: We must keep the compass opening from Step 2 the same in order to maintain the 3 centimeter radius of the circle by holding only the upper part of the compass.)

By holding the upper part of the compass, put the metallic point of the compass on point P and with the pencil point touching the paper, swing the pencil point of the compass around (through 360°) to draw a circle.

Upper part of the compass.

P

We can draw a diameter to the circle by drawing a line segment through the center of the circle at point P such that the line segment should touch the two opposite sides of the circle at points A and B.

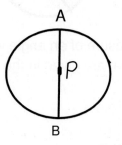

A

P

B

Analysis of the Group Exercise.

1. Use a ruler to measure the diameter AB. Is the diameter 3 cm.? Note that the diameter AB of the circle in this book is not 3 cm. because the circle is not drawn to scale and also note that the book just shows you how to draw a circle with any

specific radius.

2. Could you show that the relationship between the radii AP and PB and the diameter AB of a circle by measuring the radii AP and PB and the diameter AB. The relationship is:

$$\text{Diameter} = 2 \times \text{radius}$$

━━━━━━━━━━━━━ The notes and the generous examples have provided me with the conceptual understanding and the computational fluency to do my homework.

Exercises

1. A circle has a radius of 20 cm. How long is the diameter? Hint: See Example 2.

2. Draw a circle with each of the radius using a compass. Measure each diameter.

   (**a**) **2 cm..**   (**b**) 2 ins.   (**c**) 1 in.

   Hint: See the steps under the section "How to Draw a Circle."

Challenge Questions

4. Given the following diameter of a circle, find the radius.

   (a) 100 cm.   (b) 50 ins.   (c) 15 cm.   (d) 21 cm.

5. Given the following radius of a circle, find the diameter.

   (a) 5 cm.   (b) 9 ins.   (c) 2 cm.   (d) 11 cm.

Sum of the Measure of the Angles in a Circle

The sum of the measure of the angles in a circle is 360^0. The sum of the measures of the angles in a circle is similar to the sum of the measures of the angles at a point. The sum of the angles of the circle is: $w^0 + x^0 + y^0 + z^0 = 360^0$.

Rule 1: To find the unknown measure of an angle in a circle, find the sum of the measure of the angles that are given in the circle, and then subtract that sum from 360^0.

Example 3

Find the value of x^0 in each diagram.

(a)

 (b)

Solution

(a) The sum of the measure of the angles in a circle $= 360^0$, and therefore,

$$x^0 + 85^0 + 205^0 = 360^0$$
$$x^0 + 290^0 = 360^0 \qquad (85^0 + 205^0 = 290^0)$$
$$x^0 + 290^0 - 290^0 = 360^0 - 290^0$$

(Subtract 290^0 from each side of the equation in order to eliminate the 290^0 at the left side of the equation and also to obtain the value of x^0.) This is also the application of Rule 1.

$$x^0 + 0 = 70^0 \qquad (290^0 - 290^0 = 0, 360^0 - 290^0 = 70^0)$$
$$x^0 = 70^0$$

(b) The sum of the measure of the angles in a circle $= 360^0$, and therefore,

$$x^0 + 118^0 + 62^0 + 129^0 = 360^0$$
$$x^0 + 309^0 = 360^0 \qquad (118^0 + 62^0 + 129^0 = 309^0)$$
$$x^0 + 309^0 - 309^0 = 360^0 - 309^0$$

(Subtract 309^0 from each side of the equation in order to eliminate the 309^0 at the left side of the equation and also to obtain the value of x^0. This is also the application of rule 1.)

$$x^0 + 0 = 51^0 \qquad (309^0 - 309^0 = 0, 360^0 - 309^0 = 51^0)$$
$$x^0 = 51^0$$

The notes and the generous examples have provided me with the conceptual understanding and the computational fluency to do my homework.

Exercises

1. Find the unknown angle measure of each circle.

Let the unknown angle measure be x^0. Hint: See Example **3**.

(a)   (b)   (c)

Challenge Questions

2. Find the unknown angle measure of each circle.

(a)   (b)   (c)

Answers to Selected Questions

1(a) 110^0 **2(b)** 73^0

Mixed Review

1. Two lines that intersect to form right angles are called perpendicular lines. True or False?

2. Reduce each fraction to the lowest term.

   (a) $\dfrac{3}{9}$ (b) $\dfrac{5}{25}$ (c) $\dfrac{6}{36}$

3. What is the difference between an acute angle and an obtuse angle?

4. Solve:

   (a) $-2 - 6 =$ (b) $-9 \div 3 =$ (c) $-12 \times 2 =$

5. Solve:

   (a) $27 - 2 \times 4 + 3 =$ (b) $2 + 18 - 4 \times 2 =$ (c) $3^2 \times 2^3 =$

6. Explain what is meant by a regular hexagon.

7. What is the sum of the measure of the angles in a triangle?

8. What is the sum of the measure of the angles in a quadrilateral?

9. What is the sum of the measure of the angles formed in a circle?

10. To divide a number by a fraction, we have to multiply the number by the reciprocal of the fraction. True or False?

11. Solve:

   (a) $6 \div \dfrac{1}{3} =$ (b) $\dfrac{3}{4} \div \dfrac{1}{8} =$ (c) $3 - 1\dfrac{1}{5}$ (d) $\dfrac{2}{3} \times \dfrac{3}{2} =$

716

CHAPTER 32

CIRCUMFERENCE

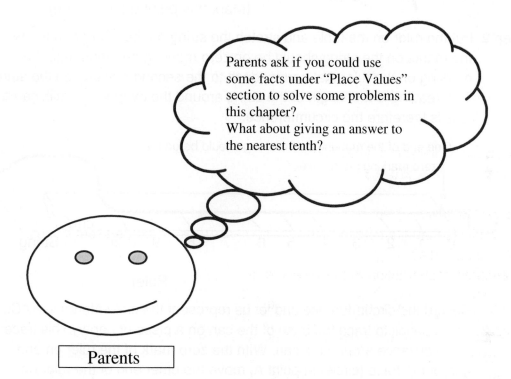

Parents ask if you could use some facts under "Place Values" section to solve some problems in this chapter?
What about giving an answer to the nearest tenth?

Parents

The **circumference** is the distance around a circle or a circular object. The ratio of the circumference to the diameter of a circle is called pi which has a symbol π. The value of $\pi = \dfrac{22}{7}$ **which is approximately 3.14.**

Find the Distance Around an Evaporated Milk Can and the Value of π.
Group Exercise.
Step 1. The materials needed for the exercise are a can, a string, a ruler, and a pen.

Each group should take a can and wrap a string around the can.
Make a mark on the string at a point where the string first overlaps.

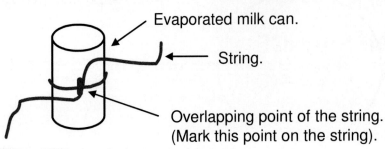

Evaporated milk can.

String.

Overlapping point of the string.
(Mark this point on the string).

Step 2. Put the ruler on the table and stretch the string on the ruler so that one of the marks on the string should be on zero marking and then read the marking on the ruler that corresponds to the second marking on the string. This reading is the length of the string around the evaporated milk can and this is therefore the circumference.

One end of the marking on the string should be on the zero marking on the ruler.

0 1 2 3 4 5 6 7 8 9 10   cm   String

Ruler

Record the circumference and let us represent the circumference by C.

Step 3. Use a pencil to trace the base of the can on a piece of paper. This trace is the distance around the can. With the zero mark of the ruler on one part of the trace (circle) at point A, move the other end of the ruler on the other side of the trace until you can find the longest distance on the ruler that coincides with the other side of the trace at point B. This distance is the diameter because we can recall that the **longest chord of a circle is the diameter**.

$\overline{AB}$ is the longest chord, which is the diameter. Record the length of the diameter, and let us represent the diameter by the letter d.

Place the zero mark on the ruler on one part of the trace (circle).

Trace the base of the can.

Ruler

Step 4. Find the ratio of the circumference to the diameter of the circle by dividing the circumference by the diameter which is $= \dfrac{c}{d}$. Record your value for the ratio $\dfrac{c}{d}$. Is your answer approximately 3.14?

Step 5: Find the circumference, the diameter and then the ratio of the circumference to the diameter of four more different size cans using steps 1 to 4 and record all the data for the group project in the table as shown:

Can type	Circumference(c)	Diameter(d)	Ratio $= \dfrac{c}{d}$
1			
2			
3			
4			
5			

Conclusion: The standard ratio $\dfrac{c}{d}$ is approximately $= 3.14 = \pi$.

Therefore, $\mathbf{c = \pi d}$ **(Important formula)**
(circumference $= \pi \times$ diameter where π is called pi)

Example 1
Find the circumference of a circle that has a diameter of 5 cm.
Solution
The circumference of a circle is given by the formula:

    $C = \pi d$, where C is the circumference, $\pi = 3.14$ and d = diameter.
    $C = \pi d$ ———————————— [A]
    $C = 3.14 \times 5$ cm   (Substitute $\pi = 3.14$, and d = 5 cm into equation [A].)
    $C = 15.7$ cm

Example 2
The circumference of a circle is 18.84 in. (**a**) Find the diameter. (**b**) Find the radius.

Solution

(a) The circumference of a circle is given by the formula:

$$C = \pi d \quad\text{———————————————}\quad [A]$$

$$18.84 = 3.14 \times d \qquad \text{(Substitute } C = 18.84 \text{ in. and } \pi = 3.14 \text{ into equation } [A].)$$

$$\frac{18.84}{3.14} = \frac{3.14}{3.14} \times d \qquad \text{(Divide each side of the equation by 3.14 in order to}$$

obtain the value of d.)

$$\frac{\overset{6}{\cancel{18.84}}}{\underset{1}{\cancel{3.14}}} = \frac{\overset{1}{\cancel{3.14}}}{\underset{1}{\cancel{3.14}}} \times d \qquad \text{(You may use the calculator to divide)}$$

$$(18.84 \div 3.14 = 6, \ 3.14 \div 3.14 = 1)$$

$$6 = d$$

Diameter = 6 in.

(b) Diameter ÷ 2 = radius. Therefore, the radius = 6 in. ÷ 2 = 3 in.

The notes and the generous examples have provided me with the conceptual understanding and the computational fluency to do my homework.

Exercises

1. Find the circumference of a circle that has the following diameter to the nearest tenth. Hint: See Example 1 and review the chapter/section on "Place Values."

(**a**) 3 cm　　　　　(**b**) 4 ft　　　　　(**c**) 6 in.　　　　　(**d**) 2.4 cm

2. The circumference of a circle is 9.42. Find the diameter of the circle.
Hint: See Example 2.

3. Find the diameter of a circle that has a circumference of 6.28 cm.
Hint: See Example 2.

Challenge Questions

4. Find the diameter of a circle that has a circumference of 31.4 cm.

5. Find the circumference of a circle that has a radius of 2.3 cm.
Hint: Change the radius to the diameter first.

6. Find the circumference of each circle.

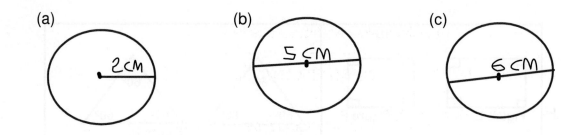

(a) 2CM

(b) 5 CM

(c) 6 CM

Answer to a Selected Question
1(a). 9.42 cm

CHAPTER 33

SIMILAR AND CONGRUENT FIGURES

New Terms: **similar**, **congruent**, **corresponding sides**, **corresponding angles**

Similar figures are figures that have the same shape but they do not necessarily have to be the same size. In the diagrams, Figure A is similar to Figure B because they have the **same shape** but do not have the **same size**. The symbol ∼ means "is similar to." In the diagram, Figure A is similar to Figure B because they have the same shape but not the same size. Similarly, Figure C is similar to Figure D because they have the same shape but not the same size.

Figure A   Figure B   60º 60º 60º Figure C   60º 60º 60º Figure D

Congruent figures are figures that have the same shape and size. In the diagrams, Figure E is congruent to Figure F because they have the same shape and size. The symbol ≅ means "is congruent to."

721

Figure E   Figure F   Figure G   Figure H

In the diagram, Figure I and Figure J are neither similar nor congruent because they have different shapes and different sizes. Similarly, Figure K and Figure L are neither similar nor congruent because they have different shapes and different sizes.

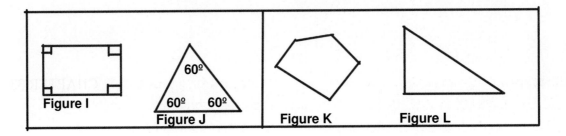

Figure I   Figure J   Figure K   Figure L

Critical Conclusions

1. Figures E and F or Figures G and H show that congruent figures are also similar figures.
2. Figures A and B or Figures C and D show that similar figures are not necessarily congruent figures.

Writing Similar Figures and Congruent Figures Using Symbols

The symbol for a triangle is △.

1. We can write that triangle ABC is similar to triangle DEF by using the symbols as follows: △ABC ~ △DEF

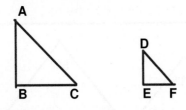

2. We can write that triangle PQW is congruent to triangle XYZ by using symbols as shown: △PQW ≅ △XYZ

Group Discussion

Triangles ABC and triangles DEF are similar.

Similar polygons have corresponding angles and corresponding sides.

Note that when two figures are similar, for each part of one figure, there is a corresponding part on the other figure. To determine the corresponding angles and the corresponding sides of similar polygons, compare the shape of the polygons and then determine how each pair of angles and each pair of sides form corresponding parts as shown:

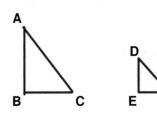

Corresponding Angles

∠A corresponds to ∠D

∠B corresponds to ∠E

∠C corresponds to ∠F

∠ is the symbol for angle.

Corresponding sides

$\overline{AB}$ corresponds to $\overline{DE}$

$\overline{BC}$ corresponds to $\overline{EF}$

$\overline{AC}$ corresponds to $\overline{DF}$

Note that the angles in △ABC are congruent to the corresponding angles in △DEF and the length of the sides of △DEF are about twice the length of the corresponding sides in △ABC.

Conclusion: Note that in similar figures the **corresponding angles are congruent** (the same measure of angles), and the ratio of the lengths of the corresponding sides are **equal**.

Group Exercise

Given that △ABC is similar to △DEF, copy and complete the statements:

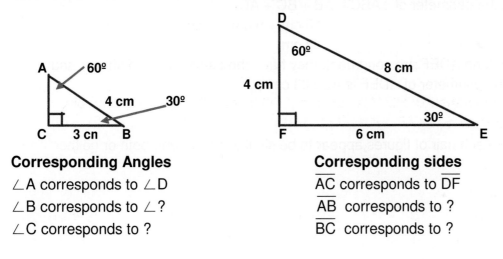

Corresponding Angles

∠A corresponds to ∠D

∠B corresponds to ∠?

∠C corresponds to ?

Corresponding sides

$\overline{AC}$ corresponds to $\overline{DF}$

$\overline{AB}$ corresponds to ?

$\overline{BC}$ corresponds to ?

723

Example 1

Given that the trapezoid ABCD is similar to the trapezoid EFGH, list all the pairs of the corresponding sides.

Solution

By comparing the shapes of the trapezoids ABCD and EFGH,

$\overline{AB}$ corresponds to $\overline{EF}$

$\overline{BC}$ corresponds to $\overline{FG}$

$\overline{CD}$ corresponds to $\overline{GH}$

$\overline{DA}$ corresponds to $\overline{HE}$

Example 2

Given that △ABC is congruent to △DEF,

a. What side of △DEF corresponds to side $\overline{AC}$?

b. What is the perimeter of △DEF ?

c. What is the length of $\overline{DF}$?

Solution

a. By comparing the shapes of △ABC and △DEF, $\overline{DF}$ corresponds to $\overline{AC}$.

b. The perimeter of △ABC is the distance around △ABC.

Therefore, the perimeter of △ABC = $\overline{AB}$ + $\overline{BC}$ + $\overline{AC}$

$$= 10 \text{ cm} + 5 \text{ cm} + 8 \text{ cm}$$

$$= 23 \text{ cm}$$

Since △ABC and △DEF are congruent, they have the same size and shape, and therefore, the perimeter of △DEF is also 23 cm.

Example 3

Write whether each pair of figures appear to be similar, congruent, both or neither.

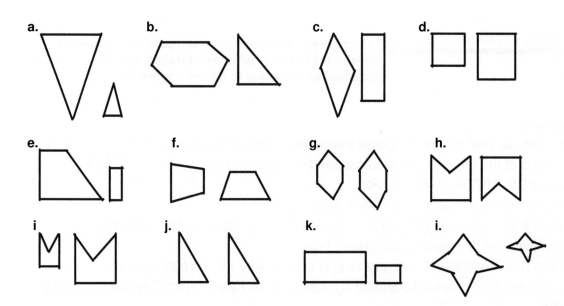

Solution

a. The two triangles appear to be similar because they have the same shape but not the same size.

b. The hexagon and the triangle are neither similar nor congruent because they have neither the same shape nor the same size.

c. The rhombus and the rectangle are neither similar nor congruent because they have neither the same shape nor the same size.

d. The two rectangles appear to be similar because they have the same shape but not the same size.

e. The trapezoid and the rectangle are neither similar nor congruent because they have neither the same shape nor the same size.

f. The two quadrilaterals appear to be similar and congruent because they have the same shape and the same size.

g. The two hexagons appear to be similar because they have the same shape but not the same size.

h. The two figures appear to be similar and congruent because they have the same shape and the same size.

i. The two figures appear to be similar because they have the same shape but not the same size.

j. The two triangles are similar and congruent because they have the same shape and the same size.

k. The two rectangles appear to be similar because they have the same shape but not the same size.

l. The two figures appear to be similar because they have the same shape but not the same size.

725

The notes and the generous examples have provided me with the conceptual understanding and the computational fluency to do my homework.

Exercises

1. We can say that in similar figures the corresponding angles are c _____ and the ratio of the lengths of the corresponding sides are e _____. Hint: See the section on "Group Discussion."

2a. Explain what is meant by similar figures.

2b. Sketch two similar right triangles. Hint: A right triangle has one right angle.

3a. Explain what is meant by congruent figures.

3b. Sketch two congruent rectangles and explain why they are congruent.

4. Congruent figures are also similar figures. True or False? Hint: See the preceding notes.

5. Similar figures are not necessarily congruent figures. True or False? Hint: See the preceding pages.

6. Two figures are neither similar nor congruent because they have different sh___ and different si____.

7a. What is the symbol for a triangle?

7b. What is the symbol for "is similar to?"

7c. What is the symbol for "is congruent to?"
    Hint: See the preceding pages.

8. Using symbols, write that:
   a. triangle XYZ is similar to triangle ABC.
   b. triangle ABC is congruent to triangle XYZ.
   Hint: See the preceding pages.

9. Similar polygons have corresponding angles and corresponding sides. True or False? Hint: See the preceding pages.

10. When two figures are similar, for each part of one figure, there is a corresponding p____ on the other figure.
    Hint: See the preceding pages.

11. In similar figures, the corresponding ang___ are congruent (the same measure of angles), and the ratio of the r____ of the corresponding s____ are equal. Hint: See the preceding pages.

12. Trapezoid WXYZ is similar to trapezoid ABCD. List all the pairs of corresponding sides. Hint: See Example **1.**

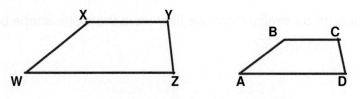

13. Given that △ABC ≅ △XYZ.

   (**a**) What side of △XYZ corresponds to side $\overline{YZ}$?

   (**b**) What is the perimeter of △XYZ?

   (**c**) What is the length of $\overline{XY}$?

   Hint: See Example **2**.

14. Write whether each pair of figures appear to be similar, congruent, both or neither and give the reason for your choice.

   Hint: See Example **3**.

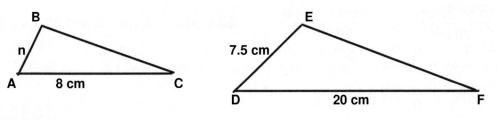

How to Use Proportion to Solve Similar Figure Problems.

What is a proportion? A **proportion** is an equation that states that **two ratios are equal**. Therefore, the **cross products** of a proportion are **equal**. Examples 1, 2, and 3 show and explain how a proportion and the cross products of a proportion can be used to solve similar figure problems.

Example 1

Given that the two figures are similar, write and solve the proportion to find the length of n.

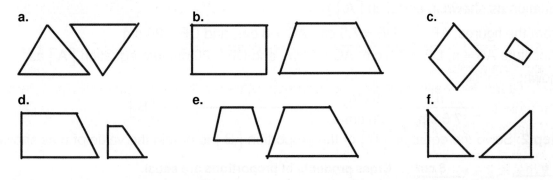

Solution

By observing the shape of the figures,

   $\overline{AB}$ corresponds to $\overline{DE}$

   $\overline{AC}$ corresponds to $\overline{DF}$

We can find the value of n by using the fact that in similar figures, the ratios of the corresponding sides are equal.

Step 1: We can therefore write two ratios or a proportion as shown:

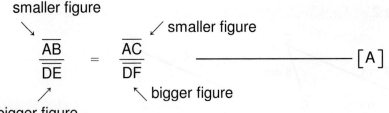

smaller figure

smaller figure

$$\frac{\overline{AB}}{\overline{DE}} = \frac{\overline{AC}}{\overline{DF}} \quad\rule{3cm}{0.4pt}\ [A]$$

bigger figure

bigger figure

(Note: It is very important to remember the order of the two ratios so that for this specific example, the smaller figure value divides the bigger value on both sides of the equation as shown in equation $[A]$.)

From the figures, $\overline{AB}$ = n, $\overline{DE}$ = 7.5 cm, $\overline{AC}$ = 8 cm, and $\overline{DF}$ = 20 cm.

Substitute $\overline{AB}$ = n, $\overline{DE}$ = 7.5 cm, $\overline{AC}$ = 8 cm, and $\overline{DF}$ = 20 cm into equation $[A]$ as shown:

$$\frac{n}{7.5 \text{ cm}} = \frac{8 \text{ cm}}{20 \text{ cm}} \quad\rule{2cm}{0.4pt}\ [B]$$

Step 2: Solve the equation $[B]$ or the proportion $[B]$ to obtain the value of n as shown:

$$\frac{n}{7.5 \text{ cm}} \times \frac{8 \text{ cm}}{20 \text{ cm}}$$

Cross products of proportions are equal.
Hint: Review the chapter/section on proportion.

$$n \times 20 \text{ cm} = 7.5 \text{ cm} \times 8 \text{ cm} \quad\rule{2cm}{0.4pt}\ [C]$$

Divide each side of the equation $[C]$ by 20 cm in order to obtain the value of n as shown:

$$\frac{n \times 20 \text{ cm}}{20 \text{ cm}} = \frac{7.5 \text{ cm} \times 8 \text{ cm}}{20 \text{ cm}}$$

$$\frac{n \times 20 \overset{1}{\cancel{\text{cm}}}}{20 \underset{1}{\cancel{\text{cm}}}} = \frac{7.5 \text{ cm} \times 8 \overset{2}{\cancel{\text{cm}}}}{20 \underset{5}{\cancel{\text{cm}}}}$$

$20 \div 20 = 1,\ 8 \div 4 = 2$ and $20 \div 4 = 5$

$$n = \frac{7.5 \text{ cm} \times 2}{5}$$

$$n = \frac{7.5 \text{ cm} \times 2}{\underset{1}{\cancel{5}}}^{1.5}$$

Divide by 5, $7.5 \div 5 = 1.5,\ 5 \div 5 = 1$.

$$n = 1.5 \text{ cm} \times 2$$
$$n = 3.0 \text{ cm}$$

Example 2

The two figures are similar. Find the length of n.

Solution

By observing the shape of the two figures, $\overline{AD}$ corresponds to $\overline{WZ}$ and $\overline{DC}$ corresponds to $\overline{ZY}$. We can find the value of n by using the fact that in similar figures, the ratios of the corresponding sides are equal.

Step 1: We can therefore, write two ratios or a proportion as shown:

Bigger figure

Bigger figure

$$\frac{\overline{AD}}{\overline{WZ}} = \frac{\overline{DC}}{\overline{ZY}} \quad\text{———————— [A]}$$

Smaller figure

Smaller figure

(Note: It is very important to remember the order of the two ratios so that for this specific example, the bigger figure value divides the smaller figure value on both sides of the equation [A] as shown.)

From the figures, $\overline{AD} = 4.5$ cm, $\overline{WZ} = n$, $\overline{DC} = 9$ cm, and $\overline{ZY} = 3$ cm.

Substitute $\overline{AD} = 4.5$ cm, $\overline{WZ} = n$, $\overline{DC} = 9$ cm, and $\overline{ZY} = 3$ cm into equation [A] as shown:

$$\frac{4.5 \text{ cm}}{n} = \frac{9 \text{ cm}}{3 \text{ cm}} \quad\text{———————— [B]}$$

Step 2: Solve the equation [B] or the proportion [B] to obtain the value of n as shown:

Cross products of a proportion are equal.
Hint: Review the chapter/section on proportion.

$$n \times 9 \text{ cm} = 4.5 \text{ cm} \times 3 \text{ cm} \quad\text{——————— [C]}$$

Divide both sides of equation [C] by 9 cm in order to obtain the value of n as

shown:

$$\frac{n \times 9 \text{ cm}}{9 \text{ cm}} = \frac{4.5 \text{ cm} \times 3 \text{ cm}}{9 \text{ cm}}$$

$$\frac{n \times 9\overset{1}{\cancel{\text{cm}}}}{\underset{1}{\cancel{9 \text{ cm}}}} = \frac{4.5 \text{ cm} \times \overset{1}{\cancel{3 \text{ cm}}}}{\underset{3}{\cancel{9 \text{ cm}}}}$$

9 can divide the left hand side of the equation and 3 can divide the right hand side of the equation.

$$n = \frac{4.5 \text{ cm}}{3}$$

$$n = 4.5 \div 3 = 1.5 \text{ cm} \qquad \text{(You may use a calculator.)}$$
$$n = 1.5 \text{ cm}.$$

Example 3
The two figures are similar. Find the length of n.

Solution
By observing the shape of the figure,

$\overline{AB}$ corresponds to $\overline{IJ}$

$\overline{AH}$ corresponds to $\overline{IP}$

We can find the value of n by using the the fact that in similar figures, the ratios of the corresponding sides are equal.

Step 1: We can therefore write two ratios or a proportion as shown:

(Note: It is very important to remember the order of the ratios so that for this specific example, the smaller figure value divides the bigger figure value on both sides of the

730

equation [A] as shown.)

From the figures, $\overline{AB} = 3$ cm, $\overline{IJ} = n$, $\overline{AH} = 1.6$ cm, and $\overline{IP} = 4.8$ cm.

Substitute $\overline{AB} = 3$ cm, $\overline{IJ} = n$, $\overline{AH} = 1.6$ cm, and $\overline{IP} = 4.8$ cm into equation [A] as shown:

$$\frac{3 \text{ cm}}{n} = \frac{1.6 \text{ cm}}{4.8 \text{ cm}} \quad\rule{8cm}{0.4pt}\text{[B]}$$

Step 2: Solve equation [B] or the proportion [B] to obtain the value of n as shown:

$$\frac{3 \text{ cm}}{n} \diagdown \frac{1.6 \text{ cm}}{4.8 \text{ cm}}$$

Cross products of a proportion are equal.
Hint: Review the chapter/section on proportion.

$$n \times 1.6 \text{ cm} = 3 \text{ cm} \times 4.8 \text{ cm} \quad\rule{5cm}{0.4pt}\text{[C]}$$

Divide both sides of equation [C] by 1.6 cm in order to obtain the value of n as shown:

$$\frac{n \times 1.6 \text{ cm}}{1.6 \text{ cm}} = \frac{3 \text{ cm} \times 4.8 \cancel{\text{cm}}}{1.6 \text{ cm}}$$

$$\frac{n \times 1.6 \cancel{\text{cm}}^{1}}{1.6 \cancel{\text{cm}}_{1}} = \frac{3 \text{ cm} \times 4.8 \cancel{\text{cm}}}{1.6 \cancel{\text{cm}}} \qquad 1.6 \div 1.6 = 1$$

$$n = \frac{14.4 \text{ cm}}{1.6} \qquad\qquad 3 \times 4.8 \text{ cm} = 14.4 \text{ cm}$$

$$n = 14.4 \div 1.6 = 9 \text{ cm} \qquad \text{(You may use a calculator.)}$$

$$n = 9 \text{ cm}.$$

The notes and the generous examples have provided me with the conceptual understanding and the computational fluency to do my homework.

Exercise

1. Each pair of figures are similar. Write and solve the proportion to find the length n.
   Hint: See Example **1**.

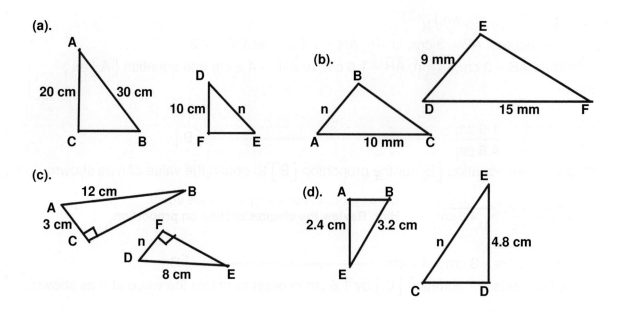

(a).

A

20 cm   30 cm

C   B

D

10 cm   n

F   E

(b).

9 mm

E

B

n

A   10 mm   C

D   15 mm   F

(c).

12 cm   B

A

3 cm

C

F

n

D

8 cm   E

(d).   A   B

2.4 cm   3.2 cm

E

E

n   4.8 cm

C   D

2. Each pair of figures are similar. Write and solve the proportion to find the length n.
Hint: See Example **2**.

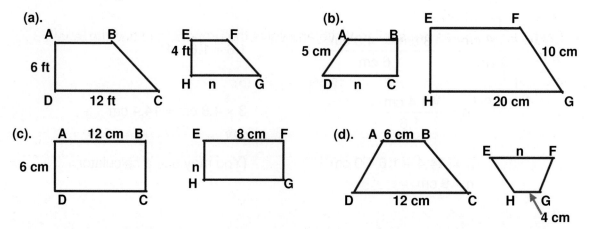

(a).

A   B

6 ft

D   12 ft   C

E   F

4 ft

H   n   G

(b).

A   B

5 cm

D   n   C

E   F

10 cm

H   20 cm   G

(c).   A   12 cm   B

6 cm

D   C

E   8 cm   F

n

H   G

(d).   A 6 cm B

D   12 cm   C

E   n   F

H   G

4 cm

3. Each pair of figures are similar. Write and solve the proportion to find the length n.
Hint: See Example **3**.

Answers to Selected Questions

1c. 2 cm   **2d.** 8 cm   **3d.** 4.5 cm

Challenge Questions

4. Each pair of figures are similar. Write and solve the proportion to find the length of n.

REAL WORLD APPLICATIONS - WORD PROBLEMS
How to Use Proportion to Solve Similar Figure Problems

Example 1

1. A man 6 feet tall casts a 4-foot shadow. A lady who is standing next to the man casts a 3-foot shadow. How tall is the lady?
Solution

We assume that both the man and the lady form right angles with the horizontal floor. We can then use pairs of similar right triangles to find how tall the lady is as shown: Let the height of the lady be n

Step 1: Sketch the diagram.

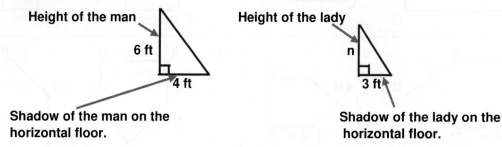

Step 2: The right triangles are similar, and therefore, write a ratio relating the shadow of the man and the shadow of the lady and also write a ratio relating the height of the man and the height of the lady because the ratios of the corresponding sides of similar figures are equal as shown:

(Note: It is very important to remember the order of the ratios so that for this specific example, the lady's height is divided by the man's height and the lady's shadow is divided by the man's shadow as shown in the equation [A].)

Step 3: Solve the proportion as shown:

Cross products of a proportion are equal.
Hint: Review the chapter/section on proportion.

$$n \times 4 \text{ ft} = 6 \text{ ft} \times 3 \text{ ft} \underline{\hspace{6cm}} [B]$$

Divide both sides of equation [B] by 4 ft in order to obtain the value of n as shown:

$$\frac{n \times 4 \text{ ft}}{4 \text{ ft}} = \frac{6 \text{ ft} \times 3 \text{ ft}}{4 \text{ ft}}$$

$$\frac{n \times \overset{1}{4} \text{ ft}}{\underset{1}{4} \text{ ft}} = \frac{\overset{3}{6} \text{ ft} \times 3 \text{ ft}}{\underset{2}{4} \text{ ft}}$$

$(4 \div 4 = 1 , 4 \div 2 = 2 , 6 \div 2 = 3)$

$$n = \frac{3 \times 3 \text{ ft}}{2} = \frac{9 \text{ ft}}{2} = 4.5 \text{ ft.}$$

$$n = 4.5 \text{ ft.}$$

━━━━━━━━━━ **The notes and the generous examples have provided me with the conceptual understanding and the computational fluency to do my homework.**

Exercises

Hint: Use the solution method for Example 1 (pair of similar right triangles) to solve the following problems. Give your answer to the nearest tenths.

1. A girl 5 ft tall casts a 3 ft shadow, a boy who is standing next to her casts a shadow of 2 ft. How tall is the boy?
2. A tower is 20 meters high and casts a shadow which is 5 meters. How tall is a nearby building that casts a 3-meter shadow?
3. When a tree casts a 6-meter shadow, a man 2 meters tall casts a 1.4-meter shadow. How tall is the tree?
4. When a 2.5-meter sign post casts a 4.2-meter shadow, a man nearby casts a 3.2-meter shadow. How tall is the man?
5. John is 6.2 ft tall and casts a 10 ft shadow. A stop sign post nearby casts a 12 ft shadow. How tall is the stop sign post?

Answer to a Selected Question

1. 3.3 ft

CHAPTER 34

SYMMETRIC FIGURES

A geometric figure that can be divided into two identical parts is **symmetric**
The line that divides the geometric figure into two identical parts is called the
line of symmetry. If the geometric figure is folded along the line of symmetry,
the two halves will match exactly. **A line of symmetry divides a geometric figure
into exactly two matching halves.**
A figure has symmetry if it can be folded into two matching halves exactly.
A geometric figure can have any number of lines of symmetry as shown in the
following diagrams.

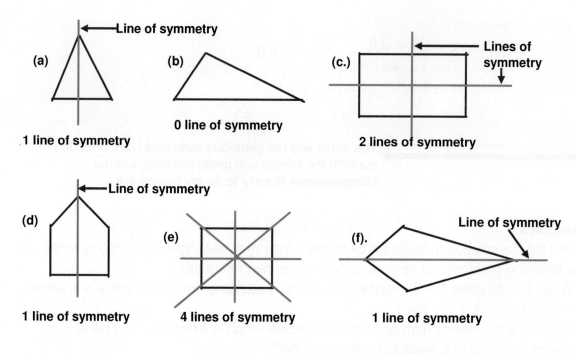

(a) 1 line of symmetry

(b) 0 line of symmetry

(c.) 2 lines of symmetry

(d) 1 line of symmetry

(e) 4 lines of symmetry

(f). 1 line of symmetry

Group Project

Obtain a kite, fold it into two matching halves similar to diagram (f).

- Are you able to fold the kite into exactly two matching halves?
- Can you conclude that a kite has symmetry?
- Compare an airplane to the kite. Does the airplane have symmetry? Sketch an airplane and draw the line of symmetry.

Symmetry of Letters

The diagrams below show some lines of symmetry of some letters as shown:

(a)

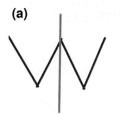

1 line of symmetry

(b)

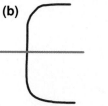

1 line of symmetry

(c.)

0 line of symmetry

The notes and the generous examples have provided me with the conceptual understanding and the computational fluency to do my homework.

Exercises

1. Explain what is meant by:

   a. symmetry

736

b. line of symmetry

c. number of lines of symmetry

2. In each diagram, is the dashed line along the line of symmetry? Explain your answer. Hint: See the notes provided.

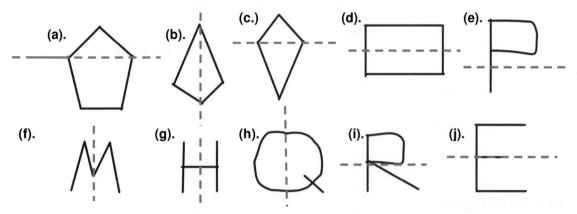

3. Sketch the following diagrams and draw all the possible lines of symmetry. Hint: See the notes provided.

Answer to selected questions

2a. The dashed line is not along the line of symmetry because the dashed line does not divide the figure exactly into two matching halves.

Cumulative Review

1. 95% of 20 =

2. 4% of 50 =

3. 6% of 16.2 =

4. .09% of 100 =

5. 900 − 398 =

6. What is an acute angle?

7. The sum of the measures of the angles in a triangle =

8. The sum of the measures of the angles on a line =

9. $4^2 - 2^2 =$

10. $24 - 2 \times 4 + 1 =$

11. The sum of the measures of the angles in a rectangle =

12. Find the missing angle.

13. Sketch and label a figure for each symbol.

a. $\angle ABC$ **b.** $\overrightarrow{DC}$ **c.** $\overleftrightarrow{XY}$ **d.** $\overline{AR}$

CHAPTER 35

FACTORS

New Term: Factor

A **factor** is a number that can divide another number evenly. For example, 2 can divide 4 evenly, and therefore, 2 is a factor of 4. A **factor** can also be said to be a number that can be multiplied by another number to obtain a product. For example, the factors of 12 are 1, 2, 3, 4, 6, and 12 because:

$$1 \times 12 = 12$$
$$2 \times 6 = 12$$
$$3 \times 4 = 12$$

Rule 1: A number will always have 1 and itself as a factor, and therefore, always begin the factors with 1, and then check in order for pairs of factors.

Rue 2: To find all the factors of a number, list all the numbers that can divide into it evenly including 1 and the number itself. List the factors from the least to the greatest.

Example 1
What are the factors of 9?
Solution
Using Rules 1 and 2, the factors of 9 are:

$$1 \times 9 = 9$$
$$3 \times 3 = 9$$

Note that the factor 3 pairs with itself, such that $3 \times 3 = 9$ and that 9 is also one of the factors, and therefore, 3 is used once as a factor instead of twice.

Therefore, the factors of 9 are 1, 3, and 9.

Example 2

What are the factors of 24?

Solution

Using Rules 1 and 2, the factors of 24 are:

$$1 \times 24 = 24$$
$$2 \times 12 = 24$$
$$3 \times 8 = 24$$
$$4 \times 6 = 24$$

The factors of 24 are 1, 2, 3, 4, 6, 8, 12, and 24.

Exercises

1. List all the factors of each number. Hint: See Examples 1 and 2 and Rules 1 and 2.

(a) 10	(b) 4	(c) 16	(d) 21	(e) 14
(f) 25	(g) 13	(h) 11	(i) 27	(j) 45
(k) 32	(l) 7	(m) 17	(n) 20	(o) 28

2. Explain what is meant by a factor?

Common Factors and Greatest Common Factor (GCF).

Two or more numbers can have factors that are the same and these factors are called **common factors**.

The **greatest common factor** (**GCF**) of two or more numbers is the greatest factor shared by the numbers.

Example 1

Find the (a) factors of 12 and 16.

(b) common factors of 12 and 16. Show your solution on a Venn diagram.

(c) greatest common factor of 12 and 16

Solution

(a) Using rules 1 and 2, the factors of 12 and 16 are as shown:

$$1 \times 12 = 12 \qquad 1 \times 16 = 16$$
$$2 \times 6 = 12 \qquad 2 \times 8 = 16$$
$$3 \times 4 = 12 \qquad 4 \times 4 = 16$$

Note that the factor 4 pairs with itself, such that $4 \times 4 = 16$ and that 16 is also one of the factors, and therefore, 4 is used once as a factor instead of twice.

From the factors above, the factors of 12 are 1, 2, 3, 4, 6, 12.

From the factors above, the factors of 16 are 1, 2, 4, 8, 16.

(b) Comparing the factors of 12 and 16, the factors that are common to both 12 and 16 are 1, 2, and 4, and therefore, the common factors of 12 and 16 are 1, 2, and 4 and this can be put in a Venn diagram as shown:

The overlapping region has the factors 1, 2, and 4 which are common to both 12 and 16.

This circle contains the factors of 16 which are 1, 2, 4, 8, and 16.

This circle contains the factors of 12 which are 1, 2, 3, 4, 6, and 12.

The diagram above is called Venn diagram

(c) From solution (b), the common factors of 12 and 16 are 1, 2, and 4. The greatest common factor from the common factors 1, 2, and 4 is 4. Therefore, the greatest common factor (GCF) of 12 and 16 is 4.

Example 2
Find the (a) factors of 8, 10, and 15.
(b) common factors of 8, 10, and 15.
(c) greatest common factors of 8, 10, and 15.

Solution
(a) Using Rules 1 and 2, the factors of 8, 10, and 15 are as shown:

Factors of 8	Factors of 10	Factors of 15
$1 \times 8 = 8$	$1 \times 10 = 10$	$1 \times 15 = 15$
$2 \times 4 = 8$	$2 \times 5 = 10$	$3 \times 5 = 15$

From the factors above, the factors of 8 are 1, 2, 4, and 8.
From the factors above, the factors of 10 are 1, 2, 5, and 10.
From the factors above, the factors of 15 are 1, 3, 5, and 15.

(b). Comparing the factors of 8,10, and 15, the factors that are common to 8, 10, and 15 is just 1.

(c). From the solution of (b), the common factor of 8, 10, and 15 is 1, and therefore, the greatest common factor (GCF) of 8, 10, and 15 is 1.

Rule 3: To find the greatest common factor (GCF) of two or more numbers, follow the three steps as shown:
1. Find the factors of the numbers.
2. Find the common factors of the numbers.
3. Select the greatest common factor (GCF) from the common factors.

Check for Understanding
(a) A number will always have itself and 1 as factors. True or False?
(b) To find all the factors of a number list all the numbers that can divide into it evenly

including 1 and itself. True or False?

Exercises

1. Explain how you can find the factors of two numbers .
2. Explain how you can find the common factors of two numbers.
3. Explain how you can find the greatest common factor(GCF) of two numbers.
4. Find the factors, common factors, and the greatest common factor (GCF) of each set of numbers. Hint: See Example 1.

(a) 4 and 12	(b) 9 and 18	(c) 12 and 18
(d) 18 and 24	(e) 12 and 18	(f) 8 and 15
(g) 12 and 16	(h) 7 and 12	(i) 11 and 19
(j) 25 and 15	(k) 3 and 10	(l) 13 and 5
(m) 16 and 20	(n) 21 and 7	(0) 8 and 20

5. Find the greatest common factor (GCF) of 24 and 42 and show your solution on a Venn diagram. Hint: See Example 1.
6. Find the factors, common factors and the greatest common factors (GCF) of each set of numbers. Hint: See Example 2.

(a) 6, 8, and 10	(b) 4, 12, and 16	(c) 8, 12, and 15
(d) 12, 18, and 24	(e) 8, 12, and 24	(f) 12, 16, and 24
(g) 7, 9, and 11	(h) 5, 10, and 15	(i) 11, 16, and 21

Challenge Questions

7. Show the solutions to question 4(a) to 4(c) on a Venn diagram.
8. Find the factors, common factors, and the greatest common factor (GCF) of each set of numbers:

(a) 5, 12, and 13	(b) 9 and 15	(c) 10, 16, and 21
(d) 8, 16, and 24	(e) 12 and 15	(f) 3 and 14

Answers to Selected Questions

4(a) GCF is 4   5. GCF is 6

PRIME FACTORIZATION

Every composite number can be expressed as the product of prime factors and this product is the **prime factorization** of the number. Recall from the chapter on the "prime numbers and composite numbers" that a composite number is a number (other than 0) that has more than two factors, that is, a composite number has more than 1 and itself as factors.

Rule 1: To write a composite number as a product of prime numbers is to write the prime factorization of the number.

What is a factor tree? A **factor tree** is a step-by-step method for factoring a number by using a diagram as shown in Example 1.

Example 1

Use a factor tree to find the prime factorization of 24. Express your answer in the exponential form.

Solution

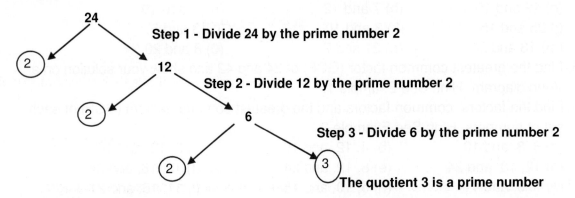

Step 1 - Divide 24 by the prime number 2

Step 2 - Divide 12 by the prime number 2

Step 3 - Divide 6 by the prime number 2

The quotient 3 is a prime number

The prime factorization of 24 is 2 · 2 · 2 · 3 which can be written in the exponential form as $2^3 \cdot 3^1$ or simply $2^3 \cdot 3$. The exponent 3 tells how many times the base 2 is used as a factor. Review the chapter on "the power of numbers".

The exponent 3 tells how many times the base 2 is used as a factor.

The exponent 1 tells how many times the base 3 is used as a factor.

Base 2

Base 3

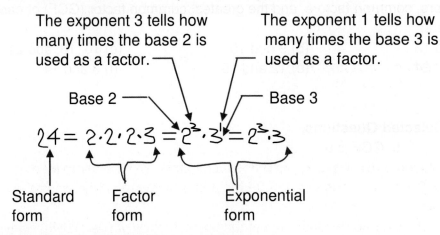

Standard form

Factor form

Exponential form

From the solution of Example 1 note that:

(a) 24, 12, and 6 are all divided by the least possible prime number of 2 until we obtain the final quotient of 3 which is a prime number.

(b) When 6 is divided by 2, the quotient is 3 and 3 is a prime number, and therefore, the division cannot go on any further.

(c) All the factors are prime.

Rule 2: To find the prime factorization of any number, divide the number by prime numbers only in order starting from the least possible prime number until

the final quotient is a prime number.

Example 2

Use a factor tree to find the prime factorization of 60. Express your answer in the exponential form.

Solution

Using rule 2, we can write the prime factorization of 60 as shown:

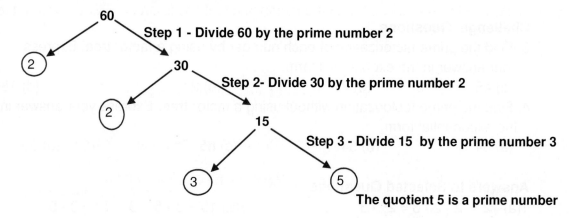

The prime factorization of 60 is $2 \cdot 2 \cdot 3 \cdot 5$ which is written in the exponential form as $2^2 \cdot 3 \cdot 5$. See the explanation for the exponential form in Example 1.

Example 3

(a) From the solution of Example 2, complete the prime factorization:
$$60 = 2 \cdot 2 \cdot 15$$
$$= 2 \cdot 2 \cdot ? \cdot 5$$

(b) Complete the prime factorization:
$$54 = 2 \cdot 27$$
$$= 2 \cdot 3 \cdot 9$$
$$= 2 \cdot 3 \cdot ? \cdot 3$$

Solution

(a) From the solution of Example 2, the prime factorization can be completed as follows:

$60 = 2 \cdot 2 \cdot 3 \cdot 5$ because one of the prime factors of 15 is missing which is 3

(b) The prime factorization of 54 is:

$54 = 2 \cdot 3 \cdot 3 \cdot 3$ because one of the prime factors of 9 is missing, which is 3.

Exercises

1. Give the prime factorization of each number by using the factor tree. Express your answer in the exponential form. Hint: See Examples 1 and 2.

    (a) 12   (b) 18   (c) 20   (d) 28

    (e) 44   (f) 32   (g) 58   (h) 48

(i) 64	(j) 36	(k) 45	(l) 50
(m) 25	(n) 54	(o) 49	(p) 30
(q) 34	(r) 65	(s) 42	(t) 27

2. Find the prime factorization without using a factor tree. Express your answer in the exponential form. Hint: See Example 3.

(a) 15	(b) 16	(c) 21	(d) 35
(e) 9	(f) 35	(g) 40	(h) 26

Challenge Questions

3. Find the prime factorization of each number by using a factor tree. Express your answer in the exponential form.

(a) 45	(b) 72	(c) 27	(d) 180

4. Find the prime factorization without using a factor tree. Express your answer in the exponential form.

(a) 64	(b) 54	(c) 85	(d) 90

Answers to Selected Questions

$1(a)\ 12 = 2 \cdot 2 \cdot 3 = 2^2 \cdot 3$ $2(a)\ 15 = 3 \cdot 5 = 3^1 \cdot 5^1 = 3 \cdot 5$

Cumulative Review

1. What is a factor tree?
2. What does PERMDAS stands for?
3. Explain the following terms:

a. median	b. scientific notation
c. mode	d. mean
e. average	f. sum
g. dividend	h. quotient

   Hint: Review the Math Teaching Series for grade 5.
4. What is the sum of the measures of the angles in a triangle?
5. What is the sum of the measures of the angles in a rectangle?
6. Mary said that the opposite sides of a rectangle are parallel. Is her statement correct? Explain. Review the Math Teaching Series for grade 5.

(The answers to the above Cumulative Review problems can also be found in the Math Teaching Series for grade 5. Refer to the Table of Contents and the Index.)

CHAPTER 36

POWER OF NUMBERS

In the grid diagram, there are 5 rows and 5 columns of blocks. The total number of blocks in the grid can be written as 5 · 5 where the dot (·) means multiplication.

One block

Total number of blocks = 5 x 5 = 25

The total number of the blocks is 5×5 which may be written as 5 · 5 which may further be written as 5^2 where the 5 is the base and 2 is the exponent as shown below:

$$5 \cdot 5 = 5^{\text{exponent}}$$
$$5 \cdot 5 = 5^2 \quad \text{base}$$

The **exponent** 2 shows how many times the base 5 is used as a factor
5^2 is known as "5 squared" or 5 to the second power. Similarly, instead of writing the same factor several times, the factor can be written once and the exponent can be used as shown:

$$5 \cdot 5 \cdot 5 = 5^3 \qquad \text{which is 5 to the third power.}$$
$$5 \cdot 5 \cdot 5 \cdot 5 = 5^4 \qquad \text{which is 5 to the fourth power.}$$
$$5 \cdot 5 \cdot 5 \cdot 5 \cdot 5 = 5^5 \qquad \text{which is 5 to the fifth power.}$$

In general, $n \cdot n \cdot n \cdot n \cdot n \cdot n \cdot \ldots = n^x$ which is n to the xth power.

Rule 1: The value of any number or any representation of a number such as a, b, n, x, or y to the power 0 is 1. For example, $1^0 = 1$, $2^0 = 1$, $100^0 = 1$, $n^0 = 1$, $x^0 = 1$, and $y^0 = 1$.

Example 1
How do you read 10^4 ?
Solution
10^4 is read as "10 to the power 4."

Example 2
(a) Write 8 in the exponential form.
(b) Write 24 in the exponential form.
(c) Write 60 in the exponential form.
Solution
(a) Use the prime factorization method under the section of prime factorization to find

the prime factors of 8 as shown:

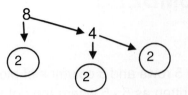

The prime factorization of 8 is 2 · 2 · 2.

Factor form

Therefore, $8 = 2 \cdot 2 \cdot 2 = 2^3$

Standard form.   Exponential form

(b) From the chapter on Prime Factorization, Example 1, the prime factors of 24 are:

2 · 2 · 2 · 3

Therefore, the exponential form of 24 is:

Factor form

$24 = 2 \cdot 2 \cdot 2 \cdot 3 = 2^3 \cdot 3$

Standard form   Exponential form

(c) From the chapter on prime factorization, Example 2, the prime factors of 60 are:

2 · 2 · 3 · 5.

Therefore, the exponential form of 60 is:

$60 = 2 \cdot 2 \cdot 3 \cdot 5 = 2^2 \cdot 3 \cdot 5$

Standard form.   Exponential form

Example 3
(a) Find the value of 4^3
(b) Find the value of 3^4
(c) Find the value of $2 \cdot 3^2$
(d) $2 \cdot 3^2 \cdot 4^2 =$
(e) Find the value of $2^2 \cdot 3 \cdot 5^2$

Solution
(a) $4^3 = 4 \times 4 \times 4 = 64$
(b) $3^4 = 3 \times 3 \times 3 \times 3 = 81$
(c) $2 \cdot 3^2 = 2 \times 3 \times 3 = 18$
(d) $2 \cdot 3^2 \cdot 4^2 = 2 \times 3 \times 3 \times 4 \times 4 = 288$

(e) $2^2 \cdot 3 \cdot 5^2 = 2 \times 2 \times 3 \times 5 \times 5 = 300$

Example 4
(a) Find the value of 6^1
(b) Find the value of 4^0
(c) Find the value of $6^1 \cdot 4^0 \cdot 2^2$
(e) Find the value of $3^0 \cdot 20^0 \cdot x^0$

Solution
(a) $6^1 = 6$

(b) $4^0 = 1$ **Notice that any number to the power of 0 is equal to 1, therefore, $4^0 = 1$.**

(c) $6^1 \cdot 4^0 \cdot 2^2 = 6 \times 1 \times 2 \times 2 = 24$ Note $4^0 = 1$

(d) $2^0 \cdot 5^1 \cdot 6^2 = 1 \times 5 \times 6 \times 6 = 180$ Note $2^0 = 1$

(e) $3^0 \cdot 20^0 \cdot x^0 = 1 \times 1 \times 1 = 1$ Note $3^0 = 1$, $20^0 = 1$, $x^0 = 1$

Example 5
Complete each equation

(a) $a \cdot a \cdot b \cdot b \cdot b = a^2?$ (b) $2 \cdot 2 \cdot 3 \cdot 5 \cdot 5 = 2^2 \cdot 3?$

(c) $2 \cdot x \cdot 4 \cdot y \cdot x = 8x^2?$ (d) $3 \cdot x \cdot y \cdot 2 \cdot y = ?x?$

(e) $a^0 \cdot 4 = ? \cdot 4$ (f) $a^0 \cdot b^0 \cdot 3 \cdot 3 \cdot 4 = ? ? 3^2 \cdot 4$

Solution
(a) $a \cdot a \cdot b \cdot b \cdot b = a^2b^3$ (b^3 because there are 3 bases of b).
                                      (a^2 because there are 2 bases of a).

(b) $2 \cdot 2 \cdot 3 \cdot 5 \cdot 5 = 2^2 \cdot 3 \cdot 5^2$ (5^2 because there are 2 bases of 5).
                                      (2^2 because there are 2 bases of 2).
                                      (3 because there is 1 base of 3).

(c) $2 \cdot x \cdot 4 \cdot y \cdot x = 8x^2y$ (y because there is 1 base of y).
                                      (x^2 because there are 2 bases of x).
                                      (8 because $2 \cdot 4 = 8$).

(d) $3 \cdot x \cdot y \cdot 2 \cdot y = 6xy^2$ (6 and y^2 because $3 \times 2 = 6$ and there are 2 bases of y).
                                      (x because there is 1 base of x).

(e) $a^0 \cdot 4 = 1 \cdot 4$ (Note: $a^0 = 1$)

(f) $a^0 \cdot b^0 \cdot 3 \cdot 3 \cdot 4 = 1 \cdot 1 \cdot 3^2 \cdot 4$ (Note: $a^0 = 1$, and $b^0 = 1$)
                                      (3^2 because there are 2 bases of 3).

Exercises
1. Explain what is meant by the base and the exponent of a number in the

exponential form.

2. How do you read the following: Hint: See Example 1.
   (a) 2^5　　　　　(b) 3^4　　　　　　　(c) 10^3　　　　　(d) 100^2

   (e) 9^1　　　　　(f) 12^3　　　　　　　(g) 5^3　　　　　(h) 2^6

3. Write the following in the exponential form. Hint: See Example 2.
   (a) 9　　　(b) 12　　　(c) 16　　　(d) 18　　　(e) 20
   (f) 32　　　(g) 45　　　(h) 25　　　(i) 36　　　(j) 27
   (k) 21　　　(l) 27　　　(m) 35　　　(n) 99　　　(o) 64

4. Find the following values. Hint: See Example 3.
   (a) 2^4　　　(b) 8^2　　　(c) $2^3 \cdot 3^2$　　　(d) $3^2 \cdot 4^2$

   (e) $2 \cdot 3^2 \cdot 5^2$　　(f) $2^2 \cdot 4 \cdot 5^2$　　　(g) $2 \cdot 3^2 \cdot 4$　　　(h) $2^3 \cdot 3 \cdot 4^2$

   (i) $3 \cdot 4 \cdot 5^2$　　(j) $2 \cdot 3^2 \cdot 6$　　　(k) $2 \cdot 2 \cdot 4^2$　　　(l) $2^2 \cdot 3^2 \cdot 4$

   (m) 10^2　　　(n) 9^2　　　　(o) $2 \cdot 10^3$　　　(p) $3^2 \cdot 8^2$

5. Find the following values. See Example 4.
   (a) 100^0　　　　　(b) 9^1　　　　　　(c) $2^0 \cdot 3^2$　　　　(d) $2^2 \cdot 4^0 \cdot 5^1$

   (e) $2^2 \cdot 3 \cdot 4^2$　　(f) $2^3 \cdot 3^0 \cdot 4^2$　　(g) $3^2 \cdot 5^0 \cdot 6^2$　　(h) $4^0 \cdot 2^2 \cdot 3^2$

   (i) $2^0 \cdot 3^1 \cdot 5^0$　　(j) $6^0 \cdot 10^0 \cdot 15^0$　　(k) $2^0 \cdot 3^0 \cdot 5^0$　　(l) $2^2 \cdot 6^2 \cdot 9^0$

   (m) $3^2 \cdot 5^0 \cdot 8^0$　　(n) $2^3 \cdot 3^2 \cdot 4^0$　　(o) $100^0 \cdot 200^0 \cdot 300^0$　　(p) $10^2 \cdot 4^2$

6. Complete each equation. See Example 5.
   (a) $a \cdot a \cdot b \cdot b = a^2\ ?$　　　　(b) $2 \cdot 3 \cdot 3 \cdot 5 = 2 \cdot ? \cdot 5$　　(c) $2 \cdot 2 \cdot 2 \cdot x \cdot x = ?\ x^2$
   (d) $3 \cdot x \cdot 2 \cdot y \cdot x = ? \cdot x^2 \cdot y$　(e) $2 \cdot a \cdot b \cdot 3 \cdot a \cdot = 6\ ?\ b$　(f) $4 \cdot x \cdot y \cdot 2 \cdot y = 8\ x\ ?$
   (g) $a \cdot a \cdot a \cdot b = ?\ b$　　　　　(h) $3 \cdot a \cdot x \cdot 4 \cdot a \cdot x = ?\ a^2\ ?$　(i) $a^0 \cdot b^0 \cdot 2 \cdot 2 = 1\ ?\ 2^2$
   (j) $2 \cdot 2 \cdot 4^0 \cdot a^0 = 2^2 \cdot ? \cdot 1$　(k) $x^0 \cdot y^0 \cdot z^0 = ?\ ?\ ?$　(l) $4 \cdot y \cdot x \cdot b \cdot 2 \cdot y \cdot b = ?\ ?\ x\ y^2$

Challenge Questions

7. Find each value.
   (a) $7^2 \cdot 9^0 =$　　　(b) $150^0 =$　　　(c) $2^0 \cdot 5^2 \cdot 7^0 =$　　(d) $5^2 \cdot a^0 \cdot b^2 =$

8. Complete the equation.
   (a) $3 \cdot a \cdot b \cdot a \cdot b = 3a^2?$　　　　(b) $4 \cdot a \cdot b \cdot 3 \cdot a \cdot b = ?\ a^2 b^2$

Answers to Selected Questions.

   3(a). 3^2　　　　　4(a). 16　　　　5(a). 1

CHAPTER 37

RATIOS

Kofi and Ama have 12 pencils. They have agreed to divide the pencils such that Kofi will have 8 pencils and Ama will have the remaining 4 pencils. To find out how many times more pencils Kofi has than Ama, divide 8 by 4.

$$8 \div 4 = 2$$

Therefore, Kofi has twice as many pencils as Ama. In the above statement we are comparing two quantities which are the number of Kofi's pencils and the number of Ama's pencils by division. Similarly, **a ratio is the comparison of two quantities by division**. The ratio of the number of Kofi's pencils to Ama's pencils can be expressed in three ways as shown:

1). Using "to" method (8 to 4).

2). Using fraction method $(\frac{8}{4})$.

3). Using a colon(:) method (8 : 4).

The ratio $\frac{8}{4}$ can be reduced to the simplest form as $\frac{2}{1}$ by dividing both the numerator and the denominator by 4. Note carefully that a ratio should always have a denominator, and therefore, if the denominator is 1, we must always write the denominator as 1.

Rule 1: To find the ratio of one number to another number, write the first number as the numerator and the second number as a denominator, and then reduce to lowest term if possible. For example, the ratio of x to y is $\frac{x}{y}$ or x : y and y is a non-zero number.

More Ratio Concepts.
Recall from the section on fractions that reducing a fraction to the lowest terms, the value of the fraction is not changed, and similarly, reducing a ratio to lowest term does not change the value of the ratio.

REAL WORLD APPLICATIONS - WORD PROBLEMS
Example 1

749

A class consists of 13 girls and 12 boys.

(a) What is the ratio of the girls to the boys?

(b) What is the ratio of the boys to the girls?

(c) What is the ratio of the boys to the whole class?

(d) What is the ratio of the girls to the whole class?

(e) What is the ratio of the total class to the number of girls?

(f). What is the ratio of the total class to the number of boys?

Solution

(a) The number of girls = 13

The number of boys = 12

Using Rule 1, which states, " To find the ratio of one number to another number, write the first number as the numerator and the second number as the denominator and then reduce to the lowest term if possible," the ratio of the girls to the boys is:

$$\frac{\text{Number of girls}}{\text{Number of boys}} = \frac{13}{12} \text{ or } 13:12$$

(b) Using Rule 1, the ratio of the boys to the girls is:

$$\frac{\text{Number of boys}}{\text{Number of girls}} = \frac{12}{13} \text{ or } 12:13$$

(c) The total number of students in the whole class = 12 + 13 = 25

Using Rule 1, the ratio of the number of boys to the whole class is:

$$\frac{\text{Number of boys}}{\text{Total number of students}} = \frac{12}{25} \text{ or } 12:25$$

(d) The total number of students in the whole class = 12 + 13 = 25.

Using Rule 1, the ratio of the number of the girls to the whole class is:

$$\frac{\text{Number of girls}}{\text{Total number of students}} = \frac{13}{25} \text{ or } 13:25$$

(e) The total number of students in the whole class is 12 + 13 = 25.

Using Rule 1, the ratio of the whole class to the number of girls is:

$$\frac{\text{Total number of students}}{\text{Number of girls}} = \frac{25}{13} \text{ or } 25:13$$

(f). The total number of students in the whole class is 12 + 13 = 25.

Using Rule 1, the ratio of the whole class to the number of boys is:

$$\frac{\text{Total number of students}}{\text{Number of boys}} = \frac{25}{12} \text{ or } 25 : 12$$

Example 2

The ratio of rabbits to birds in a small zoo is 7 : 3.

If the total population of the rabbits and the birds at the zoo is 30,

(a) how many rabbits are in the zoo?

(b) how many birds are in the zoo?

Solution

Step 1: Find the total ratio.

Total ratio $= 7 + 3 = 10$

Step 2: Find the fractions of the rabbits and the birds.

$$\text{The fraction of the rabbits} = \frac{\text{The ratio of the rabbits}}{\text{Total ratio}} = \frac{7}{10}$$

$$\text{The fraction of the birds} = \frac{\text{The ratio of the birds}}{\text{Total ratio}} = \frac{3}{10}$$

(a)

Step 3: To find the number of rabbits in the zoo, multiply the fraction for the rabbits by the total population of the zoo.

Therefore, the number of rabbits at the zoo $= \dfrac{7}{10} \times 30$

$$= \frac{7}{\underset{1}{\cancel{10}}} \times \overset{3}{\cancel{30}} \quad \text{Divide the numerator and the denominator by 10.}$$

$$= 7 \times 3 = 21 \text{ rabbits}$$

(b)

Step 4: To find the number of birds at the zoo, multiply the fraction for birds by the total population of the zoo.

Therefore, the number of birds at the zoo $= \dfrac{3}{10} \times 30$

$$= \frac{3}{\underset{1}{\cancel{10}}} \times \overset{3}{\cancel{30}} = 9 \text{ birds.} \quad \text{Divide the numerator and the denominator by 10.}$$

$$= 3 \times 3 = 9 \text{ birds}$$

Example 3

Mr. Jones is 45 years old. His son is 10 years old.

What is the ratio of Mr. Jones age to his son's age?

Solution

Using Rule 1, the ratio of Mr. Jones' age to his son's age is:

$$\frac{45}{10} \text{ or } 45:10$$

$$= \frac{\overset{9}{\cancel{45}}}{\underset{2}{\cancel{10}}} \qquad \text{Reduce } \frac{45}{10} \text{ to lowest term by dividing by 5.}$$

$$= \frac{9}{2}$$

Therefore, the ratio of Mr. Jones' age to his son's age is $\frac{9}{2}$ or $9:2$

Example 4

What is the ratio of 7 days to 3 weeks?

Solution

Before a ratio can be written, make sure that both the numerator and the denominator of the ratio have the same unit. In this example, the units are days and weeks. We cannot express days as a ratio of weeks. Convert 7 days to 1 week by dividing 7 days by 7 because 7 days = 1 week .

Solution

Using Rule 1, the ratio of 7days to 3 weeks is :

$$\frac{7 \text{ days}}{3 \text{ weeks}} = \frac{1 \text{ week}}{3 \text{ weeks}}$$

$$= \frac{1 \text{ week}}{3 \text{ weeks}}$$

$$= \frac{1}{3} \text{ or } 1:3$$

Therefore, the ratio of 7 days to 3 weeks $= \frac{1}{3}$ or $1:3$

Note: A ratio also compares more than two numbers by division as shown in Example 5.

Rule 2: To find a number which is equivalent to a ratio when the total number is given, multiply the fraction of the ratio by the total number.

Example 5

John, Eric, and Janet had a joint business, and they shared the profit of the business which was $150.00 in the ratio 2 : 3 : 5 respectively.
(a) What are the fractions of the shares of John, Eric, and Janet in the profit?
(b) What is John's share of the profit?
(c) What is Eric's share of the profit?
(d) What is Janet's share of the profit?

Solution

(a) The word "respectively" in the problem means that the ratios are matched with the names John, Eric, and Janet in order.

Since the total ratio = 2 + 3 + 5 = 10, and the ratio parts are 2, 3, and 5, the ratio 2 : 3 : 5 can also be written as a fraction as $\dfrac{2}{10}$, $\dfrac{3}{10}$, and $\dfrac{5}{10}$.

(b) The total ratio $= 2 + 3 + 5 = 10$

Using Rule 2, John's share of the profit $= \dfrac{2}{10} \times \$150$

$$= \dfrac{2}{\overset{1}{\underset{}{10}}} \times \overset{15}{\$150} \qquad \text{Divide by 10}$$

$$= 2 \times \$15 = \$30$$

Using Rule 2, Eric's share of the profit $= \dfrac{3}{10} \times \$150$

$$= \dfrac{3}{\overset{1}{\underset{}{10}}} \times \overset{15}{\$150} \qquad \text{Divide by 10}$$

$$= 3 \times \$15 = \$45$$

Using Rule 2, Janet's share of the profit $= \dfrac{5}{10} \times \$150$

$$\overset{15}{}$$

753

$$= \frac{5}{\cancel{10}} \times \$1\cancel{50} \qquad \text{Divide by 10}$$
$$1$$

$$= 5 \times \$15 = \$75$$

Exercises

1. Explain what is meant by the ratio of two numbers.
2. Change each expression to a ratio in a fraction form, and reduce to lowest term if possible. Hint: See Examples 1(a) and 1(b).
   (a) 4 to 7   (b) 5 to 8   (c) 3 to 9   (d) 5 to 20
   (e) 15 : 25   (f) 12 : 4   (g) 16 : 4   (h) 27 : 3
   (i) 49 : 7   (j) 3 to 36   (k) 18 to 3   (l) 24 : 4
   (m). 25 : 75   (n) 75 :35   (0). 11 : 99   (p) 64 : 8
3. A class consists of 10 boys and 13 girls.
   (a) What is the ratio of the number of boys to the number of girls? Hint: See Examples 1(a) and 1(b).
   (b) What is the ratio of the number of girls to the number of boys? Hint: See Examples 1(a) and 1(b).
4. A company has 50 employees. The ratio of the number of the men to the number of women is 2 : 3, find:
   (a) the number of men working for the company. Hint: See Example 2.
   (b) the number of women working for the company. Hint: See Example 2 .
5. A clinic has 3 male nurses and 7 female nurses. What is the ratio of the:
   (a) male nurses to the female nurses?
   (b) female nurses to the male nurses?
   (c) female nurses to the total number of nurses at the clinic?
   (d) male nurses to the total number of nurses at the clinic?
   (e) total number of nurses to the male nurses?
   (f) total number of nurses to the female nurses?
     Hint: See Example 1.
6. Judith scored 100% on a test, John scored 95% on the same test. What is the ratio of the test score of Judith to that of John? Reduce your answer to lowest term. Hint: See Example 3.
7. What is the ratio of 10 minutes to 1 hour? Hint: The units of a ratio must be the same, 60 minutes =1 hour, see Example 4.
8. What is the ratio of 2 feet to 6 inches? Hint: The unit of a ratio must be the same, 12 inches = 1 foot, see Example 4.
9. What is the ratio of 3 weeks to 3 months? Hint: The unit of a ratio must be the same, 4 weeks = 1 month, see Example 4 .
10 Nick, Jones, and George shared $250 in the ratio 5 : 12 : 8, respectively.

(a) What is the total ratio?
(b) What is the fraction of the money that Nick received?
(c) What is the fraction of the money that Jones received?
(d) What is the fraction of the money that George received?
(e) What is the money that Nick received?
(f) What is the money that Jones received?
(g) What is the money that George received?
Hint: See Example 5.

Challenge Questions
1. What is the ratio of 2 hours to 30 minutes?
2. What is the ratio of 6 feet to 10 inches?
3. A woman is 35 years old and her son is 5 years old. What is the ratio of the woman's age to the son's age?
4. There are 600 students in a certain school. The ratio of the girls to the boys at the school is 6 : 4.
   (a) Find the fraction of the student population that are girls?
   (b) Find the fraction of the student population that are boys?
   (c) How many students are girls in the school?
   (d) How many students are boys in the school?
5. What is the ratio of 2 weeks to 2 months?
6. Three students shared $100.00 in the ratio 6 : 3 : 1. How much did each student receive?
7. What is the ratio of 6 inches to 2 feet?

EQUIVALENT RATIOS

Equivalent ratios are ratios that represent the same thing or the same value. For example, the ratios $\frac{1}{2}$, $\frac{2}{4}$, and $\frac{4}{8}$ are equivalent ratios because all of them represent the same value of $\frac{1}{2}$ when all the ratios are reduced to lowest terms.

Understanding the Concept of Equivalent Ratios.
The concept of the equivalent ratios can further be explained by observing the equal areas of the squares of figure 1, figure 2, and figure 3. In figure 1, the square is divided into two parts and the area of the triangle BCD represents $\frac{1}{2}$ of the area of the square ABCD. The square ABCD in figure 2 is divided into 4 parts and the same

area triangle BCD is now represented by 2 parts(areas of triangles BCE and CDE) which can be written as $\frac{2}{4}$ parts of the same square ABCD which can be reduced to lowest term to obtain $\frac{1}{2}$. The square ABCD in figure 3 is divided into 8 parts and the same triangle BCD is now represented by 4 parts which can be written as $\frac{4}{8}$ parts of the same square ABCD which can be reduced to lowest term to obtain $\frac{1}{2}$.

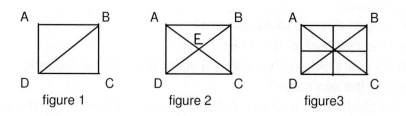

figure 1   figure 2   figure3

The logic is the fact that the same area of triangle BCE is represented as $\frac{1}{2}$ in figure 1 and it is represented as $\frac{2}{4}$ in Figure 2 and it is represented as $\frac{4}{8}$ in Figure 3, and therefore, all the ratios of $\frac{1}{2}$, $\frac{2}{4}$, and $\frac{4}{8}$ represent the same area of the triangle BCD, similarly equivalent ratios are ratios that represent the same thing or value. Equivalent ratios can be expressed or written as equivalent fractions. Cross products of equivalent fractions are equal and this will help us to solve many problems as illustrated in the following examples.

Rule 1: Equivalent ratios can be expressed or written as equivalent fractions and the cross products of equivalent fractions are equal.

Example 1
a). There are 205 animals and 37 birds at a certain zoo. Write the ratio of the number of the birds to the number of the animals in 3 different ways.

b). Complete to get equivalent or equal ratios: $\frac{3}{2} = \frac{12}{?}$

c). Complete to get equivalent or equal ratios: 4 : 1 and ? : 4

Solution

The number of birds = 37, the number of animals = 205.

Ratios can be written in three different ways by using "to," a fraction bar, or a colon.

The ratio of the birds to the animals is: 37 to 205, $\frac{37}{205}$, or 37 : 205.

b). There are two methods to solve this problem. They are by "cross products," or by inspection.

Cross Products Method:

$\dfrac{3}{2} = \dfrac{12}{?}$ can be written as $\dfrac{3}{2} = \dfrac{12}{y}$ so that we can solve for y.

Cross products of equivalent ratios or fractions are equal, and therefore,

$\dfrac{3}{2} \diagdown \dfrac{12}{y}$ is $3 \times y = 2 \times 12$

$$3y = 24 \quad\text{———————}\quad [A]$$

Divide each side of equation $[A]$ by 3 to obtain y as shown:

$$\dfrac{3y}{3} = \dfrac{24}{3}$$

$$\begin{array}{cc} y & 8 \\ \dfrac{3y}{3} & \dfrac{24}{3} \\ 1 & 1 \end{array}$$

$$y = 8$$

Therefore, the equivalent ratios of $\dfrac{3}{2} = \dfrac{12}{?}$ are $\dfrac{3}{2} = \dfrac{12}{8}$.

Inspection Method

Let us inspect the ratio $\dfrac{3}{2}$ and $\dfrac{12}{?}$ and find out how the numerator 3 can be changed to the numerator 12. We should find that the numerator 3 is multiplied by 4 to obtain the numerator of 12 and similarly we have to multiply the denominator of 2 by the same number 4 to give us a denominator of 8.

multiply by the same number.

$$\dfrac{3}{2} = \dfrac{3 \times ?}{2 \times ?} = \dfrac{3 \times 4}{2 \times 4} = \dfrac{12}{8}$$

multiply by the same number.

Therefore, the equivalent ratio $\dfrac{3}{2} = \dfrac{12}{?}$ should be $\dfrac{3}{2} = \dfrac{12}{8}$

c). In order for 4 : 1 and ? : 4 to be equal ratios, then 4 : 1 = ? : 4 and the ratio

can be written in a fraction form as $\dfrac{4}{1} = \dfrac{?}{4}$

There are two methods to solve this problem which is by "cross products " or by inspection.

Cross Products Method

The cross product of equivalent ratios or fractions are equal, and therefore:

$$\frac{4}{1} \diagup\!\!\!\!\diagdown \frac{?}{4} \quad \text{is } 4 \times 4 = 1 \times ?$$

$$16 = ?$$

Therefore, the equivalent ratio of $\frac{4}{1} = \frac{?}{4}$ is $\frac{4}{1} = \frac{16}{4}$

Inspection Method

Let us inspect the equivalent ratio $\frac{4}{1} = \frac{?}{4}$ to find out how the denominator 1 in the first ratio changes to the denominator 4 in the second ratio. The denominator 1 is multiplied by 4 to get the denominator 4 in the second ratio and similarly, the numerator 4 of the first ratio should be multiplied by the same number 4 to obtain the numerator of 16 in the second ratio as shown:

$$\frac{4}{1} = \frac{?}{4} \quad , \qquad \frac{4}{1} = \frac{4 \times ?}{1 \times ?} = \frac{4 \times 4}{1 \times 4} = \frac{16}{4}$$

↗ multiply by the same number.

↘ multiply by the same number.

↑ ↑
1st ratio   2nd ratio

Therefore, the equivalent ratio is $\frac{4}{1} = \frac{16}{4}$.

Example 2

a). State four ways to show that one ratio is equivalent to the other?

b). Show that $\frac{2}{4}$ and $\frac{4}{8}$ are equivalent ratios.

Solution

a). The four ways to show that one ratio is equivalent to another ratio are:
by multiplying each term in the smaller ratio by the same number that will be equal to the bigger ratio, by dividing each term of the bigger ratio by the same number that will be equal to the smaller ratio, by reducing each ratio to lowest term or by finding the cross products of the ratios. The cross product of equivalent ratios are equal.

b). Let us use each of the four methods in solution (a) to solve the problem.

Method 1:

What same number can multiply the terms of the smaller ratio (the smaller ratio is $\frac{2}{4}$) in order to obtain the bigger ratio (the bigger ratio is $\frac{4}{8}$)? This can be expressed as shown:

what number that can multiply 2 to obtain 4?

$$\frac{2}{4} = \frac{2 \times ?}{4 \times ?} = \frac{4}{8}$$

smaller ratio ↗   ↖ bigger ratio

what number can multiply 4 to obtain 8?

Since the terms of the smaller ratio can be multiplied by the same number, which is 2 to obtain the bigger ratio, the two ratios are equivalent.

Note: Recall that when the terms of a ratio are multiplied by the same number, the value of the ratio does not change, and that equivalent ratios have equivalent fractions.

Method 2:

What same number can divide the terms of the bigger ratio (the bigger ratio is $\frac{4}{8}$)

in order to obtain the smaller ratio. This can be expressed as shown:

what number can divide 4 to obtain 2?

$$\frac{4}{8} = \frac{4 \div ?}{8 \div ?} = \frac{2}{4}$$ smaller ratio

bigger ratio ↗   ↖ what number can divide 8 to obtain 4?

$$\frac{4}{8} = \frac{4 \div 2}{8 \div 2} = \frac{2}{4}$$

Since the terms of the bigger ratio can be divided by the same number, which is 2 to obtain the smaller ratio, the two ratios are equivalent.

Note: Recall that when the terms of a ratio are divided by the same number, the value of the ratio does not change, and that equivalent ratios have equivalent fractions.

Method 3:

Reduce each ratio to lowest term, and if the lowest terms are equal, then the ratios are equivalent.

Reduce $\frac{2}{4}$ to lowest term by dividing the terms by 2 .

Therefore, $\frac{2}{4} = \frac{\overset{1}{2}}{\underset{2}{4}} = \frac{1}{2}$

759

Reduce $\dfrac{4}{8}$ to lowest term by dividing the terms by 4.

Therefore, $\dfrac{4}{8} = \dfrac{\overset{1}{\cancel{4}}}{\underset{2}{\cancel{8}}} = \dfrac{1}{2}$

Since $\dfrac{2}{4} = \dfrac{1}{2}$ and $\dfrac{4}{8} = \dfrac{1}{2}$, both ratios are equivalent.

Method 4:

The cross products of equivalent fractions are equal, and therefore,

$$\dfrac{2}{4} \bowtie \dfrac{4}{8}$$

$$2 \times 8 = 16$$
$$4 \times 4 = 16$$

Since the cross products of the fractions are equal, the fractions are equivalent fractions, and therefore, the ratios are equivalent ratios.

Example 3

It is a fact that equivalent ratios can be written as equivalent fractions. Show that the ratio 15 : 6 is equivalent to 5 : 2.

Solution

The ratios 15 : 6 and 5 : 2 can be written as fractions as shown:

$$15 : 6 = \dfrac{15}{6} \text{ and } 5 : 2 = \dfrac{5}{2}$$

The fractions $\dfrac{15}{6}$ and $\dfrac{5}{2}$ are equivalent because the terms in $\dfrac{15}{6}$ can be divided by 3 to obtain $\dfrac{5}{2}$ as shown:

$$\dfrac{\overset{5}{\cancel{15}}}{\underset{2}{\cancel{6}}} = \dfrac{5}{2} \quad \text{or} \quad \dfrac{15}{6} = \dfrac{15 \div ?}{6 \div ?} = \dfrac{5}{2}$$

Therefore, the ratio 15 : 6 is equivalent to 5 : 2. Note that the style of the solution to Example 2(b) Method 2 is used to solve this problem.

Alternative Method

This problem can simply be solved by using Rule 1, which states that the equivalent ratios can be written as equivalent fractions and the cross products of equivalent fractions are equal.

Let us check if the cross products of the equivalent fractions are equal or not, as shown:

$$\frac{15}{6} = \frac{5}{2},$$ and the cross products are:

$$\frac{15}{6} \diagup\!\!\!\!\!\diagdown \frac{5}{2}$$

Therefore, $15 \times 2 = 30$, $6 \times 5 = 30$

Since the cross products are equal the ratios are equivalent.

Example 4

Are the ratios $\dfrac{1}{6}$ and $\dfrac{5}{31}$ equivalent?

Solution

The ratios $\dfrac{1}{6}$ and $\dfrac{5}{31}$ are already written in the fraction form, and therefore, let us find out if the two fractions $\dfrac{1}{6}$ and $\dfrac{5}{31}$ are equivalent or not. We should find what same number that can multiply the terms of $\dfrac{1}{6}$ in order to obtain the ratio $\dfrac{5}{31}$ as shown:

$$1 \times 5 = 5$$

$$\frac{1}{6} = \frac{1 \times \ ?}{6 \times \ ?} = \frac{5}{31}$$

$$6 \times 5 = 30. \text{ Note that } 30 \text{ is not } 31.$$

Since 5 can not be multiplied by the terms of $\dfrac{1}{6}$ which are 1 and 6 in order to obtain 5 and 31, $\dfrac{1}{6}$ and $\dfrac{5}{31}$ are not equivalent fractions, and therefore, the ratios $\dfrac{1}{6}$ and $\dfrac{5}{31}$ are not equivalent ratios.

Alternative Method

This problem can simply be solved by using Rule 1 which states that " Equivalent ratios can be written as equivalent fractions and the cross products of equivalent fractions are equal." Let us check if the cross products of the equivalent fractions are equal or not, as shown:

$$\frac{1}{6} = \frac{5}{31}$$

$1 \times 31 = 31$

$6 \times 5 = 30$ Note that 30 is not equal to 31.

Since the cross products are 31 and 30, and $31 \neq 30$, the ratios $\frac{1}{6}$ and $\frac{5}{31}$ are not equivalent. Note that the symbol $\neq$ means "is not equal to."

Example 5

Find a ratio that is equivalent to $\frac{6}{9}$ and explain your reasons.

Solution

There are two ways to solve this problem. One way is to divide the numerator and the denominator of $\frac{6}{9}$ by the same number and the quotient will give us the solution to the problem as shown:

$$\frac{6}{9} = \frac{6 \div 3}{9 \div 3} = \frac{2}{3}$$

Therefore, the equivalent of $\frac{6}{9}$ is $\frac{2}{3}$

Alternative Method

Another way to solve the problem is to multiply the numerator and the denominator of $\frac{6}{9}$ by the same number as shown:

$$\frac{6}{9} = \frac{6 \times ?}{9 \times ?} = \frac{6 \times 2}{9 \times 2} = \frac{12}{18}$$

Note: Both the numerator and the denominator are multiplied by the same number 2.

Therefore, the equivalent of $\frac{6}{9}$ is $\frac{12}{18}$

Exercises

1. Ratios can be written in three ways using "to," "colons," or fractions. Write each of the following ratio statements in three ways. Hint: See Example 1.
   (a) A class consists of 11 boys and 13 girls. What is the ratio of boys to girls?
   (b) There are 2 oranges and 6 apples in a room. What is the ratio of apples to oranges?
   (c) There are 4 vans and 9 cars at the school. What is the ratio of the vans to the cars?

2. State the four ways by which it can be shown that one ratio is equivalent to another ratio. Hint: See Example 2(a).

3. Complete the following statement:
   Equivalent ratios can be written as ———————————— Hint: See Rule 1.

4. Explain what is meant by equivalent ratios.

5. Explain what is meant by equivalent fractions.

6. Show that the following ratios are equivalent, use the cross products method. Hint: See Examples 2 and 3.

   (a) 1 : 2 and 2 : 4   (b) 2 : 4 and 4 : 8   (c) 2 : 4 and 8 : 16

   (d) 3 : 6 and 9 : 18   (e) 3 : 9 and 9 : 27   (f) 6 : 12 and 12 : 24

   (g) $\dfrac{9}{15}$ and $\dfrac{3}{5}$ (h) $\dfrac{3}{5}$ and $\dfrac{12}{20}$ (i) $\dfrac{1}{6}$ and $\dfrac{2}{12}$

   (j) $\dfrac{3}{4}$ and $\dfrac{9}{12}$ (k) $\dfrac{12}{16}$ and $\dfrac{3}{4}$ (l) $\dfrac{5}{15}$ and $\dfrac{10}{30}$

7. Are the ratios $\dfrac{1}{2}$ and $\dfrac{2}{5}$ equivalent? Hint: See Example 4.

8. Determine if the following ratios are equivalent or not. Hint: See Examples 3 and 4.

   (a) $\dfrac{1}{2}$ and $\dfrac{8}{16}$ (b) $\dfrac{1}{3}$ and $\dfrac{3}{8}$ (c) $\dfrac{3}{2}$ and $\dfrac{9}{6}$

   (d) 6 : 2 and 12 : 4   (e) 1 : 3 and 2 : 6   (f) 2 :3 and 5 : 6

   (g) 1 : 5 and 2 : 10   (h) 4 : 1 and 16 : 3   (i) 4 : 2 and 8 : 4

   (j) $\dfrac{2}{3}$ and $\dfrac{4}{6}$ (k) $\dfrac{5}{2}$ and $\dfrac{25}{10}$ (l) $\dfrac{7}{2}$ and $\dfrac{21}{3}$

Challenge Questions

9. A class has 6 girls and 5 boys.
   (a) What is the ratio of the boys to the girls?
   (b) What is the ratio of the girls to the boys?
   (c) What is the ratio of the boys to the number of students in the whole class?

10. Show that the following ratios are equivalent:

   (a) $\dfrac{5}{1}$ and $\dfrac{25}{5}$ (b) $\dfrac{1}{4}$ and $\dfrac{4}{16}$ (c) $\dfrac{2}{7}$ and $\dfrac{6}{21}$

   (d) 8 : 2 and 16 : 4   (e) 3 : 7 and 9 : 21   (f) $\dfrac{4}{3}$ and $\dfrac{12}{9}$

763

11. Determine which ratios are equivalent or not:

(a) $\dfrac{1}{3}$ and $\dfrac{2}{7}$

(b) $\dfrac{8}{1}$ and $\dfrac{64}{8}$

(c) $\dfrac{2}{3}$ and $\dfrac{1}{2}$

(d) $\dfrac{2}{9}$ and $\dfrac{6}{27}$

(e) 4 : 3 and 12 : 9

(f) 2 : 1 and 6 : 3

12. Complete the equations to obtain equivalent or equal ratios:

(a) $\dfrac{2}{4} = \dfrac{?}{8}$

(b) $\dfrac{4}{3} = \dfrac{8}{?}$

(c) $\dfrac{?}{2} = \dfrac{5}{6}$

(d) $\dfrac{3}{8} = \dfrac{9}{?}$

(e) $\dfrac{4}{?} = \dfrac{12}{15}$

(f) $\dfrac{1}{3} = \dfrac{?}{9}$

INDEX

A

B

C

E

F

G

H

I

K

L

M

T

U

APPLICATION OF TECHNOLOGY BY USING TI-15 - REFERENCE

After the logic of mathematics is understood, students may use calculators and other computer softwares as applications of technology. Some of the applications of the TI-15 are shown. Refer to the manual of your calculator or computer program for detail applications.

Basic Operations

Keys

1. ⊞ adds.

2. ⊟ subtracts.

3. ⊠ multiplies.

4. ÷ divides. The result may be displayed as a decimal or fraction depending on the mode setting you have selected.

5. Int÷ divides a whole number by a whole number and displays the result as a quotient and remainder.

6. Enter completes the operation.

7. (−) lets you enter a negative number.

Notes

- The examples on the transparency masters assume all default settings.

- The result of Integer Divide Int÷ always appears as quotient and remainder (__ r __).

- The maximum number of digits for quotient or remainder (**r**) is 5. Quotient, remainder, and the **r** character cannot total more than 10 characters.

- If you use the result of integer division in another calculation, only the quotient is used. The remainder is dropped.

- All numbers used with Int÷ must be positive whole numbers.

- If you attempt to divide by 0, an error message is displayed.

- ⊞, ⊟, ⊠, ÷, Enter, and Int÷ work with the built-in constants.

Display, Scrolling, Order of Operations, and Parentheses

Keys

1. ⧼(⧽ opens a parenthetical expression. You can have as many as 8 parentheses at one time.

2. ⧼)⧽ closes a parenthetical expression.

3. ◄ and ► move the cursor left and right.

   ▲ and ▼ move the cursor up and down through previous entries and results.

Notes

- The examples on the transparency masters assume all default settings.

- The EOS™ transparency master demonstrates the order in which the TI-15 completes calculations.

- When using parentheses, if you press ⧼Enter⧽ before pressing ⧼)⧽, **Syn Error** is displayed.

- Operations inside parentheses are performed first. Use ⧼(⧽ or ⧼)⧽ to change the order of operations and, therefore, change the result.

  Example: $1 + 2 \times 3 = 7$
  $(1 + 2) \times 3 = 9$

- The first and second lines display entries up to 11 characters plus a decimal point, a negative sign, and a 2-digit positive or negative exponent. Entries begin on the left and scroll to the right. An entry will always wrap at the operator.

- Results are displayed right-justified. If a whole problem will not fit on the first line, the result will display on the second line.

Equation Operating System

Priority	Functions
1 (first)	( )
2	Frac
3	^ √
4	(−)
5	× ÷
6	+ −
7	U$\frac{n}{d}$↔$\frac{n}{d}$ F↔D
8 (last)	Enter

Because operations inside parentheses are performed first, you can use ( ) to change the order of operations and, therefore, change the result.

Basic operations

$2 + 54 - 6 =$

Press	Display
2 ⊞ 54 ⊟ 6 [Enter]	┌─────────────────┐ │ 2+54-6= 50 │ └─────────────────┘

$3 \times 4 \div 2 =$

Press	Display
3 ⊠ 4 ⊡ 2 [Enter]	┌─────────────────┐ │ 3×4÷2= 6 │ └─────────────────┘

Order of Operations

$1 + 2 \times 3 =$

Press	Display
1 [+] 2 [×] 3 [Enter]	$1 + 2 \times 3 = \qquad 7$

$(1 + 2) \times 3 =$

Press	Display
[(] 1 [+] 2 [)] [×] 3 [Enter]	$(1 + 2) \times 3 = \qquad 9$

Division with remainders

Chris has 27 pieces of gum.
He wants to share the pieces evenly among himself and 5 friends. How many pieces will each person get? How many pieces will be left over?

Press	Display
27 [Int÷] 6 [Enter]	$27 \div 6 = \qquad 4\,r\,3$

Add

[+]

Multiply

[×]

Parentheses

[(] [)]

Integer Divide

[Int÷]

Division with decimal result

Set the division display option to decimal and divide 27 by 6.

Press   Display

(Mode) [Enter]

.   n/d

(Mode)

27 ÷ 6 [Enter]

27÷6=   4.5

Division with fractional result

Set the division display option to fraction and divide 27 by 6.

Press   Display

(Mode) ➡ [Enter]

.   n/d

(Mode)

$\frac{n}{d}$

27 ÷ 6 [Enter]

$\frac{n}{d}$

27÷6=   4 $\frac{5}{10}$

[Simp] [Enter]

$\frac{n}{d}$

4 $\frac{5}{10}$ 4 $\frac{1}{2}$

Divide

÷

Divide

÷

Quick Reference to Keys

A

Key	Function
(On/Off)	Turns on the calculator. If already on, turns the calculator off.
(Clear)	Clears display and error condition.
(On/Off) (Clear)	To reset the calculator, hold down (On/Off) and (Clear) simultaneously for a few seconds and release. **MEM CLEARED** shows on the display. This will completely clear the calculator, including all mode menu settings, all previous entries in history, all values in memory, and the display. All default settings will be restored.
→ ←	Moves the cursor right and left, respectively, so you can scroll the entry line or select a menu item.
	Moves the cursor up and down, respectively, so you can see previous entries or access menu lists.
←	Deletes the character to the left of the cursor before [Enter] is pressed.
(Mode)	Displays menu to select format of results of division: . n/d
(Mode) ▼	Displays menu to show or hide (?) in Op1 or Op 2: +1 Op ?
(Mode) ▼ ▼	Displays menu to clear Op1 or Op2: Op1 Clear Op2
(Mode) ▼ ▼ ▼	Displays menu to reject or accept Reset: N Y
[0][1][2][3][4][5] [6][7][8][9]	Enters the numerals 0 through 9.
[+]	Adds.
[−]	Subtracts.
[×]	Multiplies.
[÷]	Divides.
[Enter]	Completes operations. Enters the equal sign or tests a solution in Problem Solving.
[.]	Inserts a decimal point.
[(−)]	Enters a negative sign. Does not act as an operator.
[(]	Opens a parenthetical expression.
[)]	Closes a parenthetical expression.

Key	Function
Int÷	When you divide a positive whole number by a positive whole number using Int÷, the result is displayed in the form **Q r R**, where **Q** is the quotient and **R** is the remainder. If you use the result of integer division in a subsequent calculation, only the quotient is used; the remainder is dropped.
n	When pressed after entering a number, designates the numerator of a fraction. The numerator must be an integer. To negate a fraction, press (-) before entering numerator.
d	When pressed after entering a number, designates the denominator of a fraction. The denominator of a fraction must be a positive integer in the range 1 through 1000. If you perform a calculation with a fraction having a denominator greater than 1000, or if the results of a calculation yield a denominator greater than 1000, the TI-15 will convert and display the results in decimal format.
Unit	Separates a whole number from the fraction in a mixed number.
Frac	Displays a menu of settings that determine how fraction results are displayed. • **U n/d** (default) displays mixed number results. • **n/d** displays results as a simple (improper) fraction. If **N/d→n/d** is displayed after you convert a fraction to a mixed number, you can further simplify the fractional portion of the mixed number.
Frac ◄	Displays a menu to select the method of simplifying fractions: • **Man** (default) allows you to simplify manually (step-by-step). • **Auto** automatically reduces fraction results to lowest terms.
Simp	Enables you to simplify a fraction.
Fac	Displays the factor that was used to simplify a fraction.
$U\frac{n}{d} \leftrightarrow \frac{n}{d}$	Converts a mixed number to an improper fraction or an improper fraction to a mixed number.
F↔D	Converts a fraction to a decimal, or converts a decimal to a fraction, if possible. Converts π to a decimal value.
%	Enters a percentage.

Display Indicators ┃ B

Indicator	Meaning
◈	Calculator is in Problem Solving mode.
■.	Calculator is in place-value mode.
Fix	The calculator is rounding to a specified number of places.
M	Indicates that a value other than zero is in memory.
▶M	Value is being stored to memory. You must press $+$, $-$, $\times$, $\div$, or Enter to complete the process.
Op1, Op2	An operator and operand is stored.
Auto	In calculator mode, **Auto** simplification of fractions to lowest terms is selected. In ◈, Problem Solving function is in **Auto** mode.
I	Integer division function has been selected (appears only when cursor is over division sign).
n/d ÷	Division results will be displayed as fractions.
N//d→n/d	The fraction result can be further simplified.
↑ ↓	Previous entries are stored in history, or more menus are available. Press ▬ to access history. Press ▬ and ▬ to access additional menu lists.
← →	You can press ◀ and ▶ to scroll and select from a menu. You must press Enter to complete the selection process.

Quick Reference to Keys (Continued) | A

Key	Function
▶%	Converts a decimal or a fraction to a percent.
√	Calculates the square root of a number.
∧	Raises a number to the power you specify.
π	Enters the value of π. It is stored internally to 13 decimal places (3.141592653590). In some cases, results display with symbolic π, and in other cases as a numeric value.
▶M	Stores the displayed value for later use. If there is already a value in memory, the new one will replace it. When memory contains a value other than 0, **M** displays on the screen. (Will not work while a calculation is in process.)
MR/MC	Recalls the memory value for use in a calculation when pressed once. When pressed twice, clears memory.
Op1 Op2	Each can store one or more operations with constant value(s), which can be repeated by pressing only one key, as many times as desired. To store an operation to **Op1** or **Op2** and recall it: • Press Op1 (or Op2), enter the operator and the value, and press Op1 (or Op2) to save the operation. • Press Op1 (or Op2) to recall the stored operation. To clear the contents of **Op1** or **Op2**, press Mode ◄ ◄, select **Op1** or **Op2**, and press Enter. New operations can now be stored for repeated use.
Fix 1000.	Rounds off results to the nearest thousand.
Fix 100.	Rounds off results to the nearest hundred.
Fix 10.	Rounds off results to the nearest ten.
Fix 1.	Rounds off results to the nearest one.
Fix 0.1	Rounds off results to the nearest tenth.
Fix 0.01	Rounds off results to the nearest hundredth.
Fix 0.001	Rounds off results to the nearest thousandth.
Fix ·	Removes fixed-decimal setting and returns to floating decimal.